# Gay, Lesbian, Bisexual, Transgender Events

## 1848-2006

# Gay, Lesbian, Bisexual, Transgender Events

## 1848-2006

### Volume 1
1848-1983

*Editorial Board*

**Lillian Faderman,** California State University, Fresno
**Horacio Roque Ramírez,** University of California, Santa Barbara
**Yolanda Retter,** University of California, Los Angeles
**Stuart Timmons,** AUTHOR, *The Trouble with Harry Hay*
**Eric C. Wat,** AUTHOR, *The Making of a Gay Asian Community*

SALEM PRESS
Pasadena, California      Hackensack, New Jersey

*Editor in Chief:* Kenneth T. Burles

| | |
|---|---|
| *Editorial Director:* Christina J. Moose | *Research Supervisor:* Jeffry Jensen |
| *Acquisitions Editor:* Mark Rehn | *Cover and Page Design:* James Hutson |
| *Project Editor:* Desiree Dreeuws | *Photo Editor:* Cynthia Breslin Beres |
| *Production Editor:* Andrea E. Miller | *Editorial Assistant:* Dana Garey |

*Cover photos* (pictured clockwise, from top left): AIDS ribbon (AP/Wide World Photos); Stand Up & Represent (AP/Wide World Photos); Lesbian Rights NOW (Hulton Archives/Getty Images); rainbow flag (Kurt/Dreamstime.com); Rosie O'Donnell and Kelli Carpenter (AP/Wide World Photos)

Some of the essays in this work originally appeared in *GLBT Life with Full Text*, an online subscription database distributed by EBSCO Publishing.

### Library of Congress Cataloging-in-Publication Data

Great events from history. Gay, lesbian, bisexual, transgender events,
    1848-2006 / editorial board, Lillian Faderman ... [et al.].
      p. cm.
    Includes bibliographical references and index.
    ISBN-13: 978-1-58765-263-9 (set : alk. paper)
    ISBN-13: 978-1-58765-264-6 (v. 1 : alk. paper)
    ISBN-13: 978-1-58765-265-3 (v. 2 : alk. paper)
    ISBN-10: 1-58765-263-3 (set : alk. paper)
    ISBN-10: 1-58765-264-1 (v. 1 : alk. paper)
    ISBN-10: 1-58765-265-X (v. 2 : alk. paper)
    1. Sexual minorities--History. 2. Gays--History. 3. Gay rights--History.
    4. Gay community--History. I. Faderman, Lillian. II. Title: Gay, lesbian, bisexual, transgender events, 1848-2006.

HQ73.G74 2007
306.7609--dc22

        2006028400

First Printing

# CONTENTS

# CONTENTS

# Publisher's Note

*Great Events from History: Gay, Lesbian, Bisexual, Transgender Events, 1848-2006,* chronicles important historical events from around the world that have identified, defined, and legally established the rights of gays, lesbians, bisexuals, and transgender persons. In editorially defining the content of this two-volume set, we adopted the thinking expressed by historian Jonathan Ned Katz in the preface to the revised edition (1992) of his edited collection *Gay American History: Lesbians and Gay Men in the U.S.A.:*

> As the major terms defining our object of study, "homosexual" and "heterosexual," applied to a past society, may obscure the very different ways in which same-sex and different-sex pleasures were organized and constructed under different social conditions. Our modern concepts, applied uncritically to the past, simply project our present social organization of eroticism, procreation, and gender onto that past, distorting our ability to see it as it was to those who lived it. Applied to the past, "homosexuality" and "heterosexuality" may deny the difference of past and present, and may deny us a subtle, sophisticated sense of historical diversity.

Our chronology thus begins in the mid-nineteenth century, when German journalist Karl Maria Kertbeny, an advocate for the repeal of sodomy laws, coined the terms "homosexual" and "heterosexual."

We also have attempted to select events that help to mark the definition of "gender," the emergence of social, cultural, and political movements, and the struggles to gain civil rights. In some cases, one event represents and offers discussion of many. For example, the article on Illinois becoming the first state to abolish its laws against consensual homosexual acts in 1961 also discusses the effect of this action on other states. In particular, essays also include "see also" cross-references to related articles within the set.

Most of the essays published here were originally commissioned by Salem Press for inclusion in *GLBT Life with Full Text,* an online subscription database distributed by EBSCO Publishing. Salem Press retained the rights to publish this material with the addition of newly commissioned materials, primary source documents, and photographs and illustrations as a print reference book.

## Essay Length and Format

This set in gay, lesbian, bisexual, and transgender (GLBT) history joins other titles in Salem Press's *Great Events from History* sets. As in the chronological references to worldwide events in Salem's other history sets, we have approached the discussion of each historical event with a uniform essay format. Each essay, which has an average length of 1,000 words (2-3 pages), prominently displays the following:

- the most precise *date* (or date range) of the event
- the *common name* of the event
- a brief *summary* of the event and its significance
- where appropriate, an *also known as* name for the event or organization
- the *locale*, or where the event occurred
- the *categories*, or the type of event covered, from the Arts to Government and politics, HIV-AIDS, Race and ethnicity, Science, Sports, and Transgender/transsexuality
- the *key figures* of the event, with birth and death dates, where available, and a brief descriptor

The text of each essay is divided into the following sections:

- *Summary of Event:* Describes the event chronologically and includes discussion to place the event in context
- *Significance:* Describes the event's historical impact, influence, and significance
- *Byline:* Name of the contributor who wrote the essay
- *Further Reading:* Sources for further study appropriate and accessible to librarians, students, and the general public; includes some Web sites
- *See also:* Lists related essays within the GLBT set

## Special Features

We have supplemented the essays with more than 135 sidebars that will add to the reader's understanding of the topics discussed. Sidebars include quotations from primary source documents. Seventy-five essays include extracts from primary source documents such as court decisions, mission statements, laws, and important supporting texts. More than 25 essays include biographical profiles of individuals who were key to the event, tables, a filmography, and other critical information that will deepen a reader's knowledge of GLBT history. The two volumes are illustrated with more than 100 photographs and other illustrations, including news photos and photographic portraits, and images of book and magazine covers, book title pages, government documents, and movie posters.

Because the set is ordered chronologically, a Keyword List of Contents appears in the front matter to both volumes and alphabetically lists all essays, permuted by all keywords in the essay's title, to assist in locating events by name. Both volumes also include a List of Sidebars.

The back matter in Volume 2 contains a number of reference tools to help readers further explore GLBT history. The general, annotated *Bibliography*, organized by category, directs readers to accessible sources, mainly books, for further study. The *Electronic Resources* section guides readers to Web sites that aid research in GLBT history and issues. The *Chronological List of Entries* organizes contents chronologically in one place for easy reference. The *Category Index* provides access to the individual essays through the 20 broad areas of interest. The *Personages Index* directs users to events in which a particular individual plays a role. The *Subject Index* provides access to the individual essays and their content through multiple access points.

## THE CONTRIBUTORS

Salem Press extends its appreciation to all who have been involved in the development and production of this work. Special thanks go to the editorial board: Lillian Faderman, Horacio Roque Ramírez, Yolanda Retter, Stuart Timmons, and Eric C. Wat. The essays were written by academic specialists as well as independent scholars, whose expert contributions made this interdisciplinary project possible. A full list of their names and affiliations appears in the front matter of this volume.

# CONTRIBUTORS

Corinne Andersen
*Peace College*

Karen E. Antell
*University of Oklahoma*

Julia Balén
*California State University, Channel Islands*

Shelley Bannister
*Northeastern Illinois University*

Catherine P. Batza
*University of Illinois at Chicago*

Pablo Ben
*University of Chicago*

Alvin K. Benson
*Utah Valley State College*

Amy L. Besnoy
*University of San Diego*

Cynthia A. Bily
*Adrian College*

Jay Blotcher
*Independent Scholar*

Michael J. Bosia
*Northwestern University*

Ellen Bosman
*New Mexico State University Library*

John Boyd
*Appalachian State University*

Christy Burbidge
*Independent Scholar*

Matthew Steven Carlos
*Independent Scholar*

Keith Carson
*Atlantic Cape Community College*

Jamie Patrick Chandler
*City University of New York—Hunter College*

Anne Charles
*University of New Orleans*

Patricia E. Clark
*State University of New York at Oswego*

Bud Coleman
*University of Colorado at Boulder*

Mary L. Cutler
*University of North Dakota*

Lisa Dalton
*New Mexico State University*

tatiana de la tierra
*University at Buffalo*

Gwendolyn Alden Dean
*Cornell University*

M. Casey Diana
*University of Illinois at Urbana-Champaign*

Kathrin Dodds
*Mississippi State University*

L. Mara Dodge
*Westfield State College*

James M. Donovan
*University of Georgia*

Bruce E. Drushel
*Miami University*

Nikolai Endres
*Western Kentucky University*

Raja Farah
*Helem Center*

Emily Ferrara
*University of Massachusetts Medical School*

Charles H. Ford
*Norfolk State University*

Marcia M. Gallo
*Lehman College*

William R. Glass
*Mississippi University for Women*

Charles W. Gossett
*California State Polytechnic University, Pomona*

Mitchell Santine Gould
*LeavesofGrass.org*

Michael E. Graydon
*Carleton University*

Ellen Greenblatt
*University of Colorado at Denver*

Andrew Grossman
*Independent Scholar*

Scot M. Guenter
*San Jose State University*

N. Y. Gulley
*Long Beach City College*

Kim Hackford-Peer
*University of Utah*

Donald P. Haider-Markel
*University of Kansas*

Jan Hall
*National Leather Association: International*

Brian Eugenio Herrera
*Yale University*

Liz Highleyman
*Independent Scholar*

Robert Hill
*University of Georgia*

Lara Hoke
*Massachusetts Interfaith Power & Light*

Ski Hunter
*University of Texas, Arlington*

Melynda Huskey
*Washington State University*

Robin Imhof
*University of the Pacific Library*

Sarah Ivy
*Verge Magazine*

Robert Jacobs
*Central Washington University*

Dawn Elizabeth B. Johnston
*University of Calgary*

Diana Kardia
*Kardia Consulting*

Bassam Kassab
*Massachusetts Institute of Technology*

Hubert Kennedy
*Independent Scholar*

Beth D. Kivel
*California State University, Sacramento*

Nicole LaViolette
*University of Ottawa*

Andrew Lesk
*University of Toronto*

Thomas Tandy Lewis
*St. Cloud State University*

Kathleen Liddle
*University of Toronto*

Malinda Lo
*Independent Scholar*

Dan Luckenbill
*University of California, Los Angeles*

Michael A. Lutes
*University of Notre Dame*

Loralee MacPike
*California State University, San Bernardino*

Mark Miller
*Valley Village, California*

Mitsunori Misawa
*University of Georgia*

Benjamin Munson
*University of Minnesota*

Alice Myers
*Simon's Rock College of Bard*

Daniel-Raymond Nadon
*Kent State University, Trumbull Campus*

Caryn E. Neumann
*Ohio State University, Newark*

Joy Novak
*University of California, Los Angeles*

Daniel J. Nugent
*Yale University*

David W. Pantalone
*University of Washington*

Matthew Parfitt
*Boston University*

Pauline Park
*New York Association for Gender Rights Advocacy*

Blaise Astra Parker
*University of Georgia*

William A. Peniston
*The Newark Museum*

Robert F. Phillips
*University of California, Irvine*

Mark Pope
*University of Missouri—St. Louis*

Jessie Bishop Powell
*Independent Scholar*

Nicole C. Raeburn
*University of San Francisco*

Horacio N. Roque Ramírez
*University of California, Santa Barbara*

Yolanda Retter
*University of California, Los Angeles*

Robert Ridinger
*Northern Illinois University*

Jenn Rosen
*Service Employees International Union*

Sandra Rothenberg
*Framingham State College*

Glenda M. Russell
*New Leaf: Services for Our Community Institute for Gay and Lesbian Strategic Studies*

Michael Ryan
*University of Maryland*

Sam See
*University of California, Los Angeles*

Jennifer Self
*University of Washington*

Ashley T. Shelden
*Tufts University*

Leah Sheppard
*Vanderbilt University*

R. Baird Shuman
*University of Illinois at Urbana-Champaign*

Jennifer A. Smith
*Western Michigan University*

Liberty Smith
*Independent Scholar*

Tom Smith
*New Mexico State University*

Glenn Ellen Starr Stilling
*Appalachian State University*

Amy Stone
*University of Michigan*

Mary F. Stuck
*State University New York at Oswego*

K. Surkan
*Massachusetts Institute of Technology*

Ira Tattelman
*Independent Scholar*

J. T. Todd
*Drew University*

Daniel C. Tsang
*University of California, Irvine*

Ruth Vanita
*University of Montana*

Mary Ware
*State University of New York, College at Cortland*

Patricia Nell Warren
*Wildcat Press*

David W. Webber
*AIDS & Public Policy Journal*

Meredith L. Weiss
*DePaul University*

Stephen Paul Whitaker
*Emory University*

Susan J. Wurtzburg
*University of Utah*

# KEYWORD LIST OF CONTENTS

# LIST OF SIDEBARS

## July 19-20, 1848
# SENECA FALLS WOMEN'S RIGHTS CONVENTION

*The history of the Seneca Falls Convention, the first national conference for women's rights in the United States, is not complete without acknowledging the critical work of lesbian organizers and leaders.*

**LOCALE:** Seneca Falls, New York
**CATEGORIES:** Feminism; organizations and institutions; cultural and intellectual history; publications

### KEY FIGURES
*Lucretia Mott* (1793-1880),
*Elizabeth Cady Stanton* (1815-1902),
*Jane C. Hunt*,
*Mary Ann McClintock*, and
*Martha C. Wright*, convention organizers and leaders
*Frederick Douglass* (1817?-1895), editor of the Rochester *North Star*

### SUMMARY OF EVENT
The Seneca Falls Convention of 1848 is considered by most historians to be the birth of the organized women's rights movement in the United States and also of first-wave feminism. The convention was conceived on July 13, 1848, when Lucretia Mott visited her sister, Martha C. Wright, in Waterloo, New York. The sisters had held a gathering with Jane C. Hunt, Mary Ann McClintock, and Elizabeth Cady Stanton from nearby Seneca Falls. The women, with the exception of Stanton, all embraced Quakerism, a Christian religious denomination that permitted a degree of sexual equality within its meetings and affirmed the spark of the divine in all persons regardless of gender. Mott was a recognized minister in the Society of Friends. All of the women were familiar with antislavery efforts, temperance meetings, and other liberal reform movements.

The women resolved to declare their equality and enumerate women's grievances with men at a convention planned for July 19-20, 1848. Stanton was assigned the task of drafting a document, the Declaration of Sentiments and Resolutions, to be debated, discussed, and ratified by the convention delegates. Stanton modeled the Sentiments on the Declaration of Independence, and its structure and diction parallel Thomas Jefferson's 1776 text. In the Sentiments, Stanton declares "the causes that impel" her and four Quaker women to launch the long struggle for women's rights. Stanton also spells out a list of women's grievances concerning the "absolute tyranny" of men over women. The number of "injuries and usurpations" noted in the document—eighteen in total—is equal to the number of grievances presented to King George III of England in the Declaration of Independence.

Stanton concluded the Sentiments with a list of eleven resolutions to be considered by the convention delegates. The most controversial resolution was the ninth, a call for women "to secure to themselves their sacred right to the elective franchise." The delegates unanimously approved ten of Stanton's eleven resolutions in addition to a twelfth introduced by Mott on the floor of the convention. The only resolution to pass without unanimity was the resolution supporting women's right to vote. Sixty-eight women and thirty-two men signed the Sentiments. The full text of the document, and a list of its one hundred signatories, was printed in the July 28, 1848, edition of the Rochester *North Star*, edited by abolitionist Frederick Douglass, who attended the convention and argued in favor of voting rights for women.

### SIGNIFICANCE
The Seneca Falls Convention of 1848 and its Declaration of Sentiments represent the weaving together of several strands of U.S. history and culture, including the struggle for political rights and suffrage, demands for economic and social equality, feminism, and gender differences, reflecting larger trends in Western civilization as a whole. The convention marked the challenges faced by abolition-

*A contemporary illustration of seven women who attended the Seneca Falls Convention in 1848.* (Library of Congress)

ists, feminists, suffragists, and other progressives as they pressed forward with their various reform agendas. Seneca Falls also had underscored conflicts between the ideals expressed in revolutionary documents and the realities of political organization in the nineteenth century.

Seneca Falls was the culmination of many cultural and social forces that had been gathering since the birth of the republic. Much of the idealism of its leaders—women such as Elizabeth Cady Stanton, who looked at Jefferson's work for guidance in penning the Sentiments—was inspired by the nation's founding premise that all human beings are created equal.

The democratic idealism and natural rights ex-

pressed in the Declaration of Independence had been to early America what the Declaration of the Rights of Man and of the Citizen (1789) had been to Europe. Just as the United States struggled to accommodate, compromise, and contain abolition, sexuality, slavery, suffrage, temperance movements, and worker unions, so too did Europe.

Already in an economic downturn in 1848, Europe had been rocked by a series of revolutions. Unrest erupted in Austria, Bavaria, Berlin, Frankfurt, Hungary, Milan, Naples, Piedmont, the Rhineland, Rome, Saxony, Sicily, and Venice. Calls for constitutional rights, universal suffrage, and national unification reverberated in the revolutionary fervor.

The early women's rights movement, the first wave of feminism, set against this dramatic backdrop of nationalism and revolution in the Western world, was preoccupied with the question of political rights, or women's suffrage. Seneca Falls, despite negative media portrayals of a republic of petticoats, was the impetus that launched organized efforts to secure the right to vote for women; it was a right that would not be secured in the United States until nearly three-quarters of a century later with the passage of the Nineteenth Amendment to the United States Constitution in 1920. More broadly, the convention awakened among some middle-class, liberal reformers, a wide array of concerns that women struggled with in the nineteenth century and, in many ways, still struggle with. These concerns ranged from equal rights and fair labor practices to the ordination of women and to family-life issues.

By 1920, the women's movement launched by the convention of 1848 had morphed into second-wave feminism, especially the struggle for cultural legitimacy and socioeconomic equality. Among the issues that have divided feminists are differences surrounding socioeconomic status and sexuality, particularly lesbian sexuality. Some scholars have questioned the sexual orientation of the leaders of the Seneca Falls Convention, including that of Lucretia Mott. However, the role played by sexual orientation in the lives of historical figures continues to be a topic of heated scholarly debate. It is difficult to imagine how the sexuality of reformers and other leaders of the convention would have no impact on their work in the same way that it is impossible to understand the significance of James Baldwin's fiction without considering the complex nature of his literary, racial, and sexual inheritances. Nevertheless, many traditionalists in academia continue to obstruct scholarship on the impact, meaning, and significance of human sexuality on the lives and work of women such as Jane Hunt, Mary Ann McClintock, Lucretia Mott, Elizabeth Cady Stanton, and Martha Coffin Wright, who were pivotal in the development, growth, and evolution of universal human rights.

—*Keith Carson*

## FURTHER READING

Ginzberg, Lori D. *Untidy Origins: A Story of Women's Rights in Antebellum New York*. Chapel Hill: University of North Carolina Press, 2006.

Gurko, Miriam. *Ladies of Seneca Falls*. Studies in the Life of Women. New York: Pantheon, 1987.

Library of Congress. Seneca Falls Convention Exhibit. American Treasures of the Library of Congress. http://www.loc.gov/exhibits/treasures/trr040.html.

Welman, Judith. *The Road to Seneca Falls: Elizabeth Cady Stanton and the First Women's Rights Convention*. Urbana: University of Illinois Press, 2004.

SEE ALSO: May 1, 1970: Lavender Menace Protests Homophobia in Women's Movement; Mar. 22, 1972-June 30, 1982: Equal Rights Amendment Fails State Ratification; Nov. 7, 1972: Jordan Becomes First Black Congresswoman from the South; Jan. 22, 1973: *Roe v. Wade* Legalizes Abortion and Extends Privacy Rights; Nov. 18-21, 1977: National Women's Conference Convenes.

## July 4, 1855
# WHITMAN PUBLISHES *LEAVES OF GRASS*

*In his classic book-length poem* Leaves of Grass, *Walt Whitman established a masculine gay identity, portraying "manly love" as an expression of God's love.*

**LOCALE:** New York, New York
**CATEGORIES:** Literature; publications

## KEY FIGURES

*Walt Whitman* (1819-1892), American poet
*Elias Hicks* (1748-1830), American Quaker theologian
*Rufus W. Griswold* (1815-1857), American journalist
*Charles Fourier* (1772-1837), French social theorist and socialist
*Edward Carpenter* (1844-1929), English writer, gay rights leader, and socialist
*Horace L. Traubel* (1858-1919), American author, socialist, and Whitman's literary executor

## SUMMARY OF EVENT

Walt Whitman's *Leaves of Grass*, published in July of 1855, is a collection of sprawling poems that offers a fully masculine gay voice, a sexual celebration transcending any single orientation, interrupted narratives that engage the reader in an affectionate conversation, and reassurance that "manly love" is

## "I SING THE BODY ELECTRIC"

O my body! I dare not desert the likes of you in other men and women, nor the likes of the parts of you, I
believe the likes of you are to stand or fall with the likes of the soul, (and that they are the soul,) I believe the
likes of you shall stand or fall with my poems, and that they are my poems, . . .
The voice, articulation, language, whispering, shouting aloud,
Food, drink, pulse, digestion, sweat, sleep, walking, swimming,
Poise on the hips, leaping, reclining, embracing, arm-curving and tightening,
The continual changes of the flex of the mouth, and around the eyes,
The skin, the sunburnt shade, freckles, hair,
The curious sympathy one feels when feeling with the hand the naked meat of the body,
The circling rivers the breath, and breathing it in and out,
The beauty of the waist, and thence of the hips, and thence downward toward the knees,
The thin red jellies within you or within me, the bones and the marrow in the bones,
The exquisite realization of health;
O I say these are not the parts and poems of the body only, but of the soul,
O I say now these are the soul!

God's love. In October of 1855, *The New York Times* exposed the Progressive Union, a secret "free love" society. Its officers included Whitman's close friend and ally Henry Clapp. The Progressive Union taught that sexual impulses could be entrusted to the guidance of "God within"—a cornerstone of Quaker theology also known as "the inner light."

One month later, Rufus W. Griswold published an important review of *Leaves of Grass*. He compared the book to the spectacle of sex radicals emerging "out from behind the screen" (as Whitman later put it). "Unless we admit this exhibition to be beautiful," fumed Griswold, "we are at once set down for non-progressive conservatives, destitute of the 'inner light.'"

It is possible that Whitman had been inspired to write *Leaves of Grass* after reading the work of French socialist Charles Fourier, who wrote, "the Law of Attraction rules the universe, from the blade of grass, from the insect, to the stars revolving in their appointed orbits." Whitman's epic "Song of Myself," in *Leaves of Grass*, had translated Fourier's notion of attraction into maritime language. Whitman wrote, "A kelson [or keel] of the creation is love." *Leaves of Grass* is replete with references to ships and sailors, and, according to American historian Jonathan Ned Katz, the long voyages of sailing ships normalized male sexual encounters.

Like Fourier, Whitman constantly extolled the power of personal attraction. In "States!" he suggested that male-male "adhesiveness" could bind the nation like "hoops of iron."

Whitman employed the word "grass" in a third way, equally important to "Song of Myself," and offered it as a symbol of the immortal soul. He wrote, "[I]t seems to me the beautiful uncut hair of graves . . . the smallest sprout shows there is really no death." This poem was tailored to appeal to spiritualist reformers; in fact, Whitman tried to become a medium himself but failed to contact the spirits of the dead. Shortly after the appearance of *Leaves of Grass*, a satire called *Lucy Boston* harshly ridiculed spiritualism's attraction for gay males.

Ultimately, Whitman symbolized "grass" in a fourth way. After gathering the opinions of his readers, he revised and expanded *Leaves of Grass*. Comparing himself to Jesus in the garden, sweating drops of blood ("Trickle Drops"), he decided to "unbare" his "broad breast" ("Scented Herbage of My Breast") and include even more dangerous poems. Originally, in "Song of Myself" he likened the phallus to a "sweet flag." With the third edition of *Leaves of Grass* (1860), he expanded this metaphor into the "Calamus" poems "of comrades and of love." Calamus is an aromatic grass that bears a phallic cone.

Whitman skillfully used a literary sort of sleight of hand. He crosscut sexual situations with one or more literary metaphors (fire, leaves, electricity, and so on). He identified his loving bedfellow as his own "soul" or even as God. This erotic impressionism proved equally suggestive to the English gay rights leader Edward Carpenter and even to former U.S. president William Jefferson Clinton, who both were inspired by the work. Such a reach among sexualities has enabled Whitman's book and his reputation to survive periodic skirmishes with censorship for more than 150 years.

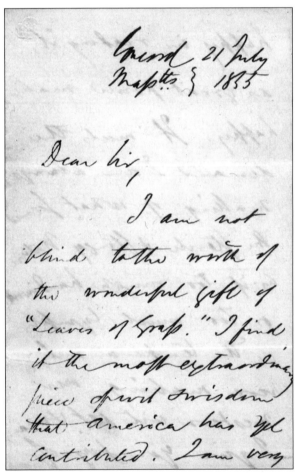

Ralph Waldo Emerson, in a letter to Whitman dated July 21, 1855, writes, upon reading Leaves of Grass, "Dear Sir, I am not blind to the worth of the wonderful gift of 'Leaves of Grass.' I find it the most extraordinary piece of wit + wisdom that America has yet contributed. (Library of Congress)

*Walt Whitman.* (Library of Congress)

## SIGNIFICANCE

Until his death in 1892, Whitman frequently expanded and expurgated his poems. By this time, he had established a liberating masculine alternative for gay men. "No dainty dolce affettuoso I," yawped Whitman, in "Starting from Paumanok," "Bearded, sun-burnt, gray-neck'd, forbidding, I have arrived, to be wrestled with as I pass. . . ." This muscular, working-man construct lay at the heart of Whitman's success. Oscar Wilde, however, resurrected the jaded playboy stereotype during the 1890's, nearly canceling the "revolution" by playing into the hands of evangelical opportunists.

Edward Carpenter, who twice visited Whitman's home in Camden, New Jersey, seems to have received Whitman's spiritual torch. Resorting to anthropological and sexological arguments, Carpenter tried to propagate Whitman's message against a swelling tide of "homosexualist" cures by Freudian opportunists. However, the great refuge for comrades and love—isolated sailing ships—had been swept away by the use of steam. Prior to World War I, Whitman and Carpenter were both regarded as religious leaders by some parts of the gay community.

In the United States, Whitman's legacy passed largely to socialist Horace Traubel, but Traubel's anarchist politics threatened the legacy's credibility. One respected author, however, may have been more successful than either Carpenter or Traubel in legitimizing *Leaves of Grass* among intellectuals: William James. In his *Varieties of Religious Experience* (1902), James praised Whitman's "religion of healthy-mindedness."

During the 1960's Stonewall era, the individual who best harnessed Whitman's legacy to the cause of gay rights was Jack Nichols of the Washington Mattachine Society. As a leading activist and journalist, he brought Whitman's ideas to life for an entire generation coming "out from the dark confinement." Before Whitman, it may have seemed that the whole world agreed that "manly love" could lead only to Hell. *Leaves of Grass* asserted that it leads to God.

—*Mitchell Santine Gould*

## FURTHER READING

Brock, William Hall. "The 'Insanity' of American Fourierism." Chapter 2 of Brock's *Phalanx on a Hill: Responses to Fourierism in the Transcendentalist Circle.* http://www.billbrock.net/fch00.

Brown, Tony, ed. *Edward Carpenter and Late Victorian Radicalism.* London: Frank Cass, 1990.

Erkkila, Betsy, and Jay Grossman, eds. *Breaking Bounds: Whitman and American Cultural Studies.* New York: Oxford University Press, 1996.

Katz, Jonathan Ned, ed. *Gay/Lesbian Almanac: A New Documentary.* New York: Harper & Row, 1983.

Maslan, Mark. *Whitman Possessed: Poetry, Sexuality, and Popular Authority.* Baltimore: Johns Hopkins University Press, 2001.

Pollak, Vivian R. *The Erotic Whitman.* Berkeley: University of California Press, 2000.

Schmidgall, Gary. *Walt Whitman: A Gay Life.* New York: Dutton, 1997.

SEE ALSO: May 25, 1895: Oscar Wilde Is Convicted of Gross Indecency; 1924: Gide Publishes the Signed Edition of *Corydon*; 1939: Isherwood Publishes *Goodbye to Berlin*; 1947-1948: Golden Age of American Gay Literature; 1956: Baldwin Publishes *Giovanni's Room*; 1963: Rechy Publishes *City of Night*; June, 1971: The Gay Book Award Debuts; 1974: *The Front Runner* Makes *The New York Times* Best-Seller List; 1975: First Novel About Coming Out to Parents Is Published; 1980-1981: Gay Writers Form the Violet Quill; May, 1987: *Lambda Rising Book Report* Begins Publication; June 2, 1989: Lambda Literary Award Is Created; 1993: Monette Wins the National Book Award for *Becoming a Man*.

## November 11, 1865
# MARY EDWARDS WALKER IS AWARDED THE MEDAL OF HONOR

*Cross-dressing physician, Civil War hero, feminist, and social reformer Mary Edwards Walker is the only woman to have received the Medal of Honor, the United States's highest military award. She was also the first female doctor of the Army Medical Corps.*

**LOCALE:** Washington, D.C.

**CATEGORIES:** Military; transgender/ transsexuality; feminism; organizations and institutions; health and medicine

**KEY FIGURES**

*Mary Edwards Walker* (1832-1919), American physician, dress reformer, suffragist, Civil War contract surgeon, and prisoner of war

*Andrew Johnson* (1808-1875), U.S. president, 1865-1869

**SUMMARY OF EVENT**

Born in Oswego, New York, in 1832, Mary Edwards Walker was raised in a progressive family that espoused radical feminist views for the time, including those of dress reform and education for women. Encouraged by her parents to seek a profession, Walker attended Syracuse Medical School and graduated in 1855, the only woman in her class. Shortly thereafter, she married fellow classmate Albert Miller, in a ceremony considered unusual for the time because Walker omitted the word "obey" from her wedding vows. She also refused to take her husband's name. The couple set up practice in Rome, New York, but the community did not easily accept a woman as a physician, especially one that dressed in nontraditional attire, and the couple eventually divorced.

When the American Civil War began, Walker moved to Washington to offer her services to the Union Army in the hopes of securing a commission as a medical officer. Unsuccessful, she served as an unpaid volunteer at Indiana Hospital (an improvised infirmary located in the Patent Office building) and helped organize the Woman's Relief Association. Walker persisted in petitioning for a commission, and in September, 1863, she was appointed as a contract assistant surgeon to the 52nd Ohio Infantry, then fighting in Tennessee. She treated civilians as well as soldiers, and during one of her visits away from the Army camp, she was captured by the Con-

*Mary Edwards Walker.* (National Institutes of Health)

## Andrew Johnson's Presentation Speech

Whereas it appears from official reports that Dr. Mary E. Walker, a graduate of medicine, "has rendered valuable service to the Government and her efforts have been earnest and untiring in a variety of ways," and that she was assigned to duty and served as an assistant surgeon in charge of female prisoners at Louisville, Ky., upon the recommendation of Major Generals Sherman and Thomas, and faithfully served as contract surgeon in the service of the United States, and has devoted herself with much patriotic zeal to the sick and wounded soldiers, both in the field and hospitals, to the detriment of her own health, and has also endured hardships as a prisoner of war four months in a Southern prison while acting as contract surgeon; and

Whereas by reason of her not being a commissioned officer in the military service, a brevet or honorary rank cannot, under existing laws, be conferred upon her; and

Whereas in the opinion of the President an honorable recognition of her services and sufferings should be made:

It is ordered, That a testimonial thereof shall be hereby made and given to the said Dr. Mary E. Walker, and that the usual medal of honor for meritorious services be given her.

Given under my [President Andrew Johnson] hand in the city of Washington, D.C., this 11th day of November, A.D. 1865.

federates and sent to Castle Thunder, a prison in Richmond, Virginia. She was released in a prisoner-of-war exchange on August 12, 1864, after four months in wretched conditions that ostensibly affected her eyesight for the rest of her life. Walker continued in government service through the end of the war, serving as the Surgeon in Charge of the Louisville Female Military Prison in Kentucky and later at an orphanage in Clarksville, Tennessee.

On November 11, 1865, President Andrew Johnson signed a citation awarding Walker the Congressional Medal of Honor in recognition of her service to the Union during the Civil War; she received the award a few months later, on January 24, 1866. When the medal was redesigned in 1907, she received an additional medal. However, in 1917, Congress revised the award criteria to include service that was meritorious only in a combat situation with an enemy, and then appointed a board to review all previously awarded medals. The board rescinded Walker's medal along with the medals of more than nine hundred others. Walker refused to relinquish either medal and proudly wore at least

one each day for the rest of her life. On June 10, 1977, the Department of the Army announced it would reinstate Walker's medal, attributing the earlier repeal to sex discrimination. President Jimmy Carter restored the medal the following day.

After the war, Walker turned her energies to various reform movements, including those relating to temperance and woman suffrage. However, she is perhaps best known for her lifelong efforts to encourage dress reform. She believed that contemporary women's clothing, consisting of constrictive corsets and heavy hoop skirts, was detrimental to women's health. She put her principles into action, and her style of dress evolved over time to become increasingly masculine.

During the Civil War, she dressed in a military-like uniform consisting of a tunic with a green surgeon's sash worn over gold-striped trousers, and after the war she appeared in public in black pants, a starched white shirt, a black frock coat, and a top hat. In the decades between the Civil War and her death shortly after World War I, Walker was arrested several times for dressing in men's clothing (or for disturbing the peace, based on public reaction to her appearance).

Although a popular lecturer in the years immediately following the Civil War—likely as much for the notoriety stemming from her war exploits and her uncommon mode of dress as for the content of her speeches—as time passed, people viewed Walker less as a hero and more as an eccentric, and her speaking venues changed from lecture halls to sideshows and dime museums. Walker died in relative obscurity at her home in Oswego at the age of eighty-six.

### Significance

Mary Edwards Walker's contributions have been

formally recognized through the issue in 1982 of a twenty-cent postage stamp commemorating her as an Army surgeon and a Medal of Honor recipient. One wonders what Walker would have made of this particular honor, though, because the stamp shows her in the "proper" feminine attire of Victorian women of the time, with no hint of her preference for masculine attire. In 1997, the Women in Military Service to America Memorial at Arlington National Cemetery in Virginia paid homage to Walker's military service in its Hall of Honor, featuring a photograph of her with her Medal of Honor proudly displayed on her typical frock coat.

Defying the conventions of her time, Walker's contributions paved the way for following generations of women to enter professions such as military service and medicine. Her unwavering dedication to dress reform liberated many women from the confining costume of the day, and inspired them to pursue more masculine occupations with confidence and without hindrance.

*—Ellen Greenblatt*

**FURTHER READING**

Katz, Jonathan Ned. "1902: Drs. Robert Shufeldt, Mary Walker, and Others; Dr. Mary Walker: 'The Most Distinguished Sexual Invert in the United States.'" *Gay American History: Lesbians and Gay Men in the U.S.A.* New York: Thomas Y. Crowell, 1976.

Leonard, Elizabeth D. "'A Thing That Nothing but the Depraved Yankee Nation Could Produce': Mary Walker, M.D., and the Limits of Tolerance." *Yankee Women: Gender Battles in the Civil War.* New York: W. W. Norton, 1994.

"Medal of Honor Is Restored to Civil War Woman Doctor." *Washington Post,* June 11, 1977, p. A3.

Spiegel, Allen D., and Peter B. Suskind. "Mary Edwards Walker, M.D.: A Feminist Physician a Century Ahead of Her Time." *Journal of Community Health* 21, no. 3 (June, 1996): 211-235.

Williams, Rudi. "Only Woman Medal of Honor Holder Ahead of Her Time." 1999. U.S. Department of Defense News Archive and Armed Forces Information Service. http://www.defenselink.mil/news/Apr1999/.

**SEE ALSO:** 1912-1924: Robles Fights in the Mexican Revolution.

## August 29, 1867
# KARL HEINRICH ULRICHS SPEAKS PUBLICLY FOR GAY AND LESBIAN RIGHTS

*Judge Karl Heinrich Ulrichs publicly proclaimed his homosexual orientation and spoke in favor of legal and civil rights for gays, marking perhaps the first time anyone had called for gay rights publicly in modern Europe.*

**LOCALE:** Munich, Germany

**CATEGORIES:** Laws, acts, and legal history; literature; organizations and institutions; health and medicine

**KEY FIGURE**

*Karl Heinrich Ulrichs* (1825-1895), German judge and freelance journalist

**SUMMARY OF EVENT**

Most of the German states and Austria had laws in 1867 against homosexuality, and the few that did not have these laws offered no formal recognition of gay rights. Karl Heinrich Ulrichs, a native of Hanover (which had no law against homosexuality), had been forced to resign his position as a civil servant and judge in 1854 after his sexuality became known to local authorities. He remained a member of the Congress of German Jurists, however, and hoped to use its podium to plead for legal changes.

Ulrichs was permitted to speak at the plenary session of some five hundred members at the Sixth Congress of German Jurists in Munich on August

*A contemporary illustration of Karl Heinrich Ulrichs.*

29, 1867, but was shouted down and not allowed to finish his speech on gay rights. The congress would not listen to his arguments. A short time later, Ulrichs published his speech in the sixth booklet of what eventually became twelve booklets: *Forschungen über das Räthsel der mannmännlichen Liebe* (1864-1879; *The Riddle of "Man-Manly" Love*, 1994).

Although Ulrichs's first five booklets were published under a pseudonym (Numa Numantius), his later booklets, which were published after his speech before the congress, contained his real name. Thus, his 1867 speech marked the first time that an out gay person publicly spoke for gay legal and civil rights. This was not the only first for Ulrichs, however. In his first five booklets of 1864-1865, he formulated the first scientific theory of homosexuality, arguing that a gay man has a male body and a female psyche (and that a lesbian woman has a female body and a male psyche).

Ulrichs's courageous act in Munich,

passed over in silence at the time, became a rallying point for later generations of gays and lesbians in Germany. In 1998, a square in Munich was dedicated to Ulrichs and named Karl-Heinrich-Ulrichs-Platz; a plaque in the square contains the following words:

> By publicly speaking up for the empire-wide legal freedom of same-sex relations at the Congress of German Jurists in 1867 in Munich he fundamentally contributed to the legal and civil equality of homosexuals.

### Significance

Ulrichs's actions had no direct effect on the various laws against homosexuality of his time, despite his continued efforts. Indeed, with the formation of the new German Empire in 1871, harsh Prussian law was extended to all of Germany. Ulrichs, however, was the inspiration for a new generation of activists who, under the leadership of sexologist Magnus Hirschfeld (1868-1935) in Berlin, formed in 1897 the first organization for gay liberation, the Wissenschaftlich-humanitäre Komitee (Scientific-Humanitarian Committee). Furthermore, in a new edition of Ulrichs's writings in 1898, Hirschfeld called him "the first and noblest of those who have striven with courage and strength in this field to

---

### URNING NATURE

The oppressed and abused recognize no right of oppression by naked force, nor a right of abuse. Therefore our position is everywhere on the side of the oppressed and abused, whether he is called Pole, Hanoverian, Jew, Catholic, or is an innocent creature who is "disreputable" to people for being so immoral as to be born outside of wedlock, just as we were so immoral as to be born with an Urning [homosexual] nature, or who is a poor "fallen woman," whom the highly moral barbarism of the nineteenth century drives to acts of despair, child murder, abortion, or even to suicide. We who know what it means to be oppressed and martyred, we can from the heart take the side of those whom we see in a similar position.

*Source:* Karl Heinrich Ulrichs, from *Prometheus*, 1870.
Translated by Michael A. Lombardi-Nash.

help truth and charity gain their rightful place."

The theoretical writings of Ulrichs on homosexuality, in particular his third-sex theory, directly influenced the discussion of homosexuality by the doctors and psychiatrists of the nineteenth century, who quickly acted to assume control of what was called the "treatment" of homosexuals. The term "third sex" has been a staple of the scientific and popular literature for more than one century, despite the literature's essential refutation.

What makes Ulrichs so outstanding and memorable is not only his action in Munich and his other efforts for gay liberation but also his anticipating later civil rights movements, including the abolition of the death penalty, national and religious tolerance, and women's rights. Also, Ulrichs coined the terms *uranismus*, derived from Urania, the Greek goddess of love Aphrodite; *urning*, to describe gay men; and *urninds*, to describe lesbians. "Homosexual" was coined earlier by German journalist and translator Karl Maria Kertbeny (1824-1882) in 1869, in an anonymously published pamphlet, and was never used by Ulrichs.

Ulrichs believed that the nature of the urning was inborn, so that every individual must follow his or her own nature and should be judged accordingly. Love between men is a riddle of nature, Ulrichs believed, but he insisted that the riddle be solved by science and not "by blindly striking with the so-called sword of justice, which already all too often with regard to heretics, Jews, and witches has shown itself to be a sword of injustice."

—*Hubert Kennedy*

## FURTHER READING

Kennedy, Hubert. *Karl Heinrich Ulrichs: Leben und Werk*. 2d ed. Hamburg, Germany: MännerschwarmSkript Verlag, 2001.

_____. *Ulrichs: The Life and Works of Karl Heinrich Ulrichs, Pioneer of the Modern Gay Movement*. Boston: Alyson, 1988. Revised edition (2002) available at http://home.pacbell.net/hubertk/.

Ulrichs, Karl Heinrich. *Forschungen über das Räthsel der mannmännlichen Liebe*. Edited by Hubert Kennedy. 4 vols. Berlin: Verlag rosa Winkel, 1994.

_____. *The Riddle of "Man-Manly" Love: The Pioneering Work on Male Homosexuality*. Translated by Michael A. Lombardi-Nash. 2 vols. Buffalo, N.Y.: Prometheus Books, 1994.

SEE ALSO: May 6, 1868: Kertbeny Coins the Terms "Homosexual" and "Heterosexual"; 1869: Westphal Advocates Medical Treatment for Sexual Inversion; 1896: *Der Eigene* Is Published as First Journal on Homosexuality; 1896: Raffalovich Publishes *Uranisme et Unisexualité*; 1897: Ellis Publishes *Sexual Inversion*; May 14, 1897: Hirschfeld Founds the Scientific-Humanitarian Committee; 1906: Friedlaender Breaks with the Scientific-Humanitarian Committee; 1908: Carpenter Publishes *The Intermediate Sex*; Dec. 10, 1924: Gerber Founds the Society for Human Rights; 1933-1945: Nazis Persecute Homosexuals; 1950: Mattachine Society Is Founded.

May 6, 1868

# Kertbeny Coins the Terms "Homosexual" and "Heterosexual"

*Karl Maria Kertbeny, working against antisodomy law in Germany, coined the terms "homosexual" and "heterosexual," first in a letter to a friend and then in pamphlets arguing for repeal of the law. The clinical-sounding term "homosexual," which also has a negative connotation, has evolved over the years and has, for the most part, been replaced by the more affirming terms "lesbian," "gay," "bisexual," and, for some, "queer."*

**Locale:** Berlin, Germany

**Categories:** Cultural and intellectual history; laws, acts, and legal history; publications

## Key Figures

*Karl Maria Kertbeny* (1824-1882), German advocate for the repeal of antisodomy law

*Richard von Krafft-Ebing* (1840-1902), German psychiatrist and sexologist

## Summary of Event

Karl Maria Kertbeny was born in Vienna in 1824 as Karl Maria Benkert. His family later moved to Budapest, Hungary. Kertbeny began a vocation as a bookseller but later decided to become a writer. He changed his name from the German "Benkert" to the Hungarian "Kertbeny" in 1847, the name used for his writings.

A pivotal event in Kertbeny's life was the suicide of a friend who had been blackmailed because of his "abnormal tastes." His friend's death inspired him to take up issues of injustice against homosexual men. After traveling widely between 1846 and 1868, he settled in Berlin. In 1869, he published anonymously a pamphlet titled "Paragraph 143 of the Prussian Penal Code of 14 April, 1851 and Its Reaffirmation as Paragraph 152 in the Proposed Penal Code for the North German Confederation." A second anonymous pamphlet on the same topic

followed quickly in the same year.

Paragraph 143 was the Prussian antisodomy law, which made sexual contact between members of the same gender punishable with one to four years in prison. After William I, king of Prussia, was made emperor of Germany on January 18, 1871, the German kingdoms were united into the federal state that is now known as Germany. In April of the same year, the new German Empire created a constitution and penal code that was based on the Prussian model and included Paragraph 143. The only thing that changed about Paragraph 143 was its name: Paragraph 143 came to be called Paragraph 175, the same law used by the Nazis some sixty years later to justify rounding up and incarcerating homosexuals in concentration camps. While in the camps, they were forced to wear pink triangles on their clothing to indicate they were homosexual, much as the Jews had to wear the Star of David to identify them as Jewish. In reference to the penal code, homosexual prisoners were referred to as the 175ers.

In his pamphlets, Kertbeny advocated the repeal of the sodomy law, arguing that the state had no right to intervene in the private life of any citizen. He claimed that Paragraph 143 violated "the rights of man" as formulated in documents of the French Revolution. He proposed the alternate model based on the liberal French criminal code of 1791, which decriminalized homosexual acts. He felt that men had the right to do what they wanted with their bodies as long as no one was hurt in the process. He also claimed that all sexual propensities were inborn and that if men who had sex with other men acted out of natural tendencies, they could not be moral failures. He believed that his friend's death by suicide came about because of Paragraph 143. In effect, Paragraph 143 made it easy for blackmailers to extort money from homosexuals. In addition, many men who had sex with other men were imprisoned. If the sodomy laws were removed, incarceration and

*Karl Maria Kertbeny, c. 1850.*

blackmail would end. He demanded freedom from penal sanctions for homosexual men in Prussia and the Prussian-dominated North German Confederation. Paragraph 143, now 175, however, remained on the German law books until 1969.

Kertbeny first used the term "homosexuality," or, more precisely, Homosexualisten in German, in a private letter dated May 6, 1868, to Karl Heinrich Ulrichs, a pioneering German sexologist, and again in the two pamphlets in 1869. He used it in place of Ulrichs's term, *urning*, and variations thereof, from the name Urania, the Greek goddess of love, to describe homosexual men. He derived Homosexualisten from the Greek *homos* (the same) and the Latin root *sexualis* (sex or sexual). Homosexualisten was not used again until 1880, in a text written by Kertbeny that was published in a popular-science book by Gustav Jäger called *Discovery of the Soul*. Also in the same volume, the term Heterosexualitat (heterosexuality) first appeared. The use of the term increased after its inclusion in the 1880

book, and near the end of the nineteenth century, both terms moved from German to other European languages.

Richard von Krafft-Ebing, one of the most significant medical writers on sex and sexuality of the last part of the nineteenth century, also adopted and popularized the term "homosexuality." He used the word in the second edition of his *Psychopathia sexualis*, a study on "deviant" sexual practices published in 1887. The word was used by Albert Moll in his work, *Contrary Sexual Feeling*, published in 1891. Havelock Ellis and Magnus Hirschfeld also adopted and popularized this term. In 1900, an excised chapter on homosexuality by Kertbeny appeared in Hirschfeld's journal, *Jahrbuch für sexuelle Zwischenstufen* (yearbook of intermediate sexual stages), which began publishing in 1899.

Kertbeny intended the term "homosexuality" to be used as a neutral, nonprejudicial word within legal arguments centered on the concept of equal rights and the protection of minorities. It gradually replaced other terms for same-sex/same-gender desire, such as "sodomite" or "degenerate" and with words that associated homosexuality with sin, depravity, vice, pathology, and crime.

Kertbeny spent so many years campaigning against the German law code that penalized sex between men, that many believed that he, too, was homosexual, but he denied this. He returned to Budapest in 1875 and died in 1882. His writings are available only in German, although excerpts are frequently translated.

### SIGNIFICANCE

The term Homosexualisten (homosexual) was not the only word created to reflect positively on same-gender desire, but it opened the door to the development of other positive and descriptive words. For example, "homophile" and "homophilia" came to be used in a positive way. Coming from the Greek, these terms mean "loving the same." Homophilia is the emotional component of same-gender love that also de-emphasizes the sexual or clinical aspect suggested by the word "homosexuality," but the term still covers both sexual and nonsexual relationships.

The term "homophile" was adopted by the post-

*Richard and Marie Luise von Krafft-Ebing.*

the term "homosexual" that identified them with sin or sickness and began to identify with a social status (gay). Although the term "homosexual" reigned for more than a century, the term "gay" began to overtake it, and by the 1980's it was a standard term used in the gay and lesbian community. Eventually, the media began to replace "homosexual" with "gay" in news reports. Many women, however, rejected "gay" during the women's movement in the 1970's and began to use the term "lesbian." "Gay" most often implies "gay men," to the exclusion of lesbians, much like the terms "man" or "mankind" brings to mind a man or men, to the exclusion of women. Lesbians wanted a name that represented their distinct and separate experiences as lesbians and as women. "Bisexual," though not a term chosen by the community it represents, seems to be an acceptable term to contemporary bisexual men and women.

The medical establishment also imposed clinical terms on transgender persons, such as "transvestite," "transsexual," and "sexual dysphoria" or "gender dysphoria," which implied a pathological state. The use of a more neutral term, "transgender," began in the 1990's (coming into widespread use around 1994).

The terms "gay," "lesbian," "bisexual," and "transgender" are currently the standard terms in use, but words and their meanings rise and fall in popularity and vary in different social and political situations. "Queer" has been an unpopular and derogatory term historically but has been rising in popularity since the 1980's. Furthermore, a self-named "queer" movement emerged in the 1980's, but the movement gave "queer" a new meaning: One could be sexually dissident but not necessarily (or exclusively) gay, lesbian, or bisexual. Some GLBT and heterosexual persons whose sexuality does not fit into the cultural standard of monogamous hetero-

World War II political movements that developed in Europe and the United States to increase understanding of gays and lesbians and to combat their social and legal persecution. Historical accounts sometimes call the years between 1950 and 1969 the "homophile period." Yet, despite these other terms, the term "homosexual" prevailed until the Stonewall Rebellion in New York in 1969. This term would come to be dismissed because of its link with negative stereotypes and because of its use as a pathological diagnosis. When opportunities increased for collective organizing and socializing, there occurred a phenomenon of self-identification as gay and lesbian instead of homosexual.

Though its origins are unknown, the term "gay" was in widespread use by the late 1960's. Although "homophile" was not a negative term, gays and lesbians did not want to use the term because it did not fit the times. They chose "gay" instead. They refused

sexual marriage have adopted the queer label.

"Queer" is meant to be an inclusive term, but there is no groundswell for using it in lesbian and gay communities, largely because many lesbians and gays who grew up when the term was used as a term of deprecation and degradation dismiss it as hostile and hurtful. The growing acceptance of this term among some lesbians and gays represents a likely generational shift, as the younger GLBT generation did not necessarily experience the problems associated with the term "queer" and, thus, tend to be the ones who accept the term.

In academic circles, "queer" often is associated with queer theory. Although queer theory is a product of universities, it is allied with the broader queer movement in GLBT communities. It has goals that differ from those of early gay-liberation leaders. The gay-liberation movement of the 1970's fought to create a place for sexual minorities. This represented the politics of convention, which holds that once heterosexuals recognize that gay and lesbian persons are "just like them," they will grant them civil liberties and civil rights. Queer politics, however, defines itself largely by difference and by its stance against normalization and the heterosexual and gay and lesbian mainstream. The aim of queer politics is to destabilize cultural ideas of normality and sexuality and to reclaim terms such as "heterosexual" and "homosexual." Queer theory aims to undermine the status quo.

Although Kertbeny coined the term "homosexual" as part of his interest in human rights and used a modern argument for these rights (inborn, natural), the term became a "medical" one and was used in a negative way. Between the late nineteenth century and the 1970's, the medical terminology represented homosexuals as pathological, degenerate, or ill, but Kertbeny is respected for rejecting this medical/pathological model. He was a forerunner of the modern GLBT movement. On June 29, 2002, the Ambad Budapest Gay Fellowship erected a tombstone in the Fiumei Street National Graveyard to commemorate Kertbeny's achievements.

—*Ski Hunter*

## Further Reading

Anderson, J. "Beyond Identity: Queer Values and Community." *Journal of Gay, Lesbian, and Bisexual Identity* 4 (1999): 293-326.

Denny, Dallas. "Transgender in the United States: A Brief Discussion." *Siecus Report* 28 (1999): 8-13.

Herdt, G. H., and A. Boxer. "Introduction: Culture, History, and Life Course of Gay Men." In *Gay Culture in America: Essays from the Field*, edited by G. Herdt. Boston: Beacon Press, 1992.

Herzer, M. "Kertbeny and the Nameless Love." *Journal of Homosexuality* 12 (1985): 1-26.

Jeffreys, Sheila. "The Queer Disappearance of Lesbians: Sexuality in the Academy." *Women's Studies International Forum* 17 (1994): 459-472.

Katz, Jonathan Ned. *The Invention of Heterosexuality*. New York: Penguin Books, 1995.

Livia, Anna, and Kira Hall, eds. *Queerly Phrased: Language, Gender, and Sexuality*. New York: Oxford University Press, 1997.

**See also:** 1869: Westphal Advocates Medical Treatment for Sexual Inversion; 1885: United Kingdom Criminalizes "Gross Indecency"; Jan. 12, 1939: *Thompson v. Aldredge* Dismisses Sodomy Charges Against Lesbians; Sept. 4, 1957: The *Wolfenden Report* Calls for Decriminalizing Private Consensual Sex; 1961: Illinois Legalizes Consensual Homosexual Sex; Jan. 22, 1973: *Roe v. Wade* Legalizes Abortion and Extends Privacy Rights; Aug., 1973: American Bar Association Calls for Repeal of Laws Against Consensual Sex; Oct. 18, 1973: Lambda Legal Authorized to Practice Law; Nov. 17, 1975: U.S. Supreme Court Rules in "Crimes Against Nature" Case; 1986: *Bowers v. Hardwick* Upholds State Sodomy Laws; Jan. 1, 1988: Canada Decriminalizes Sex Practices Between Consenting Adults; 1992-2006: Indians Struggle to Abolish Sodomy Law; June 26, 2003: U.S. Supreme Court Overturns Texas Sodomy Law.

# 1869
# WESTPHAL ADVOCATES MEDICAL TREATMENT FOR SEXUAL INVERSION

*Karl Friedrich Otto Westphal developed a psychiatric diagnosis for same-gender sexual attraction that he called "contrary sexual feeling," or "sexual inversion," and thus advocated medical treatment rather than criminal punishment for those diagnosed as sexual inverts.*

**LOCALE:** Berlin, Germany
**CATEGORIES:** Health and medicine; science; laws, acts, and legal history; organizations and institutions

## KEY FIGURES

*Karl Friedrich Westphal* (1833-1890), German neuropsychiatrist
*Karl Heinrich Ulrichs* (1825-1895), German lawyer and writer, who influenced Westphal and others working in sexology
*Richard von Krafft-Ebing* (1840-1902), professor of psychiatry, who promoted a medical-psychiatric theory of homosexuality
*Havelock Ellis* (1859-1939), British psychologist, who pioneered studies in the psychology of sex and sexual inversion
*Sigmund Freud* (1856-1939), Austrian psychiatrist, who wrote on sexual nature and development

## SUMMARY OF EVENT

Karl Friedrich Westphal, a German neuropsychiatrist, published an article in 1869 in the prestigious medical journal *Archiv für Psychiatrie und Nervenkrankheiten* (archive for psychiatry and nervous diseases), which described a phenomenon he termed "contrary sexual feeling," a newly identified psychiatric diagnosis for people attracted to members of their own gender. In his article describing two case histories—one male and one female—he advanced the theory that homosexuality was the result of a congenital "reversal of sexual feeling."

According to Westphal, male inverts exhibited effeminate behaviors and were sexually attracted to other men, while female inverts displayed masculine characteristics and were sexually attracted to women.

Because he believed that the mental disorder was congenital in most cases, he advocated for the medicalization of homosexuality and the elimination of laws against same-gender sexual practices. He believed also that patients with the diagnosis of "contrary sexual feeling" typically had other associated mental illnesses. Westphal's publication legitimized discussion of this "new" medical condition, opening the floodgates to other medical and scientific works on homosexuality.

Westphal's approach to sexual "inverts" was more humane in the context of a society that considered individuals who engaged in same-gender sex to be criminals. Inverts were thought to have acquired same-gender sexual desire because of, for example, early masturbation. Westphal and other physicians interested in sexology in the late nineteenth century were heavily influenced by the writings of German lawyer Karl Heinrich Ulrichs, who is credited with being the first homosexual to advocate, publicly, for gay civil and legal rights. Ulrichs wrote a series of pamphlets advocating theories that homosexuality was caused by congenital anomalies, was as natural as heterosexuality, and should not only be tolerated but also decriminalized.

An interesting aspect of this piece of gay history is the evolution of terms used to describe the mental disorder that Westphal named "contrary sexual feeling" in 1869. In 1871, in a review appearing in an English medical journal, Westphal's term was translated as "inverted proclivity." In 1878, in an Italian translation, the German term was translated *inversione sessuale*. Translated from the Italian into English, the term "sexual inversion" became the most widely used technical psychiatric term in the

*Title page of Richard von Krafft-Ebing's* Psychopathia sexualis *(1886).*

late nineteenth century. Richard von Krafft-Ebing, author of *Psychopathia sexualis*, an influential book of case histories published in 1886, used the phrase "contrary sexual instinct" in 1892 to advance the belief that homosexuality is a congenital anomaly and a natural biological variation. In 1897, the book *Sexual Inversion* was published by the English psychologist Havelock Ellis as part of his seven-volume series, *Studies in the Psychology of Sex*. Ellis's book ultimately became popular with general audiences, extending the term from strictly medical usage to popular usage.

Sigmund Freud's groundbreaking work, *Three Essays on the Theory of Sexuality* (1910), his earliest (first published in German, 1905) and major statement on the nature and development of sexuality and on theories of inversion, differs from the work of Westphal. Freud first used the word "inversion" in this text. By 1915, however, the term "sexual inversion" mostly had been replaced in psychiatric literature by the term "homosexual," preferred by Freud and coined in 1868 by German journalist and translator Karl Maria Kertbeny in a letter to Ulrichs.

## SIGNIFICANCE

Karl Westphal's public stance on contrary sexual feeling as a medical condition, along with the beliefs of other sexologists of his era, stimulated a trend away from the criminalization and one toward the medicalization of the condition that first came to be called sexual inversion and, then, homosexuality. This shift from the legal-moral model to the medical-scientific model is significant, though not surprising in the social context of the late nineteenth century. Westphal's efforts to diagnose and classify new mental disorders fit with the progressive movement toward the professionalization of psychiatry, a field of medicine based on scientific inquiry into "illnesses of the nerves and brain."

This medical approach also had its downside, however, as it set in motion a period of more than one hundred years during which homosexuality was viewed as pathological and therefore medically treatable. Aversion therapy by shock treatment was one such method developed to "help" inverts change their behaviors; the first recorded aversion therapy treatment for homosexuality was reported in 1935. In 1952, the American Psychiatric Association (APA) included homosexuality as a "sociopathic personality disturbance" in its first official list of mental disorders, but then recategorized the diagnosis as a "sexual deviation" in 1968. In 1973, the APA officially stated that homosexuality did not meet the criteria for being a psychiatric disorder. Twenty years later, in 1993, the World Health Organization withdrew "homosexuality" from its list of diseases, and the American Medical Association made it clear that it opposed medical treatments thought to "cure" lesbians and gays.

—*Emily Ferrara*

## FURTHER READING

Bayer, Ronald. *Homosexuality and American Psychiatry: The Politics of Diagnosis.* 1981. Reprint. Princeton, N.J.: Princeton University Press, 1987.

Bland, Lucy, and Laura Doan, eds. *Sexology in Culture: Labelling Bodies and Desires.* Chicago: University of Chicago Press, 1998.

Bullough, Vern L. *Science in the Bedroom: A History of Sex Research.* New York: Basic Books, 1994.

Ellis, Havelock. *Studies in the Psychology of Sex: Sexual Inversion*. Seattle, Wash.: University Press of the Pacific, 2001.

Krafft-Ebing, Richard von. *Psychopathia Sexualis: With Especial Reference to the Antipathic Sexual Instinct, a Medico-Forensic Study*. Burbank, Calif.: Bloat, 1999.

Mondimore, Francis Mark. *A Natural History of Homosexuality*. Baltimore: Johns Hopkins University Press, 1996.

Rosario, Vernon A. *Science and Homosexualities*. New York: Routledge, 1996.

Terry, Jennifer. *An American Obsession: Science, Medicine, and Homosexuality in Modern Society*. Chicago: University of Chicago Press, 1999.

**SEE ALSO:** Aug. 29, 1867: Karl Heinrich Ulrichs Speaks Publicly for Gay and Lesbian Rights; May 6, 1868: Kertbeny Coins the Terms "Homosexual" and "Heterosexual"; 1897: Ellis Publishes *Sexual Inversion*; May 14, 1897: Hirschfeld Founds the Scientific-Humanitarian Committee; 1905: Freud Rejects Third-Sex Theory; 1929: Davis's Research Identifies Lesbian Sexuality as Common and Normal; 1948: Kinsey Publishes *Sexual Behavior in the Human Male*; 1952: APA Classifies Homosexuality as a Mental Disorder; 1953: Kinsey Publishes *Sexual Behavior in the Human Female*; 1953-1957: Evelyn Hooker Debunks Beliefs That Homosexuality Is a "Sickness"; Mar. 7, 1967: CBS Airs *CBS Reports: The Homosexuals*; Oct. 31, 1969: *Time* Magazine Issues "The Homosexual in America"; Dec. 15, 1973: Homosexuality Is Delisted by APA; Apr. 20, 2001: Chinese Psychiatric Association Removes Homosexuality from List of Mental Disorders.

# 1885
# UNITED KINGDOM CRIMINALIZES "GROSS INDECENCY"

*In 1885, the British parliament passed the Criminal Law Amendment Act, which legally classified and normalized acceptable and unacceptable forms of human sexuality in the nation's criminal code. By shifting legal emphasis and scrutiny from the criminality of an act (such as sodomy) to the criminalization of the actor as "gross indecency," the act broadened the net that law enforcement authorities and the courts could cast to arrest, prosecute, and imprison homosexuals.*

**LOCALE:** London, England
**CATEGORIES:** Laws, acts, and legal history; crime

**KEY FIGURES**
*Henry Du Pré Labouchere* (1831-1912), journalist, editor, and liberal member of the House of Commons, 1880-1906

*William Ewart Gladstone* (1809-1898), Tory member of Parliament who helped establish the Liberal Party in 1859, and British prime minister, 1868-1874, 1880-1885, 1886, and 1892-1894

*Lord Granville* (Granville George Leveson-Gower; 1815-1891), Whig member of the House of Lords

*Ernest Boulton* (Lady Stella Clinton; Stella; Star of the Strand; b. c. 1848), actor, courtesan, and cross-dresser

*Frederick Park* (Miss Fanny Winifred Park; b. 1847/1848), actor, law student, and cross-dresser

*William Thomas Stead* (1849-1912), journalist, author, and editor

*Oscar Wilde* (1854-1900), author, critic, playwright, and poet

## SUMMARY OF EVENT

Attempts to regulate human sexuality date back to the biblical story of Sodom and Gomorrah mentioned in the Book of Genesis. The definition of "sodomy" illustrates the nuanced meaning of words and the difficulty of precise legal definition. It has been defined as any of various acts of copulation; however, it is more often specifically defined as anal or oral sex and carries with it the stigma of being unnatural. In other instances it includes acts of autoeroticism and bestiality. In Western civilization, sodomy laws have been used by governments and by religion to normalize heterosexual relations and to promote the institution of heterosexual marriage especially for, but not limited to, the purpose of procreation.

In 1533, when King Henry VIII separated the Church of England from the Roman Catholic Church in Rome so that he could divorce Catherine of Aragon, he converted Catholic doctrine into a legal code that recognized sodomy both as a crime and a sin. The laws of England codified the crime of sodomy, carrying with it the penalty of death until 1861, spreading the proscription worldwide through the common law's extension under the British colonial system. This included the original thirteen British colonies in North America.

Throughout history, punishment for sodomy has been brutal, harsh, and unforgiving. Punishment for sodomy, especially for "homosexual" sodomy, has varied from burning at the stake or burying alive during the Middle Ages to hanging under the British Buggery Act of 1533. Sodomy was removed from the list of English capital offenses in 1861, yet punishment remained severe: usually up to two years' hard labor in prison. In the United States, state sodomy statutes were upheld as constitutional as late as 1986 in the U.S. Supreme Court ruling in *Bowers v. Hardwick* (1986). Sodomy finally was abolished as a punishable crime in all U.S. states, territories, and jurisdictions in 2003 by order of the Supreme Court in the case of *Lawrence v. Texas* (2003).

In June of 1885 the ruling Liberal Party of British prime minister William Ewart Gladstone had faced a vote of no confidence in Parliament that forced the prime minister to dissolve the govern-

ment. By the end of June, a new coalition led by Lord Salisbury had formed, and the Parliament, as usual, recessed for its summer holiday. On July 6, the editor of the *Pall Mall Gazette*, William Thomas Stead, had published the first in a series of articles collectively titled "The Maiden Tribute of Modern Babylon." This exposé purported to uncover an allegedly widespread child prostitution network and Caucasian slavery ring operating in London.

The sensationalism provoked by Stead's report sent members of Parliament scurrying back to London from their summer vacations to debate and pass reform bills aimed at remedying the reputed abuses. Among the proposed laws was the Criminal Law Amendment Act of 1885 (CLAA), formally titled "An Act to Make Further Provision for the Protection of Women and Girls, the Suppression of Brothels, and Other Purposes"—otherwise known as the Labouchere amendment—after liberal member of Parliament Henry Du Pré Labouchere—or the Blackmailer's Charter.

The CLAA was first introduced in Parliament by Lord Granville in 1881. At his request, the House of Lords created a select committee to investigate the matter. The final report of the committee recommended a slew of reforms that included raising the age of consent and levying stiffer penalties for criminal assault, for promoting overseas prostitution, and for admission of a minor into any premises for reason of sexual intercourse. The committee's endorsements became the basis of the Criminal Law Amendment legislation. The part of the CLAA that dealt with sodomy was another amendment tacked onto the final bill by Labouchere as Section II.

---

### CRIMINAL LAW AMENDMENT ACT (1885)

Any male person who, in public or private, commits, or is a party to the commission of, or procures, or attempts to procure the commission by any male person of, any act of gross indecency, shall be guilty of misdemeanour, and being convicted shall be liable at the discretion of the Court to be imprisoned for any term not exceeding two years, with or without hard labour.

## SIGNIFICANCE

The Labouchere amendment defined "gross inde-cency" as a misdemeanor between two men punish-able by a maximum of two years' hard labor. The cumulative effect of the amendment was to make il-legal all male homosexual acts and all homosexual "procuring." The overall effect was cultural, legal, political, and social. Moral reformers, like Stead, sought to marry the state's police powers to con-stricting codes of acceptable conduct.

The United Kingdom, in the aftermath of a series of sex scandals beginning with the 1870 arrest and trial of Ernest Boulton and Frederick Park for con-spiracy to commit sodomite acts, and out of possi-ble public concern over the removal of sodomy from the list of English capital offenses in 1861, sought to codify homosexuality as criminal behav-ior. The CLAA was enacted by Parliament to le-gally classify and normalize acceptable and unac-ceptable forms of human sexuality. This legal and linguistic turn from criminalizing an act (sodomy) to the criminalization of the actor (gross indecency) broadened the law enforcement net.

The turn represented a dangerous slide from criminalizing particular acts to criminalizing sexual identity. Gross indecency was sufficiently broad, and vague, to enable prosecutors to try and convict any homosexual for almost any reason. The La-bouchere amendment was most famously used to prosecute Irish author, critic, dramatist, playwright, poet, and wit Oscar Wilde. Wilde was prosecuted in the spring of 1895 on charges of sodomy and gross indecency at the Central Criminal Court, Oxford, by Edward Carson, lead counsel for John Sholto Douglas, marquis of Queensberry, against whom Wilde had brought charges of libel. Queensberry was the father of Wilde's lover, Lord Alfred "Bosie" Douglas (1870-1945), who seemed to have urged Wilde to level the charges against the elder Douglas. However, during the course of Wilde's trials at the Old Bailey, it became increasingly evi-dent that gross indecency extended to everything from sodomy to literature itself. Wilde would be convicted and sentenced to two years' hard labor as retribution to the state.

In 1938 there were nearly 150 prosecutions for sodomy in England. In 1952 there were almost seven hundred. On August 24, 1957, nearly seventy-five years to the day that the CLAA was enacted, the British parliament appointed a commission of fif-teen individuals to study homosexual offenses and the penalties exacted by those found guilty of com-mitting such crimes. Not surprisingly, the commis-sion was also charged with studying offenses re-lated to prostitution. On September 4, 1957, the Wolfenden Committee issued its report of the De-partmental Committee on Homosexual Offences and Prostitution, simply, if erroneously, labeled by the press as the "Vice Report." It suggested, among other things, decriminalizing homosexuality and declassifying homosexuality as a disease.

*—Keith Carson*

## FURTHER READING

Cohen, Edward. "Legislating the Norm: From Sod-omy to Gross Indecency." In *Displacing Homo-phobia: Gay Male Perspectives in Literature and Culture*, edited by Ronald Butters, John M. Clum, and Michael Moon. Durham, N.C.: Duke University Press, 1989.

Committee on Homosexual Offences and Prostitu-tion. *The Wolfenden Report*. Authorized Ameri-can ed. Introduction by Karl Menninger. New York: Stein and Day, 1963.

Holland, Merlin, ed. *The Real Trial of Oscar Wilde: The First Uncensored Transcript of the Trial of Oscar Wilde v. John Douglas (Marquess of Queensberry), 1895*. New York: HarperCollins, 2003.

Payne, Jennifer. "The Criminal Law Amendment Act of 1885 and Sexual Assault on Minors." http://www.geocities.com/Athens/Aegean/ 7023/Consent.html#N_1_. August 24, 1998.

Summersgill, Bob, ed. "Sodomy Laws Around the World." http://www.sodomylaws.org.

Weeks, Jeffrey. "Inverts, Perverts, and May-Annes: Male Prostitution and the Regulation of Homo-sexuality in England in the Nineteenth and Early Twentieth Centuries." In *Hidden from History: Reclaiming the Gay and Lesbian Past*, edited by George Chauncey, Jr., Martin Duberman, and Martha Vicinus. New York: Meridian, 1990.

**SEE ALSO:** May 6, 1868: Kertbeny Coins the Terms "Homosexual" and "Heterosexual"; May 25, 1895: Oscar Wilde Is Convicted of Gross Indecency; Jan. 12, 1939: *Thompson v. Aldredge* Dismisses Sodomy Charges Against Lesbians; Jan. 1, 1957: United Kingdom's Sexual Offences Act Becomes Law; Sept. 4, 1957: The *Wolfenden Report* Calls for Decriminalizing Private Consensual Sex; 1961: Illinois Legalizes Consensual Homosexual Sex; July 27, 1967: United Kingdom Decriminalizes Homosexual Sex; Jan. 22, 1973: Roe v. Wade Legalizes Abortion and Extends Privacy Rights; Aug., 1973: American Bar Association Calls for Repeal of Laws Against Consensual Sex; Oct. 18, 1973: Lambda Legal Authorized to Practice Law; Nov. 17, 1975: U.S. Supreme Court Rules in "Crimes Against Nature" Case; 1986: *Bowers v. Hardwick* Upholds State Sodomy Laws; Jan. 1, 1988: Canada Decriminalizes Sex Practices Between Consenting Adults; 1992-2006: Indians Struggle to Abolish Sodomy Law; June 26, 2003: U.S. Supreme Court Overturns Texas Sodomy Law.

## January-June, 1886
# TWO-SPIRIT AMERICAN INDIAN VISITS WASHINGTON, D.C.

*The life of Zuni Pueblo Indian We'wha, who had adopted the Zuni-recognized gender role of a* lhamana, *or two-spirit person, was one of the most well-documented of the nineteenth century. His life inspired later interest in the experiences of gay and lesbian American Indians and in the concepts of third gender and transgender in indigenous cultures.*

**LOCALE:** Washington, D.C.
**CATEGORIES:** Transgender/transsexuality; race and ethnicity; cultural and intellectual history

**KEY FIGURES**
*We'wha* (1849-1896), Zuni pueblo two-spirit person
*Matilda Coxe Stevenson* (1850-1915), American anthropologist

**SUMMARY OF EVENT**
The social role of a *lhamana* (a Zuni term for a person, most often born male, who adopts the clothing, social roles and obligations, and customary duties of an other gender) is a widely documented cultural practice in more than one hundred American Indian societies, each culture naming the *lhamana* differently. Western European immigrants to North America had no knowledge of such a gender category. For western Europeans, biological sex and social, or gender, identity were, and still are, considered equivalent.

French explorers of North America used the term "berdache" (male homosexual or prostitute) to describe persons such as the *lhamana*, but berdache has since been rejected by American Indians and others as a pejorative. "Berdache," in French and other languages, traditionally meant a passive homosexual partner or "catamite," a younger person (usually a boy) in a sexual relationship with a man, a relationship connoting pederasty.

Beyond the stories from the few contacts on an individual level with settlers, soldiers, or missionaries, little accurate information existed about the *lhamana*. Their home cultures were faced with destruction and massive changes because of the military and cultural pressures exerted by the expansionist United States. It is known that an *lhamana* was a two-spirit person, one who possessed aspects of both male and female souls and was thus capable of spiritual fulfillment only by having this duality recognized and acknowledged through distinctive dress and activities, often but not exclusively ritual in nature.

One distinctive American Indian culture that had

*A rare image of We'wha.* (Courtesy, Catherine Lavender/CUNY)

resisted assimilation included the pueblo communities of New Mexico. Among the residents of the western settlement of Zuni, the category of *lhamana* had specific characteristics, dress, and duties. For a period of six months in 1886, anthropologist Matilda Coxe Stevenson, who had been conducting fieldwork with the Zuni pueblo in western New Mexico for the Smithsonian Institution's Bureau of Ethnology, returned to Washington. Accompanying Stevenson as a cultural ambassador for his people was her friend and informant We'wha, who many years earlier had adopted the socially acceptable role of a *lhamana* in Zuni culture. His ease of adaptation to white American urban culture and society were commented upon favorably by Washington society, within whose circles he moved freely; he was even asked to participate in a public ceremonial performance. On June 23, 1886, We'wha, in full ceremonial dress, called on President Grover Cleveland at the White House, who thus became the first American president to meet a *lhamana*.

## SIGNIFICANCE

Several factors contributed to the prominent coverage given to We'wha's visit to Washington, among them the absence of American Indian women in the delegations that had up to that time paid formal visits to the United States capitol. As a *lhamana*, We'wha likely was considered a legitimate American Indian women "representative." Other factors included the prominent social status of We'wha's hosts within Washington social and scientific circles, the desire of the Bureau of Ethnology to capitalize on a rare opportunity to work with a member of Zuni culture, and the curiosity of the city's residents about someone they considered to be an "exotic" American Indian.

During his six months in Washington, We'wha received significant social notice and the attention of many journalists. He also adapted quickly to the mores of local society and mastered a sufficient degree of English to be able to converse. At the request of the bureau, We'wha demonstrated the use of a backstrap loom and the techniques of weaving, and performed a prayer ceremony at Stevenson's home during the solstice.

Accepted as a woman during his trip to Washington, We'wha also had become one of the most documented cross-gender or two-spirit persons in the literature of North American anthropology. His life experience provided a basis for the later resurgence of interest in gay and lesbian and cross- or transgender individuals within Native American culture, not without debate, however. He was referenced in standard anthropological works such as American anthropologist Ruth Benedict's *Patterns of Culture* (1934). His sexuality, however, was not commented upon by anthropologist Stevenson, and has been the subject of speculation since his death in 1896.

—*Robert Ridinger*

## FURTHER READING

Brown, Lester B., ed. *Two Spirit People: American Indian Lesbian Women and Gay Men*. New York: Harrington Park Press, 1997.

Lang, Sabine. *Men As Women, Women As Men: Changing Gender in Native American Cultures*. Austin: University of Texas Press, 1998.

Roscoe, Will. *Changing Ones: Third and Fourth Genders in Native North America.* New York: St. Martin's Press, 1998.

_____. *Living the Spirit: A Gay American Indian Anthology.* New York: St. Martin's Press, 1988.

_____. *The Zuni Man-Woman.* Albuquerque: University of New Mexico Press, 1991.

Williams, Walter L. *The Spirit and the Flesh: Sexual Diversity in American Indian Culture.* 1986. New ed. Boston: Beacon Press, 1992.

SEE ALSO: Nov. 11, 1865: Mary Edwards Walker Is Awarded the Medal of Honor; 1869: Westphal Advocates Medical Treatment for Sexual Inversion; Nov. 21, 1966: First Gender Identity Clinic Opens and Provides Gender Reassignment Surgery; 1975: Gay American Indians Is Founded; 1986: Paula Gunn Allen Publishes *The Sacred Hoop*; Jan. 21, 1989: Death of Transgender Jazz Musician Billy Tipton; 1996: Hart Recognized as a Transgender Man.

## January, 1892-July, 1892
# ALICE MITCHELL FOUND GUILTY OF MURDERING HER LOVER

*A Memphis teenager murdered her female lover after a planned elopement failed. Newspapers, the courts, and public opinion were forced to grapple with and address female homosexuality, same-gender crimes of passion, and insanity.*

**LOCALE:** Memphis, Tennessee
**CATEGORIES:** Crime; publications

### KEY FIGURES

*Alice Mitchell* (1872-1898), Freda Ward's lover and murderer
*Freda Ward* (1875-1892), murdered by her lover, Alice Mitchell
*Jo Ward*, Freda Ward's sister
*Lillie Johnson*, Alice Mitchell's friend and codefendant at trial

### SUMMARY OF EVENT

On January 25, 1892, at about 3:00 P.M., nineteen-year-old Alice Mitchell cut the throat of her seventeen-year-old lover Freda Ward as Ward, her sister Jo, and their friend Christina Purnell were about to board a riverboat to return to their home in Golddust, Tennessee, after a month's visit in Memphis.

Alice and Freda had been neighbors and high school classmates; after the Wards moved to Golddust, the two girls had become romantically involved. In February, 1891, they became "engaged" and began to plan an elopement to St. Louis, where Alice would assume the name Alvin G. Ward and the two would be married. Freda's older sister, Ada Volkmar, with whom she lived, discovered the plan and insisted on the immediate termination of all contact between the girls. Freda returned to Memphis in January, 1892, for a visit with another family friend, Mrs. Kimbrough. Freda wrote to Alice on January 18, affirming her continued love and her sister's insistence that the two never meet or speak again.

On the morning of the January 25, Alice picked up her closest friend, Lillie Johnson, and Lillie's six-year-old nephew, to take them for a buggy drive. Lillie and Jo Ward had been close friends, but when Freda had been forbidden to see Alice again, her sister had also interdicted the friendship between Lillie and Jo, on the grounds that Lillie was "wild," a flirt who sought the attention of young men, and one who had corresponded under a false name with a man she did not know. Lillie and Alice spent the morning looking for and then following the Ward party around Memphis. When they finally saw the young women walking to the steamboat, Lillie, Alice, and her nephew got out of the buggy

## THE PSYCHOLOGY OF THE MITCHELL MURDER CASE

*British psychologist Havelock Ellis, who pioneered studies in the psychology of sex, wrote about the Alice Mitchell case in his book* Sexual Inversion *(1897):*

It is, moreover, noteworthy that a remarkably large proportion of the cases in which homosexuality has led to crimes of violence, or otherwise come under medico-legal observation, has been among women. It is well known that the part taken by women generally in open criminality, and especially in crimes of violence, is small as compared with men. In the homosexual field, as we might have anticipated, the conditions are to some extent reversed. Inverted men, in whom a more or less feminine temperament is so often found, are rarely impelled to acts of aggressive violence, though they frequently commit suicide. Inverted women, who may retain their feminine emotionality combined with some degree of infantile impulsiveness and masculine energy, present a favorable soil for the seeds of passional crime, under those conditions of jealousy and allied emotions which must so often enter into the invert's life.

The first conspicuous example of this tendency in recent times is the Memphis case (1892) in the United States. . . . In this case a congenital sexual invert, Alice Mitchell, planned a marriage with Freda Ward, taking a male-name and costume. This scheme was frustrated by Freda's sister, and Alice Mitchell then cut Freda's throat. There is no reason to suppose that she was insane at the time of the murder. She was a typical invert of a very pronounced kind. Her mother had been insane and had homicidal impulses. She herself was considered unbalanced, and was masculine in her habits from her earliest years. Her face was obviously unsymmetrical and she had an appearance of youthfulness below her age. She was not vicious, and had little knowledge of sexual matters, but when she kissed Freda she was ashamed of being seen, while Freda could see no reason for being ashamed. She was adjudged insane.

and passed them on the sidewalk. Alice then left Lillie and the small boy to follow Freda down the boardwalk, where she committed the murder. She returned to the buggy, and a dazed Lillie drove Alice home, advising her to tell her mother what she had done.

Newspaper coverage of the crime and subsequent trial was extensive. Lillie's hearing was held on February 23: She had been charged with murder, on the grounds that she had known Alice Mitchell's intention to kill Freda Ward and failed to prevent the murder. On February 28, Lillie was released on bail, despite the judge's determination that she was clearly guilty of aiding and abetting Alice in an "atrocious and malignant" crime.

On July 18, a so-called inquisition of lunacy was held—a court proceeding to determine Alice's mental status. Her lawyers entered a plea of incompetence, owing to present insanity, arguing that her mental state after the murder made it impossible for her to stand trial. The defense marshaled five physicians to testify that Alice suffered from hereditary mental illness, erotomania, and paranoia, supporting that diagnosis with Alice's own testimony that she loved Freda Ward, intended to marry her, and live with her as husband and wife. The medical professionals also emphasized that there was no sexual element to the girls' relationship, focusing instead on what they saw as Alice's delusional belief that she could have passed as a man. Popular media coverage was skeptical of this claim; coverage in the more sensational papers emphasized the sexual possibilities of the girls' relationship.

On July 30, Alice was found to be "presently insane and dangerous," and on August 1, she was committed to the Western Hospital for the Insane in Bolivar, Tennessee. She died there on March 31, 1898, apparently of tuberculosis.

### SIGNIFICANCE

Alice Mitchell's criminal trial crystallizes a number of significant threads in late nineteenth- and early twentieth century discourses on homosexuality. Particular characteristics of the emergent discourse coming out of the trial was the use of medical and psychiatric specialists to diagnose Alice's condition; emphases on gender confusion, sexuality, heredity, and criminality; and the role of the press in both creating and managing public discourse about the crime.

Alice was profiled as one of the case studies in Havelock Ellis's *Sexual Inversion* (1897), enshrining her as a "type" of inversion, a standard by which other cases might be examined. Sexologists, physicians, and psychiatrists studied Alice's symptoms, the letters she and Freda exchanged, and expert commentaries to construct "diagnostic" criteria for understanding same-gender desire between women. Alice and Freda were simultaneously constructed as, and constructors of, the robust stereotypes of the pathologically jealous and violent butch (masculine) lesbian and her weak, easily manipulated, and only contingently lesbian femme (feminine) partner.

The relationship between Alice and Freda also was interpreted as a consequence of Alice's hereditary mental illness: Her mother's "puerperal insanity" (probably severe postpartum depression, and described as including hallucinations, paranoia, and delusions) was carefully documented as part of the court proceedings. Likewise, Alice was described as gender-variant, with friends and neighbors contributing memories of "inappropriate" friendships, choices of toys and games, and behavior. The case and its coverage offer particularly clear and accessible examples of the medical and psychological paradigms available to late nineteenth century professionals to describe and interpret same-gender desire.

—*Melynda Huskey*

**FURTHER READING**

Duggan, Lisa. *Sapphic Slashers: Sex, Violence, and American Modernity*. Durham, N.C.: Duke University Press, 2000.

_____. "The Trials of Alice Mitchell: Sensationalism, Sexology, and the Lesbian Subject in Turn-of-the-Century America." *Signs: Journal of Women in Culture and Society* 18, no. 4 (Summer, 1993): 791-814. Reprinted in *Sexual Borderlands: Constructing an American Sexual Past*, edited by Kathleen Kennedy and Sharon Ulman (Columbus: Ohio State University Press, 2003).

Katz, Jonathan Ned. *Gay American History: Lesbians and Gay Men in the U.S.A., a Documentary History*. Rev. ed. New York: Meridian, 1992.

Lindquist, Lisa J. "Image of Alice: Gender, Deviancy, and a Love Murder in Memphis." *Journal of the History of Sexuality* 6, no. 1 (Winter, 1995): 30-61.

**SEE ALSO:** May 25, 1895: Oscar Wilde Is Convicted of Gross Indecency; 1897: Ellis Publishes *Sexual Inversion*.

**May 25, 1895**
# OSCAR WILDE IS CONVICTED OF GROSS INDECENCY

*Oscar Wilde, famed Irish author, poet, and playwright, was convicted of indecent conduct for his sexual relationships with men, most notably Lord Alfred "Bosie" Douglas, and was sentenced to two years of hard labor. The scandal surrounding his trial and conviction ended his career as a writer.*

**LOCALE:** London, England
**CATEGORIES:** Laws, acts, and legal history; crime; literature

**KEY FIGURES**
*Oscar Wilde* (1854-1900), Irish author, poet, and playwright
*Lord Alfred "Bosie" Douglas* (1870-1945), third son of John Douglas and Oscar Wilde's lover
*John Douglas* (1844-1900), marquis of Queensbury and father of Lord Alfred

**SUMMARY OF EVENT**
When Oscar Wilde met Lord Alfred "Bosie" Douglas in 1891, he could never have fathomed, with all his cleverness and wit, the outcome of what turned out to be a volatile relationship. At the time, Wilde was an established literary sensation and a principal celebrity of London's social scene, entertaining whoever happened into his company with his famous quips.

Douglas, sixteen years younger than Wilde and twenty-one years old when the two were first introduced, was an undergraduate at Oxford University and extremely handsome, although he was also vicious and petulant. Initially connecting over Douglas's admiration of Wilde's novel *The Picture of Dorian Gray* (1891), the two men met sporadically over the next year and were inseparable by May of 1892.

Although Douglas's father, John Douglas, found himself charmed by Wilde's wit, he soon began to disapprove of his son's close relationship, as rumors of the author's private life began to circulate through the London social scene. Although the elder Douglas threatened to cut off his son's allowance if he failed to end his relationship with Wilde, Bosie rebelled against his often tyrannical father, sending him into a rage and prompting him to follow the two men around town. Bosie's father attempted to sneak into the St. James Theatre on February 14, 1895, the opening night of Wilde's play *The Importance of Being Earnest* (pr. 1895, pb. 1908), with a basket of rotting vegetables, but was denied entrance. Fuming, he left a card at Wilde's hotel on February 18 that was addressed, "For Oscar Wilde posing somdomite [sic]."

Against the advice of close friends, Wilde sued

*Oscar Wilde, right, with Alfred "Bosie" Douglas, 1894.*

Bosie's father for libel on February 20, 1895, setting in motion a series of three trials that would result in Wilde's financial and personal ruin. Wilde's trial against John Douglas began on April 3 and played to an immense crowd of barristers, reporters, and curious onlookers. The case quickly turned against Wilde as John Douglas's leading counsel Edward Carson questioned Wilde on the morality of his art and presented a mountain of evidence that he and his private investigators had obtained to justify the charge of sodomy against Wilde, including testimony from young men who had engaged in sexual relations with Wilde.

Wilde withdrew his case against John Douglas on the third day of the trial, but Carson continued to present his evidence, evidence that would result inevitably in Wilde's arrest on April 5 under Section 11 of the 1885 Criminal Law Amendment Act, for "committing acts of gross indecency with other male persons." Although Wilde's offense was classified as a misdemeanor only, bail was not granted.

Wilde's first trial against the English crown began on April 26 in the Old Bailey courthouse, and quickly became a news sensation. Most newspapers printed long and detailed descriptions of each day's proceeding. While feigning shock and indignation at Wilde's purported immorality, the press printed every possible lurid detail, virtually convicting Wilde before the trial even began. To pay for his debts, incurred both by the trials and by his and Bosie's excessive spending, all of the items in Wilde's home were sold at auction two days before the trial began, and his name was removed from theater programs and billboards in both New York and London.

The trial ended in a hung jury, and although Wilde's reputation was all but demolished and the

---

## WILDE FROM PRISON

I have lain in prison for nearly two years. Out of my nature has come wild despair; an abandonment to grief that was piteous even to look at; terrible and impotent rage; bitterness and scorn; anguish that wept aloud; misery that could find no voice; sorrow that was dumb. I have passed through every possible mood of suffering. Better than Wordsworth himself I know what Wordsworth meant when he said "Suffering is permanent, obscure, and dark And has the nature of infinity."

But while there were times when I rejoiced in the idea that my sufferings were to be endless, I could not bear them to be without meaning. Now I find hidden somewhere away in my nature something that tells me that nothing in the whole world is meaningless, and suffering least of all. That something hidden away in my nature, like a treasure in a field, is Humility. . . .

All trials are trials for one's life, just as all sentences are sentences of death; and three times have I been tried. The first time I left the box to be arrested, the second time to be led back to the house of detention, the third time to pass into a prison for two years. Society, as we have constituted it, will have no place for me, has none to offer; but Nature, whose sweet rains fall on unjust and just alike, will have clefts in the rocks where I may hide, and secret valleys in whose silence I may weep undisturbed. She will hang the night with stars so that I may walk abroad in the darkness without stumbling, and send the wind over my footprints so that none may track me to my hurt: she will cleanse me in great waters, and with bitter herbs make me whole.

*Source:* Oscar Wilde, *De Profundis* (London: Methuen, 1905).

---

law had no obligation to continue with the prosecution, another trial was conducted. The Crown prevailed in the second trial, which was much more aggressive than the first, and handed down on May 25 Wilde's conviction for gross indecency with a sentence of two years' hard labor in Reading Gaol. Reportedly, prostitutes near the Old Bailey courthouse celebrated with cheers and dancing as Wilde's conviction was pronounced.

### SIGNIFICANCE

The public humiliation Wilde suffered during his trials proved to be mild compared to the horrific conditions he would face during his imprisonment in Reading Gaol. He endured constant diarrhea because he was fed rotten food, he slept on a bare plank, and he was not provided with a latrine. Furthermore, Wilde was granted one twenty-minute visit every three months only, but talking was not

*Closing scenes of Oscar Wilde's indecency trial and the sale of his personal belongings, published in* The Illustrated Police News, *May 4, 1895.*

allowed among prisoners. While in prison, Wilde composed *De Profundis* (1905), a letter to John Douglas that condemns his self-centered behavior but which also provides a meditation on Wilde's own self-destructive actions and a raw confession of his soul.

Because Wilde's reputation in London was disgraced and his name was forever tainted by the vicious character assassination performed both by the court and the newspapers, he traveled immediately to Paris after his release on May 19, 1897. He was never again allowed to see his two sons, and all but the most devoted of his friends abandoned him. Wilde lived in destitute poverty and isolation in a Paris hotel, where he died on November 30, 1900; he was only forty-six years old.

As it became clear to Wilde that he would be con-

victed for his sexual relations, he began to defend what he famously called "the love that dare not speak its name" more directly and aggressively under cross-examination. In addition, after his release from prison, he openly discussed his homosexuality with the few friends who remained by his side and readily acknowledged his affection for men. As Wilde's defense of homosexuality became more widely known and the conditions of his prosecution and imprisonment were revealed, Wilde became a posthumous hero for gays and lesbians, and his tombstone in Paris has become a shrine visited by thousands of people each year, some of whom kiss the gray stone in tribute.

—*Jennifer A. Smith*

**FURTHER READING**

Foldy, Michael S. *The Trials of Oscar Wilde: Deviance, Morality, and Late-Victorian Society.* New Haven, Conn.: Yale University Press, 1997.

Gilbert, Brian, director. *Wilde.* Motion picture. Columbia/Tristar, 1998. Performances by Stephen Fry and Jude Law.

Holland, Merlin. *The Real Trial of Oscar Wilde: The First Uncensored Transcript of the Trial of Oscar Wilde Versus John Douglas (Marquess of Queensbury), 1895.* New York: HarperCollins, 2003.

Keane, Robert N., ed. *Oscar Wilde: The Man, His Writings, and His World.* New York: AMS Press, 2003.

**SEE ALSO:** July 4, 1855: Whitman Publishes *Leaves of Grass*; 1885: United Kingdom Criminalizes "Gross Indecency"; 1924: Gide Publishes the Signed Edition of *Corydon*; 1939: Isherwood Publishes *Goodbye to Berlin*; 1947-1948: Golden Age of American Gay Literature; 1956: Baldwin Publishes *Giovanni's Room*; 1963: Rechy Publishes *City of Night*; Fall, 1967: Oscar Wilde Memorial Bookshop Opens as First Gay Bookstore; June, 1971: The Gay Book Award Debuts; 1974: *The Front Runner* Makes *The New York Times* Best-Seller List; 1975: First Novel About Coming Out to Parents Is Published; 1980-1981: Gay Writers Form the Violet Quill.

# 1896
# *DER EIGENE* IS PUBLISHED AS FIRST JOURNAL ON HOMOSEXUALITY

Der Eigene, *the first journal to focus on the gay experience, began publication in Berlin, Germany. A companion organization, Gemeinschaft der Eigenen, formed around the journal and celebrated ancient Greek male and masculine culture.*

LOCALE: Berlin, Germany

CATEGORIES: Publications; organizations and institutions; laws, acts, and legal history; literature

## KEY FIGURES
*Adolf Brand* (1874-1945), German founder and editor of *Der Eigene*
*Benedict Friedlaender* (1866-1908), wealthy German scholar
*John Henry Mackay* (1864-1933), German poet
*Fidus* (Hugo Höppener; 1868-1948), German illustrator
*Karl Meier* (1897-1974), Swiss actor and editor of the journal *Der Kreis*

## SUMMARY OF EVENT

Edited by founder Adolf Brand, *Der Eigene* began as an anarchist journal in the direction of Max Stirner, the nineteenth century German philosopher of egoism. The journal's title and the leading article of the first issue (1896) reflect Stirner's philosophy of egoism and the absolute autonomy of the individual. Stirner had given the term *eigen* a particular meaning ("self-owner") in his magnum opus *Der Einzige und sein Eigentum* (1845; *The Ego and His Own*, 1907), insisting not on individualism as self-interest but as "ownness" (Eigenheit), as self-mastery. Many of the journal's authors shared this perspective on egoism and individuality, especially John Henry Mackay, who was Stirner's biographer.

*Der Eigene*'s content was not focused explicitly on homosexuality until 1898, but before that date, much of the work could be interpreted as focusing on the gay experience. *Der Eigene* came into existence prior to the *Jahrbuch für sexuelle Zwischenstufen* (yearbook of intermediate sexual stages), the second journal to focus on homosexuality. It began publishing in 1899, also in Berlin, and was edited by the noted German sexologist Magnus Hirschfeld.

*Der Eigene* opposed the larger movement for gay liberation represented by Hirschfeld's Wissenschaftlich-humanitäre Komitee (Scientific-Humanitarian Committee) (formed in 1897). Supporters of *Der Eigene* formed their own organization, the Gemeinschaft der Eigenen (community of self-owners) in May of 1903. The Gemeinschaft der Eigenen, whose members were men and were often married, wanted to revive the male culture of ancient Greece—and for some this also included sexual relationships with boys. The group had about one dozen cofounders, including the scholar Benedict Friedlaender, whose book was written around the time of the group's founding.

Friedlaender's *Renaissance des Eros Uranos: Die physiologische Freundschaft, ein normaler Grundtrieb des Menschen und eine Frage der männlichen Gesellungsfreiheit* (1904; renaissance of the Uranian eros: the physiological friendship, a normal, fundamental drive of man, and a question of the freedom of males to join together) celebrates the Greek "culture of the male." The work includes beautiful illustrations of nudes by Hugo Höppener (known as Fidus), drawings that had appeared in *Der Eigene*. He is best known for his illustrations in the journal *Die Jugend*, however, which gave its name to the art movement called Jugendstil (or Art Nouveau).

Hirschfeld's committee, in contrast to the Gemeinschaft der Eigenen, believed gay men to be distinguished by feminine traits, had worked with the women's movement, and had been willing to accept a relatively high age of consent if necessary to gain revision of Germany's Paragraph 175, which out-

*The front page of the first issue of* Der Eigene, *1896.*

lawed sex between males (enacted 1871). The Gemeinschaft der Eigenen celebrated masculinity, believed women should be subordinate to men, and wanted an age of consent that would be low enough to accommodate their interest in boys. Legal revision, however, was a secondary consideration for them, whereas it was primary for Hirschfeld's committee.

### SIGNIFICANCE

*Der Eigene* was often highly literary. John Henry Mackay's "boy-love" poetry, for example, was first published in *Der Eigene* under the pseudonym Sagitta, the name that Mackay used for all of his boy-love writings. As Sagitta, Mackay is perhaps best known for his 1926 novel *Der Puppenjunge* (*The Hustler*, 1985). British-born American writer Christopher Isherwood had said about the book that it "gives a picture of the Berlin sexual underworld early in this century which I know, from my own experience, to be authentic."

Even if the impact of *Der Eigene* on the gay movement of the early twentieth century was limited, it did comfort or inspire many individuals. Swiss actor Karl Meier, who was engaged in provincial tours in Germany from 1924 to 1932, wrote an essay for *Der Eigene* in 1929, using the pseudonym Rolf, the name he used during the many years (1943-1967) he was editor of the Swiss journal *Der Kreis* (the circle or ring). *Der Kreis* had been the only trilingual gay journal, featuring regular contributions in German, French, and English. During the Nazi years, it was the only surviving gay-focused journal.

The historical significance of the Gemeinschaft der Eigenen is its ideological aversion to contemporary medical theories on male homosexuality, especially the view that homosexuality is a biological phenomenon, that is, that gay men differ from heterosexual men. Despite differences, sporadic cooperation did exist among members of Brand's Gemeinschaft der Eigenen and Hirschfeld's committee; but so did conflict, between Brand and Hirschfeld. Friedlaender also was a member of Hirschfeld's committee, but he, too, fell out with Hirschfeld, in 1906, and formed a rival group called the Secession of the Scientific-Humanitarian Committee. Friedlaender's death in 1908 also meant the end of much financial support for the Secession.

With the rise of the Nazis, all efforts for legal reform came to an end. Paragraph 175 was not to be repealed until 1994, nearly one hundred years after *Der Eigene* was first published. Mackay's writings under pseudonym were placed on the Nazi's list of forbidden books. Although *Der Eigene* had to cease publication, Brand himself was not subjected to persecution. He survived in Berlin until 1945 when, ironically, he was killed by bombs dropped by the Allies during World War II.

—*Hubert Kennedy*

### FURTHER READING

Hohmann, Joachim S., ed. *Der Eigene: Ein Blatt für männliche Kultur: Das Beste aus der ersten Homosexuellenzeitschrift der Welt.* Frankfurt, West Germany: Foerster Verlag, 1981.

Keilson-Lauritz, Marita. *Die Geschichte der eigenen Geschichte: Literatur und Literaturkritik in den*

*Anfängen der Schwulenbewegung am Beispiel des Jahrbuchs für sexuelle Zwischenstufen und der Zeitschrift Der Eigene.* Berlin, Germany: Verlag rosa Winkel, 1997.

Kennedy, Hubert. *Anarchist of Love: The Secret Life of John Henry Mackay.* Rev. ed. New York: North American Man/Boy Love Association, 1996.

Mackay, John Henry. *The Hustler: The Story of a Nameless Love from Friedrich Street.* Translated by Hubert Kennedy. Boston: Alyson, 1985.

Oosterhuis, Harry, ed. *Homosexuality and Male Bonding in Pre-Nazi Germany: The Youth Movement, the Gay Movement, and Male Bonding Before Hitler's Rise, Original Transcripts from "Der Eigene," the First Gay Journal in the World.* Translated by Hubert Kennedy. New York: Harrington Park Press, 1991.

Porter, Jack Nusan. *Sexual Politics in Nazi Germany, the Persecution of the Homosexuals During the Holocaust: Essays, Biographical Sketches, Biographies, Bibliographies, Photos, and Charts on Sexology, Homosexuality, Nazism, and Magnus Hirschfeld.* 3d ed. Newton, Mass.: Spencer Press, 2003.

SEE ALSO: Aug. 29, 1867: Karl Heinrich Ulrichs Speaks Publicly for Gay and Lesbian Rights; May 6, 1868: Kertbeny Coins the Terms "Homosexual" and "Heterosexual"; 1869: Westphal Advocates Medical Treatment for Sexual Inversion; 1896: Raffalovich Publishes *Uranisme et Unisexualité*; 1897: Ellis Publishes *Sexual Inversion*; May 14, 1897: Hirschfeld Founds the Scientific-Humanitarian Committee; 1906: Friedlaender Breaks with the Scientific-Humanitarian Committee; 1908: Carpenter Publishes *The Intermediate Sex*; Dec. 10, 1924: Gerber Founds the Society for Human Rights; 1933-1945: Nazis Persecute Homosexuals; 1950: Mattachine Society Is Founded.

## 1896
# RAFFALOVICH PUBLISHES *URANISME ET UNISEXUALITÉ*

*Poet and sexologist Marc-André Raffalovich, in his work* Uranisme et Unisexualité, *defended homosexuality as an innate trait that has served certain individuals well in the arts, the humanities, and the sciences.*

**LOCALE:** Paris, France
**CATEGORIES:** Literature; publications

**KEY FIGURE**
*Marc-André Raffalovich* (1864-1934), Russian-born poet and sexologist

**SUMMARY OF EVENT**

In the 1880's, Marc-André Raffalovich—a wealthy Russian Jew who had grown up in France but who had settled in Russia—established a reputation as a minor poet among the Decadents. By the 1890's, he had formed a lasting friendship with John Gray, another minor Decadent poet. Also, he had converted to Catholicism and had taken up the serious study of homosexuality.

In *Uranisme et Unisexualité: Étude sur différentes manifestations de l'instinct sexuel* (1896), Raffalovich argued against the prevailing medical opinion that homosexuality was an innate degenerative condition that resulted in mental illnesses. He believed that the experts had based their theories on far-too-limited case studies focusing on just one "type" of homosexual. He proposed a complex taxonomy of types, from the ultra-masculine homosexual to the extremely effeminate homosexual. He also elaborated a similar gradation of types for heterosexuals—a term that he himself used.

To prove his theory, Raffalovich turned to history, pointing out that homosexuality had existed in all places and at all times. The Greeks had known it, and many of them had practiced it. However, following Plato, some had developed a means of dealing with it through a process of sublimation that had led many individuals to make significant contributions to their civilization.

Christianity had replaced philosophy with religion, but it, too, upheld the same process of sublimation during the Middle Ages as the means by which some individuals, including homosexuals, could achieve spiritual enlightenment. The Renaissance and the Enlightenment saw many famous homosexuals as well, and these individuals had achieved remarkable success in the arts, the humanities, and the sciences. Even in the nineteenth century, homosexuals had played important roles in their societies by concentrating on their intellectual pursuits.

By historicizing homosexuality, Raffalovich was trying to normalize it. He agreed with the medical field that homosexuality was an innate trait, but he disagreed with medical professionals who labeled homosexuality a degenerative trait. Instead, Raffalovich believed fervently that many homosexuals had an innate predisposition for the spiritual or intellectual life, but he believed equally that, to attain this life, they had to practice a form of chastity. Homosexuals who could obtain this level of chastity could channel their energy into constructive projects. Ultimately, Raffalovich separated the person, whom he believed deserved respect, from the act, which he believed deserved condemnation.

## SIGNIFICANCE

*Uranisme et Unisexualité* was an eccentrically produced book that did not gain wide circulation, not has it been translated into English. However, by publishing it as a medical treatise, Raffalovich confronted the medical discourse directly, and he established himself as one of the leading experts on this subject. He broadened the study of homosexuality by pointing out that homosexuals did not conform to the medical stereotype, although he did agree that such effeminate individuals did exist.

In contrast, however, he analyzed famous men and women from the past who had made significant social contributions. His emphasis on the cultural contribution of these individuals influenced other thinkers throughout the twentieth century, who be

gan to look at the intersection between one's sexuality and one's cultural products. In addition, his advocacy of chastity, which grew out of his own conversion to the Roman Catholic faith, had an important impact on other religious thinkers, who adopted the principle of tolerating the individual but condemning the act. In the final analysis, his defense of homosexuality was an idealization of romantic friendship but not of sexuality per se.

—*William A. Peniston*

## FURTHER READING

Mendès-Leite, Rommel, and Pierre-Olivier de Busscher, eds. *Gay Studies from the French Cultures: Voices from France, Belgium, Brazil, Canada, and the Netherlands*. New York: Haworth Press, 1993.

Roden, Frederick S. *Same-Sex Desire in Victorian Religious Culture*. New York: Palgrave Macmillan, 2002.

Sewell, Brocard. *Footnote to the Nineties: A Memoir of John Gray and André Raffalovich*. London: Cecil & Amelia Woolf, 1968.

_____, ed. *Two Friends, John Gray and André Raffalovich: Essay Biographical and Critical*. Aylesford, England: St. Albert's Press, 1963.

Smith, Timothy d'Arch. *Love in Earnest: Some Notes on the Lives and the Writings of the English "Uranian" Poets from 1889 to 1930*. London: Routledge & Kegan Paul, 1970.

SEE ALSO: Aug. 29, 1867: Karl Heinrich Ulrichs Speaks Publicly for Gay and Lesbian Rights; May 6, 1868: Kertbeny Coins the Terms "Homosexual" and "Heterosexual"; 1869: Westphal Advocates Medical Treatment for Sexual Inversion; 1896: *Der Eigene* Is Published as First Journal on Homosexuality; 1897: Ellis Publishes *Sexual Inversion*; May 14, 1897: Hirschfeld Founds the Scientific-Humanitarian Committee; 1906: Friedlaender Breaks with the Scientific-Humanitarian Committee; 1908: Carpenter Publishes *The Intermediate Sex*; Dec. 10, 1924: Gerber Founds the Society for Human Rights; 1933-1945: Nazis Persecute Homosexuals; 1950: Mattachine Society Is Founded.

# 1897
# ELLIS PUBLISHES *SEXUAL INVERSION*

Sexual Inversion *was the first social scientific work to describe homosexuality in neutral terms, avoiding moralistic, legal, and pathological representations. The text was regarded as radical by contemporary sexologists because it considered homosexuality to be hereditary and normal.*

**LOCALE:** Leipzig, Germany
**CATEGORIES:** Science; publications

**KEY FIGURES**
*Havelock Ellis* (1859-1939), English sexologist and physician
*John Addington Symonds* (1840-1893), English historian, poet, and translator, who collaborated with Ellis on *Sexual Inversion*
*Sigmund Freud* (1856-1939), Viennese psychiatrist and founder of psychoanalysis
*Magnus Hirschfeld* (1868-1935), German physician and sexologist
*Richard von Krafft-Ebing* (1840-1902), German psychiatrist and sex researcher

*Karl Maria Kertbeny* (1824-1882), German writer, coined term "homosexual" in 1868
*Albert Moll* (1862-1939), German physician and sexologist
*Karl Heinrich Ulrichs* (1825-1895), German lawyer and theologian

**SUMMARY OF EVENT**
Western civilization in the nineteenth century witnessed the development, growth, and evolution of the social sciences, that is, the application of scientific methods to the study of human attitudes, beliefs, behaviors, emotions, and knowledge. One of these new sciences was sexology, or the study of human sexuality. The abstraction of human sexuality as a particular field of study presented sexologists with unique problems of categorization, and the study of sexuality led to the question, How are various forms of human sexual expression and identity to be conceived?

A variety of practitioners beginning in 1875 published their research and studies on human sexual

---

## AN INTRODUCTION TO *SEXUAL INVERSION*

There can be no doubt that a peculiar amount of ignorance exists regarding the subject of sexual inversion. I know medical men of many years' general experience who have never, to their knowledge, come across a single case. We may remember, indeed, that some fifteen years ago the total number of cases recorded in scientific literature scarcely equaled those of British race which I have obtained, and that before my first cases were published not a single British case, unconnected with the asylum or the prison, had ever been recorded. Probably not a very large number of people are even aware that the turning in of the sexual instinct toward persons of the same sex can ever be regarded as inborn, so far as any sexual instinct is inborn. And very few, indeed, would not be surprised if it were possible to publish a list of the names of sexually inverted men and women who at the present time are honorably known in church, state, society, art, or letters. It could not be positively affirmed of all such persons that they were born inverted, but in most the inverted tendency seems to be instinctive, and appears at a somewhat early age. In any case, however, it must be realized that in this volume we are not dealing with subjects belonging to the lunatic asylum, or the prison. We are concerned with individuals who live in freedom, some of them suffering intensely from their abnormal organization, but otherwise ordinary members of society. In a few cases we are concerned with individuals whose moral or artistic ideals have widely influenced their fellows, who know nothing of the peculiar organization which has largely molded those ideals.

*Source:* From the preface to the first edition of *Sexual Inversion*, vol. 2 in *Studies in the Psychology of Sex*, 3d rev. ed. (Philadelphia: Davis, 1921).

## WHAT IS SEXUAL INVERSION?

Is it, as many would have us believe, an abominably acquired vice, to be stamped out by prison? or is it, as a few assert, a beneficial variety of human emotion which should be tolerated or even fostered? Is it a diseased condition which qualifies its subject for the lunatic asylum? or is it a natural monstrosity, a human "sport," the manifestations of which must be regulated when they become antisocial? There is probably an element of truth in more than one of these views. Very widely divergent views of sexual inversion are largely justified by the position and attitude of the investigator. It is natural that the police-official should find that his cases are largely mere examples of disgusting vice and crime. It is natural that the asylum superintendent should find that we are chiefly dealing with a form of insanity. It is equally natural that the sexual invert himself should find that he and his inverted friends are not so very unlike ordinary persons. We have to recognize the influence of professional and personal bias and the influence of environment. . . .

In dealing with it [sexual inversion] I have sought to avoid that attitude of moral superiority which is so common in the literature of this subject, and have refrained from pointing out how loathsome this phenomenon is, or how hideous that. Such an attitude is as much out of place in scientific investigation as it is in judicial investigation, and may well be left to the amateur. The physician who feels nothing but disgust at the sight of disease is unlikely to bring either succor to his patients or instructions to his pupils.

*Source:* Excerpt from *Sexual Inversion*, vol. 2 in *Studies in the Psychology of Sex*, 3d rev. ed. (Philadelphia: Davis, 1921).

difference and variation. Together these books formed the early fundamental literature on sexology. The core sexological texts included Karl Heinrich Ulrichs's *Forschungen über das Räthsel der mannmännlichen Liebe* (1864-1879; *The Riddle of "Man-Manly" Love*, 1994), a series of pamphlets), Richard von Krafft-Ebing's *Psychopathia sexualis* (1886), and Albert Moll's *Untersuchungen über die Libido sexualis* (1897). The definitive sexology textbook, the five-volume *Geschlechtskunde auf Grund dreissigjähriger Forschung und Erfahrung* (sexual knowledge) was written by Magnus Hirschfeld between 1926 and 1930.

The late nineteenth century interest in sexology, however, was overshadowed by the early twentieth century fascination with psychology. Sigmund Freud's voluminous groundbreaking works in the field of psychiatry, including *Die Traumdeutung* (1900; *The Interpretation of Dreams*, 1913) and his *Vorlesungen Einführung in die Psychoanalyse* (1916-1917; *A General Introduction to Psychoanalysis*, 1920), attracted more attention than did sexology and diminished the overall prestige of the fledgling discipline.

In 1896, Havelock Ellis published his work on "sexual inversion," or "contrary sexual feeling,"

first in German translation, as *Das konträre Geschlechtsgefühl* (*Sexual Inversion*, 1897). Ellis chose to publish the book in Germany rather than his native England because of the fear of censorship generated by the sensationalism surrounding the 1895 trials of Oscar Wilde in London for sodomy and gross indecency. British publishers were frightened to print any works dealing with homosexuality in the aftermath of Wilde's well-publicized prosecution and conviction, regardless of the seriousness of the scholarship. Ellis's decision to publish first in Germany instead of England would hold unintended consequences for the future of sexological research.

John Addington Symonds, who died in 1893, before *Sexual Inversion* was published, coauthored part of the work. Symonds's death forced Ellis to complete the book on his own. Only the first German edition, however, acknowledges Symonds as a coauthor. The first English edition of *Sexual Inversion* appeared the following year, and it was published in London. It was privately censored and distribution was largely curtailed. A second English edition was published in the United States (Philadelphia) in 1901.

## Significance

Previous works in sexology had dealt with homosexuality as a form of degeneracy and as a disease of the mind, or a psychological disorder. Freud thought that homosexuality was a stage of human sexual development and saw its manifestation in adult males as cases of arrested development. Others, such as Krafft-Ebing and Moll, believed also that homosexuality was a psychological and medical pathology.

The term "homosexuality" was coined only in the latter half of the nineteenth century and did not come into widespread usage until the 1870's. Karl Heinrich Ulrichs did not have the benefit of access or reference to the term when writing his pamphlets. Instead, Ulrichs referred to homosexuality as "uranism" and to homosexuals as "uranians." The actual word "homosexual" appears to have been coined by Karl Maria Kertbeny in his 1869 open letter to the Prussian government, condemning reform of the criminal code, which proposed defining male homosexuality as illegal and punishable. Despite such opposition, efforts to criminalize homosexuality succeeded when the Reichstag adopted Paragraph 143 of the Prussian criminal code, which included also a provision against bestiality. Paragraph 143 (changed to Paragraph 175) was widely used by the Nazis to arrest and punish homosexuals during the Third Reich.

Ellis's work is notable for discussing homosexuality in philosophical terms. His sensitivity toward homosexuality may have been conditioned by his wife, Edith Lees, who was a lesbian. Whereas Krafft-Ebing and Freud spoke of homosexuals in terms of psychopathology and abnormal sexual development, Ellis's *Sexual Inversion* was revolutionary in its humane and nonjudgmental scientific approach toward human sexuality research. Deviating from contemporary attitudes toward homosexuality as abnormal, criminal, degenerate, immoral, or pathological, the work presented homosexuality as hereditary and as a normal variation in a spectrum of sexual orientations. Ellis was instrumental in developing a taxonomy of human sexual behavior and classification. He also described differences in homosexual behavior (situational homosexuality versus innate, or latent, homosexuality), and distinguished between male and female homosexuality and bisexuality. *Sexual Inversion* remains a foundational text of modern sex research.

*—Keith Carson*

## Further Reading

Ellis, Havelock. *Studies in the Psychology of Sex: Sexual Inversion.* Seattle, Wash.: University Press of the Pacific, 2001.

Hirschfeld, Magnus. *The Homosexuality of Men and Women.* 1920. Reprint. Amherst, N.Y.: Prometheus Books, 2000.

Krafft-Ebing, Richard von. *Psychopathia Sexualis.* 1886. Reprint. Burbank, Calif.: Bloat, 1999.

Moll, Albert. *Libido Sexualis: Studies in the Psychosexual Laws of Love Verified by Clinical Sexual Case Histories.* New York: American Ethnological Press, 1933.

Ulrichs, Karl Heinrich. *The Riddle of "Man-Manly" Love: The Pioneering Work on Male Homosexuality.* Translated by Michael A. Lombardi-Nash. 2 vols. Buffalo, N.Y.: Prometheus Books, 1994.

**See also:** May 6, 1868: Kertbeny Coins the Terms "Homosexual" and "Heterosexual"; 1869: Westphal Advocates Medical Treatment for Sexual Inversion; Jan., 1892-July, 1892: Alice Mitchell Found Guilty of Murdering Her Lover; May 14, 1897: Hirschfeld Founds the Scientific-Humanitarian Committee; 1905: Freud Rejects Third-Sex Theory; 1929: Davis's Research Identifies Lesbian Sexuality as Common and Normal; 1948: Kinsey Publishes *Sexual Behavior in the Human Male*; 1952: APA Classifies Homosexuality as a Mental Disorder; 1953: Kinsey Publishes *Sexual Behavior in the Human Female*; 1953-1957: Evelyn Hooker Debunks Beliefs That Homosexuality Is a "Sickness"; Mar. 7, 1967: CBS Airs *CBS Reports: The Homosexuals*; Oct. 31, 1969: *Time* Magazine Issues "The Homosexual in America"; Dec. 15, 1973: Homosexuality Is Delisted by APA; Apr. 20, 2001: Chinese Psychiatric Association Removes Homosexuality from List of Mental Disorders.

## May 14, 1897
# HIRSCHFELD FOUNDS THE SCIENTIFIC-HUMANITARIAN COMMITTEE

*Magnus Hirschfeld established the Scientific-Humanitarian Committee to work for repeal of Paragraph 175 of the German criminal code, which prohibited sexual acts between men, and to advocate for a wide range of sexual rights.*

**LOCALE:** Germany

**CATEGORIES:** Organizations and institutions; government and politics; laws, acts, and legal history

### KEY FIGURES

*Magnus Hirschfeld* (1868-1935), German sexologist and physician, who founded the committee and the Institute for Sexual Science

*Kurt Hiller* (1885-1972), German writer and lawyer, headed the committee before it was outlawed by the Nazis

*Adolf Brand* (1874-1945), German activist and editor, who criticized the committee as assimilationist

*Ernst Rohm* (1887-1934), German Nazi leader of the Sturmabteilung (SA), which destroyed Hirschfeld's institute in 1933

### SUMMARY OF EVENT

Magnus Hirschfeld was born in Prussia, and he studied philology and medicine. Considered the "Einstein of sex," he was one of the founding scholars in the discipline of human sexuality. With other pioneering sex researchers, Hirschfeld helped establish sexology: the science and study of human sexuality.

Hirschfeld founded the Wissenschaftlich-humanitäre Komitee, or Scientific-Humanitarian Committee (SHC), on May 14, 1897, to advocate for individual sexual rights. He was particularly distressed by the treatment of homosexuals, or what he had called the "third sex," a biological category intermediate to males and females. His view, how-ever, of homosexuality as a third, or intermediate, sex constituting a "female soul trapped in a male body," or a "male soul trapped in a female body," is regarded now as prima facie false. Because he believed in the biological basis of homosexuality, Hirschfeld is considered to be an essentialist, that is, he believes sexuality is innate.

Intersexuality (another term at the time for homosexuality) was considered a natural intermediate category of human sexuality and was not, therefore, an errant aberration, biological defect, or the result of moral degeneracy. Hirschfeld's presupposition that homosexual behavior was just one form of behavior on a continuum of human sexuality was considered radical at the time. Sexology, however, was overshadowed by the revolutionary work simultaneously conducted in the fledgling fields of human psychology and psychoanalysis by Sigmund Freud and others.

The chief objective of the SHC had been the repeal of Paragraph 175 of the German criminal code. As modern nation-states developed throughout Europe in the nineteenth century, the relationship between the individual and the state evolved and governments attempted to reconcile standards of behavior with prevailing, often constricting, notions of the moral good. Such efforts to regulate sexual conduct were part of the process of organizing the modern state and of defining and distinguishing between the public and private realms,

---

**GERMAN CRIMINAL CODE, PARAGRAPH 175, VERSION OF 1871**

*Unnatural Fornication*

Unnatural fornication, whether between persons of the male sex or of humans with beasts, is to be punished by imprisonment; a sentence of loss of civil rights may also be passed.

criminal and legal activities, and moral degeneracy and health.

Although Hirschfeld was a scientist, his political instincts and social activism demonstrated he also was savvy and sophisticated in the realms of politics and society. Apparently, he understood that neither the prevailing atmosphere of sexual tolerance in Germany nor his work there in sexology were guaranteed. The Weimar renaissance could be threatened by contemporary legal statutes, political pressure, and social repression.

*The board of the Scientific-Humanitarian Committee in 1901. From left, Georg Plock, Ernst Burchard, Magnus Hirschfeld, and Baron von Teschenberg.*

Hirschfeld's approach was two-pronged and is best represented by the two organizations with which his name is most often associated: the SHC and the Institute for Sexual Science (Institut für Sexualwissenschaft). The Institute for Sexual Science, established by Hirschfeld in Berlin in 1919, was a professional, scholarly organization based on the scientific model of inquiry. The earlier SHC had been an advocacy group that sought to advance gay and lesbian rights, promote legal reform, and encourage understanding of the diversity of human sexuality. Its model was based on advocacy, education, and public awareness. In many ways these organizations complemented one another, but both, however, had distinct purposes.

As a professional establishment, the Institute for Sexual Science offered, for example, marriage and sexual counseling, a library and research, and expert legal advice and testimony. The institute's primary professional practice broached the fields of law, medicine, and scholarship.

The SHC engaged in human rights advocacy, political activism, and social justice within the established political process. Its primary mission centered on legal reform, most notably the campaign to repeal Paragraph 175. The SHC's movement to strike down Paragraph 175 in the Reichstag focused national attention on the issue of gay rights. The committee was criticized by some homosexual activists, such as Adolf Brand, and by pederasts and German nationalists as bourgeois and effeminate in its goals of assimilating gays and lesbians into existing mainstream institutions and middle-class structures, such as marriage and the modern family.

## SIGNIFICANCE

The impact of Hirschfeld's work was as controversial as it was revolutionary. Essentially a pioneer in the modern science of human sexuality and a champion of gay rights, Hirschfeld was viewed as a hero by some and a villain by others.

Paragraph 175 was bound up with the history of German nationhood. When Germany unified in 1871, Kaiser William I adopted the conservative Prussian criminal code over the liberal Napoleonic code that many German principalities had subscribed to prior to nationalizing. Indeed, the Scientific-Humanitarian Committee's creed, "justice through science," belied Enlightenment principles, and some of its members even took up the revolutionary motto of France, but added a twist: "Liberte, Fraternite, Egalite, Homosexualite!"

Legal reform, though, proved more difficult, evasive, and fleeting in spite of the enthusiasm of some SHC members. With the mounting political influence of the National Socialist German Workers' Party (NSDAP), the SHC's destiny was becoming increasingly unclear.

By 1933, with the rising political fortunes of the NSDAP's leader, Adolf Hitler, the demise of the

*The cover of a 1922 tract opposing Paragraph 175 of the German criminal code, which outlawed homosexuality. The title translates as the "ignominy" or "scandal" "of the century."*

SHC was ensured. The forces of extremism and intolerance converged in Berlin on May 6, 1933, when Nazi thugs in Ernst Rohm's SA, or Brown Shirts, stormed the Institute for Sexual Science, eventually burning and destroying much of its library holdings and other contents. In the aftermath of the violence and devastation wrought in 1933, many SHC members left Berlin and sought exile from Germany. Hirschfeld emigrated to France, where he died in Nice in 1935.

Hirschfeld's relationship with the NSDAP was in some ways complicated by the prevalence of homosexuals in the ranks of Nazi leadership. Rohm, who was gay, subscribed to the elitist view of homosexuality that saw "Greek love," or pederasty, as the highest form of love, or eros. According to the elite theory of homosexuality proposed by Brand, gay sex, especially sex between men and boys, was celebrated as the purest expression of masculinity and national strength. Strands of the elite theory can be glimpsed in Nazi anti-Semitism and the pseudo-science of racial purity, which exulted in a virile, penile, and impudent militarism. The Aryan warrior was bred to defend through valor and violence the honor of the fatherland. Hirschfeld rejected the elite theory of homosexuality and specifically denounced pederasty.

The legacy of Hirschfeld's Scientific-Humanitarian Committee is mixed. During its existence it was a strong proponent of human sexual rights, although it failed to achieve its major objective: the repeal of Paragraph 175. Clearly, however, Hirschfeld's scholarship inspired future sex researchers, such as Alfred Kinsey, a sexologist at Indiana University–Bloomington, whose studies of male and female sexual behavior remain revolutionary and controversial.

While scholarship in human sexuality has gradually advanced—although it remains curtailed and limited in significant ways—reform of criminal law concerning homosexuality proceeded even more slowly. Kurt Hiller, for example, after escaping Nazi internment at the Brandenburg and Sachsenhausen concentration camps and eluding capture by communists in Eastern Europe following World War II, received virtually no support in his efforts to continue the work of the Scientific-Humanitarian Committee in Hamburg, West Germany, in the 1950's nor in his attempt to reestablish it in 1962. Furthermore, Paragraph 175 of the German criminal code remained in effect until March 10, 1994.

—*Keith Carson*

### FURTHER READING

Bauer, J. Edgar. "On the Nameless Love and Infinite Sexualities: John Henry Mackay, Magnus Hirschfeld and the Origins of the Sexual Emancipation Movement." *Journal of Homosexuality* 50, no. 1 (2005): 1-26.

Epstein, Rob, and Jeffrey Friedman, producers and directors. *Paragraph 175.* Documentary film. New Yorker Films, 2000.

Grau, Gunter, ed. *Hidden Holocaust? Gay and Lesbian Persecution in Germany, 1933-45.* Translated by Patrick Camiller. Chicago: Fitzroy Dearborn, 1995.

Hirschfeld, Magnus. *The Homosexuality of Men and Women*. 1920. Reprint. Amherst, N.Y.: Prometheus Books, 2000.

Magnus Hirschfeld Archive for Sexology, Humboldt-Universität, Berlin. http://www2.berlin.de/sexology/.

Magnus Hirschfeld Society, Centre for Research on the History of Sexual Science. http://www.hirschfeld.in-berlin.de.

Wolff, Charlotte. *Magnus Hirschfeld: A Portrait of a Pioneer in Sexology*. Topsfield, Mass.: Salem House, 1987.

**SEE ALSO:** May 6, 1868: Kertbeny Coins the Terms "Homosexual" and "Heterosexual"; 1869: Westphal Advocates Medical Treatment for Sexual Inversion; 1897: Ellis Publishes *Sexual Inversion*; 1905: Freud Rejects Third-Sex Theory; 1929: Davis's Research Identifies Lesbian Sexuality as Common and Normal; 1948: Kinsey Publishes *Sexual Behavior in the Human Male*; 1952: APA Classifies Homosexuality as a Mental Disorder; 1953: Kinsey Publishes *Sexual Behavior in the Human Female*; 1953-1957: Evelyn Hooker Debunks Beliefs That Homosexuality Is a "Sickness"; Mar. 7, 1967: CBS Airs *CBS Reports: The Homosexuals*; Oct. 31, 1969: *Time* Magazine Issues "The Homosexual in America"; Dec. 15, 1973: Homosexuality Is Delisted by APA; Apr. 20, 2001: Chinese Psychiatric Association Removes Homosexuality from List of Mental Disorders.

## c. 1899
# TRANSGENDER REPORTER COVERS SPANISH-AMERICAN WAR REVOLTS

*Elvira Mugarrieta, a female-to-male transgender reporter better known as Babe Bean, traveled to the Philippines in 1899 as a freelance news correspondent to report on the Filipino revolts against U.S. occupation of the country after the Spanish-American War.*

**LOCALE:** California; The Philippines
**CATEGORIES:** Transgender/transsexuality; military

### KEY FIGURE
*Babe Bean* (Elvira Mugarrieta; Jack Bee Garland; 1869-1936), freelance reporter

### SUMMARY OF EVENT
In the late nineteenth century, Americans, much like their European counterparts, had acquired an appetite for colonial possessions. Cuba and the Philippines, both in the middle of revolts against Spanish colonial rule, acquired American aid after the United States declared war against Spain in 1898.

The fighting in the Spanish-American War lasted a few months only. In the Treaty of Paris (1898), which ended the conflict, the United States obtained Cuba, Guam, Puerto Rico, and all of the Philippines. Filipinos, however, not wanting to exchange Spanish masters for American ones, revolted in 1899. A freelance reporter named Babe Bean, born Elvira Mugarrieta, was determined to cover the Filipino revolt as a male reporter, sure to get a different perspective on the war because of his gender. Bean dressed as a man and then traveled to the Philippines. The Filipino insurrection had continued for seven years, until Filipino insurgents were overwhelmed by U.S. forces. It is not known, however, how long Bean had stayed in the region.

Born in the Russian Hill section of San Francisco, Muggarieta came from an upper-class family. At some point in her childhood, Mugarrieta frightened her parents with her rebellious ways, including being a "tomboy," and was sent to a convent. To escape the Roman Catholic Church and the nunnery, at the age of fifteen, she married her brother's best friend, possibly named "Bean." Within a few months, the couple divorced, and Mugarrieta adopted a man's name to match her masculine attire. Now known as Babe Bean, she passed for a man in hobo camps, in the mountains, and on city streets. Male attire protected Bean from sexual assault and allowed Bean entry into all-male enclaves, including the realm of war.

In the years before he began war reporting (during the summer of 1897), Bean was arrested by police in Stockton, California, after police had received reports of a young woman "posing" as a man. Officers spent two weeks trying to track down the "wrongdoer" and finally apprehended Bean in August. His clothing—a large hat, a boy's long suit-jacket with padded shoulders, long vest, tie, and oversized shoes—disguised the curves and build of a woman about 5 feet 2 inches tall and weighing a mere 104 pounds. His high-pitched voice could give him away, so he claimed to be unable to speak after being injured in an accident. Bean would "speak" to police and newspaper reporters by means of writing. The Stockton police released him. Bean remained in Stockton but never hid, never stopped wearing male clothing, and never again faced arrest.

Bean would become a local celebrity as a transgender person, with contemporary newspaper accounts showing that he received affectionate treatment from the people of Stockton, including the local bachelor club, which made him an honorary member; this is all the more interesting because Bean presented himself as a gay man. Later, the *Stockton Evening Mail* hired him as a reporter. Called "Jack" by his neighbors, Bean lived on a houseboat on McLeod's Lake until the start of the Spanish-American War in 1898. Determined to see the conflict from the point of view of one treated as a man, he wrangled passage in 1899 on the troop transport *City of Para* to Manila in the Philippines. In addition to working as a news correspondent, Bean worked as a field hospital aide before returning to the port of San Francisco (the date is uncertain).

Bean took up residence in San Francisco and briefly resumed wearing women's clothing, but discovered, not surprisingly, that the attire still limited his freedom; he once again donned a man's suit. In 1903, San Francisco had passed an ordinance banning the wearing of opposite-gender apparel. Fearing arrest, Bean adopted his mother's family name to become Jack Bee Garland.

Garland died on September 18, 1936, in San Francisco, of generalized peritonitis following the perforation of a peptic ulcer. He had been suffering from abdominal pains for some time, but, like many transgender men, feared that a physician would expose him as a "cross-dresser." Garland collapsed on a sidewalk and soon died in a hospital. Predictably, the autopsy surgeon discovered Garland's birth gender and publicized his findings.

## SIGNIFICANCE

Appearing in public in dress contrary to one's birth gender was long illegal in many countries, including the United States. Masculine gender roles have historically been valued over female gender roles, and masculinity is typically associated with authority, assertiveness, and the warranting of respect. Females, such as Babe Bean, who dress in masculine attire sometimes enjoy privileges not afforded to women and girls. Accessing privileges traditionally reserved for one gender and not the other has led to the condemnation of transgender individuals by religion, the state, the medical profession, and society in general.

To many people in the nineteenth and twentieth centuries, transgenderism was considered a sexual perversion. By 1952, the American Psychiatric Association listed male, but not female, transvestism as an illness in its *Diagnostic and Statistical Manual of Mental Disorders*. Only in the late twentieth century did this label come under heavy attack by transgender activists. As part of the so-called sexual revolution of the 1960's, transvestites and cross-dressers began to organize. Women who dressed as men or dressed in masculine attire—usually "butch" lesbians—found support within the emerging transgender/transsexual communities. A general relaxation in clothing standards in the late twentieth century has made it somewhat acceptable for women to dress in masculine attire, to a point. For the person wearing "opposite-gender" attire—especially if that person's gender expression is ambiguous to begin with—and for society at large, transgender expression remains an issue of curiosity, derision, misunderstanding, and, at its worst, verbal taunting, physical violence, or both.

—*Caryn E. Neumann*

**FURTHER READING**

Bullough, Vern L., and Bonnie Bullough. *Cross Dressing, Sex, and Gender*. Philadelphia: University of Pennsylvania Press, 1993.

Rupp, Leila J. *A Desired Past: A Short History of Same-Sex Love in America*. Chicago: University of Chicago Press, 1999.

San Francisco Lesbian and Gay History Project. "'She Even Chewed Tobacco': A Pictorial Narrative of Passing Women in America." In *Hidden from History: Reclaiming the Gay and Lesbian Past*, edited by Martin Duberman, Martha Vicinus, and George Chauncey, Jr. New York: Penguin, 1989.

Sullivan, Louis. *From Female to Male: The Life of Jack Bee Garland*. Boston: Alyson, 1990.

**SEE ALSO:** Jan.-June, 1886: Two-Spirit American Indian Visits Washington, D.C.; 1912-1924: Robles Fights in the Mexican Revolution; Sept. 24, 1951: George Jorgensen Becomes Christine Jorgensen; Nov. 21, 1966: First Gender Identity Clinic Opens and Provides Gender Reassignment Surgery; Jan. 21, 1989: Death of Transgender Jazz Musician Billy Tipton; 1992: Transgender Nation Holds Its First Protest; Dec. 24, 1993-Dec. 31, 1993: Transgender Man Brandon Teena Raped and Murdered; June 17, 1995: International Bill of Gender Rights Is First Circulated; 1996: Hart Recognized as a Transgender Man; Nov. 20, 2003: Transgender Day of Remembrance and Remembering Our Dead Project; May 17, 2004: Transsexual Athletes Allowed to Compete in Olympic Games.

---

## November 17, 1901
# POLICE ARREST "LOS 41" IN MEXICO CITY

*Police arrested forty-one gay men at a dance in Mexico City, creating a media sensation that challenged the concepts of sexual and gender identity and led to social debate about homosexuality, gender expression, and even Mexican identity in general.*

**ALSO KNOWN AS:** Party of the 41
**LOCALE:** Mexico City, Mexico
**CATEGORIES:** Civil rights; government and politics; crime

**SUMMARY OF EVENT**

Mexico's history of sexuality documents the case of the famous "Los 41." A small network of gay men agreed to organize a fiesta, promoting it among their friends and through invitations delivered to select men in the cantinas of Mexico City. On the evening of November 17, 1901, police officers dressed as civilians entered the party; after some hours had passed, the police raided the place and arrested forty-one men.

Unlike many other "scandals" involving same-gender sexuality, the Party of the 41, as it came to be called, became a major event. The Mexico City newspapers reported on the raid and the men's punishment. José Guadalupe Posada illustrated the event and wrote comic poems about it for the general public. Many *corridos* (poetic songs) and fictional accounts, including a novel, circulated in the following months.

The event became so significant that the number

41 became a metaphor for homosexuality, a metaphor that continues to this day, even though the event with which it is associated has been all but forgotten. Robert McKee Irwin, in an article on the party, states that the open discussion in the media was associated with the fear such an event posed to Mexican identity. Unlike other countries of Latin America, where scandals were hidden and homosexuality was portrayed as foreign, Mexico allowed journalists and writers to describe the forty-one queer men as Mexican. This created concern about Mexican national identity, because same-gender sexuality was seen as an obstacle to building this identity. This fear continued throughout the twentieth century in the work of famous Mexican intellectuals who wrote about the fate of the nation. For example, Octavio Paz, in *El laberinto de la soledad: Vida y pensamiento de México* (1950; *The Labyrinth of Solitude: Life and Thought in Mexico*, 1961), gendered all social relations, illustrating how the fear of emasculation is a major determinant in daily interactions.

The fictionalization of the Party of the 41 in the newspapers and in literary accounts, together with contradicting versions, obscured what is known about the event. According to many accounts, the police publicly ridiculed half the men because they were in drag. They were forced to sweep the streets in their female attire while onlookers laughed. This public humiliation was depicted in illustrations and became known even among those who could not read. Although many of the men at the party belonged to privileged families, the scandal's magnitude prevented their families from helping them. No legal code in Mexico had established a punishment for cross-dressing or practicing same-gender sexuality. Just the same, the Party of the 41 was punished by being enlisted in the military. They were sent by train first to Veracruz and then to Yucatán, where they joined the Mexican army and fought against a Mayan uprising.

Cross-dressing was common practice in the theater and other forms of popular amusement of the time, and the Mexican government tolerated it. However, the men suffered not only from the stigma of their own sexual and gender identities but also from Mexicans' association of ball dances with immorality. Public opinion pressured the government to inflict harsh punishment. Newspapers such as *El País*, *El Universal*, *El Popular*, and *El Hijo del Ahuizote* covered the event widely, and they called for official action against the men, who had violated sex and gender norms. The more conservative media used the party to condemn the government, associating the liberalism of the state with the "libertinage" of the fiesta of the 41. Others criticized the government for sending to the army people who had "abdicated their sex."

## SIGNIFICANCE

According to scholar Robert McKee Irwin, an analysis of the different accounts of this event suggests that two contradictory paradigms about same-gender sexuality existed in Mexico at the time. On one side, any same-gender sexual practice implies homosexuality; on the other, homosexuality includes only those who "invert" their gender roles, playing the "feminine role," and who desire to be penetrated by men. The coexistence of these views is complex, and it creates the possibility of multiple forms of queer identity. Although many scholars have argued that Mexican gay men are always identified as effeminate, Irwin argues that the masculine men in the Party of the 41 were also labeled "homosexuals."

Considering the coexistence of the two views on homosexuality opens the possibility of comparing Mexico's similarities to and differences from its northern neighbor. Those who identify Mexican homosexuality as inevitably associated with effeminacy may contribute to the idea of Latin America as an exotic place, without recognizing that the cultural interchange with the United States has strongly shaped both cultures.

On the centenary of "Los 41," Tulane University organized a conference on Latin American sexuality to memorialize the event. Carlos Monsivais and other Mexican scholars who had written about the 41 and the history of sexuality in Mexico were invited to participate. Monsivais denounced the lack of a commemoration in Mexico City, and he referred to the silencing of the history of the 41 in Mexican historiography. As a result of this conference, a book was published that includes primary sources and papers about sexuality in Mexico in the early twentieth century.

—*Pablo Ben*

## FURTHER READING

Franco, Jean. *Plotting Women: Gender and Representation in Mexico*. New York: Columbia University Press, 1989.

Irwin, Robert McKee. "The Famous 41: The Scandalous Birth of Modern Mexican Homosexuality." *GLQ* 6, no. 3 (2000): 353-376.

_____. *Mexican Masculinities*. Minneapolis: University of Minnesota Press, 2003.

Irwin, Robert McKee, Edward J. McCaughan, and Michelle Rocio Nasser, eds. *The Famous 41: Sexuality and Social Control in Mexico, c. 1901*. New York: Palgrave Macmillan, 2003.

Lancaster, Roger. "Sexual Positions: Caveats and Second Thoughts on 'Categories.'" *Americas* 54 (1997): 1-16.

Monsivais, Carlos. "El mundo soslayado." In *La estatua de sal*, edited by Salvador Novo. Mexico City: Consejo Nacional Para la Cultura y las Artes, 1998.

Paz, Octavio. *El laberinto de la soledad*. Mexico City: Fondo de Cultura Económica, 1989.

_____. *The Labyrinth of Solitude: Life and Thought in Mexico*. Translated by Lysander Kemp. New York: Grove Press, 1961.

**SEE ALSO:** 1907-1909: The Eulenburg Affair Scandalizes Germany's Leadership; 1912-1924: Robles Fights in the Mexican Revolution; 1933-1945: Nazis Persecute Homosexuals; June 30-July 1, 1934: Hitler's Night of the Long Knives; 1939: Isherwood Publishes *Goodbye to Berlin*; Nov., 1965: Revolutionary Cuba Imprisons Gays; 1969: Nuestro Mundo Forms as First Queer Organization in Argentina; June 27-July 2, 1969: Stonewall Rebellion Ignites Modern Gay and Lesbian Rights Movement; Oct. 14-17, 1987: Latin American and Caribbean Lesbian Feminist Network Is Formed; June 19, 2002: Gays and Lesbians March for Equal Rights in Mexico City; Apr., 2003: Buenos Aires Recognizes Same-Gender Civil Unions; Jan., 2006: Jiménez Flores Elected to the Mexican Senate.

## 1903
# STEIN WRITES *Q.E.D.*

*Based on a student love affair, Q.E.D. is Gertrude Stein's first and most overtly lesbian text and the first modern lesbian novel by any author. Q.E.D. also is one of the queerest novels of the early twentieth century, although it was not published until 1950.*

**ALSO KNOWN AS:** *Things as They Are* (1950)
**LOCALE:** Paris, France
**CATEGORIES:** Literature; publications

## KEY FIGURES

*Gertrude Stein* (1874-1946), American expatriate author

*Alice B. Toklas* (1877-1967), American expatriate in Paris who was Stein's lifelong partner

*May Bookstaver*, student at Johns Hopkins University and the love interest depicted in *Q.E.D.*

*Mable Haynes*, Stein's rival for Bookstaver's affections and the third member of *Q.E.D.*'s *love triangle*

## SUMMARY OF EVENT

While attending Johns Hopkins Medical School, Gertrude Stein began a love affair with fellow student May Bookstaver. Stein was mystified by the tacit rules of May's social circle of largely short-term "romantic friends" and was ultimately rejected by May in favor of her more experienced lover, Mable Haynes. In response, Stein spent much of the following year (1903) contemplating this failure and writing about it explicitly in the novella, *Q.E.D.* Despite the importance of this relationship and text for Stein's personal and literary development, it was her "marriage" to Alice B. Toklas from 1908 until Stein's death in 1946 that defined her as one of the foremothers of modern feminism and lesbianism as well as of literary modernism.

Given the controversial nature of the novella, Stein claimed to have forgotten about it until 1932, when she asked a publisher for advice on the work. Given the continued atmosphere of sexual oppression, however, *Q.E.D.* did not appear in Stein's lifetime. Toklas, as she did with so many other works by Stein, was finally successful in getting *Q.E.D.* into print; it was published in 1950 by Bayam Press under the title *Things as They Are*, although it bore its original title in subsequent editions.

*Q.E.D.* is divided into three sections named for the three fictional representations of the members of the romantic triangle: book 1, Adele (Stein); book 2, Mabel Neathe (Mable); and book 3, Helen (May). While this predictable structure and the novella's straightforward language make it Stein's least experimental work and largely a holdover from narrative traditions of the nineteenth century, the text also reflects a faith in science primarily associated with twentieth century literary and cultural modernism.

The title itself suggests this modern turn. Standing for the Latin phrase *quod erat demonstrandum* (literally, "which was to be demonstrated" or "proved"), the abbreviation often occurs at the end of a mathematical or logical proof to signal its completion. Used for this novella, the title reflects Stein's attempt here and in subsequent writing (notably in *The Making of Americans*, 1925—begun in the same year as *Q.E.D.*) to make a nearly scientific study of "bottom nature," or the forces and rhythms that define personality and determine all human interaction.

### SIGNIFICANCE

The importance of this text's composition must be measured both in terms of its role in Stein's development as an icon of lesbian and gay culture and an innovator in modernism and in terms of its more direct and literal historical impact. In the first case, this novella was most obviously important for Stein as it figured in her developing sexuality. After the ill-fitting relationships she saw and experienced in May's social circle of romantic friends, she and Toklas, like the butch and femme lesbians who followed them, created a very different kind of relationship in the relative openness and stability of their lesbian "marriage."

---

## GERTRUDE STEIN

Gertrude Stein's greatest achievement was her wily and strong independence, which revealed itself as much in the way she lived her life as it did in her work. She was a creative person with a strong personality, a gift for conversation, and a good ear, and her home became a center for the avant-garde circle of artists in Paris during the early twentieth century. Perhaps this salon would not be so famous were it not for the fact that those associated with it were later accepted as the outstanding figures of the modern art world. In time, artists as different as Ernest Hemingway, Sherwood Anderson, Virgil Thomson, Guillaume Apollinaire, Henri Matisse, and Pablo Picasso became associated with Stein and were drawn into the discussions and activities that took place in her home. Among contemporaries she was recognized as a fascinating individual with strong opinions and definite views, and a lively intelligence and vibrant mind; among the cultural historians who came later, she was acknowledged to be a person of enormous creative influence and an empowering force.

Stein's work, however, has never been easily accessible to the reader. During her lifetime, her work was both ridiculed and celebrated, and indeed these two attitudes continue to prevail among Stein's readers. Historical distance has provided a supportive context for Stein's work, though, and now that readers can see Stein in a milieu of highly creative artists devoted to wrenching art from the restrictions of realism and verisimilitude, her work is more easily appreciated for the inroads it makes against conventions, although perhaps not more easily understood. Stein was a powerful initiator, a ruthless experimenter, and a bold and forthright manipulator of words.

*Alice B. Toklas, left, and Gertrude Stein.*

(published as *Stanzas in Meditation, and Other Poems, 1929-1933*, 1956), from before and after the discovery of *Q.E.D.*, scholar Ulla Dydo has shown that Stein significantly revised it, probably in response to Toklas's anger. Specifically, Dydo demonstrates that the author edited out nearly all of the poem's many uses of the word "may."

More significantly still, it seems likely that even Stein's most famous piece, *The Autobiography of Alice B. Toklas* (1933), was begun the year of *Q.E.D.*'s discovery, at least in part as another gesture to appease Toklas. *The Autobiography of Alice B. Toklas* and the U.S. book tour that it inspired were crucial factors in creating Stein-the-icon and in bringing the Stein-Toklas relationship to the public eye.

Approaching its impact more directly, as the first modern lesbian novel, the importance of *Q.E.D.* as a milestone in GLBT culture cannot be denied. In this sense, the text represents a kind of time capsule, depicting in the sexual anxieties and silences of its characters those of its historical moment. A phrase from the novella suggests this sense best: Like the silences surrounding issues of fidelity in the text's romantic triangle, the moment was full of "the atmosphere of the unasked question" regarding sexuality. The importance of *Q.E.D.* is that it gave voice to that question.

—*Liberty Smith*

The text is also prominent in Stein's development as a writer, reappearing in or influencing many of the most important of Stein's later works. For example, Stein rewrites the novella as the 1905 short story "Melanctha," or "Each One as She May," in the *Three Lives* trilogy (1909). Well known for its use of dialect and repetition in depicting the rhythm of its (apparently heterosexual) African American characters, this text marks the emergence of Stein's more experimental modern voice. It also represents one instance of the kind of deployment of racial others for which both white GLBT culture and modernism have been criticized.

In 1932, Toklas's anger at discovering that Stein had kept *Q.E.D.* from her for thirty years dramatically impacted two of Stein's most important works. Comparing manuscripts of the long poem she was writing at the time, *Stanzas in Meditation*

### FURTHER READING

Dydo, Ulla E. "Reading the Hand Writing: The Manuscripts of Gertrude Stein." In *A Gertrude Stein Companion: Content with the Example*, edited by Bruce Kellner. New York: Greenwood, 1990.

Hovey, Jaime. "Sapphic Primitivism in Gertrude Stein's *Q.E.D.*" *Modern Fiction Studies* 42 (1996): 547-569.

Katz, Leon. Introduction to Gertrude Stein's *"Fernhurst," "Q.E.D.," and Other Early Writings*, edited by Donald Gallup. New York: Liveright, 1971.

Kostelanetz, Richard, ed. *The Gertrude Stein Reader: The Great American Pioneer of Avantgarde Letters*. New York: Cooper Square Press, 2002.

Souhami, Diana. *Gertrude and Alice*. London: Pandora, 1991.

Stein, Gertrude. *Q.E.D.* In *"Fernhurst," "Q.E.D.," and Other Early Writings*, edited by Donald Gallup. New York: Liveright, 1971.

_____. *Three Lives*, edited by Linda Wagner-Martin. Bedford Cultural Editions. Boston: Bedford/St. Martin's Press, 2000.

_____. *"Three Lives"; and "Q.E.D.": Authoritative Texts, Contexts, Criticism*, edited by Marianne DeKoven. Norton Critical Edition. New York: W. W. Norton, 2006.

SEE ALSO: July 4, 1855: Whitman Publishes *Leaves of Grass*; May 25, 1895: Oscar Wilde Is Convicted of Gross Indecency; 1896: *Der Eigene* Is Published as First Journal on Homosexuality; 1896: Raffalovich Publishes *Uranisme et Unisexualité*; Oct., 1909: Barney Opens Her Paris Salon; 1924: Gide Publishes the Signed Edition of *Corydon*; 1928: Hall Publishes *The Well of Loneliness*; 1939: Isherwood Publishes *Goodbye to Berlin*; 1947-1948: Golden Age of American Gay Literature; 1956: Foster Publishes *Sex Variant Women in Literature*; 1973: Brown Publishes *Rubyfruit Jungle*; 1975: Rule Publishes *Lesbian Images*; 1981: Faderman Publishes *Surpassing the Love of Men*; 1982: Lorde's Autobiography *Zami* Is Published.

# 1905
# FREUD REJECTS THIRD-SEX THEORY

*Sigmund Freud rejected the idea that persons with same-gender sexual attraction constituted a biological "third sex," arguing instead that all humans are inherently bisexual.*

**LOCALE:** Vienna, Austria

**CATEGORIES:** Science; health and medicine; publications; cultural and intellectual history

### KEY FIGURES

*Sigmund Freud* (1856-1939), Austrian physician, developed psychoanalysis

*Karl Heinrich Ulrichs* (1825-1890), German writer, proposed the third-sex theory

*Magnus Hirschfeld* (1868-1935), German neurologist and sex researcher, promoted the third-sex theory

### SUMMARY OF EVENT

"Third sex" is a term that was first used by Plato in his *Symposium*, a philosophical dialogue on the nature of love. Plato wrote that the earliest human ancestors were made up of three sexes: female-female, male-male, and male-female. Punished by the mythical god Zeus, each human "pairing" had been divided in half. Countless generations later, Plato argued, descendants continue to strive to reunite the pairings, which defines erotic love. If a person's ancient ancestor was male-female, that person will be attracted to members of the opposite gender. Descendants of male-male or female-female ancestors seek wholeness through attraction to members of the same gender.

The term "third sex" resurfaced in Europe in the nineteenth century in novels and poems with homosexual themes. In the 1860's, lawyer and writer Karl Heinrich Ulrichs explored the reasons for homosexual love. Ulrichs believed that the human embryo begins with both male and female sex organs, but that as the embryo develops it retains the organs of only one gender. In some cases, the selection process is incomplete, and thus a person may have the mind of one gender and the body of another. Ulrichs reasoned that the existence of a biological third sex established homosexuality as normal, and therefore it should be considered morally and legally acceptable.

In *Drei Abhandlungen zur Sexualtheorie* (1905; *Three Essays on the Theory of Sexuality*, 1910),

Freud rejected the idea of a third sex. He did not believe that the existence of homosexuality required a distinct sex (or gender, to use the more modern term), but that human sexuality occurs along a spectrum, that all people are born with bisexual *tendencies* (a bisexuality that is not a biological necessity).

In early life, Freud believed, children respond to certain stimuli that shape their eventual mature sexual orientation. A child who develops normally will be a heterosexual adult, because societies impose a structure that prefers a male-female dichotomy, but various traumas that occur during childhood could lead one to homosexuality. For example, a young boy's fear of castration might lead him in later life to become homosexual. A young man with an Oedipus complex might, in fixating on his mother, become so identified with her that he seeks a man as a sex partner. Conversely, a woman obsessed with her father might seek a woman as a sex partner as a way of substituting herself for her father.

Implied in Freud's theories is that sexual orientation is neither completely biological (nature) nor completely learned (nurture). Furthermore, since homosexuals are in all other ways able to survive and to function in society, their deviation from the norm should not be classified as degenerate. In other words, homosexuality is not "appropriate" because it does not lead to procreation, but neither is it dangerous nor a choice that can be unmade or corrected. Therefore, homosexuality should not be condemned, nor can it (or should it) be "cured." To criminalize homosexual behavior is to punish people for acting on impulses that are beyond their control.

Overall, Freud's ideas about homosexuality were rather vague and contradictory. Freud emphasized that homosexuality was not a perversion of sexuality, but he did consistently refer to it as a variation or a deviation of the norm. Five years after *Drei Abhandlungen zur Sexualtheorie*, Freud published again on sexuality, this time focusing on Renaissance artist Leonardo da Vinci. He observed also that certain homosexual men and women in the scientific community, particularly the sexologist Magnus Hirschfeld, referred to themselves as members of a third sex, but he again rejected the validity of the claim.

## SIGNIFICANCE

Freud's theories about homosexuality emphasize that sexual orientation is neither wrong nor sick, and that it is beyond a person's control. This idea that sexual orientation is at least partially inherent, and not chosen, had become an important part of legal and moral debates of the early twentieth century, debates that continue unabated.

Although Freud did not believe that homosexuals could be "cured" of their homosexuality, many

*Sigmund Freud.* (Library of Congress)

---

## PLATO ON THIRD SEX

Aristophanes professed to open another vein of discourse; he had a mind to praise Love in another way, unlike that either of Pausanias or Eryximachus. Mankind; he said, judging by their neglect of him, have never, as I think, at all understood the power of Love. For if they had understood him they would surely have built noble temples and altars, and offered solemn sacrifices in his honour; but this is not done, and most certainly ought to be done: since of all the gods he is the best friend of men, the helper and the healer of the ills which are the great impediment to the happiness of the race. . . .

Each of us when separated, having one side only, like a flat fish, is but the indenture of a man, and he is always looking for his other half. Men who are a section of that double nature which was once called Androgynous are lovers of women; adulterers are generally of this breed, and also adulterous women who lust after men: the women who are a section of the woman do not care for men, but have female attachments; the female companions are of this sort. But they who are a section of the male follow the male, and while they are young, being slices of the original man, they hang about men and embrace them, and they are themselves the best of boys and youths, because they have the most manly nature. Some indeed assert that they are shameless, but this is not true; for they do not act thus from any want of shame, but because they are valiant and manly, and have a manly countenance, and they embrace that which is like them. And these when they grow up become our statesmen, and these only, which is a great proof of the truth of what I am saying. When they reach manhood they are loves of youth, and are not naturally inclined to marry or beget children,—if at all, they do so only in obedience to the law; but they are satisfied if they may be allowed to live with one another unwedded; and such a nature is prone to love and ready to return love, always embracing that which is akin to him. And when one of them meets with his other half, the actual half of himself, whether he be a lover of youth or a lover of another sort, the pair are lost in an amazement of love and friendship and intimacy, and would not be out of the other's sight, as I may say, even for a moment: these are the people who pass their whole lives together; yet they could not explain what they desire of one another. For the intense yearning which each of them has towards the other does not appear to be the desire of lover's intercourse, but of something else which the soul of either evidently desires and cannot tell. . . .

*Source:Symposium*, 388-368 B.C.E.

---

of his followers in psychoanalysis, psychology, and medicine disagreed. They argued that if childhood trauma led to homosexuality, as Freud posited, then it seemed reasonable to believe that the "damage" from the trauma could be undone. Psychoanalytical and even surgical treatments for "improper" sexual orientation became prevalent in the 1930's and 1940's, counter to Freud's advice. In 1952, the American Psychiatric Association's *Diagnostic and Statistical Manual of Mental Disorders* (DSM) listed "homosexuality" for the first time as a personality disorder. Freud's belief that homosexuality was a sexual variation—and not a perversion—still, unwittingly perpetuated intolerant ideologies and attitudes. References to homosexuality as a mental illness, however, were removed from the manual in 1973.

Freud's theory of human development as directly linear and unwavering limited Western understandings of sexual orientation for decades, because researchers following his principles tended to look at sexuality through a narrow lens. That is, rather than seeing that ideas about sexuality, and sexuality itself, might change within and across cultures and might change through time, researchers interpreted the sexual development and sexual behavior of persons in other societies using Freud's unwavering, universalizing theory as the standard. This led them to determine what behavior was essentially "normal" and what behavior was essentially "abnormal," regardless of a person's cultural or social settings or backgrounds.

—*Cynthia A. Bily*

### FURTHER READING

Freud, Sigmund. *Three Essays on the Theory of Sexuality*. Translated and edited by James Strachey. New York: Basic Books, 2000.

Herdt, Gilbert, ed. *Third Sex, Third Gender: Beyond Sexual Dimorphism in Culture and History.* New York: Zone Books, 1996.

Kennedy, Hubert C. "The 'Third Sex' Theory of Karl Heinrich Ulrichs." *Journal of Homosexuality* 6, nos. 1-2 (1982): 103-111.

LeVay, Simon. *Queer Science: The Use and Abuse of Research Into Homosexuality.* Cambridge, Mass.: MIT Press, 1996.

Rubenstein, William B. *Cases and Materials on Sexual Orientation and the Law.* St. Paul, Minn.: West, 1997.

**SEE ALSO:** May 6, 1868: Kertbeny Coins the Terms "Homosexual" and "Heterosexual"; 1869: Westphal Advocates Medical Treatment for Sexual Inversion; 1897: Ellis Publishes *Sexual Inversion*; May 14, 1897: Hirschfeld Founds the Scientific-Humanitarian Committee; 1929: Davis's Research Identifies Lesbian Sexuality as Common and Normal; 1948: Kinsey Publishes *Sexual Behavior in the Human Male*; 1952: APA Classifies Homosexuality as a Mental Disorder; 1953: Kinsey Publishes *Sexual Behavior in the Human Female*; 1953-1957: Evelyn Hooker Debunks Beliefs That Homosexuality Is a "Sickness"; Dec. 15, 1973: Homosexuality Is Delisted by APA; 1991: LeVay Postulates the "Gay Brain"; Apr. 20, 2001: Chinese Psychiatric Association Removes Homosexuality from List of Mental Disorders.

# 1906
# FRIEDLAENDER BREAKS WITH THE SCIENTIFIC-HUMANITARIAN COMMITTEE

*Benedict Friedlaender's split with the Scientific-Humanitarian Committee underscored philosophical differences, strategic disagreements, and diversity of opinion in the early German movement for gay and lesbian emancipation. Some in the movement believed sexuality was inborn, and others believed sexuality to be shaped by society.*

**LOCALE:** Berlin, Germany

**CATEGORIES:** Organizations and institutions; civil rights; cultural and intellectual history; science; government and politics; laws, acts, and legal history

## KEY FIGURES

*Benedict Friedlaender* (1866-1908), German scholar, cofounded opposition group

*Adolf Brand* (1874-1945), German activist and editor, cofounded opposition group

*Wilhelm Janzen*, cofounded opposition group

*Magnus Hirschfeld* (1868-1935), German sexologist and physician, founded the Scientific-Humanitarian Committee

*Karl Heinrich Ulrichs* (1825-1895), German writer, proposed the third-sex theory of homosexuality

*William II* (1859-1941), emperor of Germany and king of Prussia, r. 1888-1918

*Maximilian Harden* (1861-1927), German journalist

## SUMMARY OF EVENT

Benedict Friedlaender was an activist, anarchist, and writer who participated in the pre-Nazi homosexual rights movement in Germany. Along with Adolf Brand and philosopher Max Stirner—publisher of *Der Eigene*, the first-known homosexual journal—Friedlaender was a founding patron of the movement. He also cofounded in 1902, with Brand and Wilhelm Janzen, the Gemeinschaft der Eigenen, variously translated as the "community of self-owners" or "community of the elite."

Friedlaender and members of the Gemeinschaft der Eigenen opposed the third-sex hypothesis developed by Karl Heinrich Ulrichs and later advocated by Magnus Hirschfeld, who believed homosexuals made up a third sex. The third-sex theory conceived homosexuality as an intermediate sex (or, to use the more modern term, "gender") that existed between men and women and envisioned a gay or lesbian individual as an inversion: a man trapped in a woman's body (a gay man), or a woman trapped in a man's body (a lesbian). The comparison of sexual inversion to physical disability, implying biological "defectiveness," repulsed the elites, who considered the masculine homosexual as the ideal of German perfection and that homosexuality was a fundamental masculinity: superior to effete homosexuals, heterosexual men, and females. The elitists believed that the third-sex theory promoted a picture of gay men as campy, eccentric, effeminate, and middle class.

The elitists extolled ancient Hellenic virtues and recast them into early twentieth century gay life. The Spartan values of control, discipline, and militarism, and, most significantly, the Spartan soldier's habit of bonding and fostering esprit de corps through homosexual relationships with his fellow warriors, suited the elitists well while emphasizing the superior masculine traits they found so attractive. Greek masculinity, the idealization of classical beauty, the adoption of man-boy love, and other Hellenic practices and customs, combined with a Teutonic heritage of chivalry, kinship, obedience to the tribal chieftain, loyalty to clan, and the resolving of conflicts through violence resulted in an attitude that homosexual men were superior, privileged, and had sexual license.

The egotism of such elitist perspectives, which were elevated and generalized to a national level, had political consequences for an immature, insecure, untested modern nation-state where unification was within the memory of the living generation. Some German pederasts justified their sexual activity with young boys as beneficial to the social good. They argued that by encouraging man-boy love, society was relieved of irresponsible sexual behavior that could result in unintended, negative social consequences, such as teenage pregnancy. By having sex with older, experienced men, young males were initiated into responsible sexual conduct and were given a sense of heightened masculinity that would aid them as future national leaders.

Friedlaender and many of the intellectuals whose theories of human sexuality lent support to homosexual elitism believed in expectations of privacy, natural rights, and acceptance for homosexuals. They called for direct action to remove criminal and societal constraints on homosexuality. Hirschfeld and other third-sex theorists understood homosexuality through a medical, rational, and scientific model and sought tolerance. They, too, desired social change and the removal of certain limits, but they advocated assimilation, acculturation, and absorption into the mainstream, not confrontation and conflict with the majority.

In 1897, when Hirschfeld founded the Wissenschaftlich-humanitäre Komitee (Scientific-Humanitarian Committee, or SHC) to repeal Paragraph 175 of the German criminal code, which outlawed sexual acts between men, the staff of *Der Eigene* joined with Hirschfeld to support German legal reform. Common ground soon gave way to tension between Hirschfeld and supporters of Ulrichs's third-sex theory, and Brand and his followers, who, like Friedlaender, scorned Hirschfeld's conception of an intermediate sex. Brand and Friedlaender thought Hirschfeld was selling out the German movement for homosexual liberation because he was advocating tolerance alone, rather than social equality through cultural acceptance.

Events separated Friedlaender from Hirschfeld and the SHC as much as did ideological considerations. Friedlaender's cofounding of the Gemeinschaft der Eigenen, Hirschfeld's publication of *Berlins drittes Geschlecht* (1905; Berlin's third sex), the Eulenburg affair of 1906-1909, and the subsequent stalling of repeal of Paragraph 175 in the Reichstag were all factors in Friedlaender's decision to dissociate from Hirschfeld and leave the Scientific-Humanitarian Committee.

When Hirschfeld published *Berlins drittes Geschlecht*, Friedlaender's suspicions were confirmed: Hirschfeld considered homosexuality a form of sexual inversion, even implying biological degeneration. Although qualified, inquiring, and methodical in tone, and aiming toward a scientific narrative, Hirschfeld's book alluded to an abstract system of sexual categorization that many—including Friedlaender—regarded as the biological fictionalization and medicalization of homosexuality. Elitists decried the pathologizing of sexual orientation.

Finally, the impact of the Eulenburg scandal and its accompanying trial on the movement to repeal Paragraph 175, a trial in which Hirschfeld participated as an expert witness, irrevocably split Friedlaender and the Scientific-Humanitarian Committee. In 1906, several trusted advisers and intimates to Kaiser William II, including Count Kuno von Moltke, the military commandant of Berlin, and Philipp, prince of Eulenburg-Hertefeld, were named by a conservative newspaper reporter, Maximilian Harden, as homosexual. Moltke brought a libel suit against Harden, who in turn produced testimony, including a statement by the plaintiff's former wife, that Eulenburg and Moltke had indeed engaged in homosexual activities. Hirschfeld also testified as an expert witness at trial claiming Moltke exhibited homosexual personality attributes.

Although Harden was acquitted of the libel charge at the first trial, Hirschfeld's expertise was called into question and subject to public ridicule when Moltke's former wife retracted her statements and Harden renounced his initial accusation and was convicted of libel during a subsequent lawsuit.

Because of the sensationalism and public fascination with the Eulenburg affair, and, more important, because of its proximity to the imperial court, Kaiser William II, in reaction to the scandal and in an effort to distance himself from the German homosexual emancipation movement, pulled from the floor of the Reichstag the bill to repeal Paragraph 175. Hirschfeld's expertise did little to improve the matter. The public outcry against Hirschfeld in the aftermath of the affair ranged from the comic to outright denunciations of his theories and scientific work as fraudulent propaganda and mad science. No doubt the kaiser's judgment to squash the proposed repeal was influenced also by Hirschfeld's involvement in the scandal.

## SIGNIFICANCE

The failure to achieve reform of the German criminal code by repeal of Paragraph 175 had adverse consequences for the German homosexual rights movement. The diverse Berlin gay and lesbian community's inability to persuade the German parliament to repeal the law exposed divisions within the gay and lesbian rights movement.

Those divisions were already fomenting at the fin de siècle, but they became more pronounced and less reconcilable in the aftermath of the Eulenburg scandal and the resultant defeat of the effort to repeal Paragraph 175 in the Reichstag.

The split revealed ideological differences over the nature of homosexuality between essentialists—or those, like Hirschfeld, who believed in a biological basis for homosexuality—and nominalists, or those, like Friedlaender, who believed sexual orientation is conditioned by society.

In addition to causes, the philosophical rift also emphasized disagreements over the methods and outcome of homosexual activism. That is, does activism need to embrace direct action or would activism be better served by a conciliatory approach emphasizing compromise and reform? Is the objective of activism acceptance, equality, and inclusion, or is it acculturation and assimilation? These questions remain relevant into the twenty-first century, and they are still debated.

—*Keith Carson*

## FURTHER READING

Hirschfeld, Magnus. *The Homosexuality of Men and Women.* 1920. Reprint. Amherst, N.Y.: Prometheus Books, 2000.

Jones, James W. *"We of the Third Sex": Literary Representations of Homosexuality in Wilhelmine Germany.* New York: Peter Lang, 1990.

Oosterhuis, Harry, ed. *Homosexuality and Male Bonding in Pre-Nazi Germany: The Youth Movement, the Gay Movement, and Male Bonding Before Hitler's Rise, Original Transcripts from "Der Eigene," the First Gay Journal in the World.* Translated by Hubert Kennedy. New York: Harrington Park Press, 1991.

Porter, Jack Nusan. *Sexual Politics in Nazi Germany, the Persecution of the Homosexuals During the Holocaust: Essays, Biographical Sketches, Biographies, Bibliographies, Photos, and Charts on Sexology, Homosexuality, Nazism, and Magnus Hirschfeld.* 3d ed. Newton, Mass.: Spencer Press, 2003.

**SEE ALSO:** May 6, 1868: Kertbeny Coins the Terms "Homosexual" and "Heterosexual"; 1869: Westphal Advocates Medical Treatment for Sexual Inversion; 1896: *Der Eigene* Is Published as First Journal on Homosexuality; 1897: Ellis Publishes *Sexual Inversion*; 1905: Freud Rejects Third-Sex Theory; 1929: Davis's Research Identifies Lesbian Sexuality as Common and Normal; 1953-1957: Evelyn Hooker Debunks Beliefs That Homosexuality Is a "Sickness"; Dec. 15, 1973: Homosexuality Is Delisted by APA; 1991: LeVay Postulates the "Gay Brain."

## 1907-1909
# THE EULENBURG AFFAIR SCANDALIZES GERMANY'S LEADERSHIP

*The Eulenburg affair involved accusations of homosexuality among the entourage of German kaiser William II and set in motion a series of sensational trials. The affair had lasting political, legal, and cultural consequences, including increased public discussion of homosexuality, most of which was negative.*

**LOCALE:** Germany
**CATEGORIES:** Government and politics; laws, acts, and legal history

**KEY FIGURES**
*Philipp, prince of Eulenburg-Hertefeld* (1847-1921), German diplomat, writer, playwright, and composer
*Kuno von Moltke* (1847-1923), military commandant of Berlin
*William II* (1859-1941), emperor of Germany and king of Prussia, r. 1888-1918
*Maximilian Harden* (1861-1927), German journalist

**SUMMARY OF EVENT**
Philipp, prince of Eulenburg-Hertefeld, grew up in a noble Prussian family, prodded by an austere father toward a "manly" career and balanced by an ar-

*Philipp, prince of Eulenburg-Hertefeld.*

*Kuno von Moltke, 1900.*

tistically gifted mother who encouraged his more "feminine" sensibilities, including his poetry and writing of music and plays. Eulenburg married a Swedish countess and produced eight children but never cared for his wife.

In 1886, Eulenburg met Crown Prince William, soon to be Kaiser William II, and became part of a close-knit group of homoerotically inclined generals, civilians, diplomats, politicians, and lawmakers, known as the Liebenberg circle, a group named after Eulenburg's retreat. (Liebenberg means the "mountain of love.") Eulenburg's meteoric rise included appointments as envoy to Bavaria and ambassador to Austria-Hungary. He was given the title of prince in 1900.

Trouble was ahead, however. Earlier, Eulenburg's brother had been outed as homosexual. Emperor William immediately ordered Eulenburg to denounce his sibling and sever all ties with him,

which Eulenburg refused to do. In 1902, Eulenburg retired from politics—prompted in part by blackmail and imminent exposure. Aggravating circumstances included revelations that Friedrich Alfred Krupp, heir to Germany's largest industrial magnate, had been consorting with boys on the island of Capri (Krupp committed suicide in 1902); a staggering number of gay-related suicides, resignations, and military courts-martial; a cross-dressing evening at court, where the military ballerina dropped dead from a heart attack; and the political fallout caused by a French spy who had abused Eulenburg's confidence.

Starting in 1906, Maximilian Harden, in the weekly *Die Zukunft* (the future), which he founded and edited, accused the group of deviant sexuality, targeting, in particular, Kuno von Moltke, the military commandant of Berlin. (In the late 1890's, Moltke's wife had sued for divorce because of his homosexuality.) Later, Moltke challenged Harden to a duel, but Harden refused, leading Moltke to sue him for libel in civil court. Harden was acquitted, but the case was retried in criminal court. In this second trial, Harden was found guilty, but once again, the verdict was overturned.

Another trial followed. With the possibility of appeal, the sensational scandal was likely to drag on, so Harden eventually agreed to an out-of-court settlement (the government secretly paid for his expenses). Harden later dropped a bombshell: He accused Eulenburg of having had sex with two men who were completely out of his class.

Eulenburg's health was rapidly declining, and thus another trial against him, this time for alleged perjury, was postponed several times and was never completed. Friends had counseled Eulenburg to commit suicide during the long ordeal. He died in 1921, abandoned by almost everyone.

Unfortunately, prosecutorial evidence and transcripts of Eulenburg's trials were destroyed by German authorities in 1932; earlier, in 1907, correspondence between Moltke and Eulenburg had been hastily burned; and World War II destroyed whatever documents survived the purge.

## SIGNIFICANCE

Politically, the trials proved disastrous. Emperor William distanced himself from men who often mitigated his emotional outbursts, firebrand politics, and rash decisions. Some maintain that Eulenburg and his friends could have steered William's militancy in a different direction.

Culturally, the affair fostered a climate of disgust and distrust. Even the kaiser was no longer above suspicion. In 1886, William—however innocently—had sailed on the Starnberger Sea with the very fisherman who claimed to have had sex with Eulenburg. Indeed, the epistolary correspondence between Moltke and Eulenburg revealed a titillating term for the emperor: Liebchen, a diminutive of the word "darling."

At the same time, pioneer sexologists, such as Magnus Hirschfeld, founder of the Wissenschaftlich-humanitäre Komitee (Scientific-Humanitarian Committee), who had testified in court, met with more denial and denigration. Furthermore, just a decade after the trials of Oscar Wilde, the revelations prompted German police to enforce Paragraph 175 (which earlier had been interpreted as defining anal intercourse only) more strictly, even extending it to women.

Moreover, the cause célèbre had implications for the history of sexuality. Isabel Hull quotes a letter by Eulenburg, composed shortly after the scandal.

> In the moment when the freshest example of the modern age, a Harden, criticized our nature, stripped our ideal friendship, laid bare the form of our thinking and feeling which we had justifiably regarded all our lives as something obvious and natural, in that moment, the modern age, laughing cold-bloodedly, broke our necks.... The new concepts of sensuality and love stamp our nature as weak, even unhealthily weak.

The medicalization and criminalization of homosexuality was in full swing then, having dealt the final blow to Platonic love, romantic friendship, and homosocial bonding.

Historian James Steakley sums up the affair thus:

> Despite its [alleged] role in the outbreak of World War I, despite the campaign for moral rearma-

ment, the anti-Semitic undertones, the heightening of military discipline, the concern about decadence, and the exhortations to middle-class morality, a subtle dialectic was at work tending to proliferate sexual practices and identities.

Finally, the word "homosexual" was established as the standard term, replacing the earlier, derogatory terms "pederasty" and "unnatural vice" and the clinical/medical terms "intermediate type" or "third sex." In literary circles, the Eulenburg scandal affected the lives and writings of Thomas Mann, Marcel Proust, André Gide, and Felix Paul Greve (Frederick Philip Grove), among others.

—*Nikolai Endres*

## FURTHER READING

Cavell, Richard. "Felix Paul Greve, the Eulenburg Scandal, and Frederick Philip Grove." *Essays on Canadian Writing* 62 (Fall, 1997): 12-45.

Hull, Isabel V. *The Entourage of Kaiser Wilhelm II, 1888-1918.* New York: Cambridge University Press, 1982.

Jones, James W. *"We of the Third Sex": Literary Representations of Homosexuality in Wilhelmine Germany.* New York: Peter Lang, 1990.

Röhl, John C. G. *The Kaiser and His Court: Wilhelm II and the Government of Germany.* Translated by Terence F. Cole. New York: Cambridge University Press, 1994.

Steakley, James D. "Iconography of a Scandal: Political Cartoons and the Eulenburg Affair in Wilhelmin Germany." In *Hidden from History: Reclaiming the Gay and Lesbian Past*, edited by Martin Duberman, Martha Vicinus, and George Chauncey, Jr. New York: NAL Books, 1989.

Young, Harry F. *Maximilian Harden, Censor Germaniae: The Critic in Opposition from Bismarck to the Rise of Nazism.* The Hague, the Netherlands: Martinus Nijhoff, 1959.

SEE ALSO: May 6, 1868: Kertbeny Coins the Terms "Homosexual" and "Heterosexual"; 1885: United Kingdom Criminalizes "Gross Indecency"; May 25, 1895: Oscar Wilde Is Convicted of Gross Indecency; May 14, 1897: Hirschfeld Founds the

Scientific-Humanitarian Committee; 1906: Friedlaender Breaks with the Scientific-Humanitarian Committee; Mar. 15, 1919-1921: U.S.Navy Launches Sting Operation Against "Sexual Per- verts"; 1933-1945: Nazis Persecute Homosexuals; June 30-July 1, 1934: Hitler's Night of the Long Knives.

# 1908
# CARPENTER PUBLISHES *THE INTERMEDIATE SEX*

*Poet and social activist Edward Carpenter's* The Intermediate Sex *was the first book in English on homosexuality to receive wide distribution, both nationally and abroad.*

**LOCALE:** London and Manchester, England
**CATEGORIES:** Literature; publications

**KEY FIGURE**
*Edward Carpenter* (1844-1929), English writer, poet, and social philosopher

**SUMMARY OF EVENT**
*The Intermediate Sex: A Study of Some Transitional Types of Men and Women* was published simultaneously in English in 1908 by Swan Sonnenschein in London and S. Clarke in Manchester. Though the book already had appeared in German (*Das Mittelgeschlecht*) in 1907 and as articles or pamphlets earlier, publication in book form in English made Carpenter's writings on homosexuality available to the general English reader for the first time, and for almost two decades it stood alone in providing a sympathetic treatment of homosexuality as a congenital disposition.

Especially in the first half of the book, Carpenter adopts the stance of a disinterested observer, that of an ethnologist or psychologist taking a fresh look at an ancient social "problem." He makes a brief survey of "homogenic" (that is, homosexual) love throughout history and into modern times, deliberately blurring the customary distinction between passionate same-gender friendships and explicitly sexual relationships. Eventually his concern for the rights of this misunderstood sexual minority comes

to the fore, but he continues, perhaps for strategic reasons, to downplay the importance of sexual acts, explaining that while homogenic love "has its physical side," it is more essentially marked by "spiritual" qualities such as affection, commitment, and common purpose. He remarks that work by Euro-

*Edward Carpenter, c. 1875.*

## "The Intermediate Sex"

"Urning men and women, on whose book of life Nature has written her new word which sounds so strange to us, bear such storm and stress within them, such ferment and fluctuation, so much complex material having its outlet only towards the future; their individualities are so rich and many-sided, and withal so little understood, that it is impossible to characterise them adequately in a few sentences." (Otto de Joux)

In late years (and since the arrival of the New Woman amongst us) many things in the relation of men and women to each other have altered, or at any rate become clearer. The growing sense of equality in habits and customs—university studies, art, music, politics, the bicycle, etc.—all these things have brought about a rapprochement between the sexes. If the modern woman is a little more masculine in some ways than her predecessor, the modern man (it is to be hoped), while by no means effeminate, is a little more sensitive in temperament and artistic in feeling than the original John Bull. It is beginning to be recognised that the sexes do not or should not normally form two groups hopelessly isolated in habit and feeling from each other, but that they rather represent the two poles of one group—which is the human race; so that while certainly the extreme specimens at either pole are vastly divergent, there are great numbers in the middle region who (though differing corporeally as men and women) are by emotion and temperament very near to each other. We all know women with a strong dash of the masculine temperament, and we all know men whose almost feminine sensibility and intuition seem to belie their bodily form. Nature, it might appear, in mixing the elements which go to compose each individual, does not always keep her two groups of ingredients—which represent the two sexes—properly apart, but often throws them crosswise in a somewhat baffling manner, now this way and now that; yet wisely, we must think—for if a severe distinction of elements were always maintained the two sexes would soon drift into far latitudes and absolutely cease to understand each other. As it is, there are some remarkable and (we think) indispensable types of character in whom there is such a union or balance of the feminine and masculine qualities that these people become to a great extent the interpreters of men and women to each other.

*Source:* Edward Carpenter, *The Intermediate Sex*, 1908, reprint (London: Allen and Unwin, 1930).

pean sexologists such as Karl Heinrich Ulrichs, Albert Moll, and Richard von Krafft-Ebing indicates that *uranism*, as homosexuality was called, is a congenital disposition, and more common than generally thought.

Carpenter further argues, however, that "comrade lovers" can make a vital contribution to society. Drawing on "A Problem in Greek Ethics," a privately printed pamphlet by John Addington Symonds, he suggests that, just as in the ancient world comrade lovers defended the state against tyranny, so today they might devote themselves to fighting social ills. If "the slaughter of tyrants" may no longer be required, modern society does confront "hydra-headed monsters at least as numerous as the tyrants of old, and more difficult to deal with, and requiring no little courage to encounter." Quoting Walt Whitman's essay "Democratic Vistas," he suggests that comradeship can bring about the spiritualization of democracy and defend it from sinking into crass materialism.

Three of *The Intermediate Sex*'s five chapters had also appeared in English previously. Chapter 2, "The Intermediate Sex," first appeared as "An Unknown People" in the Labour Party magazine *The Reformer* in July and August, 1897, and Carpenter had incorporated a slightly revised version into the fifth (1906) edition of his best-selling book on relations between the sexes, *Love's Coming of Age*. Chapter 3, "The Homogenic Attachment," was a revised version of a fifty-one-page pamphlet titled *Homogenic Love: And Its Place in a Free Society* that Carpenter had privately printed in 1894 as one of a series of pamphlets on sexual problems. Chapter 4, "Affection in Education," had appeared in the *International Journal of Ethics* in July, 1899.

The fact that only a small portion of *The Intermediate Sex* was completely new and that Carpenter was held in high regard as a social philosopher and poet made it difficult for authorities to prosecute him for committing "obscene libel," though government officials did seriously consider bringing charges.

Carpenter had studied mathematics at Cambridge University and briefly served as an assistant clergyman, but after reading Whitman's poetry and traveling in Germany, he decided to join the Cambridge University Extension Movement to bring education to working men and women in the industrial cities of England's Midlands. Associating with workers politicized Carpenter, and he became active in the socialist movement, joining the Sheffield Socialists, the Fabian Society, and the Fellowship of the New Life. Carpenter's socialism was utopian, however, and as the program of the labor movement became more pragmatic, aiming to win seats in Parliament, he found himself increasingly on the margins. This fact, and the strength of his domestic partnership with George Merrill, persuaded him to speak out more boldly on behalf of homosexuals.

Carpenter's work is remembered less for its originality than for its influence in his own time. Through a steady stream of articles, lectures, and poems, he proved to be a skillful and effective popularizer of "advanced ideas" concerning not only homosexuality but also vegetarianism, animal rights, smoke pollution, women's rights, Hindu philosophy, and spiritualism. He corresponded with progressive thinkers worldwide, including Mohandas K. Gandhi and Leo Tolstoy. Though as much an anarchist as a socialist, he was widely read and admired. His farm at Millthorpe became a destination of pilgrimage for all those interested in social reform.

## SIGNIFICANCE

England imposed no official censorship on books as it did plays, but the system of prosecuting work thought to be "obscene" made it extremely hazardous to publish on the subject of homosexuality. The few who did would generally print their work privately, for distribution only to friends and colleagues. As a result, Carpenter's *The Intermediate Sex* was in its time the only work on homosexuality that ordinary readers could obtain. The value of the book for gays and lesbians of the period is inestima-

ble, though the testimony of contemporary readers such as E. M. Forster, Robert Graves, Siegfried Sassoon, and Edith Lees suggests that it profoundly affected many individual lives.

The majority of reviews were surprisingly favorable, and the book sold well, running through five editions between 1908 and 1918, and six more reprints between 1918 and 1930—about eleven thousand copies in all. In the 1920's, interest in the work of Sigmund Freud and psychoanalysis diminished the influence of Carpenter's work. By his death in 1929, Carpenter's ideas, even about "homogenic love," already seemed to belong to a bygone time.

—*Matthew Parfitt*

## FURTHER READING

Brown, Tony, ed. *Edward Carpenter and Late Victorian Radicalism*. Special issue, *Prose Studies: History, Theory, Criticism* 13, no. 1 (May, 1990).

Carpenter, Edward. *The Intermediate Sex: A Study of Some Transitional Types of Men and Women*. In *Selected Writings*. London: GMP/Heretic, 1984. Available at http://www.edwardcarpenter.net.

_____. *My Days and Dreams*. London: George Allen & Unwin, 1916.

Hynes, Samuel. "Science, Seers, and Sex." In *The Edwardian Turn of Mind*. Princeton, N.J.: Princeton University Press, 1968.

Rowbotham, Sheila, and Jeffrey Weeks. *Socialism and the New Life: The Personal and Sexual Politics of Edward Carpenter and Havelock Ellis*. London: Pluto Press, 1977.

Tsuzuki, Chushichi. *Edward Carpenter, 1844-1929: Prophet of Human Fellowship*. New York: Cambridge University Press, 1980.

**SEE ALSO:** May 6, 1868: Kertbeny Coins the Terms "Homosexual" and "Heterosexual"; 1869: Westphal Advocates Medical Treatment for Sexual Inversion; 1896: *Der Eigene* Is Published as First Journal on Homosexuality; 1896: Raffalovich Publishes *Uranisme et Unisexualité*; 1897: Ellis Publishes *Sexual Inversion*; May 14, 1897: Hirschfeld Founds the Scientific-Humanitarian Committee; 1903: Stein Writes *Q.E.D.*; 1905: Freud Rejects Third-Sex Theory; 1906: Friedlaender Breaks with the Scientific-Humanitarian Committee; Dec. 10, 1924: Gerber Founds the Society for Human Rights; 1928: Hall Publishes *The Well of Loneliness*; 1933-1945: Nazis Persecute Homosexuals; 1950: Mattachine Society Is Founded.

## October, 1909
# BARNEY OPENS HER PARIS SALON

*Natalie Clifford Barney opened her Left Bank home in Paris to some of the most prominent artists and intellectuals of the twentieth century, initiating what was to become a weekly salon, or literary gathering, of women and men of all sexualities.*

**LOCALE**: Paris, France
**CATEGORIES:** Cultural and intellectual history; literature; feminism

**KEY FIGURE**
*Natalie Clifford Barney* (1876-1972), expatriate American writer and salon host

**SUMMARY OF EVENT**
Drawing on the long French history of the successful operation of salons, a tradition that started during the Renaissance, and on her flamboyant personal history as a host, expatriate heir Natalie Clifford Barney opened the doors of her home in the Left Bank area of Paris to a range of artists, writers, bohemians, aristocrats, and freethinkers in October of 1909. The gesture made her address, 20 Rue Jacob, synonymous with unorthodox thought, avant-garde creativity, and heterogeneous internationalism.

Barney's lesbian sexuality provided her legendary Friday night salons with a warm acceptance of sexual diversity, as she and many of her friends drew on classical Greek models of love between women for artistic inspiration. Strikingly, Barney's property on Rue Jacob featured a Doric-columned edifice on which the word "Temple of Friendship" had been carved in French. The temple stood in a wild garden, which provided a sense of natural abandon in the heart of the city. This environment provided the setting for countless amateur theatricals and masquerades in which Barney and friends performed, many celebrating the ancient poet Sappho and her circle.

Though these parties occurred regularly in the garden, a different kind of gathering began to de-

*Natalie Clifford Barney, 1892.*

## NATALIE CLIFFORD BARNEY

Natalie Clifford Barney, a wealthy American writer, muse, and salon host, was a striking presence among the literary circles of Paris. Known as "the wild girl from Cincinnati" and "the Amazon," Barney was also notable for never having hid the fact that her sexual preference was for women.

Barney, born in 1876 in Dayton, Ohio, was one of two daughters born to Alice Pike and Albert Clifford Barney. After the family moved to Washington, D.C., Albert wanted nothing more than for his wife and daughters to participate in respectable society. Alice, however, was determined to cultivate her considerable artistic talent and often took the girls on extended trips to Paris. What Alice did not know was that many of the models who posed for her paintings also were lovers of her daughter Natalie.

After her father's death, Barney moved permanently to Paris. Like so many independent women artists and writers of the early twentieth century, Barney found that Paris was the one place where she could live and express herself as she pleased. While in Paris, she came across a translation of Sappho's poetry, which captivated her. Barney and British-born poet Renée Vivien, in an attempt to revive the culture of Sappho, envisioned a kind of women's artist colony. This failed idea was nonetheless the first in a series of significant efforts on Barney's part to bring women together in an artistic community.

Barney's female lovers were legion. Along with Vivien, the American painter Romaine Brooks was one of her greatest loves. Barney, though, had insisted on pursuing her amorous affairs in spite of her partners' protests. At the age of eighty-eight, on a park bench, she met for the last time the woman who also would be her last love. Brooks, after enduring fifty-five years of Barney's infidelities, bitterly ended their relationship. The next year, Brooks died without reconciliation. Barney died in Paris in 1972 at the age of ninety-five, having, as she put it, "got more out of life . . . perhaps more than it contained."

Rue Jacob salon had welcomed an impressive array of twentieth century luminaries, but a relatively small group who were to become regulars appeared at the first few Friday gatherings. Probable attendees at the opening included Count Robert de Montesquiou, the model for Baron de Charlus in French writer Marcel Proust's *Á la recherche du temps perdu* (1913-1927; *Remembrance of Things Past*, 1922-1931); novelist and poet Lucie Delarue-Mardrus and her husband Joseph Charles Mardrus, translator of Sir Richard Francis Burton's edition of *The Arabian Nights' Entertainments* (1885) into French; and memoirist Elizabeth de Gramont, the duchess of Clermont-Tonnerre. Interestingly, both women of this group had been Barney's lovers and Montesquiou was gay, but salon guests' sexualities were heterogeneous. At the time the salon ended, its visitors had included heterosexual, bisexual, lesbian, and gay cultural figures and artists, including Paul Claudel, Auguste Rodin, George Antheil, Sylvia Beach, Rainer Maria Rilke, André Gide, Rabindranath Tagore, James Joyce, Gertrude Stein, Anatole France, Ezra Pound, Isadora Duncan, Paul Valéry, and Gabriele D'Annunzio.

This partial guest list disproves the myth that Barney's salon presented a woman-only space, although in 1927, with the inauguration of Barney's Académie des Femmes (academy of women), the salon took a decidedly feminist turn. Having long toyed with the idea of forming an alliance of women writers, Barney finally executed the plan in 1927 by forming an association designed for women to read their works and pay tribute to one another. The name of the association shows that Barney was con-

velop within the walls of Barney's Rue Jacob residence. Having been warned that the floors of her house were not sturdy enough to tolerate much dancing, Barney began to formulate plans for calmer entertainment: She thought of the salon. Thus, beginning in 1909, from five to eight on every Friday evening that Barney was in town, members of the Parisian literati and avant-garde could be found partaking of generous offerings of pastries, sandwiches, libations (both alcoholic and otherwise) and, above all, conversation. The number of guests ranged from the average of thirty to thirty-five up to two hundred for special events.

Before its closing at Barney's death in 1972, the

sciously providing an alternative to the exclusive Académie Française (French Academy), a French cultural institution that excluded women writers until it finally admitted modernist writer Marguerite Yourcenar (also a friend of Barney) in 1980. Despite the Académie des Femmes' feminist goal of providing support and exposure to women writers, men were invited to its special events and, as in the case of Ezra Pound, were occasionally subsidized by the association.

Although the regular salon had little official direction, the meetings of the Académie des Femmes held a series of special Friday evenings, each honoring a woman of letters. On January 14, 1927, writer Colette performed selected scenes from her work *La Vagabonde* (1911; *The Vagabond*, 1954). The academy then honored writer Gertrude Stein in February with more than two hundred people in attendance. Stein also had hosted a salon in Paris in the early part of the century, which attracted mostly men, in contrast to Barney's salon. Though the women's academy faded after 1927, it honored important female modernists such as Mina Loy and Djuna Barnes and talents of the time such as Rachilde, Lucie Delarue-Mardrus, and Elizabeth de Gramont, the duchess of Clermont-Tonnerre.

## SIGNIFICANCE

A fictionalized version of Barney's salon is included in Radclyffe Hall's classic lesbian novel *The Well of Loneliness*, published in 1928. That same year, Djuna Barnes released *Ladies Almanack*, a privately printed spoof on Barney and her lesbian circle. Barney not only appears in a range of memoirs and novels but also is the author of twelve published books of various genres. In part because Barney wrote in French, much of her work is only slowly being recovered, translated, and made available to the non-French-reading public.

Though Barney's salon was selective in that a person had to be invited or brought by a guest to attend, and although Barney reportedly aligned with fascism during World War II, her legend and her famous salon also live on in the hearts and minds of lesbians and gays seeking a dynamic, unapologetic predecessor who, for more than sixty years, entertained, provoked, and supported some of the greatest talents of her time.

*—Anne Charles*

## FURTHER READING

Barney, Natalie Clifford. *Adventures of the Mind.* Translated by John Spalding Gatton. New York: New York University Press, 1992.

Crane, Sheila. "Mapping the Amazon's Salon: Symbolic Landscapes and Topographies of Identity in Natalie Clifford Barney's Literary Salon." In *Gender and Landscape: Renegotiating Morality and Space*, edited by Lorraine Dowler, Josephine Carubia, and Bonj Szczygiel. New York: Routledge, 2005.

Jay, Karla. *The Amazon and the Page.* Bloomington: Indiana University Press, 1988.

Rodriguez, Suzanne. *Wild Heart: A Life.* New York: HarperCollins, 2002.

Wickes, George. *The Amazon of Letters: The Life and Loves of Natalie Barney.* New York: Popular Library, 1978.

**SEE ALSO:** July 4, 1855: Whitman Publishes *Leaves of Grass*; May 25, 1895: Oscar Wilde Is Convicted of Gross Indecency; 1903: Stein Writes *Q.E.D.*; 1924: Gide Publishes the Signed Edition of *Corydon*; 1928: Hall Publishes *The Well of Loneliness*; 1939: Isherwood Publishes *Goodbye to Berlin*; 1947-1948: Golden Age of American Gay Literature; 1956: Foster Publishes *Sex Variant Women in Literature*.

## 1912-1924
# ROBLES FIGHTS IN THE MEXICAN REVOLUTION

*Carmen Amelia Robles, who preferred the name Amelio Robles and chose to live as a man, joined Emiliano Zapata's revolutionary army and not only fought in the Mexican Revolution but also led male troops in battle.*

**LOCALE:** Mexico
**CATEGORIES:** Transgender/transsexuality; military

**KEY FIGURE**
*Amelio Robles* (1889-1984), cavalry colonel during Mexican Revolution

**SUMMARY OF EVENT**

The Mexican Revolution was a bloody civil war that began in 1910 with the overthrow of dictator Porfirio Díaz and lasted for more than one decade. Women participated in this conflict, and those who fought as *soldaderas* (female soldiers) did so for a variety of reasons. Some had strong political beliefs, others wanted to accompany a significant other, some had been assaulted during the war and fighting was a self-protective response, while some thought fighting was an opportunity for adventure they would not have under normal circumstances. A number of the *soldaderas* led battalions, were promoted to the rank of officer, and a few were later decorated by the Mexican government.

While there is little information on most of the women, researchers have begun to "rescue" some of them from the dustbin of history. Among those now remembered are Dionisia Villarino, Margarita Neri, Maria de la Luz Espinoza Barrera, Eucaria Apresa, Petra Ruiz, and Carmen Amelia Robles, who preferred to be called Amelio and to live as a man.

Biographical sources on Robles provide varying and sometimes conflicting accounts of her life, of why she joined the revolution, and why she preferred to pass or live as a man. Robles was born Carmen Amelia Robles on November 3, 1889, in Xochipala (state of Guerrero). She was the daughter of a middle-class rancher who died when Amelio was three. As a young child, she preferred to ride horses, shoot guns, and engage in other cross-gender activities.

After her mother remarried, Amelio found herself at odds with her stepfather. In 1912, she joined the Ejército Libertador del Sur, Emiliano Zapata's army. While her (or *his*, as she was likely living as a man by this point) motives for joining the army are not clear, they perhaps came out of the conflicts with her stepfather. One source suggests that her mother encouraged her to join so that she would be less vulnerable to the sexual violence that was part of the war. Scholar Gabriela Cano quotes Robles as saying that the military life drew her because it provided a "feeling of complete liberty."

Robles had been a fierce fighter and a skilled horseback rider who served in the cavalry. She fought in various battles, including Chilpancingo, Tixtla, and Chilapa, and was wounded several times. She was known for a quick temper and once shot and killed a drunken *coronel* (colonel) who insisted on slapping a painful leg wound she had sustained. She was placed in command of male troops on more than one occasion. Coronel Esteban Estrada, who also fought in the revolution, remembered that Robles had come down from the mountains in 1918 at the head of a battalion of three hundred men.

After serving in Zapata's army until 1918, Robles returned home, but several years later, she rejoined the revolution and did not retire until 1924. She provided researcher Olga Cardenas Trueba with a list of seventy military encounters in which she had participated, but Cardenas thought that the true number was greater. After her retirement, Robles continued to dress in male attire and dedicated herself to ranching. She also served as an advocate for local townspeople, worked against logging interests, helped to build a local highway, and advocated for veterans of the Mexican Revolution.

She had one last military "hurrah" when she joined an uprising to protest voting fraud in her district in 1940.

Robles insisted on being treated as a man. Her hometown at first rejected her cross-gender behavior, so she moved to Iguala, where she found a more tolerant climate. She returned to Xochipala in her later years to live with her nephew. Robles's longtime companion was identified by Cano as Angelita Torres. Cano notes that Robles and Torres raised an adopted daughter together. Several photographs of Robles exist; in one photo she is wearing boots, a hat, trousers, and a gun and holster. In another photo taken by Agustin Victor Casasola, two women dressed in military attire and posing with male soldiers are identified as Amelio and Carmen Robles. One source explains that this identification is in error and that Carmen Amelia is one person and the other woman's name is unknown.

## SIGNIFICANCE

Amelio Robles's gender identity provides a rich subject for those interested in the construction of gender. Some would say Robles was a male-identified transgender person who might have chosen to be transsexual (and thus have reassigned her gender) had she had the opportunity to do so. Some lesbians might argue that she was a woman who identified as a man so that she might do the things that men could do, including "courting a girl." Others might argue that she identified outside the stereotypical standards of her day and chose to express herself as freely as possible without support from social movements or academic theories. Some Mexican feminists claim her as an independent woman who defied cultural expectations but who ironically (for them) denied her female self.

Over the years, Robles had granted a number of interviews. Some who wrote about her saw her as a curiosity, while others sang her praises as a brave woman who refused to fit into the gender expectations of her culture.

For several decades, Robles petitioned for a pension and the recognition of her rank as a *coronel*. Gabriela Cano suggests that Robles received some form of pension or payout, but that her rank of *coronel* went unacknowledged by the Mexican government. She died in 1984, and her last wishes were to be accorded the honors due to a soldier and to be buried in a dress to make peace with God. A museum in her honor was later established in Xochipala.

—*Yolanda Retter*

## FURTHER READING

Cano, Gabriela. "El Coronel Robles: Una combatiente zapatista." *Fem*, April, 1988, 22-24.

Cárdenas Trueba, Olga. "Amelia Robles y la revolución zapatista en el estado de Guerrero." In *Estudios Sobre el Zapatismo*, edited by Laura Espejel López. México D.F.: Instituto Nacional de Antropología e Historia, 2002.

Linhard, Tabea Alexa. *Fearless Women in the Mexican Revolution and the Spanish Civil War.* Columbia: University of Missouri Press, 2005.

Salas, Elizabeth. "The Soldadera in the Mexican Revolution: War and Men's Illusions." In *Women of the Mexican Countryside, 1850-1990: Creating Spaces, Shaping Transition*, edited by Heather Fowler-Salamini and Mary Kay Vaughan. Tucson: University of Arizona Press, 1994.

SEE ALSO: Nov. 11, 1865: Mary Edwards Walker Is Awarded the Medal of Honor; c. 1899: Transgender Reporter Covers Spanish-American War Revolts; Nov. 17, 1901: Police Arrest "Los 41" in Mexico City; Nov., 1965: Revolutionary Cuba Imprisons Gays; Nov. 21, 1966: First Gender Identity Clinic Opens and Provides Gender Reassignment Surgery; 1969: Nuestro Mundo Forms as First Queer Organization in Argentina; 1975-1983: Gay Latino Alliance Is Formed; Oct. 14-17, 1987: Latin American and Caribbean Lesbian Feminist Network Is Formed; Jan. 21, 1989: Death of Transgender Jazz Musician Billy Tipton; 1996: Hart Recognized as a Transgender Man; June 19, 2002: Gays and Lesbians March for Equal Rights in Mexico City; Apr., 2003: Buenos Aires Recognizes Same-Gender Civil Unions; Jan., 2006: Jiménez Flores Elected to the Mexican Senate.

# March 15, 1919-1921
# U.S. Navy Launches Sting Operation Against "Sexual Perverts"

*High-ranking U.S. Navy officials tasked young enlisted men, mostly teenagers, as undercover decoys and solicitors of gay sex to "trap" unsuspecting men seeking sex with other men.*

**Locale:** Newport, Rhode Island
**Categories:** Military; government and politics; laws, acts, and legal history

## Key Figures

*Josephus Daniels* (1862-1948), secretary of the Navy under President Woodrow Wilson
*Franklin D. Roosevelt* (1882-1945), assistant secretary of the Navy
*Samuel Neal Kent*, Episcopal chaplain of the Naval Hospital in Newport
*Edward H. Campbell*, naval captain and commander of the Newport Naval Training Station
*Erastus Mead Hudson*, naval lieutenant and physician serving in the Medical Corps
*Ervin Arnold*, former private detective and machinist's mate
*Richard Leigh*, naval captain and acting chief of the Bureau of Navigation
*James DeWolf Perry* (b. 1871), Episcopal bishop of Rhode Island, 1911-1946
*A. Mitchell Palmer* (1872-1936), attorney general under Wilson

## Summary of Event

To American elites in 1919, a most disturbing scandal was the U.S. Navy's undercover operations to "trap" gay men soliciting sex with other men, in and around a Navy training station and at a Young Men's Christian Association (YMCA) site in Newport, Rhode Island.

In late nineteenth century America, conventional wisdom associated homosexuality with either alien, decadent aristocrats or desperately poor and single immigrants from Europe. Red-light districts were designed to contain this foreign "vice," among other activities, such as prostitution and narcotics, from contaminating surrounding families and neighborhoods. Progressives such as Woodrow Wilson, Josephus Daniels, and Franklin D. Roosevelt wanted to cleanse their cities of corruption once and for all; now in power, they embarked upon quixotic crusades to make bourgeois domesticity and thus "real men" safe from ubiquitous temptation.

Progressives discovered more than they bargained for, however. While being the best customers of what red-light districts had to offer, middle-class, native-born Anglo-Saxon men were thought to be largely immune from "unnatural" same-gender desires and relationships. Yet a number of exposés beginning with a raid on the YMCA in Portland, Oregon, in 1912, and culminating in the Newport sting seven years later, unmasked seemingly straight men as homosexual far outside the notorious saloon or seedy theater.

Cleared by the same attorney general, A. Mitchell Palmer, who was the architect of the first Red Scare, the Newport sting against "queers" began as an attack on heterosexual prostitution. In 1917, Daniels, as Navy secretary, was concerned about the corrosive effects of Newport brothels upon the training and readiness of naval personnel. He urged and got local authorities to scare away prostitutes from the base, deploying military police officers in front of identified houses of ill repute to keep uniformed sailors from going inside.

Two years later, after conditions had failed to improve on the heterosexual front, Secretary Daniels was even more incensed about new and frequent reports about homosexual activity among the sailors and townspeople. Daniels was unable to handle this "problem" himself because he had to attend a postwar Allied Powers naval conference in Europe, but he charged Captain Edward H. Campbell, the Newport Naval Training Station's commandant, with establishing a court of inquiry to "disinfect" his base specifically against homosexuality. The earlier concern with heterosexual prostitution had been eclipsed by this new need to protect new recruits from succumbing to intricate and long-established networks of gay men meeting in the gyms, parks, beaches, and wharves of this famous resort and port.

On March 15, 1919, following Daniels's directive, Captain Campbell established a four-man panel chaired by Lieutenant Erastus Mead Hudson of the Medical Corps. Even before the panel had been named, however, Campbell had Hudson conduct a preliminary investigation in which Hudson contacted Ervin Arnold, a machinist's mate and former private detective. It was Arnold who persuaded Hudson and then the panel that the best way to fight secretive homosexuals would be to draft a group of equally cagey, attractive, young recruits to be approached by the shadowy "perpetrators." By late March, Arnold had thirteen newly enlisted sailors lined up to do his dirty work, which he oversaw from a room provided to him by the American Red Cross.

The decoys got right to business, ensnaring at least eighteen comrades in April. Even though some of the decoys actually went so far as to accept fellatio willingly from their victims, they were praised by Hudson's court for being serviced. The disgraced perpetrators were shown no mercy, however. Nearly all were court-martialed or dishonorably discharged, facing the full weight of naval justice.

Yet policing the ranks did nothing to stem the endless tide of civilians who tempted "innocent" servicemen into homosexuality. Eager to please his absent boss and political patron, assistant secretary of the Navy Franklin Roosevelt had Hudson and Arnold widen their witch hunt to include civilians engaging in furtive sex with sailors stationed in Newport. By June, Hudson was working out of Roosevelt's office and was funded by the assistant secretary's own discretionary funds. Nevertheless, worried about the legality of their methods of en-

trapment, Hudson insisted upon clearance from Palmer and the U.S. Justice Department and upon advice from a local attorney. Hudson got what he wanted to hear. Now underwritten by Roosevelt's office, the decoys grew in number to forty-one by July, nearly a quarter of who were just teenagers.

After a second wave of undercover operations that arrested sixteen civilians, Hudson and Roosevelt ran into political and legal difficulties themselves. Disciplining common sailors was one thing, but exposing privileged members of Newport society as homosexual was another. Among those arrested was Samuel Neal Kent, the Episcopal chaplain of the Naval Hospital in Newport. Kent had been one of those impeccable, upper-class gentlemen whom Progressives felt would never stoop to this level of depravity. He was acquitted in a local trial on August 23, but he immediately suffered a nervous breakdown and never recovered fully. Nevertheless, Kent's well-connected friends then campaigned to expose the entrapment and to show the chaplain as the inherently innocent victim of foul play. They complained to Richard Leigh, the acting chief of the Bureau of Navigation, who went on to urge further investigation of Hudson's methods and eventually sent the Episcopal bishop of Rhode Island, James DeWolf Perry, to pressure Secretary Daniels.

This counterattack, in turn, led Daniels and Roosevelt to praise Hudson and his henchmen unconditionally. Palmer's Justice Department then completely absolved Daniels and Roosevelt; to make matters worse, in a parting shot, Kent was rearrested on the same "crime," this time for breaking a wartime federal statute regarding lewdness near a military base. Joined by local newspapers, Kent's allies rallied, winning a pyrrhic victory by getting the Senate Naval Affairs Committee to denounce the questionable tactics pursued by Hudson, Roosevelt, and Daniels. A decade before the New Deal, Roosevelt was shown to be a traitor to his class, but the elite Episcopalian horror at the scandal failed to hurt him within his own Democratic Party, which, in the 1920's, was the haven of social conservatives.

## Significance

The 1919 naval sting operation was a harbinger of abuses of power in the name of exposing homosexuality among soldiers, sailors, marines, and civilians in the twentieth century. Roosevelt's ease in dispelling legal concerns about entrapment led to a cottage industry of vice cops deployed to catch and detain men seeking sex with other men.

Roosevelt would later regret his role in the making of the national security state. In the decade after his death during the second red scare, a security state would come to see homosexuality not just as an impediment to military effectiveness but as treason itself.

—*Charles H. Ford*

## Further Reading

Chauncey, George, Jr. "Christian Brotherhood or Sexual Perversion? Homosexual Identities and the Construction of Sexual Boundaries in the World War I Era." In *Hidden from History: Reclaiming the Gay and Lesbian Past*, edited by Martin B. Duberman, Martha Vicinus, and George Chauncey, Jr. New York: New American Library, 1989.

Gustav-Wrathall, John Donald. *Take the Young Stranger by the Hand: Same-Sex Relations and the YMCA*. Chicago: University of Chicago Press, 1998.

Murphy, Lawrence R. "Cleaning Up Newport: The U.S. Navy's Prosecution of Homosexuals After World War I." *Journal of American Culture* 7 (Fall, 1984): 57-64.

Shilts, Randy. *Conduct Unbecoming: Gays and Lesbians in the U.S. Military*. 1994. New ed. New York: St. Martin's Griffin, 2005.

Ward, Geoffrey C. *A First-Class Temperament: The Emergence of Franklin Roosevelt*. New York: Harper & Row, 1989.

**See also:** Nov. 17, 1901: Police Arrest "Los 41" in Mexico City; 1933-1945: Nazis Persecute Homosexuals; June 30-July 1, 1934: Hitler's Night of the Long Knives; July 3, 1975: U.S. Civil Service Commission Prohibits Discrimination Against Federal Employees; 1976-1990: Army Reservist Ben-Shalom Sues for Reinstatement; May-Aug., 1980: U.S. Navy Investigates the USS *Norton Sound* in Antilesbian Witch Hunt; May 3, 1989: *Watkins v. United States Army* Reinstates Gay Soldier; 1990, 1994: *Coming Out Under Fire* Documents Gay and Lesbian Military Veterans; Aug. 27, 1991: *The Advocate* Outs Pentagon Spokesman Pete Williams; Oct., 1992: Canadian Military Lifts Its Ban on Gays and Lesbians; Nov. 30, 1993: Don't Ask, Don't Tell Policy Is Implemented; Jan. 12, 2000: United Kingdom Lifts Ban on Gays and Lesbians in the Military.

## February 19, 1923
# THE GOD OF VENGEANCE OPENS ON BROADWAY

The God of Vengeance, *the controversial English-language version of Sholem Asch's 1907 Yiddish play, was the first drama on Broadway to include a lesbian love scene. The play's producer and cast, and the theater owner, were arrested and found guilty of obscenity.*

LOCALE: New York, New York
CATEGORIES: Arts; cultural and intellectual history; crime

KEY FIGURES
*Sholem Asch* (1880-1957), Yiddish novelist, essayist, short–story writer, and playwright
*Joseph Silverman*, rabbi who denounced the play
*Harry Weinberger*, play's producer on Broadway
*Michael Selwyn*, owner of the theater where the play was produced
*Rudolph Schildkraut*, play's director

SUMMARY OF EVENT
Broadway's first lesbian love scene was presented in a play that had already been produced in a dozen languages in at least eight countries. Indeed, *Got fun Nekomeh* (pr. 1907; *The God of Vengeance*, 1918) had already been performed off and on for a decade and a half in New York City Yiddish theaters without incident. However, when *The God of Vengeance* appeared on Broadway in 1923 in an English-language translation, *The Daily News* fumed that the play presented "an ugly story" that was "hopelessly foreign to our Anglo-Saxon taste and understanding." The cast would be arrested and charged with promoting obscenity days after the play opened.

The basic action of the play consists of the efforts of a Polish brothel owner, Yekel Tchaftchovitch, to protect the innocence of his seventeen-year-old daughter Rivkele and marry her off to a respectable young man. To safeguard his daughter from the sins of her parents (her mother, Sore, is a former prostitute), Yekel makes a generous donation to his local synagogue to obtain a copy of the Torah, which he places in Rivkele's bedroom. Even though she is forbidden to have contact with the prostitutes who live and work directly beneath her home, she is in fact a lover of one of them, Manke. Meanwhile, another prostitute, Hindel, is anxious to marry a pimp and establish her own brothel. Hindel convinces Manke that the only way that she and Rivkele can be together is for them to leave the Tchaftchovitch house and join her new brothel.

Rivkele accepts Hindel's advice and leaves home.

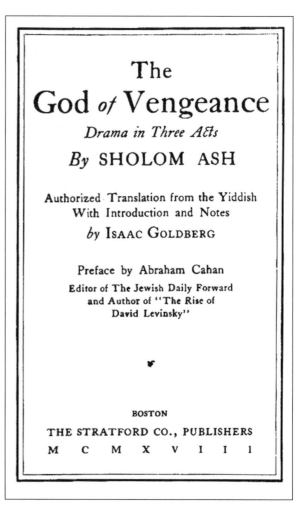

The title page of The God of Vengeance *(1918).*

*Sholem Asch.* (Library of Congress)

for "presenting an obscene, indecent, immoral and impure theatrical production." The fourteen defendants posted $300 bail and were back at the theater to give a matinee performance. The publicity was great for business; *The God of Vengeance* ran for 133 performances before it closed.

Written in Yiddish in 1906 and first published in that language in 1907, *The God of Vengeance* is, according to scholar Alisa Solomon, "one of the toughest and most self-critical plays in the Yiddish canon," tackling domestic violence, rabbinic hypocrisy, and the collision between modern and traditional worlds. While the message in this moral melodrama is very clear—

Her flight, however, is discovered; when she is brought back home her father asks if she is "still as pure as when you left this house." She responds that she "doesn't know." When the matchmaker arrives with the prospective groom's father in order to finalize the marriage arrangements, Yekel goes crazy, banishing his daughter and wife to the brothel located below their home and placing the Holy Scroll in the arms of the bewildered matchmaker.

The Broadway production was met with controversy: A group of private citizens, the Society for the Suppression of Vice, attacked the play for being "obscene, indecent, disgusting, and tending to corruption of the morals of youth." Joseph Silverman, rabbi of Temple Emanuel, caught the attention of the district attorney. An outspoken member of the religious community, Silverman was convinced that the play was indecent and blasphemous, and he was especially offended that all the characters in the brothel (prostitutes, lesbian prostitutes, and johns) were Jewish.

Fifteen days after *The God of Vengeance* opened on Broadway, the cast, producer Harry Weinberger, and theater owner Michael Selwyn were arrested

a life of sin leads Yekel to lose what he values most—the play also contains trenchant social commentary, especially in regard to the plight of women whose only option is to be sold as prostitutes or brides.

The love between Manke and Rivkele is not presented as shocking or perverse; in fact, they are the only couple in the play whose relationship is not marred by violence and emotional brutality. There is no analysis or even discussion of same-gender desire by any of the characters. What is explicit is that the two women have an emotional and physical relationship. At the end of act 1, they kiss on stage; in act 2, after frolicking in a warm spring rain, Manke delights in Rivkele's body.

> I uncovered your breasts and washed them with the rain water that ran into my hands. So white and firm, your breasts, and the blood in them cools under the hand like white snow. And their fragrance is like the smell of grass in the meadows.

The playwright wrote in the play's Broadway program that the love between the two characters "is not only an erotic one. It is unconscious mother love of which they are deprived . . . rather than the sensuous, inverted love of one woman for another." While some audience members might have come away from the play with Asch's interpretation, others could just as easily applaud the love these two women obviously have for one another.

Most of the New York critics made no mention of the lesbian plot in their reviews. Some were obtuse, *The Evening Telegram* allowing "The terrible details need not be recorded here, they are almost too terrible to look upon in the theatre." Producer Alice Kauser trimmed the lesbian love scenes for the English-language presentation when it opened on December 20, 1922, in the Off-Broadway Provincetown Playhouse, and most historians assume that more cuts were made to the play before it moved from Greenwich Village to Broadway, where it opened at the Apollo Theatre on 42nd Street on February 19, 1923.None of the critics who covered the play in its December or February opening explained to their readers that *The God of Vengeance* was the first play to introduce lesbian characters to English-language audiences.

After the play closed, the obscenity case against the play's cast, producers, and the theater owner went to trial. Despite the testimony of numerous rabbis in support of the play, the judge ruled against it, fining actor-director Rudolph Schildkraut and producer Weinberger $200 each; the rest of the cast were given suspended sentences. Suspended or not, these sentences marked the first time in American theater that a jury found performers guilty of presenting obscene material. The New York State Court of Appeals reversed the convictions in January, 1925, on the grounds that the manuscript of the play had not been allowed in evidence at the trial.

## SIGNIFICANCE

Even as some critics held that *The God of Vengeance* is the greatest drama of the Yiddish theater, its English-language productions continued to cause controversy. In 1946, the British play reader assigned to the English-language play suggested that London's chief rabbi be asked to assess the play before it was granted a license to be performed. Rabbi Harris M. Lazarus was firm when he wrote,

[T]he theme is offensive and not fit for the public stage. . . . This play could not have been intended for the stage either in Russia or in any other Jewish centre. It is a sordid theme, repulsive in personnel and diction, and offensive to any feeling of decency in the use of the Scroll for such purpose.

Rabbi Lazarus did not know that the Yiddish play had already been performed in London, that its first production in St. Petersburg in 1908 (in Russian) was a rousing success, and that by the 1930's it had been performed by virtually every Yiddish theater company in the world.

---

### SHOLEM ASCH

Sholem Asch, born in Poland in 1880, was one of the most important authors writing in Yiddish in the early twentieth century. He was one of fifteen children born to Moishe, a businessman, and Malka Asch. He was educated in the local Hebrew school and later taught Hebrew.

In 1899, Asch moved to Warsaw, where he became the protégé of the famous writer I. L. Peretz. Following Peretz's advice, Asch began to write in Yiddish and was soon publishing in Yiddish newspapers. In 1901, Asch married Matilde Spiro, and in 1902 their first child was born. His first novel, *The Little Town*, was published in 1905, and three years later, with the successful production of *The God of Vengeance*, he secured an international reputation as a major Yiddish writer.

Concerned about the safety of his four young children in Poland, Asch moved with his family to New York in 1914, where he continued to write and publish plays and novels. His novels were serialized in the *Jewish Daily Forward* before being published in book form.

Although he had become an American citizen, Asch moved his family to Nice, France, in 1925. His books began to appear in best-selling English translations, but his fame could not protect him and his family from the threatening political situation in Europe. In 1938 he returned to the United States but returned to Europe with his wife in 1953. During a stay in Israel, Asch suffered a stroke. He returned to London for medical care but died there on July 10, 1957.

Pulitzer Prize-winning playwright Donald Margulies crafted his own adaptation of Asch's play in 2000. Streamlining the play by reducing it from three to two acts, he accomplished what Alisa Solomon described as a "crossover success, making *The God of Vengeance* a profoundly compelling American play."

*—Bud Coleman*

**FURTHER READING**

Asch, Sholem. *The God of Vengeance*. Translated by Isaac Goldberg, preface by Abraham Cahan. Boston: Stratford, 1918.

Berkowitz, Joel, ed. *Yiddish Theatre: New Approaches*. Portland, Oreg.: Littman Library of Jewish Civilization, 2003.

Bordman, Gerald. *American Theatre: A Chronicle of Comedy and Drama, 1914-1930*. New York: Oxford University Press, 1995.

Curtin, Kaier. *"We Can Always Call Them Bulgarians": The Emergence of Lesbians and Gay Men on the American Stage*. Boston: Alyson, 1987.

Margulies, Donald. *God of Vengeance*. Adapted from the play by Sholem Asch. Translated by Joachim Neugroschel, introduced by Alisa Solomon. New York: Theatre Communications Group, 2004.

Siegel, Ben. *The Controversial Sholem Asch: An Introduction to His Fiction*. Bowling Green, Ohio: Bowling Green University Popular Press, 1976.

**SEE ALSO:** 1928: Hall Publishes *The Well of Loneliness*; 1929: *Pandora's Box* Opens; Mar. 20, 1988: *M. Butterfly* Opens on Broadway.

## 1924
# GIDE PUBLISHES THE SIGNED EDITION OF *CORYDON*

*Popular French novelist André Gide published a signed commercial edition of his Socratic dialogues,* Corydon, *a work on the virtues of homosexuality. Soon after* Corydon *was published, Gide acknowledged in his autobiography that he was gay.*

**LOCALE:** Paris, France
**CATEGORIES:** Literature; publications

**KEY FIGURE**
*André Gide* (1869-1951), French novelist

**SUMMARY OF EVENT**
In 1911, André Gide first published anonymously, and in an incomplete form, a collection of dialogues on homosexuality in a private edition of twelve. He republished this pamphlet, titled *Corydon*, in its complete form in 1920, but again only in a private edition, this time of twenty-one copies. The signed commercial edition did not appear until 1924 (and the English translation did not appear until 1950). In it, Gide argued that homosexuality was not only natural but also beneficial to society.

*Corydon* opens when a rather naïve narrator comes to see his old friend, Corydon, a successful doctor, about a homosexual scandal reported in the press. They agree to discuss a book that Corydon is writing, called *A Defense of Pederasty*. Corydon explains that he discovered his sexual inclination while he was engaged, during his internship at the hospital. At first he could not understand why he did not feel any physical desire for his fiancé, although he did feel love. Later he realized that his affections for her younger brother went beyond mere friendship, and he concluded that his attraction to him was quite natural and even praiseworthy.

In the second dialogue, Corydon advocates a new theory on sexual attraction that rejects the idea that the sexual instinct attracts males to females for the sake of reproduction. Instead, he believes that the sexual instinct pushes males and females to seek pleasure in a number of different ways, which includes the contact of males with males and of females with females. In other words, homosexuality is an entirely natural phenomenon. "To obtain pleasure, this joining together of the two sexes is not indispensable," Corydon tells his visitor.

Corydon continues in the next dialogue with the idea that society has developed artificial means of attraction that are less spontaneous, less naïvely innocent, and, in short, less natural than the simple beauty of the human body, especially of the male body. Such artificial means of attraction have often produced immoral and unethical behavior among both homosexual and heterosexual men and women. In its purest form, sexual behavior, whether homosexual or heterosexual, is neither moral nor immoral, neither ethical nor unethical. He writes,

> In homosexuality, just as in heterosexuality, there are all shades and degrees, from Platonic love to lust, from self-denial to sadism, from radiant health to sullen sickliness, from simple expansiveness to all the refinements of vice.

In the final dialogue, Corydon argues that the love of an older man for an adolescent boy can be more beneficial for the emotional development of the young man than can the charms of an older woman. After all, the young adolescent is usually unsure of his sexual inclinations, is more willing to explore his sexuality, and is more in need of the affections of an older man, who "can understand an adolescent boy's troubles better than a woman can." He believes that "such a lover will jealously watch over him, protect him, and himself exalted, purified by this love, will guide him toward those radiant heights, which are not to be reached without love."

## ANDRÉ GIDE

André Gide was awarded the Nobel Prize in Literature in 1947, an event that terminated a debate that had for many decades been carried on in France regarding whether Gide, a writer of great talent and diversity, should be given official sanction and recognition with membership in the French Academy.

During much of his career, Gide was suspect because of his revelation in *Corydon* (1924), which is essentially a defense of homosexuality, of his own sexual orientation. His whole career, in a way that is more typical of France than of most other countries, was a constant theme for debate and speculation. Did aesthetic excellence mean that one should overlook a writer's challenge to conventional social patterns?

The events of Gide's life are a record of the publication of many books and of wide-ranging travels in Europe and Africa that were in accord with his restless spirit. In his early years he found the cultures of North Africa particularly attractive. Toward the end of the 1920's he was strongly attracted by the social experiments of the Soviet Union and finally traveled in that country. His report, in 1936, on what he found there—the triumph of an unimaginative dictatorship over the social aspirations of the 1917 revolution—aroused almost as much controversy as the personal avowals of *Corydon*. Because of his censures of Russia, Gide was the center of a storm that did not abate until the beginning of World War II. This experience convinced him that artists take an unwise risk when they involve themselves in current problems.

Gide was strongly drawn, as Justin O'Brien points out in his *Portrait of André Gide* (1953), by ancient myths as well as by scriptural narratives, convinced that the old tales are naïve only on the surface; actually, they offer the modern writer inexhaustible suggestions for creation. Indeed, the tales are richer than the codes readers have associated with them; his defenders consider that he was successful, in part, because he detached himself from the codes and sought the reality, whether in ancient myth or in the sorrow and delight of his own life and art.

### SIGNIFICANCE

Gide's defense of homosexuality in *Corydon* was an eloquent plea for toleration based on his belief that homosexuality is natural. Society's attempts to regulate sexual activity is, in and of itself, unnatural and consequently the source of immoral and unethical behavior, among both homosexuals and heterosexuals.

Soon after *Corydon*, Gide published his autobiography *Si le grain ne meurt* (1926; *If It Die . . .*, 1935), in which he explicitly acknowledged his own homosexuality. Together with *Corydon*, *Si*

*André Gide.* (The Nobel Foundation)

impetus that led him to write, that gave meaning to his life, and that he passed on to others through his own reflections.

—*William A. Peniston*

**FURTHER READING**

Gide, André. *Corydon*. Paris: Gallimard, 1924. Translated by Richard Howard. New York: Farrar, Straus, Giroux, 1983.

_____. *Si le grain ne meurt*. Paris: Gallimard, 1926. Translated by Dorothy Bussy as *If It Die . . .* London: Secker and Warburg, 1950.

Lucey, Michael. *Gide's Bent: Sexuality, Politics, Writing*. New York: Oxford University Press, 1995.

Martin du Gard, Roger. *Notes on André Gide*. Translated by John Russell. New York: Helen Marx, 2005.

Pollard, Patrick. *André Gide: The Homosexual Moralist*. New Haven, Conn.: Yale University Press, 1991.

Segal, Naomi. *André Gide: Pederasty and Pedagogy*. Oxford, England: Clarendon Press, 1998.

Sheridan, Alan. *André Gide: A Life in the Present*. Cambridge, Mass.: Harvard University Press, 1999.

**SEE ALSO:** July 4, 1855: Whitman Publishes *Leaves of Grass*; May 25, 1895: Oscar Wilde Is Convicted of Gross Indecency; 1903: Stein Writes *Q.E.D.*; 1928: Hall Publishes *The Well of Loneliness*; 1939: Isherwood Publishes *Goodbye to Berlin*; 1947-1948: Golden Age of American Gay Literature; 1956: Baldwin Publishes *Giovanni's Room*; 1963: Rechy Publishes *City of Night*; June, 1971: The Gay Book Award Debuts; 1974: *The Front Runner* Makes *The New York Times* Best-Seller List; 1975: First Novel About Coming Out to Parents Is Published; 1980-1981: Gay Writers Form the Violet Quill; May, 1987: *Lambda Rising Book Report* Begins Publication; June 2, 1989: Lambda Literary Award Is Created; 1993: Monette Wins the National Book Award for *Becoming a Man*.

*le grain ne meurt* caused quite a sensation. Gide was denounced by many members of the intellectual elite, but others found his arguments thoughtful and reasonable. His public stance gave homosexuals in France the courage to live their lives openly and honestly.

Gide's defense of homosexuality is significant not so much because of the ideas he advocated— many of which are still popular arguments—but because he had the courage to confront the issue without deceiving himself or others. This courage, which allowed him to portray his sexual identity in positive terms, was not something that came about suddenly. It was the result of a long personal struggle that had developed over the course of his childhood, his marriage, and his literary career. It was the

## December 10, 1924
# Gerber Founds the Society for Human Rights

*The Society for Human Rights, a nonprofit social justice organization and the first documented gay rights organization in the United States, was created in an effort to spearhead a U.S. gay rights movement. Although the organization was short-lived, it is said to have inspired the founding in 1950 of the Mattachine Society, the better-known gay rights group for men.*

**Locale:** Chicago, Illinois

**Categories:** Organizations and institutions; civil rights; government and politics; publications

**Key Figures**

*Henry Gerber* (1895-1972), Bavarian-born founder and secretary of the society, U.S. postal worker

*John T. Graves*, African American clergyman and president of the society

*Al Meininger*, the society's vice president, whose extramarital homosexual affair ultimately led to his imprisonment with Gerber and Graves

**Summary of Event**

The state of Illinois, on December 10, 1924, issued a charter to a new human rights organization, a non-profit corporation with the stated objective "to promote and protect the interests of people who by reasons of mental and physical abnormalities are abused and hindered in the legal pursuit of happiness." Called the Society for Human Rights, the group was formed by Henry Gerber, who served with the Army of Occupation in Germany after World War I. He founded the society, according to its charter, as a means "to combat the public prejudices . . . by dissemination of factors according to modern science among intellectuals of mature age." Gerber wanted the society to help promote social equality and encourage acceptance of "alternative" sexual lifestyles. He had arranged for the Reverend John T. Graves to sign the society's charter as president, along with Al Meininger as vice president. While these two men

assisted Gerber in running the organization, ultimately it was Gerber who did most of the work and bore all the costs for its maintenance.

In early 1925, Gerber created the first publication in the United States intended for a gay audience. *Friendship and Freedom*'s goal was to attract members to the society and act as a forum for discussing the difficulties faced by early twentieth century urban homosexuals. However, very few individuals were willing to receive *Friendship and Freedom*, fearing the publication would make it easy for police to find and target them as criminals. Persons engaging in same-gender sexual relations were considered criminals by law in 1920's America. In this era, U.S. postal censors cooperated with local law enforcement to identify what were then called "sex deviants."

Because of widespread apprehension within the gay community, and because of low membership, the society foundered. Chicago police, though, dealt the group its final blow soon after the initial production of *Friendship and Freedom*. Gerber, Graves, and Meininger were jailed after Meininger's wife approached a social worker about her husband's involvement in a homosexual organization. The social worker in turn informed police.

Soon after, the three leaders of the society were arrested, along with a young man who, according to a news story, was in Meininger's bedroom at the time of Meininger's arrest. Gerber said that the Chicago *Herald and Examiner* reported the society's breakup under the headline "Strange Sex Cult Exposed." (Historian Jonathan Ned Katz, in his 1976 book *Gay American History*, wrote in a footnote that this article could not be located by a researcher. He adds, though, that the article might have appeared at an earlier time.)

During the trial for the three men, the prosecution maintained that the society's publication *Friendship and Freedom* violated federal laws regarding the mailing of obscene materials through the U.S. postal service. The "obscenity" in question

## SOCIETY FOR HUMAN RIGHTS, CHARTER (1924)

[T]o promote and to protect the interests of people who by reasons of mental and physical abnormalities are abused and hindered in the legal pursuit of happiness which is guaranteed them by the Declaration of Independence, and to combat the public prejudices against them by dissemination of facts according to modern science among intellectuals of mature age. The Society stands only for law and order; it is in harmony with any and all general laws insofar as they protect the rights of others, and does in no manner recommend any acts in violation of present laws nor advocate any matter inimical to the public welfare.

*Source:* Jonathan Ned Katz, *Gay American History: Lesbians and Gay Men in the U.S.A.* Rev. ed. (New York: Meridian Books, 1992).

was the discussion of homosexuality. Eventually, upon reassignment of a new judge, the case was dismissed. Yet Gerber's legal defense still cost him his life savings. Meininger pled guilty to disorderly conduct and was fined. All undistributed copies of *Friendship and Freedom* were confiscated, and the Society for Human Rights was disbanded.

### SIGNIFICANCE

It is difficult to assess the historical impact of an organization when its message had been so poorly received by the demographic to which it was geared. The Society for Human Rights sought bring together and empower the homosexual community of early twentieth century Chicago, yet widespread fear inhibited the realization of the society's goals.

Nonetheless, the founding and then dismantling of the society had significantly impacted Henry Gerber's life. The turmoil of the event made him bitter toward homosexuals, and, ultimately, he also resented trying to rally gays to fight for equality. This sense of animosity shaped Gerber's future social justice endeavors and his outlook on civil rights.

While the society did not have an immediate impact on gays and lesbians living in 1920's Chicago (aside from publicly embarrassing three gay men in the media), the organization's existence is a historical barometer of the social and cultural conditions that gays endured at the time. Furthermore, scholars could use this moment in history to understand the sense of community and collectivized pride, or lack thereof, germinating among gays in the era.

As the first gay rights and advocacy organization of its kind, however, the society helped clear a path for future gay and lesbian rights groups and organizations to follow. The society is believed to have inspired and influenced the creation in 1950 of the successful and long-running Mattachine Society.

—*Daniel J. Nugent*

### FURTHER READING

Bullough, Vern L., ed. *Before Stonewall: Activists for Gay and Lesbian Rights in Historical Context*. New York: Harrington Park Press, 2002.

Chauncey, George. *Gay New York: Gender, Urban Culture, and the Making of the Gay Male World, 1890-1940*. New York: Basic Books, 1994.

Gerber, Henry. "The Society for Human Rights—1925." *ONE* 10, no. 9 (1962): 5-11.

Haeberle, E. J. "A Movement of Inverts: An Early Plan for a Homosexual Organization in the United States." *Journal of Homosexuality* 1/2 (1984): 127-133.

Heap, Chad. *Homosexuality in the City: A Century of Research at the University of Chicago*. Chicago: University of Chicago Press, 2000.

Katz, Jonathan Ned. *Gay American History: Lesbians and Gay Men in the U.S.A., a Documentary History*. 1976. Rev. ed. New York: Meridian, 1992.

_____. *Homosexual Emancipation Miscellany, c. 1835-1952*. New York: Arno Press, 1975.

SEE ALSO: 1906: Friedlaender Breaks with the Scientific-Humanitarian Committee; 1950: Mattachine Society Is Founded; 1952: ONE, Inc., Is Founded; 1955: Daughters of Bilitis Founded as First National Lesbian Group in United States; Feb. 19-20, 1966: First North American Conference of Homophile Organizations Convenes; Aug. 11-18, 1968: NACHO Formally Becomes the First Gay Political Coalition.

## February, 1927
# WALES PADLOCK LAW CENSORS RISQUE THEATER

*Often considered the first and only major censorship law covering the theater in the United States, the Wales Padlock Law targeted plays considered risque, namely those dealing with homosexuality and prostitution. The law remained on the books until 1967.*

**LOCALE:** New York, New York
**CATEGORIES:** Laws, acts, and legal history; arts

**KEY FIGURES**
*Mae West* (1893-1980), playwright and actor
*James "Jimmy" Walker* (1881-1946), mayor of New York
*Joseph V. "Holy Joe" McKee* (1889-1956), acting mayor of New York
*B. Roger Wales* (b. 1879), New York state senator
*Joab H. Banton* and
*Charles H. Dodd*, New York district attorneys

**SUMMARY OF EVENT**
The 1920's in New York City was a decade of contrasts. While liquor prohibition was in effect and moral crusades were plentiful, the speakeasy culture was entrenched and the moral order was being challenged by Broadway theater. Expecting big profits, playwright and actor Mae West chose to press the boundaries of public decency. Her vaudeville-inspired play *Sex* was financially successful and prompted playwrights and theater owners to tackle more sexual themes. Her friendly relationship with the city's mayor, Jimmy Walker, encouraged her to be more sexually explicit in her plays.

However, on February 9, 1927, Mayor Walker was on vacation, and acting Mayor Joseph V. McKee, known as "Holy Joe," staged a politically motivated raid on three "indecent" plays. West's *Sex*, William Francis Dugan's unsuccessful comedy *The Virgin Man*, and Éduard Bourdet's lesbian drama *The Captive* were each halted at intermission. The first two plays were considered lewd but nonthreatening. However, *The Captive*, a sensitive, restrained look at a lesbian relationship, was considered dangerous. As a result, the cast and crew of each show were arrested, jailed, and subsequently fined.

The raids renewed the resolve of socially conservative forces in the New York State Assembly. Their response came in less than two weeks. During the last few hours of a legislative session, the Republicans in Albany introduced legislation amending the Penal Code of 1909, a code regulating indecent materials. Two new provisions were added to the law. The first prohibited plays "depicting or dealing with the subject of sex degeneracy, or sex perversion." The second and more troubling provision, Section 1140A, directed that theater owners who chose to produce a show that could "tend to the corruption of youth or others" could have their playhouses padlocked and closed for the course of one year.

District attorneys Joab H. Banton of New York and Charles H. Dodd of Brooklyn had suggested the law, and Senator B. Roger Wales had sponsored it in the legislature. The entire legislature was sensitive to the public outcry for censorship leading up to the 1927 raids. As a result, the Wales Padlock Law was passed, giving New York officials the authority to arrest and prosecute producers and actors associated with any "immoral drama."

Opponents of the bill felt that it gave too much power to the district attorney or assistant district attorney, and they circulated a petition to repeal the law. The petition had been sent to Governor Alfred E. Smith, but the law remained in effect until 1967.

**SIGNIFICANCE**
The adoption of the Wales Padlock Law began a forty-year period of extreme self-censorship on the part of the U.S. theater community, especially in New York and particularly where depictions of gay and lesbian characters and themes were concerned. Because the law targeted theater owners and producers, who supported the theater financially, few playwrights, directors, or actors would or could challenge it in a meaningful way.

## MAE WEST

Mae West was born August 17, 1893, in Brooklyn, the first child of a boxer and a corset model. Her mother, Matilda, instilled ambition and self-confidence in Mae, and by age seven, she became a vaudeville and burlesque star.

In an attempt to secure roles for herself, West began writing plays. She merged her bawdy and sexually charged vaudevillian characters with a realistic playwriting style. Her first endeavor, *Sex* (1926), led to her widely publicized trial on obscenity charges, culminating in her incarceration. Subsequent plays, including *The Drag* (1927), *Diamond Lil* (1928), *Pleasure Man* (1928), *The Constant Sinner* (1928), and *Catherine Was Great* (1944), sealed her controversial reputation.

When theatrical censorship became pervasive, West turned to film, where she attempted to tone down her work. Even so, she battled with the Hays code over her positive depictions of female sexuality. She starred with leading men, such as Cary Grant and W. C. Fields. Her films include *Night After Night* (1932), *She Done Him Wrong* (1933), *I'm No Angel* (1933), *Go West Young Man* (1936), and *My Little Chickadee* (1940).

When the censors began to ease their actions, West returned to film in *Myra Breckenridge* (1970) and *Sextette* (1978). In May, 1977, acknowledgments of her contributions to the sexual revolution began to surface when the lesbian and gay publication *After Dark* awarded its Ruby Award to West, "Whose bold comic brilliance has taught us to laugh at our own puritanical heritage."

West suffered a series of strokes that led to her death on November 22, 1980, in Hollywood, California.

---

In 1928, the first drama to be affected by the law, Simon Gantillon's *Maya*, set a chilling example for years to come. In this case, the district attorney began receiving protests about the play. Then, acting on the suggestion made in an assistant's review, he closed the play after only fifteen performances. The producers, knowing the Wales Padlock Law could close their theater, did not appeal the case.

In 1930, the first legal challenge to the law was filed by Mae West. It was an attempt to dismiss obscenity charges against her gay-themed play *Pleasure Man*, formerly titled *The Drag*. Surprisingly, the case ended in a hung jury, which caused the judge to dismiss the charges. As a result of this challenge, an amendment was attached to the Wales Law that assured that, from that point on, only the writers and producers and not the cast or crew of a production would be held responsible for material deemed obscene or immoral.

The insidious self-censorship encouraged by the Wales Law was its primary impact; only a small number of little-known plays were actively removed from the stage between 1927 and 1967. Attempts to remove classic plays such as Ben Jonson's *Volpone* (pr. 1605) and Eugene O'Neill's *Strange Interlude* (pr. 1928) in the late 1920's were unsuccessful. Producer-director Herman Shumlin, tired of the threat of the padlock, challenged the law in 1934 with Lillian Hellman's lesbian classic *The Children's Hour* (pr. 1934). Though not well supported in the theater community, the play opened successfully on Broadway. Another lesbian drama, Dorothy and Howard Baker's *Trio*, was closed by the Shuberts in 1944 to avoid the law's sanctions. During the 1950's, the McCarthy years, few gay or lesbian plays were attempted for fear of the padlock. In the 1960's the law was ignored, and by 1970 the depiction of gay and lesbian characters on stage began to be commonplace.

In 1967, the U.S. Supreme Court finally granted freedom of speech status to the legitimate theater. Only one year later, Mart Crowley's *The Boys in the Band* (pr. 1968) would launch the GLBT theater revolution.

*—Daniel-Raymond Nadon*

### FURTHER READING

Clum, John. *Acting Gay: Male Homosexuality in Modern Drama*. New York: Columbia University Press, 1992.

Curtin, Kaier. *"We Can Always Call Them Bulgarians": The Emergence of Lesbians and Gay Men on the American Stage*. Boston: Alyson, 1987.

DeJongh, Nicholas. *Not in Front of the Audience: Homosexuality on Stage*. New York: Routledge, 1992.

Friedman, Andrea. *Prurient Interests: Gender, Democracy, and Obscenity in New York City, 1909-1945*. New York: Columbia University Press, 2000.

Hanna, David. *Come Up and See Me Sometime: An Uncensored Biography of Mae West*. New York: Belmont Tower Books, 1976.

Latham, Angela J. "The Right to Bare: Containing and Encoding American Women in Popular Entertainments of the 1920's." *Theatre Journal* 49, no. 4 (1997): 455-473.

Laufe, Abe. *The Wicked Stage: A History of Theatre Censorship and Harassment in the United States*. New York: Ungar, 1978.

West, Mae. *Goodness Had Nothing to Do with It.* New York: Avon, 1959.

**SEE ALSO:** Feb. 19, 1923: *The God of Vengeance* Opens on Broadway; 1928: Hall Publishes *The Well of Loneliness*; 1929: *Pandora's Box* Opens; 1930's-1960's: Hollywood Bans "Sexual Perversion" in Films; Mar. 20, 1988: *M. Butterfly* Opens on Broadway; 1989-1990: Helms Claims Photographs Are Indecent; 1990-1993: Artists Sue the National Endowment for the Arts; Dec. 3, 1998-Feb. 25, 1999: Screening of *Fire* Ignites Violent Protests in India.

# 1928
# HALL PUBLISHES *THE WELL OF LONELINESS*

*Radclyffe Hall's* The Well of Loneliness *was the first novel in English that dealt openly with a self-realized lesbian identity. The book, published in Paris to avoid British censors, was banned and then tried for obscenity in England and tried in the United States but found to be legal as written. Hall's work set the stage for the writing and publishing of lesbian-themed novels.*

**LOCALE:** Paris, France; London, England; and New York, New York

**CATEGORIES:** Literature; publications; laws, acts, and legal history

**KEY FIGURES**

*Radclyffe Hall* (1880-1943), English author

*Chartres Biron* (1883-1940), chief magistrate in London

*Morris Ernst* (1888-1976), American lawyer who successfully defended Hall's novel

**SUMMARY OF EVENT**

Noted author and literary prize winner Radclyffe Hall published her novel *The Well of Loneliness* in

*Radclyffe Hall, 1926.*

1928, marking a milestone in the history of lesbian literature. *The Well of Loneliness* was the first novel in English to openly and realistically address lesbian sexuality, which Hall called "sexual inversion" in the novel, the accepted term used also by sexologists of the time. In the book, Hall sympathetically chronicles protagonist Stephen Gordon's realization that she is lesbian, a self-awareness Gordon developed during childhood and then confronted and accepted as an adult.

Although received by many critics in the English press as a novel of literary merit and a tactfully treated work on a controversial subject, the novel was brought to the English court on a charge of obscenity. Hall and her publisher Jonathan Cape were defendants in the case. Despite a letter of support by an impressive list of literary figures such as George Bernard Shaw and T. S. Elliot, the chief judge for the case, Chartres Biron, found the book obscene and ordered its destruction. The judge declared that the work was especially subversive and obscene, a declaration likely made because the book was an earnest account of lesbian sexuality and the characters were depicted in an attractive and sympathetic light. The book's publisher, Jonathan Cape, had *The Well of Loneliness* printed in Paris (and printed in English) by Pegasus Press, and it had been smuggled into Great Britain from Paris by the intelligentsia.

In 1928, Jonathan Cape sold the American rights to *The Well of Loneliness* to the American publisher Covici Friede. Understanding the book's legal reception in England, Covici Friede knew that it would be charged with obscenity in the United States as well, so the publisher hired a lawyer, Morris Ernst, who was opposed to censorship. Ernst had a successful record of defending several controversial books.

Sales in the United States of *The Well of Loneliness* were tremendous, even though the price of the book, $5.00, was high for the time. A number of critics in the United States, as they had in England, gave the work positive reviews, and a distinguished list of persons of letters, including Theodore Dreiser and Upton Sinclair, signed their names in support of the novel.

## The Well of LONELINESS

By RADCLYFFE HALL
With a Commentary
by HAVELOCK ELLIS

Blue Ribbon Books, Garden City, New York

*The title page of* The Well of Loneliness *(1928).* (Blue Ribbon Books)

The U.S. trial in 1929 proceeded differently from its English counterpart, primarily because of Ernst's defense strategy. Ernst had read the work of sexologists Richard von Krafft-Ebing and Havelock Ellis (a supporter of Hall) and defended the novel's subject matter—lesbian sexuality—as a scientific phenomenon. He also decided to construct his case in relation to other literary works that depicted lesbian sexuality and had been cleared of obscenity in other legal cases.

Ernst also argued that *The Well of Loneliness* possessed dignity, social value, and significance because it shed light on a sensitive subject in a serious way. Ernst argued that there were no indecent scenes, nor "dirty" words, in the novel. He argued that Hall wrote with a large amount of restraint and was less explicit than other novelists who depicted lesbian sexuality, novelists whose works had been, in turn, acquitted of obscenity.

The lower court found *The Well of Loneliness* obscene, but the Court of Special Sessions in New York City cleared it of obscenity charges by finding that it dealt with a delicate social "problem" in a way that was not in violation of the law. That is, the book was not obscene as written. The publisher was thus able to reprint and circulate the novel without legal sanction.

## SIGNIFICANCE

The obscenity trials in England and the United States against *The Well of Loneliness* had subsequent social and cultural consequences. The controversy surrounding the bans and trials turned the novel into an underground best seller in the United States and in France. Though it was banned in England, demand for the novel continued as well. Also, the book has been read by many as either a "bible" for lesbians or as a horror story, a story of shame and capitulation. *The Well of Loneliness* and its trial of vindication in the United States also paved the way for the writing, publishing, and circulating of lesbian literature in the United States.

—*Sandra Rothenberg*

## FURTHER READING

Brittain, Vera. *Radclyffe Hall: A Case of Obscenity?* New York: A. S. Barnes, 1968.

Cline, Sally. *Radclyffe Hall: A Woman Called John.*

New York: Overlook Press, 1997.

Doan, Laura, and Jay Prosser, eds. *Palatable Poison: Critical Perspectives on "The Well of Loneliness."* New York: Columbia University Press, 2001.

Hall, Radclyffe. *The Well of Loneliness.* Introduction by Diana Souhami. London: Weidenfeld & Nicolson, 1998.

Souhami, Diana. *The Trials of Radclyffe Hall.* New York: Doubleday, 1999.

Taylor, Leslie A. "'I Made Up My Mind to Get It': The American Trial of *The Well of Loneliness*, New York City, 1928-1929." *Journal of the History of Sexuality* 10, no. 2 (2001): 250-286.

SEE ALSO: July 4, 1855: Whitman Publishes *Leaves of Grass*; May 25, 1895: Oscar Wilde Is Convicted of Gross Indecency; 1896: *Der Eigene* Is Published as First Journal on Homosexuality; 1896: Raffalovich Publishes *Uranisme et Unisexualité*; 1903: Stein Writes *Q.E.D.*; Oct., 1909: Barney Opens Her Paris Salon; 1924: Gide Publishes the Signed Edition of *Corydon*; Feb., 1927: Wales Padlock Law Censors Risque Theater; 1939: Isherwood Publishes *Goodbye to Berlin*; 1947-1948: Golden Age of American Gay Literature; 1956: Foster Publishes *Sex Variant Women in Literature*; 1973: Brown Publishes *Rubyfruit Jungle*; 1975: Rule Publishes *Lesbian Images*; 1981: Faderman Publishes *Surpassing the Love of Men*.

**1929**

# DAVIS'S RESEARCH IDENTIFIES LESBIAN SEXUALITY AS COMMON AND NORMAL

*A first-of-its-kind longitudinal sex survey found that 50 percent of unmarried women and 33 percent of married women had experienced sexual or emotional desire for women. Katharine Davis's study set the stage for research, including that of the better-known sexologist Alfred Kinsey, on lesbian and gay lives in the United States.*

**LOCALE:** New York, New York
**CATEGORIES:** Science; cultural and intellectual history

**KEY FIGURES**
*Katharine Bement Davis* (1860-1935), prison reformer, social worker, and author of survey
*John D. Rockefeller, Jr.* (1874-1960), philanthropist who helped fund the survey

**SUMMARY OF EVENT**
In 1920, scholars could not legitimately study the sexual desires and experiences of the general public. Religious and cultural views defined normal behavior; unacceptable behavior was considered uncommon, present only among social deviants. Attempts to counter this moral stronghold with data were met with derision and political blockades.

Homosexuality in men was recognized among a small stereotyped group of men, but homosexuality in women was a definite threat. The early 1900's and World War I brought growing social and economic independence for women, with lesbian sexuality regarded as threatening to erode marriage and family. Higher education especially was coming under fire for "uselessly" preparing women for roles outside the domestic sphere and for its assumed tendency to foster "unnatural" desires among women.

Within this context, penologist and social worker Katharine Bement Davis launched an in-depth and revealing survey of women's sexuality. The survey's report, *Factors in the Sex Life of Twenty-two Hundred Women*, contained more than two hundred statistical tables as well as charts and case studies, and was published in 1929.

Davis had by this time distinguished herself from the norm in many arenas. She was one of the first women in the United States to earn a social sciences doctorate and the first woman in New York City government to hold a top position. Davis studied social deviants: women in the penal system of New York. As superintendent of the state reformatory for women, she developed systems for psychological, moral, and physical evaluations of convicted women. Through this system, shorter sentences were given to women identified as easily rehabilitated while lengthier terms were given to those identified as incorrigible offenders in order to prevent "defective" women from perpetuating their kind (in keeping with Davis's eugenicist principles).

Davis asserted that deviance could not be understood without a thorough understanding of "the norm," defined as women able to adjust satisfactorily to their social group. She devised a lengthy questionnaire on the sex lives of women, including autoerotic practices, frequency of sexual desire, use of contraceptives, frequency of intercourse, premarital sex, extramarital sex, and emotional and physical intimacy with other women.

Her study was funded by the Rockefeller Foundation through the Bureau of Social Hygiene. John D. Rockefeller, Jr., founded the bureau in the hope of funding sex research. However, leadership within the bureau defined a more moderate agenda, consisting of the study of crime, especially related to drugs and prostitution, with a smaller emphasis on birth control, maternal health, and sex education. Davis became general secretary and member of the board of directors of the bureau in 1918, and it was from this role that she began her study.

Questionnaires were distributed through women's club and college alumnae lists as part of a search for women who had graduated from college no more than five years before the start of the study. The study focused on upper-middle-class, educated, predominantly white women, who were considered to have greater intelligence, and thus more social importance, than the population at large; they thus had the social capital to be considered "normal." Investigating college graduates, both married and unmarried, also would allow Davis to confront suspicions that lesbian sexuality and the higher education of women were threats to the American family.

Across the seven years that the study was active, one thousand married women and twelve hundred single women, ages twenty-one to eighty-three, responded to the questionnaires. Davis's findings normalized many types of sexual expression: 71 percent of married respondents reported sex before marriage; 60 percent of respondents had masturbated. Approximately 50 percent of single women and 33 percent of married women reported intense emotional feelings for other women, and half of these identified these feelings as sexual. More important, analyses identified few statistical differences between married and single women who reported these feelings and few differences between this combined group and the other women in the study. Sex with women was not associated with any decrease in overall happiness, and married women with lesbian experience prior to marriage adjusted to marital sex as well as did other women. Thus, Davis framed lesbian sexuality as a common trait among women rather than as an exclusive identity that undermined "family values."

Davis encountered significant resistance to her study. The publication of its results came with the bureau's request for Davis's retirement in 1928. The study sold well in popular and scholarly circles but the results were given select attention. Statistics on premarital and marital sex were cited heavily, but little notice was given to Davis's overall conclusions. Her findings on sex without men and on women's sexual desires was routinely ignored.

## Significance

At a time when normalcy was defined primarily by moral imperative, Davis countered with an emphasis on actual behavior and statistical normalcy. In this way, she was able to redefine lesbian sexuality and place it within the norm of mainstream womanhood rather than within the category of deviant behavior on the margins.

Also, Davis's survey paved the way for the field of sex research in the United States. In 1922, the Committee for Research in Problems of Sex (CRPS) was founded through support by the Rockefeller Foundation, and it operated in cooperation with Davis's Bureau of Social Hygiene. Alfred Kinsey joined the CRPS in 1941, and his work was initially funded through this organization. Kinsey's work continued Davis's foundational work in normalizing homosexuality through statistical accounting (for example, Kinsey's 1948 book *Sexual Behavior in the Human Male* reported that 37 percent of males had experienced at least one sexual encounter with another male).

Both Davis and Kinsey are considered forerunners of the work of Masters and Johnson, who, in the 1950's, were the first to study sex in a laboratory setting. Kinsey's work also became the catalyst for Harry Hay's founding of the Mattachine Society by providing evidence that gays and lesbians existed in large enough numbers to be an organizable minority.

—*Diana Kardia*

## Further Reading

Davis, Katharine Bement. *Factors in the Sex Life of Twenty-two Hundred Women*. New York: Harper and Bros., 1929.

Deegan, Mary Jo, ed. *Women in Sociology: A Bio-bibliographical Sourcebook*. New York: Greenwood Press, 1991.

Ericksen, Julia A., and Sally A. Steffen. *Kiss and Tell: Surveying Sex in the Twentieth Century*. Cambridge, Mass.: Harvard University Press, 1999.

Faderman, Lillian. *To Believe in Women: What Lesbians Have Done for America—A History*. Boston: Houghton Mifflin, 1999.

Fitzpatrick, Ellen. *Endless Crusade: Women Social Scientists and Progressive Reform in America, 1830-1930.* New York: Oxford University Press, 1990.

_____, ed. *Katharine Bement Davis, Early Twentieth-Century American Women, and the Study of Sex Behavior.* New York: Garland, 1987.

**SEE ALSO:** May 6, 1868: Kertbeny Coins the Terms "Homosexual" and "Heterosexual"; 1869: Westphal Advocates Medical Treatment for Sexual Inversion; 1897: Ellis Publishes *Sexual Inversion*; May 14, 1897: Hirschfeld Founds the Scientific-Humanitarian Committee; 1905: Freud Rejects Third-Sex Theory; 1948: Kinsey Publishes *Sexual Behavior in the Human Male*; 1952: APA Classifies Homosexuality as a Mental Disorder; 1953: Kinsey Publishes *Sexual Behavior in the Human Female*; 1953-1957: Evelyn Hooker Debunks Beliefs That Homosexuality Is a "Sickness"; Dec. 15, 1973: Homosexuality Is Delisted by APA; Apr. 20, 2001: Chinese Psychiatric Association Removes Homosexuality from List of Mental Disorders.

# 1929
# *PANDORA'S BOX* OPENS

*German director G. W. Pabst's film* Die Büchse der Pandora, *or* Pandora's Box, *features what is likely the first lesbian character in cinematic history.*

**LOCALE:** Germany; United States
**CATEGORIES:** Arts; cultural and intellectual history

**KEY FIGURES**
*Georg Wilhelm Pabst* (1885-1967), German film director
*Frank Wedekind* (1864-1918), German playwright
*Louise Brooks* (1906-1985), American actor
*Alice Roberts*, Belgian actor

**SUMMARY OF EVENT**
"Lulu is not a real character," German playwright Frank Wedekind said of his creation. Instead, Lulu is "the personification of primitive sexuality who inspires evil unaware." As an archetypal femme fatale, Lulu was originally conceived as an insatiable male fantasy figure, possessing an irresistible eroticism that leads her lovers to their doom. The so-called "Lulu plays," *Erdgeist* (Earth spirit) and *Die Büchse der Pandora* (*Pandora's Box*), were well known by Berlin theatergoers when they opened in 1929.

German film director G. W. Pabst condensed the plays into a single film. Pabst, however, transformed the character of Lulu from Wedekind's

*Louise Brooks, c. 1927.*

## LOUISE BROOKS

With her trademark black bob, and even with just a handful of films to her credit, Louise Brooks, born in Cherryville, Kansas, in 1906, remains one of the most recognizable stars in cinema history. Brooks began her professional career at age fifteen with the influential Denishawn Dance Company but was soon dismissed for having a "superior attitude." This attitude would continue to bristle Brooks's employers throughout her short film career.

In 1925, Brooks moved to New York and joined the Ziegfeld Follies. At the height of the Roaring Twenties, Brooks was the quintessential flapper. Her unapologetic sexuality, intelligence, and strong personality captivated many in the film industry; in 1926 she signed with Paramount. Brooks also captured the attention of G. W. Pabst, the German director who was looking for an actor to play the lead in his next film. Brooks's entire film reputation rests on *Pandora's Box* and *Diary of a Lost Girl*, the two motion pictures she made with Pabst. Although Pabst had plans for Brooks to become a major international star, Brooks was bored with Berlin and returned to the United States.

Around the time of her return, Hollywood had been transitioning to sound films, and Paramount wanted Brooks to do some voice-overs; she refused. Rumor quickly spread that she did not record well, and this effectively sealed her fate with the Hollywood studio system.

Brooks returned to New York in 1938 and survived by doing a variety of odd jobs and by the generosity of a few benefactors. In the early 1950's, her Pabst films were seen by a new generation of film enthusiasts. James Card, the curator of Eastman House, invited her to move to Rochester, New York, and be a guest speaker at the film archive. She became a frequent contributor to film journals, and her collected essays were published in 1982 as *Lulu in Hollywood*. She remained in Rochester until her death in 1985 from a heart attack.

turn-of-the-century man-eater into a modern "New Woman," freely expressing her sexuality without thought of the consequences. To embody this modern spirit, Pabst searched for the ideal actor who would be able to radiate both a childlike innocence and a smoldering sensuality. After a two-year search, he found these qualities and more in the American actor Louise Brooks.

Pabst's choice was controversial. Marlene Dietrich, who coveted the part, was rejected by Pabst because he thought her "too old and too obvious." German audiences were appalled that "their" Lulu would be played by an American actor, but Pabst knew what he was doing. He was looking to extend his film beyond the traditional German expressionist style of filmmaking into a more modernist piece, and the twenty-two-year-old Brooks, with her sleek black bob and androgynous slenderness, had the look he was seeking.

In *Pandora's Box*, Lulu attracts potential lovers regardless of gender. Belgian actor Alice Roberts portrays the countess Anna Geschwitz, who is passionately in love with Lulu. Though Lulu impetuously agrees to marry Dr. Schön, she continues her love affair with Geschwitz. The most overt scene features the countess and Lulu dancing together cheek-to-cheek on Lulu's wedding night. By her loving gazes at Lulu and her jealous glares at rival male suitors, the countess leaves no doubt in the mind of the audience of her sexual orientation. In her splendid collection of essays, *Lulu in Hollywood*, Brooks recounted Alice Roberts's uneasiness portraying same-gender desire during the filming.

> She [Roberts] came on the set looking chic in her Paris evening dress and [was] aristocratically self-possessed. Then Mr. Pabst began explaining the action of the scene in which she was to dance the tango with me. Suddenly, she understood that she was to touch, to embrace, to make love to another woman. Her blue eyes bulged and her hands trembled.

Pabst then whisked Roberts away and told her that he would position himself in such a way so that she could gaze lovingly at *him*, and he would return the loving looks to her off camera. This seemed to calm Roberts's panic, and Brooks acknowledged the silliness of this. Brooks wrote, "Out of the funny complexity of this design Mr. Pabst extracted his tense portrait of sterile lesbian passion, and Mme Roberts satisfactorily preserved her reputation."

Brooks, it seems, had her own concerns about the public confusing her on-screen persona with her private life. "At the time," Brooks said,

> I thought her conduct was silly. The fact that the public could believe an actress' private life to be like the one in a role in a film did not come home to me until I was visited by a French student last year. Explaining why the young people of Paris loved Lulu, he put an uneasy thought in my head. "You talk as if I were a lesbian in real life," I said. "But of course!" he answered in a way that made me laugh to realize I had been living in cinematic perversion for thirty-five years.

Brooks, however, was notoriously inconsistent when discussing her lesbian acquaintances, and to the degree she participated with these women sexually is anyone's guess. Though she admitted to preferring men's bodies, in her biography there are references to trysts with Greta Garbo, Tallulah Bankhead, and Marion Davies' niece, Pepi Lederer. Sexuality, on or off screen, was certainly not something Brooks was squeamish about, and she was savvy enough to know that by cultivating an image of bisexuality, she was following in the footsteps of other notable screen sirens of the era.

### SIGNIFICANCE

Upon its initial release, *Pandora's Box* was unenthusiastically received both in Europe and in the United States. Nearly one-third of the film was cut to appease the censors. U.S. audiences would not even see the film in its entirety until a restored version was released thirty years later.

Brooks was pulled from obscurity by the declaration of Henri Langlois, director of the Cinema Française, who said, "There is no Garbo! There is no Dietrich! There is only Louise Brooks!" During this period, the film and its star underwent a major revival, and many film critics consider *Pandora's Box* a masterpiece of world cinema. It has secured its place in GLBT history with the inclusion of the first-known, explicitly drawn lesbian character in film history.

*—Robin Imhof*

### FURTHER READING

Atwell, Lee. *G. W. Pabst*. Boston: Twayne, 1977.

Brooks, Louise. *Lulu in Hollywood*. Minneapolis: University of Minnesota Press, 2000.

Elsaesser, Thomas. "Lulu and the Meter Man: Pabst's *Pandora's Box* (1929)." In *German Film and Literature: Adaptations and Transformations*, by Eric Rentschler. New York: Methuen, 1986.

Paris, Barry. *Louise Brooks: A Biography*. Minneapolis: University of Minnesota Press, 2000.

Vajda, Ladislaus, and Joseph R. Fliesner. *Pandora's Box (LuLu): A Film by G. W. Pabst*. New York: Simon and Schuster, 1971.

SEE ALSO: Feb. 19, 1923: *The God of Vengeance* Opens on Broadway; 1928: Hall Publishes *The Well of Loneliness*; 1985: Lesbian Film *Desert Hearts* Is Released; 1990, 1994: *Coming Out Under Fire* Documents Gay and Lesbian Military Veterans; 1992-2002: Celebrity Lesbians Come Out; Mar. 21, 2000: Hollywood Awards Transgender Portrayals in Film; Mar. 5, 2006: *Brokeback Mountain, Capote,* and *Transamerica* Receive Oscars.

**1930's-1960's**
# HOLLYWOOD BANS "SEXUAL PERVERSION" IN FILMS

*Hollywood studios enacted the Motion Picture Production Code, which prohibited all references in film to homosexuality or "sex perversion." The code was strengthened in 1934 under pressure from the Catholic-led Legion for Decency, and it remained in force until the mid-1960's.*

**ALSO KNOWN AS:** Motion Picture Production Code; Hays code
**LOCALE:** Los Angeles, California
**CATEGORIES:** Arts; cultural and intellectual history; organizations and institutions; religion

## KEY FIGURES

*Will H. Hays* (1879-1954), head of the Motion Picture Producers and Distributors Association
*Daniel A. Lord* (1885-1955), Catholic priest and educator largely responsible for writing the production code
*Joseph Breen* (1890-1965), Catholic layperson and journalist who was the first head of the Production Code Administration

## SUMMARY OF EVENT

Reeling from scandals, criticisms that movies corrupted America's youth, and threats to establish more local and state censorship boards, the heads of the major studios in 1922 hired Will H. Hays, U.S. president William Harding's postmaster general and a Presbyterian, to head the Motion Picture Producers and Distributors Association (MPPDA). Hays successfully stalled efforts to impose external controls on the content of movies, and he encouraged the members of the association to recognize that the best way to defeat such efforts was for Hollywood to regulate itself.

In 1930, the MPPDA ratified the Motion Picture Production Code (sometimes called, inaccurately, the Hays code), pledging its members to abide by its guidelines on what was and was not appropriate content for film. Homosexuality was not a significant feature in the scandals and criticisms, nor did it receive elaborate consideration in the code. One terse sentence, however, banned homosexuality from the screen: "Sex perversion or any inference to it is forbidden."

Most of the code was written by Father Daniel A. Lord, a professor of drama at St. Louis University. Recognizing the power of film, Lord felt that chances to shape society by producing films that glorified morality had been lost. Lord and his coauthors made the code into more that just a set of do's and don'ts; they described film's unique place in popular culture and argued for its ability to promote moral values. The authors, however, soon felt betrayed because Hollywood ignored the code in the early 1930's, filling films with sex and violence in an effort to turn a profit in the days of the Great Depression.

To pressure Hollywood, the Roman Catholic Church created its Legion of Decency to rate films and encourage a boycott of those condemned for immorality. In response, Hays, in 1934, got the MPPDA to approve the creation of the Production Code Administration (PCA), an office that had absolute control over whether a film met the code. To head the PCA, Hays hired Joseph Breen, a print journalist associated with the authors of the code and the establishment of the Legion of Decency. For the next thirty years, until the code was replaced in the mid-1960's with a new ratings system, the United States had a Catholic layperson enforcing a code (written by a Catholic priest) over mostly Jewish movie moguls, who made films for a Protestant majority.

## SIGNIFICANCE

Breen and the PCA were largely successful in keeping the open and direct portrayal of the lives of gays and lesbians off the screen, even when a film's historical, literary, or theatrical source had queer content. When faced with the code's prohibition, filmmakers often made substitutions. In *These Three*, for example, a 1936 adaption of Lillian Hellman's hit play *The Children's Hour* in which two female teachers of a girls' school were lesbians, became the story of a rumor that one teacher was having a heterosexual affair with the fiancé of the other teacher.

In adapting a novel into the film *The Lost Weekend* (1945), director and screenwriter Billy Wilder turned the main character's confusion about his sexuality into a man with writer's block. A killer's rage against homosexuals in the novel *The Brick Foxhole* became anti-Semitism in the movie *Crossfire* (1947). In *Tea and Sympathy* (1956), a schoolboy's concern about being gay was turned into a story about the boy doubting his ability to make a woman love him. Under pressure from the PCA, filmmakers sanitized their adaptations of Tennessee Williams's plays *Streetcar Named Desire* (1951) and *Cat on a Hot Tin Roof* (1958).

Gays and lesbians, though, were not completely absent from the screen, though their orientation was never directly acknowledged nor portrayed in a positive or sympathetic way. At best, they were confused about their gender identity, as in *Calamity Jane* (1953). At worst, same-gender desire was coded in such a way to make the villain more villainous. These villains include the sinister housekeeper tormenting the new Mrs. DeWinter in *Rebecca* (1940) or Bruno in *Strangers on a Train* (1951), who offered to swap murders with a tennis star aspiring to marry a senator's daughter.

By the early 1960's, the PCA's ability to shape the presentation of certain topics was diminishing. Nonetheless, the office still moved to keep homosexuality off the screen, even in the vaguest of references. One of the more noted examples was when the PCA required director Stanley Kubrick to delete the scene in *Spartacus* (1960) where the Roman general Crassus questions his slave about the slave's preference for oysters or snails. Nevertheless,

under pressure from studios wishing to include adult material in a responsible way, the PCA amended the code: "In keeping with the culture, the mores and values of our time, homosexuality and other sexual aberrations may now be treated with care, discretion and restraint." This openness, however, did not represent an improvement. Those characters who acknowledged or acted on their desire were fated to meet an untimely end. In a 1961 remake of *The Children's Hour*, one of the teachers hangs herself after confessing her desire for the other teacher. In *Suddenly, Last Summer* (1959) a man is punished for his homosexuality by being cannibalized by his tricks, while in *Advise and Consent* (1962) a senator slits his throat when he learns he is about to be blackmailed for a youthful homosexual indiscretion.

Cataloging Hollywood's misrepresentation of queer lives addresses only the most obvious impact of the production code's ban on depictions of homosexuality. More subtly, and more deadly, the

---

## FROM THE MOTION PICTURE PRODUCTION CODE (1930)

*Section II. Sex*
The sanctity of the institution of marriage and the home shall be upheld. Pictures shall not infer that low forms of sex relationship are the accepted or common thing.

1. Adultery, sometimes necessary plot material, must not be explicitly treated, or justified, or presented attractively.
2. Scenes of Passion
   a. They should not be introduced when not essential to the plot.
   b. Excessive and lustful kissing, lustful embraces, suggestive postures and gestures, are not to be shown.
   c. In general passion should so be treated that these scenes do not stimulate the lower and baser element.
3. Seduction or Rape
   a. They should never be more than suggested, and only when essential for the plot, and even then never shown by explicit method.
   b. They are never the proper subject for comedy.
4. Sex perversion or any inference to it is forbidden.
5. White slavery shall not be treated.
6. Miscegenation (sex relationships between the white and black races) is forbidden.
7. Sex hygiene and venereal diseases are not subjects for motion pictures.
8. Scenes of actual child birth, in fact or in silhouette, are never to be presented.
9. Children's sex organs are never to be exposed.

films made under the code meant that for more than thirty years, according to the documentary film *The Celluloid Closet* (1995), "Hollywood . . . taught straight people what to think about gay people, and gay people what to think about themselves."

—*William R. Glass*

**FURTHER READING**

Barrios, Richard. *Screened Out: Playing Gay in Hollywood, from Edison to Stonewall.* New York: Routledge, 2002.

Black, Gregory D. *Hollywood Censored: Morality Codes, Catholics, and the Movies.* New York: Cambridge University Press, 1994.

Miller, Frank. *Censored Hollywood: Sex, Sin, and Violence on Screen.* Atlanta: Turner, 1994.

Russo, Vito. *The Celluloid Closet: Homosexuality in the Movies.* Rev. ed. New York: Harper & Row, 1987.

Tyler, Parker. *Screening the Sexes: Homosexuality in the Movies.* New York: Da Capo Press, 1993.

**SEE ALSO:** Feb., 1927: Wales Padlock Law Censors Risque Theater; Mar. 7, 1967: CBS Airs *CBS Reports: The Homosexuals*; 1979-1981: First Gay British Television Series Airs; 1985: GLAAD Begins Monitoring Media Coverage of Gays and Lesbians; 1985: Lesbian Film *Desert Hearts* Is Released; July 25, 1985: Actor Hudson Announces He Has AIDS; 1988: *Macho Dancer* Is Released in the Philippines; 1992-2002: Celebrity Lesbians Come Out; Mar. 21, 2000: Hollywood Awards Transgender Portrayals in Film; Sept. 7, 2001: First Gay and Lesbian Television Network Is Launched in Canada; Mar. 5, 2006: *Brokeback Mountain, Capote,* and *Transamerica* Receive Oscars.

# 1933-1945
# NAZIS PERSECUTE HOMOSEXUALS

*Between 1933 and 1945, an estimated 100,000 homosexuals were arrested and prosecuted under Paragraph 175 of a revised version of the German Penal Code. Between 10,000 and 15,000 of these Holocaust victims died in Nazi internment camps.*

**LOCALE:** Germany

**CATEGORIES:** Laws, acts, and legal history; government and politics

**KEY FIGURES**

*Adolf Hitler* (1889-1945), German dictator, 1933-1945

*Heinrich Himmler* (1900-1945), head of the Schutzstaffel, or SS

**SUMMARY OF EVENT**

Soon after Adolf Hitler took office in 1933, his storm troopers raided gay institutions and gathering places, closing all gay bars and social organizations as part of his campaign to rid Germany of those perceived to threaten Nazi beliefs. Nazi ideology centered on male dominance and racial purity, and homosexuality was inconsistent with those ideals. The Nazis hoped to combat the declining birth rate through selective reproduction and to increase the purity of its citizens' bloodline by eradicating all people deemed undesirable or those considered enemies of the state. Official Nazi policy was to not eradicate homosexuals but to transform them into heterosexuals through "re-education" or to isolate them from the rest of society.

On June 28, 1935, Hitler sanctioned the revision of Paragraph 175, a portion of the German Penal Code that had been on the books since 1871. Paragraph 175 originally prohibited "unnatural fornication, whether between persons of the male sex or of humans with beasts." The newly amended statute

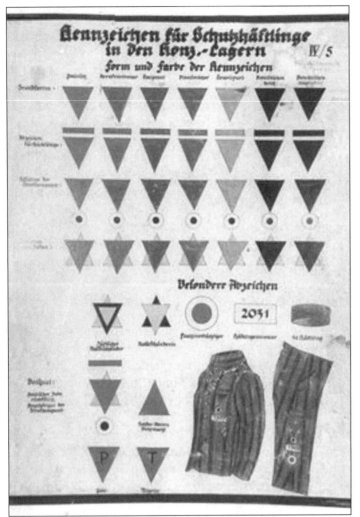

*Homosexual men were marked with the "pink triangle" badge in the concentration camps of the Holocaust. This undated chart is titled, in translation, "Distinguishing Marks for Protective Custody of Prisoners." Variations of the pink triangle were issued to homosexuals who also were Jewish, repeat offenders, or prisoners in punishment battalions. Lesbians were marked with the black triangle. (Courtesy, USHMM)*

rested men were seized and a network of informers was created to compile lists of names and make arrests. Those arrested were beaten and tortured in order to secure additional names of suspects. Many were given no trial and were sent to prisons, mental hospitals, or internment camps or were "voluntarily" castrated. Although numbers are unsubstantiated, an estimated 100,000 gay men were arrested and prosecuted; 10,000 to 15,000 of these men were sent to internment camps, where they were starved, beaten, or died from disease, exhaustion, exposure, brutality, and medical experimentation.

Heinrich Himmler, head of the Schutzstaffel (SS), the elite Nazi bodyguard forces that controlled the police and concentration camps, was the person most responsible for the Nazi persecution of homosexuals and for much of the antigay propaganda. His hatred for homosexuality directly influenced the purging of gays from the Nazi ranks. He ordered that gay SS men be expelled, court-martialed, and imprisoned for the maximum period allowed by Paragraph 175. Privately, he instructed his generals to take these soldiers to concentration camps, where they were to be "shot while attempting to escape." On April 4, 1938, the Gestapo (state police) issued a direct decree allowing for incarceration of men convicted of homosexuality. In 1941, Himmler sent a confidential order to the SS generals and police stating that "any member of the SS or the police who engaged in indecent behavior with another man or permits himself to be abused by him for indecent purposes will be condemned to death and executed."

Using a system of color-coded patches worn on prisoner uniforms, the Nazis were able to identify different groups of prisoners. The symbols for homosexuals were varied—including a large black dot and a large "175" drawn on the back of a pris-

included arrest on the grounds not only of homosexual behavior but also gossip, innuendo, gestures, touches, and looks. Under this expanded law, prosecutions increased dramatically. All local police departments were required to submit lists of suspected homosexuals to the Nazi authorities. It quickly became dangerous for homosexuals to meet in public or even to recognize each other publicly.

As police raids increased, address books of ar-

## GERMAN CRIMINAL CODE, PARAGRAPH 175, VERSION OF 1935

### Lewdness Between Men

I. A man who engages as the active or passive partner in lewdness with another man is to be punished by imprisonment.

II. With an involved party who at the time of the act had not yet reached the age of twenty-one years, the Court can refrain from punishment in mild cases.

### Severe Lewdness

A punishment of up to ten years in the penitentiary, and even with mitigating circumstances no less than three months imprisonment for:

1. A man, who by force or by threat of harm to life and limb forces another man to engage in such an act as either the active or passive partner;

2. A man, who by abusing a dependency founded in a service-, work-, or employment-based relationship coerces another man into engaging in such an act as either the active or passive partner;

3. A man over twenty-one years old who entices a male under twenty-one years old to engage in such an act as either the active or passive partner;

4. A man who professionally offers himself for such an act as either the active or passive partner.

oner's jacket. Later, a pink triangle patch was used. Fearing that homosexuality would "spread" to other inmates and guards, prisoners bearing the pink triangle were often segregated, singled out for harsher treatment, given dangerous and deadly work assignments, and humiliated by guards. Because the homosexual community outside the camps had been virtually destroyed, communication and support among those wearing the pink triangles was nearly nonexistent. Other prisoners, indoctrinated by Nazi propaganda, treated homosexuals with disgust, making those bearing pink triangles the "lowest" prisoners in the camps.

Believing homosexuality was a sickness that could be corrected, the Nazis devised methods for "curing" gays of their supposed illness through harsh treatment, exhausting work, cruel experimentation, and castration. Castration was used first as a voluntary measure but ultimately at the discretion of Nazi leaders. The life expectancy of a pink-triangle prisoner in an internment camp was only three months.

## SIGNIFICANCE

After the war ended, homosexuality remained a crime, and many convicted under Paragraph 175 were sent directly to prison. Homosexual prisoners of concentration camps had not been acknowledged as victims of Nazi persecution until 2002, and they have yet to receive reparations for their time in the camps. The 1935 version of Paragraph 175 remained in effect until 1969, when the law was revised to decriminalize homosexual relations between men over the age of twenty-one.

Many homosexual survivors of the Nazi persecutions never discussed their experiences, and some entered into heterosexual marriages. In May, 2002, the German government pardoned convicted "175ers," and gay victims of the Holocaust were finally recognized in 2004 at a memorial service held at the site of the former Sachsenhausen concentration camp. Little was said or written about gay Holocaust survivors until the early twenty-first century when, through continued efforts to make their suffering known, the few remaining survivors began to speak out about their experiences.

—*Kathrin Dodds*

## FURTHER READING

Epstein, Rob, and Jeffrey Friedman, producers and directors. *Paragraph 175*. Documentary film, narrated by Rupert Everett. New York: New Yorker Films, 2000.

Gellately, Robert, and Nathan Stoltzfus, eds. *Social Outsiders in Nazi Germany*. Princeton, N.J.: Princeton University Press, 2001.

Grau, Gunter, ed. *Hidden Holocaust? Gay and Lesbian Persecution in Germany, 1933-45*. Translated by Patrick Camiller. Chicago: Fitzroy Dearborn, 1995.

Heger, Heinz. *The Men with the Pink Triangle: The*

*True, Life-and-Death Story of Homosexuals in the Nazi Death Camps*. Translated by David Fernbach. Introduction by Klaus Müller. Boston: Alyson, 1994.

Herzog, Dagmar. *Sexuality and German Fascism*. Austin: University of Texas Press, 2002.

Johannson, Warren, and William Percy, trans. "Homosexuals in Nazi Germany." *Simon Wiesenthal Center Annual* 7 (1990). http://www.ushmm.org/research/library/bibliography/gays/paragraph175.htm.

Lautmann, Rudiger, Erhard Vismar, and Jack Nusan Porter. *Sexual Politics in the Third Reich: The Persecution of the Homosexuals During the Holocaust*. Translated by Page Brubb, edited by Jack Nusan Porter. Newton, Mass.: Spencer Press, 1997.

Plant, Richard. *The Pink Triangle: The Nazi War Against Homosexuals*. New York: Henry Holt, 1986.

U.S. Holocaust Memorial Museum. "Nazi Persecution of Homosexuals, 1933-1945." http://www.ushmm.org/museum/exhibit/focus/homosexuals_02/.

**SEE ALSO:** Nov. 17, 1901: Police Arrest "Los 41" in Mexico City; 1907-1909: The Eulenburg Affair Scandalizes Germany's Leadership; Mar. 15, 1919-1921: U.S. Navy Launches Sting Operation Against "Sexual Perverts"; June 30-July 1, 1934: Hitler's Night of the Long Knives; Nov., 1965: Revolutionary Cuba Imprisons Gays; June 27-July 2, 1969: Stonewall Rebellion Ignites Modern Gay and Lesbian Rights Movement; Dec. 31, 1977: Toronto Police Raid Offices of *The Body Politic*; Nov. 27, 1978: White Murders Politicians Moscone and Milk; May-Aug., 1980: U.S. Navy Investigates the USS *Norton Sound* in Antilesbian Witch Hunt; Feb. 5, 1981: Toronto Police Raid Gay Bathhouses.

## June 30-July 1, 1934
# HITLER'S NIGHT OF THE LONG KNIVES

*Adolf Hitler purged gay men from the leadership structure of the Sturmabteilung, better known as the SA, or Brown Shirts, which led to a stronger law against homosexuality in Germany, the destruction of German gay and lesbian culture, and the beginning of Hitler's rise to power.*

**LOCALE:** Germany

**CATEGORIES:** Government and politics; military; laws, acts, and legal history

**KEY FIGURES**

*Adolf Hitler* (1889-1945), German dictator and chancellor, 1933-1945

*Ernst Rohm* (1887-1934), leader of the Sturmabteilung

*Joseph Goebbels* (1897-1945), Reich minister for public enlightenment and propaganda

*Hermann Göring* (1893-1946), Reich minister for the air forces

*Heinrich Himmler* (1900-1945), chief of the Schutzstaffel

*Reinhard Heydrich* (1904-1942), general and second-in-command of the Schutzstaffel

*Paul von Hindenburg* (1847-1934), German president, 1925-1932, 1932-1934

**SUMMARY OF EVENT**

Beginning June 30, 1934, and continuing until the following morning, German chancellor Adolf Hitler ordered the murder of Ernst Rohm and Rohm's leadership circle of the Sturmabteilung (SA), a large quasi-military organization with some two million members. The SA, also called the Brown Shirts, was fiercely and loyally attached to National Socialism and sought to supplant the regular Ger-

*German SA (Brown Shirts) leader Ernst Rohm, second from right, was assassinated by Hitler's SS in the summer of 1934, allegedly because Rohm was homosexual. Hitler stands to Rohm's right in this photograph from 1923.*

man army as the true military force to lead a socialist revolution.

Despite Rohm's early usefulness to Hitler's rise to power, Rohm and the SA soon became a liability. Hitler's growing popularity required him to think on a larger scale. He needed to build stronger support for his programs across an expanded base of traditional political elites, capitalists, and regular army generals. The SA's violent history of extortion and intimidation scared the average German, and Rohm's candid homosexuality opened Hitler to potential attacks from his opposition.

Hitler publicly tolerated Rohm's sexual openness for quite some time, and he took an ambiguous public position on rumors of homosexual activity within the SA. By 1934, however, Hitler's campaign for president of Germany demanded he take a more conformist stance, one that would appeal to broader elements of German society. In February, 1934, Hitler held a meeting with the SA and the regular German army. He announced that the SA would cede its military ambitions and limit its future political involvement to certain peripheral activities.

Rohm agreed with Hitler, but by April, 1934, Rohm's frustration with the SA's loss of power would become public. Rohm announced at a press conference that the SA was the true military source of the National Socialist revolution. Recognizing an opportunity to capitalize on Rohm's eventual downfall, Schutzstaffel (SS) chief Heinrich Himmler, military officers Reinhard Heydrich and Her-

mann Göring, and Reich minister Joseph Goebbels devised a plan for Hitler to act against Rohm.

On June 4, Hitler and Rohm had a heated, five-hour meeting, during which Rohm had threatened to go public with Hitler's own alleged homosexuality. Hitler calmed Rohm and then convinced him to take a vacation and send the SA on a monthlong furlough. Hitler also ordered Rohm to hold an SA conference near Munich on June 30, where Rohm and Hitler would sort out the SA's future role in German politics.

Hitler's true intention, however, was to isolate Rohm from his security forces. A few days after Hitler and Rohm's meeting, the SA intelligence group was disbanded, and on June 21, Hitler obtained German president Paul von Hindenburg's approval to proceed against the SA by force. At the same time, Himmler spread false rumors that the SA was planning a revolution, and so made a secret deal with the army generals. The army was to support the SS with equipment and weapons but was to remain off the streets while SS officers conducted their plan against the SA. On June 25, General Werner von Blomberg, the defense minister, placed the German army on alert after Goebbels gave a long, angry speech on German radio accusing the SA of planning a violent putsch, that is, a secretly plotted attempt to overthrow the German government.

Between June 25 and 29, SA forces took to the streets in Munich as rumors circulated of an imminent police action against them. On June 29, Hitler traveled to Munich to confront Rohm and the SA face-to-face. On the morning of June 30, Hitler arrived in Munich and ordered the arrest of the SA officers who had massed inside the Nazi Party headquarters. Then, along with several SS troops, Hitler went to the resort town of Bad Wiesse and arrested Rohm. Rohm was then transferred to Stadelheim prison outside Munich and given the choice of taking his own life or being executed. He refused to kill himself and was later shot by the SS.

Later that morning, Hitler contacted Göring in Berlin and ordered SS execution squads to capture and kill SA leaders and other political enemies of Hitler. By 4:00 A.M., July 1, the Night of the Long Knives (*Nacht der langen Messer*) was over. The purge had been called *Nacht der langen Messer* by Hitler in a speech to the Reichstag on July 13. The exact number of SA killed, estimated to have been between 150 and 1,000, has not been determined, but a large percentage of those killed were either homosexual or suspected of being homosexual.

Goebbels gave a radio speech portraying the purge as a brilliant move to suppress a dangerous conspiracy. Hitler immediately launched a public campaign to legally justify the purge and executions, a campaign that included his speech to the Reichstag. In the speech, he argued that

> If anyone reproaches me and asks why I did not resort to the regular courts of justice, then all I can say is this: In this hour I was responsible for the fate of the German people, and thereby I became the supreme judge of the German people. . . . Everyone must know for all future time that if he raises his hand to strike the State, then certain death is his lot.

## SIGNIFICANCE

It is believed that the Night of the Long Knives, in addition to stopping enemies of Hitler and the Nazi regime, allowed Hitler to eliminate witnesses and thousands of incriminating documents regarding his alleged homosexuality: Rohm and his associates could have blackmailed Hitler about his private life.

German gay and lesbian culture, too, suffered significantly after the Night of the Long Knives, as Hitler took quick action to eliminate any possible links to his gay past. In 1937, he strengthened Paragraph 175 of the Penal Code and enabled abusive police procedures against suspected homosexuals.

By 1939, thousands of homosexuals had been either under surveillance or imprisoned in Nazi concentration camps.

—*Jamie Patrick Chandler*

## FURTHER READING

Beaumont, Roger. *The Nazis March to Chaos: The Hitler Era Through the Lenses of Chaos-Complexity Theory.* London: Praeger, 2000.

Gallo, Max. *The Night of Long Knives.* Translated by Lily Emmet. New York: Da Capo Press, 1997.

Heger, Heinz. *The Men with the Pink Triangle: The True, Life-and-Death Story of Homosexuals in the Nazi Death Camps.* Translated by David Fernbach. Introduction by Klaus Müller. Rev. ed. Boston: Alyson, 1994.

Machtan, Lothar. *The Hidden Hitler.* New York: Basic Books, 2001.

Plant, Richard. *The Pink Triangle: The Nazi War Against Homosexuals.* New York: H. Holt, 1986.

Waite, Robert G. L. *The Psychopathic God: Adolf Hitler.* New York: Da Capo Press, 1993.

Wheeler-Bennett, John W. *The Nemesis of Power: The German Army in Politics, 1918-1945.* New York: St. Martin's Press, 1954.

SEE ALSO: Nov. 17, 1901: Police Arrest "Los 41" in Mexico City; 1907-1909: The Eulenburg Affair Scandalizes Germany's Leadership; Mar. 15, 1919-1921: U.S. Navy Launches Sting Operation Against "Sexual Perverts"; 1933-1945: Nazis Persecute Homosexuals; Nov., 1965: Revolutionary Cuba Imprisons Gays; June 27-July 2, 1969: Stonewall Rebellion Ignites Modern Gay and Lesbian Rights Movement; Dec. 31, 1977: Toronto Police Raid Offices of *The Body Politic*; Nov. 27, 1978: White Murders Politicians Moscone and Milk; May-Aug., 1980: U.S. Navy Investigates the USS *Norton Sound* in Antilesbian Witch Hunt; Feb. 5, 1981: Toronto Police Raid Gay Bathhouses.

**1939**
# ISHERWOOD PUBLISHES *GOODBYE TO BERLIN*

*The gay characters and the character of free-spirited Sally Bowles of* Goodbye to Berlin *were an inspiration to gay men and others, as was Christopher Isherwood himself. Isherwood was one of the early prominent gays to come out and live openly with his partner, artist Don Bachardy.*

**LOCALE:** London, England; New York, New York

**CATEGORIES:** Literature; publications

**KEY FIGURES**

*Christopher Isherwood* (1904-1986), English-born American writer

*Don Bachardy* (b. 1934), American artist and Isherwood's longtime companion

**SUMMARY OF EVENT**

Beginning in 1928, Christopher Isherwood's books all alluded to gay themes or had gay characters. *Goodbye to Berlin* (1939) was Isherwood's first to place gay characters and a homosexual affair in the larger context of world politics, thus departing from the usual practice of writing a "gay" novel as a problem novel.

*Goodbye to Berlin* also was Isherwood's first novel to use "Christopher Isherwood" as the first-person narrator. At the story's beginning, a young English writer sits in Berlin and writes in his diary, "I am a camera with its shutter open, quite passive, recording, not thinking." In the novel Christopher moves from this objective stance, increasingly identifying with Berlin and understanding its citizens as they adapt to the Nazis.

The novel is composed of two diaries and four story segments. "Sally Bowles," the most famous segment, depicts a young expatriate Englishwoman who paints her fingernails green, eats prairie oysters for breakfast, and sings, not too well, in an arty bar. Her mishaps in choosing lovers form her story as the significance of the political events going on around her elude her understanding.

The segment "On Ruegen Island (Summer 1931)" depicts the young gay Englishman Peter Wilkinson's attraction to the young bisexual Berliner Otto Nowak. Christopher observes the affair during a vacation they all share away from Berlin. In this story, as in the others, individual conflicts mirror the larger clash of social forces in German politics and in the world just before World War II. The book's focus on ordinary people and not the larger political scene mark it as one of the most sophisticated works of political fiction of the twentieth century.

A scene late in the novel occurs in a gay bar called the Salomé. Gawking American tourists sus-

*The cover of Isherwood's* Goodbye to Berlin *(1939).* (Minerva)

## CHRISTOPHER ISHERWOOD

Christopher Isherwood, considered by some critics to be one of the most important English writers of the 1930's, visited Berlin in 1929 with W. H. Auden, whom he had met while they were both students at St. Edmund's School. Isherwood and Auden remained lifelong friends, and during the 1930's, they collaborated on a travel book and three plays. From 1930 to 1933, Isherwood taught English in Berlin, where he met Heinz Neddermayer, a working-class youth. The two traveled together between 1934 and 1937, while Heinz tried to avoid being drafted into the German army.

Isherwood's experiences in Berlin during the 1930's provided material for his three most successful works: *The Last of Mr. Norris* (1935), *Sally Bowles* (1937), and *Goodbye to Berlin* (1939), known collectively as the "Berlin stories." Literary critics and historians alike consider these works, especially *Goodbye to Berlin*, to be among the most significant political fiction of the twentieth century.

In 1939, Isherwood settled in Southern California with Auden. Shortly afterward, he cut all ties with his Christian past and embraced Vedantism, one of the numerous forms of Hinduism. He had always felt an inner conflict between the Christian teachings of his youth and his homosexuality. His conversion to Vedantism enabled him to resolve, or at least escape, the conflict, since Vedantism views both heterosexuality and homosexuality as valid choices. The move to California marked the beginning of what critics term Isherwood's American, or Vedantic, years. During the late 1940's, he worked as a scriptwriter in Hollywood and edited a periodical, *Vedanta and the West*. His first American novel, *Prater Violet* (1945), which is actually set in London, explored the two themes that were becoming increasingly dominant in his work—homosexuality and Vedantism.

pect that the place is "queer" and direct hostile questions at Christopher and his heterosexual companion, who replies using the broader sense of the term "queer," saying, "Eventually we're all queer." Christopher states that he is "very queer indeed." This was a bold acknowledgment at the time.

Isherwood's greatest gay-themed work is *A Single Man* (1964), published five years before the Stonewall Rebellion in New York City. *A Single Man* delineates a loving relationship between two men—George, an expatriate from England and an English professor—and takes place during one day in Los Angeles in 1962. The story is even more moving because the younger man had died prior to the action of the novel. The novel embodies the nascent thinking that homosexuals are a political minority who deserve civil rights. George rails at the "annihilation by blandness" that homosexuals suffer at the hands of even well-meaning liberals who pity homosexuals but would not want to know details of their love lives.

If, in *A Single Man*, George is preoccupied with daily and political concerns, the novelist Isherwood places him in the context of beliefs learned from Isherwood's study of Vedanta, a religion based on Hinduism. Isherwood's thought is a precursor of what has been termed "gay spirit" by writer Mark Thompson and others.

### SIGNIFICANCE

*Goodbye to Berlin* was adapted as the drama and the film *I Am a Camera* (1951; 1955) and as the musical play and Academy Award-winning film *Cabaret* (1966; 1972). The musical used the sexual license of Weimar Berlin and its cabaret culture to create metaphors for the blur of traditional sexual identities, in turn signaling other breakdowns that paved the way for the Nazi rise to power. Isherwood thought aspects of the popular film to be "antigay," and critic Linda Mizejewski has termed it "homophobic."

Isherwood was part of a group of Los Angeles researchers and thinkers that included fellow gay British expatriate Gerald Heard and Evelyn Hooker a research psychologist at the University of California, Los Angeles. They all were at times connected with Los Angeles's ONE Institute. ONE was founded and incorporated in 1952 and was loosely modeled on Magnus Hirschfeld's Institute for Sexual Science in Berlin, which Isherwood knew in the 1930's. At great personal danger, Hirschfeld had lobbied for a change in the laws on homosexuality.

Isherwood pioneered in rewriting his already very autobiographical work to include more details

*Christopher Isherwood, left, and W. H. Auden.* (Library of Congress)

about his gay life. In 1971 he used letters and diaries of his mother and father to form a work that was named for them, *Kathleen and Frank: The Autobiography of a Family*, although he admitted that the book was "chiefly about Christopher." In this work he became one of the first writers of his stature to come out in print. As early as 1973, in an interview in the gay liberation journal *Gay Sunshine*, Isherwood began to tell the "truth" about the stories in *Goodbye to Berlin* and revealed that he, and not the fictional Peter Wilkinson, was the lover of "Otto." Isherwood collected more true stories about his Berlin period, including details about Hirschfeld and the destruction of his library and institute by the Nazis in May of 1933, in *Christopher and His Kind: 1929-1939* (1976).

In 1948, Isherwood had written that successful homosexual relationships "raise our collective morale." Perhaps as early as 1951, Isherwood met Don Bachardy, then a teenager, and they lived together from 1953 until Isherwood's death in 1986. Bac-

hardy, benefiting from Isherwood's mentoring and sensitive attention to their relationship, became a noted artist and famous portraitist. Even before the 1970's, Isherwood and Bachardy appeared in public together, thus providing an early and rare visible example of a committed and enduring gay couple. They are depicted together in their Santa Monica Canyon (Los Angeles area) living room in an iconic portrait painted by their friend, British artist David Hockney, in 1968.

In his literary production, his political and religious thought and work, and his sexual politics and daily life, Christopher Isherwood was a pioneer gay figure for a great part of the twentieth century. He remains an iconic figure into the twenty-first century as well.

*—Dan Luckenbill*

## FURTHER READING

Berg, James J., and Chris Freeman, eds. *The Isherwood Century: Essays on the Life and Work of Christopher Isherwood*. Madison: University of Wisconsin Press, 2000.

Isherwood, Christopher. *The Berlin Stories*. New York: New Directions, 1945.

_____. *Christopher and His Kind: 1929-1939*. New York: Farrar Straus Giroux, 1976.

_____. "Christopher Isherwood Interviewed by (I) Winston Leyland (II) Roger Austen." In *Gay Sunshine Interviews*. Vol. 1, edited by Winston Leyland. San Francisco, Calif.: Gay Sunshine Press, 1978.

_____. *Kathleen and Frank: The Autobiography of a Family*. New York: Simon and Schuster, 1972.

_____. *A Single Man*. New York: Simon and Schuster, 1964.

Mizejewski, Linda. *Divine Decadence: Fascism, Female Spectacle, and the Makings of Sally Bowles*. Princeton, N.J.: Princeton University Press, 1992.

Summers, Claude J. *Christopher Isherwood*. New York: Ungar, 1980.

_____. *Gay Fictions, Wilde to Stonewall: Studies in a Male Homosexual Literary Tradition*. New York: Continuum, 1990.

Thompson, Mark. "Double Reflections: Isherwood

and Bachardy on Art, Love, and Faith." In *Gay Spirit: Myth and Meaning*, edited by Mark Thompson. New York: St. Martin's Press, 1987.

**SEE ALSO:** July 4, 1855: Whitman Publishes *Leaves of Grass*; May 25, 1895: Oscar Wilde Is Convicted of Gross Indecency; 1924: Gide Publishes the Signed Edition of *Corydon*; 1947-1948: Golden Age of American Gay Literature; 1956: Baldwin Publishes *Giovanni's Room*; 1963: Rechy Publishes *City of Night*; June, 1971: The Gay Book Award Debuts; 1974: *The Front Runner* Makes *The New York Times* Best-Seller List; 1975: First Novel About Coming Out to Parents Is Published; 1980-1981: Gay Writers Form the Violet Quill; May, 1987: *Lambda Rising Book Report* Begins Publication; June 2, 1989: Lambda Literary Award Is Created; 1993: Monette Wins the National Book Award for *Becoming a Man*.

---

## January 12, 1939
# *THOMPSON V. ALDREDGE* DISMISSES SODOMY CHARGES AGAINST LESBIANS

*The Georgia Supreme Court found that the definition of "sodomy" as outlined in Georgia state law cannot be applied to sex between women. The law remained on the books until 1968, when the state amended its criminal code and included oral sex between women in its legal definition of sodomy. Sodomy remained illegal in Georgia and many other states until the U.S. Supreme Court, in 2003, ruled that private, consensual sex between adults, including oral sex, was legal.*

**LOCALE:** Georgia
**CATEGORY:** Laws, acts, and legal history

**KEY FIGURES**
*Ella Thompson*, found guilty of sodomy
*J. C. Aldredge*, sheriff of Fulton County, Georgia
*Warren Grice*, justice of the Georgia Supreme Court and author of the *Thompson v. Aldredge* decision

**SUMMARY OF EVENT**
Georgia was a relative latecomer in defining and prosecuting illegal sexual behavior. In 1791, when the U.S. Bill of Rights was adopted, the only colony of the thirteen colonies without laws regulating consensual sex was Georgia. An 1817 Georgia law did order a life sentence for those convicted of sod-

omy, but the acts covered under the term "sodomy" were not described. Beginning in 1833, Georgia common law defined sodomy as "the carnal knowledge and connection against the order of nature, by man with man, or in the same unnatural manner with woman."

Although Georgia's definition was rather vague, it was more specific than those of many states and territories. In general, it was understood that the behaviors forbidden were heterosexual or homosexual anal intercourse. Oral sex was neither mentioned nor implied, and it does not appear to have occurred to the drafters that two women might engage in sexual acts. In a 1904 decision, the Supreme Court of Georgia amended the sodomy laws to include oral sex performed on a man, reasoning that oral contact with the penis was "baser" than anal contact, and would have been specifically forbidden if the act had been more common at the time of the original law. In 1917, the court ruled that a man performing oral sex on a woman had also committed sodomy. Although this act does not appear to fit the definition in the 1833 codes, the majority of the justices argued that the connection was implied.

In 1939, Ella Thompson and a female partner were arrested and accused of engaging in oral sex, albeit private and consensual. Legal records do not explain how they were discovered in a sexual act, and the name of Thompson's partner never was revealed. Fulton County sheriff J. C. Aldredge filed charges against Thompson and her partner, including the crime of sodomy, and the two were found guilty. Thompson appealed, claiming that under Georgia law two women could not commit sodomy. Her case made it to the Georgia Supreme Court, where the guilty verdict was overturned.

Although Justice Warren Grice wrote that the acts committed by Thompson and her partner were "just as loathsome" as sex between two men, the judges nevertheless found unanimously that the definitions then on the books did not specifically include the acts the women were accused of performing, and so the women could not be guilty of sodomy. The drafters of the law had not included prohibiting sex between two women, and the court believed it was not justified to read into the definition something that was not explicitly stated. The decision by Judge Paul S. Etheridge of the Superior Court, Fulton County, was reversed.

## SIGNIFICANCE

After *Thompson v. Aldredge*, there were no prosecutions for private consensual homosexual sodomy (female or male) in Georgia for several decades. It is reasonable to conclude that the courts recognized that the language of the codes was sufficiently vague to make prosecutions difficult, and yet there was a resistance among legislators to taint legal documents with more specific and precise language describing sexual acts.

A 1949 revision of the sodomy laws in Georgia decreased the penalty from life imprisonment to one-to-ten years in prison. In spite of the *Thompson v. Aldredge* decision, the revision did not add language addressing sexual behavior between women. In 1968, the criminal code again was revised. The new language was more explicit in describing sexual acts, and for the first time it included oral sex between women.

In 1986, the U.S. Supreme Court agreed to rule on another Georgia case, *Bowers v. Hardwick*. In that suit, Michael Hardwick challenged the constitutionality of the Georgia statute that defined consensual oral sex between two men as sodomy. In the majority opinion, the court upheld Georgia's code, finding that based on the country's history and tradition, there is no constitutional right to privacy that would override a state's right to criminalize homosexual behavior.

Oral arguments in *Bowers v. Hardwick* referred to *Thompson v. Aldredge*, and the state acknowledged that it had not prosecuted anyone for consensual sodomy since that case. Hardwick believed that because there had been no further prosecutions, this indicated that the people of the state had little interest in criminalizing private consensual sexual activity. The court ruled, though, that the lack of prosecutions did not affect the constitutionality of the statutes.

In 2003, however, the U.S. Supreme Court, in *Lawrence v. Texas*, ruled that private, consensual sex, heterosexual *and* homosexual, between adults was protected behavior, thus overturning Georgia's sodomy laws and the sodomy laws of all U.S. states.

—*Cynthia A. Bily*

## FURTHER READING

Cain, Patricia A. *Rainbow Rights: The Role of Lawyers and Courts in the Lesbian and Gay Civil Rights Movement*. Cambridge, Mass.: Westview Press, 2000.

Curry, Lynne. *The Human Body on Trial: A Handbook with Cases, Laws, and Documents*. Santa Barbara, Calif.: ABC-CLIO, 2002.

Harris, John B., ed. *A History of the Supreme Court of Georgia: A Centennial Volume*. Macon, Ga.: J. W. Burke, 1948.

*Harvard Law Review. Sexual Orientation and the Law*. Cambridge, Mass.: Harvard University Press, 1990.

Hickey, Adam. "Between Two Spheres: Comparing State and Federal Approaches to the Right to Privacy and Prohibitions Against Sodomy." *Yale Law Review* 111, no. 4 (January, 2002): 993-1030.

Murdoch, Joyce, and Deb Price. *Courting Justice: Gay Men and Lesbians v. the Supreme Court*. New York: Basic Books, 2001.

Richards, David A. J. *The Case for Gay Rights: From Bowers to Lawrence and Beyond*. Lawrence: University Press of Kansas, 2005.

Rubenstein, William B. *Cases and Materials on Sexual Orientation and the Law*. St. Paul, Minn.: West, 1997.

"Supreme Court of Georgia: *Thompson v. Aldredge, Sheriff.*" *Southeastern Reporter* 200 (1939): 799-800.

Williams, Walter L., and Yolanda Retter. *Gay and Lesbian Rights in the United States: A Documentary History*. Westport, Conn.: Greenwood Press, 2003.

**SEE ALSO:** May 6, 1868: Kertbeny Coins the Terms "Homosexual" and "Heterosexual"; 1885: United Kingdom Criminalizes "Gross Indecency"; Sept. 4, 1957: The *Wolfenden Report* Calls for Decriminalizing Private Consensual Sex; 1961: Illinois Legalizes Consensual Homosexual Sex; Jan. 22, 1973: *Roe v. Wade* Legalizes Abortion and Extends Privacy Rights; Aug., 1973: American Bar Association Calls for Repeal of Laws Against Consensual Sex; Oct. 18, 1973: Lambda Legal Authorized to Practice Law; Nov. 17, 1975: U.S. Supreme Court Rules in "Crimes Against Nature" Case; 1986: *Bowers v. Hardwick* Upholds State Sodomy Laws; Jan. 1, 1988: Canada Decriminalizes Sex Practices Between Consenting Adults; 1992-2006: Indians Struggle to Abolish Sodomy Law; June 26, 2003: U.S. Supreme Court Overturns Texas Sodomy Law.

---

## 1947-1948
# GOLDEN AGE OF AMERICAN GAY LITERATURE

*New works by several popular and critically acclaimed writers, including Gore Vidal, Truman Capote, and Tennessee Williams, began to popularize gay sensibility by portraying gay lives and loves realistically and sympathetically.*

**LOCALE:** New York, New York
**CATEGORIES:** Literature; publications

**KEY FIGURES**

*Gore Vidal* (b. 1925), American novelist and essayist

*Truman Capote* (1924-1984), American novelist and journalist

*Tennessee Williams* (1911-1983), American playwright

**SUMMARY OF EVENT**

Gay themes are largely absent from American fiction prior to the "golden age" of 1947-1948, and the few earlier novels that mention homosexuality are riddled with stereotypes and literary flaws. Typically, these early works relegate their gay characters to minor roles and portray them unsympathetically, usually describing homosexuality as an illness that renders gay characters incapable of forming fulfilling relationships. In some works, gay characters are depicted as villainous figures who prey upon "normal" young men. The most scorn is reserved for characters with feminine characteristics, who are typically portrayed as unhappy,

---

**FROM *THE CITY AND THE PILLAR***

"We'd be a lot happier if we were less frightened."

The fat man looked at him, his eyes were understanding. "Yes. . . . But we must have some conventions, some order, or, my gracious, everyone would be running around committing murder and all that."

"One could keep those conventions; the ones to discard are the sexual taboos, the neurotic fears of frustrated people who don't dare live out their dreams because of self-made conventions and who become the zealots of normality—whatever freakish state that is."

*Source:* Gore Vidal, *The City and the Pillar* (New York: Dutton, 1948).

unsuccessful, and morally repugnant.

Three works that appeared in 1947-1948 altered this literary landscape dramatically: Gore Vidal's novel *The City and the Pillar* (1948, revised 1965), Truman Capote's novel *Other Voices, Other Rooms* (1948), and, to a lesser extent, Tennessee Williams's play *A Streetcar Named Desire* (pr., pb. 1947) marked a change in several ways. *The City and the Pillar* was the first American novel by a prominent writer in which homosexuality was a central theme and gay characters were portrayed as multidimensional human beings. Perhaps most significantly, its gay main character, Jim Willard, is physically attractive in a typically masculine way. Athletic, strong, and square-jawed, to a mainstream audience Jim compared favorably with more feminine gay characters who had been derided as "pansies" and "fairies." Jim's portrayal as "normal" in both appearance and outward behavior lent support to the novel's theme that the taboo on homosexuality was an unnecessary burden preventing people from living their lives to the fullest. Vidal depicts Jim's awakening sexuality and his several love affairs with both sympathy and realism, presenting

for the first time in American literature a fully developed gay character whose only "abnormality" is that he is not free to be himself in mainstream culture.

Capote's *Other Voices, Other Rooms* introduced homosexual themes to the Southern gothic genre in the story of Joel Knox, a thirteen-year-old New Orleans boy sent to a rural southern town, Skully's Landing, to live with a father he has never known. When he arrives, Joel learns that his father is paralyzed and capable only of saying a few words, so Joel is left in the care of his ineffectual stepmother and her cross-dressing, homosexual cousin Randolph. In this bizarrely nightmarish situation, Randolph's lavish compliments and sexual advances are the only tenderness available to Joel. However, like Randolph's gender and sexual identity, the novel's ending is deeply ambiguous: Joel ultimately rejects Randolph and leaves Skully's Landing, presumably to return to New Orleans. The ambiguity lies in Joel's sexuality: Having come of age and rejected Randolph, it is still unclear whether Joel has also rejected Randolph's sexual orientation. Critics are divided on this point; what really matters is not Joel's sexual orientation but that he has begun creating his own destiny by walking away from the gothic horror of Skully's Landing.

*Other Voices, Other Rooms* is groundbreaking in its introduction of homosexual themes to the standard Southern gothic genre and the coming-of-age story. Although the main gay character, Randolph, is portrayed as a predatory and effeminate gay man, the story ultimately is Joel's story, and his grappling with his own emerging sexuality introduces an original and pioneering theme to the coming-of-age genre.

Homosexuality is also a significant theme in Williams's *A Streetcar Named Desire*. The

*Truman Capote.* (Library of Congress)

## VIDAL "ON PRETTINESS"

In the fifteenth century the adjective "pretty" joined the English language (derived from the Old Teutonic noun *pratti* or *prata*, meaning trick or wile). At first everyone thought the world of pretty. To be a pretty fellow was to be clever, apt, skillful; a pretty soldier was gallant and brave; a pretty thing was ingenious and artful. It was not until the sixteenth century that something started to go wrong with the idea of prettiness. Although women and children could still take pleasure in being called pretty, a pretty man had degenerated into a fop with a tendency to slyness. Pretty objects continued to be admired until 1875 when the phrase "pretty-pretty" was coined. That did it. For the truly clever, apt, and skillful, the adjective pretty could only be used in the pejorative sense, as I discovered thirty years ago while being shown around King's College by E. M. Forster. As we approached the celebrated chapel (magnificent, superb, a bit much), I said, "Pretty." Forster thought I meant the chapel when, actually, I was referring to a youthful couple in the damp middle distance. A ruthless moralist, Forster publicized my use of the dread word. Told in Fitzrovia and published in the streets of Dacca, the daughters of the Philistines rejoiced; the daughters of the uncircumcised triumphed. For a time, my mighty shield was vilely cast away.

*Source: Gore Vidal: United States, Essays, 1952-1992* (New York: Random House, 1992).

play's main character, Blanche DuBois, is best characterized as an aging Southern belle who has witnessed the loss of her family's plantation as well as the suicide of her husband, a gay poet. "Her fundamental regret . . . is not that she happened to marry a homosexual [but that] she brought on the boy's suicide by her unqualified expression of disgust." Blanche's reminiscence about discovering the truth of her husband's sexual orientation highlights the tragedy of both lost love and her failure to extend love in the way it was needed.

> There was something different about the boy . . . tenderness which wasn't like a man's. . . . He came to me for help . . . and all I knew was I'd failed him in some mysterious way. . . . [O]n the dance-- floor—unable to stop myself—I'd suddenly said— "I saw! I know! You disgust me!"

Although critics disagree about the extent to which Blanche is culpable for her husband's suicide, one thing remains clear: Her regret about failing to accept her husband's homosexuality was a new perspective in American literature and marks one of the first calls for tolerance.

## SIGNIFICANCE

The golden age of gay literature, as heralded by the three works discussed here, had both an immediate

and a long-term effect on American attitudes toward homosexuality and its depiction in literature. All three works were widely reviewed and received mixed critical reception. Without a doubt, these works paved the way for the pioneering gay literature that was to come in the following decades.

Although some contemporary reviewers expressed moral repugnance, several prescient critics welcomed the openness with which these works treated the variety of human sexuality. Perhaps most indicative of these works' future impact was Richard McLaughlin's review of Vidal's *The City and the Pillar* in the *Saturday Review* ("Precarious Status," January 10, 1948). With great insight, McLaughlin noted that *Sexual Behavior in the Human Male* (commonly known as the Kinsey Report), also published in 1948, supported the naturalism with which Jim Willard's love affairs were described.

> And with the help of the astounding revelations in the first report of the Kinsey group, a great many more people are soon going to be forcefully enlightened on the variety and changes in the American sex patterns and, furthermore, the necessity for greater public and private tolerance of the vast differences in the sex habits of Americans. . . . Mr. Vidal . . . launches on his own . . . campaign against those same myths and delusions. . . . It should . . . prove to be a happy juxtaposition for both publications.

The publication of these three literary works in 1947-1948 marked a turning point in American literature: With the publication of important works by prominent and gifted writers, gay themes came out of the closet and into mainstream literature.

—*Karen E. Antell*

## FURTHER READING

Berkman, Leonard. "The Tragic Downfall of Blanche DuBois." *Modern Drama* 10, no. 2 (December, 1967): 249-257.

Bloom, Harold. *Truman Capote*. Philadelphia: Chelsea House, 2003.

Capote, Truman. *Other Voices, Other Rooms*. New York: Random House, 1948.

Levin, James. *The Gay Novel in America*. New York: Garland, 1991.

Mengeling, Marvin E. "*Other Voices, Other Rooms*: Oedipus Between the Covers." In *The Critical Response to Truman Capote*, edited by Joseph J. Waldmeir and John C. Waldmeir. Westport, Conn.: Greenwood, 1999.

Paller, Michael. *Gentlemen Callers: Tennessee Williams, Homosexuality, and Mid-Twentieth-Century Broadway Drama*. New York: Palgrave Macmillan, 2005.

Phillips, Gene D. "Blanche's Phantom Husband: Homosexuality on Stage and Screen." *Louisiana Literature: A Review of Literature and Humanities* 14, no. 2 (Fall, 1997): 36-47.

Summers, Claude Jay. "*The City and the Pillar* as Gay Fiction." In *Gore Vidal: Writer Against the Grain*, edited by Jay Parini. New York: Columbia University Press, 1992.

Vidal, Gore. *The City and the Pillar*. New York: Dutton, 1948.

_____. *Gore Vidal, Sexually Speaking: Collected Sex Writings*. Edited by Donald Weise. San Francisco, Calif.: Cleis Press, 1999.

Williams, Tennessee. *A Streetcar Named Desire*. New York: New Directions, 1947.

**SEE ALSO:** July 4, 1855: Whitman Publishes *Leaves of Grass*; May 25, 1895: Oscar Wilde Is Convicted of Gross Indecency; 1924: Gide Publishes the Signed Edition of *Corydon*; 1939: Isherwood Publishes *Goodbye to Berlin*; 1956: Baldwin Publishes *Giovanni's Room*; 1963: Rechy Publishes *City of Night*; June, 1971: The Gay Book Award Debuts; 1974: *The Front Runner* Makes *The New York Times* Best-Seller List; 1975: First Novel About Coming Out to Parents Is Published; 1980-1981: Gay Writers Form the Violet Quill; May, 1987: *Lambda Rising Book Report* Begins Publication; June 2, 1989: Lambda Literary Award Is Created; 1993: Monette Wins the National Book Award for *Becoming a Man*.

## June, 1947-February, 1948
# *VICE VERSA* IS PUBLISHED AS FIRST LESBIAN PERIODICAL

*Two years after the end of World War II, a young writer, Lisa Ben, created the first known lesbian publication in the United States, a newsletter by and for lesbians called* Vice Versa.

**LOCALE:** Los Angeles, California
**CATEGORIES:** Publications; civil rights

**KEY FIGURE**
*Lisa Ben* (b. 1921), pseudonym for the creator, writer, and distributor of *Vice Versa*

**SUMMARY OF EVENT**
While working as a typist for the Hollywood movie studio RKO in 1947, the twenty-six-year-old Lisa Ben (anagram of "lesbian") had discovered the lesbian bar scene in postwar Los Angeles and recognized her own attraction to women. Told by her boss that the important thing was to "look busy" on the job despite slow periods, she decided to create a newsletter. Ben noticed that while there were many different kinds of magazines available for all sorts of people, there was nothing for lesbians. A budding poet and writer, she knew she could include some of her own work as well as solicit pieces written by friends.

Ben named her new effort *Vice Versa* and subtitled it *America's Gayest Magazine* because, as she said in interviews conducted many years later, at the time she started, homosexuality was considered a vice. She wanted to challenge that concept and instead celebrate "the gay life." Appealing to "nonconformists," she promised her readers spontaneity and entertainment.

Secrecy also was an all-important concern for the creator of *Vice Versa*. Ben's fears of being found out were so great that not only did she write and publish *Vice Versa* anonymously but she also typed originals—two sets at a time, with five carbon copies of each, making a total of twelve copies. She would then type two more sets of originals. She could have used the still-laborious but much faster mimeographing process, but that would have left evidence of her magazine and its contents. Not trusting the mail, she handed out copies to friends and friends of friends that she met at the bars or through the small lesbian social circles in the Los Angeles area.

Ben worked on *Vice Versa* from June, 1947, to February, 1948, writing most of the copy herself or retyping and republishing material she found elsewhere. Issues contained everything from show business reviews to poems and political commentary. Despite a positive response from the women who received it, the Valentine's Day, 1948, issue would be the last one she would produce.

Most accounts of Ben's life attribute the demise of *Vice Versa* to the tediousness and isolation of the work. However, one account complicates that picture, quoting Ben as saying that the real reason she stopped producing the newsletter was that she had lost her job at RKO and lost access to the resources and privacy it had provided her.

In addition to creating the newsletter, Ben had been one of the earliest lesbian celebrities in the 1960's. As the "first gay folk singer," she reworked popular songs, giving them overtly same-gender meanings ("the girl that I marry will probably be/ As butch as a hunk of machinery . . ."). Ben's songs were recorded and, through the homophile groups that had formed in the 1950's, they were sold to lesbians and gays around the country. She also performed at functions and parties, and she had a regular show at a Los Angeles club, the Flamingo, which featured gay events on Sunday afternoons in the early 1960's.

**SIGNIFICANCE**
In 1958, ten years after Lisa Ben stopped publishing *Vice Versa*, the San Francisco-based lesbian organization Daughters of Bilitis (DOB), founded by Phyllis Lyon, Del Martin, and six other lesbians as a "secret" social club, formed a chapter in Los Angeles. Ben was one of its original members. She

served as a local officer, taking on the position of secretary for the first few years of the chapter's existence. Ben also contributed her poetry and fiction to the DOB newsletter, *The Ladder*, which was started in 1956 as a way to encourage women to join the organization. From the beginning, the women of DOB and the staff of *The Ladder* recognized their debt to Ben, and they paid tribute to her in its pages. They knew that Ben had provided an important foundation for their later efforts.

Most women (and some men) who wrote for *The Ladder* used the protection of a pseudonym or pen name. Ben adopted her unique pseudonym at the urging of *The Ladder*'s first editor, Phyllis Lyon. Ben still prefers the pseudonym in accounts of her lesbian activism. Her initial choice for her pen name, she said, was "Ima Spinster," but, she added, her DOB colleagues did not appreciate the joke.

Lesbians and gays in the 1940's, 1950's, and 1960's had known that most people in the United States—including important opinion makers such as religious and political leaders, psychiatrists, judges, and ordinary women and men—considered them sick and immoral, and their behavior illegal. Lesbians and gays feared, correctly, that the discovery of their homosexuality could cost them their families, jobs, and friends. It was difficult enough to attend a meeting of lesbians and gays or a public forum on the issue of homosexuality; many people were too afraid to risk being identified publicly in a magazine for lesbians or gays.

Ben's efforts in 1947 and 1948 to provide a written source of information for lesbians helped launch a revolution in not only the lesbian and gay movement but also the larger world of publishing and public opinion. For the next three decades, Ben continued to be part of the lesbian and gay movement at the local and national level, even after she stopped performing and writing regularly. Ben and her story are included in the award-winning documentary *Before Stonewall* and in other works featuring early pioneers of the movements for lesbian and gay rights.

—*Marcia M. Gallo*

**FURTHER READING**

Cain, Paul. "Lisa Ben." In *Leading the Parade: Conversations with America's Most Influential Lesbians and Gay Men*. Lanham, Md.: Scarecrow Press, 2002.

Fleischman, Florine, with Susan Bullough. "Lisa Ben." In *Before Stonewall: Activists for Gay and Lesbian Rights in Historical Context*, edited by Vern L. Bullough. Binghamton, N.Y.: Harrington Park Press, 2002.

Streitmatter, Rodger. *Unspeakable: The Rise of the Gay and Lesbian Press in America*. Winchester, Mass.: Faber and Faber, 1995.

**SEE ALSO:** 1896: *Der Eigene* Is Published as First Journal on Homosexuality; 1953: *ONE* Magazine Begins Publication; 1955: Daughters of Bilitis Founded as First National Lesbian Group in United States; 1967: *Los Angeles Advocate* Begins Publication; 1971: *Lesbian Tide* Publishes Its First Issue; Nov., 1971: *The Body Politic* Begins Publication; Oct., 1974: *Lesbian Connection* Begins Publication; Jan., 1986: South Asian Newsletter *Trikone* Begins Publication.

# 1948
# KINSEY PUBLISHES *SEXUAL BEHAVIOR IN THE HUMAN MALE*

*Alfred Kinsey published a revolutionary report that suggested that 4 percent of Anglo-American men were exclusively homosexual. In addition to raising a topic that traditionally had been discussed only behind closed doors, Kinsey's work made inroads into dispelling the prejudices toward and stereotypes about gays and lesbians.*

**LOCALE:** Bloomington, Indiana
**CATEGORIES:** Science; publications; organizations and institutions

**KEY FIGURE**
*Alfred Kinsey* (1894-1956), biologist and sex researcher

**SUMMARY OF EVENT**
In 1948, Alfred Kinsey released unprecedented findings about human sexuality in his work *Sexual Behavior in the Human Male*. To compile the report, Kinsey's researchers interviewed volunteers from all walks of life, though most of the data came from the input of fifty-three hundred college-aged Anglo-American men. Kinsey's highly trained face-to-face interviewers could ask as many as 521 questions, depending on the participant's specific experiences. The questions focused on sexual experiences Kinsey considered measurable, which meant that in actuality the results provided information about the behavior of given individuals at specific times. Kinsey also asked questions about erogenous zones, premarital sex, extramarital sex, oral sex, foreplay, masturbation, and orgasm. The section concerned with homosexuality made up only one area of the overall study.

Kinsey created a seven-point homosexual-heterosexual rating scale, now called the Kinsey Scale, to identify whether a participant's behavior was predominantly heterosexual, predominantly homosexual, or somewhere in between. He used this scale to measure the degree to which the participants in his study had engaged in some form of ho-

mosexual activity. A zero on the scale indicated exclusively heterosexual behavior, and a seven on the scale indicated exclusively homosexual behavior.

The work showed that 4 percent of the white men in his study were completely homosexual. This suggested that, contrary to popular belief, homosexuality was not a perverted aberration. The reports also suggested that there was middle ground between heterosexuality and homosexuality, and that there were people who were bisexual. Kinsey stated that 37 percent of the men in the sample had experienced an orgasm with another man, 10 percent were

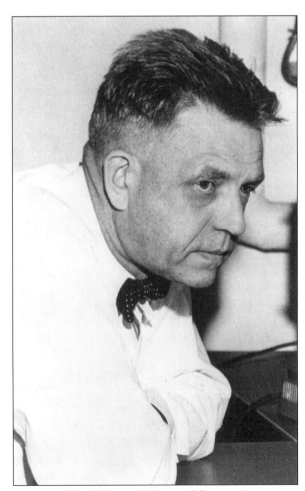

*Alfred Kinsey.* (Library of Congress)

## ALFRED KINSEY

Alfred Kinsey had climbed the academic ladder smoothly, achieving a full professorship at Indiana University in 1929. He became the world's leading authority on gall wasps, measuring and cataloging 3,500,000 specimens. He wrote a high school biology textbook (1926) that sold nearly half a million copies. In the 1930's came what proved the turning point of his career: He was asked by university administrators to coordinate a marriage course, initially to be taught in the summer of 1938. Kinsey was surprised to find no reliable statistical evidence regarding human sexual conduct. He decided that the empirical, taxonomic approach he had successfully used for his gall wasps and biology classes might also work well for sex research. He therefore began, in July, 1938, to take the sexual histories of those of his marriage course students who were willing to provide them.

Within a year, Kinsey had amassed 350 histories but in the process had aroused opposition among a few colleagues and within the conservative Bloomington community. The university's president, Herman Wells, offered Kinsey the choice of continuing either the marriage course or his case-history project. As a trained research scientist, Kinsey naturally preferred to pursue his investigative studies, and he resigned from the course. He had found a second career that was to make this unassuming, modest midwesterner world-famous: sex research.

Prior to the late 1930's, little knowledge had been factually established regarding human sexuality. Sigmund Freud (1856-1939), the founder of psychoanalysis, had studied the sexual lives of largely upper-class Viennese women. Havelock Ellis (1859-1939) had corresponded concerning sexual behavior with upper-class British men. In 1915, an American physician, M. J. Exner, had sent one thousand male college students questionnaires about their sex lives. By 1938, nineteen different studies on human sexual behavior had been reported, all of them sketchy in their topics and inadequate in their methodology.

Kinsey was particularly appalled by Freud's moralistic judgments regarding masturbation, which the Austrian condemned as infantile and neurotic. Instead, Kinsey made one principle clear above all others throughout his sexual investigations: As a scientist, he registered no objection to any kind of sexual behavior in which a subject might be involved. This written statement to a student was typical: "I am absolutely tolerant of everything in human sex behavior. It would be impossible to make an objective study if I passed any evaluation pro or con on any sort of behavior. . . . Moreover, . . . I have absolutely preserved the confidence of all individual records." In the early 1940's, Kinsey recruited three able assistants for what was to be incorporated as the Institute for Sex Research.

Kinsey and his coworkers had compiled and published a monumental amount of information regarding sexual behavior in the United States. Despite some dubious sampling techniques and perhaps an overweighting of homosexual histories, his work became the standard achievement in the empirical investigation of human sexual patterns. The tremendous scale of the research opened previously closed doors of a culture constrained by Puritan and Victorian inhibitions. Kinsey took sex research out of the realm of subjective speculation and placed it on a scholarly and respectable scientific foundation.

mostly homosexual between age sixteen and fifty-five, and 8 percent were entirely homosexual (same age range). Finally, Kinsey reported that a person's sexual orientation could change at different phases of life.

Kinsey already had begun research for this project in 1938, well before the study was published, and the research concluded in 1963, after Kinsey's death. The findings are most often considered in conjunction with the report *Sexual Behavior in the Human Female*, which Kinsey published in 1953. Because Kinsey was a well-respected researcher, and his research methods were considered scientific and objective, his findings were taken seriously by both the scientific community and the general public.

### SIGNIFICANCE

Though Kinsey's findings were taken seriously, they were not universally accepted as good. The findings about heterosexual sex were controversial enough, but the findings about homosexual sex created a maelstrom of responses. Released, as it was, during the second red scare during the Cold War and on the budding cusp of the United States' trip through the paranoia of the McCarthy era, *Sexual Behavior in the Human Male* was one of the few positive signs for gays, lesbians, and bisexuals in the United States. The report generated widespread conversation about the taboo topic of homosexuality, but many years would pass before the study's findings were used to counter negative social views of homosexuals and homosexuality.

During the second red scare, and particularly when the United States was deep in the grip of Senator Joseph McCarthy and other anticommunist "red hunters" such as the House Un-American Activities Committee, homosexuality was treated as if it were a dangerous perversion. Workers were often fired merely for any *suspicion* of homosexuality. Additionally, the few groups, such as the Daughters of Bilitis (founded 1955) and the Mattachine Society (founded 1950), which existed to support lesbians and gays operated in strict secrecy and promised their members the utmost privacy. The entire homophile movement, however, had been relying on studies such as those of Kinsey for their helpful findings that gays and lesbians accounted for a significant percentage of the population and that homosexuality was normal. These groups hoped that science would vindicate them and that superstition and bias would ultimately give way before the strength of scientific study.

Science would need to be married to activism before any degree of equality could be attained, however. After all, the American Psychiatric Association was classifying homosexuality as a mental illness, and it did so until 1973. Kinsey was attacked as a communist by a congressional committee, and the Kinsey Institute for Research in Sex, Gender, and Reproduction, which he had founded in 1947, lost some of its major private funding because of its controversial work. The institute maintained solid footing, however, and continued to make inroads into American sexual mores. As the sexual revolution and later the gay and lesbian rights movement began to change predominant social attitudes about sex and sexuality, Kinsey's findings came to be seen as visionary. The Kinsey Institute released the report *Homosexualities: A Study of Diversity Among Men and Women* in 1978, well after the GLBT rights movement was in progress.

Later studies have suggested that some of Kinsey's findings, particularly in the area of bisexuality, were exaggerated by volunteer bias. His landmark research, however, still is considered one of the catalysts that began the slow erosion of prejudice against gays and lesbians in the United States.

—*Jessie Bishop Powell*

## FURTHER READING

Bell, Alan P., and Martin S. Weinberg. *Homosexualities: A Study of Human Diversity*. Report of a Study Made by the Institute for Sex Research. New York: Simon and Schuster, 1978.

D'Emilio, John. *Sexual Politics, Sexual Communities: The Making of a Homosexual Minority in the United States, 1940-1970*. 2d ed. Chicago: University of Chicago Press, 1998.

Duberman, Martin. *About Time: Exploring the Gay Past*. New York: Meridian, 1991.

Gathorne-Hardy, Jonathan. *Sex the Measure of All Things: A Life of Alfred C. Kinsey*. Bloomington: Indiana University Press, 2000.

Jones, James H. *Alfred Kinsey: A Public/Private Life*. New York: W. W. Norton, 1997.

Kinsey, Alfred. *Sexual Behavior In the Human Female*. Bloomington: Indiana University Press, 1998.

_____. *Sexual Behavior In the Human Male*. Bloomington: Indiana University Press, 1998.

**SEE ALSO:** May 6, 1868: Kertbeny Coins the Terms "Homosexual" and "Heterosexual"; 1869: Westphal Advocates Medical Treatment for Sexual Inversion; 1897: Ellis Publishes *Sexual Inversion*; May 14, 1897: Hirschfeld Founds the Scientific-Humanitarian Committee; 1905: Freud Rejects Third-Sex Theory; 1929: Davis's Research Identifies Lesbian Sexuality as Common and Normal; 1952: APA Classifies Homosexuality as a Mental Disorder; 1953: Kinsey Publishes *Sexual Behavior in the Human Female*; 1953-1957: Evelyn Hooker Debunks Beliefs That Homosexuality Is a "Sickness"; Dec. 15, 1973: Homosexuality Is Delisted by APA; Apr. 20, 2001: Chinese Psychiatric Association Removes Homosexuality from List of Mental Disorders.

**1950**
# MATTACHINE SOCIETY IS FOUNDED

*Harry Hay and four other gay men founded the first gay organization in the United States in 1950, soon naming it the Mattachine Society. The group's creation marked the start of an unbroken history of GLBT activism in the United States.*

**LOCALE:** Los Angeles, California
**CATEGORIES:** Organizations and institutions; civil rights; publications

**KEY FIGURES**
*Harry Hay* (1912-2002),
*Rudi Gernreich* (1922-1985),
*Dale Jennings* (1917-2000),
*Bob Hull*, and
*Chuck Rowland*, cofounders of the Mattachine Society

**SUMMARY OF EVENT**
In 1948, Harry Hay, a music history teacher at the People's Educational Center in Los Angeles, was working on the Henry Wallace presidential campaign for the Progressive Party. He proposed an interest group called Bachelors for Wallace to endorse and publicize the campaign. The group did not come to fruition, but for Hay it sparked the concept of a political group for gays. Two years later, Hay, along with four gay friends, Rudi Gernreich, Bob Hull, Dale Jennings, and Chuck Rowland (all leftists politically), met to discuss forming such a group. Believing that prejudice against gays was not a problem that individuals could solve, the founders wanted to popularize the concept of a gay *minority* and develop group consciousness around this concept.

At the time, homosexuality was illegal in every U.S. state, so Mattachine Society (as the group came to be called in 1951) meetings often took place in secret and members used aliases. A cell structure was used (an idea from the American Communist Party) that was noncentralized: In case of a raid by authorities, limited information about

the group could be found at a given location.

In April, 1951, Mattachine created statements of missions and purposes, which were ratified on July 20 of the same year. There was a call to challenge antihomosexual discrimination and for building a positive, ethical gay community and culture. Discussion groups provided gays a place to share openly their thoughts and feelings and to feel self-worth. By 1953, more than one hundred discussion groups existed in Southern California. Affiliates also existed in New York, Boston, Chicago, Denver, and the District of Columbia. Mattachine also sponsored social events and fund-raisers and published newsletters, *ONE* magazine, and the *Mattachine Review. ONE* was the first homophile magazine in the United States to be distributed publicly. The group's periodicals and newsletters reached gays outside urban areas, extending Mattachine's message.

After the 1952 arrest of cofounder Dale Jennings on a sex charge following police entrapment, the Mattachine Society took on its first political battle. By defending Jennings, Mattachine also took on the notorious Los Angeles Police Department and its pattern of harassing gays. The arresting officer was caught lying, and the judge dismissed the charges. Although the outcome of the case was not reported by media, the Mattachine Society nonetheless distributed information about the case with flyers, which were placed throughout Los Angeles and mostly where gays met.

In March, 1953, a columnist for a local newspaper, the *Los Angeles Daily Mirror*, wrote that gays in Los Angeles were a "strange new pressure group" of "sexual deviates" and were banding together to wield "tremendous political power." The column also linked Mattachine to communism, saying the group's attorney was a well-known subversive and an unfriendly and uncooperative witness before the House Un-American Activities Committee. This publicity worried Mattachine members. Some called for statewide conferences to address the issue.

A strong coalition of conservative delegates

emerged at the conferences, and some were determined to get rid of the so-called communists in the leadership. The original Mattachine founders resigned on the last day of the conferences and turned over leadership to the conservatives. The result was a second Mattachine Society, which moved its headquarters to San Francisco.

The new leadership shared none of the visions of the original founders and revised Mattachine's goals drastically. They opposed social change, a separate gay culture, the political mobilization of gays, and the idea that the problems faced by gays was institutional. They preferred to conform and accommodate and to assimilate into mainstream society. Except for their sexual lives, they felt no different from heterosexuals. They wanted to present themselves as reasonable, well-adjusted persons, hoping that arbiters of public opinion (professionals such as psychiatrists) would rethink their assumptions and views about homosexuality. Membership soon declined, and a convention in May of 1954 saw only forty-two attendees. The national structure dissolved in 1961, but the New York, Los Angeles, and San Francisco chapters remained active for several more years.

## SIGNIFICANCE

The Mattachine Society would grow into a national movement, and, in conjunction with the lesbian organization Daughters of Bilitis (created in 1955), the two existed as the only civil rights organizations for gays and lesbians until the 1969 Stonewall Rebellion in New York City. Harry Hay's belief that gays are an oppressed minority was thought of as an absurd idea at the time of Mattachine's founding, but eventually the idea would be a central theme in the gay and lesbian rights movement.

After Stonewall, however, Mattachine and the Daughters of Bilitis were considered to be too traditional and politically nonconfrontational and assimilationist. Other organizations, such as the San Francisco Society for Individual Rights, the Gay Liberation Front, the Gay Activist Alliance, Lavender Menace/Radicalesbians, Lesbian Feminist Liberation, Third World Gay Revolution, and Street Transvestite Action Revolutionaries would start the GLBT movement on a different, more radical, and later more diverse, path.

—*Ski Hunter*

## FURTHER READING

Bullough, Vern L. *Before Stonewall: Activists for Gay and Lesbian Rights in Historical Context*. New York: Harrington Park Press, 2002.

D'Emilio, John E. *Sexual Politics, Sexual Communities: The Making of a Homosexual Minority in the United States, 1940-1970*. 2d ed. Chicago: University of Chicago Press, 1998.

Hay, Harry. *Radically Gay: Gay Liberation in the Words of Its Founder*. Edited by Will Roscoe. Boston: Beacon Press, 1996.

Johnson, David K. *The Lavender Scare: The Cold War Persecution of Gays and Lesbians in the Federal Government*. Chicago: University of Chicago Press, 2004.

Timmons, Stuart. *The Trouble with Harry Hay: Founder of the Modern Gay Movement*. Boston: Alyson, 1990.

Williams, Walter W., and Yolanda Retter. *Gay and Lesbian Rights in the United States*. Westport, Conn.: Greenwood Press, 2003.

SEE ALSO: Dec. 10, 1924: Gerber Founds the Society for Human Rights; 1952: ONE, Inc., Is Founded; 1955: Daughters of Bilitis Founded as First National Lesbian Group in United States; May 27-30, 1960: First National Lesbian Conference Convenes; Feb. 19-20, 1966: First North American Conference of Homophile Organizations Convenes; Apr. 19, 1967: First Student Homophile League Is Formed; Aug. 11-18, 1968: NACHO Formally Becomes the First Gay Political Coalition; July 31, 1969: Gay Liberation Front Is Formed; May 1, 1970: Radicalesbians Issues "The Woman Identified Woman" Manifesto; June 28, 1970: First Lesbian and Gay Pride March in the United States; Nov. 28, 1970: Del Martin Quits Gay Liberation Movement; 1973: National Gay Task Force Is Formed; Oct. 18, 1973: Lambda Legal Authorized to Practice Law; Apr. 22, 1980: Human Rights Campaign Fund Is Founded.

## September 24, 1951
# George Jorgensen Becomes Christine Jorgensen

*Christine Jorgensen's gender reassignment surgery marked a crucial and necessary distinction between transsexualism and homosexuality. It also changed the way medical professionals, and society in general, viewed transsexuality and the significance of gender identity to personal well-being.*

**Locale:** New York; California; Copenhagen, Denmark

**Categories:** Health and medicine; science; transgender/transsexuality

### Key Figures

*Christine Jorgensen* (1926-1989), American transsexual who had gender reassignment surgery

*Christian Hamburger*, Danish physician who performed Jorgensen's gender reassignment surgery

### Summary of Event

George William Jorgensen, Jr., received an honorable discharge from the U.S. Army in 1946 and became a woman—Christine Jorgensen—on September 24, 1951. She had taken the name Christine, a female variant of the name Christian, to honor Danish doctor Christian Hamburger, the surgeon who performed her gender reassignment surgery. Also, for more than one year before the surgery, Hamburger had supervised Christine's (George's) comprehensive—and necessary—hormone treatment.

From early childhood, George believed he was different from most boys. As he developed, he was small of stature and weighed less than one hundred pounds when he first attempted to join the Army. He had almost no body hair, his spontaneous gestures were distinctly feminine (or were interpreted as feminine), and his male organs were underdeveloped. George had been humiliated and taunted at school. He later had difficulty finding and holding jobs because of reactions to his effeminacy.

People were uncomfortable with him.

In his teens, George was deeply conflicted about his sexuality, and he denied being gay. Rather, he was convinced that he was a woman who, through some accident of birth, had been "trapped in a man's body," a common phrase that reflects society's lack of knowledge about the life experiences of those who believe their given gender at birth does not "match" the gender they feel to be. Fortunately, George had supportive and understanding parents who, although bewildered by his gender identity, did not condemn him for feeling different.

The estimated 3 percent of the population who were considered to have "gender dysphoria" generally had few places to turn for psychological counseling and adequate, professional, medical advice. Most who were thought to be gender dysphoric were considered gay or lesbian and were referred to psychologists or psychiatrists who either attempted to "convert" them to heterosexuality or tried to help them adjust to being gay or lesbian.

In 1945, George had been drafted. He served in the Army for more than one year before being honorably discharged following a life-threatening case of pneumonia. In the Army, he worked clerical jobs and did not fit in easily among his coworkers. He maintained a low profile and had little social contact with his fellow soldiers.

In high school, George had worked part time in a library, so he had access to books related to homosexuality and gender variance. He had to read the books clandestinely, though, because they were secured, which also made them difficult to get to for the reading public. He read about research in endocrinology, which suggested that hormone treatment could be used to "help" transsexuals. Subsequently, he contacted Harold Grayson, a noted endocrinologist, but Grayson referred him to a psychiatrist, who suggested a lengthy course of psychiatric treatment to address what he diagnosed as homosexuality, which was believed to be a psychiatric disorder by the American Psychiatric Association until 1973.

George could not afford this course of treatment but, more crucially, he knew it was not what he needed. He was frustrated because he could not find individuals with professional knowledge of sexuality and of gender issues. Realizing that the psychiatrist's treatment would be of little help, George rejected it and then continued on his own to study endocrinology; he also took courses in medical technology.

George first traveled to Copenhagen, Denmark, in May, 1950, after Helen Johnson, a friend he had known in Los Angeles and who had relocated to Copenhagen, told him about medical research in Scandinavia involving transsexuals. Severely strained financially, George was able to afford only a one-way ticket to Denmark. He had saved enough money to live for a few months in his new surroundings without working. Johnson put George in touch with her doctor, who then referred him to specialists on transsexuality, including Christian Hamburger. The doctor, in meeting with George, told George he was likely transsexual, not homosexual.

Because George was to participate in an experiment on the effects of human hormones, the Danish government paid for his treatment, which began in August, 1950. To be absolutely sure that the experiment was conducted according to the best medical protocols, Hamburger insisted that George consult a psychiatrist, which remains a standard of care for those considering gender reassignment surgery. After several sessions, during which the psychiatrist examined George in depth, he gave his consent to proceed with the course of treatment proposed by Hamburger. Meanwhile, Hamburger asked George to provide urine samples to test for the effects of the hormone treatment.

George had applied to the U.S. embassy in Co-

*Christine Jorgensen in 1953, speaking to reporters in New York City after returning from Denmark, where she had gender reassignment surgery.* (AP/Wide World Photos)

penhagen to obtain a new passport that would reflect his gender and name changes, and the embassy granted the new passport. Bureaucratic stumbling blocks with Danish officials, however, temporarily stalled the surgery. The Medico-Legal Council of the Danish Ministry of Justice had to approve the procedure, a requirement that was further complicated because George was not a Danish citizen. These problems were overcome, however, and on September 24, 1951, Hamburger started with the surgery, removing George's testicles. In October, 1952, the doctor removed George's penis; the following procedure involved shaping a vagina, which would be lined with sensitive penile tissue.

On June 8, 1952, George, now Christine, talked with her parents. The hormone treatments had reshaped her body so that she now had breasts and presented as a woman. Christine's father shared this news with friends at the Danish-American social club to which he belonged. One of its members sold the information to the New York *Daily News*, which triggered a huge wave of publicity. Christine's reassignment surgery was not the first such surgery performed, however. There had been at least thirty before her, from several places around the world, but Christine's was the first to generate the national and international publicity that followed the surgery.

Upon her return to the United States in 1953 following a three-year absence, Christine wrote what became a highly popular autobiography (published in 1967); she also became an entertainer, but she had been banned from making appearances in many cities and at military bases in the United States. She lived the rest of her life in California, where she died of bladder cancer in 1989.

## SIGNIFICANCE

The most significant effect of Christine Jorgensen's heroic struggle to change her gender was that it made a crucial and necessary distinction between transsexuality and homosexuality. Making such a distinction was important to her because she was fighting her battle with the medical profession in a country (the United States) in the late 1940's and the 1950's that fiercely opposed the idea of changing one's gender. Society believed gender dysphoria to be a sickness like homosexuality and not a critical aspect of a person's self-identity. Furthermore, the reassignment surgery, which at the time could be done outside the United States only, changed the way in which medical professionals, and even the general public, view transsexuality and the critical importance of gender identity to personal well-being.

The publicity that followed Christine's gender reassignment brought "out of the closet" many transsexuals who had often been considered "freaks of nature" and "one of a kind." It soon became evident, however, that substantial numbers of people are transsexual. Many had been very unhappy, severely depressed, and almost pathologically secretive until the Christine Jorgensen story was unfolded in newspapers and magazines throughout the world. News of Christine's gender reassignment opened the doors of discussion and debate concerning gender reassignment, transsexuality, and sexuality in general.

After 1953, gender reassignment clinics began to appear in many parts of the world. The Scandinavian countries, particularly Denmark and Sweden, were early centers for such treatment in Europe, with Hamburger's Statens Seruminstitut in Copenhagen among the most pioneering of such centers. In Asia, Thailand has established sexual reassignment clinics, often combined with plastic surgery clinics, throughout the country.

Many countries have made it possible for postoperative transsexuals to have their official records altered to reflect their change of gender. At one time, Christine wanted to marry but could not because her birth certificate did not reflect her postoperative gender, even though her passport and other official documents identified her as a woman. As same-gender marriage continues as a controversial issue in the United States and other countries during the early years of the twenty-first century, questions also continue regarding the legality of marriage of those who have undergone gender reassignment. In the United Kingdom, transsexuals can now legally marry. It is doubtful that prohibitions against transsexual marriage will long be supported in other Western countries.

In some countries, transsexuals who wish to marry are not forced into marriage according to their gender at birth. That is, a person named a girl at birth who reassigns her gender to that of a man is not required to marry a man in order for the marriage to be legally recognized. However, a transsexual woman (born a boy), for example, cannot legally marry a man born a boy. Judge Van der Reijt, chair of the Dutch Gender Identity Foundation, suggested that the best way to deal with the legal problems faced by transsexuals and transgender people is to ignore noting the gender of newborns on birth certificates, a notation Van der Reijt considers virtually useless.

—*R. Baird Shuman*

## FURTHER READING

Benjamin, Harry. *The Transsexual Phenomenon*. New York: Julian Press, 1966. Available at http://www.symposion.com/ijt/benjamin/.

Bullough, Vern L., ed. *Before Stonewall: Activists for Gay and Lesbian Rights in Historical Context*. New York: Harrington Park Press, 2002.

Califia, Patrick. *Sex Changes: The Politics of Transgenderism.* 2d ed. San Francisco, Calif.: Cleis Press, 2003.

Chiland, Collette. *Transsexualism: Illusion and Reality.* Translated by Philip Slotkin. Middletown, Conn.: Wesleyan University Press, 2003.

Denny, Dallas, ed. *Current Concepts in Transgender Identity.* New York: Garland, 1998.

Devor, Holly. *FTM: Female-to-Male Transsexuals in Society.* Bloomington: Indiana University Press, 1997.

Feinberg, Leslie. *Transgender Liberation: A Movement Whose Time Has Come.* New York: World View Forum, 1992.

Jorgensen, Christine. *Christine Jorgensen: A Personal Autobiography.* San Francisco, Calif.: Cleis Press, 1967.

Lev, Arlene Istar. *Transgender Emergence: Therapeutic Guidelines for Working with Gender-Variant People and Their Families.* New York: Haworth Clinical Practice Press, 2004.

**SEE ALSO:** 1952: APA Classifies Homosexuality as a Mental Disorder; Nov. 21, 1966: First Gender Identity Clinic Opens and Provides Gender Reassignment Surgery; Dec. 15, 1973: Homosexuality Is Delisted by APA; 1978: Harry Benjamin International Gender Dysphoria Association Is Founded; 1993: Intersex Society of North America Is Founded; June 17, 1995: International Bill of Gender Rights Is First Circulated; 1996: Hart Recognized as a Transgender Man; 1998: Transgender Scholarship Proliferates; Feb. 21, 2003: Australian Court Validates Transsexual Marriage; Nov. 20, 2003: Transgender Day of Remembrance and Remembering Our Dead Project; May 17, 2004: Transsexual Athletes Allowed to Compete in Olympic Games; Apr. 4, 2005: United Kingdom's Gender Recognition Act Legalizes Transsexual Marriage.

# 1952
# APA CLASSIFIES HOMOSEXUALITY AS A MENTAL DISORDER

*Homosexuality was classified as a mental disorder in the first edition of the American Psychiatric Association's* Diagnostic and Statistical Manual of Mental Disorders *(DSM), leading to attempts to "treat" persons who had same-gender sexual desires and identities. The classification also led to the founding of Christian-based organizations in support of psychiatry's claims of reparative therapy and to groups claiming to "cure" GLBT individuals.*

**LOCALE:** United States
**CATEGORIES:** Health and medicine; science; laws, acts, and legal history; organizations and institutions

**KEY FIGURES**

*Karl Friedrich Westphal* (1833-1890), credited with the first scientific study of homosexuality
*Martin Charcot* (1825-1893), first doctor to use hypnosis on lesbians and gays
*Irving Bieber* (1908-1991) and
*Sandor Rado* (1890-1972), two psychiatrists who helped develop the DSM classification on homosexuality
*Bruce Voeller* (1934-1994), biologist and member of the National Gay Task Force

**SUMMARY OF EVENT**

The *Diagnostic and Statistical Manual of Mental Disorders* (DSM) is considered the bible of psychiatry and of psychiatric illness. In its fourth edition, it contains the criteria and diagnostic tools for deter-

## FROM THE *DIAGNOSTIC AND STATISTICAL MANUAL OF MENTAL DISORDERS* (1952)

### Sexual Deviation

This diagnosis is reserved for deviant sexuality which is not symptomatic of more extensive syndromes, such as schizophrenic and obsessional reactions. The term includes most of the cases formerly classed as "psychopathic personality with pathologic sexuality." The diagnoses will specify the type of the pathologic behavior, such as homosexuality, transvestism, pedophilia, fetishism, and sexual sadism (including rape, sexual assault, mutilation).

mining all classified psychiatric disorders. The first edition of the DSM, published in 1952 by the American Psychiatric Association (APA), included the category "homosexuality" as a mental disorder under the subcategory "sexual deviation."

Sexual deviation was broadly classified as a "personality disorder." Personality disorders were further broken down into three groups: personality pattern disturbance, personality trait disturbance, and sociopathic personality disturbance. Sexual deviation (including homosexuality) was considered a sociopathic personality disturbance. The other diagnoses that fell under this subcategory were antisocial reaction and drug and alcohol addiction.

Homosexuality was characterized as a mental disorder, however, long before it was classified as such by the APA. In *Outlines of Lectures on Mental Disease* (1826), Sir Alexander Morison (1779-1866), a Scottish physician, declared that "it is a consolation to know that [homosexuality] is sometimes the consequence of insanity." Homosexuality, however, was not studied scientifically until the close of the nineteenth century. The first study, undertaken by German psychiatry professor Karl Friedrich Westphal in 1869, examined the traits of one lesbian woman over the course of several years. Westphal later expanded his study to include more than two hundred subjects, and ultimately he devised a system for classifying behaviors thought to be associated with homosexuality. In the mid-nineteenth century, French psychiatrist Martin

Charcot was the first to attempt—and fail—to cure homosexuality through hypnosis.

Diagnosing homosexuality with the guidance of the DSM was similar to that of diagnosing mental disorders in general, and "treatment" for homosexuality reflected the treatment administered for the other disorders. Though many patients were openly gay or lesbian, others were forced into treatment by family members. Because it was considered a mental disorder, treatment could not begin until the patient admitted to having a "problem."

Aside from traditional psychotherapy, a host of treatments for homosexuality became available shortly after its DSM classification. Treatments included aversion therapy, nausea-producing drugs, castration, electric shock, brain surgery, and breast amputation. Of these, aversion therapy and shock therapy were used most often. Both involved "training" the subconscious mind to associate homosexual thoughts and desires with pain. It was believed that administering a painful stimuli when a patient had homosexual desires (at what point this could be determined is unclear) would lead to the eventual disappearance of those desires. Not until the early 1970's did psychiatrists and other professionals move to abandon these and other treatments.

Prior to the 1952 DSM classification, leading psychoanalysts were optimistic about the classification and treatment of homosexuality as a mental disorder. Not surprisingly, this optimism was based on little more than conjecture. Sandor Rado was an analyst who theorized that homosexuality was a phobic response to members of the opposite gender. His "science" was to observe that lesbians choose women considered masculine and gays seek men considered feminine. Rado then concluded that heterosexual inclinations are innate and can be uncovered.

Irving Bieber, another prominent analyst, conducted an infamous study in 1962, published as *Homosexuality: A Psychoanalytic Study of Male Homosexuals*. The study has been widely criticized as inadequate because Bieber analyzed only 106 individuals; also, at least one-quarter of the subjects had previously diagnosed character disorders. Although Rado and Bieber each had a unique focus, both believed homosexuality to be unnatural and "fixable."

## SIGNIFICANCE

The inclusion of homosexuality in the DSM incited debate that has extended into the twenty-first century. After homosexuality (as a mental illness) was removed from the DSM in 1973, Bruce Voeller, biologist and founder of the National Gay Task Force (now the National Gay and Lesbian Task Force), argued that it was the moral responsibility of the APA to undo the injuries it caused by classifying homosexuality as an illness.

In addition to insisting that gays and lesbians be given rights to become foster parents, he declared firmly that high schools across America have a social obligation to reach out to GLBT teens who have been marginalized by society's pernicious ignorance. One way to reach out is to form GLBT student organizations.

Despite Voeller's call for the APA, local lawmakers, and secondary schools to act, and despite other radical moves to amend the injury caused by the APA's classification, many people continue to insist that homosexuality is a mental disorder and that it can be treated. Reparative therapy was devised in the nineteenth century, and it was based on the notion that because people were inherently heterosexual, homosexuality, therefore, could be "unlearned."

Unlike the more secular current of the era leading up to the 1950's, the latest belief in the ability to "cure" gays and lesbians is almost entirely backed by conservative Christian ministries, such as Coral Ridge and Focus on the Family. Furthermore, Exodus International, a Christian-based group, boasts large numbers of people claiming to have been "saved" from their homosexuality. In the 1990's, reparative therapy had been reintroduced and revitalized by Joseph Nicolosi and Charles Socarides of NARTH—the National Association for Research and Therapy of Homosexuality.

*—Christy Burbidge*

## FURTHER READING

Bayer, Ronald. *Homosexuality and American Psychiatry: The Politics of Diagnosis*. New York: Basic Books, 1981.

Cory, Donald Webster (pseud.), and John P. LeRoy (pseudo.). "Why Homosexuals Resist Cure." *Sexology* 30, no. 7 (1964): 480-482.

Galeano, Eduardo. "The Heresy of Difference." *The Progressive* 68 (January, 2004): 16-17.

Martin, Karen A. "Gender and Sexuality: Medical Opinion on Homosexuality." *Gender & Society* 7, no. 2 (June, 1993): 246-250.

Zucker, Kenneth J. "The Politics and Science of 'Reparative Therapy.'" *Archives of Sexual Behavior* 32 (October, 2003): 399-402.

SEE ALSO: May 6, 1868: Kertbeny Coins the Terms "Homosexual" and "Heterosexual"; 1869: Westphal Advocates Medical Treatment for Sexual Inversion; 1897: Ellis Publishes *Sexual Inversion*; May 14, 1897: Hirschfeld Founds the Scientific-Humanitarian Committee; 1905: Freud Rejects Third-Sex Theory; 1929: Davis's Research Identifies Lesbian Sexuality as Common and Normal; 1948: Kinsey Publishes *Sexual Behavior in the Human Male*; 1953: Kinsey Publishes *Sexual Behavior in the Human Female*; 1953-1957: Evelyn Hooker Debunks Beliefs That Homosexuality Is a "Sickness"; Dec. 15, 1973: Homosexuality Is Delisted by APA; Apr. 20, 2001: Chinese Psychiatric Association Removes Homosexuality from List of Mental Disorders.

# 1952
# ONE, INC., IS FOUNDED

*ONE, Inc., the longest-lived GLBT organization in the United States, began as the publisher of the landmark* ONE *magazine.* ONE *and ONE, Inc., expanded into an institute that conducted the first American gay studies classes and assembled a library that operates today as ONE National Gay & Lesbian Archives.*

**LOCALE:** Los Angeles, California
**CATEGORIES:** Organizations and institutions; publications; civil rights; cultural and intellectual history; laws, acts, and legal history

## KEY FIGURES

*Reed Erickson* (1917-1992), American female-to-male transsexual businessman and philanthropist
*W. Dorr Legg* (1904-1994), American activist and educator
*Don Slater* (1923-1997), American activist, editor, and collector
*Jim Kepner* (1923-1997), writer, collector, and cofounder of the ONE Institute of Homophile Studies
*Merritt M. Thompson*, cofounder of the ONE Institute of Homophile Studies
*Bailey Whitaker*, early Mattachine Society member who coined the institute's name

## SUMMARY OF EVENT

At the October 15, 1952, meeting of the Mattachine Society, members who wanted a more-visible gay social presence discussed creating a gay-focused magazine, which would provide the homophile movement the exposure it wanted. On November 29, 1952, at the Studio Bookshop in Hollywood, a vote of approval led to the founding of a nonprofit organization that would create and publish the magazine, soon to be called *ONE*. The magazine's parent would be ONE, Inc., incorporated in 1953. Early member Bailey Whitaker supplied the group's name, a name that was inspired by British essayist Thomas Carlyle's words, "A mystic bond of brotherhood makes all men one." Also, "one" was a campy nod that referred to someone gay as "one of us."

ONE's charter, in brief, established that the institute publish and distribute magazines and books, sponsor educational programs, and stimulate and sponsor research—all pertaining to "socio-sexual behavior." ONE first published *ONE* magazine in January, 1953; it had, at varying times, the subtitle *The Homosexual Magazine* or *The Homosexual Viewpoint*. ONE also was the first gay or lesbian group in the United States to have its own office, which was in downtown Los Angeles. The ONE office served as a prototype GLBT community center, providing an informal meeting space, lectures, and legal referrals. W. Dorr Legg, given a salary of $25 per week, was the first full-time, paid employee, likely making him also the first paid employee of any organization in a fledgling gay and lesbian rights movement.

Legg had the most influence on ONE in its early years, holding a long view of homophile history and studies and envisioning the organization in terms of an institute. Its model was sexologist Magnus Hirschfeld's Institute for Sexual Science, founded in Berlin in 1919. (Nazis had stormed the institute and burned its books in 1933.) Legg saw ONE as a center of learning and a degree-granting institution. In 1955, Legg, Jim Kepner, and Merritt M. Thompson, a retired University of Southern California (USC) professor, conceptualized what would become the ONE Institute of Homophile Studies in 1956. ONE preferred the term "homophile" to the more clinical term "homosexual" and its awkward combining of root words from two languages.

The institute was supported by academic apparatuses, including conferences, classes, a research library, and a means to publish research. These were set up professionally with Merritt's input. There were classes in the history of homosexuality, famous homosexuals, homosexuality and religion, and other topics.

In 1961, ONE moved to larger quarters at 2256 Venice Boulevard, and in 1964, businessman Reed Erickson began to provide money for ONE's educational services. ONE established the Institute for the Study of Human Resources (ISHR) as a nonprofit tax-exempt charitable arm of ONE, funded by the Erickson Educational Foundation. ONE's supporters also included researchers Evelyn Hooker and Blanche Baker and prominent gay persons such as Gerald Heard and writer Christopher Isherwood, who introduced Hooker to ONE at an ISHR fund-raiser in 1974.

In 1965, Don Slater, who by this time was a long-time editor of *ONE* magazine, in an act that has come to be called "The Heist," removed everything from the magazine's offices to another location. The magazine's library, office contents, historical files, and mailing list were taken by Slater and some of his supporters. Slater had been in conflict with Legg for various reasons, including personal and ideological. After Slater's "heist," Legg had to rely

on his memory of the mailing list to continue circulating the magazine. Lawsuits ensued, with Legg retaining the right to use the name ONE, Inc. ONE soon received a needed boost when Erickson provided the Milbank estate to the institute, an estate that had two large houses in what was once an opulent area of Los Angeles. In time, Legg and Erickson quarreled, however, leaving the use of the house and its inheritance in dispute.

## SIGNIFICANCE

In a time when few were daring enough to join a gay or lesbian organization, neither ONE nor any of the contemporary organizations had great numbers of members. They could reach more people through their magazines and newsletters, however.

Legg saw homophile studies as interdisciplinary, a view that prevails into the twenty-first century. Class attendance was sparse, although articles and publicity made it seem otherwise.

Through ISHR funding, Legg, Vern Bullough,

---

## ONE'S ARTICLES OF INCORPORATION (1953)

### A. Primary Purposes:

That the specific and primary purposes for which this corporation was formed are to publish and disseminate a magazine dealing primarily with homosexuality from the scientific, historical and critical point of view, and to aid in the social integration and rehabilitation of the sexual variant.

### B. General Purposes:

That the general purposes for which this corporation is formed, in addition to those enumerated above, are as follows:

1. To publish and disseminate magazines, brochures, leaflets, books and papers concerned with medical, social, pathological, psychological and therapeutic research of every kind and description pertaining to socio-sexual behavior.

2. To sponsor, supervise and conduct educational, programs, lectures and concerts for the aid and benefit of all social and emotional variants and to promote among the general public an interest, knowledge and understanding of the problems of such persons.

3. To stimulate, sponsor, aid, supervise and conduct research of every kind and description pertaining to socio-sexual behavior.

4. To promote the integration into society of such persons whose behavior varies from current moral and social standards and to aid the development of social and moral responsibility in all such persons.

5. To lease, purchase, hold, have, use and take possession of and enjoy any personal or real property necessary for the uses and purposes of the corporation, and to sell, lease, deed in trust, alien or dispose of the same at the pleasure of the corporation, and for the purposes and uses for which said corporation is formed and to buy and sell real or personal property and to apply the proceeds of the sale, including any and all income, to the uses and purposes of the corporation.

6. To do any and all other acts, things, business or businesses in any manner connected with or necessary, incidental, convenient, or auxiliary to any of the objects hereinbefore enumerated or calculated, directly or indirectly, to promote the interest of the corporation.

Barry Elcano, and others in 1964 began what would become *An Annotated Bibliography of Homosexuality* (1976), a two-volume compilation. The first advanced degrees in homophile studies—master's and doctorate—were given in 1984, when the institute moved to the Milbank estate. In the end, however, the rush of mainstream institutions to offer lesbian and gay studies programs of their own in the 1990's made the institute ultimately unnecessary. Legg, along with others, wrote a history of the institute's accomplishments that was to be issued just before his death.

ONE composed a lengthy draft bill of homosexual rights in 1961 that included civil rights as well. It read, in part, "Work rights. The right to employment without discrimination in either private or public capacity; the right to military service without prejudice or penalty." It formulated questions that are still germane, such as, "Can democratic voting procedures determine moral and ethical questions?" and "Does the State have authority to proscribe sex behavior?"

It is possible to see the shell of all future GLBT activism and community building in ONE's history, whether or not ONE itself was successful in that activism; ONE was not immune to many of the social concerns of the day, including the rights of women and the place of lesbians within the organization. For example, although women helped to write and design *ONE* magazine, they did not have significant input into the day-to-day running of ONE.

There was a signal achievement when the institute's library was united with the archives of Jim Kepner, who had written for *ONE* magazine. With this merger the name ONE remained and thus survives actively as the longest-lived GLBT organization in the United States. ONE, Inc.'s, name was changed in 2004 to ONE National Gay & Lesbian Archives, and it is run by a board of directors, numerous volunteers, and a full-time staff when funding is available.

—*Dan Luckenbill*

## FURTHER READING

Bullough, Vern L., Judith M. Saunders, and C. Todd White, eds. *Before Stonewall: Activists for Gay and Lesbian Rights in Historical Context.* New York: Harrington Park Press, 2002.

D'Emilio, John. *Sexual Politics, Sexual Communities: The Making of a Homosexual Minority in the United States, 1940-1970.* 2d ed. Chicago: University of Chicago Press, 1998.

Devor, Aaron H., and Nicholas Matte. "ONE Inc. and Reed Erickson: The Uneasy Collaboration of Gay and Trans Activism, 1964-2003." *GLQ: A Journal of Lesbian and Gay Studies* 10, no. 2 (2004): 179-209.

Gregory, Robert. "ONE Institute, 1955-1960: A Report." *Homophile Studies* 3 (1960): 214-220.

Legg, W. Dorr, David G. Cameron, and Walter L. Williams, eds. *Homophile Studies in Theory and Practice.* San Francisco, Calif.: ONE Institute Press and GLB Publishers, 1994.

Williams, Walter L., and Yolanda Retter, eds. *Gay and Lesbian Rights in the United States: A Documentary History.* Westport, Conn.: Greenwood Press, 2003.

**SEE ALSO:** Dec. 10, 1924: Gerber Founds the Society for Human Rights; 1950: Mattachine Society Is Founded; 1953: *ONE* Magazine Begins Publication; 1955: Daughters of Bilitis Founded as First National Lesbian Group in United States; May 27-30, 1960: First National Lesbian Conference Convenes; Apr. 19, 1967: First Student Homophile League Is Formed; May 22, 1967: U.S. Supreme Court Upholds Law Preventing Immigration of Gays and Lesbians; Aug. 11-18, 1968: NACHO Formally Becomes the First Gay Political Coalition; July 31, 1969: Gay Liberation Front Is Formed; June 28, 1970: First Lesbian and Gay Pride March in the United States; Nov. 28, 1970: Del Martin Quits Gay Liberation Movement; 1973: National Gay Task Force Is Formed; Fall, 1973: Lesbian Herstory Archives Is Founded; Oct. 18, 1973: Lambda Legal Authorized to Practice Law; Mar. 5, 1974: Antigay and Antilesbian Organizations Begin to Form; 1975: First Gay and Lesbian Archives Is Founded; Apr. 22, 1980: Human Rights Campaign Fund Is Founded; Aug., 1991: Leather Archives and Museum Is Founded.

**1952-1990**
# U.S. Law Prohibits Gay and Lesbian Immigration

*Between 1952 and 1990, U.S. immigration law prohibited lesbians and gays from visiting, immigrating to, or becoming naturalized citizens of the United States. The U.S. Supreme Court upheld this policy in 1967, and the Immigration Act of 1990 revised it to the benefit of GLBT persons.*

**ALSO KNOWN AS:** McCarran-Walter Immigration and Nationality Act
**LOCALE:** Washington, D.C.
**CATEGORIES:** Laws, acts, and legal history; civil rights

**KEY FIGURES**
*Barney Frank* (b. 1940), Democratic representative from Massachusetts
*Alan Cranston* (1914-2000), Democratic senator from California

## SUMMARY OF EVENT
Although many countries have laws criminalizing homosexual acts, between 1952 and 1990 the United States had an official policy of refusing entry to visitors and potential immigrants on the basis of their sexual orientation. Immigrants who entered the country legally but were later discovered to be homosexual were ineligible for citizenship and could be deported at any time, regardless of how many years they had lived in the United States as law-abiding residents. This strict exclusion policy was in place for decades even though the word "homosexual" never directly appeared in U.S. immigration law.

In 1952 the U.S. Congress passed the McCarran-Walter Immigration and Nationality Act, which focused on the exclusion from entry of communists, anarchists, and other alleged subversives. Although the 1952 act was the first to include homosexuals, it must be viewed in the context of long-standing policies of excluding "undesirable" races, nationalities, and minority groups. Prostitutes, polygamists, paupers, alcoholics, drug addicts, and the mentally and physically disabled, as well as those who could not prove "good moral character," were also barred from legal entry.

The homosexual exclusion policy of the new law cannot be understood apart from the Cold War context in which the "homosexual menace" was conflated with communism and un-American activities. In 1950 the U.S. Senate conducted a massive investigation into "sex perverts" in government. This investigation laid the groundwork for President Dwight D. Eisenhower's executive order banning homosexuals from federal employment, which resulted in the resignation or termination of more than one thousand employees during the following three years. Meanwhile, the military purged thousands of suspected homosexuals from its ranks each year.

In 1950 the Senate's drafting committee proposed that the new immigration law explicitly bar foreigners deemed "psychopathic personalities" or who were thought to be "homosexuals and sex perverts." However, when advised by the U.S. Public Health Service (PHS) that psychiatrists considered the term "psychopathic personality" to be "sufficiently broad" to include homosexuals, Congress omitted the phrase "homosexuals and sex perverts" from the final wording. Nevertheless, Congress clearly specified for the legislative record that the change in terminology was "not to be construed in any way as modifying the intent to exclude all aliens who are sexual deviates." Thus, even though the law never used the word "homosexual," Congress made clear its goal of preventing the entry of all such persons into the United States.

## SIGNIFICANCE
It is impossible to know how many potential visitors and immigrants had been affected by this policy, as the Immigration and Naturalization Service (INS) maintained no exact records. Moreover, most foreigners who apply for visas do so at U.S. embassies in their home countries. No records exist regarding

the degree to which embassy officials abroad grilled visa applicants on their sexual orientation. Some reports suggest that until the 1980's the INS routinely queried foreign nationals arriving in the United States regarding their sexual and criminal histories. Grounds for suspicion could include appearance, non-gender-conforming dress, unmarried status, possession of gay or lesbian literature, or plans to attend a gay rights conference. In an unusually well-publicized case from 1979, two Mexican men were refused entry, one because he was carrying what INS officials said "looked like a woman's handbag" and the other because he was wearing a gold earring.

Anecdotal evidence indicates that some INS border officials deliberately singled out suspected homosexuals. One lawyer reported that an INS officer on the Mexican border in the 1960's was responsible for the exclusion or deportation of hundreds of Mexican women for "sexual deviation." "Manish"-looking women were particularly susceptible. Canadian women attending the Michigan Womyn's Music Festival in the early 1980's reported being harassed by border officials and questioned in detail about their sex lives.

Since foreign nationals who were denied entry into the United States had no legal right to appeal their exclusion, nearly all challenges to the law involved immigrants who were granted legal entry but later faced deportation when the INS became aware of their homosexuality. Before an immigrant could leave the United States, whether for a family visit or for a trip abroad, he or she had to undergo a reentry hearing upon return. In 1961, Sara Quiroz was stopped at the U.S.-Mexico border after a family visit because her short hair and trousers aroused suspicion. At first she denied being a lesbian, but after repeated questioning she admitted she was a lesbian and was refused reentry. In her legal challenge Quiroz asserted that her homosexuality did not necessarily make her a psychopathic personality. Despite the testimony of two doctors on her behalf, a U.S. Court of Appeals, in *Quiroz v. Neelly*, rejected her argument and upheld her deportation.

In 1962, however, a different appeals court held that the term "psychopathic personality" was too vague to be indiscriminately applied to all homo-

sexuals (*Fleuti v. Rosenberg*). The court relied on medical experts who expressed the profession's growing skepticism regarding the term's usefulness and legitimacy. Unfortunately, this victory was short-lived. At the urging of both the PHS and the INS, in 1965 Congress amended the McCarran-Walter Act to exclude "aliens afflicted with psychopathic personality, or sexual deviation, or a mental defect." The congressional report made it clear that "sexual deviation" was expressly intended to include homosexuality.

In 1967, the Supreme Court held that Congress had fully intended the phrase "psychopathic personality" to exclude all homosexuals and that such an exclusion was constitutional. In this case Clive Boutilier, a Canadian national, had lived in the United States for eight years when he applied for citizenship. After the PHS determined that he was a homosexual, the INS instituted deportation hearings. The Supreme Court upheld his deportation (*Boutilier v. INS*). However, during the 1970's some judges rejected the Supreme Court's ruling. In 1971, a New York district court granted citizenship to a gay Cuban man, ruling that homosexuality per se did not preclude the finding of "good moral character" required for naturalization (*In re Labady*).

Under the 1952 act, legal immigrants also faced deportation following arrest for unspecified "crimes of moral turpitude." These typically referred to "morals offenses" such as loitering, solicitation, lewd and lascivious behavior, disorderly conduct, or vagrancy, all of which were associated with public homosexuality. Gay men, the targets of undercover police entrapment operations at places frequented by gays, were far more likely than lesbians to be deported under this provision. While homosexuality per se might go undetected, arrests for solicitation branded male resident aliens. In a representative case, a Greek immigrant was deported in 1959 after thirty-nine years in the United States. He had twice been convicted of disorderly conduct for "loiter[ing] about [a] public place soliciting men for the purpose of committing a crime against nature. . . ." Local police informed the INS, which ordered his deportation (*Babouris v. Esperdy*).

As *Babouris* suggests, police were supposed to

> ### FROM THE MCCARRAN-WALTER IMMIGRATION AND NATIONALITY ACT (1952)
>
> *General Classes of Aliens Ineligible to Receive Visas and Excluded from Admission*
>
> Sec. 212. (a) Except as otherwise provided in this Act, the following classes of aliens shall be ineligible to receive visas and shall be excluded from admission into the United States: . . .
>
> (9) Aliens who have been convicted of a crime involving moral turpitude (other than a purely political offense), or aliens who admit having committed such a crime, or aliens who admit committing acts which constitute the essential elements of such a crime; . . .
>
> (13) Aliens coming to the United States to engage in any immoral sexual act.

contact the INS following an alien's arrest. However, this occurred irregularly. In most cases the INS became aware of criminal charges indicating homosexuality from questioning during a reentry interview. For gay and lesbian immigrants, any trip abroad could exact a heavy price: denied reentry. In addition, any time resident aliens sought to change status (for example, from a student visa to permanent residency status) they had to undergo another examination, which also carried the risk of deportation. In 1965, a Filipino student sought permanent residency. After the required medical examination, the PHS physician issued a certificate classifying him as a sexual deviate. Dismissing his claim that he had not been a homosexual at the time of his original entry, the appeals court upheld his deportation (*Campos v. Immigration and Naturalization Service*, 1968). In all of these situations, the numbers of immigrants affected remain unknown.

After the American Psychiatric Association (APA) declared in 1973 that it would no longer classify homosexuality as a mental disease, APA president John Spiegel urged the INS to stop excluding and deporting homosexuals. The INS replied that it was legally obligated to uphold the law. However, in 1979, the PHS director, Surgeon General Julius

Richmond, referring to the APA's decision, told the INS that the PHS no longer viewed homosexuality as a medically certifiable condition and would no longer participate in exclusion proceedings.

The INS was caught in a bind. The 1952 act required officials to send suspected homosexuals for an interview with a PHS physician, who issued a "Certificate A" declaring that the applicant was a psychopathic personality (or sexual deviate) and thus barred from entry. Without this certificate there were no legal grounds for exclusion. In 1980 the Justice Department announced new INS guidelines for "the inspection of aliens who are suspected of being homosexual." INS inspectors would no longer ask any direct questions about an individual's sexual orientation. Nor would possession of gay literature, wearing of gay rights buttons or T-shirts, or attendance at a gay rights conference be considered grounds for further questioning. However, in the event that an individual made an "unsolicited, unambiguous . . . admission of homosexuality," he or she would be asked to sign a statement and would be referred for an exclusion hearing. Not all INS officers immediately complied with these less repressive guidelines, resulting in the increasingly arbitrary processing of suspected homosexuals.

Contradictory court decisions added to the confusion, resulting in even more inconsistent treatment. In 1983 the Ninth U.S. Circuit Court of Appeals held that the INS could not exclude an out gay person without a PHS medical certificate (*Hill v. INS*). The court went further and questioned the constitutionality of the INS exclusion policy. However, three weeks later the Fifth U.S. Circuit Court of Appeals ruled that the INS could deny citizenship to a homosexual applicant solely because he was gay. The plaintiff, a British citizen and small-business owner, had been a law-abiding resident for eighteen years and had never been charged with a crime (*Longstaff v. INS*).

As during earlier periods, the numbers affected remain unknowable. INS official statistics indicate that 172 applicants were denied entry to the United States between 1984 and 1988 under the category "aliens afflicted with psychopathic personality, or sexual deviation, or a mental defect." However, there is no breakdown that lists how many were considered gay. Moreover, as mentioned, these statistics do not include all those applying for admission to the United States, such as those who were denied visas by embassy officials abroad or those whom INS officials informally persuaded at the border not to bother applying for entry. Rather than risking an official record of denied entry, "effeminate" males or "manly" women might choose to try their luck another day.

Throughout the 1980's many fought for a total repeal. Gay U.S. representative Barney Frank (Democrat, Massachusetts) and Senator Alan Cranston (Democrat, California) led the fight in Congress while gay rights legal groups lobbied behind the scenes. In 1980, Cranston submitted the first bill to rescind the "sexual deviates" clause. The Justice Department endorsed the bill, which quickly died in committee. In 1984 and 1987 officials in the administration of President Ronald Reagan publicly endorsed an end to the exclusion policy in congressional hearings.

Finally, with very little fanfare, Congress eliminated the homosexual exclusion clause from the Immigration Act of 1990. With that, gays and lesbians gained the legal right to enter the United States as visitors, speakers, or immigrants without hiding their identities. However, because the "crimes involving moral turpitude" exclusion was not amended, even after the 1990 act lesbians and gays were at risk of deportation if convicted of sodomy or a public morality offense. Some courts continued to hold that homosexuals could be denied citizenship under the "good moral character" requirement, which remained in the 1990 act. However, after the historic *Lawrence v. Texas* decision in 2003, in which the Supreme Court finally struck down state sodomy laws as unconstitutional, the last grounds for homosexual deportation and denial of citizenship were eliminated.

In 2004, immigrants constituted 10 percent of the U.S. population, more than 30 million people—the largest number ever in the nation's history. Given that statistic, it is clear that the end of homosexual exclusion has had an enormously liberating effect on the lives of millions of gay and lesbian immigrants and their partners, families, and friends. In addition gays and lesbians won the right to seek political asylum in the United States. In 1994, Attorney General Janet Reno formalized a 1990 administrative decision that accepted sexual orientation as a basis for asylum for applicants who could document a "well-founded fear of persecution" in their home countries.

Although the INS has granted asylum to several hundred gays and lesbians, groups such as Immigration Equality express concern over the many inconsistencies uncovered in INS decision making. Applicants from the same country are often treated very differently. Moreover, other provisions of immigration law continue to discriminate against gays and lesbians. Unlike heterosexual couples, U.S. citizens or permanent residents in a same-gender relationship with a foreign national who is temporarily residing in the United States (for example, on a student visa) have no right to request legal residency for their partners. As a result, thousands of binational couples live in fear of being separated. Similarly, unlike heterosexuals, gay and lesbian immigrants do not have the right to sponsor their partners from abroad. In 2000, the Permanent Partners Immigration Act (PPIA) was first introduced in Congress; it was unsuccessful. In contrast to the United States, sixteen countries grant immigration rights to same-gender couples.

In addition to these unresolved issues, a new form of exclusion has been created. The 1993 National Institutes of Health Revitalization Act barred admission to the United States of anyone with HIV-AIDS and required mandatory testing of immigrants applying for permanent residency. Those who test positive can be deported. This has had a disproportionate impact on gays and lesbians and remains a major issue for GLBT immigration rights groups.

*—L. Mara Dodge*

## FURTHER READING

Cain, Patricia A. *Rainbow Rights: The Role of Lawyers and Courts in the Lesbian and Gay Civil Rights Movement*. Cambridge, Mass.: Westview Press, 2000.

Canaday, Margot. "'Who Is a Homosexual?' The Consolidation of Sexual Identities in Mid-Twentieth Century American Immigration Law." *Law and Social Inquiry* 28 (2003): 351-386.

Eskridge, William N. *Gaylaw: Challenging the Apartheid of the Closet.* Cambridge, Mass.: Harvard University Press, 1999.

Luibhéid, Eithne. *Entry Denied: Controlling Sexuality at the Border.* Minneapolis: University of Minnesota Press, 2002.

Murdoch, Joyce, and Deb Price. *Courting Justice: Gay Men and Lesbians v. the Supreme Court.* New York: Basic Books, 2001.

Rubenstein, William B. *Cases and Materials on Sexual Orientation and the Law: Lesbians, Gay Men, and the Law.* 2d ed. St. Paul, Minn.: West, 1997.

**SEE ALSO:** Jan. 12, 1939: *Thompson v. Aldredge* Dismisses Sodomy Charges Against Lesbians; May 22, 1967: U.S. Supreme Court Upholds Law Preventing Immigration of Gays and Lesbians; Jan. 22, 1973: *Roe v. Wade* Legalizes Abortion and Extends Privacy Rights; June 21, 1973: U.S. Supreme Court Supports Local Obscenity Laws; Aug., 1973: American Bar Association Calls for Repeal of Laws Against Consensual Sex; Nov. 17, 1975: U.S. Supreme Court Rules in "Crimes Against Nature" Case; 1981: Gay and Lesbian Palimony Suits Emerge; 1982-1991: Lesbian Academic and Activist Sues University of California for Discrimination; 1986: *Bowers v. Hardwick* Upholds State Sodomy Laws; May 1, 1989: U.S. Supreme Court Rules Gender-Role Stereotyping Is Discriminatory; Dec. 17, 1991: Minnesota Court Awards Guardianship to Lesbian Partner; 1992-2006: Indians Struggle to Abolish Sodomy Law; 1993-1996: Hawaii Opens Door to Same-Gender Marriages; Sept. 21, 1993-Apr. 21, 1995: Lesbian Mother Loses Custody of Her Child; Dec. 20, 1999: *Baker v. Vermont* Leads to Recognition of Same-Gender Civil Unions; June 28, 2000: *Boy Scouts of America v. Dale*; June 26, 2003: U.S. Supreme Court Overturns Texas Sodomy Law.

---

## 1953
# KINSEY PUBLISHES *SEXUAL BEHAVIOR IN THE HUMAN FEMALE*

*Alfred Kinsey continued his controversial sex research and found that about 2 percent of unmarried Anglo-American women and between 2 percent and 6 percent of all women between ages twenty and thirty-five—married or unmarried—were lesbians exclusively.*

**LOCALE:** Bloomington, Indiana
**CATEGORIES:** Science; publications; organizations and institutions

**KEY FIGURE**
*Alfred Kinsey* (1894-1956), biologist and sex researcher

**SUMMARY OF EVENT**
Alfred Kinsey's *Sexual Behavior in the Human Female* (1953) was released to a wondering reading public several years after his unprecedented study of the sexuality of males, *Sexual Behavior in the Human Male* (1948). Research for the men's and women's studies began and ended simultaneously, and Kinsey's findings in the area of female sexuality largely corresponded with what he had learned about men's sexuality. The findings on women's sexuality were shocking to the American public, who generally assumed that women were less sexual than men. The findings were used by feminists to promote women's sexual equality and to encourage further research into female sexual behavior.

topics ranging from premarital sex to masturbation to orgasm and to homosexual behavior.

Kinsey applied the same seven-point homosexual-heterosexual rating scale, now called the Kinsey Scale, to the women as he had for the men. The scale indicated how much the participant engaged in homosexual activity. Someone ranked with a zero was considered exclusively heterosexual, and someone ranked seven was considered exclusively homosexual.

Kinsey's work showed that between 1 and 3 percent of the unmarried white women between the ages of twenty and thirty-five in his study were completely homosexual. It also said that between 2 and 6 percent of all of the women in this age range were exclusively homosexual. This reinforced the notion created in the male study that homosexuality was not a perversion. The female report also contained the notion of bisexuality, and it found that 13 percent of the women in the sample had experienced an orgasm with another woman. Also, once *Sexual Behavior in the Human Female* had been released, its results were compared with the results of the study of men's sexuality.

*Alfred Kinsey and the "birds and bees" on the cover of* Time *magazine, August 24, 1953.* (Courtesy, Time, Inc.)

Kinsey began his research after teaching a course involving the biological elements of sex as it related to marriage. He found a dearth of information about human sexuality, so he conducted a study himself beginning in 1938.

Kinsey collected interviews with a large number of women of all races, but most of his data for *Sexual Behavior in the Human Female* came from 5,940 Anglo-American women. As with the men's study, interviewers could ask questions about as many as 521 items focused on scientifically measurable sexual experiences. It is noteworthy that Kinsey stated that it was impossible to determine how many people were homosexual; only behavior at a given time could be evaluated. Kinsey asked questions about

## SIGNIFICANCE

Kinsey's findings had a huge and immediate impact on the perception of women's sexuality. Along with *Sexual Behavior in the Human Male*, this study was at the forefront of the sexual revolution. Until the study was released, it was generally believed, and accepted, that women took little physical pleasure in sex and that they engaged in it largely in order to procreate.

Kinsey's findings about premarital sex demonstrated that young women did not, as was popularly believed and encouraged, exclusively abstain from sex before they were married. Roughly 50 percent engaged in premarital sex. Kinsey's research also challenged the notion that women who masturbated before marriage did not enjoy sex after marriage. Before the study, a woman was considered mostly disinterested in things sexual, but after the study, women were considered to be not only interested in sex but also interested in sex with other women.

At the outset, however, Kinsey's findings were more helpful to heterosexual than to homosexual women. The study was released during the second red scare, at the height of McCarthyism, and it was dangerous to be or to be assumed lesbian. A woman could lose her children in a divorce for the mere *suggestion* that she was lesbian, and there were few organized groups to support her. Indeed, homophile groups in the 1950's were generally secretive. The Mattachine Society (founded 1950) and the Daughters of Bilitis (founded 1955) promised members complete privacy. These same groups looked to studies such as those of Kinsey to demonstrate that homosexuality was normal and to change public attitudes toward lesbians and gays and bisexuals.

Gays and lesbians as a group were unable to find support for their position even in the radical activist groups of the 1950's and 1960's. The gays and lesbians who participated in the civil rights movement, the movement against the Vietnam War, and the women's movement all felt constrained on the topic of sexuality. Not until 1971, did one such group—the National Organization for Women (NOW)—admit that lesbian concerns were part of the greater women's movement. To begin the process of social change, political activism earmarked toward GLBT rights specifically would have to be in place before influential studies such as the Kinsey Reports could have positive social and cultural effects.

—*Jessie Bishop Powell*

**FURTHER READING**

Gathorne-Hardy, Jonathan. *Sex the Measure of All Things: A Life of Alfred C. Kinsey.* Bloomington: Indiana University Press, 2000.

Jones, James H. *Alfred Kinsey: A Public/Private Life.* New York: W. W. Norton, 1997.

Kinsey, Alfred. *Sexual Behavior in the Human Female.* Bloomington: Indiana University Press, 1998.

_____. *Sexual Behavior in the Human Male.* Bloomington: Indiana University Press, 1998.

Martin, Del, and Phyllis Lyon. *Lesbian/Woman.* Volcano, Calif.: Volcano Press, 1991.

Miller, Diane Helene. *Freedom to Differ: The Shaping of the Gay and Lesbian Struggle for Civil Rights.* New York: New York University Press, 1998.

**SEE ALSO:** May 6, 1868: Kertbeny Coins the Terms "Homosexual" and "Heterosexual"; 1869: Westphal Advocates Medical Treatment for Sexual Inversion; 1897: Ellis Publishes *Sexual Inversion*; May 14, 1897: Hirschfeld Founds the Scientific-Humanitarian Committee; 1905: Freud Rejects Third-Sex Theory; 1929: Davis's Research Identifies Lesbian Sexuality as Common and Normal; 1948: Kinsey Publishes *Sexual Behavior in the Human Male*; 1952: APA Classifies Homosexuality as a Mental Disorder; 1953-1957: Evelyn Hooker Debunks Beliefs That Homosexuality Is a "Sickness"; Dec. 15, 1973: Homosexuality Is Delisted by APA; Apr. 20, 2001: Chinese Psychiatric Association Removes Homosexuality from List of Mental Disorders.

## 1953
# *ONE* MAGAZINE BEGINS PUBLICATION

*ONE was the first long-term gay magazine published in the United States. In 1958, it won a landmark U.S. Supreme Court case that allowed texts with gay and lesbian themes, including magazines, to be distributed through the U.S. mail.*

ALSO KNOWN AS: *ONE: The Homosexual Magazine*; *ONE: The Homosexual Viewpoint*
LOCALE: Los Angeles, California
CATEGORIES: Publications; civil rights; cultural and intellectual history; laws, acts, and legal history; literature; organizations and institutions

KEY FIGURES

*Martin Block*, American bookseller, Jewish and gay rights activist, and first editor of *ONE*
*Joan Corbin*, American activist and *ONE* graphic designer
*Joseph Hansen* (b. 1923), American author, *ONE* fiction writer
*Eric Julber*, *ONE* magazine attorney, filed brief with U.S. Supreme Court
*Jim Kepner* (1923-1997), American collector, activist, writer, educator, and first *ONE* news columnist
*W. Dorr Legg* (1904-1994), American activist, educator, and *ONE* business manager
*Stella Russell* (b. 1925), American activist, poet, and *ONE* artist
*Don Slater* (1923-1997), American activist, archivist, and third editor of *ONE*
*Irma "Corky" Wolf*, American activist and *ONE* circulation manager
*Dale Jennings*, second editor of *ONE*

SUMMARY OF EVENT

In 1952, members of the Mattachine Society in Los Angeles discussed forming a magazine; that same year, they founded ONE, Inc., the magazine's parent. The first issue of *ONE*, dated January, 1953,

was published with the subtitle *The Homosexual Magazine*; later in its history, it carried the subtitle *The Homosexual Viewpoint*. *ONE* was one of the first three long-term gay publications in the United States; all three originated in California.

Early names associated with *ONE* include W. Dorr Legg, who was hired as business manager, and Martin Block, the first editor. The next editor was Dale Jennings, a Mattachine member, and then Don Slater. Early graphic design was done by Joan Corbin (as Eve Elloree), and Irma "Corky" Wolf (as Ann Carll Reid) was circulation manager.

The first issues were plain but had bold graphics, were typeset, and came in an odd size, almost square. This changed to a 5.5 by 8.5-inch format, which came through folding an 8.5 by 11-inch sheet of paper. It was first distributed by hand in bars but then sold at newsstands. It reached readers in all states, and its highest circulation was five thousand.

Women were represented in the pages of *ONE* as well. The first issue had a poem by Helen Ito and an article by Betty Perdue (a friend of Jim Kepner), writing as Geraldine Jackson. The February, 1954, issue was titled "The Feminine Viewpoint," and another issue featured a cover portrait of "Sten Rush" (Stella Russell). Kepner, who wrote a news column for *ONE*, was the first person to do so in a gay publication. Kepner's news columns were filled primarily with news of arrests and were taken from his own clippings and from those sent to him by readers.

In 1965, Slater, who by this time was a longtime editor of *ONE*, in an act that has come to be called "The Heist," removed everything from *ONE*'s offices to another location. The magazine's library, office contents, its historical files, and its mailing list were taken by Slater and some of his supporters. Slater had been in conflict with Legg for various reasons, including personal and ideological. After Slater's "heist," Legg had to rely on his memory of the mailing list to continue circulating the magazine. Lawsuits ensued, with Legg retaining the right to use the name ONE, Inc. Slater began another

ONE *magazine had a cover story on same-gender marriage as early as 1953.* (Courtesy, ONE National Gay & Lesbian Archives)

Olesen stopped the mailing of the October, 1954, issue. ONE sued the Postal Service but lost. ONE's lawyer, Eric Julber, appealed the decision and lost twice, and the magazine was declared "lewd, obscene, lascivious, and filthy." Julber used his own money to travel to Washington, D.C., to deliver a brief to the U.S. Supreme Court.

In January, 1958, and in a victory for gay and lesbian rights, the Court decided the case, *ONE, Inc. v. Olesen*, without a hearing. It based its decision on the earlier *Roth v. United States* ruling, in which the Court determined that the mere discussion of sexual matters was not in itself obscene. This decision, although limited, has been termed the sole victory for gays and lesbians of the 1950's, according to historian John D'Emilio, and paved the way for more lesbian and gay publications. Also in 1958, and after the Court decision, the cover of *ONE* was emblazoned with the words "I Am Glad I Am a Homosexual," an article written by Legg (as Hollister Barnes).

magazine titled *Tangents*, which also drew in Kepner and Joseph Hansen, but *Tangents* lasted only until 1970. *ONE* did not adapt to the more militant political messages of the late 1960's gay and lesbian rights movement and so published its last issue in 1969 (although it published again in 1972).

## SIGNIFICANCE

*ONE* magazine faced opposition from three sources: the U.S. Postal Service; the Federal Bureau of Investigation (FBI); and Alexander Wiley, a Republican senator from Wisconsin. Wiley had alerted the FBI to an issue of *ONE* that implied that homosexuals held key positions in the FBI. The FBI began its surveillance of *ONE* and its staff.

The Postal Service seized an issue of *ONE* and released it. Then, Los Angeles postmaster Otto

Letters from readers to the editors in the early years of *ONE* remain some of the most valuable windows into gay life in the United States at that time. Readers poured their hearts out in their communications, many for the first and only time able to communicate their innermost feelings. Many letters were published, and many others are archived as valuable resources at the ONE National Gay & Lesbian Archives in Los Angeles.

*ONE* contributors set the debate for the decades that followed the magazine's early years. A cover story in its first year asked, "Homosexual Marriage?" *ONE* treated this topic again in 1963, with the title "Let's Push Homophile Marriage." Other special topics included "Homosexual Servicemen" and "What About Religion?" *ONE* added humor with banners and cover illustrations for "Something About Sailors," "Homo Beatniks," and, "Bring Your Own Bikini."

An early edition of *ONE* also had a gay travel article, which gave information about a gay beach at Santa Monica Canyon (in Los Angeles County). Book reviews were numerous and contributed to a developing canon of gay literature. Articles also discussed transgender persons to some degree.

The most important writer of nonfiction to emerge from the magazine was Jim Kepner, who framed gay issues in ways that are still germane. The editors also persuaded well-known writer Norman Mailer to contribute "The Homosexual Villain," a piece about the gay character in his novel *The Deer Park*. Mailer had been worried that *ONE*'s readership would be repelled by the novel's villainous character. The most important writer of fiction for *ONE* was Joseph Hansen, writing as James Colton. Colton is best known for his successful Dave Brandstetter mysteries, which he wrote after his work for *ONE*.

—*Dan Luckenbill*

**FURTHER READING**

Gannett, Lewis, and William A. Percy III. "Jim Kepner (1923-1997)." In *Before Stonewall: Activists for Gay and Lesbian Rights in Historical Context*, edited by Vern L. Bullough, Judith M. Saunders, and C. Todd White. New York: Harrington Park Press, 2002.

Kepner, Jim. *Rough News, Daring Views: 1950's Pioneer Gay Press Journalism*. New York: Haworth Press, 1998.

Murdoch, Joyce, and Deb Price. *Courting Justice: Gay Men and Lesbians v. the Supreme Court*. New York: Basic Books, 2001.

Streitmatter, Rodger. *Unspeakable: The Rise of the Gay and Lesbian Press in America*. Boston: Faber and Faber, 1995.

**SEE ALSO:** 1952: ONE, Inc., Is Founded; Fall, 1973: Lesbian Herstory Archives Is Founded; 1975: First Gay and Lesbian Archives Is Founded; Aug., 1991: Leather Archives and Museum Is Founded.

## 1953-1957
# EVELYN HOOKER DEBUNKS BELIEFS THAT HOMOSEXUALITY IS A "SICKNESS"

*In a study of homosexual men and heterosexual men, Evelyn Hooker found that gay men were no more likely to be mentally ill than their heterosexual counterparts. Her work was a major factor in the development of studies of homosexuality.*

**LOCALE:** Los Angeles, California
**CATEGORIES:** Health and medicine; science

**KEY FIGURES**

*Evelyn Hooker* (1907-1996), psychologist at the University of California, Los Angeles
*John Eberhart*, chief of the National Institute of Mental Health

**SUMMARY OF EVENT**

Psychologist Evelyn Hooker began a research study in 1953 that would change the world's attitudes toward homosexuality, and in 1992, the American Psychological Association summarized her study as "revolutionary," a study that "provided empirical evidence that normal homosexuals existed, and supported the radical idea then emerging that homosexuality is within the normal range of human behavior."

Hooker's research, supported by the National Institute of Mental Health (NIMH), compared nonclinical, matched samples of homosexually oriented and heterosexually oriented men. Her findings would rock the foundations of psychological

## "HOMOSEXUALITY AS A CLINICAL ENTITY DOES NOT EXIST"

Homosexuality as a clinical entity does not exist. Its forms are as varied as those of heterosexuality. Homosexuality may be a deviation in sexual pattern, which is within the normal range, psychologically. The role of particular forms of sexual desire and expression in personality structure and development may be less important than has frequently been assumed.

*Source:* Evelyn Hooker, "The Adjustment of the Male Overt Homosexual," *Journal of Projective Techniques* 21 (1957).

assumptions and practice for counseling gay men. Those findings challenged the widespread belief that homosexuality is a psychological sickness by demonstrating that experienced clinicians using psychological tests, widely believed at the time to be appropriate, could not differentiate the nonclinical, homosexually oriented group from the nonclinical, heterosexually oriented group. She concluded that gay men were no more likely to exhibit mental illness than were their heterosexually oriented counterparts.

Until Hooker's study, psychiatrists, psychologists, counselors, and others who ministered to the mental health needs of gay men began their work assuming that homosexually oriented men were by definition neurotic, unstable, infantile, and identifiable. Most of the research published before Hooker's time came from psychiatrists who studied gay men who were seeking psychological treatment and consisted of individual case studies of their patients.

When Bruno Klopfer—with whom Hooker shared an office at the University of California, Los Angeles, and the person who wrote the definitive book on the interpretation of the Rorschach Inkblot Test—learned that Hooker was thinking about such a study, he "jumped out of his chair and said, 'You must do it, Eee-vah-leeeen! You must do it! Your friend is absolutely right. We don't know anything about people like him. The only ones we know

about are people who come to us as patients. And, of course, many of those who come to us are very disturbed, pathological. You must do it!'"

Despite the stigma associated with homosexuality and given that gays were being forced out of government jobs and were being arrested in police raids, Hooker boldly submitted her grant proposal for funding by NIMH. The reply was not long in coming. John Eberhart, then chief of the NIMH grants division, flew out to spend a day with Hooker to "make sure she was not a Lesbian." Her application, she was told, was quite extraordinary, especially because it was submitted at the height of the McCarthy era, when communists, and gays, were being purged from government service.

Hooker's research design was rigorous—and the controversial nature of her study demanded rigor. Hooker approached two gay groups, the Mattachine Society and ONE, to help her recruit seventy-four exclusively gay men who had never been in therapy or in trouble with the law. Finding volunteers for such a study during the McCarthy era was very difficult; many gay men were afraid of having their sexual orientation exposed for fear of losing their jobs. As confidentiality was imperative, Hooker insisted on conducting all of the interviews at her home office even though university officials had demanded that the research be conducted at the university.

In the study, Hooker administered three standard personality tests—the Chicago Inventory of Beliefs, the Thematic Apperception Test, and the Rorschach Inkblot Test—to two groups of thirty men. In one of the groups, the participants were gay. The two groups were matched in age, IQ, and educational level. She then had three expert clinicians examine her results. Unaware of the subjects' sexual orientation, these expert judges could not distinguish between the two groups based on the test results, and they found no discernible pathology among the gay participants.

The study was published as "The Adjustment of the Male Overt Homosexual" in the *Journal of Projective Techniques* in 1957. Like any study on a controversial issue, Hooker's was criticized by others in the field, who said she conducted the study on members of homophile groups who were fighting for gay and lesbian rights and were, thus, probably better adjusted than those not affiliated with such groups.

## SIGNIFICANCE

Despite criticism, Evelyn Hooker's study influenced the American Psychiatric Association's decision to remove homosexuality from the *Diagnostic and Statistical Manual of Mental Disorders* in 1973. She was honored with the 1991 American Psychological Association's Award for Distinguished Contributions to Psychology in the Public Interest.

In September, 1967, Stanley Yolles, director of the National Institute of Mental Health, appointed Hooker as chair of a task force on homosexuality. The task force's fifteen members included Chief Justice David Bazelon of the U.S. Court of Appeals; Judd Marmor, University of Southern California professor of psychiatry and president of the American Psychiatric Association (who led the 1973 APA's reclassification of homosexuality); Professors Jerome Frank, Morris Ploscowe, Seward Hiltner, John Money, and Edwin Schur; and other prestigious specialists. However, historian Jim Kepner recorded that

> Hooker rejected well-qualified Martin Hoffman for the committee for fear his private gayness would be thought to invalidate the committee's impartiality. On October 10, 1969, the Task Force recommended, with minor dissents, additional research and education, intensive research on possible prevention and treatment factors, repeal of legal penalties on private, adult consensual homosexual acts, and the ending of employment discrimination. The Nixon Administration buried the report and fired Dr. Yolles. The report finally appeared in ONE Institute's *Quarterly of Homophile Studies*, its last issue, number 22, in 1972.

Hooker's work was instrumental in the establishment of homosexuality as a legitimate area of study. The University of Chicago honored her for this accomplishment by establishing the Evelyn Hooker Center for the Mental Health of Gays and Lesbians. She is also the subject of a documentary film, *Changing Our Minds: The Story of Dr. Evelyn Hooker*, directed by Richard Schmiechen and produced by David Haugland in 1991. The film was nominated for an Academy Award as Best Documentary.

—*Mark Pope*

## FURTHER READING

Boxer, Andrew M., and Joseph M. Carrier. "Evelyn Hooker: A Life Remembered." *Journal of Homosexuality* 36, no. 1 (1998): 1-17.

Hooker, Evelyn. "The Adjustment of the Male Overt Homosexual." *Journal of Projective Techniques* 21 (1957): 18-31.

_____. "An Empirical Study of Some Relations Between Sexual Patterns and Gender Identity in Male Homosexuals." In *Sex Research: New Developments*, edited by John Money. New York: Holt, Rinehart & Winston, 1965.

_____. "Homosexuality: Summary of Studies." In *Sex Ways in Fact and Faith*, edited by E. M. Duvall and S. M. Duvall. New York: Association Press, 1961.

_____. "Male Homosexuality." In *Taboo Topics*, edited by N. L. Farberow. New York: Atherton, 1963.

_____. "Male Homosexuality in the Rorschach." *Journal of Projective Techniques* 23 (1958): 278-281.

_____. "Male Homosexuals and Their Worlds." In *Sexual Inversion: The Multiple Roots of Homosexuality*, edited by J. Marmor. New York: Basic Books, 1965.

Kepner, Jim. "A Memory of Dr. Evelyn Hooker." In *ONE Institute International Gay and Lesbian Archives Bulletin*. Los Angeles: ONE Institute, 1997. http://gaytoday.badpuppy.com/garchive/people/042897pe.htm.

Minton, Henry L. *Departing from Deviance: A History of Homosexual Rights and Emancipatory Science in America*. Chicago: University of Chicago Press, 2002.

Schmiechen, Richard. *Changing Our Minds: The Story of Dr. Evelyn Hooker* (1991). Documentary film. Catalog description at http://catalog frameline.org/titles/changing_our.html.

**SEE ALSO:** May 6, 1868: Kertbeny Coins the Terms "Homosexual" and "Heterosexual"; 1869: West-phal Advocates Medical Treatment for Sexual Inversion; 1897: Ellis Publishes *Sexual Inversion*; May 14, 1897: Hirschfeld Founds the Scientific-Humanitarian Committee; 1905: Freud Rejects Third-Sex Theory; 1929: Davis's Research Identifies Lesbian Sexuality as Common and Normal; 1948: Kinsey Publishes *Sexual Behavior in the Human Male*; 1952: APA Classifies Homosexuality as a Mental Disorder; 1953: Kinsey Publishes *Sexual Behavior in the Human Female*; Dec. 15, 1973: Homosexuality Is Delisted by APA; Apr. 20, 2001: Chinese Psychiatric Association Removes Homosexuality from List of Mental Disorders.

## April 27, 1953

# U.S. PRESIDENT EISENHOWER PROHIBITS FEDERAL EMPLOYMENT OF LESBIANS AND GAYS

*U.S. president Dwight D. Eisenhower's 1953 executive order prohibited the employment of gays and lesbians in federal government, an action that reflected a perceived risk to national security if gays and lesbians were to work as federal employees. The Civil Service Commission changed this discriminatory policy in 1975.*

**ALSO KNOWN AS:** Executive Order 10450: Security Requirements for Government Employment

**LOCALE:** Washington, D.C.

**CATEGORIES:** Civil rights; government and politics; laws, acts, and legal history

### KEY FIGURES

*Dwight D. Eisenhower* (1890-1969), U.S. president, 1953-1961

*Harry S. Truman* (1884-1972), U.S. president, 1945-1953

*Kenneth Spicer Wherry* (1892-1951), Republican senator from Nebraska

*Joseph Lister Hill* (1894-1984), Republican senator from Alabama

*Joseph McCarthy* (1908-1957), Republican senator from Wisconsin

*Clyde Roark Hoey* (1877-1954), Democratic senator from North Carolina

### SUMMARY OF EVENT

On April 27, 1953, President Dwight D. Eisenhower signed Executive Order 10450: Security Requirements for Government Employment. The order listed "sexual perversion" as a condition for firing a federal employee and for denying employment to potential applicants. Homosexuality, moral perversion, and communism were categorized as national security threats; the issue of homosexual federal workers had become a dire federal personnel policy concern.

Although President Harry S. Truman had set broad standards for dismissal from federal employment during his administration before Eisenhower, his policy toward dismissing homosexuals was seen as too weak. Eisenhower ordered the government to hire and retain employees only when "clearly consistent with the interests of national security."

Removing homosexuals from federal employment had been common practice. Since the nineteenth century, civil service regulations instructed the bureaucracy to deny examinations and refuse appointments to eligible applicants and to fire employees from their jobs for conduct unbecoming. Records indicate that several federal employees, including poet Walt Whitman, had been dismissed for being homosexual. Whitman had been fired for immoral behavior from a clerical position at the Interior Department in 1863, and Henry Gerber,

---

### "NOTORIOUSLY DISGRACEFUL CONDUCT" AND GOVERNMENT EMPLOYMENT

*Section 8.* (a) The investigations conducted pursuant to this order shall be designed to develop information as to whether the employment or retention in employment in the Federal service of the person being investigated is clearly consistent with the interests of the national security. Such information shall relate, but shall not be limited, to the following:

(1) Depending on the relation of the Government employment to the national security:

(i) Any behavior, activities, or associations which tend to show that the individual is not reliable or trustworthy.

(ii) Any deliberate misrepresentations, falsifications, or omissions of material facts.

(iii) Any criminal, infamous, dishonest, immoral, or notoriously disgraceful conduct, habitual use of intoxicants to excess, drug addiction, *sexual perversion* [emphasis added].

(iv) Any illness, including any mental condition, of a nature which in the opinion of competent medical authority may cause significant defect in the judgment or reliability of the employee, with due regard to the transient or continuing effect of the illness and the medical findings in such case.

(v) Any facts which furnish reason to believe that the individual may be subjected to coercion, influence, or pressure which may cause him to act contrary to the best interests of the national security.

---

founder of the gay political organization the Society for Human Rights, had been dismissed from the postal service in 1925 for "conduct unbecoming" a postal worker.

The investigations of Republican senator Joseph McCarthy moved the issue of gay federal employees to the top of the national agenda. Capitalizing on news reports about morality and communism, McCarthy claimed that a "homosexual underground" was aiding the "communist conspiracy." In June of 1950, Republican senators Kenneth Spicer Wherry and Joseph Lister Hill, with McCarthy's support, formed a subcommittee to study the effects of the Truman administration's employment policy concerning homosexuals. Expert testimony gave the senators enough evidence to argue that "moral perverts [were] bad national security risks because of their susceptibility to blackmail and threat of exposure."

The committee concluded that the bureaucracy had inadequate procedures to prevent homosexuals from resigning from one federal job and taking up employment in another part of the government. The Civil Service Commission, in response to the committee's recommendations, instructed federal agencies to document the reasons why employees left or lost their federal jobs, including any moral issues that could affect employees' suitability for reemployment. Civil Service commissioner Harry Mitchell suggested that local police departments report any "moral" arrest in detail to the Federal Bureau of Investigation (FBI) and the FBI in turn send the information to the Civil Service Commission for further action.

Senator Clyde Roark Hoey, a Democrat, followed these recommendations with an extensive investigation into the supposed reasons why homosexuals made undesirable federal employees. His committee concluded that the immorality and emotional instability of homosexual behavior, and the propensity for gays and lesbians to seduce "normal" people, especially the young and impressionable, constituted significant reasons to justify the prohibition of homosexuals from federal jobs. The committee recommended that the Civil Service Commission use arrest records more diligently to root out homosexual employees. Hoey argued that arrest records were desirable because a number of U.S. cities were in the process of conducting extensive sting operations against sexual deviants. The Washington, D.C., and Philadelphia, Pennsylvania, police forces averaged between one thousand and twelve hundred gay-related arrests per year in the early 1950's.

During his 1952 presidential campaign, Eisenhower promised to eradicate communists and other security risks from government and defense-industry employment. He suggested their presence had been too easily tolerated by the Truman administration. On February 2, 1953, during his first state of the union address, Eisenhower promised a new system "for keeping out the disloyal and dangerous." On April 27 he signed the executive order. McCarthy, who had been invited to the signing ceremony by the administration, praised the new order as a "pretty darn good program." *The New York Times* reported the next day that "The new [personnel security] program will require a new investigation of many thousands of employees previously investigated, as well as many more thousands who have had no security check."

During the 1960's and 1970's, gays and lesbians turned to the court system for protection against federal job discrimination. The court cases of *Norton v. Macy* (1969), *Vigil v. Post Office Department* (1969), *Schlegel v. United States* (1969), and *Society for Individual Rights and Hickerson v. Hampton* (1973), as well as changing public attitudes concerning homosexuals and homosexuality, helped undermine the Civil Service Commission's policy. In 1975, the commission officially ended job discrimination against lesbians and gays for most federal jobs except those within the FBI and other intelligence agencies.

## SIGNIFICANCE

President Eisenhower's order not only made it much harder for gays and lesbians to obtain and hold federal employment but also affected civilian government contractors. The order barred homosexuals from 20 percent of the nation's jobs and led to the firing of fifteen hundred and the resignation of six thousand federal employees. Many business owners and bureaucrats were so afraid of being accused of protecting "subversives" that they began to quickly dismiss homosexual workers. From 1947 to 1950, dismissals of homosexuals averaged about five per month in civilian government jobs. In 1950, there were 720 dismissals, and in 1955, there were 837 dismissals. Through the late 1950's and 1960's, dismissals fell to an average of twenty-five per year.

Although the Civil Service Commission curtailed the discriminatory policy in 1975, the United States as a nation still lacks a widespread, general sexual orientation nondiscrimination policy. In 1998, President Bill Clinton signed Executive Order 13087, which prohibited discrimination based on sexual orientation in federal civilian employment. Many U.S. states and municipal governments prohibit discrimination against lesbians and gays in areas such as employment as well, but they also prohibit discrimination in housing, health care, and other critical areas.

—*Jamie Patrick Chandler*

## FURTHER READING

Brown, Ralph S., Jr. *Loyalty and Security: Employment Tests in the United States.* New Haven, Conn.: Yale University Press, 1958.

D'Emilio, John. *Sexual Politics, Sexual Communities: The Making of a Homosexual Minority in the United States, 1940-1970.* 2d ed. Chicago: University of Chicago Press, 1998.

Johnson, David K. "'Homosexual Citizens': Washington's Gay Community Confronts the Civil Service." *Washington History* 6, no. 2 (1994): 44-63.

_____. *The Lavender Scare: The Cold War Persecution of Gays and Lesbians in the Federal Government.* Chicago: University of Chicago Press, 2004.

Koppelman, Andrew. *The Gay Rights Question in Contemporary American Law.* Chicago: University of Chicago Press, 2002.

Lewis, Gregory B. "Lifting the Ban on Gays in the Civil Service: Federal Policy Toward Gay and Lesbian Employees Since the Cold War." *Public Administration Review* 57, no. 5 (1997): 387-395.

Winfeld, Liz. *Straight Talk About Gays in the Workplace: Creating an Inclusive, Productive Environment for Everyone in Your Organization.* 3d ed. New York: Harrington Park Press, 2005.

**SEE ALSO:** 1972-1973: Local Governments Pass Antidiscrimination Laws; June 27, 1974: Abzug and Koch Attempt to Amend the Civil Rights Act of 1964; July 3, 1975: U.S. Civil Service Commission Prohibits Discrimination Against Federal Employees; 1978: Lesbian and Gay Workplace

Movement Is Founded; June 2, 1980: Canadian Gay Postal Workers Secure Union Protections; Dec. 4, 1984: Berkeley Extends Benefits to Domestic Partners of City Employees; Nov. 8, 1988: Oregon Repeals Ban on Antigay Job Discrimination; May 1, 1989: U.S. Supreme Court Rules Gender-Role Stereotyping Is Discriminatory; Sept. 29, 1991: California Governor Wilson Vetoes Antidiscrimination Bill; Sept. 23, 1992: Massachusetts Grants Family Rights to Gay and Lesbian State Workers; Apr. 2, 1998: Canadian Supreme Court Reverses Gay Academic's Firing; July, 2003: Singapore Lifts Ban on Hiring Lesbian and Gay Employees; July, 2003: Wal-Mart Adds Lesbians and Gays to Its Antidiscrimination Policy.

## 1955

# DAUGHTERS OF BILITIS FOUNDED AS FIRST NATIONAL LESBIAN GROUP IN UNITED STATES

*The Daughters of Bilitis, a social club for lesbians, became the first national lesbian organization in the United States. Through its political activism and its publication,* The Ladder, *the group challenged society's sexism, heterosexism, and homophobia and created a space for lesbians to come together for political, social, and personal empowerment.*

LOCALE: San Francisco, California
CATEGORIES: Organizations and institutions; publications; feminism

### KEY FIGURES

*Phyllis Lyon* (b. 1924),
*Del Martin* (b. 1921),
*Noni Frey*, and
*Rose Bamburger*, four founders of Daughters of Bilitis
*Helen Sandoz* and
*Stella Rush*, founders of DOB-Los Angeles
*Barbara Gittings* (b. 1932) and
*Kay Tobin Lahusen* (b. 1930), founders of DOB-New York
*Barbara Grier* (b. 1933), editor of *The Ladder*

### SUMMARY OF EVENT

In 1953, after they met and then fell in love in Seattle, Washington, Phyllis Lyon and Del Martin moved home to the San Francisco Bay Area. There they established a life together but were frustrated in their efforts to meet other lesbians. In September, 1955, they eagerly accepted an invitation to talk with six other women about forming a "secret" club for lesbians. Out of their discussions grew the Daughters of Bilitis (DOB).

From 1955 to 1970, the Daughters of Bilitis was a national organization, with local chapters, biannual conferences, and a paid membership averaging about two hundred women annually. Although small in numbers, the organization played a crucial role in the fledgling homophile movement. In addition to the DOB's main office in San Francisco, there were established DOB chapters in New York, Los Angeles, Chicago, and Boston. Local chapters—organized by activists such as Helen Sandoz and Stella Rush in Los Angeles, and Barbara Gittings and Kay Tobin Lahusen in New York—encouraged women to join by sponsoring house parties, dances, picnics, informal discussion groups, and public programs. Other cities, such as Houston, New Orleans, Philadelphia, and Providence, Rhode Island, as well as Melbourne, Australia, also had chapters for shorter periods of time. A national office in San Francisco oversaw administration and publications mainly.

The reach provided by DOB's magazine *The Ladder*, launched in 1956 to publicize the group's

*Daughters of Bilitis cofounders Phyllis Lyon, left, and Del Martin, who have been a couple for more than a half century, were legally married in California in 2004. Same-gender marriages have since been rescinded in California and other states, but legal challenges followed.* (AP/Wide World Photos)

manipulated the public's concerns about the safety and security of Americans. Some, such as U.S. senator Joseph McCarthy, alleged that U.S. institutions—from Hollywood to the state department—were in danger of being corrupted by traitors. Soon, "loyalty" was equated with "conformity," and it was not long before "subversive" was linked with "homosexual" in the public's mind. In 1953, an executive order signed by President Dwight D. Eisenhower gave the federal government the power to deny employment based on an applicant's sexual orientation. Despite the publicity given the televised interrogations of people accused of Communist Party affiliations in the early 1950's, more people were discharged from their government jobs for being suspected homosexuals than for being Communists.

From the beginning, the founders of DOB made organizational choices that enabled them to work toward their goals of self-acceptance, societal recognition, and changes in public policies regarding homosexuality. DOB membership was always open to all women interested in learning more about the "problems" of homosexuality. Even the name they chose for their new group provided protection, as it borrowed the title of an obscure nineteenth century work of erotica written possibly by one of the female lovers of the Greek poet Sappho, named Bilitis.

DOB was many things to many women. First and foremost, it was where a lesbian possibly could meet a new lover. It was a circle of friends to share good times and bad, a network of peer counselors who offered support and guidance, a resource center for questions about homosexuality, and an arena for activism. In addition to challenging American sex and gender norms of the mid-twentieth century, the group criticized the sexism faced within the ho-

efforts, also broadened the organization's impact throughout the 1950's and 1960's. Under editors Lyon, Martin, Gittings, Sandoz, and Barbara Grier, the monthly magazine became one of the most important national publications of the growing lesbian and gay rights movement, and it was read by thousands of women and men around the country and throughout the world. DOB-New York activist Lahusen was one of the movement's first photographers; her covers for *The Ladder* in the mid-1960's featured black-and-white portraits of lesbians, portraits never before made public. In its literary and political coverage and its artwork, *The Ladder* began to lift the veil of silence from lesbian lives.

The early architects of DOB may not have thought it radical to publish a magazine or organize parties and conventions for lesbians, but in those Cold War years, their acts were indeed radical. In the post-World War II period, the United States experienced precarious prosperity at home, and competition from the U.S.S.R., a former ally, abroad. Right-wing politicians, looking to regain control of Congress and the White House in the early 1950's,

The Ladder *was a longtime publication of the Daughters of Bilitis.*

mophile movement and fought against the homophobia and heterosexism encountered within the women's movement.

By 1970, already existing divisions within DOB over the significance of political ideologies such as feminism and lesbian and gay liberation, as well as organizational fragmentation, were sharpened when then-editor of *The Ladder,* Grier and national president Rita Laporte decided to sever the magazine from DOB and publish it independently. Citing fears about the organization's commitment to *The Ladder,* Grier and Laporte removed the mailing lists and production materials from DOB headquarters in San Francisco across state lines to Nevada without informing the organization's leaders. Devastated by the loss of their prized magazine, the

DOB governing board decided not to pursue expensive and time-consuming legal remedies to force the magazine's return. They also agreed to disband the national organization, giving autonomy to the local chapters operating under the DOB name. Many of the local chapters—such as those in San Francisco and New York—continued to organize activities for their members throughout the 1970's; the DOB chapter in Boston, started in 1969, is still nominally in existence.

## SIGNIFICANCE

Unlike the plethora of choices open to lesbians in the early twenty-first century—from campus groups to chat rooms to professional organizations to coffeehouses and cafés—in 1955 there was nowhere, beyond a few bars, where a lesbian could go to meet others like herself. During a culturally conservative time in the United States, when "the feminine mystique" exerted more cultural power than did feminism in reinforcing a retreat to conformity and domesticity for American women, the Daughters of Bilitis created and maintained first a local, then a national, organization that challenged homophobia and sexism. Through their dances and debates, and their publications and meetings, the Daughters of Bilitis helped build not one but two significant twentieth century movements for social justice: the lesbian and gay civil rights movement and feminism.

—*Marcia M. Gallo*

## FURTHER READING

Boyd, Nan Alamilla. *Wide Open Town: A History of Queer San Francisco to 1965.* Berkeley: University of California Press, 2003.

Bullough, Vern L., ed. *Before Stonewall: Activists for Gay and Lesbian Rights in Historical Context.* New York: Harrington Park Press, 2002.

D'Emilio, John. *Sexual Politics, Sexual Communities: The Making of a Homosexual Minority in the United States, 1940-1970.* 2d ed. Chicago: University of Chicago Press, 1998.

Faderman, Lillian. *Odd Girls and Twilight Lovers: A History of Lesbian Life in Twentieth Century America.* New York: Columbia University Press, 1991.

Gallo, Marcia M. *Different Daughters: A History of the Daughters of Bilitis and the Birth of the Lesbian Rights Movement.* New York: Carroll & Graf, 2006.

_____. "Different Daughters: The Daughters of Bilitis and the Roots of Lesbian and Women's Liberation, 1955-1970." Ph.D. dissertation, City University of New York Graduate Center, 2004.

Grier, Barbara, and Coletta Reid, eds. *The Lavender Herring: Lesbian Essays from "The Ladder."* Baltimore: Diana Press, 1976.

Martin, Del, and Phyllis Lyon. *Lesbian/Woman.* 1972. Rev. ed. Volcano, Calif.: Volcano Press, 1991.

Schultz, Gretchen. "Daughters of Bilitis: Literary Genealogy and Lesbian Authenticity." *GLQ: A Journal of Lesbian and Gay Studies* 7, no. 3 (2001): 377-389.

**SEE ALSO:** Dec. 10, 1924: Gerber Founds the Society for Human Rights; June, 1947-Feb., 1948: *Vice Versa* Is Published as First Lesbian Periodical; May 27-30, 1960: First National Lesbian Conference Convenes; Feb. 19-20, 1966: First North American Conference of Homophile Organizations Convenes; May 1, 1970: Radicalesbians Issues "The Woman Identified Woman" Manifesto; Nov. 28, 1970: Del Martin Quits Gay Liberation Movement; 1971: *Lesbian Tide* Publishes Its First Issue; Oct., 1974: *Lesbian Connection* Begins Publication; Apr., 1987: Old Lesbians Organize for Change.

## 1956
# BALDWIN PUBLISHES *GIOVANNI'S ROOM*

*James Baldwin's novel* Giovanni's Room *depicts a gay relationship in a manner strikingly more explicit than previous works of fiction. It is a groundbreaking novel not merely because it is the first explicit account of gay sex in American fiction but also because it is the first American gay novel that tells the story of a man, not a "case study" or a "type."*

**LOCALE:** New York, New York
**CATEGORIES:** Literature; publications

**KEY FIGURE**
*James Baldwin* (1924-1987), American novelist and essayist

**SUMMARY OF EVENT**
When *Giovanni's Room* appeared in 1956, James Baldwin was already a respected novelist, having enjoyed the critical and commercial success of his first novel, *Go Tell It on the Mountain*, in 1953. This first novel hints at homosexual themes in the coming-of-age story of its protagonist, fourteen-

*James Baldwin. (© John Hoppy Hopkins)*

## "But I Am Not a Housewife"

But I am not a housewife—men never can be housewives. And the pleasure was never real or deep, though Giovanni smiled his humble, grateful smile and told me in as many ways as he could find how wonderful it was to have me there. . . . Each day he invited me to witness how he had changed, how love had changed him, how he worked and sang and cherished me. I was in a terrible confusion. Sometimes I thought, but this *is* your life. Stop fighting it. Stop fighting. Or I thought, but I am happy. And he loves me. I am safe. Sometimes, when he was not near me, I thought, I will never let him touch me again.

*Source:* James Baldwin, *Giovanni's Room* (New York: Dial, 1956).

year-old John Grimes. *Giovanni's Room*, on the other hand, is explicitly about a homosexual love affair and its protagonist's tortured struggle with his sexual identity.

As the story opens, David, a white American man living in Paris, is engaged to a young woman named Hella, who is away in Spain on an extended vacation. While she is gone, David meets Giovanni, an Italian bartender at a gay bar. David and Giovanni immediately begin an intense love affair, and David moves in with Giovanni, who lives in a small rented room in a working-class section of Paris. For the many weeks that Hella is away, David and Giovanni live almost as a married couple, with Giovanni going off to work in the evenings and David taking "a kind of pleasure in playing the housewife." Whenever he leaves the room, however, David is beset by an inner struggle that goes to the core of his identity.

For David, Giovanni's room comes to represent his homosexual desires, which are a source of deep conflict for him: He is repulsed by his own behavior, even as he finds deep pleasure in sex with Giovanni. When Hella returns to Paris, David abandons Giovanni. He and Hella make plans to move together to the south of France, and they prepare for their wedding. Before Hella and David leave Paris, David visits Giovanni one last time and explains why he has returned to Hella.

"I can have a life with her. . . . What kind of life can we have in this room?—this filthy little room. What kind of life can two men have together, anyway? . . . You want to go out and be the big laborer and bring home the money, and you want me to stay here and wash the dishes and cook the food . . . and be your little *girl*. . . . And you take *me* because you haven't got the guts to go after a woman, which is what you *really* want? . . ."

"But I'm a man . . . a man! What do you think can *happen* between us?"

"You know very well," said Giovanni slowly, "what can happen between us. It is for that reason you are leaving me."

As soon as David and Hella leave Paris, David loses all sexual interest in her, and before long she realizes why. When she leaves him, David is left alone and as confused as ever, paralyzed with indecision, unable to reconcile his sexual desires with his desire for a "normal" life.

### SIGNIFICANCE

James Baldwin encountered a great deal of difficulty in getting *Giovanni's Room* published, mainly because of its sexual content. Although by no means the first major American novel to focus on a gay character or a gay love affair, *Giovanni's Room* was at the time of its publication by far the most frank and explicit account of gay sex in American fiction.

Nevertheless, despite the publishers' apparent doubts, the book was on the whole well received by critics in the mainstream press. In his review of the book for *Saturday Review* ("A Squalid World," December 1, 1956), David Karp writes, "Mr. Baldwin has taken a very special theme and treated it with great artistry and restraint [and] has managed to instil in one reader, at least, a greater tolerance, a fresher sense of pity." However, reviews in African American publications were mixed. For instance, James Ivy's review in *The Crisis*, the publication of the National Association for the Advancement of Colored People, disparaged Baldwin for "wasting" his talent on a book about a white man's gay love affair.

Critics also noted the difference between *Gio-*

vanni's Room and the gay fiction that had come before. To a number of critics, this difference made the novel superior to earlier gay literature. A reviewer for the *San Francisco Chronicle* (December 2, 1956), for example, thought that "David's struggle has dignity and compassion that raise it far above a homosexual case study like Gore Vidal's *The City and the Pillar* [1948]," and novelist Nelson Algren, writing for *The Nation* (December 1, 1956), saw the novel as "more than another report on homosexuality. It is the story of a man who could not make up his mind." *Giovanni's Room* is the story of a man, not a "case study."

*—Karen E. Antell*

**FURTHER READING**

Baldwin, James. *Giovanni's Room*. New York: Dial, 1956.

DeGout, Yasmin Y. "Dividing the Mind: Contradictory Portraits of Homoerotic Love in *Giovanni's Room*." *African American Review* 26, no. 3 (Fall, 1992): 425-435.

Escoffier, Jeffrey. "Homosexuality and the Sociological Imagination: The 1950's and 1960's." In *A Queer World: The Center for Lesbian and Gay Studies Reader*, edited with an introduction by Martin Duberman. New York: New York University Press, 1997.

Johnson-Roullier, Cyraina E. *Reading on the Edge: Exiles, Modernities, and Cultural Transformation in Proust, Joyce, and Baldwin*. Albany: State University of New York Press, 2000.

Leeming, David Adams. *James Baldwin: A Biography*. New York: Knopf, 1994.

Levin, James. *The Gay Novel in America*. New York: Garland, 1991.

Zaborowska, Magdalena J. "Mapping American Masculinities: James Baldwin's Innocents Abroad, or *Giovanni's Room* Revisited." In *Other Americans, Other Americas: The Politics and Poetics of Multiculturalism*. Aarhus, Denmark: Aarhus University Press, 1998.

**SEE ALSO:** July 4, 1855: Whitman Publishes *Leaves of Grass*; May 25, 1895: Oscar Wilde Is Convicted of Gross Indecency; 1924: Gide Publishes the Signed Edition of *Corydon*; 1939: Isherwood Publishes *Goodbye to Berlin*; 1947-1948: Golden Age of American Gay Literature; 1963: Rechy Publishes *City of Night*; June, 1971: The Gay Book Award Debuts; 1974: *The Front Runner* Makes *The New York Times* Best-Seller List; 1975: First Novel About Coming Out to Parents Is Published; 1980-1981: Gay Writers Form the Violet Quill; May, 1987: *Lambda Rising Book Report* Begins Publication; June 2, 1989: Lambda Literary Award Is Created; 1993: Monette Wins the National Book Award for *Becoming a Man*.

## 1956
# FOSTER PUBLISHES *SEX VARIANT WOMEN IN LITERATURE*

*Jeannette Foster's monumental bibliography,* Sex Variant Women in Literature, *the "foundation bible of lesbian literature," covers approximately twenty-six hundred years of lesbian writings from the beginning of publishing history to 1954.*

**LOCALE:** New York, New York
**CATEGORIES:** Publications; literature

**KEY FIGURES**
*Jeannette Howard Foster* (1895-1981), scholar and librarian
*Barbara Grier* (b. 1933), publisher and editor

**SUMMARY OF EVENT**

Jeannette Howard Foster published in 1956 what her friend Barbara Grier called *the* foundational work on the subject of lesbian literature. This is no false claim. Foster's exhaustive scholarship, published at a time when literature of this type was heavily coded or practically inaccessible, is still an invaluable resource with which to begin a historical study of lesbian literature.

From 1948 to 1952, Foster was the librarian at the Kinsey Institute for Research in Sex, Gender, and Reproduction, which provided her unique access to materials of a sexually explicit nature. She knew at first hand the difficulties of identifying, locating, and obtaining writings pertaining to lesbian sexuality. Foster writes in her introduction to *Sex Variant Women in Literature,* "No class of printed matter except outright pornography has suffered more critical neglect, exclusion from libraries, or omission from collected works than variant belles-lettres." Noting the problem of the term "lesbian," she purposely selected the more flexible term "sex variant" to include instances of same-gender relationships and desire in literary works by primarily heterosexual characters. In an interview with lesbian scholar Karla Jay, Foster humorously describes her search for a title.

As my research went on, I began to see the pattern for a book, and I worked awfully hard to find a title for it which would begin with the word "sex." As I had learned from searching bibliographies, a title beginning with the word "sex" couldn't be ignored!

Foster's bibliography is more than a collection of titles featuring lesbian themes and images; it also includes Foster's narrative critical analyses of the texts and biographical information on the authors. The scope of the work begins with biblical and ancient Greek literature and continues to 1954, the last copyright date Foster covers. The works included are primarily from works in English, French, and German, the three languages Foster could read fluently. Foster spent thirty years collecting and researching her material, finally including a total of 324 titles.

Getting *Sex Variant Women in Literature* published proved to be an even greater challenge for Foster than the massive research involved. The first editor died before the book went to press, and the editor's successor failed to uphold the contract because of the book's controversial subject matter. As there was virtually no commercial interest in such a work, Foster ultimately published her opus through a vanity press and was forced to pay $2,000 of her own money—the equivalent of one year's salary—which she never recouped. Fortunately, her work was republished in 1974 by Diana Press, and again in 1985 by Naiad Press. Foster's important contribution to the study of lesbian literature did not go unnoticed by her librarian colleagues, and in 1974 the American Library Association's Gay and Lesbian Task Force honored *Sex Variant Women in Literature* with its third annual Gay Book Award.

Born in Oak Park, Illinois, Foster received a bachelor of science degree in chemistry and engineering in 1918 during an era when few women pursued a science-based curriculum. She changed her path of study in graduate school and earned a mas-

## "I AM SOMEWAY THE LESBIAN WOMAN"

Also I am someway the Lesbian woman.

It is but one phase—one which slightly touches each other phase I own. And in it I am poetic and imaginative and worldly and amorous and gentle and true and strong and weak and ardent and shy and sensitive and generous and morbid and sweet and fine and false.

The Lesbian sex-strain as an effect is reckoned a pre-natal influence—and, as I conceive, it comes also of conglomerate incarnations and their reactions and flare-backs. Of some thus bestowed it makes strange hard highly emotional indefinably vicious woman, turbulent and brilliant of mind, mystically overborne, overwrought of heart. They are marvels of perverse barbaric energy. They make with men varied flinty friendships, but to each other they are friends, lovers, victims, preyers, masters, slaves: the flawed fruits of one oblique sex-inherence.

Except two breeds—the stupid and the narrowly feline—all women have a touch of the Lesbian: an assertion all good non-analytic creatures refute with horror, but quite, quite true: there is always the poignant intensive personal taste, the flair of inner-sex, in the tenderest friendships of women.

For myself, there is no vice in my Lesbian vein. I am too personally fastidious, too temperamentally dishonest, too eerily wavering to walk in direct repellent roads of vice in freest moods. There is instead a pleasant degeneracy of attitude more debauching to my spirit than any mere trivial trainant vice would be. And a fascination it tempers my humanness with an evil-feeling power.

I have lightly kissed and been kissed by Lesbian lips in a way which filled my throat with a sudden subtle pagan blood-flavored wistfulness, ruinous and contraband: breath of bewildering demoniac winds smothering mine.

*Source:* Mary MacLane, *I, Mary MacLane: A Diary of Human Days* (New York: Frederick Stokes, 1917). MacLane's work is discussed by Foster.

ter's degree in English and American literature in 1922, as well as both a bachelor of science and a doctorate in library science. She also served as a librarian to the President's Advisory Committee on Education. Foster's long academic career included teaching appointments in literature and library science departments in various universities. During the 1960's she contributed many articles, reviews, and poems to the groundbreaking lesbian periodical *The Ladder*. She died in a nursing home in Pocahontas, Arkansas, at the age of eighty-five.

Although Foster did not publish another research work in the field, she continued to offer assistance to those attempting to locate lesbian material by teaching them how to decipher the coded language often used in book reviews. Foster's other significant contribution to lesbian literature was a translation of a prose work by Renée Vivien, an early twentieth century Anglo-American lesbian poet who wrote exclusively in French. Foster's translation was "a present" to Naiad Press's founder, Barbara Grier, who wanted very much to read the piece but did not know French. Naiad Press published the work in 1974 as *A Woman Appeared to Me*, introducing English-speaking readers to Vivien's work for the first time.

### SIGNIFICANCE

Though the publishing of works on lesbian literature has increased exponentially since the 1950's, *Sex Variant Women in Literature* remains the cornerstone title in the field. As Barbara Grier pointed out, "When *Sex Variant Women in Literature* was first published, there was not one title in the general field of nonfiction that dealt accurately with lesbians. Now it is impossible to count the number of titles published that outline the lives of famous lesbians of the past."

—*Robin L. Imhof*

### FURTHER READING

Bullough, Vern L., ed. *Before Stonewall: Activists for Gay and Lesbian Rights in Historical Context.* New York: Harrington Park Press, 2002.

Foster, Jeannette H. *Sex Variant Women in Literature: A Historical and Quantitative Study.* Tallahassee, Fla.: Naiad Press, 1985.

Grier, Barbara. "In Fond Remembrance." *Lambda Book Report* 12 (December, 2003): 38.

Jay, Karla. "The X-Rated Bibliographer: A Spy in

the House of Sex." In *Lavender Culture*, edited by Karla Jay and Allen Young. 1979. Reprint. New York: New York University Press, 1994.

SEE ALSO: 1903: Stein Writes *Q.E.D.*; 1928: Hall Publishes *The Well of Loneliness*; June, 1971: The Gay Book Award Debuts; 1973: Brown Publishes *Rubyfruit Jungle*; 1973: Naiad Press Is Founded; 1975: Rule Publishes *Lesbian Images*; 1981: Faderman Publishes *Surpassing the Love of Men*; 1981: *This Bridge Called My Back* Is Published; Oct., 1981: Kitchen Table: Women of Color Press Is Founded; 1982: Lorde's Autobiography *Zami* Is Published; 1985: Lesbian Film *Desert Hearts* Is Released; 1986: Paula Gunn Allen Publishes *The Sacred Hoop*; 1987: Anzaldúa Publishes *Borderlands/La Frontera*; 1987: *Compañeras: Latina Lesbians* Is Published; May, 1987: *Lambda Rising Book Report* Begins Publication; June 2, 1989: Lambda Literary Award Is Created.

## January 1, 1957
# UNITED KINGDOM'S SEXUAL OFFENCES ACT BECOMES LAW

*The British parliament consolidated the law of England and Wales regarding sexual crimes. The law remained among the most severe in Europe, encapsulating British society's then-prevalent antigay attitudes. In effect, the law made what had been a crime against the person a "crime against nature."*

LOCALE: London, England
CATEGORIES: Laws, acts, and legal history; crime; civil rights

### SUMMARY OF EVENT

In 1956, the United Kingdom consolidated its existing laws governing the prosecution of sexual crimes. The new statute the "Sexual Offences Act, 1956" took effect on January 1, 1957, and addressed offenses such as intercourse by force, and with minors and "defectives," as well as prostitution and an assortment of "unnatural offences." The 1956 act remains the touchstone of English law on the subject, although it has been the object of many liberalizing amendments since its original passage.

The act signaled few obvious innovations in the law. It was enacted while Sir John Frederick Wolfenden's Departmental Committee on Homosexual Offences and Prostitution was convened and before it issued its report (known, simply, as the *Wolfenden Report*) the following September, thus suggesting that any substantial changes to the law were deliberately postponed until that group had reported. Thus, the act retained several glaring anomalies that had accreted over time in regard to how similar crimes would be punished. Among the more notable anomalies are the differences between the maximum punishments for indecent assault upon men and women (ten years and two years, respectively) and between the maximum sentences for attempted rape and attempted intercourse with a girl under thirteen (seven years and two years, respectively).

Of special relevance to the history of gay and lesbian rights are the sections on "unnatural offences," by which is meant "buggery" and "indecency between men." Buggery included both sodomy and bestiality. In general, only men can commit buggery, although women can commit buggery with animals. Conviction could bring life imprisonment, and an attempt to commit buggery could bring a sentence of as much as ten years. The 1956 section repeated the law from 1861, which had reduced the penalty from death. A hint of the antigay tenor of the nineteenth century is evident because the act of consensual sodomy was more severely punished than was rape.

In the new act, "indecency between men," also known as "gross indecency," became a crime sanctioned with a two-year prison term, as was conviction of a charge of an "attempt to procure the commission" of indecency with another man. This section reproduced language dating from 1885 and, to be violated, did not require physical contact. The act included no comparable crime of indecency between women. As a general rule, the law tended to criminalize homosexual acts between men but not between women.

Other crimes penalized by the new law that targeted male homosexuals primarily, if not exclusively, include "indecent assault on a man" and "assault with intent to commit buggery." This last charge carried a sentence of up to ten years—more than that risked by an attempted rape. Again, the act underscored the prevailing notion that sexual violence against males was a more socially injurious harm than was sexual violence against women.

### SIGNIFICANCE

The 1956 law included little that was new in terms of explicit statutory prohibitions, being in many ways more of a clerical tidying of the law than a substantive rethinking of it. The legal situations of gays and lesbians were barely changed from where they had stood before. The impact of the new statute, therefore, must be measured by something other than changes in the law.

Leslie Moran, in *The Homosexual(ity) of Law* (1996), argues that the 1956 Sexual Offences Act significantly altered the symbolic associations of these preexisting crimes. The category of "sexual offences" was itself new, constructed "out of the category of offences against the person and conjoin[ed] with other offences and [set] up in a new and distinct division of the law." This reordering fundamentally realigned the crimes from acts against persons to violations of the sexual natural order. The crime would be prosecuted not because of the personal harms the victim suffered but because of the damage it inflicted upon the moral order of human society; what had been a crime against

the person had become a "crime against nature." One would expect such an elevation of the harm's metaphysical significance to be accompanied by a heightened perception of the seriousness of the offense, with resulting increases in police interest in its prevention and punishment.

Some data suggest this is indeed what happened. As reported by Tony Honoré in *Sex Law in England* (1978), following the act's passage convictions for "indecency between men" almost doubled every five years, from 483 convictions in 1965 to 1,507 in 1975. This rate of increase appears to be significantly higher than that seen before the 1956 act: The *Wolfenden Report* shows only about a 31 percent increase in the years from 1951 to 1955. Even allowing for the obvious differences in reporting, the data support an argument that homosexual offenses became the target of more vigorous arrests and prosecutions after the act than before. This jaundiced view of homosexuality, once entrenched, would be eroded only with great difficulty, even in the face of later improvements in the formal legal status of gays and lesbians.

*—James M. Donovan*

### FURTHER READING

Great Britain. Committee on Homosexual Offences and Prostitution. *The Wolfenden Report.* Authorized American ed. Introduction by Karl Menninger. New York: Stein and Day, 1963.

Honoré, Tony. *Sex Law in England.* London: Archon Books, 1978.

Moran, Leslie F. *The Homosexual(ity) of Law.* New York: Routledge, 1996.

Orr, C. Bruce. *The Sexual Offences Act, 1956.* London: Butterworth, 1957.

Rees, J. Tudor, and Harley V. Usill, eds. *They Stand Apart: A Critical Survey of the Problems of Homosexuality.* New York: Macmillan, 1955.

Selfe, David W., and Vincent Burke. *Perspectives on Sex, Crime, and Society.* London: Cavendish, 1998.

SEE ALSO: 1885: United Kingdom Criminalizes "Gross Indecency"; May 25, 1895: Oscar Wilde Is Convicted of Gross Indecency; Sept. 4, 1957:

The *Wolfenden Report* Calls for Decriminalizing Private Consensual Sex; July 27, 1967: United Kingdom Decriminalizes Homosexual Sex; Jan. 12, 2000: United Kingdom Lifts Ban on Gays and Lesbians in the Military; Nov. 18, 2004: United Kingdom Legalizes Same-Gender Civil Partnerships.

## September 4, 1957
# THE *WOLFENDEN REPORT* CALLS FOR DECRIMINALIZING PRIVATE CONSENSUAL SEX

*A committee of fifteen individuals was appointed by the British government to study the issue of homosexual offenses in the United Kingdom. The committee's report recommended decriminalizing private sexual acts among consenting adults and recommended legal guidelines for public acts of homosexual indecency. The report led to the reversal of more than four hundred years of British sodomy laws and would have far-reaching effects around the globe.*

**LOCALE:** London, England
**CATEGORIES:** Publications; laws, acts, and legal history; crime; civil rights

**KEY FIGURES**
*Sir John Frederick Wolfenden* (1906-1985), chair of the Departmental Committee on Homosexual Offences and Prostitution and vice chancellor of Reading University
*Leo Abse* (b. 1917), member of the House of Commons
*Earl of Arran* (1910-1983), member of the House of Lords

**SUMMARY OF EVENT**
The *Wolfenden Report* was the culmination of three years of public hearings and research conducted by a fifteen-member committee led by Sir John Frederick Wolfenden. Members were drawn from the fields of law, politics, religion, and medicine. Appointed by the British government on August 4, 1954, the committee was directed to examine the law and legal practices related to homosexual crimes and prostitution, including the impact of homosexual convictions and how the legal system should treat those charged.

Impetus for the committee's work was created by public furor over the numbers of men prosecuted under sodomy and indecency statutes in the early 1950's. Caught in the legal snare were members of Parliament, aristocrats, and celebrities such as Sir John Gielgud and Jeffrey Weeks. Almost 4 percent of men in prison at the time had been incarcerated as a result of same-gender crime convictions.

Following sixty-two meetings of the committee and evidence gathered from more than two hundred individuals and organizations, the committee's findings were presented on September 3, 1957. The official title of the document, "The Report of the Departmental Committee on Homosexual Offences and Prostitution," was presented to the British parliament and published the following day. The document, nearly two hundred pages long, recommended decriminalization of consensual homosexual acts conducted in private.

The primary recommendations were that private consensual acts by men over twenty years of age were to be decriminalized and legal penalties for homosexual offenses were to be amended. Regarding prostitution, the committee distinguished between privacy and public decency. Members agreed that penalties for public "street offenses" should be raised to reduce public prostitution. Further measures to criminalize male prostitution were also suggested.

Though the *Wolfenden Report* is a prominent social document, it can best be defined as a think piece rather than a definitive study. Neither homosexuality nor prostitution was fully studied, but important issues were raised for further debate. These issues included the relations among laws, mores, and public opinion; the proper role of criminal law in society; and the relationship of scientific research and public policy. The significance of the report lies in the committee's general orientation to the criminal law and in select recommendations, among them the decriminalization of adult homosexual acts. The scope of criminal law regarding sexual behavior should be to preserve public order and decency, protect citizens from what is offensive or injurious, and provide safeguards against exploitation and corruption.

In public discussion, the report's recommendations were viewed as liberalizing, but the actual goal of the *Wolfenden Report* was to regulate homosexual acts more effectively and, in terms of private behavior, by means other than through criminal law. In general the report condemned homosexuality on grounds of immorality, as psychologically damaging to the individual, and urged research for treatment and cures. Many of the legal reforms outlined in the document pertaining to prostitution were passed nearly immediately. Meanwhile, other issues regarding homosexual legal reform lingered for years afterward. Sex between women was not a punishable offense in Britain and was not a subject of the committee's work.

Patrick Higgins, in *Heterosexual Dictatorship: Male Homosexuality in Postwar Britain* (1996), disavows the notion that the *Wolfenden Report* was the result of benevolent and progressive British governmental policy. The author denies there was a humane, liberal conclusion in British government that antiquated sex laws had to be repealed. Second, Higgins states that the period following the release of the *Wolfenden Report* was historically a time of heightened prosecution of gay men, of increasing and heinous attacks on individuals, and of the repudiation of homosexuality in British media.

In *Fear, Punishment, Anxiety, and the "Wolfenden Report"* (1959), Charles Berg states that the report, while ahead of its time in legal recommendations on homosexuality, should be considered sci-

entifically reactionary. He believed that the committee members were incapable of comprehending the issue of homosexuality because they did not understand the psychopathology and origin of attitudes, defensive mechanisms, and societal bias. Furthermore, the committee did not go far enough in separating public law and private morality, nor in proposing gay and lesbian rights to comparable to those of the heterosexual population.

## SIGNIFICANCE

The ramifications of the *Wolfenden Report* transcended the boundaries of Great Britain, impacting laws in many of the common-law, English-speaking nations around the world. The American Bar Association in 1961 drafted and approved a model penal code that omitted homosexual offenses between consenting adult males. The Canadian parliament followed suit in 1969, excluding consensual homosexual acts as punishable offenses. Further legislative impact was observed in Australia and New Zealand. The report had negligible or no effect in many former British colonies in Africa, South Asia, and the Caribbean.

In Great Britain, the report languished in Parliament until 1962. Leo Abse in the House of Commons introduced a private member's bill that advanced some of the less controversial segments of the Wolfenden Committee's recommendations but did not make adult, consensual, homosexual behavior legal. Three years later, Lord Arran persuaded the House of Lords to initiate legislation to decriminalize consensual homosexual acts. In Commons, Abse followed the earl's lead. The two members of Parliament advocated both the protection of young men from homosexuality and partial decriminalization of homosexuality.

In the summer of 1967 the Sexual Offences Act, a revision of the original 1956 law, took effect in England and Wales, but not, at that date, in Scotland and Northern Ireland. The act unfortunately did not address issues of harassment, intolerance, and discrimination against gays.

*—Michael A. Lutes*

## Further Reading

Berg, Charles. *Fear, Punishment, Anxiety, and the "Wolfenden Report."* London: George Allen & Unwin, 1959.

_____. *The Problem of Homosexuality.* New York: Citadel Press, 1958.

Chesser, Eustace. *Live and Let Live: The Moral of the "Wolfenden Report."* London: Mayfair Books, 1962.

Great Britain. Committee on Homosexual Offences and Prostitution. *The Wolfenden Report.* Authorized American ed. Introduction by Karl Menninger. New York: Stein and Day, 1963.

Higgins, Patrick. *Heterosexual Dictatorship: Male Homosexuality in Postwar Britain.* London: Fourth Estate, 1996.

Jeffrey-Poulter, Stephen. *Peers, Queers, and Commons: The Struggle for Gay Law Reform from 1950 to the Present.* New York: Routledge, 1991.

**See also:** May 6, 1868: Kertbeny Coins the Terms "Homosexual" and "Heterosexual"; 1885: United Kingdom Criminalizes "Gross Indecency"; May 25, 1895: Oscar Wilde Is Convicted of Gross Indecency; Jan. 12, 1939: *Thompson v. Aldredge* Dismisses Sodomy Charges Against Lesbians; Jan. 22, 1973: *Roe v. Wade* Legalizes Abortion and Extends Privacy Rights; Aug., 1973: American Bar Association Calls for Repeal of Laws Against Consensual Sex; Oct. 18, 1973: Lambda Legal Authorized to Practice Law; Nov. 17, 1975: U.S. Supreme Court Rules in "Crimes Against Nature" Case; 1986: *Bowers v. Hardwick* Upholds State Sodomy Laws; Jan. 1, 1988: Canada Decriminalizes Sex Practices Between Consenting Adults; 1992-2006: Indians Struggle to Abolish Sodomy Law; June 26, 2003: U.S. Supreme Court Overturns Texas Sodomy Law.

## May 27-30, 1960
# First National Lesbian Conference Convenes

*Beginning in 1960, and continuing for the next decade, the lesbian group Daughters of Bilitis organized biennial public conferences for lesbians and their supporters in major U.S. cities, the first such conferences in the United States.*

**Locale:** San Francisco, California
**Categories:** Civil rights; organizations and institutions; feminism

### Key Figures

*Del Martin* (b. 1921) and
*Phyllis Lyon* (b. 1924), National Lesbian Conference organizers

### Summary of Event

From May 27 to 30, 1960, at the Hotel Whitcomb in downtown San Francisco, the Daughters of Bilitis (DOB) sponsored a historic national conference that drew two hundred women, and a few men, for a program headlined "A Look at the Lesbian." For a registration fee of $12.50 for the weekend's activities, attendees were treated to a Friday night cocktail party at the home of DOB founders Del Martin and Phyllis Lyon, followed by a series of speakers, a luncheon, a reception, and a banquet on Saturday. Sunday featured a DOB business meeting "for members only" during the day and a dinner for members and guests (women only) held at a lesbian-owned bar, The Front.

In organizing their program, DOB activists purposely invited speakers who would be able to assert "official" (albeit negative) religious and legal views of homosexuality. In their book *Lesbian/Woman* (1972), Martin and Lyon wrote about their choice of luncheon speaker, the Reverend Fordyce Eastburn, and their desire to open dialogue with the church. The official representative of the Cali-

---

## MARTIN AND LYON IN CONVERSATION WITH THE CHURCH

The church was at the core of all our problems, and there had to be some way, somehow to reach the church. In planning DOB's first convention in 1960, we noted that both [the] Mattachine [Society] and ONE [Institute] had previously counted among their speakers clergymen who recognized the needs of homosexuals. But they spoke unofficially, out of personal conviction, and never revealed what church they belonged to. Change could only come about if we could develop a dialogue with the church itself, and we were determined to have an official representative from some particular denomination.

*Source:* Del Martin and Phyllis Lyon, *Lesbian/Woman* (Volcano, Calif.: Volcano Press, 1972).

---

fornia Episcopal Diocese told conference attendees that Episcopalians had two choices for lesbians and gays seeking acceptance by the church: change or be celibate. "We look at it this way: we've opened a door to communication with the church. And that's what we were looking for," Martin wrote in *Lesbian/Woman*. Four years later, their strategy would pay off when local ministers teamed up with DOB members and other gay and lesbian rights activists to organize the groundbreaking Council on Religion and the Homosexual in San Francisco.

The first DOB national conference in 1960 also included a debate on lesbian and gay bars between two local legal heavyweights. Attorneys Morris Lowenthal, who represented San Francisco Bay Area gay-bar owners in a number of cases, and Sidney Feinberg of California's Alcoholic Beverage Commission, had faced each other in court over the question of the legality of lesbian and gay bars not long before the conference convened. The DOB saw the issue as paramount. The founders of DOB had organized their group to provide an alternative to the bar scene, although they believed that lesbians and gays had a basic right to socialize in bars, restaurants, and nightclubs if they preferred.

Martin and Lyon wrote in *Lesbian/Woman*, "In the early days of DOB, a great deal of energy was expended in apprising Lesbians of their legal rights,

advising them of what to do in case of arrest, and obtaining legal counsel for victims of raids. *The Ladder* [DOB's newsletter] had the distinction of having its September and October 1958 issues filed with the District Court of Appeals along with an amicus curiae brief by Lowenthal and Associates in the case of an Oakland Lesbian bar called Mary's First and Last Chance." While Lowenthal's brief asserted a dichotomy between the DOB and the lesbians who patronized bars, it was true that DOB's most active members and leaders were also regular customers of the numerous nightspots catering to gays and lesbians in the San Francisco Bay Area. The program for the national conference included not just a debate on the "gay bar question" but a gay and lesbian bar tour for out-of-town visitors, complete with a map and annotated comments provided by local DOB members.

Later Daughters of Bilitis gatherings, which drew anywhere from one hundred to three hundred women (and men) at each conference, were held in San Francisco and New York (1960 and 1966 in San Francisco; 1964 and 1970 in New York). They were also held in Los Angeles (1962) and a small Colorado town, Aurora, near Denver (1968). Structured much like those organized by other homophile groups at the time, each conference featured speeches, parties, and at least one gala event. Special awards—the "S.O.B awards" (for "Sons of Bilitis") were given at each conference to men who had been helpful allies in DOB's efforts to challenge both homophobia and sexism in the gay movement and in U.S. society.

Conferences also included a DOB business meeting, during which delegates from the chapters voted on national officers and policy changes. Voting lists of eligible members, proxies, and financial statements and reports were carefully created by the national governing board and the chapters for each gathering. In this way, the DOB consciously implemented democratic structures and practices into its organizational work.

## Significance

Starting in 1960, and continuing every two years for the next decade, the DOB national conferences were the first and only national gatherings of lesbian activists and their allies in the United States, an impressive feat for a tiny, all-volunteer group.

Importantly, the conferences provided unprecedented opportunities to put the faces of the DOB before the public. As the 1960's progressed, and media interest in homosexuality increased, DOB activists—and therefore lesbians in general—saw their visibility climb as they were "discovered" by local and then national talk shows hungry for provocative and popular topics. Daughters of Bilitis members were able to sharpen their skills at working with newspaper reporters, radio hosts, and television personalities on the still-titillating topic of homosexual sex, particularly among women, without allowing themselves to be trivialized or dismissed. The appearance of a DOB member in print, over the airwaves, or on television, was of critical importance; this media exposure led many women to contact DOB for information about the organization. The conferences provided an unmatched opening for successfully approaching the local media in the host cities, and each successive conference saw an increase in media coverage.

—*Marcia M. Gallo*

## Further Reading

Boyd, Nan Alamilla. *Wide Open Town: A History of Queer San Francisco to 1965*. Berkeley: University of California Press, 2003.

Bullough, Vern L., ed. *Before Stonewall: Activists for Gay and Lesbian Rights in Historical Context*. New York: Harrington Park Press, 2002.

Faderman, Lillian. *Odd Girls and Twilight Lovers: A History of Lesbian Life in Twentieth Century America*. New York: Columbia University Press, 1991.

Gallo, Marcia M. *Different Daughters: A History of the Daughters of Bilitis and the Birth of the Lesbian Rights Movement*. New York: Carroll & Graf, 2006.

Martin, Del, and Phyllis Lyon. *Lesbian/Woman*. 1972. Reprint. Volcano, Calif.: Volcano Press, 1991.

**See also:** 1955: Daughters of Bilitis Founded as First National Lesbian Group in United States; Feb. 19-20, 1966: First North American Conference of Homophile Organizations Convenes; May 1, 1970: Lavender Menace Protests Homophobia in Women's Movement; Nov. 28, 1970: Del Martin Quits Gay Liberation Movement; Nov. 18-21, 1977: National Women's Conference Convenes; Oct. 12-15, 1979: First National Third World Lesbian and Gay Conference Convenes; Apr., 1987: Old Lesbians Organize for Change.

## 1961
# ILLINOIS LEGALIZES CONSENSUAL HOMOSEXUAL SEX

*Illinois became the first U.S. state—and for ten years the only state—to abolish its laws that prohibited consensual same-gender sex.*

**LOCALE:** Illinois
**CATEGORIES:** Laws, acts, and legal history; civil rights

### SUMMARY OF EVENT

Before 1961, Illinois, like many states, had prohibited various sexual behaviors that legislators were unwilling to define explicitly. The Illinois statute read in part, "The infamous crime against nature, either with man or beast, shall subject the offender to be punished by imprisonment in the penitentiary for a term of not less than one year and not more than ten years."

There were several problems with this law as it was written. First, the vague language did not give clear warning to potential offenders; people could not always tell beforehand what acts might be deemed "crimes against nature." The vagueness of the language led to uneven enforcement of the laws, since law enforcement officers and prosecutors were unwilling to bring charges if they could not clearly prove the illegality of certain acts. In Illinois, a judgment in court was required to determine what acts were forbidden. Other states, including Wisconsin and Louisiana, had revised their penal codes during the 1950's, and in the process they had written new, more explicit, definitions for "sodomy" and "crimes against nature."

When the Illinois penal code was revised in 1961, on the recommendation of the American Law Institute, it was noted that although the 1948 Kinsey Report on male sexuality had stated that more than one-third of adult males had participated in some form of homosexual behavior, the prosecution rate of those persons seemed to be well under 1 percent. It was particularly difficult to establish guilt in the cases of private, consensual sexual activity because corroborating witnesses almost always refused to

come forward or could not be found. However, the fear of prosecution was significant enough to make those involved in prohibited sexual activity easy targets for blackmail, and also, this fear could lead to psychological injury.

The drafters of the 1961 code focused on four goals that they believed were appropriate legislative concerns: protection from nonconsensual sex, protection of minors, protection of the public from open displays of sexual behavior, and protection of marriage. Section 11-2 of the new code included a more specific definition of the types of behaviors that were forbidden, but the code intentionally excluded all sexual acts conducted in private between consenting adults. In fact, other legislative bodies had made similar revisions to their codes, but like the American Law Institute's 1961 Model Penal Law, they protected only private consensual behavior between married couples. Illinois was alone in protecting private sexual behavior regardless of the marital status or sexual orientation of those involved.

The revised code did, however, prohibit "lewd fondling or caressing of the body of another person of the same sex," although such fondling by heterosexuals was not forbidden. The drafters felt that caressing between people of the same gender was so "disgusting and offensive" that most people would be offended to see it. Only two years later, in 1963, a new law made it illegal to publicly fondle a person of "either sex." In 1970, the Illinois constitution was amended to strengthen the right to privacy.

### SIGNIFICANCE

It took ten years before Idaho, in the process of revising its criminal code, became the second state to repeal its laws against private consensual sex. Most residents did not notice the change until a gay newspaper ran a story celebrating the repeal. A public outcry from the Mormon Church and the Roman Catholic Church led to an emergency session of the legislature and a repeal of the new code. Idaho thus became the first state to reinstate a sodomy law that it had previously discarded.

The third state to repeal its sodomy laws was Connecticut, also in 1971. Twenty-one other states, mostly in the north and the west, soon followed suit. The first southern state to exclude private consensual sexual behavior from its criminal code was Arkansas. In 1975, it made a thorough revision of its criminal codes, as several other states had done previously, and repealed its sodomy laws. In 1977, Arkansas reinstated only that part of the law that applied to homosexual sex; private consensual heterosexual sex was still protected.

By the year 2000, only fourteen states and Puerto Rico still had laws on the books that prohibited sodomy. On June 26, 2003, the U.S. Supreme Court, in *Lawrence v. Texas*, ruled that two gay men who had been charged with sodomy were denied equal protection and their right to privacy when they were arrested for having private consensual sex in their home. By a vote of 6 to 3, the Court declared all sodomy laws in the United States to be unconstitutional when they restrict noncommercial private acts between consenting adults.

—*Cynthia A. Bily*

## FURTHER READING

*Harvard Law Review. Sexual Orientation and the Law*. Cambridge, Mass.: Harvard University Press, 1990.

Rubenstein, William B. *Cases and Materials on Sexual Orientation and the Law*. St. Paul, Minn.: West, 1997.

Washington University School of Law. "Deviate Sexual Behavior Under the New Illinois Criminal Code." *Washington University Law Quarterly* (1965): 220-235.

Williams, Walter L., and Yolanda Retter. *Gay and Lesbian Rights in the United States: A Documentary History*. Westport, Conn.: Greenwood Press, 2003.

**SEE ALSO:** May 6, 1868: Kertbeny Coins the Terms "Homosexual" and "Heterosexual"; 1885: United Kingdom Criminalizes "Gross Indecency"; Jan. 12, 1939: *Thompson v. Aldredge* Dismisses Sodomy Charges Against Lesbians; Sept. 4, 1957: The *Wolfenden Report* Calls for Decriminalizing Private Consensual Sex; Jan. 22, 1973: *Roe v. Wade* Legalizes Abortion and Extends Privacy Rights; Aug., 1973: American Bar Association Calls for Repeal of Laws Against Consensual Sex; Oct. 18, 1973: Lambda Legal Authorized to Practice Law; Nov. 17, 1975: U.S. Supreme Court Rules in "Crimes Against Nature" Case; 1986: *Bowers v. Hardwick* Upholds State Sodomy Laws; Jan. 1, 1988: Canada Decriminalizes Sex Practices Between Consenting Adults; 1992-2006: Indians Struggle to Abolish Sodomy Law; June 26, 2003: U.S. Supreme Court Overturns Texas Sodomy Law.

## 1961
# SARRIA IS FIRST OUT GAY OR LESBIAN CANDIDATE FOR PUBLIC OFFICE

*Gay activist José Sarria ran for a seat on the San Francisco board of supervisors, becoming the first out gay or lesbian person to run for public office in the United States.*

**LOCALE:** San Francisco, California
**CATEGORIES:** Government and politics; civil rights

**KEY FIGURE**
*José Sarria* (b. 1923), gay rights activist and former drag queen

**SUMMARY OF EVENT**
José Sarria was born in San Francisco to a Colombian mother, whose family included members who had participated in several political revolts in Colombia. José's father's ancestors were from Spain, and some family members lived in Nicaragua. Because of his mother's health problems and his father's absence, José, as an infant, had been placed in the care of family friends, Jesserina and Charles Millen.

During World War II, although not meeting the height and weight requirements, José Sarria persuaded an officer to sign the forms that allowed him to enlist in the U.S. Army. Once inducted, he was posted in Berlin. After World War II, he returned to San Francisco, where he worked as a waiter at the Black Cat, a gay bar. What began as impromptu singing and camp commentary by Sarria as he worked in the bar became a weekly drag show that drew large audiences. Sarria used this venue to raise consciousness by challenging the passive and self-loathing attitudes of many Black Cat customers. After each drag show he gave a pep talk to the audience and ended by singing a modified version of "God Save the Queen," which he had called "God Save the Nellie Queens." George Mendenhall, a Black Cat customer, recalled that at a time when

many gays felt oppressed and powerless, "José would make these political comments about our rights as homosexuals. [Sarria's comments marked] the beginning of my awareness as a gay person."

After World War II, gays and lesbians had begun to discretely organize on behalf of their dignity and civil rights. In Los Angeles, Lisa Ben (pseudonym) published *Vice Versa*, an underground lesbian newsletter (1947-1948). In the 1950's, the first lasting gay organizations in the United States (the Mattachine Society and ONE) and the first lesbian organization (Daughters of Bilitis) were formed. In San Francisco in 1959, Daughters of Bilitis, led by Del Martin and Phyllis Lyon, was instrumental in helping to defeat a homophobic mayoral candidate. Gays and lesbians began to gain skills and confidence in the political arena.

In 1961, Sarria formed the League for Civil Education, which provided educational programs about homosexuality and support for gays who had been victimized by police entrapment. After the league folded because of internecine conflicts, Sarria helped organize the Society for Individual Rights (SIR), which provided a variety of social and legal services for the next seventeen years and was arguably the first gay community services center in the United States. In 1961, Sarria, ever the pioneer, decided to run for a seat on the San Francisco board of supervisors, becoming the first out homosexual to run for office in the United States. His campaign flyer quoted from the words engraved on the San Francisco Hall of Justice, which spoke of impartial enforcement of laws and equal justice for all.

Initially, Sarria had been one of nine candidates running for five seats on the board, but twelve hours before the filing deadline, a total of thirty-three candidates had filed. Some of the newcomers were undoubtedly drafted to weaken Sarria's position. Although Sarria lost, he received more than fifty-five hundred votes and placed ninth overall, a sign that some people were willing to vote for an out gay person.

## SIGNIFICANCE

José Sarria's run for office as an out gay person set a precedent that would inspire a new generation of activists during the following decade. After the Stonewall uprising of June, 1969, radical Gay Liberation Front groups proliferated across the United States and some out gays and lesbians decided to run for office. During the McCarthy witch hunts of the 1950's, Frank Kameny, an astronomer, had been fired from his job at a government agency because of his sexual orientation. Kameny did not go quietly. He sued the government but eventually lost his case. He became a full-time activist and an early promoter of radical, affirmative gay politics. The slogan Gay is Good is attributed to him. In 1971, he decided to run for Congress as an openly gay man. He placed fourth in a field of six candidates.

In 1973, Nancy Weschler and Jerry DeGrieck, two members of the Ann Arbor, Michigan, city council, came out. The following year was a watershed year for lesbian and gay electoral politics. Kathy Kozachenko ran as an out lesbian and won a seat on the Ann Arbor city council as well. In November, Elaine Noble, also an out lesbian, was elected to the Massachusetts House of Representatives, and Minnesota state senator Alan Spears came out. In 1977, sixteen years after José Sarria's run, Harvey Milk was the first out gay person elected to the San Francisco board of supervisors. Harvey, along with San Francisco mayor George Moscone, was assassinated in 1978 by disgruntled former San Francisco supervisor Dan White.

In the 1980's, Congressmen Gerry Studds (1983) and Barney Frank (1987), both from Massachusetts, came out as gay because of sex scandals. Republicans in the House of Representatives, Jim Kolbe (Arizona) and Steve Gunderson (Wisconsin), came out in the 1990's. The millennium ended with out lesbian Tammy Baldwin elected from Wisconsin to the U.S. House of Representatives (1998). In 2003, Ron Oden became the first African Ameri-

can (and the first gay) mayor of Palm Springs, California. One year later, out lesbian Lupe Valdéz was elected sheriff of Dallas County, Texas. In 2006, New York City councilwoman Christine Quinn was elected as speaker of the council.

In an *Echelon* magazine article in early 2006, The Victory Fund, which provides support to lesbian, gay, bisexual, transgender, and intersex (LGBTI) candidates, announced that since 1992, the number of out elected LGBT officials in the United States had grown from 49 to more than 350. Sarria, eighty-three years old in 2006 and the "grand dame" and "empress" of the court system (of drag culture) in San Francisco, has lived long enough to see the beginning of his dream of acceptance and dignity for LGBT people.

—*Yolanda Retter*

## FURTHER READING

Boyd, Nan Alamilla, ed. *Wide-Open Town: A History of Queer San Francisco to 1965*. Berkeley: University of California Press, 2003.

Bullough, Vern L., Judith M. Saunders, and C. Todd White, eds. *Before Stonewall: Activists for Gay and Lesbian Rights in Historical Context*. New York: Harrington Park Press, 2002.

D'Emilio, John. *Sexual Politics, Sexual Communities*. 2d ed. Chicago: University of Chicago Press, 1998.

*Echelon*. http://www.echelonmagazine.com/ news_ victoryfund.htm.

Gorman, Michael Robert. *The Empress Is a Man: Stories from the Life of Jose Sarria*. New York: Haworth Press, 1998.

SEE ALSO: 1971: Kameny Is First Out Candidate for U.S. Congress; Nov. 5, 1974: Noble Is First Out Lesbian or Gay Person to Win State-Level Election; July 14, 1983: Studds Is First Out Gay Man in the U.S. Congress; Nov. 6, 1984: West Hollywood Incorporates with Majority Gay and Lesbian City Council; May 30, 1987: U.S. Congressman Frank Comes Out as Gay; May 24, 1993: Achtenberg Becomes Assistant Housing Secretary.

# 1963
# RECHY PUBLISHES *CITY OF NIGHT*

*John Rechy's experiences hustling and his extraordinary literary and reporting skills led him to write his novel* City of Night, *which gave readers a hitherto unseen panorama of gay characters, places, and cultures in late 1950's and early 1960's America.*

**LOCALE:** New York, New York
**CATEGORIES:** Literature; publications

**KEY FIGURES**
*John Rechy* (b. 1934), American author and educator
*Don Merriam Allen* (1912-2004), American literary editor and anthologist

**SUMMARY OF EVENT**
*City of Night* is a novel in segments, interspersed with lyrical commentary by an unnamed first-person narrator, a male hustler. The novel is framed by the recollection of the protagonist's first loss as a child in El Paso, Texas: the death of his dog, for which he is inconsolable because he has been told that dogs cannot go to heaven. This example of life's unfairness leads the narrator to question other inequities and to empathize with the very tricks who, by selecting and paying him, empower him and allay certain identity crises.

Freedom for a gay life has often been found through travel. Although *City of Night* is set in the United States, the narrator crosses the country, giving dispatches, as it were, from most major U.S. cities. The narrator creates a travelogue of underground life from the late 1950's to the time of the novel's publication in 1963.

"City of night" refers in part to life in areas of cities that are unknown to most heterosexuals and even to those gays who do not participate in gay life at the margins. During the period when the novel takes place, the subcultures of gay life came alive at night in areas of cities rejected by straights. At the same time that characters in the novel are alienated

from mainstream venues, they are initiates of other places difficult to reach and purposely not well advertised. This inverse glamour is akin to slumming and reminiscent of the location of clubs in offbeat parts of cities, even into the twenty-first century.

The narrator moves through classes and cultures as fluidly as he moves across the physical landscape. He and his fellow hustlers are privileged to enter—though not belong to—the world of an elite Hollywood film director, for example. Middle class by birth and having chosen the life of a hustler, the narrator witnesses "the compassion that only one outcast can feel for another." Transient experiences inspire and become a permanent art, whereby he extends his compassion to his characters.

Prominent among these characters are drag queens, such as Darling Dolly Dane and Miss Destiny, whose dream is to have a lavish wedding with one of her hustler beaux. In contrast to her actual living conditions in Echo Park, a run-down area of Los Angeles in the early 1960's, Miss Destiny dreams of a life as a conventionally gendered woman. Her assertive if not aggressive dialogue stems from the daily struggles of drag queens to define themselves and their gender roles in society.

Other characters include johns who pay the narrator for specific "sexual" acts, such as sitting around naked while the john cooks dinner; skewed scenes of domesticity, traditionally denied to gay men; and scenes of intimacy between the narrator and a fellow hustler. Hustling and hustler bars do not, of course, represent gay life generally and have never been in the mainstream. In the restricted and oppressive atmosphere of the late 1950's and early 1960's, however, working-class gay bars often drew gays who were not strictly a part of the drag queen and hustler cultures, providing opportunities for johns to meet hustlers. Johns placed an emphasis on actual or perceived straightness, at a time when queens cruised military men in uniform. Johns sought hustlers who dressed according to the masculine norms of the time, with clothing styles and

## JOHN RECHY

With the publication of his first novel, *City of Night* (1963), John Rechy commenced a lifelong process of self-analysis. "My life," Rechy stated, "is so intertwined with my writing that I almost live it as if it were a novel." In particular, Rechy examines the ways in which gay sexuality, Chicano and European American heritages, and the strictures of the Roman Catholic Church struggle and sometimes harmonize with one another despite incompatibilities. Rechy writes what he calls "autobiography as fiction" in order to construct parables of spiritual salvation and damnation. Alternately remote from or near to God, family, and human connection, Rechy's protagonists struggle against self-absorption and the fear of death.

Rechy's parents immigrated to the southwestern United States during the Mexican Revolution. Rechy grew up torn between his father's stern sense of defeat in the face of anti-Mexican discrimination and his mother's intense protection of her son. The combination of his father's Scottish heritage and his mother's traditional Mexican background made Rechy intensely aware of his status as a person of mixed ancestry in the El Paso of his youth.

Conflicts and pressures at home caused him to move into a narcissistic remoteness that found comfort in the emotional distance of purchased sex. Wandering the country after high school, Rechy worked as a male prostitute in New York, Los Angeles, San Francisco, Chicago, and New Orleans. These experiences as a hustler became the material for *City of Night*. This first-person narrative of sexual and spiritual salvation combines an unapologetic depiction of the sexual underground, featuring a sympathetic protagonist's search for ultimate connection and caring.

Set against both the urban indifference of Los Angeles and the unforgiving landscape of the desert Southwest, Rechy's novels explore the thematic connections between sex, soul, and self. In subsequent works—in particular, *This Day's Death* (1970) and *The Miraculous Day of Amalia Gómez* (1991)—Rechy has extended his explorations of the spirit to the particulars of Chicano family and culture.

Rechy's autobiographical fictions chart the intersections of ethnic, sexual, regional, and religious identities. He journeys across the southwestern landscape, through sex and spirit, along the night streets of Los Angeles, and through his own memories of growing up in El Paso.

time of the Stonewall Rebellion (1969). Concomitant changes led to diversified gay male gender identities.

### SIGNIFICANCE

*City of Night* was an outgrowth of changes in the types of subject matter that could be published in the United States. After numerous court challenges, the pioneering Grove Press was able to publish and sell books formerly "published in Paris" and long sold only "under the counter." Grove Press books include *Lady Chatterley's Lover* (1928) by D. H. Lawrence (Grove Press ed., 1959), *Tropic of Cancer* (1934) by Henry Miller (Grove Press ed., 1961), and translations of works by French gay author Jean Genet.

Rechy began to publish his stories of gay life in the United States during this period of change. The first story came in the form of a letter to a friend, which appeared in the Grove Press journal *Evergreen Review* in 1958. The review's editor, Don Merriam Allen, encouraged Rechy to turn subsequently published stories into a novel and supported his decision to rewrite the book completely, even after it had been in galley proofs. Although some booksellers refused to stock the novel, it appeared on U.S. best-seller lists for more than six months and also was an international best seller, translated into twenty languages. *City of Night* is widely considered an American classic, and it appears on the required reading lists of many general literature courses as well as those of gay literature courses.

Rechy's novel gave gay readers of its day some of the first easily available pictures of themselves.

even hairstyles influenced by outlaw actors Marlon Brando and James Dean.

The hustler narrator participates sexually in what is considered the more "masculine" role. He is not penetrated in any of the sexual acts his clients hire him to perform. This division of gays into those who assume "active" roles and those who assume "passive" roles is a construction of gay sexual identities more typical of the era than it was after the

The narrator bestows a dignity on his gay characters by writing about them from inside their world and by observing them "clinically," as would a psychologist or social worker, a common practice at the time when writing about gay life.

Rechy has written numerous other works of fiction and nonfiction with breakthrough subject matter. The persona from *City of Night* cruises into the next novel, *Numbers* (1967), where the narrator is given the name Johnny Rio. Johnny's story is one in which the desire and ability of homosexuals to have multiple sexual partners, "numbers," is used as a metaphor for larger questions of sexual identity.

Rechy has also been a teacher of writers, and alumnae from his courses have published extensively in all genres. In the early 1970's, he began lecturing to classes in gay literature, and he has written numerous book reviews. He also has influenced a much younger generation of outlaw or outsider writers, such as J. T. Leroy, author of *The Heart Is Deceitful Above All Things* (2001), and Mack Friedman, author of a history of male hustlers, *Strapped for Cash* (2003).

—*Dan Luckenbill*

## Further Reading

Bredbeck, Gregory W. "John Rechy." In *Contemporary Gay American Novelists*, edited by Emmanuel S. Nelson. Westport, Conn.: Greenwood Press, 1993.

Casillo, Charles. *Outlaw: The Lives and Careers of John Rechy*. Los Angeles: Advocate Books, 2002.

Friedman, Mack. *Strapped for Cash: A History of American Hustler Culture*. Los Angeles: Alyson, 2003.

Rechy, John. *City of Night*. New York: Grove Press, 1963.

_____. *Numbers*. New York: Grove Press, 1967.

_____. *The Sexual Outlaw: A Documentary, a Non-Fiction Account, with Commentaries, of Three Days and Nights in the Sexual Underground*. New York: Grove Press, 1977.

**SEE ALSO:** July 4, 1855: Whitman Publishes *Leaves of Grass*; May 25, 1895: Oscar Wilde Is Convicted of Gross Indecency; 1924: Gide Publishes the Signed Edition of *Corydon*; 1939: Isherwood Publishes *Goodbye to Berlin*; 1947-1948: Golden Age of American Gay Literature; 1956: Baldwin Publishes *Giovanni's Room*; June, 1971: The Gay Book Award Debuts; 1974: *The Front Runner* Makes *The New York Times* Best-Seller List; 1975: First Novel About Coming Out to Parents Is Published; 1980: Alyson Begins Publishing Gay and Lesbian Books; 1980-1981: Gay Writers Form the Violet Quill; May, 1987: *Lambda Rising Book Report* Begins Publication; June 2, 1989: Lambda Literary Award Is Created; 1993: Monette Wins the National Book Award for *Becoming a Man*.

**July 2-August 28, 1963**

# Rustin Organizes the March on Washington

*Bayard Rustin, a gay African American, organized the 1963 March on Washington, the event where Martin Luther King, Jr., delivered his famous "I Have a Dream" speech, one of the most important orations in U.S. history. The march had been the largest demonstration on the nation's capital.*

**Also known as:** March on Washington for Jobs and Freedom

**Locale:** Washington, D.C.

**Categories:** Civil rights; marches, protests, and riots; organizations and institutions; race and ethnicity

**Key Figures**

*Bayard Rustin* (1910-1987), African American civil rights leader, war-resistance activist, pacifist, and organizer of the 1963 March on Washington

*Martin Luther King, Jr.* (1929-1968), civil rights leader, reverend, Nobel Peace Prize winner, and march speaker

*A. Philip Randolph* (1889-1979), African American labor leader, civil rights activist, and chair of the march

**Summary of Event**

Meeting in New York City on July 2, 1963, a coalition of key civil rights leaders planned a march on Washington, D.C. Coalition members included Martin Luther King, Jr., founder of the Southern Christian Leadership Conference (SCLC); A. Philip Randolph (founder of the Brotherhood of Sleeping Car Porters and vice president of the AFL-CIO); Roy Wilkins of the National Association for the Advancement of Colored People (NAACP); Whitney Young, Jr., of the Urban League; John Lewis from the SNCC (Student Nonviolent Coordinating Committee); and James Farmer from CORE (the Congress of Racial Equality).

After debate, the group selected Bayard Rustin,

the founder of CORE, to coordinate the march. The official March on Washington for Jobs and Freedom director, Randolph, an activist labor leader and civil rights veteran, supported Rustin to work on his behalf as chief march planner, which Bayard successfully did in only two months.

Within the first weeks of planning, Rustin had an organizing manual written and two thousand copies distributed to civil rights leaders in strategic locations throughout the United States. Funds were raised by collecting large and small donations and through sales of buttons and an official memento that consisted of a portfolio of photographs. By mid-August, 175,000 buttons had been purchased by supporters for twenty-five cents each, and 40,000 portfolios had been printed.

Randolph's and Rustin's collaboration, however, had begun in 1941, when Randolph, with Rustin's assistance, planned a March on Washington to protest racism in the U.S. armed forces. The 1941 march never materialized, however, because at the last moment, President Franklin D. Roosevelt issued an executive order protecting African American rights. Rustin continued to organize after the 1963 March on Washington, and in 1964, he was involved in the extensive New York City school boycott to protest continued segregation in the city's schools.

In the mid-1950's, lesbian writer and activist Lillian Smith pressed Rustin to assist King in developing Gandhian principles of nonviolent resistance for the Montgomery, Alabama, bus boycott. Smith was the internationally acclaimed author of the controversial 1944 novel *Strange Fruit*—the tale of lynching in a small Southern town—and was the companion of Paula Snelling, a professor at the University of Georgia. In 1964, Smith published *Our Faces, Our Words*, a work that extolled the principles of nonviolence that had become a fundamental part of the Civil Rights movement, in large part through the influence of Rustin. Smith had asked Rustin to assist King because of his under-

*Bayard Rustin at a news conference before the March on Washington in August, 1963.* (Library of Congress)

standing of nonviolence, which originated in his family's ties to the pacifist church, the Religious Society of Friends (Quakers).

Rustin's philosophy of nonviolence had deepened during his periodic travels to India and Africa between 1947 and 1952 to explore the peaceful reistance embedded in independence movements. By the late 1950's, Rustin had become a speechwriter, political adviser, and confidant of King, and he was instrumental in bringing Gandhi's protest techniques to the American Civil Rights movement.

Rustin's life as an African American as well as a gay person placed him in many tense and dangerous situations. Being gay during a fiercely homophobic and bigoted time in U.S. history led him to voice concerns about the civil rights denied to people because of their sexual orientation. As a black man he was engaged in the civil rights struggle for African

American freedom—political and economic. White segregationists such as Strom Thurmond, a U.S. senator from South Carolina, used Rustin's homosexuality to try to discredit the Civil Rights movement. The term "communist" was used by FBI director J. Edgar Hoover and others in their attempts to block the march and to discredit King.

In July, 1963, Thurmond attacked the march on the floor of the U.S. Senate, using Rustin's sexual orientation, namely his arrest on charges of public indecency in Pasadena, California, in 1953, as his main rhetorical weapon. Thurmond also attacked Rustin's pacifism (he "dodged" the draft) and his former Communist Party affiliation, all to dishonor him and the Civil Rights movement. In a similar way, Senator Jesse Helms of North Carolina later smeared Rustin's reputation.

### SIGNIFICANCE

The 1963 March on Washington, held on August 28, was the culmination of more than two decades of civil rights struggles by churches, labor organizations, and social-justice advocates. The march focused on civil rights and national economic demands and galvanized the Civil Rights movement unlike any event up to that time, bringing as many as a quarter of a million people into the streets under Rustin's organizational leadership.

Rustin was implicated in some of the political strife *within* the Civil Rights movement itself. In 1985, during an interview for an oral history project at Columbia University, he revealed that in 1960, Harlem congressmember Adam Clayton Powell threatened to expose his homosexuality. The event led King to publicly disassociate himself from Rustin for a period of time.

Like a number of other civil rights leaders, Rustin refused to take up identity politics and was labeled an "Uncle Tom" by radical militants of the Black Power movement—a charge used to show disapproval of the tactics of often older, traditional, religious African Americans.

Always controversial, Rustin alienated some in the black community because he was critical of affirmative action programs and the development of black studies departments in U.S. colleges and universities. He alienated himself from liberals because of his support of Israel. Rustin's homosexuality appears to have been particularly troublesome for Roy Wilkins, a key figure who played a major role in the preparation of *Brown v. Board of Education of Topeka* (1954), the case that led to legally mandated desegregation of schools in the United States.

For his efforts to stop segregation in interstate travel, in 1948 the Council Against Intolerance in America gave Rustin the Thomas Jefferson Award for the Advancement of Democracy. Throughout his life he was an outspoken advocate of freedom and democracy, a passion that took him to Chile, El Salvador, Grenada, Haiti, Poland, and Zimbabwe as a delegate for Freedom House, a nongovernmental organization (NGO) founded by Eleanor Roosevelt, Wendell Wilkie, and other Americans concerned with the mounting threats to peace and democracy around the world. In this capacity, Rustin helped to monitor elections and the status of human rights.

Shortly before Rustin died of cardiac arrest on August 24, 1987, at Lenox Hill Hospital in New York City, he had compared the black struggle with the fight for gay and lesbian rights. He noted one major difference: In the black struggle, gaining rights under the law had to be joined with economic relief. Citing King, he said that getting into a restaurant was only half the fight—having the money to buy food was the other part of the equation. Human rights in the African American struggle included economic *and* social rights. For gays and lesbians, Rustin felt that the struggle was about prejudice under the law only.

In the early twenty-first century, the relationship between African American civil rights and rights for sexual minorities is still being debated. One point is seldom argued, however, when comparing the struggles of people of color with those of sexual minorities—a truth found in a statement Rustin made in November, 1960. In an interview, together with Malcolm X, at radio station WRAI in New York, Bayard said, "it is quite impossible for people to struggle creatively if they do not truly believe in themselves."

In tireless toil, troubles, opprobrium, and the face of death, Bayard Rustin never stopped believing in himself—even when those around him had ceased to believe in him. This is the hallmark of Rustin, the black gay man who was at the center of the African American freedom struggle.

*—Robert Hill*

## FURTHER READING

Anderson, J. *Bayard Rustin: Troubles I've Seen—A Biography*. New York: HarperCollins, 1997.

"Bayard Rustin, African American Gay Hero." In *OUT in All Directions: An Almanac of Gay and Lesbian America*, edited by Lynn Witt, Sherry Thomas, and Eric Marcus. New York: Warner Books, 1995.

"Bayard Rustin: Obituary." *The New Republic*, September 28, 1987, 10.

*Brother Outsider: The Life of Bayard Rustin*. Nancy Kates and Bennett Singer, producers and directors. Independent Television Service, the National Black Programming Consortium, KQED. South Burlington, Vt.: California Newsreel, 2002. Video recording. http://rustin.org.

D'Emilio, John. *Lost Prophet: The Life and Times of Bayard Rustin*. New York: Free Press, 2003.

Edwin, Ed. "The Reminiscences of Bayard Rustin." In *Adam's Friends and Foes: Bayard Rustin* (February 28, 1985). New York: Columbia University, Oral History Office. http://c250.columbia.edu/c250_celebrates/harlem_history/rustin_p.html.

Gates, Henry Louis. "Blacklash." In *The Columbia Reader on Lesbians and Gay Men in Media, Society, and Politics*, edited by Larry Gross and James D. Woods. New York: Columbia University Press, 1999.

Haskins, J. *Bayard Rustin: Behind the Scenes of the Civil Rights Movement*. New York: Hyperion Press, 1997.

Kasher, Steven. *The Civil Rights Movement: A Photographic History, 1954-1968*. Foreword by Myrlie Evers-Williams. New York: Abbeville Press, 1996.

Levine, D. *Bayard Rustin and the Civil Rights Movement*. New Brunswick, N.J.: Rutgers University Press, 1999.

Rollins, Avon, Sr. "The March on Washington Remembered." http://www.crmvet.org/info/mow rolin.htm.

Rustin, Bayard. *Down the Line: The Collected Writings of Bayard Rustin*. Chicago: Quadrangle Books, 1971.

_____. *Time on Two Crosses: The Collected Writings of Bayard Rustin*. Edited by D. W. Carbado and D. Weise. San Francisco, Calif.: Cleis Press, 2003.

**SEE ALSO:** 1956: Baldwin Publishes *Giovanni's Room*; June 28, 1970: First Lesbian and Gay Pride March in the United States; Nov. 7, 1972: Jordan Becomes First Black Congresswoman from the South; July 3, 1975: U.S. Civil Service Commission Prohibits Discrimination Against Federal Employees; Apr., 1977: Combahee River Collective Issues "A Black Feminist Statement"; Oct. 12-15, 1979: First March on Washington for Lesbian and Gay Rights; 1981: *This Bridge Called My Back* Is Published; Oct., 1981: Kitchen Table: Women of Color Press Is Founded; 1982: Lorde's Autobiography *Zami* Is Published; Sept., 1983: First National Lesbians of Color Conference Convenes; May 3, 1989: *Watkins v. United States Army* Reinstates Gay Soldier; 1990: United Lesbians of African Heritage Is Founded.

## November, 1965
# REVOLUTIONARY CUBA IMPRISONS GAYS

*In bursts of nationalistic zeal, Fidel Castro's regime in 1963 began rounding up gay men, as well as priests, intellectuals, and others considered counterrevolutionary, and forced them to undertake hard labor in the infamous concentration camps called Military Units to Aid Production (UMAP). The camps were fully operational by the end of 1965.*

**LOCALE:** Cuba

**CATEGORIES:** Government and politics; military; laws, acts, and legal history; civil rights; organizations and institutions

### KEY FIGURES

*Fidel Castro* (b. 1926 or 1927), prime minister and first secretary of the Communist Party in Cuba

*Che Guevara* (1928-1967), Argentinian physician who became Castro's chief aide and later an icon of revolutionary fervor

*Reinaldo Arenas* (1943-1990), Cuban writer

### SUMMARY OF EVENT

Communism in Cuba initially triggered the systematic persecution of gay men. Like most nationalistic uprisings, the early Cuban Revolution was homophobic, associating gay men regardless of class or race with the bourgeoisie and believing them traitors helping the hated Americans to exploit their long-oppressed country. It is true that the revolution bettered conditions for women and Afro-Cubans and that it provided universal education and health care unmatched in Latin America. Yet those gains came at a price. Much of the former establishment had left for exile in Miami, so the new government targeted anyone still left with any connection, however imagined or tenuous, to the decadent nightlife of former Cuban dictator Fulgencio Batista y Zaldívar's Havana, whose regime was overthrown by Fidel Castro in 1959.

The revolutionary dictator Castro, by the middle 1960's, created his own set of indigenous gulags, or forced-labor camps, euphemistically known as Military Units to Aid Production (UMAP). Ironically reconfirming Cuba's economy as a sugar monoculture, this politically correct (to the Communists) slavery was designed to cure and contain perceived domestic threats to national security and ideological loyalty. It was also designed to keep the stalled revolution going.

## REINALDO ARENAS

Reinaldo Arenas overcame a poor rural upbringing to become a renowned novelist and short-story writer. He belongs to a generation of young writers who received literary training in official programs to promote literacy among the Cuban poor. Such training, however, also involved heavy indoctrination by political organizations that promoted only revolutionary readings. Although his career depended upon his incorporation into such political agenda, Arenas refused to take an ideological stand. His decision caused him prosecution by legal authorities, imprisonment, and exile.

A superb storyteller, Arenas, in his first novel, *Celestino antes del alba* (1967; revised as *Cantando en el pozo*, 1982; *Singing from the Well*, 1987), presents young peasant characters who find themselves in an existentialist quest. Surrounded by a bleak rural environment, these protagonists fight the absolute poverty that keeps them from achieving their dreams. They also must confront their homosexual feelings, which force them to become outcasts. Although the subject of homosexuality is not an essential theme of the novel—the subject is merely hinted at— Arenas's novel received a cold reception from Cuban critics.

*El mundo alucinante* (1969; *Hallucinations*, 1971) brought Arenas's first confrontations with revolutionary critics and political authorities. Dissatisfied with the Castro regime, Arenas in the novel equates the Cuban Revolution to the oppressive forces of the Spanish Inquisition by drawing parallels between the persecutory practices of the two institutions. He also published the novel abroad without governmental consent, a crime punishable by law. That violation caused him to lose job opportunities and made him the target of multiple attempts at indoctrination, which included his imprisonment in a forced labor camp in 1970.

In spite of constant threats, Arenas continued writing antirevolutionary works that were smuggled out of the country by friends and published abroad in French translations. The theme of these works is constant: denunciation of Castro's oppressive political practices, most significantly the forced labor camps. The novels also decry the systematic persecution of gays by military police and the relocation of gays in labor camps.

After an incarceration of almost three years (1973-1976), Arenas made several attempts to escape from Cuba illegally. He finally succeeded in 1980, when he entered the United States by means of the Mariel boat lift. In the United States he continued his strong opposition to the Castro regime and re-edited the literary work he had written in Cuba. In addition, he intensified his interest in gay characters who, like his early young characters, find themselves in confrontation with the oppressive societies that punish them because of their sexual orientation. His open treatment of homosexuality makes him a forerunner of writers on that subject in Latin American literature.

---

Both inspired and threatened by the uncompromising idealism of his chief aide Che Guevara, Castro proclaimed that the success of the revolution demanded the making of a "new man," a self-sacrificing father who would endure anything, including self-abnegation, for the common good as defined by the omnipresent state. The pesky threats who needed to be made into "new men" included Jehovah's Witnesses, Catholic priests, vagrants, transvestites, and homosexuals, "social scum" who were believed to have stemmed from either superfluous traditions or capitalistic selfishness. The regime saved its worst contempt for intellectuals, with many teachers at the University of Havana losing their jobs and homes. To Castro, real men did not speak their own minds; real men had the socialist discipline to not always be themselves and to de-

fer to their communal responsibilities of work and family. Thus, Castro's "family values" campaign was overtly anticlerical and anti-intellectual as well as homophobic. He oppressed the born again, the bookworms, and the drag queens.

Castro cast a broad net for his prey. Beginning in 1963 and in full operation by mid-1965, his secret police raided the homes and churches of those individuals he had written off as counterrevolutionary. Focusing on cities, his minions arrested thousands of men, who were detained at their local police station under the pretext of verifying their identity. From the police stations, the detainees were transferred to warehouses, stadiums, and makeshift shelters to be tortured until they confessed to counterrevolutionary activities that, among other things, included sodomy. The ones who broke down and confessed were forced to sign a written document that listed their alleged "crimes." These prisoners were then temporarily released to their families, only to be summoned a few months later to a more permanent stay at dreaded concentration camps set up in remote areas of the province of Camaguey.

Internment began in earnest in November of 1965. While not as gruesome or extensive as Hitler's Auschwitz and other concentration camps or Stalin's archipelago, the UMAP of Camaguey served the same purpose: to humiliate, starve, injure, and murder specified groups on a relatively large scale and away from the eyes of the foreign press. In a twisted ideological insistence, many of the urban residents who were jailed were forced to work on neighboring collectivized sugar plantations. Since no one, including the guards in charge, had any agricultural expertise, these cruel experiments contributed to the infamous failed harvests that never met their stated quotas.

This uniquely Cuban maltreatment was never actually designed on a practical level to turn gays, professors, and Christians into socialists. Conversion or recycling so-called human garbage was merely the rhetorical justification put forth by Castro to his party faithful. Ironically, seventy years earlier, and long before Auschwitz, the Spanish had established the very first concentration camps in colonial Cuba to combat insurgents. The concept returned to revolutionary Cuba with a vengeance and has yet to leave completely, although the official name "UMAP" was dropped from the camps in July, 1968. The high-water mark of official homophobia came three years after the renaming and eventual revamping of the camps. An infamous 1971 cultural declaration connected "homosexual deviations" with "the question of social pathology."

## SIGNIFICANCE

Persecution of gays has never really stopped in Castro's Cuba, although overt denunciations of homosexuals as counterrevolutionary died down in part to please world opinion, especially leftists abroad. Even during the 1960's within Cuba, however, there was strong resistance to the UMAP. The state-sponsored Union of Artists and Writers of Cuba (UNEAC) criticized the UMAP in 1967, a brave move that set the stage for marginally better conditions at the camps that would no longer be called UMAP.

Reinaldo Arenas, a famous author and later exile who had been imprisoned by the regime—in a forced labor camp in 1970 and again from 1973 to 1976—writes in his autobiography, *Before Night Falls* (1993), of more private and effective resistance by gay men to the official oppression. He graphically describes the promiscuity and the sexual liberation sweeping the country in the 1960's that Castro's policies failed to squelch. In fact, Arenas speculates that widespread persecution pushed many men, to whatever extent they were gay, to rebel against the bleak conformity required to be a socialist "new man." To the libertine Arenas, they had sex with each other with an enthusiasm like never before or since.

Public opinion abroad, however, and not sexual behavior domestically, changed at minimum the legal status of gays in Cuba. In the late 1980's, Castro repealed laws against open homosexuality, even if at the same time he also incarcerated those who were HIV-positive. The 1990's witnessed official funding and approval of films, such as *Strawberry and Chocolate*, which are critical of earlier Communist homophobia. Yet camps and jails remain filled with gays and others who continue to dissent in the name of expressive freedoms.

The creation of the UMAP in Cuba shows that homophobia was not restricted to political conservatives in the twentieth century, even though American policymakers linked communism with homosexuality in the 1950's and 1960's. Regardless of ideology, authoritarian governments around the world attacked creative people, the outspoken, and intellectuals, who stereotypically included many gay men and, similarly, many religious people who dared to be different. These governments tried to create new utopias but instead created dystopias.

—*Charles H. Ford*

**FURTHER READING**

Arenas, Reinaldo. *Before Night Falls*. New York: Viking Press, 1993.

Bejel, Emilio. *Gay Cuban Nation*. Chicago: University of Chicago Press, 2001.

Blazquez, Agustin, and Jaums Sutton. "UMAP: Castro's Genocide Plan." 1999. http://www .nocastro.com/archives/umapgenoc.htm.

Geyer, Georgie Ann. *Guerrilla Prince: The Untold Story of Fidel Castro*. Boston: Little, Brown, 1991.

Lumsden, Ian. *Machos, Maricones, and Gays: Cuba and Homosexuality*. Philadelphia: Temple University Press, 1996.

Matthews, Herbert L. *Revolution in Cuba: An Essay in Understanding*. New York: Charles Scribner's Sons, 1975.

Valls, Jorge. *Twenty Years and Forty Days: Life in a Cuban Prison*. New York: Americas Watch, 1986.

**SEE ALSO:** Nov. 17, 1901: Police Arrest "Los 41" in Mexico City; 1912-1924: Robles Fights in the Mexican Revolution; 1933-1945: Nazis Persecute Homosexuals; June 30-July 1, 1934: Hitler's Night of the Long Knives; 1969: Nuestro Mundo Forms as First Queer Organization in Argentina; Oct. 14-17, 1987: Latin American and Caribbean Lesbian Feminist Network Is Formed; June 19, 2002: Gays and Lesbians March for Equal Rights in Mexico City; Apr., 2003: Buenos Aires Recognizes Same-Gender Civil Unions; Jan., 2006: Jiménez Flores Elected to the Mexican Senate.

## February 19-20, 1966
# FIRST NORTH AMERICAN CONFERENCE OF HOMOPHILE ORGANIZATIONS CONVENES

*The first national meeting of gay and lesbian organizations fostered communication among a wide variety of groups from across the United States and Canada, giving structure to what had been a loose configuration of civil rights organizations focused on lesbian and gay rights. The groups would soon form into the first GLBT political action coalition, the North American Conference of Homophile Organizations, in 1968.*

**LOCALE:** Kansas City, Missouri

**CATEGORIES:** Organizations and institutions; civil rights; government and politics

**KEY FIGURES**

*Clarence Colwell*, president of the Council on Religion and the Homosexual and minister of the Northern California Conference of the United Church of Christ

*William Kelley*, officer of Mattachine Midwest

**SUMMARY OF EVENT**

In 1965, an estimated fifteen million gays and lesbians were living in the United States. The first gay or lesbian group to survive for any legitimate period of time, the Mattachine Society, had by then been in existence for nearly fifteen years. Only a handful of scattered organizations had taken shape by the end of the 1960's, while the persecution and harassment of homosexuals continued.

At the Third Annual East Coast Homophile Organizations conference in 1965, organizations discussed how little was known about each other's structure and actions, and that the lack of communication and collaboration among organizations was an impediment to the progress of the GLBT movement. In this light, a conference was planned for a central location, convenient enough so that groups from all over the United States and Canada could meet to exchange ideas and strategies. Shortly thereafter, the liaison committee of the Mattachine

Society of New York drafted a preliminary agenda and invitation list for the meeting, which was set for Kansas City, Missouri, on February 19 and 20, 1966. Each organization would be allotted three votes during the conference, and each group could send delegates with the authority to cast those votes.

Clark Polak, president of the Janus Society in Philadelphia, originally had arranged for the conference to be held in a photography studio, but numerous complaints were made that such a space would compromise the dignity of the event. Instead, the conference, held at the State Hotel, included forty individuals (eight of whom were women) representing sixteen organizations. Dick Leitsch, president of the Mattachine Society of New York, had asked William Beardemphl, president of the Society for Individual Rights in San Francisco, to moderate the event. Although Beardemphl would attend the event, he declined the honor to moderate and alternately suggested the Reverend Clarence Colwell, president of the Council on Religion and the Homosexual of San Francisco, and another person, who was not gay or lesbian; both accepted the offer.

Among the organizations present were Citizens News (San Francisco); ONE, Inc. (Los Angeles); ONE in Kansas City; Daughters of Bilitis (San Francisco, New York, and Chicago chapters); Janus Society of America (Philadelphia); Mattachine Society (San Francisco); Mattachine Midwest (Chicago); Mattachine Society of New York; Mattachine Society of Philadelphia; Mattachine Society of Florida; Mattachine Society of Washington; National League for Social Understanding (Los Angeles); Tangents (Los An-

geles); and Tavern Guild of San Francisco. William Kelley of Mattachine Midwest presided as secretary for the conference.

The first order of business had been to learn about the goals and practices of each respective organization. With the exception of the Daughters of Bilitis, every homophile organization had a predominantly male membership and, not surprisingly, directed its concern at problems believed to be faced mostly by gay men: police harassment, unequal law enforcement, and harsh penalties for practices of solicitation or public sex. The Daugh-

*Protesters carry signs outside Independence Hall in Philadelphia on July 4, 1965, in one of the first rallies of its kind for gay and lesbian rights. The early rallies helped inspire centralized political organizing by gay and lesbian groups around the country.* (Courtesy, Equality Forum)

ters of Bilitis wanted confirmation that the conference would "be as concerned about women's civil rights as [it would be about] male homosexuals' civil liberties." Additionally, groups were working to end discrimination in government employment and the military (including obtaining security clearances), to abolish sodomy laws, and to address the prevailing belief that homosexuality was a sickness. Some organizations came with the understanding that the conference was simply a forum for communication on such issues, while others came with the distinct hope to start a unified national front, but only four of the organizations granted their delegates voting authority.

Constituents agreed to establish a legal defense fund (in principle only), to hold a nationwide protest on Armed Forces Day (May 21), to publish a work on various aspects of homosexuality, and to produce a pact of cooperation to open communication and to update one another through publications, by-laws, and constitutions. The conference issued a statement to the press that "objective research projects undertaken thus far have indicated that findings of homosexual undesirability are based on opinion, value judgments or emotional reaction rather than scientific evidence or fact" and that "each homosexual should be judged as an individual." Finally, attendees agreed to hold another conference, in San Francisco, in August of the same year.

## SIGNIFICANCE

The conference in Kansas City marked the birth of the first concerted effort toward a national interorganizational GLBT rights movement. The planning conference continued to meet and became the North American Conference of Homophile Organizations (NACHO). The coalition promoted an unprecedented amount of communication and collaboration that did not see reproach. New organizations surfaced, and new individuals joined the movement after the conference. By 1967, NACHO claimed a membership of six thousand individuals and organizations. The first national day of protest was held as scheduled on May 21, and a legal defense fund was established in San Francisco.

The national day of protest, the founding of the

legal defense fund, and further intergroup actions fostered through NACHO brought attention to injustice toward gays and lesbians. Between 1966 and 1969, for cases concerning dismissals from civil service, courts started to demand from prosecutors evidence other than the charge of "immoral conduct" between consenting adults in private.

NACHO would convene five more times: San Francisco in 1966, Washington, D.C., in 1967, Chicago in 1968, Kansas City in 1969, and San Francisco in 1970. The organization had fostered an environment that emboldened young leaders and laid the groundwork for a more radical GLBT movement, which was sparked into action by the 1969 Stonewall Rebellion in New York City.

—Sarah Ivy

## FURTHER READING

Blasius, Mark, and Shane Phelan. *We Are Everywhere*. New York: Routledge, 1997.

DeLeon, David, ed. *Leaders from the 1960's: A Biographical Sourcebook of American Activism*. Westport, Conn.: Greenwood Press, 1994.

D'Emilio, John. *Sexual Politics, Sexual Communities: The Making of a Homosexual Minority in the United States, 1940-1970*. 2d ed. Chicago: University of Chicago Press, 1998.

Duberman, Martin B. *Stonewall*. New York: Dutton, 1993.

Marcus, Eric. *Making Gay History: The Half Century Fight for Lesbian and Gay Equal Rights*. New York: HarperCollins, 2002.

Rimmerman, Craig A., Kenneth D. Wald, and Clyde Wilcox, eds. *The Politics of Gay Rights*. Chicago: University of Chicago Press, 2000.

SEE ALSO: Dec. 10, 1924: Gerber Founds the Society for Human Rights; 1950: Mattachine Society Is Founded; 1952: ONE, Inc., Is Founded; 1955: Daughters of Bilitis Founded as First National Lesbian Group in United States; May 27-30, 1960: First National Lesbian Conference Convenes; Apr. 19, 1967: First Student Homophile League Is Formed; Aug. 11-18, 1968: NACHO Formally Becomes the First Gay Political Coalition; July 31, 1969: Gay Liberation Front Is

Formed; June 28, 1970: First Lesbian and Gay Pride March in the United States; Nov. 28, 1970: Del Martin Quits Gay Liberation Movement; 1973: National Gay Task Force Is Formed; Oct. 18, 1973: Lambda Legal Authorized to Practice Law; Mar. 5, 1974: Antigay and Antilesbian Organizations Begin to Form; Apr. 22, 1980: Human Rights Campaign Fund Is Founded.

## August, 1966
# QUEER YOUTH FIGHT POLICE HARASSMENT AT COMPTON'S CAFETERIA IN SAN FRANCISCO

*An uprising by transgender and gay street youth at Compton's Cafeteria in San Francisco's impoverished Tenderloin neighborhood is thought to be the earliest militant expression of queer resistance by any age group to police harassment and societal oppression. The incident led to new social services for transgender individuals in San Francisco and inspired the transgender rights movement of the following decades.*

**LOCALE:** San Francisco, California
**CATEGORIES:** Marches, protests, and riots; civil rights; transgender/transsexuality

**KEY FIGURES**
*Ted McIlvenna*, social worker and later progressive minister with Glide Memorial Methodist Church
*Cecil Williams*, reverend at Glide Memorial Methodist Church

**SUMMARY OF EVENT**
The youth uprising at Compton's Cafeteria in San Francisco's Tenderloin district came at a time in San Francisco with an already well-established homophile community that included groups such as the Daughters of Bilitis, the Tavern Guild, and the Society for Individual Rights. In 1964, riding the decade's wave of progressive activism and civil rights organizing, radical ministers from Glide Memorial Methodist Church—including the Reverend Cecil Williams and Ted McIlvenna, a young social worker—joined representatives of the homophile groups to organize the Council on Religion and the Homosexual (CORH).

While the established homophile organizations had succeeded in reducing police harassment of gay bar patrons and had made inroads into the city's political establishment, disadvantaged queer youth were largely left out of the picture, since they were too young to frequent the bars and because members of the adult-focused organizations were worried that they would be charged with corrupting minors.

In the mid-1960's, ministers from Glide, homophile leaders, and neighborhood activists came together to form the Central City Citizen's Council, which succeeded in obtaining federal poverty program funds. Some of this money went toward providing services for the burgeoning population of gay, lesbian, and transgender youth—many of them runaways and hustlers—who called the streets of the Tenderloin district home. In the summer of 1966, with McIlvenna's help, local queer youth formed their own organization, Vanguard, which had a style and politics at odds with the "respectable" older groups.

Compton's Cafeteria (part of a small local chain), located at the corner of Taylor and Turk Streets, was a popular all-night gathering place for the Tenderloin's queer youth, including transgender prostitutes and young hustlers who frequented the diner between tricks and drag queens and street kids who had few other indoor places to hang out. In the spring of 1966, following the death of a gay night manager who tolerated the queer youth, the incoming management decided to discourage the young patrons, who often spent long hours, but little money, at the diner. The cafeteria hired security guards who, along with local police, harassed and intimidated the youths. One of the first actions organized by Vanguard, in July of 1966, was a picket at the diner to protest the discrimination and harassment.

One warm night in August—the exact date remains unclear—Compton's Cafeteria erupted in chaos. The incident was never well documented, and details remain scarce. According to available accounts, a police officer, late at night, tried to grab one of the young drag queens. Rather than tolerating the affront, the youth threw a cup of coffee in the officer's face. Mayhem ensued as the enraged young queers threw dishes at the police and guards, broke the cafeteria's windows, and burned down a nearby newspaper stand. The management closed the diner, and as the youth exited, police tried to grab them. This led to a general melee, with street kids hitting cops in the groin and drag queens pummeling them with their purses. The next day, Compton's banned drag queens from the establishment. That night, the queer youth—reportedly joined this time by some older, more conservative gays—set up a picket line outside the diner, and the establishment's newly repaired front window was once again smashed.

## SIGNIFICANCE

Although New York City's 1969 Stonewall Rebellion, which also was carried out largely by young drag queens, gay and lesbian street youth, and transgender persons, most often is credited with sparking the gay and lesbian liberation movement, the rebellion was not the first incident of its kind. The Compton's Cafeteria uprising was likely the first ever in which queers fought back physically against police harassment. A police raid on a New Year's Eve fund-raising ball in San Francisco in 1964, sponsored by CORH, produced outrage and prompted liberal ministers to speak out publicly against gay and lesbian oppression, but it did not lead to a physical altercation.

Other early protests against police intimidation followed a crackdown on bars and cruising spots in

the Los Angeles area beginning in the early morning hours of New Year's Day in 1967. Protests included a demonstration at a police station during which protesters "pelted" the cops with flowers. It was not until Stonewall, however, that gay, lesbian, and transgender demands entered public consciousness and the LGBT liberation movement took hold in a sustained manner.

The Compton's Cafeteria uprising can be regarded as the first glimmer of an incipient transgender movement as well, a moment when the transgender community first became politicized and began demanding its rights. Historian Susan Stryker, whose research was used for the 2005 documentary about the incident, *Screaming Queens: The Riot at Compton's Cafeteria*, argues that the formation of Vanguard gave the Tenderloin's transgender youth a new sense of empowerment.

Also around this time, street queens became aware of advances in the care of transsexuals, advances that were pioneered mainly by Harry Benjamin, who had an office in the Tenderloin, and improved procedures for gender reassignment surgery, which provided a new feeling of hope. Soon after the altercation at Compton's, new social services were put in place for transgender individuals, including city-funded clinics.

In the 1960's and 1970's, the focus was on helping transsexuals permanently transition and embark upon a new life as heterosexual and traditionally feminine or masculine members of their new gender. It was not until the 1990's that transgender activists began to demand their inclusion within the gay and lesbian community and to demand their right to occupy all positions on the gender spectrum.

*—Liz Highleyman*

## FURTHER READING

Anonymous. "History of Christopher Street West, San Francisco." In the San Francisco Gay Pride program book. June 25, 1972.

Anonymous. "Young Homos Picket Compton's Restaurant." *Cruise News & World Report* 2, no. 8 (August, 1966).

Carter, David. *Stonewall: The Riots That Sparked*

*the Gay Revolution*. New York: St. Martin's Press, 2004.

Feinberg, Leslie. "California Resistance Predated Stonewall Rebellion." http://www.workers .org/ 2006/us/lavender-red-62/.

Gay and Lesbian Historical Society of Northern California. "MTF Transgender Activism in the Tenderloin and Beyond, 1966-1975: A Commentary and Interview with Elliot Blackstone." *GLQ: A Journal of Lesbian and Gay Studies* 4, no. 2 (1998): 349-372.

Hernandez-Bolden-Kramer Productions. *Queer Geography: Mapping Our Identities, Detailing the Experiences of Four Queer Youth*. Video recording. A project of the Mission High School Health Science Academy. San Francisco, Calif.: Frameline, 2001.

Huegel, Kelly. *GLBTQ: The Survival Guide for Queer and Questioning Teens*. Minneapolis, Minn.: Free Spirit, 2003.

"The Riot at Compton's Cafeteria: Coming Soon to a Theater near You!" *Transgender Tapestry* no. 105 (Spring, 2004).

Silverman, Victor, and Susan Stryker, producers. *Screaming Queens: The Riot at Compton's Cafeteria*. Documentary. San Francisco, Calif.: Frameline, 2005.

**SEE ALSO:** June 27-July 2, 1969: Stonewall Rebellion Ignites Modern Gay and Lesbian Rights Movement; July 31, 1969: Gay Liberation Front Is Formed; Oct. 12-15, 1979: First March on Washington for Lesbian and Gay Rights; 1982: Lesbian and Gay Youth Protection Institute Is Founded; Mar., 1987: Radical AIDS Activist Group ACT UP Is Founded; May, 1988: Lavender Youth Recreation and Information Center Opens; Dec. 10, 1989: ACT UP Protests at St. Patrick's Cathedral; Mar. 20, 1990: Queer Nation Is Founded; Apr. 24, 1993: First Dyke March Is Held in Washington, D.C.

# November 21, 1966
# FIRST GENDER IDENTITY CLINIC OPENS AND PROVIDES GENDER REASSIGNMENT SURGERY

*The Johns Hopkins University School of Medicine established the first medical clinic to address gender identity and the medical concerns of transsexuals and those seeking gender reassignment. In the year before the clinic opened, the medical school performed the first gender reassignment surgery in the United States.*

**LOCALE:** Baltimore, Maryland
**CATEGORIES:** Health and medicine; transgender/ transsexuality; organizations and institutions

## KEY FIGURES

*Harry Benjamin* (1885-1986), endocrinologist, expert on transsexuality, and author of *The Transsexual Phenomenon*

*Milton T. Edgerton* (b. 1921), plastic surgeon and professor at Johns Hopkins

*John E. Hoopes* (b. 1931), assistant professor of plastic surgery and chair of the Johns Hopkins Gender Identity Clinic

*John Money* (b. 1921), associate professor of medical psychology and pediatrics at Johns Hopkins

## SUMMARY OF EVENT

On November 21, 1966, a ten-member team of physicians, psychiatrists, and psychologists at the Johns Hopkins University School of Medicine announced that they had formed the university's Gender Identity Clinic "to deal with the problems of the transsexual, physically normal people who are psychologically the opposite sex." Chaired by John E. Hoopes, the group also included Milton Edgerton, who had previously performed surgery on transsexual patients, and John Money, a psychologist known for his work on hermaphroditism, psychoendocrinology, and childhood sexual development. With funding from the Erickson Educational Foundation, the group had been meeting since late 1965, and it already had begun taking patients by the time the public was notified of the clinic's opening.

The first patient to receive full gender reassignment surgery at Johns Hopkins was a male-to-female transsexual in her twenties who was referred by Harry Benjamin, a New York physician widely recognized as the first endocrinologist to specialize in the medical treatment of transsexuals. The patient had surgery in February, 1965, and one year later made news when she was mentioned in a gossip column in the *New York Daily News* on October 4, 1966. A second gender reassignment surgery was performed on a male-to-female transsexual, also in her twenties, in the fall of 1966.

Although Johns Hopkins was the first hospital in the United States to initiate surgical treatment of transsexuals, by 1966 it was reported that approximately two thousand male-to-female surgeries had already been performed abroad, in Casablanca, Europe, Japan, and Mexico. Of those, some five hundred Americans were thought to have had the surgery. Female-to-male procedures for genital surgery were less common, primarily because techniques for the successful construction of a penis had not been developed. Money noted, in the book *Transsexualism and Sex Reassignment* (1969), that by 1966, his colleague Edgerton "had already attended to the surgical needs of two female-to-male transsexuals," but it is not clear whether those were attempts at genital surgery or the more "routine" procedures of mastectomy and hysterectomy.

There had been four known sites in the United States in the mid-1960's where transsexuals could seek medical treatment: the Harry Benjamin Foundation in New York, Johns Hopkins Hospital in Baltimore, the University of Minnesota Medical Center in Minneapolis, and the University of California, Los Angeles, Medical Center. However, of

these, only Johns Hopkins and the University of Minnesota were performing gender reassignment surgery. At Minnesota, doctors formed a committee on gender in October, 1966, consisting of two surgeons, an obstetrician-gynecologist, a psychologist, a senior nurse, a hospital administrator, and a psychiatrist. Two months later, in December, 1966, the university hospital saw its first gender reassignment surgery.

At issue for medical professionals was the question of liability and the possibility of prosecution. At Johns Hopkins, a previous case involving the criminal prosecution of a seventeen-year-old boy (G. L.) for stealing a purse, women's clothing, and "eight-hundred dollars worth of wigs" established a connection between the legal system and medical experts treating the boy for psychosexual problems. The juvenile requested gender reassignment surgery after his May, 1964, arrest, and the court later issued an order for medical intervention, but the surgery was never performed. The doctors at Johns Hopkins felt that the G. L. case had established "a liaison between medicine and the law in the event that elective surgical conversion should be challenged in the future."

At the University of Minnesota, doctors interested in developing a gender program consulted with legal experts and university administrators before offering gender reassignment surgery to twenty male-to-female transsexual "candidates." Central to the decision to offer the surgery was the removal of a "mayhem" statute in 1963 from the Minnesota criminal code. Mayhem statutes, derived from English common law, define as a criminal offense the specific malicious intent to maim or disfigure the body. Originally, these statutes were designed to prevent men from avoiding military service by damaging or otherwise injuring a body part, usually fingers or toes. Doctors feared that with such a law on the books, they would be at risk of criminal prosecution for performing gender reassignment surgeries.

### SIGNIFICANCE

The establishment of the Gender Identity Clinic at Johns Hopkins University and a committee on gender at the University of Minnesota gave a limited number of transsexuals (predominantly male-to-female) access to gender reassignment surgery in the United States in the mid-1960's. The ensuing press coverage resulted in hundreds of letters from transsexuals all over the world who wrote to inquire about having the surgery. Prior to 1965, a person seeking genital reconstructive surgery had to travel outside the United States for the procedure.

—*K. Surkan*

**FURTHER READING**

Buckley, Thomas. "A Changing of Sex by Surgery Begun at Johns Hopkins." *The New York Times*, November 21, 1966, 1, 32.

"Change of Gender." *Newsweek*, December 5, 1966, 73.

Denny, Dallas, ed. *Current Concepts in Transgender Identity*. New York: Garland, 1998.

Green, Richard, and John Money, eds. *Transsexualism and Sex Reassignment*. 1969. New printing. Baltimore: Johns Hopkins University Press, 1975.

Meyerowitz, Joanne. *How Sex Changed: A History of Transsexuality in the United States*. Cambridge, Mass.: Harvard University Press, 2002.

Money, John, and Florence Schwartz. "Public Opinion and Social Issues in Transsexualism: A Case Study in Medical Sociology." In *Transsexualism and Sex Reassignment*, edited by Richard Green and John Money. Baltimore: Johns Hopkins University Press, 1975.

"Sex-Change Operations at a U.S. Hospital." *U.S. News and World Report*, December 5, 1966.

"Surgery: A Body to Match the Mind." *Time*, December 2, 1966, 52-53.

**SEE ALSO:** 1869: Westphal Advocates Medical Treatment for Sexual Inversion; Sept. 24, 1951: George Jorgensen Becomes Christine Jorgensen; 1978: Harry Benjamin International Gender Dysphoria Association Is Founded; Jan. 21, 1989: Death of Transgender Jazz Musician Billy Tipton; 1992: Transgender Nation Holds Its First Protest; 1993: Intersex Society of North America Is Founded; 1996: Hart Recognized as a Transgender Man; 1998: Transgender Scholarship Proliferates.

# 1967
# *LOS ANGELES ADVOCATE* BEGINS PUBLICATION

The Advocate, *a well-known gay and lesbian biweekly magazine with an international circulation, was first published in 1967 as a newsletter called the* Los Angeles Advocate. *The magazine remains a widely circulated periodical with a broad readership.*

**LOCALE:** Los Angeles, California
**CATEGORIES:** Publications; organizations and institutions

**KEY FIGURES**

*Dick Michaels* (c. 1930's-1997), journalist, civil libertarian, chemist, and newsletter cofounder
*Bill Rand*, journalist and newsletter cofounder

*Sam Winston*, artist, cartoonist, and newsletter cofounder

**SUMMARY OF EVENT**

Five hundred copies of the *Los Angeles Advocate*, a newsletter, were published in 1967 in the basement of the headquarters of ABC television by an ABC employee. The newsletter sold for twenty-five cents in the gay bars of Los Angeles. It is less clear when the newsletter became the popular magazine now called *The Advocate*. According to a 1997 article in *The Advocate* itself, the magazine started publishing in 1967. Another source, however, shows that it was first published in 1969, and yet another believes the first magazine was published in 1970.

A brutal police raid of the Black Cat Bar in Los Angeles on New Year's Day, 1967, galvanized members of the local gay activist group PRIDE (Personal Rights in Defense and Education). PRIDE had published a newsletter that was a precursor to the *Los Angeles Advocate*. Dick Michaels, the first editor of the newsletter but not a member of PRIDE, was in the Black Cat when it was raided. He was arrested by vice cops and then charged with lewd conduct, simply for being in the bar. It was his arrest that propelled him to begin working on the newsletter.

Michaels, Bill Rand, and Sam Winston created the *Los Angeles Advocate* to improve upon PRIDE's existing newsletter. In 1968, Michaels and Rand paid PRIDE one dollar for ownership of the new newsletter (a legal maneuver to protect them from PRIDE debts). By July of 1968, the newsletter changed to a newspaper format, increased its range of coverage to circulate nationally, and had one full-time employee (a news editor) and a telephone; by 1969, it abbreviated its name to *The Advocate*.

One year after the first five hundred issues of the *Los Angeles Advocate* had been sold in local gay bars, fifty-five hundred copies of *The Advocate* were in circulation in Southern California. It is clear the publication found an avid audience given the tenfold increase in circulation in just one year.

Michaels had been aware that any social movement trying to effect social change needed a newspaper of its own. As he stated, "the gay community needed . . . a publication with widespread circulation, some way to get the word out about what was happening." The original intention was to have the newspaper provide a service to the local gay community. Initially it published articles on issues such as how to protect oneself during a police raid, and it called for basic civil rights for gays, including demands for the military to end its antigay policy, subjects that laid the foundation for the gay and lesbian rights movement of the 1970's.

## SIGNIFICANCE

From its very beginning, *The Advocate* (as a newsletter, as a newspaper, and in its present forms as a glossy magazine and a Web site) has made extraordinary contributions to the gay and (later) lesbian, bisexual, and transgender communities. The magazine addresses GLBT civil and legal rights and makes visible the lives of all kinds of gays and lesbians—from the person in the street to the men and women in Congress. The magazine also publishes editorials and articles on current affairs; health news; interviews with prominent gay and lesbian individuals and allies; features on GLBT film, music, theater, and television; summaries of nationwide legislation affecting GLBT people; and book reviews.

Mainstream companies advertise regularly in *The Advocate*. They include Movado, Miller Brewing Company, Jeep, Audi, American Express Travel and Financial Services, and Subaru, to name but a few.

In 1990, *The Advocate* added "lesbian" to its subtitle: "The National Gay & Lesbian Newsmagazine." Prior to 1990, its content and emphasis was directed primarily at white, middle- and upper- middle-class, gay men. In July, 1996, the magazine named its first female editor in chief, Judith Wieder.

*The Advocate* remains the most prominent GLBT-owned, GLBT-run, and GLBT-themed magazine in the United States, and probably in the world, outliving many competitors. It is published biweekly, except for monthlies in January and August, and has a Web site (www.advocate.com). In effect, *The Advocate* is a synchronous history of the ongoing lesbian and gay rights movement; it helps define the issues that are critical to GLBT communities.

—*Mary F. Stuck*

## FURTHER READING

Benwell, Bethan, ed. *Masculinity and Men's Lifestyle Magazines*. Oxford, England: Blackwell/ Sociological Review, 2003.

Kaiser, Charles. *The Gay Metropolis, 1940-1996*. Boston: Houghton Mifflin, 1997.

Sender, Katherine. "Gay Readers, Consumers, and a Dominant Gay Habitus: Twenty-Five Years of *The Advocate* Magazine." *Journal of Communication* 51, no. 1 (2001).

Streitmatter, Rodger. *Sex Sells! The Media's Jour-*

*ney from Repression to Obsession.* Cambridge, Mass.: Westview Press, 2004.

_____. *Unspeakable: The Rise of the Gay and Lesbian Press in America.* Boston: Faber and Faber, 1995.

Thompson, Mark, ed. *Long Road to Freedom: "The Advocate" History of the Gay and Lesbian Movement.* New York: St. Martin's Press, 1994.

**SEE ALSO:** 1896: *Der Eigene* Is Published as First Journal on Homosexuality; June, 1947-Feb., 1948: *Vice Versa* Is Published as First Lesbian Periodical; 1953: *ONE* Magazine Begins Publication: Oct. 31, 1969: *Time* Magazine Issues "The Homosexual in America"; Nov. 28, 1970: Del Martin Quits Gay Liberation Movement; 1971: *Lesbian Tide* Publishes Its First Issue; Nov., 1971: *The Body Politic* Begins Publication; Oct., 1974: *Lesbian Connection* Begins Publication; Dec. 31, 1977: Toronto Police Raid Offices of *The Body Politic*; Jan., 1986: South Asian Newsletter *Trikone* Begins Publication; May, 1987: *Lambda Rising Book Report* Begins Publication; Aug. 27, 1991: *The Advocate* Outs Pentagon Spokesman Pete Williams; 1992-2002: Celebrity Lesbians Come Out; 1995: *The Advocate* Outs Oscar Nominee Nigel Hawthorne.

## March 7, 1967
# CBS AIRS *CBS REPORTS: THE HOMOSEXUALS*

CBS Reports: The Homosexuals *was the first U.S. network television program to feature self-identified gays. Though the program's tone was generally sympathetic, it nevertheless focused on views of homosexuality as a social and psychological problem.*

**LOCALE:** United States
**CATEGORY:** Cultural and intellectual history

**KEY FIGURES**

*Mike Wallace* (b. 1918), CBS news correspondent and report narrator

*Warren Adkins*, pseudonym of a gay man interviewed for the report

*Albert Goldman*, author and social critic, interviewed for the report

*Gore Vidal* (b. 1925), author and screenwriter, interviewed for the report

*James Braxton Craven* (1918-1977), U.S. district judge, who was included in the report

*Charles Socarides* (b. 1922), professor, Albert Einstein School of Medicine, who was included in the report

**SUMMARY OF EVENT**

When *CBS Reports: The Homosexuals* finally aired on March 7, 1967, the documentary already had been on a nearly three-year journey through two network news presidents, two producers, canceled air dates, and several re-edits. The hour-long program that audiences saw likely struck viewers as fact-based, comprehensive, balanced, and even sympathetic. By early twenty-first century standards, however, viewers can see that the program focuses on homosexuality as socially deviant and pathological; also, it omits mention of women almost entirely. According to insiders, the program that was broadcast was considerably less sympathetic than the version the network originally planned to broadcast.

The documentary was narrated by Mike Wallace, who would later become a long-time *60 Minutes* coanchor, and Wallace conducted most of the interviews. The first two interviews presented sharply contrasting views of the self-perceptions of gays. A young man identified as Warren Adkins, who was a member of the Mattachine Society, appeared confident and well adjusted, and was accepted by his family. He was followed by a second, unidentified young man whose face was obscured by a large houseplant.

He had been in and out of jail, was unable to hold a job, and said he believed he was sick.

A second pair of interviews at the end of the documentary emphasized divergent views of the impact of homosexuality on culture. Author Albert Goldman, famous for disparaging biographies of cultural icons such as Elvis Presley, John Lennon, and Lenny Bruce, accused gays in the arts and in the fashion industry of having a distorted view of life, a view that was manifested as distorted visions of masculinity and femininity. Author and screenwriter Gore Vidal countered that the problem with American culture was its emphasis on outdated social institutions such as marriage.

Indeed, although it was evident that CBS attempted to provide two sides to many of the issues raised in the documentary, it is also evident that the network did not provide balanced viewpoints. Wallace, for instance, reported results of an in-house survey that found most Americans favored criminal punishment for homosexual acts between consenting adults. That was juxtaposed with a clip of U.S. district court judge James Braxton Craven comparing sentences for sodomy to those for other crimes, and then wondering aloud if homosexual acts are twice as bad as second-degree murder, since the sentences for sodomy are twice as long as those for second-degree murder.

Considerable airtime was devoted to homosexual behavior as a crime, which perhaps was not surprising given that, in 1967, most U.S. states still had antisodomy statutes. A dramatic sequence shows the arrest of a nineteen-year-old military man who left his girlfriend to have sex with another man in a restroom in a public park. The audience never sees his face, but it hears him express concern that the arrest will ruin his life. It also hears his halting efforts to explain the incident since, after all, he loves his girlfriend. The sequence is juxtaposed with a sound bite from a Los Angeles Police Department inspector talking about the number of gays arrested for public sex.

The perspective of the mental health community in the documentary was much more one-sided. Charles Socarides, at the time of the documentary a professor at Yeshiva University's Albert Einstein School of Medicine, tells students during a lecture that homosexuality is a mental illness that had reached epidemic proportions and that people were not born homosexual; homosexuality was a behavior learned early in life. Ironically, twenty-five years later, Socarides' out gay son Richard would join the presidential campaign of Bill Clinton and serve as Clinton's liaison to the lesbian and gay community during his presidency. Another psychologist can be heard on the broadcast saying that male homosexuality is the result of an overly protective mother and an emotionally detached father. Furthermore, Socarides, with Joseph Nicolosi in the 1990's, would lead the argument for the use of "reparative therapy" to "cure" gays and lesbians.

Little of the original filming for the TV program, most of which was done in 1964 and 1965, made the final cut. Scenes that did make the cut included street scenes and the interior of a gay bar. Those images served as backdrop to Wallace's explanation for why gays were attracted to big cities (their anonymity and permissiveness) and his assessment of their romantic lives (they are promiscuous and incapable of lasting relationships).

The last interview of the program is of a thirty-one-year-old psychology professor—shown in silhouette—whose wife indicates she is aware of his homosexuality. He seems matter-of-fact about his physical attraction to men, though he says that he does not believe in having a long-term love relationship with another man.

For those in the audience who might have missed the point, Wallace's closing sentences clearly mark gays as the problematic "other":

> The dilemma of the homosexual. Told by the medical profession he is sick. By the law that he is a criminal. Shunned by employers. Rejected by heterosexual society. Incapable of a fulfilling relationship with a woman or for that matter with a man. At the center of his life he remains anonymous. . . . A displaced person. An outsider.

## SIGNIFICANCE

Though the program's audience was not large— network news specials then, as now, typically were not viewer magnets—it did provide for the vast majority of its viewers what they assumed to be their first exposure to real, self-identified gays. Also, while the politics surrounding the program's production and eventual broadcast made its message less positive than was originally intended, its timing was significant: By March of 1967, the growing gay and lesbian rights movement was increasing public visibility of lesbians and gays, particularly in metropolitan areas, but not necessarily their media exposure. A few big-city stations had included gays in discussions of "the homosexual problem" on locally produced late-night talk shows, but lesbians and gays had remained absent from the networks and from prime time.

A little more than two years after the broadcast, patrons of the Stonewall Inn, a gay bar in lower Manhattan, rebelled over several nights because of ongoing harassment by police, something the media could not completely ignore. Increased media visibility was a positive step, but only a first one. For the next quarter century, lesbians and gays still would be represented largely as everything from leather-clad or bare-breasted freaks at pride rallies to tragic, stereotyped, and marginalized characters on situation comedies and dramas. These images are slowly changing, as media coverage has expanded its range to include positive portrayals of GLBT characters (in sitcoms, in TV dramas, and in film) and coverage of issues regarding GLBT families, same-gender marriage, politics, and culture.

—*Bruce E. Drushel*

**FURTHER READING**

Alwood, Edward. *Straight News: Gays, Lesbians, and the News Media.* New York: Columbia University Press, 1996.

Capsuto, Steven. *Alternate Channels: The Uncensored Story of Gay and Lesbian Images in Radio and Television, 1930's to the Present.* New York: Ballantine Books, 2000.

Gross, Larry. *Up from Invisibility: Lesbians, Gay Men, and the Media in America.* New York: Columbia University Press, 2001.

Tropiano, Stephen. *The Prime Time Closet: A History of Gays and Lesbians on TV.* New York: Applause Theatre & Cinema Books, 2002.

Walters, Suzanna Danuta. *All the Rage: The Story of Gay Visibility in America.* Chicago: University of Chicago Press, 2001.

**SEE ALSO:** Oct. 31, 1969: *Time* Magazine Issues "The Homosexual in America"; 1979-1981: First Gay British Television Series Airs; June 5 and July 3, 1981: Reports of Rare Diseases Mark Beginning of AIDS Epidemic; 1985: GLAAD Begins Monitoring Media Coverage of Gays and Lesbians; 1985: Lesbian Film *Desert Hearts* Is Released; July 25, 1985: Actor Hudson Announces He Has AIDS; 1988: *Macho Dancer* Is Released in the Philippines; 1992-2002: Celebrity Lesbians Come Out; Mar. 21, 2000: Hollywood Awards Transgender Portrayals in Film; Sept. 7, 2001: First Gay and Lesbian Television Network Is Launched in Canada; Mar. 5, 2006: *Brokeback Mountain, Capote,* and *Transamerica* Receive Oscars.

**April 19, 1967**
# FIRST STUDENT HOMOPHILE LEAGUE IS FORMED

*Stephen Donaldson formed the first gay and lesbian college group, the Student Homophile League, at Columbia University in New York City. In the ensuing years, student groups would become a large and vibrant component of the GLBT movement.*

LOCALE: New York, New York
CATEGORIES: Organizations and institutions; marches, protests, and riots; civil rights

**KEY FIGURE**
*Stephen Donaldson* (Robert Martin; 1946-1996), founder of the first chapter of the Student Homophile League, Columbia University

**SUMMARY OF EVENT**
Given a young person's propensity to explore his or her sexuality, institutions of higher learning provide a natural opportunity for gay, lesbian, bisexual, transgender, queer, and questioning students to gather with others like themselves. Although informal queer student networks no doubt existed in the past, the first formal college gay and lesbian groups formed in the latter half of the 1960's. The emergence of these early student groups occurred during an era when the homophile organizations of the 1950's were beginning to give way to the gay and lesbian rights movement of the late 1960's and early 1970's.

The first gay student organization, the Student Homophile League (SHL), was formed at Columbia University in New York City by sophomore Stephen Donaldson (born Robert Martin), who envisioned the group as "a vehicle for students of all orientations to combat homophobia." The group, which originally consisted of twelve members, began meeting in the fall of 1966; it took several months of struggle with the university's administration before the SHL was officially recognized by the university on April 19, 1967. Although the chartering of the group garnered a mention on the front

page of *The New York Times*, the *Columbia Spectator* reported that some students thought the SHL was an April Fools' Day joke.

Donaldson played a key leadership role in the gay and lesbian movement of the late 1960's, despite his identifying as bisexual, and had romantic relationships with women (including Martha Shelley, the head of the New York chapter of the Daughters of Bilitis). In addition to founding the SHL, Donaldson was also involved with the New York chapter of the Mattachine Society and the Sexual Freedom League, and in 1968 was elected an officer of the North American Conference of Homophile Organizations (NACHO).

Donaldson joined the Navy after graduating from Columbia, and he was among the first to fight a dishonorable discharge from the military for homosexual behavior; his discharge was eventually upgraded to honorable. In 1973, after he was arrested for trespassing on the White House lawn during a protest of the bombings in Cambodia, Donaldson was repeatedly gang-raped in a Washington, D.C., jail. Upon his release, he became the first man to speak out publicly about his experiences and later served as president of Stop Prisoner Rape.

Starting in the 1980's, Donaldson wrote a column for the punk rock magazine *Maximum Rock N Roll* under the name "Donny the Punk" and later was coeditor with Wayne Dynes of the *Encyclopedia of Homosexuality* (1990) and the Studies in Homosexuality series. In the mid-1990's, he was a coplaintiff in the case of *ACLU v. Reno*, which challenged the Communications Decency Act, later overturned by the U.S. Supreme Court in 1997. Donaldson died on July 18, 1996, from complications related to AIDS. A memorial plaque bearing his name hangs in the lounge at Columbia's Furnald Hall.

Following in the wake of the original SHL chapter at Columbia, chapters were soon formed at other universities, in some cases by activists who would

*The Student Homophile League at MIT, formed in 1969, distributed this flyer, likely in 1970. Students included a contact phone number on the flyer as well, a bold move for the time.* (Courtesy, Boston Intercollegiate Lesbian and Gay Alliance)

become well-known names in the GLBT movement. Writer Rita Mae Brown, who later became a leader in the lesbian-feminist and women's rights movements and who has written many novels, including the popular lesbian novel *Rubyfruit Jungle* (1973), started an SHL chapter at New York University the following year. In 1968, Jearld Moldenhauer, who would go on to open Glad Day bookstore in Toronto, Canada, formed an SHL chapter at Cornell University in Ithaca, New York, with radical Catholic priest Daniel Berrigan acting as the first faculty adviser. That year also saw the establishment of a chapter at Stanford University in California.

In 1969, an SHL group was started at the Massachusetts Institute of Technology by Stan Tillotson, who had read about the Columbia chapter in the *Village Voice*. Tillotson later recalled that he could not convince the required five gay undergraduates to sign the group's charter, and instead prevailed upon some straight friends to do so as a favor. Also in 1969, San Francisco State University and Rutgers University in New Jersey gained chapters, the latter started by an African American student, Lionel Cuffie. The University of Massachusetts, Amherst, followed in 1970. The local SHL chapters were organized into a national network, with Donaldson serving as chair. Other early campus gay groups outside the SHL network included the Boston University Homophile Committee, Fight Repression of Erotic Expression (FREE) at the University of Minnesota, and Homosexuals Intransigent at the City College of New York.

The early student gay groups typically adopted more radical politics than those of the earlier homophile organizations, like the larger radical youth counterculture sweeping the nation. The mission statement of the Amherst chapter, for example, stated that the SHL "is working to free the person with a homosexual orientation from the oppression of the heterosexual society and to help realize the revolution within our society that will allow every individual to express all the facets of his/her personality and reach his/her full potential as a human being." Lesbian and gay students also were involved with other causes, including the free speech, antiwar, and Black Power movements.

After the Stonewall Rebellion in June of 1969 in New York City, Gay Liberation Front chapters started on several campuses, including one in Boston that evolved out of MIT's SHL chapter. A similar phenomenon occurred in the early 1990's when ACT UP and Queer Nation had a strong presence on some campuses. A queer-student group called SQUISH, Strong Queers United in Stopping Heterosexism, was formed in the early 1990's by students at California State University, Northridge, using Queer Nation and ACT UP as models. In addition to political activism, GLBT student groups—then and now—sponsored educational forums, held speakers' bureaus, held consciousness-raising sessions (now called support groups), provided assistance to students coming out, and organized social events such as dances and parties.

According to historian Brett Beemyn, by 1971, more than 175 colleges and universities had gay and lesbian student organizations, and countless more sprang up in the ensuing decades. During the 1970's, students on some campuses seeking to form gay and lesbian groups had to battle university administrations, which at the time took a more paternalistic attitude toward their students than is the case today. Other schools were more supportive, including the University of Michigan, which in 1971 became the first college to hire staff to offer services to GLBT students.

GLBT graduate students and professors also began to organize in the 1970's. The Gay Academic Union (GAU), the first professional association of academics working in gay and lesbian studies (later called, also, queer studies or queer theory), was formed in November of 1973. Among GAU's early members were historians Martin Duberman, John D'Emilio, and Jonathan Ned Katz, and professor and writer Joan Nestle, who founded the Lesbian Herstory Archives, now in Brooklyn. GAU members, along with undergraduate and graduate students on some campuses, were instrumental in establishing gay and lesbian studies programs beginning in the late 1970's and queer studies in the 1990's. The first dedicated lesbian, gay, and bisexual studies department was established at the City College of San Francisco in 1989, followed by the Center for Lesbian and Gay Studies at the City University of New York and the Lesbian and Gay Studies Center at Yale University.

The earliest college gay groups consisted largely of gays, and lesbians were often left out and made to feel unwelcome. Lesbian activist and writer Karla Jay, then a student at Barnard College (Columbia's "sister" school), later recalled that Columbia University's SHL chapter had "the off-putting air of a men's club." She continued, "I could see why I was the only woman present at the one meeting I attended." In this climate—and as happened within the gay movement as a whole—lesbian students began holding their own social events and organizing separate campus groups throughout the 1970's and early 1980's. Many also belonged to feminist groups on campus and worked with campus women's centers.

A similar dynamic repeated itself in the late 1980's and 1990's, as bisexual and then transgender students began to form their own distinct organizations. In addition, during the same period, many formerly gay and lesbian student groups expanded their mandates to include bisexuals and transgender individuals.

## SIGNIFICANCE

Into the early twenty-first century, student organizations had made up one of the largest and most vibrant segments of the GLBT movement, with thousands of groups across the United States A few of the early Student Homophile League groups, having gone through numerous reorganizations and name changes, are still in existence, including the Columbia Queer Alliance.

Some larger and more progressive campuses have multiple GLBT organizations. The University of California, Berkeley, has about one dozen, including groups for queer students of color or those in a particular field of study. Even many conservative and religious colleges have at least one GLBT group, sometimes established after a long struggle. A few student GLBT groups produce their own publications, such as the newspaper *Ten Percent* at the University of California, Los Angeles (UCLA). A national fraternity called Delta Lambda Phi was organized in 1986 in Washington, D.C., offering social, service, and recreational activities for "gay, bisexual, and progressive gentlemen." In 1988, the first national sorority for lesbians, Lambda Delta Lambda, was founded and chartered at UCLA.

Often free for the first time from the strictures of families and hometowns, many college students find the opportunity to explore their sexuality. Studies show that young people are more accepting of GLBT people than their elders, making many college campuses relatively friendly places to come out. Young people in general tend to be more flexible about their sexual orientation—and, increasingly, their gender identity—and have been at the forefront of progressive activism and rethinking of identity categories. This tendency is apparent in the field of queer studies, which emphasizes the socially constructed and fluid nature of sexuality and gender.

In the late 1990's and early twenty-first century, a growing number of student groups sprang up at high schools and middle schools, as queer youth embraced their sexuality at ever-earlier ages. There are more than two thousand GLBT/straight alliances, many of them started by students who had to go to a court of law to win their right to gather. An umbrella organization, the Gay-Straight Alliance Network, also exists. Even as sexual orientation and gender boundaries become increasingly blurred, students continue to recognize the value of gay, lesbian, bisexual, transgender, queer, and questioning groups made up of their peers.

—*Liz Highleyman*

**FURTHER READING**

Beemyn, Brett. "The Silence Is Broken: A History of the First Lesbian, Gay, and Bisexual College Student Groups." *Journal of the History of Sexuality* 12, no. 2 (April, 2003).

Broberg, Susan. "Gay/Straight Alliances and Other Controversial Student Groups: A New Test for the Equal Access Act." *Brigham Young University Education & Law Journal* (Summer, 1999).

D'Emilio, John. *The World Turned.* Durham, N.C.: Duke University Press, 2002.

Donaldson, Stephen. "The Bisexual Movement's Beginnings in the 70's: A Personal Retrospective." In *Bisexual Politics: Theories, Queries, and Visions,* edited by Naomi Tucker. New York: Haworth Press, 1995.

Howard, Kim, and Annie Stevens, eds. *Out and About Campus: Personal Accounts by Lesbian, Gay, Bisexual, and Transgendered College Students.* Los Angeles: Alyson Books, 2000.

Jay, Karla. *Tales of the Lavender Menace.* New York: Basic Books, 1999.

Kissack, Terence. "Freaking Fag Revolutionaries: New York's Gay Liberation Front, 1969-1971." *Radical History Review* 62 (Spring, 1995): 104-134.

Shepard, Curtis F., Felice Yeskel, and Charles Outcalt. *Lesbian, Gay, Bisexual, and Transgender Campus Organizing: A Comprehensive Manual.* National Gay and Lesbian Task Force. 1995. Available at http://www.lgbtcampus.org/resources/books.html.

**SEE ALSO:** 1950: Mattachine Society Is Founded; 1952: ONE, Inc., Is Founded; 1955: Daughters of Bilitis Founded as First National Lesbian Group in United States; May 27-30, 1960: First National Lesbian Conference Convenes; Feb. 19-20, 1966: First North American Conference of Homophile Organizations Convenes; Aug. 11-18, 1968: NACHO Formally Becomes the First Gay Political Coalition; July 31, 1969: Gay Liberation Front Is Formed; June 28, 1970: First Lesbian and Gay Pride March in the United States; Nov. 28, 1970: Del Martin Quits Gay Liberation Movement; 1973: National Gay Task Force Is Formed; Oct. 18, 1973: Lambda Legal Authorized to Practice Law; Mar. 5, 1974: Antigay and Antilesbian Organizations Begin to Form; 1976: Katz Publishes First Lesbian and Gay History Anthology; Apr. 22, 1980: Human Rights Campaign Fund Is Founded.

## May 22, 1967
# U.S. Supreme Court Upholds Law Preventing Immigration of Gays and Lesbians

*The U.S. Supreme Court ruled that Congress had the right to bar gays and lesbians from entering the United States and could deny citizenship to, and deport, any foreign national who was gay or lesbian.*

**Also known as:** *Boutilier v. INS*
**Locale:** Washington, D.C.
**Categories:** Laws, acts, and legal history; civil rights; government and politics

**Key Figures**

*Clive Michael Boutilier* (1933-2003), Canadian citizen deported from the United States because he was gay
*Blanch Freedman*, Boutilier's attorney
*Earl Warren* (1891-1974), chief justice of the United States, 1953-1969

**Summary of Event**

On November 10, 1968, thirty-five-year-old Clive Michael Boutilier, a Canadian citizen, was deported from the United States, having lost his immigration case before the U.S. Supreme Court. Boutilier had grown up in Nova Scotia, the oldest son in a large, Irish Catholic farming family. In 1955, at the age of twenty-one, he legally entered the United States as a permanent resident. He arrived with several siblings and his mother, who had recently remarried, this time to a U.S. citizen. Comfortably settled in New York City, Boutilier worked steady jobs and applied for U.S. citizenship in 1963. This is when his legal troubles began.

In 1952, Congress had passed the McCarran-Walter Immigration and Nationality Act, which excludes Communists, anarchists, and other alleged subversives from the United States. The law's original draft also explicitly excluded all foreigners who were "psychopathic personalities, homosexuals, or sex perverts." However, the U.S. Public

Health Service (PHS) advised the U.S. Senate that the term "psychopathic personality" was "sufficiently broad" to include homosexuals. Accordingly, the phrase "homosexuals, or sex perverts" was omitted from the final wording of the law. Congress made sure to specify that the change in terminology was "not to be construed in any way as modifying the intent to exclude all aliens who are sexual deviates."

When Boutilier applied for citizenship in 1963, he admitted that he had been arrested for sodomy four years previously, although the charge had been dismissed when the complainant failed to appear in court. The Immigration and Naturalization Service (INS) examiner closely interrogated Boutilier on the exact details of the sexual encounter, as well as on his entire sexual history. Boutilier admitted that his "first homosexual experience" took place when he was fourteen years old, and that he had had sex with men three to four times per year while living in Canada (and, less frequently, sex with women). On the basis of this confession, the PHS diagnosed Boutilier as "afflicted with a class A condition, namely, psychopathic personality, sexual deviate" at the time he was admitted to the United States.

Boutilier, facing deportation, sought legal help and was represented by Blanch Freedman, a radical civil rights lawyer. He also received support from the Homosexual Law Reform Society and the American Civil Liberties Union. In 1965 the INS's Board of Immigration Appeals ruled against Boutilier, as did the Second Circuit Court of Appeals in 1966. However, in two previous decisions, the Ninth Circuit Court of Appeals had ruled that the term "psychopathic personality" was too vague to be indiscriminately applied to all homosexuals. It was now up to the U.S. Supreme Court, in *Boutilier v. INS*, to resolve the conflict, and it did so in favor of the U.S. government, ruling against Boutilier on May 22, 1967.

## SIGNIFICANCE

*Boutilier v. INS* was the first major case in which the Supreme Court considered the rights of homosexuals. In a 6-3 decision, the Court held that one, by "psychopathic personality," Congress had fully *intended* to prohibit all homosexuals from entering the United States; two, Congress had the constitutional *right* to bar any group from the United States; and three, the INS had clearly proven that Boutilier was "afflicted with homosexuality" long before entering the United States. Hence, he had been ineligible for legal entry and could now be deported.

In upholding Boutilier's deportation, the Court's decision had a chilling impact. Although the 1952 immigration law never explicitly used the word "homosexual," Congress nevertheless made clear its intent to deny homosexuals all rights: from short-term tourist visas, to permanent residency status, to citizenship. Instead of protecting a minority group, the Court affirmed Congress's right to discriminate on the basis of sexual orientation. From 1952 until 1990, foreign nationals who were legally admitted but later found to be homosexual had been subject to deportation, regardless of the time they had lived in the United States as law-abiding, legal residents. Ironically, when discussing the Warren Court, legal scholars traditionally have ignored this particular case, but they have not ignored the Court's sexually "liberalized" rulings involving issues such as birth control, obscenity, and interracial marriage.

In *Boutilier* the majority also dismissed concerns that the phrase "psychopathic personality" was unconstitutionally vague. It also failed to recognize a denial of human rights when it concluded, "The petitioner is not being deported for conduct engaged in after his entry into the United States, but rather for characteristics he possessed *at the time of* his entry. Here, when petitioner first presented himself at our border for entrance, he was already afflicted with homosexuality. The pattern was cut, and under it he was not admissible."

Yet, the three dissenting justices likewise failed to offer a positive view of homosexuality. In their assessment, "The homosexual is one, who by some freak, is the product of an arrested development." However, they made a distinction between conduct and character, reasoning that even though Boutilier had participated in occasional homosexual acts, he was not "afflicted with homosexuality." And even if he were homosexual, they argued that not all homosexuals should be classified as "psychopathic personalities."

Shortly after he lost his case, Boutilier was hit by a bus while crossing a street in New York City. He was in a coma for one month and emerged from the coma brain-damaged and mentally disabled. For the rest of his life he spoke haltingly and walked as if drunk, although he could perform basic daily functions such as dressing and eating. Family lore speculated that the accident may have been a suicide attempt. Boutilier had been extremely distraught by the legal proceedings against him and overwhelmed by mounting legal costs. The INS waited one year after his accident to deport him. Because he now needed long-term care, his mother and stepfather also returned to Canada, caring for him as long as they were able. In the 1990's he was moved to a group home for the disabled. In 2003 he died from complications related to a heart condition. No obituary noted his passing nor the tragic part he had played in GLBT legal history.

Congress finally eliminated the homosexual exclusion clause, but not until the Immigration Act of 1990. Gays and lesbians finally gained the right to legally enter the United States and become naturalized citizens.

—*L. Mara Dodge*

## FURTHER READING

Canaday, Margot. "'Who Is a Homosexual?' The Consolidation of Sexual Identities in Mid-Twentieth Century American Immigration Law." *Law and Social Inquiry* 28 (2003): 351-386.

Luibheid, Eithne. *Entry Denied: Controlling Sexuality at the Border.* Minneapolis: University of Minnesota Press, 2002.

Murdoch, Joyce, and Deb Price. *Courting Justice: Gay Men and Lesbians v. the Supreme Court.* New York: Basic Books, 2001.

Stein, Marc. "Boutilier and the Supreme Court's Sexual Revolution." *Law and History Review* 23, no. 3 (Fall, 2005): 491-536.

_____. "Crossing the Border to Memory: In Search of Clive Michael Boutilier, 1933-2003." *Torquere* 6 (2004): 91-115.

_____. "Forgetting and Remembering a Deported Alien." *History News Network*, November 3, 2003. http://hnn.us/articles/1769.html.

**SEE ALSO:** Jan. 12, 1939: *Thompson v. Aldredge* Dismisses Sodomy Charges Against Lesbians; 1952-1990: U.S. Law Prohibits Gay and Lesbian Immigration; Jan. 22, 1973: *Roe v. Wade* Legalizes Abortion and Extends Privacy Rights; June 21, 1973: U.S. Supreme Court Supports Local Obscenity Laws; Aug., 1973: American Bar Association Calls for Repeal of Laws Against Consensual Sex; Nov. 17, 1975: U.S. Supreme Court Rules in "Crimes Against Nature" Case; 1981: Gay and Lesbian Palimony Suits Emerge; 1982-1991: Lesbian Academic and Activist Sues University of California for Discrimination; 1986: *Bowers v. Hardwick* Upholds State Sodomy Laws; May 1, 1989: U.S. Supreme Court Rules Gender-Role Stereotyping Is Discriminatory; Dec. 17, 1991: Minnesota Court Awards Guardianship to Lesbian Partner; 1992-2006: Indians Struggle to Abolish Sodomy Law; 1993-1996: Hawaii Opens Door to Same-Gender Marriages; Sept. 21, 1993-Apr. 21, 1995: Lesbian Mother Loses Custody of Her Child; Dec. 20, 1999: *Baker v. Vermont* Leads to Recognition of Same-Gender Civil Unions; June 28, 2000: *Boy Scouts of America v. Dale*; June 26, 2003: U.S. Supreme Court Overturns Texas Sodomy Law.

## July 27, 1967
# UNITED KINGDOM DECRIMINALIZES HOMOSEXUAL SEX

*The decriminalization of homosexual acts conducted in private between consenting adults was a major British civil rights milestone, but the new law failed to fully protect the civil rights of gays and lesbians throughout the United Kingdom and even led to increased prosecutions. Nevertheless, the act would significantly impact U.S. law as well because of the two nations' shared legal traditions.*

**ALSO KNOWN AS:** 1967 Sexual Offences Act
**LOCALE:** London, England
**CATEGORIES:** Laws, acts, and legal history; civil rights; crime

### KEY FIGURES
*Sir John Frederick Wolfenden* (1906-1985), chair of the Committee on Homosexual Offences and Prostitution
*Leo Abse* (b. 1917), member of the House of Commons

*Earl of Arran* (1910-1983), member of the House of Lords

### SUMMARY OF EVENT
Even as Great Britain passed one of Europe's most restrictive sex laws in 1956, a committee of Parliament invited testimony on possible legal reforms regarding homosexuality. Charged in 1954, the Committee on Homosexual Offences and Prostitution based its work on the principle that

> the function of the criminal law . . . is to preserve public order and decency, to protect the citizen from what is offensive or injurious, and to provide sufficient safeguards against exploitation and corruption of others, particularly those who are specially vulnerable because they are young, weak in body or mind, inexperienced, or in a state of special physical, official or economic dependence.

In keeping with this dictum, the final product of the committee's investigations, known as the *Wolf-*

*enden Report* for the committee's chair, Sir John Frederick Wolfenden, included recommendations that "homosexual behavior between consenting adults in private be no longer a criminal offence" and that the maximum penalties for buggery and gross indecency be revised.

The Wolfenden recommendations did not flow from a wellspring of sympathy for gays. The committee reasoned that more men would seek psychological treatment if they did not fear prosecution. In any event, it seemed irrational to maintain the criminality of male homosexuality while adultery, fornication, and lesbian sex all remained outside the criminal purview, contradicting any argument that the ban needed to be maintained to preserve the moral basis of civilization.

Lawmakers did not react well to the committee's logic, fearing that decriminalization of homosexuality would unleash a torrent of homosexual contagion. As attitudes began to liberalize during the 1960's, however, reforms were enacted in several areas touching on sexual life. The death penalty was abolished, and divorce and abortion laws were modernized. Within this milieu, revising the laws on homosexuality no longer seemed unthinkable.

In 1966, Leo Abse, a member of the House of Commons, and the earl of Arran, of the House of Lords, introduced legislation, nicknamed "William," to revise the 1956 Sexual Offences Act and decriminalize selected homosexual acts. The final statute became the new 1967 Sexual Offences Act. Section 1 of the new act contains the heart of the proposed reforms of the *Wolfenden Report*, legalizing homosexual acts conducted in private between consenting adults over the age of twenty-one. Other parts of the law, however, criminalized sex in which more than two people participated. Punishment for buggery was reduced from life to ten years, and charges became subject to a statute of limitations of twelve months.

The earlier 1956 law had targeted male homosexuality much more harshly than female homosexuality. The 1967 revision did little to balance treatment of the two types of sexuality. As a rule, lesbian sexual acts remained legal unless a partner did not consent.

## SIGNIFICANCE

From its inception the 1967 Sexual Offences Act was a compromise measure. Although a major milestone in the advance of civil rights for gays and lesbians, the details of the law did not ensure complete protection. For example, the armed services were expressly exempted from the legalization of homosexual acts, and the statute enforced a higher age of consent for homosexual acts than for heterosexual ones: twenty-one instead of sixteen. Equal ages of consent were not achieved until the 2000 Sexual Offences Act. A final, surprising limitation of the 1967 act is found in Section 11(5), which withheld the new reforms from Scotland and Northern Ireland. In 1981 the European Commission found this limitation to be a breach of the European Convention.

The most controversial amendment to the bill, however, concerned the privacy of the sexual acts. The law allowed consenting adults to engage in homosexual acts in private. However, it also defined a situation as "private" when no more than two people were present. On its face, this stipulation preserved the criminality of group sex. Interpretations further limited the meaning of "private." "Public," the antithesis of "private," became defined as any place where third parties might be present. If two men had sex alone in a room behind an unlocked door, they were having sex in public because another person could walk in.

Because of these limitations on the new formal liberties, prosecutions for homosexual offenses reportedly have increased since the passage of the 1967 law. A similar pattern exists in the United States. The formally "liberalized" military posture toward homosexuals—encapsulated in the Don't Ask, Don't Tell policy—has led to an *increase* in discharges for homosexuality.

Despite these drawbacks, the 1967 Sexual Offences Act represents a milestone in Anglo-American common law. Although other societies, especially those practicing the civil law tradition, had long since abolished criminal sanctions against homosexuality, the later action by Great Britain would have a deeper influence on attitudes in the United States.

—*James M. Donovan*

## Further Reading

Abse, Leo. "The Sexual Offences Act." *British Journal of Criminology* 8 (1968): 86-88.

Great Britain. Committee on Homosexual Offences and Prostitution. *The Wolfenden Report.* Authorized American ed. Introduction by Karl Menninger. New York: Stein and Day, 1963.

Higgins, Patrick. *Heterosexual Dictatorship: Male Homosexuality in Postwar Britain.* London: Fourth Estate, 1996.

Honoré, Tony. *Sex Law in England.* London: Archon Books, 1978.

Jeffrey-Poulter, Stephen. *Peers, Queers, and Commons: The Struggle for Gay Law Reform from 1950 to the Present.* New York: Routledge, 1991.

Lafitte, François. "Homosexuality and the Law: The 'Wolfenden Report' in Historical Perspective." *British Journal of Delinquency* 9 (1958): 8-19.

Moran, Leslie F. *The Homosexual(ity) of Law.* London: Routledge, 1996.

**See also:** 1885: United Kingdom Criminalizes "Gross Indecency"; May 25, 1895: Oscar Wilde Is Convicted of Gross Indecency; Jan. 1, 1957: United Kingdom's Sexual Offences Act Becomes Law; Sept. 4, 1957: The *Wolfenden Report* Calls for Decriminalizing Private Consensual Sex; Jan. 12, 2000: United Kingdom Lifts Ban on Gays and Lesbians in the Military; Nov. 18, 2004: United Kingdom Legalizes Same-Gender Civil Partnerships.

---

**Fall, 1967**

# Oscar Wilde Memorial Bookshop Opens as First Gay Bookstore

*The Oscar Wilde Memorial Bookshop was the first bookshop to specialize in books of interest mostly to gay men. The store provided a communal gathering place, helping to advance gay pride and political activism. Other gay, as well as lesbian-feminist, bookstores soon opened around the United States.*

**Locale:** New York, New York

**Categories:** Economics; literature; publications

## Key Figures

*Craig Rodwell* (1940-2003), gay rights activist who founded the Oscar Wilde Memorial Bookshop

*Larry Lingle*, who purchased the bookstore in 1969

*Deacon Maccubbin*, founder of Lambda Rising Bookshop in Washington, D.C., who bought the Oscar Wilde bookstore in 2003

## Summary of Event

The Oscar Wilde Memorial Bookshop, the oldest gay bookshop in the United States and quite possibly the first such bookshop anywhere, opened in the fall of 1967 at 291 Mercer Street in New York City, in Greenwich Village near New York University. Providing titles in its early days mainly for gay men, the shop was named for the nineteenth century Irish playwright Oscar Wilde, who had been imprisoned for sodomy.

When the bookshop opened, it had less than one hundred titles, and it had a large window decal that proclaimed "Gay is Good." The store began its service as an activist center two years before the Stonewall Rebellion in 1969. Indeed, what was the first of many pride marches commemorating Stonewall began at the Oscar Wilde Memorial Bookshop in 1970.

In 1973, the store moved to a row house at 15 Christopher Street, in the West Village at the intersection of Christopher and Gay Streets, close to the renowned, although by this time closed, Stonewall Inn bar, which was the scene of the Stonewall Rebellion.

Craig Rodwell, a gay activist and former lover of San Francisco city and county supervisor Harvey Milk, founded the Oscar Wilde Memorial Bookshop as quite possibly the first business not related somehow with either sex or alcohol (as in, for example, bathhouses and bars) that was geared toward gays and lesbians. Rodwell opened the store with very few titles because he refused to carry pornography, which effectively brought to light the scarcity of gay- and lesbian-oriented literature and other works. In addition, from its earliest days, the Oscar Wilde Memorial Bookshop served as a community center, and its books provided queer people with personal insights and affirmations of their identity.

Bookstores featuring lesbian and lesbian-feminist titles soon opened as well. Amazon Bookstore, in Minneapolis, Minnesota, opened in 1970. Others followed. Deacon Maccubbin, at his Lambda Rising bookstore in Washington, D.C., which opened in 1974, began selling *The Advocate*, the well-known GLBT newsmagazine, and a small number of books. Lambda Rising became a hub of radical activism, housing at different times the Gay Switchboard as well as the *Gay Blade* (later the *Washington Blade*) newspaper. Other bookshops, such as Giovanni's Room in Philadelphia, We Think the World of You in Boston, Outwrite Books in Atlanta, and the Walt Whitman Bookshop in San Francisco, opened their doors. A Different Light opened in Los Angeles in 1979. Before long, other gay and lesbian bookshops sprang up in other cities. Many of these stores, like the Oscar Wilde, also became community centers and sites for activism.

Rodwell sold the Oscar Wilde in 1996 to Larry Lingle, stating financial reasons for his decision. After thirty years in business, it looked as if Lingle would have to permanently close the famous bookshop's doors as well, in January, 2003. Fortunately, the shop was purchased by Maccubbin.

## SIGNIFICANCE

Unfortunately, only a few GLBT bookstores remain in New York City, and many others around the United States have had to close their doors because, as some owners have said, the GLBT community is not supporting them. Books are being purchased at often discounted prices at large chain stores such as Barnes and Noble and Borders. Gay and lesbian literature started to go mainstream at the end of the twentieth century, and with this mainstreaming of GLBT titles came the national chain stores featuring sections devoted exclusively to gay and lesbian literature and nonfiction as well as GLBT works in other sections. The chains often are able to sell books at lower prices because of their high sales volume, much higher than the smaller, specialized bookstores.

GLBT migration out of urban areas and into suburban neighborhoods also has led to diminishing sales at GLBT bookshops. Also, Amazon.com, Abebooks.com, and other Web-based businesses are able to sell a wide variety of new and used GLBT titles to a wide-ranging group of readers online, further taking away business from GLBT bookshops. Also, because many GLBT authors now are more likely to read and sign their work at the larger national chain stores, which advertise prominently and attract far larger audiences, resulting in larger author profits, the GLBT bookstore suffers.

In an attempt to outwit the large, chain, corporate bookshops, several GLBT bookshops have issued catalogs and have established mail-order businesses, but the sense of community that once thrived at GLBT stores continues to diminish. However, even with ongoing economic challenges, many GLBT bookshops are determined to stay open, striving to remain not just bookstores but also community-oriented institutions.

—*M. Casey Diana*

## FURTHER READING

Bronski, Michael. "The Paradox of Gay Publishing." *Publishers Weekly* 249, no. 34 (August 26, 2000): 18-20.

Carter, David. *Stonewall: The Riots That Sparked the Gay Revolution*. New York: St. Martin's Press, 2004.

Gluckman, Amy, and Betsy Reed, eds. *Homo Economics: Capitalism, Community, and Lesbian and Gay Life*. New York: Routledge 1997.

Liddle, Kathleen. "More than a Bookstore: The Continuing Relevance of Feminist Bookstores for the Lesbian Community." *Journal of Lesbian Studies* 9, nos. 1/2 (2005).

Santora, Mark. "Plot Twist for a Gay Bookstore: The Last Chapter Actually Isn't." *The New York Times*, February 4, 2003, p. B3.

Tobin, Kay, and Randy Wicker. *The Gay Crusaders*. New York: Arno, 1975.

**SEE ALSO:** May 25, 1895: Oscar Wilde Is Convicted of Gross Indecency; 1970: Amazon Bookstore Opens as First Feminist-Lesbian Book Shop; June, 1971: The Gay Book Award Debuts; 1973: Brown Publishes *Rubyfruit Jungle*; 1973: Naiad Press Is Founded; 1974: *The Front Runner* Makes *The New York Times* Best-Seller List; 1975: First Novel About Coming Out to Parents Is Published; 1980: Alyson Begins Publishing Gay and Lesbian Books; Oct., 1981: Kitchen Table: Women of Color Press Is Founded; May, 1987: *Lambda Rising Book Report* Begins Publication; June 2, 1989: Lambda Literary Award Is Created; 1993: Monette Wins the National Book Award for *Becoming a Man*.

## August 11-18, 1968
# NACHO FORMALLY BECOMES THE FIRST GAY POLITICAL COALITION

*The North American Conference of Homophile Organizations, or NACHO, was formally created as a formal body with a mission to unify the homophile movement at a national level in terms of philosophy, ideals, and action. The founding of this first gay political coalition set the stage for the militant era of the lesbian and gay rights movement that soon followed.*

**LOCALE:** Chicago, Illinois
**CATEGORIES:** Organizations and institutions; civil rights

**KEY FIGURES**
*Robert Warren Cromey*, vicar of St. Aidan's Episcopal Church in San Francisco, California
*Stephen Donaldson* (Robert Martin; 1946-1996), founder of the first Student Homophile League at Columbia University, New York
*Franklin Kameny* (b. 1925), executive director of the Mattachine Society of Washington, D.C.

**SUMMARY OF EVENT**
Between August 11 and 18, just one week prior to the Democratic National Convention in 1968, the fourth meeting of the North American Conference of Homophile Organizations (NACHO), known earlier as the National Planning Conference of Homosexual Organizations, convened in Chicago. The meetings were held in a closed bar that temporarily had its liquor license revoked. Previous meetings had established various committees to deal with such issues as security clearances for homosexuals, government employment, military service, developing new organizations, reaching out to youth, circulating publications, religion, accreditation, and forming a national organization.

By the time of the Chicago meeting, NACHO had made a significant shift, from simply being a convention for communications (as it was in Kansas City in 1966) to becoming a "loose federation" with articles of confederation (San Francisco, 1966) to proclaiming itself as "a duly constituted continuing body with the ultimate goal of establishing a legitimate homophile movement on a national scale" (Washington, D.C., 1967). The Chicago conference was a turning point for NACHO. It had legitimately matured into what a few visionary leaders had first intended: a formal, united body. It was thought that national unity would expand and strengthen the homophile movement by projecting an image of gays that would necessarily demand respect and a serious hearing. Regardless of many groups' disparate views on the direction the movement should take and wide disapproval of the credentials committee's subjective stance toward applicants (in fact, a few groups were threatening withdrawal over the committee's actions), the affiliates met in Chicago and established a formal structure for NACHO.

The conference chairman, the Reverend Robert Cromey, moderated the event. The Committee on Unity, chaired by Stephen Donaldson, was perhaps the most active body that week. On August 13, 1968, the committee submitted a draft of "standing rules" that proposed the operation of an administrative body with an executive committee and council. The document stated that the convention was still the supreme organ and would overrule any decisions made by any faction of the NACHO constituency. It was further decided that the conference would subdivide into regions—East, West, and Midwest—to allow frequent communications and intergroup activities that would not contradict the policies of the national office.

The important studies of Evelyn Hooker, psychologist at the University of California, Los Angeles, had recently been published; she had provided valid evidence that homosexuals are not inherently sick individuals. Much of the conference lent itself to discussion surrounding this issue. At the time, the general retort from homophile groups to the ominous condemnation that "gay is bad" was that "gay is *not* bad." Franklin Kameny took this retort a step further with a slogan he crafted prior to the conference, the radically positive affirmation that "Gay Is Good." Two years earlier, NACHO had been able to agree only on a watered-down, self-oppressed statement that "each homosexual should be judged as an individual." Now they adopted Kameny's slogan to be used on the national front.

The conference also focused on issuing a "homosexual bill of rights" from the now-national homophile coalition. The proclamation can be summarized by saying that homosexuals were no longer pleading for but instead demanding that they receive equal treatment and protection under the law in matters of employment, federal security clearances, citizenship, and service in the military. They demanded a cessation of entrapment and sodomy laws as they pertained to consensual adults in private. They agreed, furthermore, that all political candidates should be held accountable to their homosexual constituencies and declare their views on issues concerning gay and lesbian rights.

## SIGNIFICANCE

It is ironic that what ultimately led to the demise of NACHO was a failure to embrace a characteristic inherent in the homophile community at large. The homophile community is rich with diversity; it is not and never will be composed of a single race or ethnicity, gender, or creed of persons. Charged predominantly by white men, NACHO failed to incorporate lesbian issues in the forefront of its cause, failed to reach out to other groups fighting the battle for civil rights, and refused to abandon its conservatism in a climate that called for radical reform.

In 1968, the Eastern Regional Conference of Homophile Organizations was officially overrun by radical youth, an event that proved to be only the beginning of a trend that gained strength through the 1969 Stonewall Rebellion and its aftermath, including the birth of the Gay Liberation Front. Stephen Donaldson was at the forefront of the radical youth movement and in many ways led the Gay Liberation Front's infiltration into NACHO.

NACHO's accomplishments may have fallen short of expectations, but they nonetheless were real. Promoting a breakthrough in communication and collaboration, the movement proclaimed an idea that was radical for its time—"Gay Is Good"— and loosened the grip of self-oppression on many gays, effectively opening the issue of homosexuality and encouraging large numbers of gays to join the movement. It will always remain to be proven whether Stonewall would have happened in 1969 if not for NACHO and the radical increase in the visibility and interconnectivity of homosexuals that it created.

*—Sarah Ivy*

## FURTHER READING

Blasius, Mark, and Shane Phelan. *We Are Every-where*. New York: Routledge, 1997.

D'Emilio, John. *Sexual Politics, Sexual Communities: The Making of a Homosexual Minority in the United States, 1940-1970*. 2d ed. Chicago: University of Chicago Press, 1998.

Duberman, Martin B. *Stonewall*. New York: Dutton, 1993.

Johnson, David. "Frank Kameny." In *Leaders from the 1960's: A Biographical Sourcebook of American Activism*, edited by David DeLeon. Westport, Conn.: Greenwood Press, 1994.

Marcus, Eric. *Making Gay History: The Half Century Fight for Lesbian and Gay Equal Rights*. New York: HarperCollins, 2002.

Marotta, Toby. *The Politics of Homosexuality*. Boston: Houghton Mifflin, 1981.

**SEE ALSO:** Dec. 10, 1924: Gerber Founds the Society for Human Rights; 1950: Mattachine Society Is Founded; 1952: ONE, Inc., Is Founded; 1955: Daughters of Bilitis Founded as First National Lesbian Group in United States; May 27-30, 1960: First National Lesbian Conference Convenes; Feb. 19-20, 1966: First North American Conference of Homophile Organizations Convenes; Apr. 19, 1967: First Student Homophile League Is Formed; July 31, 1969: Gay Liberation Front Is Formed; June 28, 1970: First Lesbian and Gay Pride March in the United States; Nov. 28, 1970: Del Martin Quits Gay Liberation Movement; 1971: Kameny Is First Out Candidate for U.S. Congress; 1973: National Gay Task Force Is Formed; Oct. 18, 1973: Lambda Legal Authorized to Practice Law; Mar. 5, 1974: Antigay and Antilesbian Organizations Begin to Form; Apr. 22, 1980: Human Rights Campaign Fund Is Founded.

## October 6, 1968
# METROPOLITAN COMMUNITY CHURCH IS FOUNDED

*The Reverend Troy Perry founded the first church for lesbians, gays, bisexuals, and transgender individuals, sparking a new Christian movement that is one of the world's largest GLBT organizations.*

**LOCALE:** Los Angeles, California
**CATEGORIES:** Religion; organizations and institutions

## KEY FIGURES

*Troy Perry* (b. 1940), Pentecostal minister and founder of the Metropolitan Community Church, or MCC

*Willie Smith*, housemate of Troy who encouraged his ministry

*Richard Ploen*, Presbyterian minister who became an early MCC leader

*Freda Smith*, first woman to be ordained to the MCC ministry

## SUMMARY OF EVENT

In the late 1960's, most churches in the United States were openly hostile to gays and lesbians, believing homosexuality to be a transgression against Christian teachings. Many lesbians and gays viewed, and still view, religion as one of the most intractable obstacles to equal rights.

In 1968, the Reverend Troy Perry founded a movement that proclaimed the compatibility of gay and Christian identities. Perry, a high school dropout from the rural south and an ordained minister in the Church of God of Prophecy, denied his sexual desires for many years. He married, became the father of two sons, and moved to Santa Ana, California, to serve a church there. In 1963, when he was twenty-three years old, Perry acknowledged to himself, his church supervisor, and his wife that he was gay. His marriage ended, and so did his career as a Pentecostal minister.

After a brief tour of duty in the U.S. Army, Perry

---

**METROPOLITAN COMMUNITY CHURCH:
STATEMENT OF FAITH**

This is the simple declaration of what MCC believes, as stated in our By-Laws, and accepted by our General Conference:

Christianity is the revelation of God in Jesus Christ and is the religion set forth in the scriptures. Jesus Christ is foretold in the Old Testament, presented in the New Testament, and proclaimed by the Christian Church in every age and in every land.

Founded in the interest of offering a church home to all who confess and believe, Metropolitan Community Churches moves in the mainstream of Christianity.

Our faith is based upon the principles outlined in the historic creeds: Apostles and Nicene.

*We believe:*

In one triune God, omnipotent, omnipresent and omniscient, of one substance and of three persons: God—our Parent-Creator; Jesus Christ, the only begotten son of God, God in flesh, human; and the Holy Spirit—God as our Sustainer.

That the Bible is the divinely inspired Word of God, showing forth God to every person through the law and the prophets, and finally, completely and ultimately on earth in the being of Jesus Christ.

That Jesus . . . the Christ . . . historically recorded as living some 2,000 years before this writing, is God incarnate, of human birth, fully God and fully human, and that by being one with God, Jesus has demonstrated once and forever that all people are likewise Children of God, being spiritually made in God's image.

That the Holy Spirit is God making known God's love and interest to all people. The Holy Spirit is God, available to and working through all who are willing to place their welfare in God's keeping.

Every person is justified by grace to God through faith in Jesus Christ.

---

came out into the burgeoning gay world of West Hollywood, California. A failed love affair led Perry to attempt suicide, a crisis that ended when he realized it was possible to be both gay and a faithful Christian. He claims to have received a mandate from God to found a new church with a particular ministry to gays and lesbians.

In the fall of 1968, Perry placed an advertisement in *The Advocate*, a gay monthly magazine based in Los Angeles, announcing the organization of what he called the Metropolitan Community Church (MCC), its first service to be held on October 6, 1968, in Perry's home in the Huntington Park area of Los Angeles. On that Sunday, Perry set up chairs in his living room and dressed in a borrowed clerical robe. The ad in *The Advocate* drew three guests

only; most of the twelve attendees were Perry's friends. Perry's housemate, Willie Smith, who went on to become MCC's first music director, led the assembly in singing hymns. Perry's sermon, entitled "Be True to You," drew from Shakespeare's *Hamlet* and the biblical stories of Job's sufferings and David's triumph over Goliath, as Perry encouraged his small congregation to believe in their own self-worth and to believe in God. After celebrating communion, Perry collected an offering of $3.18, delivered a closing prayer, and invited his small congregation to stay for coffee and cake.

Within weeks, the tiny church began to grow, and the increasingly crowded services required a shift in venue. MCC moved from Perry's living room to the Encore Theater in Hollywood, where Willie Smith worked as a projectionist. The Reverend Richard Ploen, a Presbyterian minister and former missionary in Africa, joined Perry as a leader in the new church. From the beginning, MCC was an ecumenical Christian church, drawing gays, mostly, who came from Catholic and Protestant churches.

**SIGNIFICANCE**

Driven by an evangelical impulse to share a gay-friendly version of Christianity, MCC spread rapidly and successfully. Perry, like many Pentecostal preachers before him, preached in unlikely venues, but he was surely the first to proselytize in gay bars and restaurants. Within two years of Perry's first service, Metropolitan Community Churches were established in Los Angeles, San Francisco, Chicago, San Diego, and Honolulu. These five churches formed the core of what became, in 1970, a new Protestant denomination, the Universal Fellowship of Metropolitan Community Churches (UFMCC), the term "universal" signaling Perry's conviction that the Christian gospel was intended for all people. By 1972, the UFMCC included thirty-one congregations in the United States, Canada, and the United Kingdom.

Although women were a minority in the earliest years, lesbians gained influence in the movement throughout the 1970's, as they demanded and received a greater voice in the church's leadership. The Reverend Freda Smith became the first woman ordained in the UFMCC in 1973. In that same year, arson destroyed the mother church in Los Angeles, and in subsequent years suspicious fires plagued other UFMCC churches.

From the beginning, the UFMCC presented itself as a Christian movement that was conservative in theological terms, abiding by the historic creeds of Christianity and proclaiming the authority of the Bible and the divinity of Jesus Christ. The UFMCC's major innovation, rooted in Perry's experience and resonant in the lives of so many others, has been its message of the compatibility of Christianity and homosexuality. The message that Perry and other UFMCC ministers preach might be summed up with the phrase "God made you gay, so be thankful and be proud."

Like many Protestant churches, the UFMCC has an active social justice agenda, which includes ministries in prisons and hospitals. Its particular mission to sexual minorities can be seen in the leading role the church played in helping to organize the 1979 and 1993 GLBT marches on Washington, D.C., in responding to the HIV-AIDS crisis, and in demanding equal marriage rights for lesbians and gays. MCC has blessed couples in a service it calls Holy Unions since its founding.

Perry retired as the denomination's moderator (presiding minister) in 2005. With headquarters in West Hollywood, the UFMCC has 275 churches in 25 nations, including Nigeria and Bulgaria, with a total membership of about fifty thousand individuals, making it one of the largest GLBT organizations in the world.

—*J. T. Todd*

## FURTHER READING

Perry, Troy. *Don't Be Afraid Anymore: The Story of the Rev. Troy Perry and the Metropolitan Community Churches*. New York: St. Martin's Press, 1990.

_____. *The Lord Is My Shepherd and He Knows I'm Gay*. Los Angeles: Nash, 1972.

Warner, R. Stephen. "The Metropolitan Community Churches and the Gay Agenda: The Power of Pentecostalism and Essentialism." In *Sex, Lies, and Sanctity: Religion and Deviance in Contemporary North America*, edited by David Bromley. Greenwich, Conn.: JAI Press, 1995.

Wilcox, Melissa M. *Coming Out in Christianity: Religion, Identity, and Community*. Bloomington: Indiana University Press, 2004.

_____. "Of Markets and Missions: The Early History of the Universal Fellowship of Metropolitan Community Churches." *Religion and American Culture* 11 (Winter, 2001): 83-108.

**SEE ALSO:** Mar., 1972-Mar., 1973: First Gay and Lesbian Synagogue in the United States Is Formed; June 25, 1972: First Out Gay Minister Is Ordained; Oct. 9-12, 1998: First International Retreat for Lesbian and Gay Muslims Is Held; Mar. 7, 2004: Robinson Becomes First Out Gay Bishop in Christian History; Nov. 29, 2005: Roman Catholic Church Bans Gay Seminarians.

# 1969
# NUESTRO MUNDO FORMS AS FIRST QUEER ORGANIZATION IN ARGENTINA

*In a climate of social protest and rebellion, Nuestro Mundo, the first queer organization in Argentina, was founded by former workers' union activists.*

**ALSO KNOWN AS:** Frente de Liberación Homosexual

**LOCALE:** Buenos Aires, Argentina

**CATEGORIES:** Organizations and institutions; civil rights

**KEY FIGURE**

*Héctor Anabitarte*, founder of Nuestro Mundo

## SUMMARY OF EVENT

Nuestro Mundo (our world) was the first organization specifically for lesbians and gays in Argentina. Although Nuestro Mundo existed without support and had only a few members, its emergence marked a change in Argentine society. By the end of the 1960's, a great number of left-wing groups and social protesters were trying to radically transform society. The climate of criticism resulted from decades of struggles between unions and dictatorial governments. Between 1958 and 1966, governments were democratically elected, but Peronism, a form of socialism that was instituted by former Argentine president Juan Perón, was forbidden.

In 1966, Argentina faced a coup d'état, with the support of the United States; under the resulting dictatorship, all political parties were forbidden. Resistance was defeated consistently until a 1969 rebellion in Córdoba, the second largest city in the country and one of the most important industrial centers at the time. A great number of underground movements suddenly went public and began to demonstrate against the dictatorship. Nuestro Mundo was part of this social uprising, and, in fact, many of the activists in the organization had previously been active in the workers' unions.

Although Perón had been democratically elected as president in 1946 and again in 1952, he was a general in the Argentine army, and he had been part of the previous military government. He won the first elections with a coalition that included the army and the Roman Catholic Church, and his views on sexuality were extremely conservative. Among other issues, Perón promoted legally controlled female heterosexual prostitution as a means to prevent the "spread" of homosexuality. Machismo was key to the propaganda of the Perón regime, and he represented himself as the most masculine of men who could master any sport and maintain a courageous approach to politics.

Despite the homophobic social context of the 1950's, Argentina was becoming an industrialized country where urban anonymity, social mobility, educational possibilities, and other modern social conditions encouraged the emergence of a lesbian and gay intellectual subculture. During this period, a small group of lesbians and gays began to write and publish homophile texts. During the 1960's new currents of thought began to spread among intellectuals and activists. With the emergence of Peronism, leftist politics, and feminism, there also emerged new attitudes toward sexuality. The creation of Nuestro Mundo was part of this new social milieu.

Nuestro Mundo had its first meetings in a small kitchen of a poor suburban house in greater Buenos Aires. Some neighbors suspected that underground political meetings were taking place, and the group was denounced. Nuestro Mundo continued its meetings in a station house, where every fifteen minutes its members had to hide from train passengers. Despite the obstacles the group faced, Nuestro Mundo had an ambitious goal: to make lesbians and gays politically conscious of their oppression. To fulfill this goal, the group distributed information about homosexual oppression to the press. Héctor Anabitarte, the founder of the group, explained that journalists had been surprised to receive this message from a masculine man whom they would never have expected to be homosexual; they also had been shocked that he was willing to express his homosexuality in an open manner.

Anabitarte had been a unionist and a Communist. In 1967, he had gone to Moscow to celebrate the fiftieth anniversary of the Bolshevik Revolution. He was assured that there were no homosexuals in Soviet Russia. After being ousted from the Communist Party for being an out homosexual, Anabitarte tried to organize a queer group on his own. In 1969, he met several gay and lesbian workers who were willing to join him in creating Nuestro Mundo.

As part of the strategy to reach lesbians and gays, Nuestro Mundo published a mimeographed newsletter to promote its views. While the group was courageous and promoted forms of activism unknown at the time, the newsletter made clear that the organization's goal was not to "promote" homosexuality. Fearing the consequences of their activism in an age of dictatorial rule, Nuestro Mundo members, according to their writings, wanted only to represent the life of homosexual people realistically and to correct distortions and stereotypes. The group published biographies of famous queer intellectuals as well as film reviews, news, and interviews with married homosexuals who felt they had no choice but to hide their true sexuality.

The group also promoted intellectual discussions at the University of Buenos Aires. In 1970, during the dictatorship, two gays participated on equal terms for the first time in a roundtable discussion with two professors who were specialists on the subject of homosexuality. These activities increased the audience for Nuestro Mundo, and eventually a group of young lesbian and gay activists from left-wing parties decided to join the queer group. The new activists were university students, and they gave a new tone to the group. They promoted a direct challenge for lesbian and gay rights, and they asked for a change in the name of the group to Frente de Liberación Homosexual (FLH, the Homosexual Liberation Front). José "Pepe" Bianco, an intellectual and writer who had been skeptical about the battle for queer rights, offered his house as a meeting place and translated articles about the queer movement in the United States.

## SIGNIFICANCE

In the early 1970's, Frente de Liberación Homosexual played an important role in politics, even as it was rejected by the left. However, in 1976 a military dictatorship gained power in Argentina, and the group was dissolved in an environment in which some thirty thousand people, accused of being subversives, were killed.

As part of the effort to remember and vindicate Nuestro Mundo, an Argentine gay pride parade is celebrated the first Saturday of every November, the same date on which Nuestro Mundo, the first lesbian and gay group in Argentina, was founded.

*—Pablo Ben*

## FURTHER READING

Adam, Barry D., Willem Jan Duyvendak, and André Krouwel, eds. *The Global Emergence of Gay and Lesbian Politics: National Imprints of a Worldwide Movement*. Philadelphia: Temple University Press, 1999.

Balderston, Daniel, and Donna Guy. *Sex and Sexuality in Latin America*. New York: New York University Press, 1997.

Bazán, Osvaldo. *Historia de la homosexualidad en la Argentina: De la conquista de América al siglo XXI*. Buenos Aires: Marea, 2004.

Berco, Cristian. "Silencing the Unmentionable: Non-reproductive Sex and the Creation of a Civilized Argentina, 1860-1900." *The Americas* 58, no. 3 (January, 2002): 419-441.

Brown, Stephen. "'Con discriminación y represión no hay democracia.' The Lesbian and Gay Movement in Argentina." *Latin American Perspectives* 29, no. 2 (March, 2002): 119-138.

Guy, Donna. *Sex and Danger in Buenos Aires: Prostitution, Family, and Nation in Argentina*. Lincoln: University of Nebraska Press, 1991.

Rapisardi, Flavio, and Alejandro Modarelli. *Fiestas, baños y exilios: Los gays porteños en la última dictadura*. Buenos Aires: Sudamericana, 2001.

**SEE ALSO:** Nov. 17, 1901: Police Arrest "Los 41" in Mexico City; 1912-1924: Robles Fights in the

Mexican Revolution; Nov., 1965: Revolutionary Cuba Imprisons Gays; Oct. 14-17, 1987: Latin American and Caribbean Lesbian Feminist Network Is Formed; 1990: International Gay and Lesbian Human Rights Commission Is Founded; June 19, 2002: Gays and Lesbians March for Equal Rights in Mexico City; Apr., 2003: Buenos Aires Recognizes Same-Gender Civil Unions; Jan., 2006: Jiménez Flores Elected to the Mexican Senate.

## 1969-1973
# GAY CATHOLICS FIND DIGNITY

*Founded as a counseling group, Dignity became a national organization of gay and lesbian Roman Catholics, the first organization of its kind in the United States. In 1972 the National Federation of Priests Councils passed a resolution that formed a task force to develop a Christian ministry model for outreach to gay and lesbian parishioners. That ministry model has influenced other Christian outreach programs for ministry to lesbians and gays.*

**LOCALE:** San Diego and Los Angeles, California
**CATEGORIES:** Organizations and institutions; religion

### KEY FIGURES
*Patrick X. Nidorf* (b. 1932), Augustinian priest, psychologist, and founder of Dignity
*Bob Fournier*, Dignity's first general chairman and drafter of Dignity's original Statement of Position and Purpose
*Joe Gilgamesh*, president of Dignity in 1972
*John J. McNeill* (b. 1925), expelled from the Jesuit order but continued to minister to gay and lesbian Catholics

### SUMMARY OF EVENT
The relationship between gays and lesbians and the Roman Catholic Church has often been tenuous at best. In 1969, Father Patrick X. Nidorf, an Augustinian priest and psychologist in San Diego, California, had noticed a trend with his gay clients. He wrote,

The Catholic gay people whom I had met were frequently bothered by ethical problems and identity with the Church. It seemed obvious that the Church was not meeting the needs of the gay community. In counseling gay Catholics, there always seemed to be an excessive and unreal problem of guilt that was sometimes reinforced in the confessional instead of being resolved. (Dignity Archives, 2004)

Nidorf, not content merely to sit with this understanding, wrote a paper proposing the creation of a group for gay Catholics and presented it during a provincial meeting. The majority of priests expressed favor for the concept and encouraged him to form a group. Thus began Dignity, a counseling group for gay and lesbian Catholics.

News of the group's founding spread primarily by word of mouth, but soon Nidorf began placing ads in the *Los Angeles Free Press*. The ads stated that members must be twenty-one years of age. Before each meeting, Nidorf asked for completed applications, fees of $5.00 per year, and personal interviews to keep religious zealots from Dignity's safe space; Nidorf understood the vulnerability of the individuals with whom he was working. The group he created began to gain momentum. Eventually, meetings moved to Los Angeles and were held in private homes; the first meeting in Los Angeles was held on February 28, 1970. Nidorf started the Dignity newsletter earlier in February, alerting members to meeting times and places and to topics for conversation. Within months, Bob Fournier had drafted the first Dignity statement of purpose and had become the first general chair of Dignity.

By 1971, Dignity membership had grown strong and vocal, all at a time when being gay was still classified as a mental disorder by the American Psychiatric Association. Members urged Nidorf to request recognition from the Los Angeles Diocese. Against his better judgment, Nidorf sent a letter to the diocese. On February 11, 1971, he was called before the archbishop of the diocese, who found offense that Nidorf was working in his diocese without permission. The archbishop further stated that Dignity's principles were untenable and demanded that Nidorf disassociate himself from the group. Nidorf complied, and on February 20, 1971, he announced his resignation to the nearly ninety group members. The group was emboldened by Fournier to continue its work as a mission led by lay people.

Over the course of the next two years, Dignity flourished, publishing its first national newsletter, calling for new chapters outside Los Angeles (Dignity/Louisville being the first), and organizing its chapters into a national organization. On February 19, 1972, at the first annual meeting of Dignity, members elected new officers and announced that Dignity then served nearly two hundred members, half from Los Angeles and the other half from the Philippines, Australia, Canada, the West Indies, England, the Netherlands, and Switzerland. New president Joe Gilgamesh traveled the United States encouraging other Catholics to join the Dignity movement. He also gained permission from Father John McNeill to reprint articles from his work, which provided the basis for Dignity's statement of purpose.

The movement had an impact. In March, 1972, the National Federation of Priests Councils passed a resolution that formed a task force with the duty of developing a Christian ministry model for outreach to gays and lesbians. Dignity chapters formed in the District of Columbia, Baltimore, New York, and Boston. Dignity was growing so quickly that an administrative services group was formed to oversee the affairs of the group that fell outside Los Angeles, and in December, Dignity's statement of purpose was sent out on national-office letterhead, signaling the birth of a national organization. Dignity held its first biennial convention in the summer of 1973, and by the end of that year its national headquarters had relocated to Boston from Los Angeles. DignityUSA found its national home in Washington, D.C., in 1980.

## DignityUSA: Statement of Position and Purpose

We believe that gay, lesbian, bisexual and transgender Catholics in our diversity are members of Christ's mystical body, numbered among the People of God. We have an inherent dignity because God created us, Christ died for us, and the Holy Spirit sanctified us in Baptism, making us temples of the Spirit, and channels through which God's love becomes visible. Because of this, it is our right, our privilege, and our duty to live the sacramental life of the Church, so that we might become more powerful instruments of God's love working among all people.

We believe that gay, lesbian, bisexual and transgender persons can express their sexuality in a manner that is consonant with Christ's teaching. We believe that we can express our sexuality physically, in a unitive manner that is loving, life-giving, and life-affirming. We believe that all sexuality should be exercised in an ethically responsible and unselfish way.

Dignity is organized to unite gay, lesbian, bisexual and transgender Catholics, as well as our families, friends and loved ones in order to develop leadership, and be an instrument through which we may be heard by and promote reform in the Church.

To be such an organization, we accept our responsibilities to the Church, to our Catholic heritage, to society, and to individual gay, lesbian, bisexual and transgender Catholics.

*Source:* http://www.dignityusa.org.

### Significance

Dignity's lasting impact has been threefold: It provides ministry and spaces of compassion and understanding to gay and lesbian Catholics, it encourages the Catholic Church to reflect on the way in which the church provides ministry to its gay and lesbian members, and it has led the way for other Christian churches to reevaluate the light in which they cast their gay and lesbian members. In the early twenty-first century, Dignity-USA has seen more than sixty chapters in the United States, its Web site is visited by more than ten thousand people each month, it advocates on behalf of gay and lesbian Catholics, and it provides education, resources, and comfort to its constituents.

Dignity led the way in breaking the silence of Christian churches with regard to their gay and lesbian members, and the relationship of Christian denominations with gays and lesbians has shifted since the group's founding. Many denominations, such as the More Light Presbyterians, the Metropolitan Community Churches, and Lutherans Concerned, reach out and minister to gays and lesbians. As the gay rights movement continues to gain momentum, other religions have opened their doors to gay and lesbian people, and groups representing gay and lesbian Jews, Buddhists, and Muslims (Al-Fatiha) have formed. Though religion and religious proscriptions remain sources of pain and confusion for gays and lesbians, more people of faith and communities of faith are expressing deeper love and compassion for all their people.

—*Jennifer Self*

---

> ## "OUR OBLIGATION TO LOVE PEOPLE"
>
> Members of DIGNITY:
> It is a pretty great thing to get a group of sensitive intelligent people together who are truly awair [sic], who have a broad capacity for helping others and themselves, and who want to enrich their lives. If DIGNITY becomes great, it will not be due to Fr. Pat [Nidorf], but to our members.
>
> Perhaps to summarize a few themes we discussed at our past meeting would be helpful. The big cop-out: "I'm gay and rejected" is a little too convenient to be real. Our obligations, not only as Catholics and Christians, but as human beings is not lessened because we are gay, if anything, it may be increased. Our obligation is simply to love people. So easy to say but at times so difficult to accomplish. . . .
>
> The fact is that we have so much to give—we can't let anything stand in the way of our giving. And this must be our moral concentration: not self-devaluation and browbeating because we hopped into bed with a buddy again, but rather a realistic self-searching as to simply how Christ-like we are in our every day dealings with people . . . [ellipses in original] ordinary people. . . .
>
> We all stand alone in the center of the world, because we are gay doesn't mean that we corner the market on loneliness. The more egocentric and selfish we are, the more keenly do we feel the pain of our loneliness. If that pain becomes unbearable, it is because we ourselves have become unbearable. We have stopped giving. . . .
>
> Our next meeting will be in L.A. . . . Two topics to be discussed are: age and how to handle it; the advantages or disadvantages of telling the "world" you are gay. Be thinking. . . .
>
> *Source: Dignity*, February, 1970, newsletter. http://www.dignityusa .org/archives/history.html.

---

### FURTHER READING

Balka, Christie, and Andy Rose, eds. *Twice Blessed: On Being Lesbian, Gay, and Jewish.* Boston: Beacon Press, 1989.

Curb, Rosemary, and Nancy Manahan, eds. *Lesbian Nuns: Breaking Silence.* London: Women's Press, 1993.

Dillon, Michele. *Catholic Identity: Balancing Reason, Faith, and Power.* New York: Cambridge University Press, 1999.

Glaser, Chris. *Coming Out to God: Prayers for Lesbians and Gay Men, Their Families, and Friends.* Louisville, Ky.: Westminster/John Knox Press, 1991.

Helminiak, Daniel A. *What the Bible Really Says About Homosexuality.* Foreword by John S. Spong. Millennium ed., updated and expanded. Tajique, N.Mex.: Alamo Square Press, 2000.

Liuzzi, Peter J. *With Listening Hearts: Understanding the Voices of Lesbian and Gay Catholics.* New York: Paulist Press, 2001.

McNeill, John. *Both Feet Firmly Planted in Midair: My Spiritual Journey.* Louisville, Ky.: Westminster/John Knox Press, 1998.

_____. *The Church and the Homosexual.* 1976. 4th ed. Boston: Beacon Press, 1993.

Maher, Michael J. S., Jr. *Being Gay and Lesbian in*

a *Catholic High School: Beyond the Uniform*. New York: Harrington Park Press, 2001.

Stuart, Elizabeth. *Gay and Lesbian Theologies: Repetitions with Critical Difference*. Burlington, Vt.: Ashgate, 2002.

White, Mel. *Stranger at the Gate: To Be Gay and Christian in America*. New York: Simon & Schuster, 1994.

**SEE ALSO:** Oct. 6, 1968: Metropolitan Community Church Is Founded; Mar., 1972-Mar., 1973: First Gay and Lesbian Synagogue in the United States Is Formed; June 25, 1972: First Out Gay Minister Is Ordained; Oct. 9-12, 1998: First International Retreat for Lesbian and Gay Muslims Is Held; Mar. 7, 2004: Robinson Becomes First Out Gay Bishop in Christian History; Nov. 29, 2005: Roman Catholic Church Bans Gay Seminarians.

## June 27-July 2, 1969
# STONEWALL REBELLION IGNITES MODERN GAY AND LESBIAN RIGHTS MOVEMENT

*GLBT patrons at the Stonewall Inn, a bar in New York City, spontaneously rebelled against a police raid that had been preceded by years of police raids of gay bars in the city. For the first time, sexual minorities rebelled in numbers and with force against systematic oppression, inspiring pride and sparking the modern movement for lesbian, gay, bisexual, and transgender rights.*

**ALSO KNOWN AS:** Stonewall riot
**LOCALE:** Greenwich Village, New York
**CATEGORIES:** Marches, protests, and riots; civil rights

### KEY FIGURES
*Seymour Pine*, deputy inspector, New York City Police Department
*Howard Smith*, reporter for *The Village Voice*
*Dick Leitsch*, executive director of the Mattachine Society of New York, who reported on the rebellion for *The Advocate*

### SUMMARY OF EVENT
In New York City in 1969, the rights of gays and lesbians to congregate and to express their sexuality in public were at best tentative. It was not unusual that gay and lesbian bars were raided and then closed for a period of up to three weeks. The Stonewall Inn, a GLBT bar in Lower Manhattan's Greenwich Village, came under the jurisdiction of the New York Police Department's new commanding officer for the sixth precinct, a commander who soon initiated the raid on the Stonewall Inn.

Said to be the only gay bar in the city at the time that allowed same-gender dancing, the Stonewall Inn, located at 53 Christopher Street, near Sheridan Square, drew a diverse crowd: students, drag queens and kings, young African American and Latino drag queens, and some businessmen and older people. The bar was rumored to have ties with organized crime, something not uncommon in big cities on the East Coast.

Around midnight on Friday, June 27, two plainclothes detectives and two undercover female police officers from the sixth precinct entered the Stonewall Inn to observe the employees. At about 1:20 A.M. on Saturday, June 28, Deputy Inspector Seymour Pine, head of the public morals section, presented management with a search warrant, confiscated cases of liquor, announced the closure of the bar, and began expelling the club's two hundred or so customers with his force of eight officers. Police paddy wagons came to haul away the bartender, the doorman, and others, including those in full

*The Stonewall Inn, Christopher Street, New York City, 1969.* (National Park Service)

parking meter and used it to batter down the doors. A number of burning objects were tossed into the bar, and the place erupted into flames. The police used a fire hose from inside the bar to put out the fire and to deter the crowd. It was then that Tactical Patrol Force units arrived and began dispersing the crowd.

Eventually, the police gained control over the neighborhood. Thirteen men were arrested on charges of harassment, disorderly conduct, and resisting arrest. Four police officers were injured in the melee; the most serious injury was a broken wrist. The uprising itself began shortly after 3:00 A.M. and lasted about forty-five minutes.

The following evening, Saturday, June 28, throngs of young men congregated at the site of the burned-out bar to read a condemnation of police behavior. Graffiti on the boarded-up windows read "Support Gay Power" and "Legalize Gay Bars." Tensions mounted as the night progressed, and, by midnight, several hundred people gathered to resume the protest against police.

Police from the Charles Street Station House were unable to control the crowds, and so Tactical Patrol Force units again were called in to help. The units poured into the area shortly after 2:00 A.M. They broke through a line of protesters and, linking arms in a line of their own, swept up and down Christopher Street between Sixth and Seventh Avenues to disperse the crowds. Estimates of the number involved in the disturbance were as high as four hundred police and two thousand protesters. Eventually, the crowd dispersed, and police left the area at approximately four in the morning. Three men were arrested on charges of harassment and disorderly conduct. By the following Wednesday, the initial eruption at the Stonewall Inn died down, but a movement was born.

### SIGNIFICANCE

Those two nights outside the Stonewall Inn set in motion the modern movement for gay and lesbian rights. The impulse to fight for equal rights in American society had been strong but latent; the Stonewall Rebellion was a major catalyst that created an immediate and extensive response.

drag. As patrons were herded into the streets, they began to chant, attracting attention and swelling in numbers as friends and passersby joined in the chant.

The last customer to be guided out, a lesbian, put up a struggle. As the police subdued her, the crowd grew unruly and exploded into rebellion. A rain of coins was released on the police, suggesting the financial payoffs they were rumored to receive. Some threw beer bottles and pulled cobblestones from the street, tossing them in all directions. The eight police officers, severely outnumbered, sought refuge in the empty bar; reporter Howard Smith, of *The Village Voice*, went in the bar with the police. They locked the front doors, but protesters uprooted a

*A commemorative flyer with news stories covering the Stonewall Rebellion.* (Courtesy, Stonewall Veterans' Association)

On Sunday, June 29, New York's Mattachine Society, led by Dick Leitsch, handed out leaflets calling for organized resistance to police and societal harassment of gays. By Tuesday, July 1, those advocating a more aggressive form of protest had organized the Gay Liberation Front; the group would meet at New York's Alternative University.

The uprising received cursory coverage in the interior pages of *The New York Times* on Sunday and Monday, June 29 and 30. The coverage there and in *The Village Voice*, while scornful, fueled awareness and commitment among not only gays, lesbians, and transgender people but also the people of New York City who supported the cause.

The gay and lesbian rights movement developed with rapid speed. Gay Liberation Front chapters were established and organized in New York and San Francisco, and branches were soon founded in major cities and universities in not only the United States but also Canada, Europe, and Australia. The uprisings at the Stonewall Inn and environs in June of 1969 permanently changed the way GLBT people cope with and confront societal attitudes concerning sexuality and also changed the way society understands and accepts sexual minorities and same-gender sexuality. Also, the rebellion led to mandated sensitivity training for the New York Police Department.

—*Kenneth T. Burles*

**FURTHER READING**

Carter, David. *Stonewall: The Riots That Sparked the Gay Revolution.* New York: St. Martin's Press, 2004.

D'Emilio, John. *Sexual Battles, Sexual Communities: The Making of a Homosexual Minority in the United States, 1940-1970.* 2d ed. Chicago: University of Chicago Press, 1998.

Duberman, Martin B. *Stonewall.* New York: Dutton, 1993.

Marcus, Eric. *Making History: The Struggles for Gay and Lesbian Equal Rights, 1945-1990: An Oral History.* New York: HarperCollins, 1992.

Miller, Neil. *Out of the Past: Gay and Lesbian History from 1869 to the Present.* New York: Vintage Books, 1995.

Stonewall Veteran's Association. http://www.stonewallvets.org. An excellent resource that includes media clippings and personal testimony from those who were part of the rebellion.

Williams, Walter, and Yolanda Retter. *Gay and Lesbian Rights in the United States: A Documentary History.* Westport, Conn.: Greenwood Press, 2003.

**SEE ALSO:** Nov. 17, 1901: Police Arrest "Los 41" in Mexico City; Mar. 15, 1919-1921: U.S. Navy Launches Sting Operation Against "Sexual Perverts"; June 30-July 1, 1934: Hitler's Night of the Long Knives; Aug., 1966: Queer Youth Fight Police Harassment at Compton's Cafeteria in San Francisco; July 31, 1969: Gay Liberation

Front Is Formed; June 28, 1970: First Lesbian and Gay Pride March in the United States; Dec. 31, 1977: Toronto Police Raid Offices of *The Body Politic*; Oct. 12-15, 1979: First March on Washington for Lesbian and Gay Rights; Feb. 5, 1981: Toronto Police Raid Gay Bathhouses; Oct. 11, 1987: Second March on Washington for Lesbian and Gay Rights; Apr. 24, 1993: First Dyke March Is Held in Washington, D.C.; Apr. 25, 1993: March on Washington for Gay, Lesbian, and Bi Equal Rights and Liberation; June, 1994: Stonewall 25 March and Rallies Are Held in New York City; June 19, 2002: Gays and Lesbians March for Equal Rights in Mexico City.

## July 31, 1969
# GAY LIBERATION FRONT IS FORMED

*Harnessing the political energy that came out of the Stonewall Rebellion of June, 1969, the founding of the Gay Liberation Front heralded a new era not only of mainstream liberal but also radical GLBT activism across the United States and the world.*

**LOCALE:** New York, New York
**CATEGORIES:** Civil rights; marches, protests, and riots; organizations and institutions

**KEY FIGURES**
*Jim Fouratt*, cofounder of Gay Liberation Front and Gay Activists Alliance
*Dick Leitsch*, head of the Mattachine Society
*Jim Owles* (1946-1993), cofounder of Gay Liberation Front and first president of Gay Activists Alliance
*Marty Robinson*, cofounder of Gay Liberation Front and Gay Activists Alliance
*Martha Shelley* (b. 1943), cofounder of Gay Liberation Front and Lavender Menace/ Radicalesbians

**SUMMARY OF EVENT**
In the days after the 1969 rebellion at the Stonewall Inn, a GLBT bar in New York City, tensions ran high among those inspired by this confrontation. While homophile organizations had worked to change social, legal, and political norms for decades, their efforts tended toward an assimilationist approach, emphasizing mere acceptance of lesbians and gays. The idea of assimilation conflicted with the goals of a new generation of lesbians and gays who were trained to be more radical by being part of the Civil Rights movement, namely the Black Panthers, the antiwar movement, and other causes. The radical wing of the lesbian and gay movement advocated linking sexual expression and the struggle for gay and lesbian rights with the struggles and politics of the radical, inclusive New Left movement of the 1960's.

These tensions surfaced repeatedly during July of 1969, when groups met to formulate a new response to GLBT oppression. While the Mattachine Society, led by Dick Leitsch, organized the early gatherings, those who flocked to the meetings were angered by the old vanguards' temperate (and sexist) approach to politics (including the guideline

*A Gay Liberation Front decal from 1970.* (William J. Canfield Papers, Northeastern University Library)

---

### "A Gay Manifesto"

Where once there was frustration, alienation, and cynicism, there are new characteristics among us. We are full of love for each other and are showing it; we are full of anger at what has been done to us. And as we recall all the self-censorship and repression for so many years, a reservoir of tears pours out of our eyes. And we are euphoric, high, with the initial flourish of a movement.

We want to make ourselves clear: our first job is to free ourselves; that means clearing our heads of the garbage that's been poured into them. This article is an attempt at raising a number of issues, and presenting some ideas to replace the old ones. It is primarily for ourselves, a starting point of discussion. If straight people of good will find it useful in understanding what liberation is about, so much the better.

It should also be clear that these are the views of one person, and are determined not only by my homosexuality, but my being white, male, middle class. It is my individual consciousness. Our group consciousness will evolve as we get ourselves together—we are only at the beginning.

*I. On Orientation*

1. What homosexuality is: Nature leaves undefined the object of sexual desire. The gender of that object is imposed socially. . . .

*II. On Women*

1. Lesbianism: It's been a male-dominated society for too long, and that has warped both men and women. So gay women are going to see things differently from gay men; they are going to feel put down as women, too. Their liberation is tied up with both gay liberation and women's liberation. . . .

*III. On Roles*

1. Mimicry of straight society: We are children of straight society. We still think straight: that is part of our oppression. . . .

*IV. On Oppression*

It is important to catalog and understand the different facets of our oppression. There is no future in arguing about degrees of oppression. . . .

*V. On Sex*

1. What sex is: It is both creative expression and communication: good when it is either, and better when it is both. . . .

*Conclusion: An Outline of Imperatives for Gay Liberation*

1. Free ourselves: come out everywhere; initiate self defense and political activity; initiate counter community institutions.

2. Turn other gay people on: talk all the time; understand, forgive, accept.

3. Free the homosexual in everyone. . . .

4. We've been playing an act for a long time, so we're consummate actors. Now we can begin to be, and it'll be a good show!

*Source:* Carl Wittman, 1970. http://www.freedomroad.org/content/view/313/63/.

---

that women wear skirts to protests). Following a legendary confrontation between Leitsch and Jim Fouratt (a leader from the Yippie movement, later called the Youth International Party, and colleague of radical 1960's activist Abbie Hoffman), dozens of participants walked out of a meeting and recongregated at what was called Alternative U, or Alt U (alternative university), home to the city's radical political and cultural groups.

Martha Shelley took the lead in organizing a rally in Washington Square Park in late July, which drew between five hundred and two thousand participants (reports vary). While both the Mattachine Society and the Daughters of Bilitis cosponsored the rally, this was to be their last formal association with the redefined movement. Amid the rally activities, flyers were circulated carrying the slogan Do You Think Homosexuals Are Revolting? You Bet Your Sweet Ass We Are! They advertised a meeting to take place four days later, July 31, 1969, at Alt U.

Fifty people attended the meeting, almost none representing the established homophile movement.

The name Gay Liberation Front (GLF) was agreed upon, and a new organization was born—one in which members would apply the political analysis and energies they had devoted to other causes to their own oppression as gay and lesbian people.

GLF's New Left roots were reflected in its organizational structures. Meetings were nonhierarchical, operated by consensus, and they devoted significant time to consciousness-raising and to coming-out stories. The meetings also became a place for the critique of the politics, participants, and strategies of the homophile movement. Discussion and debate included topics on social issues and concerns ranging from closing the Pentagon to legalizing abortion to ending poverty, and all were linked with gay and lesbian rights. As such, meetings were often highly emotional, conflicted, and chaotic.

By 1970, GLF was publishing theoretical pamphlets and a gay and lesbian newspaper called *Come Out!*; sponsoring demonstrations, protests, and dances; organizing parades and conferences; and establishing a community center. Its activities were often characterized as exuberant and sometimes campy, as they creatively confronted politicians, the media, and dominant social structures through "gay-ins," "kiss-ins," dancing, and guerrilla theater.

In the year after GLF began in New York, GLF chapters were formed across the United States in Berkeley, Chicago, Philadelphia, Los Angeles, Minnesota, Detroit, Madison, and San Francisco. Within a few years, GLF was active in thirty-five states and appeared also outside major metropolitan areas. GLF organizations also arose in Vancouver and Sydney, as well as London, Paris, Berlin, and other European cities. Meanwhile, the older homophile organizations folded: Daughters of Bilitis dissolved in 1970, and the Mattachine Society disbanded in 1971.

The initial entity that was GLF survived until 1972 and fractured many times during its short existence. Within its first six months, GLF members Jim Fouratt, Jim Owles, Marty Robinson, and oth-

*Gay Liberation Front members join the gay and lesbian pride march in Hollywood, California, on June 29, 1970. (AP/ Wide World Photos)*

ers broke with GLF to create the Gay Activists Alliance (GAA), a more tempered and formal organization focused on the concerns of gays and lesbians exclusively. Tensions within GLF and GAA, both of which were made up mostly by white, middle-class gay men, also led to the creation of organizations focused on lesbians, people of color, transsexuals, and transgender people. These new groups included Gay Liberation Front Women, Lavender Menace/Radicalesbians, Lesbian Feminist Liberation, Third World Gay Revolution, and Street Transvestite Action Revolutionaries.

## Significance

The Gay Liberation Front was at the center of a new radical visibility and energy devoted to the rights of LGBT people. Less polite, less interested in acceptance and understanding, and less isolationist in approach, GLF worked toward social transformation, not assimilation.

GLF also fostered a new level of self-definition within the LGBT community by being the first group to use the word "gay" in its name instead of the word "homosexual." The mainstream media was so resistant to this change that even the progressive periodical *The Village Voice* refused to use "gay" in advertising copy submitted by GLF to publicize its meetings. By protesting at the offices of *The Village Voice* and other media outlets, the community increasingly demanded and won the right to self-definition and encouraged the use of the term "gay" by the media. This legacy of self-definition was furthered in later years when protests at American Psychiatric Association meetings successfully challenged the practice of listing "homosexuality" as a psychiatric disorder.

Finally, the nonhierarchical, "power to the people" approach of GLF allowed for thoughts and ideas, experiences, and identities in a manner that was unprecedented in the old homophile movement. Although GLF splintered, it created the forums through which participants articulated their racial, political, and gendered experiences, and it invented the new alliances, caucuses, and organizations that carried forward the movement's work.

—*Diana Kardia*

## Further Reading

Clendinene, Dudley, and Adam Nagourney. *Out for Good: The Struggle to Build a Gay Rights Movement in America*. New York: Simon & Schuster, 1999.

Duberman, Martin B. *Stonewall*. New York: Dutton, 1993.

Kissack, Terence. "Freaking Fag Revolutionaries: New York's Gay Liberation Front, 1969-1971." *Radical History Review* 62 (Spring, 1995): 104-134.

McGarry, Molly, and Fred Wasserman. *Becoming Visible*. New York: Penguin Putnam, 1998.

Marcus, Eric. *Making Gay History: The Half Century Fight for Lesbian and Gay Equal Rights*. New York: HarperCollins, 2002.

Rimmerman, Craig A. *From Identity to Politics: The Lesbian and Gay Movements in the United States*. Philadelphia: Temple University Press, 2002.

Thompson, Mark, ed. *Long Road to Freedom: The Advocate History of the Gay and Lesbian Movement*. New York: St. Martin's Press, 1994.

**See also:** 1950: Mattachine Society Is Founded; 1952: ONE, Inc., Is Founded; 1955: Daughters of Bilitis Founded as First National Lesbian Group in United States; May 27-30, 1960: First National Lesbian Conference Convenes; Feb. 19-20, 1966: First North American Conference of Homophile Organizations Convenes; Apr. 19, 1967: First Student Homophile League Is Formed; Aug. 11-18, 1968: NACHO Formally Becomes the First Gay Political Coalition; June 28, 1970: First Lesbian and Gay Pride March in the United States; Nov. 28, 1970: Del Martin Quits Gay Liberation Movement; 1973: National Gay Task Force Is Formed; Oct. 18, 1973: Lambda Legal Authorized to Practice Law; Mar. 5, 1974: Antigay and Antilesbian Organizations Begin to Form; Apr. 22, 1980: Human Rights Campaign Fund Is Founded; Mar., 1987: Radical AIDS Activist Group ACT UP Is Founded; Mar. 20, 1990: Queer Nation Is Founded.

**August 26, 1969**
# CANADA DECRIMINALIZES HOMOSEXUAL ACTS

*Amendments to the Canadian criminal code legalized private sexual acts, including same-gender sexual acts, between consenting adults over the age of twenty-one.*

**LOCALE:** Ottawa, Canada
**CATEGORIES:** Laws, acts, and legal history; civil rights; crime

## KEY FIGURES

*Everett George Klippert*, Canadian found guilty of gross indecency
*Pierre Trudeau* (1919-2000), federal minister of justice and prime minister of Canada

## SUMMARY OF EVENT

On August 24, 1965, Everett George Klippert, of Pine Point, Northwest Territories, was sentenced to three years in prison for "gross indecency" for sexual acts committed with other men in private. The following year, Klippert was declared a "dangerous sexual offender," subject to incarceration indefinitely. He appealed this decision to the Supreme Court of Canada, but the appeal was rejected on November 7, 1967. The case nevertheless spawned extensive commentary critical of laws making homosexual acts a crime.

The month after Klippert lost his appeal, Pierre Trudeau, then the federal minister of justice, introduced a sexual offenses reform bill. Although this bill had been expected, it was Trudeau's charisma that gave the proposed bill a sense of being up-to-date. After introducing the legislation, which most famously relaxed penalties for sexual acts by two consenting adults in private, Trudeau said, "The state has no place in the bedrooms of the nation." These reforms were included in the 1969 omnibus criminal reform bill, C-150, which was passed on May 14.

It is debatable if the Klippert affair had any bearing on Trudeau's decision, as much as it was likely that Trudeau wanted to drag Canada, fresh from celebrating its centenary but still socially backward in some respects, into the dynamic era that was the latter part of the twentieth century. Still, Trudeau, as justice minister, could not have been unaware of Klippert's case. One of the justices in the Klippert case said that laws regarding homosexuality needed clarification and that, in any case, it was not the court's intention to keep gays in jail indefinitely, detention that had been legal at the time. Trudeau was asked in the House of Commons, on November 7, 1967, about the arbitrary nature of preventive detention measures, a clear reference to Klippert. The question was ruled out of order, and Trudeau did not reply. The next day, however, he did gesture to legal amendments that might be pursued in the Ouimet committee on penal reform. (Klippert was not paroled until July 20, 1971.) C-150 was introduced in the House of Commons on December 21.

## SIGNIFICANCE

Not unlike the Sexual Offences Bill of 1967 in the United Kingdom, Canada's C-150 had little to say on homosexuality but did declare that gross indecency and buggery were not criminal if done in private by two consenting persons age twenty-one years or older. More than two people made such acts public and, thus, illegal. Buggery and gross indecency remained on the books, and they were still crimes; they applied to homosexual acts except when committed by two consenting adults in private.

In June of the following year, an antigay campaign took special aim against Trudeau in the run-up to the June 25, 1968, general election. A number of ultraconservative groups called Trudeau a "beast of Sodom." He was elected prime minister anyway. In the same year, the Canadian Bar Association and a research group at Toronto's Clarke Institute of Psychiatry both recommended that gross indecency, as set out in C-150, required closer definition. The bill was debated in the house from April 16 to May 14, 1969, and then easily passed in a 149 to 55 vote on May 14. Bill C-150 went into effect on August 26, 1969.

This legislative victory for Canada's progressive, civil rights movement contrasted sharply with a better-known happening south of the Canadian border. On the night of June 27, 1969, the New York Police Department launched a bar raid on Greenwich Village's Stonewall Inn, inciting an uprising that is now widely considered to be the genesis of the modern gay and lesbian rights movement.

*—Andrew Lesk*

**FURTHER READING**

Lahey, Kathleen A. *Are We "Persons" Yet? Law and Sexuality in Canada*. Buffalo, N.Y.: University of Toronto Press, 1999.

MacDougall, Bruce. *Queer Judgements: Homosexuality, Expression, and the Courts in Canada*. Buffalo, N.Y.: University of Toronto Press, 2000.

McLeod, Donald W. *Lesbian and Gay Liberation in Canada: A Selected Annotated Chronology, 1964-1975*. Toronto, Ont.: ECW Press/Homewood Books, 1996.

Miller, Neil. *Out of the Past: Gay and Lesbian History from 1869 to the Present*. New York: Vintage Books, 1995.

Pedersen, Lyn. "Germany, Canada Pass 'Consenting Adults' Laws." *The Advocate*, June, 1969, 3.

Smith, Miriam. *Lesbian and Gay Rights in Canada: Social Movements and Equality Seeking, 1971-1999*. Buffalo, N.Y.: University of Toronto Press, 1999.

Warner, Tom. *Never Going Back: A History of Queer Activism in Canada*. Buffalo, N.Y.: University of Toronto Press, 2002.

**SEE ALSO:** 1885: United Kingdom Criminalizes "Gross Indecency"; 1972-1973: Local Governments Pass Antidiscrimination Laws; Aug., 1973: American Bar Association Calls for Repeal of Laws Against Consensual Sex; Nov. 17, 1975: U.S. Supreme Court Rules in "Crimes Against Nature" Case; Dec. 19, 1977: Quebec Includes Lesbians and Gays in Its Charter of Human Rights and Freedoms; June 2, 1980: Canadian Gay Postal Workers Secure Union Protections; 1986: *Bowers v. Hardwick* Upholds State Sodomy Laws; Jan. 1, 1988: Canada Decriminalizes Sex Practices Between Consenting Adults; Dec. 30, 1991-Feb. 22, 1993: Canada Grants Asylum Based on Sexual Orientation; Apr. 27, 1992: Canadian Government Antigay Campaign Is Revealed; Oct., 1992: Canadian Military Lifts Its Ban on Gays and Lesbians; Apr. 2, 1998: Canadian Supreme Court Reverses Gay Academic's Firing; June 17, 2003, and July 19, 2005: Canada Legalizes Same-Gender Marriage; June 26, 2003: U.S. Supreme Court Overturns Texas Sodomy Law.

## October 31, 1969
# *TIME* MAGAZINE ISSUES "THE HOMOSEXUAL IN AMERICA"

*A cover story on gay and lesbian rights in* Time, *a leading newsmagazine, suggested a broadening of attitudes in the United States in discussing, defining, and dealing with same-gender sexuality.*

**LOCALE:** New York, New York
**CATEGORIES:** Publications; civil rights

**KEY FIGURES**
*Evelyn Hooker* (1907-1996), psychologist who chaired the National Institute of Mental Health's Task Force on Homosexuality
*Franklin Kameny* (b. 1925), astronomer, out candidate for Congress, founding president of the Mattachine Society of Washington who and contributor to *Time* cover story
*Wardell Pomeroy*, psychologist who coauthored the Kinsey Reports on men and women, and contributor to *Time* cover story

**SUMMARY OF EVENT**
In the mid-twentieth century, before the rise of the Internet or cable television news channels, weekly newsmagazines wielded considerable influence in U.S. society, and among these the most influential was *Time*. This publication was satirized by Allen Ginsberg in his 1956 poem "America" for its pervasive influence over the flow of ideas and interpretive values for mainstream America. As late as January 21, 1966, in an unsigned *Time* editorial, homosexuality was described as "a pitiable flight from life" that deserved "no encouragement, no glamorization, no rationalization, no fake status as minority martyrdom, no sophistry about simple differences in taste—and above all, no pretense that it is anything but a pernicious sickness."

The October 24, 1969, issue, however, in the column "Behavior," showed a somewhat progressive step forward, based on a new report by the National Institute of Mental Health's Task Force on Homosexuality. The fourteen-member NIH panel, after a thorough two-year study led by University of Cali-

fornia, Los Angeles, psychologist Evelyn Hooker, became the first U.S. government-sponsored group to formally call for a reevaluation of and change in social attitudes toward homosexuality. The panel urged states to abolish all laws making homosexuality a crime for consenting adults in private, and it called upon employers to stop discriminating against competent homosexuals in the workplace. Reflecting upon these suggestions, the unsigned 1969 *Time* column concluded that Americans could now come to understand that "an undesirable handicap does not necessarily make everyone afflicted with it undesirable."

The following week, the periodical took an even bigger step: The October 31, 1969, issue of *Time* ran the cover story "The Homosexual in America." Dated on Halloween, the article noted Halloween's special significance of masking and role-playing in the visible urban gay subcultures celebrating it in such cities as San Francisco, New York, Los Angeles, Houston, and St. Louis, Missouri. The article described the growing political movement and increasing influence of "homophile" organizations clamoring for civil rights, and it noted the similar rise in attention to gay and lesbian perspectives in literature, theater, and cinema available to the general public. At the same time, though, the article noted a Harris poll taken just a week earlier that indicated 63 percent of the nation believed homosexuals were "harmful to American life."

*Time* worked to dispel some misconceptions and myths about homosexuality. It pointed out that gays and lesbians are no more likely than heterosexuals to be child molesters, and that gays and lesbians are more likely to be victimized by crime than to commit crimes themselves. *Time* suggested that only 10 percent of the males who had experienced same-gender sex in the United States fit the definition of the easily identifiable and stereotypical limp-wristed sissy; the other 90 percent were labeled "secret lifers," those who passed as heterosexual in daily life but still actively participated in "secret"

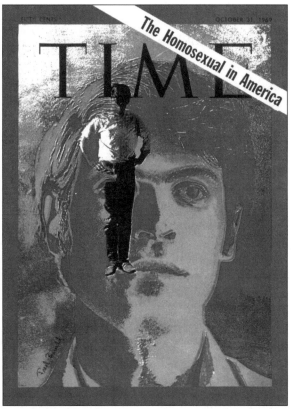

*The cover of* Time *magazine's "The Homosexual in America" issue (October 31, 1969).* (Hulton Archive/ Getty Images)

homosexual activities. Diversity in sexual practices was addressed by such summary categories as "The Desperate," "The Adjusted," "The Bisexual," and "The Situational-Experimental," the latter referring to men who have sex with men without any deep homosexual motivation.

The report on gay life and culture included a review of the then-prevalent idea that homosexuality must be a learned behavior because gender identity is a learned behavior, while it admitted there were no simple answers for what makes a person gay or lesbian. Despite offering some trepidation that, historically, greater acceptance of homosexuality seemed often to be related to the decline, then demise, of earlier societies, in the end the *Time* cover story called for greater tolerance of gays and lesbians with these words: "While homosexuality is a serious and sometimes crippling maladjustment, research has made clear that it is no longer necessary or morally justifiable to treat all inverts as outcasts."

*Time* also invited eight acknowledged experts on homosexuality to discuss the topic "Are Homosexuals Sick?" Excerpts from this exchange were published as an addendum to the cover story. Included in the group were openly gay Franklin Kameny and psychoanalyst Wardell Pomeroy. Kameny argued that homophobic social attitudes are detrimental to gays just as racist social attitudes are detrimental to racial minorities. Pomeroy noted that he did encounter "sick" homosexuals in his practice, but in his twenty years of research outside the analyst's office he had also encountered hundreds of "happy homosexuals" living successful lives with no desire for therapy. When leading heterosexual psychoanalysts on the panel agreed that homosexuals deserved civil rights but maintained homosexuality must definitely be declared an emotional illness, Kameny refused to accept this label, and *Time* allowed him the last word in the printed exchange.

## Significance

Coming a few months after the Stonewall Rebellion in New York City, this cover story in *Time* signaled that a formerly taboo discussion topic, the issue of civil rights for gays and lesbians, was not only permissible but also, perhaps, needed, for the good of gays and lesbians as well as for the common good of society. The tone of the article was respectful of the findings of Hooker's NIH task force and cognizant of the many injustices gays and lesbians face in their daily lives. This broadening of the public discourse to include gay and lesbian concerns and perspectives was part of a larger social phenomenon activated by the rise of the 1960's counterculture, but its impact on mainstream society was undeniable.

Furthermore, Frank Kameny would be vindicated in 1973, when the American Psychiatric Association formally removed "homosexual" from its *Diagnostic and Statistical Manual of Mental Disorders*. Other changes took more time: It was not until 2003 that the U.S. Supreme Court overturned antisodomy laws, which traditionally had been the legal argument for police harassment of homosexuals.

—*Scot M. Guenter*

**FURTHER READING**

Bull, Chris, ed. *Come Out Fighting: A Century of Essential Writing on Gay and Lesbian Liberation.* New York: Thunder's Mouth Press/Nation Books, 2001.

Gross, Larry. *Up from Invisibility: Lesbians, Gay Men, and the Media in America.* New York: Columbia University Press, 2001.

Gross, Larry, and James D. Woods, eds. *The Columbia Reader on Lesbians and Gay Men in Media, Society, and Politics.* New York: Columbia University Press, 1999.

Hooker, Evelyn. "Reflections of a Forty-Year Exploration: A Scientific View of Homosexuality." *American Psychologist* 48, no. 4 (1993): 450-454.

Loughery, John. *The Other Side of Silence: Men's Lives and Gay Identities, a Twentieth Century History.* New York: H. Holt, 1998.

McGarry, Molly, and Fred Wasserman. *Becoming Visible: An Illustrated History of Lesbian and Gay Life in Twentieth Century America.* New York: Penguin Studio, 1998.

Smith, Patricia Juliana. *The Queer Sixties.* New York: Routledge, 1999.

**SEE ALSO:** 1929: Davis's Research Identifies Lesbian Sexuality as Common and Normal; 1953-1957: Evelyn Hooker Debunks Beliefs That Homosexuality Is a "Sickness"; Mar. 7, 1967: CBS Airs *CBS Reports: The Homosexuals*; 1971: Kameny Is First Out Candidate for U.S. Congress; Dec. 15, 1973: Homosexuality Is Delisted by APA; 1979-1981: First Gay British Television Series Airs; June 5 and July 3, 1981: Reports of Rare Diseases Mark Beginning of AIDS Epidemic; 1985: GLAAD Begins Monitoring Media Coverage of Gays and Lesbians; 1985: Lesbian Film *Desert Hearts* Is Released; July 25, 1985: Actor Hudson Announces He Has AIDS; 1988: *Macho Dancer* Is Released in the Philippines; 1992-2002: Celebrity Lesbians Come Out; Mar. 21, 2000: Hollywood Awards Transgender Portrayals in Film; Sept. 7, 2001: First Gay and Lesbian Television Network Is Launched in Canada; Mar. 5, 2006: *Brokeback Mountain, Capote,* and *Transamerica* Receive Oscars.

## 1970
# AMAZON BOOKSTORE OPENS AS FIRST FEMINIST-LESBIAN BOOK SHOP

*Amazon Bookstore—the oldest and likely the first U.S. feminist bookstore, which also includes books by, for, and about lesbians—opened in Minneapolis in 1970. In addition, feminist bookstores like Amazon have provided safe gathering spaces for women.*

**ALSO KNOWN AS:** Amazon Bookstore Cooperative

**LOCALE:** Minneapolis, Minnesota

**CATEGORIES:** Cultural and intellectual history; literature; organizations and institutions; publications; feminism; economics

**KEY FIGURES**

*Rosina Richter Christy*, store cofounder

*Julie Morse Quist*, store cofounder

*Cindy Hanson* and

*Karen Browne*, store co-owners in the early 1970's

*Jo den Boer*,

*Donna Niles*,

*Barb Wieser*, and

*Kathy Sharp*, store management team members

*Irene Whitney*, provided a new location for the store in 1985

## Summary of Event

In 1970, Rosina Richter Christy and Julie Morse Quist lived in a women's collective in Minneapolis. They began selling books written by and for women from the porch of their house. At the time, thanks to the burgeoning women's movement, more books about women's issues were becoming available. However, mainstream publishers and booksellers were reluctant to produce and distribute them. Feminist bookstores were one segment of what came to be known as the women in print movement. Comprising feminist authors, publishers, printers, distributors, and booksellers, this movement attempted to rectify the absence of women's voices in the publishing industry. In particular, these activists wanted to see more books written by and for lesbians and women of color. Many, if not most, of these enterprises were run by lesbians

In the early 1970's, Christy and Quist sold their inventory to Cindy Hanson and Karen Browne, who moved it to the now-defunct Lesbian Resource Center. After two more moves, Amazon relocated to a neighborhood that offered more parking and easier access to public transportation. The business began to grow, drawing a mix of lesbians and heterosexual women. However, the neighborhood soon began attracting upscale businesses, and the owners of Amazon's space raised the rent. The bookstore's future was uncertain until the help of Irene Whitney. With her husband, Whitney owned a building across from Loring Park. Despite its location in a prime real estate area, Whitney arranged for Amazon to rent it at the same rate that Amazon had been paying at the previous location. The store moved to the new site and expanded in 1985.

Around 1990, Amazon created a four-member management team, including Jo den Boer, Donna Niles, Barb Wieser, and Kathy Sharp. By 1995, Amazon boasted a staff of fourteen and annual sales of $600,000. However, the mid-1990's also brought a new set of challenges. As the neighborhood became increasingly popular, parking became more difficult. Increasing numbers of large chain bookstores and a growing conglomeration of publishers made it difficult for independent bookstores in general to survive. Further complications were tied to the emergence of online bookseller Amazon.com (unrelated) in 1995. In addition to the competition posed by the on-line retailer, staff time at Amazon Bookstore was absorbed by dealing with phone calls, packages, and e-mails meant for Amazon.com. Other people made purchases at Amazon.com, thinking they were supporting the feminist bookstore. Throughout this period, sales dropped.

In 1999, the five-member collective of worker-owners took Amazon.com to court over trademark infringement. They reached an out-of-court settlement in the spring of 2000. As a result of the settlement, the original Amazon had to call itself Amazon Bookstore Cooperative. Three months later, the store relocated to a space next to Chrysalis, a nonprofit women's resource center.

## Significance

In the early 1970's, feminist bookstores sold the few books, pamphlets, and periodicals available that dealt with social issues relating to women, and to lesbians. As more books became available, the stores expanded their inventories to include a variety of genres. Many stores sell a variety of products other than books, such as buttons, bumper stickers, music, T-shirts, jewelry, and crafts made by women. While many of these products are available from other sources, feminist bookstores continue to bring women-focused items together in a safe space.

Besides selling merchandise, feminist bookstores have always served in part as community centers for feminists, lesbians, and other women. Amazon Bookstore Cooperative and other stores across the country offer special events such as author readings, book groups, and discussion groups. Bulletin boards provide a place for women to post announcements, find roommates, and learn about community resources. Lesbians, in particular, visit feminist bookstores both to find books relevant to their lives and to make connections with the community. Many report their first visit to a feminist bookstore as being a significant event in their coming-out process.

Feminist bookstores have typically received strong support from their surrounding communities. Many stores rely in part on volunteer assistance. In times of dire need, local women may offer direct financial support. For example, after the terrorist attacks on September 11, 2001, Amazon Bookstore Cooperative's sales declined, and it received an unexpected property tax bill. After holding a fund-raising dance and through direct appeals, the store raised $30,000, mostly from small individual contributions.

Historically, when feminist publishers had trouble finding stores willing to sell their books, feminist bookstores began to spring up across the country. For many years, these stores were the most likely places to find feminist and lesbian titles produced by small presses. While very few books were available in the early 1970's, the number grew quickly, and eventually even mainstream presses began publishing in these areas. As mainstream bookstores became more willing to carry these titles and as large bookstore chains proliferated (including those that are Web-based), feminist bookstores—along with independent bookstores in general—began to decline. Those that have survived continue to serve their communities by providing access to books written by, for, and about women. They also continue to serve as gathering places for the local feminist and lesbian communities.

—*Kathleen Liddle*

**FURTHER READING**

Amazon Bookstore Cooperative. http://www.amazonbookstorecoop.com/.

Kirch, Claire. "The Struggle Continues: Amazon Bookstore Cooperative's Financial and Psychological Turnaround Through Grassroots Support." *Publishers Weekly*, October 13, 2003, 20.

Liddle, Kathleen. "More than a Bookstore: The Continuing Relevance of Feminist Bookstores for the Lesbian Community." *Journal of Lesbian Studies* 9, nos. 1/2 (2005).

Norman, Rose. "Support Your Feminist Bookseller: She Supports You." *NWSAction: National Women's Studies Association* 13, no. 1 (2001): 30-32.

Seajay, Carol. "Twenty Years of Feminist Bookstores." *Ms.* 3, no. 1 (1992): 60-61.

_____, ed. *Feminist Bookstore News* (now defunct). See Books to Watch Out For! http://www.btwof.com/index.html.

**SEE ALSO:** Fall, 1967: Oscar Wilde Memorial Bookshop Opens as First Gay Bookstore; June, 1971: The Gay Book Award Debuts; 1973: Naiad Press Is Founded; 1980: Alyson Begins Publishing Gay and Lesbian Books; Oct., 1981: Kitchen Table: Women of Color Press Is Founded.

## May 1, 1970
# Lavender Menace Protests Homophobia in Women's Movement

*Lesbian-feminist protesters at the second Congress to Unite Women in New York challenged their exclusion from the program as well as the disparaging comments about lesbians made by Betty Friedan, founder of the National Organization for Women, or NOW. Wearing T-shirts emblazoned with the words "Lavender Menace," nearly two dozen activists mocked Friedan's fears that NOW was threatened by lesbian visibility.*

**Locale:** New York, New York
**Categories:** Marches, protests, and riots; organizations and institutions; feminism

**Key Figures**

*Betty Friedan* (1921-2006), journalist and a cofounder of NOW
*Aileen Hernandez* (b. 1926), former EEOC commissioner and a cofounder of NOW
*Rita Mae Brown* (b. 1944), novelist and activist
*Karla Jay* (b. 1947), scholar and activist
*Del Martin* (b. 1921), cofounder of the Daughters of Bilitis
*Phyllis Lyon* (b. 1924), cofounder of the Daughters of Bilitis

**Summary of Event**

Under pressure from such prominent female Democratic Party leaders as former first lady Eleanor Roosevelt, President John F. Kennedy established, shortly after his election, a national commission to evaluate the status of women in the United States. By 1963, after accumulating mountains of data from women around the country, the new commission issued a report reaffirming women's traditional roles as wives and mothers while documenting the economic inequities they experienced.

Inspired by the national commission's work, local feminists organized state commissions on the status of women and began holding national conferences to discuss their goals and objectives. Women such as labor activist and National Association for the Advancement of Colored People (NAACP) leader Addie Wyatt began calling for a women's organization modeled on the NAACP to fight for gender equality.

By 1966, despite the passage of two significant pieces of legislation (the 1963 Equal Pay Act and the 1964 Civil Rights Act, which created the landmark Equal Employment Opportunity Commission, or EEOC), feminists who had been working within the structures of government were disenchanted with the results. When the new EEOC ruled in August, 1965, that sex-segregated help-wanted ads were legal and refused to take action to rectify widespread sex discrimination in the United States, legislators such as Martha Griffiths, civil rights attorney and legal scholar Pauli Murray, former EEOC commissioner Aileen Hernandez, journalist Betty Friedan, and other activists formed a new women's rights group, the National Organization for Women (NOW), in Washington, D.C., in October, 1966.

Friedan had become a spokesperson for gender equity after publishing her landmark book *The Feminine Mystique* in 1963, when she exposed "the problem that has no name": the intense dissatisfaction felt by well-educated middle-class white women who were unfulfilled by their socially prescribed roles as wives and mothers. Friedan assumed leadership of the new organization, with former EEOC commissioners Hernandez and Richard Graham serving as vice presidents. The new organization's statement of purpose consciously included men and declared the group's commitment to "equal partnership of the sexes." In its first few years, NOW received little serious media attention while it went about its work of organizing, lobbying, and litigating on behalf of women's rights, focusing on economic equity.

*Betty Friedan was the focus of the Lavender Menace's protest of homophobia in the women's movement.*

Despite the organization's resistance to embracing their issues, lesbians had been active in NOW from the beginning. San Franciscans Del Martin and Phyllis Lyon, founders in 1955 of the first national lesbian organization in the United States, the Daughters of Bilitis (DOB), joined NOW immediately upon hearing a radio interview with NOW organizer Inca O'Hanrahan in 1966. Martin and Lyon availed themselves of NOW's "couple's membership"—the first lesbian couple to do so—and inadvertently caused a crisis among the new group's leadership. The joint membership option was quickly rescinded.

In New York, chapter president Ivy Bottini worked to challenge the homophobia of the national NOW leadership but finally was driven from her post in 1969. Lesbian author and activist Rita Mae Brown also felt silenced in NOW. When DOB's name was omitted from a NOW press release listing the sponsors for the first national feminist Congress to Unite Women in 1969, Brown left NOW and joined the newly formed Gay Liberation Front (GLF), where many "refugees" from the women's movement hoped to find a home. Soon, a number of lesbian-feminist activists had formed a collective. After an article appeared in *The New York Times Magazine* by Susan Brownmiller, quoting Friedan's comments in the early days of the movement that lesbians constituted a "lavender menace" to feminism, the collective planned a protest for an upcoming women's conference.

At the second Congress to Unite Women, held in New York City on May 1, 1970, lesbian activists including Karla Jay, Martha Shelley, Brown, and more than two dozen other women staged a historic confrontation. On the opening night of the congress, while hundreds of people waited for the beginning of a scheduled panel session, the auditorium suddenly plunged into darkness. When the lights were turned on, seventeen women wearing purple T-shirts proclaiming themselves the Lavender Menace stood on stage. The hall was decorated with signs proclaiming The Women's Movement Is a Lesbian Plot and similar slogans.

The group of women, who soon began calling themselves the Radicalesbians, also distributed a statement they had drafted titled "The Woman Identified Woman." The drama of the protest and the clarity and strength of the women's demands first shocked the attendees but eventually carried the day; the Lavender Menace got a resolution passed by the end of the weekend conference calling for the validation and affirmation of lesbians and lesbian sexuality. Friedan herself was not present when the protest took place, but news of it quickly reached her and others who had been determined to keep the issue of women's sexuality off NOW's agenda.

## SIGNIFICANCE

As Martin and Lyon recounted in their book *Lesbian/Woman* in 1972, the 1970 Lavender Menace action helped break through NOW's nervousness about lesbianism, due in large part to the collaboration between local activists and new national leadership from a black woman who understood the importance of inclusion. Aileen Hernandez, the seasoned San Francisco labor and civil rights activist who had been named by President Lyndon Johnson in 1965 as the only woman member of the U.S. Equal Employment Opportunity Commission, was a friend of Martin and Lyon and a mentor in the women's movement. She had asked Martin and Lyon to help organize educational programs on lesbians and lesbian sexuality for the national NOW conference held in Los Angeles in 1971.

Martin and Lyon agreed, and as the conference opened, they found in the official packets "a beautiful statement" from the host chapter about the importance of lesbians to NOW. There were many statements of support from NOW chapters all over the country, from Atlanta to Detroit to Los Angeles, testifying to the crucial role lesbians had played in the organization at the local level. According to Lyon and Martin, "They said lesbianism was pro-feminism and [NOW] couldn't throw out lesbians and still have a movement."

Although Friedan maintained her personal and public opposition—continuing to fight lesbian leadership in the organization and even questioning whether the Lavender Menace action was designed by U.S. government agents to undermine NOW—the attendees at the 1971 NOW conference had produced a resolution affirming the importance of lesbian rights. The largest national women's rights organization in the United States had for the first time expressed solidarity with lesbians, although it would take several more years before it would take action on lesbian issues.

—*Marcia M. Gallo*

## FURTHER READING

Brown, Rita Mae. "Take a Lesbian to Lunch." In *The Lavender Herring: Lesbian Essays from "The Ladder,"* edited by Barbara Grier and Coletta Reid. Baltimore: Diana Press, 1976.

Jay, Karla. *Tales of the Lavender Menace: A Memoir of Liberation.* New York: Basic Books, 1999.

Martin, Del, and Phyllis Lyon. *Lesbian/Woman.* 1972. Reprint. Volcano, Calif.: Volcano Press, 1991.

Rosen, Ruth. *The World Split Open: How the Women's Movement Changed America.* New York: Viking Press, 2000.

SEE ALSO: July 19-20, 1848: Seneca Falls Women's Rights Convention; 1955: Daughters of Bilitis Founded as First National Lesbian Group in United States; May 27-30, 1960: First National Lesbian Conference Convenes; May 1, 1970: Radicalesbians Issues "The Woman Identified Woman" Manifesto; Nov. 28, 1970: Del Martin Quits Gay Liberation Movement; Nov. 7, 1972: Jordan Becomes First Black Congresswoman from the South; Nov. 18-21, 1977: National Women's Conference Convenes.

## May 1, 1970
# RADICALESBIANS ISSUES "THE WOMAN IDENTIFIED WOMAN" MANIFESTO

*Angered by the homophobia and heterosexism of the resurgent women's movement, a small group of lesbian-feminist activists "zapped" a women's rights conference in New York in 1970. At the protest, they distributed copies of their manifesto, "The Woman Identified Woman," which argued that lesbianism was central to feminism. The manifesto remains one of the classic works of lesbian-feminist theory, activism, and history.*

**LOCALE:** New York, New York

**CATEGORIES:** Cultural and intellectual history; marches, protests, and riots; organizations and institutions; publications; feminism

**KEY FIGURES**

*Rita Mae Brown* (b. 1944),
*Karla Jay* (b. 1947),
*Martha Shelley* (b. 1943),
*Sydney Abbott*,
*Barbara Love*,
*Lois Hart*,
*Ellen Shumsky*,
*Cynthia Funk*, and
*March Hoffman*, key founders of Radicalesbians, "zap" protesters, and distributors of the manifesto

**SUMMARY OF EVENT**

In the mid- to late 1960's and early 1970's, many young lesbian activists—some of whom had been involved in the pioneering lesbian group the Daughters of Bilitis (DOB) or had published essays in DOB's monthly magazine *The Ladder*—were forming or joining local and national women's groups, from New York Radical Women to the National Organization for Women (NOW). The women often found that while their organizational talents and political skills were appreciated in these organizations, their sexuality and sexual identity were disparaged or ig-

nored. Some of the women were veterans of battles over sexism within gay rights groups; they now found themselves fighting homophobia and heterosexism in the women's movement.

After a few years of trying to change within NOW the oppression of lesbians and the suppression of issues of same-gender sexuality, and after numerous women (including New York chapter president Ivy Bottini) resigned or were "purged" from its leadership, many lesbian activists began to look for other groups to join. Some NOW members, such as writer and activist Rita Mae Brown, quit NOW for the Gay Liberation Front (GLF).

Brown's break with liberal feminism came in 1969 after the name of the New York chapter of the DOB had been left off the press release announcing the first national Congress to Unite Women. While still part of GLF, Brown and former DOB-New York member (and *The Ladder* essayist) Martha Shelley, along with Karla Jay, Sydney Abbott, Barbara Love, Lois Hart, Ellen Shumsky, Cynthia Funk, March Hoffman (Artemis March), and other lesbian feminists, began organizing smaller groups of women to discuss their experiences as lesbians separately from the larger GLF mixed-gender group.

An article by writer Susan Brownmiller, downplaying the importance of lesbians in NOW, appeared in *The New York Times Magazine* in March, 1970, igniting a protest for the opening night (May 1, 1970) of the second Congress to Unite Women, held in New York City during the first few days of May. Wearing hand-dyed purple T-shirts with the words "Lavender Menace" stenciled on them, Brown, Shelley, Jay, and more than one dozen other women launched a surprise protest. They addressed NOW president Betty Friedan's comments that the presence of lesbians in the women's movement would harm the movement. As they prepared for the protest, they began to write a statement that would

## "A LESBIAN IS THE RAGE OF ALL WOMEN"

What is a lesbian? A lesbian is the rage of all women condensed to the point of explosion. She is the woman who, often beginning at an extremely early age, acts in accordance with her inner compulsion to be a more complete and freer human being than her society—perhaps then, but certainly later—cares to allow her. These needs and actions, over a period of years, bring her into painful conflict with people, situations, the accepted ways of thinking, feeling and behaving, until she is in a state of continual war with everything around her, and usually with her self. She may not be fully conscious of the political implications of what for her began as personal necessity, but on some level she has not been able to accept the limitations and oppression laid on her by the most basic role of her society—the female role. . . .

It should first be understood that lesbianism, like male homosexuality, is a category of behavior possible only in a sexist society characterized by rigid sex roles and dominated by male supremacy. Those sex roles dehumanize women by defining us as a supportive/serving caste in relation to the master caste of men, and emotionally cripple men by demanding that they be alienated from their own bodies and emotions in order to perform their economic/political/military functions effectively. Homosexuality is a by-product of a particular way of setting up roles (or approved patterns of behavior) on the basis of sex; as such it is an inauthentic (not consonant with "reality") category. In a society in which men do not oppress women, and sexual expression is allowed to follow feelings, the categories of homosexuality and heterosexuality would disappear. . . .

But lesbianism is also different from male homosexuality, and serves a different function in the society. "Dyke" is a different kind of put-down from "faggot," although both imply you are not playing your socially assigned sex role . . . are not therefore a "real woman" or a "real man." The grudging admiration felt for the tomboy, and the queasiness felt around a sissy boy point to the same thing: the contempt in which women—or those who play a female role—are held. And the investment in keeping women in that contemptuous role is very great. Lesbian is a word, the label, the condition that holds women in line. . . .

It is the primacy of women relating to women, of women creating a new consciousness of and with each other, which is at the heart of women's liberation, and the basis for the cultural revolution. Together we must find, reinforce, and validate our authentic selves. As we do this, we confirm in each other that struggling, incipient sense of pride and strength, the divisive barriers begin to melt, we feel this growing solidarity with our sisters. We see ourselves as prime, find our centers inside of ourselves. We find receding the sense of alienation, of being cut off, of being behind a locked window, of being unable to get out what we know is inside. We feel a realness, feel at last we are coinciding with ourselves. With that real self, with that consciousness, we begin a revolution to end the imposition of all coercive identifications, and to achieve maximum autonomy in human expression.

*Source:* Radicalesbians, "The Woman Identified Woman." Duke University, Special Collections Library, Documents from the Women's Liberation Movement. http://scriptorium.lib.duke.edu/wlm/womid/.

be distributed to conference attendees, explaining their lesbian-feminist philosophy.

The "zap," or surprise political action, took the conference by storm. It also produced a commitment from NOW by the end of the conference to officially recognize the importance of lesbians to the women's movement. In her memoir *Tales of the Lavender Menace*, Karla Jay writes that a handful of the women involved in the Lavender Menace action worked to draft the collective statement they distributed at the protest. (However, in the August/September, 1970, issue of *The Ladder*, where the manifesto was published just two months after it

was distributed at the New York meeting, "The Woman Identified Woman" manifesto shows Rita Mae Brown's signature only.)

Starting with the now-famous words "What is a lesbian? A lesbian is the rage of all women condensed to the point of explosion," the manifesto was intended to educate heterosexual women about the revolutionary nature of being lesbian and of lesbian sexuality. Placing their emphasis on the political and personal importance of women loving themselves and one another, whether as sexual partners, friends, or comrades, the Lavender Menace women—who adopted the name Radicalesbians shortly after their protest action—called upon the women's movement to create a revolutionary political sensibility, starting with their most intimate, personal relationships.

"The Woman Identified Woman" manifesto called upon women to work together to develop their "authentic selves" as well as build their collective power, promising a radical new way of thinking and being.

For the next year, Radicalesbians in New York continued to meet, organize consciousness-raising groups, and work to create a nonhierarchical organization that relied on decision making by consensus. Radicalesbian groups also formed outside New York City—including ones in Philadelphia, Pennsylvania, and Madison, Wisconsin—for short periods of time. The intensity of the group members' radical demands upon one another, including their increasing separatism from gay and heterosexual men, bisexuals, and heterosexual women, began to cause difficulties. Some members moved to other cities or drifted back to other lesbian and gay or women's rights groups. By the end of 1971, the group had disbanded.

## SIGNIFICANCE

The Radicalesbians' groundbreaking manifesto, "The Woman Identified Woman," challenged feminists and other activists to name and examine their heterosexism, that is, the institutional and ideological dominance of opposite-gender sexuality and re-lationships. The manifesto, with its emphasis on the social construction of sexuality and sexual and gender roles, helped define the causes and effects of homophobia, heterosexism, bigotry, and discrimination against lesbians and gays. "The Woman Identified Woman" also helped explain how systems of male supremacy are maintained by denying women, and all sexual nonconformists, self-definition and agency.

*—Marcia M. Gallo*

## FURTHER READING

Freedman, Estelle B. *No Turning Back: The History of Feminism and the Future of Women.* New York: Ballantine, 2002.

Jay, Karla. *Tales of the Lavender Menace: A Memoir of Liberation.* New York: Basic Books, 1999.

Miller, Neil. *Out of the Past: Gay and Lesbian History from 1869 to the Present.* New York: Vintage Books, 1995.

Radicalesbians. "The Woman Identified Woman." Duke University, Special Collections Library. http://scriptorium.lib.duke.edu/wlm/womid/.

SEE ALSO: May 27-30, 1960: First National Lesbian Conference Convenes; July 31, 1969: Gay Liberation Front Is Formed; May 1, 1970: Lavender Menace Protests Homophobia in Women's Movement; Mar. 22, 1972-June 30, 1982: Equal Rights Amendment Fails State Ratification.

## June 28, 1970
# FIRST LESBIAN AND GAY PRIDE MARCH IN THE UNITED STATES

*New York City hosted the first lesbian and gay pride march in the United States. The march commemorated the 1969 Stonewall Rebellion in Greenwich Village, an uprising that many believe sparked the modern GLBT rights movement in the United States.*

**ALSO KNOWN AS:** Christopher Street Liberation Day
**LOCALE:** New York, New York
**CATEGORIES:** Marches, protests, and riots; organizations and institutions; civil rights

### KEY FIGURES

*John O'Brien*, march organizer and a cofounder the Gay Liberation Front, New York
*Jim Owles* (1946-1993), march organizer and president of the Gay Activists Alliance, New York
*Marc Rubin*, march organizer and cofounder of the Gay Activists Alliance, New York

### SUMMARY OF EVENT

To commemorate the one year anniversary of the Stonewall Rebellion, gay and lesbian activists organized the first GLBT pride march in the United States. The march was held in New York City on June 28, 1970, and similar, though smaller, marches were also held in other U.S. cities, most notably Los Angeles.

The New York City parade, which began near Waverly Place in Greenwich Village and continued along Fifth Avenue to Central Park, drew about two thousand people. The Christopher Street Liberation Day Committee was largely responsible for instituting a sense of organization and cohesiveness to the march. The committee, which had come together soon after the Stonewall Rebellion, named the pride event "Christopher Street Liberation Day."

Gay activists of the time, including John O'Brien

of the Gay Liberation Front, along with Jim Owles and Marc Rubin of the Gay Activists Alliance, organized the 1970 New York march. Activist Morris Kight was influential in carrying out a similar march in Los Angeles that same year.

Numerous accounts of the march have been recorded. In one case, historian Martin Duberman, in his book *Stonewall* (1994), provides an especially poignant quotation from one participant in the march: "By the time the kick-off came, at about two-fifteen, everyone . . . was scared to death. As they fell in under their organizational banners—the GAA [the Gay Activist Alliance] notably resplendent in blue T-shirts with gold lambda crests, and the GLF [the Gay Liberation Front] crowded under a banner adorned with same-sex symbols—they shouted encouragement at each other, hugged their neighbors fiercely, raised clenched fists in the air, and spread their fingers in the V sign. For many, it was less a gesture of absolute defiance than a cover for embarrassment, an antidote for fear."

Christopher Street Liberation Day laid the groundwork for the GLBT pride parades and festivals that have continued into the twenty-first century. Each year beginning in May and June, and extending into the early fall, pride festivals and parades are held across the United States to commemorate the birth of the modern gay and lesbian civil rights movement.

### SIGNIFICANCE

Christopher Street Liberation Day generated a sense of pride within the GLBT community while reaffirming the idea of collective empowerment. The first pride march in New York City not only served as a springboard for later gay movements but also set the tone for how movements for GLBT rights would come to celebrate gay pride.

The ideas of "pride" and "celebration," galvanized by the 1970 march, have come to define the

*Marchers in New York City at the annual Christopher Street Liberation Day in 1971.* (AP/Wide World Photos)

way many GLBT communities fight discrimination and social inequality. Consequently, the first Stonewall commemoration march has served not only to acknowledge the courage of the GLBT individuals who fought the police on June 28, 1969, but also to inculcate such courage and determination in future generations. Furthermore, the first pride march brought national attention to what had been considered a primarily northeast United States and California urban phenomenon. Pride marches prompted a national discourse that reached out from the traditional peripheries of large liberal cities and into typically insular small towns and communities, which would come to hold their own marches and festivals in the years following Stonewall.

Pride marches also encouraged gays and lesbians to plan and execute socially and politically charged events. Such practice in galvanizing the diverse and disparate queer community, while also helping to promote an agenda of tolerance and acceptance, would later prove immeasurable for GLBT movements such as opening military service to gays and lesbians and legalizing same-gender marriage and civil unions.

—*Daniel J. Nugent*

## FURTHER READING

Carter, David. *Stonewall: The Riots That Sparked the Gay Revolution*. New York: St. Martin's Press, 2004.

D'Emilio, John. *Sexual Politics, Sexual Communities: The Making of a Homosexual Minority in the United States*. Chicago: University of Chicago Press, 1998.

Duberman, Martin. *About Time: Exploring the Gay Past*. New York: Meridian, 1991.

_____. *Stonewall*. New York: Plume Books, 1994.

Katz, Jonathan Ned. *Gay American History: Lesbians and Gay Men in the U.S.A., A Documentary History. 1976. Rev. ed. New York: Meridian, 1992.

_____. Gay/Lesbian Almanac: A New Documentary. New York: Harper & Row, 1983.

McDarrah, Fred W. Gay Pride: Photographs from Stonewall to Today. Chicago: A Cappella Books, 1994.

Nelson, Lisa. "Marches and Parades." In Gay Histories and Cultures, edited by George E. Haggerty. New York: Garland, 2000.

SEE ALSO: July 2-Aug. 28, 1963: Rustin Organizes the March on Washington; June 27-July 2, 1969: Stonewall Rebellion Ignites Modern Gay and Lesbian Rights Movement; July 31, 1969: Gay Liberation Front Is Formed; Oct. 11, 1987: Second March on Washington for Lesbian and Gay Rights; Apr. 25, 1993: March on Washington for Gay, Lesbian, and Bi Equal Rights and Liberation; June, 1994: Stonewall 25 March and Rallies Are Held in New York City.

## November 28, 1970
# DEL MARTIN QUITS GAY LIBERATION MOVEMENT

*Lesbian and gay rights activist Del Martin wrote a letter published in the gay newsmagazine* The Advocate, *denouncing the sexism of gay men in cogender activist groups, a sentiment shared by other lesbians in the gay rights movement. She changed her focus to the feminist and women's movements, which, however, had rejected in its early years out lesbians as detrimental to the cause of women's rights.*

**LOCALE:** United States
**CATEGORIES:** Feminism; organizations and institutions; publications

**KEY FIGURE**
*Del Martin* (b. 1921), lesbian rights activist and cofounder of Daughters of Bilitis

**SUMMARY OF EVENT**
When the movement for gay rights began after World War II, lesbians felt motivated to join forces with gays on behalf of LGBT civil rights and against homophobia. The first long-lasting gay activist groups in the United States were the Mattachine Society (founded 1950) and ONE (founded 1952). Both groups were overwhelmingly made up of white men. The first lesbian organization, the Daughters of Bilitis (DOB) had been cofounded in 1955 by eight lesbians. Two of the founders were women of color and six were white, including Del Martin. Shortly after its founding, DOB split over issues of class, race, and whether the group should be social or activist. In 1959, DOB had been instrumental in helping to defeat a homophobic San Francisco mayoral candidate.

By the mid-1960's, some lesbians were actively objecting to the sexism of gays. In Philadelphia, several lesbians formed the cogender activist group Homosexual Action League (HAL). HAL had less overt sexism because lesbians were in leadership positions. In 1969, the Stonewall uprising galvanized a new generation of activists. Radical Gay Liberation Front (GLF) groups sprang up around the United States, and in the middle of a national wave of social movements, hopes were high for social change.

Soon after this first wave, however, lesbians, who were angry about the sexism they had experienced in "progressive" cogender social movements, and those who had been exposed to the new wave of feminism, began to oppose the sexism of the GLF groups. Some lesbians formed women's caucuses within GLF groups, but eventually most of them left to establish autonomous lesbian groups. The pattern was the same in many cities. In 1972, for example, the Lesbian Liberation Committee of the Gay Activist Alliance in New York City became Lesbian Feminist Liberation. In Los Angeles, Gay Liberation Front women first formed a women's caucus and then left to form Lesbian Feminists of Los Angeles. Lesbian groups proliferated and a new national movement had been born.

The lesbian manifesto "The Woman Identified Woman," which had been drafted by the group New York Radicalesbians in 1970, was a rallying cry for lesbian-feminist activism. The now-familiar first sentence of the document expressed lesbian frustration with sexism in all areas of society: "What is a lesbian?" the manifesto asks rhetorically. "A lesbian is the rage of all women condensed to the point of explosion. . . ." The manifesto called for women to work together for a better world: "It is the primacy of women relating to women, of women creating a new consciousness of and with each other, which is at the heart of women's liberation, and the basis for the cultural revolution. . . ."

The rage of homophile women had also increased. In the November 28, 1970, issue of *The Advocate*, Del Martin wrote a farewell letter to her "brothers" in the homophile movement.

> After fifteen years of working for the homophile movement . . . I have been torn apart. I am bereft. For I have been forced to the realization that I have no brothers in the homophile movement. . . . As they cling to their old ideas and their old values in a time that calls for radical change, I must bid them farewell. There is so much to be done, I have neither the stomach nor the inclination to stand by and watch them self destruct. . . .

Martin then listed many of the issues that she as a lesbian took exception to, including how women in cogender gay and lesbian groups were expected to be secretaries and makers of coffee rather than makers of policy; the time spent by men defending washroom sex and pornographic movies; homophile publications that looked like "magazines for male nudist colonies"; and exaggerated "swishing" that in the public mind became the stereotype of gays. Martin added that she felt no hate, only disappointment. She had expected more. She said she

was leaving for an environment where there was hope and possibility of personal and collective growth—the women's movement. In her final paragraph, Martin delivered a parting salvo, saying she was leaving "each of you to your own device. Take care of it, stroke it gently . . . fondle it. As the center of your consciousness, it's really all you have."

After separating from the sexism of the gay rights movement, lesbians hoped to find allies in the women's movement. As part of their activism, lesbians supported and led projects that benefited a wide spectrum of women including abortion rights, rape hotlines, self-help clinics, battered women's shelters, and campaigns against media violence. Instead of welcoming their lesbian sisters, however, many heterosexual feminists, who were afraid of being identified as lesbians and compromising the women's movement, distanced themselves from what feminist icon Betty Friedan labeled the "lavender menace."

Friedan was a cofounder of the National Organization for Women (NOW), and although many lesbians were active in NOW, the organization initially rejected lesbians, especially if they were out. In 1970, out lesbian activists such as Ivy Bottini and Rita Mae Brown were "purged" from the organization. One year later, the Los Angeles chapter of NOW, working with members of Lesbian Feminists of Los Angeles, were instrumental in persuading the national NOW membership to support lesbian rights.

## SIGNIFICANCE

At the same time that lesbian feminists were seeking acceptance from heterosexual feminists, they were rejecting veterans of the homophile movement. Ideological conflicts between lesbian feminists and homophile-era lesbians may have been based partly on differences in political identity development. At the time, "lesbian feminism" had been the term of choice for most if not all lesbians in the movement, but in retrospect, two very different points of view, which could be called "lesbian feminist" and "feminist lesbian," were at play. Lesbian feminists had more often been heterosexual, then feminist, and then lesbian. Their self-identity could be called "plastic" or "fluid" in the sense of having been modified in significant ways. The latter (feminist lesbians) had been lifelong lesbians who had been influenced by feminism. This difference in identity development led to internal conflicts over issues such as gender roles (butch and femme), monogamy, and whether lesbians were born lesbian or whether lesbian sexuality was "socially constructed" or simply a "choice."

In addition to issues of identity in lesbian groups, there also were unaddressed issues of race and class. While white lesbians enjoyed a new sense of agency in these new women-only groups, the few lesbians of color in lesbian and feminist groups were faced with the racist attitudes of their white sisters. Eventually, lesbians of color would set up ethnic caucuses within white lesbian and cogender people of color groups. Like the women's caucuses in the GLF groups, forming caucuses had been a stop-gap measure only. Many lesbians of color eventually left both types of groups to form groups for lesbians of color specifically, where they would be free from sexism and racism.

The issues of race and gender would continue to impact lesbian, gay, bisexual, transgender, and intersex (LGBTI) groups. In the 1990's, for example, the radical group Queer Nation, whose name implied a commitment to "difference" (queer) and "inclusiveness" (nation), soon lost momentum as a group over issues of sexism and racism. In contemporary LGBTI groups and organizations, the absence of lesbians and people of color often signals the presence of racism and sexism. While racism, in general, has not been addressed within LGBTI communities, the struggle against sexism has fared better. In the 1980's, some groups, such as the National Gay Task Force and the Los Angeles Gay Community Services Center added "lesbian" to their names. Beginning in the 1990's, lesbians increasingly gained positions of leadership within LGBTI cogender organizations. Some of these gains came partly because of the loss of so many gay leaders to the AIDS virus. More than thirty-five years after Del Martin had sent her letter to *The Ad-*

*vocate*, and more than fifty years after she had begun working on behalf of lesbian and gay rights, Martin and her longtime partner Phyllis Lyon continue to advocate for lesbian rights. They were the first LGBTI couple to be married by Republican mayor Gavin Newsom of San Francisco, California, in 2004, during the challenge to heterosexual-only marriage laws.

—*Yolanda Retter*

**FURTHER READING**

Bunch, Charlotte. "Lesbians in Revolt: Male Supremacy Quakes and Quivers." *The Furies: Lesbian/Feminist Monthly*, January, 1972, 8-9. Available at http://scriptorium.lib.duke.edu/wlm/furies/.

Martin, Del. "Good-Bye, My Alienated Brothers." In *Long Road to Freedom: The Advocate History of the Gay and Lesbian Movement*, edited by Mark Thompson. New York: St. Martin's Press, 1994. Originally published in *The Advocate*, October 28, 1970, 21-22.

Radicalesbians. "The Woman Identified Woman." 1970. http://scriptorium.lib.duke.edu/wlm/womid.

Russell, Valerie. "Racism and Sexism, a Collective Struggle: A Minority Woman's Point of View." (n.d.) http://scriptorium.lib.duke.edu/wlm/racesex/.

**SEE ALSO:** 1950: Mattachine Society Is Founded; 1952: ONE, Inc., Is Founded; 1955: Daughters of Bilitis Founded as First National Lesbian Group in United States; May 27-30, 1960: First National Lesbian Conference Convenes; Feb. 19-20, 1966: First North American Conference of Homophile Organizations Convenes; Aug. 11-18, 1968: NACHO Formally Becomes the First Gay Political Coalition; July 31, 1969: Gay Liberation Front Is Formed; May 1, 1970: Lavender Menace Protests Homophobia in Women's Movement; May 1, 1970: Radicalesbians Issues "The Woman Identified Woman" Manifesto.

# 1971
# KAMENY IS FIRST OUT CANDIDATE FOR U.S. CONGRESS

*After years of activism in the gay and lesbian rights movement, Franklin Kameny became the first out gay person—male or female—to run for U.S. Congress.*

**LOCALE:** Washington, D.C.
**CATEGORY:** Government and politics

**KEY FIGURE**
*Franklin Kameny* (b. 1925), astronomer and gay rights activist

**SUMMARY OF EVENT**

After returning from combat in World War II, Franklin Kameny studied astronomy at Harvard University, earning his Ph.D. in 1956. Kameny anticipated a career in science and moved to Washington, D.C., becoming part of the faculty at Georgetown University. After a year of teaching, Kameny accepted a civil service position as an astronomer with the U.S. Army Map Service in July of 1957.

That fall, after just a few months on the job, Kameny was fired from his position with the Map Service because of his homosexual conduct. Kameny also was barred from any other employment in the civil service or the federal government because of his homosexuality. This injustice drove Kameny away from a career in science and into a life of activism on behalf of gay, lesbian, and bisexual Americans. "My dismissal amounted to a declaration of war against me by the government," Kameny said.

Kameny's activism started with a long series of legal battles—or his "war"—to get his government job back. This four-year legal struggle included many appeals and culminated with his filing a petition to the U.S. Supreme Court, a petition that was rejected by the Court in 1961. Kameny then moved from this personal, individual advocacy to organizing and advocating on behalf of a larger gay and lesbian rights movement. "The time had come to fight collectively," Kameny said.

Kameny took a page from the Civil Rights movement and decided to adopt a direct, assertive, grassroots strategy on behalf of gays and lesbians. He began by cofounding a Washington, D.C., branch of the Mattachine Society with his friend Jack Nichols, later in 1961. This was the first gay organization in the nation's capitol, and Kameny became its first president.

Under his leadership, the group took on the ban of gays and lesbians from civil service employment, and, in 1965, they organized the first gay and lesbian demonstration at the White House. For this demonstration, the group dressed conservatively—men in suits and women in dresses—and held signs with slogans such as Civil Service Commission is Un-American. (Kameny's knack for creating slogans continued when he coined the phrase "Gay is Good" in 1966. This slogan was adopted by the North American Conference of Homophile Organizations, or NACHO, in 1968.) Just a few months after this demonstration, the U.S. Court of Appeals held that rejecting an application for federal employment because of homosexual conduct was "too vague" and did not adequately explain how homosexual conduct was related to competence in employment.

In 1971, Kameny became the first openly gay person to run for Congress. He had entered the race for the District of Columbia's nonvoting delegate seat in the U.S. House of Representatives. He finished in fourth place, out of six, collecting just 1.6 percent of the vote. In 1975, Kameny became the first openly gay person in Washington, D.C., to receive a mayoral appointment when he became the commissioner of the D.C. Commission on Human Rights.

**SIGNIFICANCE**

While Franklin Kameny's Washington, D.C., branch of the Mattachine Society has been overshadowed by other gay and lesbian rights groups following the 1969 Stonewall Rebellion, it was mainly his strategy that set the stage for the GLBT rights movement of the twenty-first century. Kameny's grassroots strategy of dealing directly with politicians and those in power, rather than hiding behind the scenes, was a direct precursor to the more militant activism of GLBT rights groups in the late twentieth century. Although Kameny made the conscious decision to not take on HIV-AIDS activism, ACT UP (AIDS Coalition to Unleash Power) and other HIV-AIDS advocates in the 1980's and 1990's borrowed from—and built upon—Kameny's unapologetic, "Gay is Good" style.

Kameny had indeed embraced the post-Stonewall, radicalized gay and lesbian rights movement, but he continued to urge gay and lesbian activists to struggle in the mainstream of politics, nevertheless. This "assertive yet respectable" approach has proven successful over time. Although Kameny did not succeed in his 1971 bid for Congress, his campaign helped to mobilize the gay and lesbian voting bloc in D.C. Furthermore, the Gay Activists Alliance was also mobilized by aiding Kameny's 1971 campaign for Congress. Kameny later cofounded the National Gay Rights Lobby, which paved the way for the largely mainstream Human Rights Campaign (formerly the Human Rights Campaign Fund). He also was involved in the 1972 formation of the National Gay Task Force (now the National Gay and Lesbian Task Force). In the early twenty-first century, the Human Rights Campaign and the National Gay and Lesbian Task Force are the two prime, national GLBT lobbying groups.

Kameny's own activism did have direct results. A decade after the Kameny-led protest at the White House—and eighteen years after he was fired for his homosexual conduct—the U.S. Civil Service Commission amended its antihomosexual policy in 1975, saying that it would no longer bar lesbians and gays from federal employment. In 1995, President Bill Clinton announced that sexual orientation could no longer be the basis for denying a security clearance to federal employees. Only the controversial Don't Ask, Don't Tell policy and the ban on out gays and out lesbians in the U.S. Armed Services remain.

Finally, Kameny's run for Congress did foreshadow successful campaigns. In 1974, Elaine No-

ble, an out lesbian, was elected to the Massachusetts General Assembly, the first lesbian to win a statewide election. In 1977, Harvey Milk, an out gay man, was elected to the San Francisco board of supervisors. In 1983, U.S. Representative Gerry Studds of Massachusetts came out as gay after his censure for sexual improprieties with a male page; in so doing, Studds became the first out gay member of Congress. In 1984, Studds was re-elected, becoming the first out gay man to run for and win a seat in Congress. In 1998, U.S. Representative Tammy Baldwin of Wisconsin became the first out lesbian to be elected to Congress. The Reverend Walter Fauntroy, who defeated Kameny in the 1971 bid for Congress, sits on the board of advisers for the Alliance for Marriage, an organization seeking to amend the U.S. Constitution to ban same-gender marriage.

*—Lara Hoke*

## FURTHER READING

Clendinen, Dudley, and Adam Nagourney. *Out for Good: The Struggle to Build a Gay Rights Movement in America.* New York: Simon & Schuster, 1999.

D'Emilio, John. *Sexual Politics, Sexual Communities: The Making of a Homosexual Minority in the United States, 1940-1970.* 2d ed. Chicago: University of Chicago Press, 1998.

D'Emilio, John, William B. Turner, and Urvashi Vaid, eds. *Creating Change: Sexuality, Public Policy, and Civil Rights.* New York: St. Martin's Press, 2002.

Gross, Larry, and James D. Woods, eds. *The Columbia Reader on Lesbians and Gay Men in Media, Society, and Politics.* New York: Columbia University Press, 1999.

Johnson, David K. *The Lavender Scare: The Cold War Persecution of Gays and Lesbians in the Federal Government.* Chicago: University of Chicago Press, 2004.

Marcus, Eric. *Making History: The Struggle for Gay and Lesbian Equal Rights, 1945-1990.* New York: HarperCollins, 1992.

Tobin, Kay, and Randy Wicker. *The Gay Crusaders.* New York: Arno Press, 1975.

Vargas, Jose Antonio. "Signs of Progress: Franklin Kameny Keeps Mementos of His Activism in the Attic, Not the Closet." *The Washington Post*, July 23, 2005. Available at http://www.washingtonpost.com/wp-dyn/content/article/2005/07/22/AR2005072202010.html.

**SEE ALSO:** Aug. 11-18, 1968: NACHO Formally Becomes the First Gay Political Coalition; Oct. 31, 1969: *Time* Magazine Issues "The Homosexual in America"; 1973: National Gay Task Force Is Formed; Dec. 15, 1973: Homosexuality Is Delisted by APA; Nov. 5, 1974: Noble Is First Out Lesbian or Gay Person to Win State-Level Election; July 3, 1975: U.S. Civil Service Commission Prohibits Discrimination Against Federal Employees; Nov. 27, 1978: White Murders Politicians Moscone and Milk; Oct. 12-15, 1979: First March on Washington for Lesbian and Gay Rights; Apr. 22, 1980: Human Rights Campaign Fund Is Founded; July 14, 1983: Studds Is First Out Gay Man in the U.S. Congress; Nov. 30, 1993: Don't Ask, Don't Tell Policy Is Implemented.

## 1971
# *LESBIAN TIDE* PUBLISHES ITS FIRST ISSUE

*The* Lesbian Tide *was the first all-news periodical for lesbians and the first with a specifically lesbian-focused editorial policy. Along with editorials, it published news articles and features on topics such as politics, personal appearance, sexuality, pornography, and lesbian separatism, setting a reporting standard for the lesbian press that followed.*

**ALSO KNOWN AS:** *Tide*
**LOCALE:** Los Angeles, California
**CATEGORIES:** Publications; feminism

**KEY FIGURE**
*Jeanne Cordova* (b. 1948), founder and publisher of the *Lesbian Tide*

**SUMMARY OF EVENT**
The *Lesbian Tide* began as a newsletter for the Los Angeles chapter of the national lesbian organization Daughters of Bilitis. Soon it formed into an independent, lesbian-feminist newsmagazine published by Jeanne Cordova.

The magazine's regular and contributing staff averaged twenty women. Featuring news stories, editorials, interviews, summer-vacation directories, and cultural-events listings, the *Lesbian Tide* (or *Tide*) provided a forum for lesbians throughout the United States. Financially supported by private funds and donations, but also by some advertising, the *Tide* was published sporadically between 1971 and 1975 and on a bimonthly, uninterrupted schedule between 1975 and 1980.

The *Tide* touched upon issues relevant to lesbians from all backgrounds. There were frequent stories on lesbian musicians, including the article "The Jazz-grass of Robin Flower" from the May/June, 1980, issue. The article discusses the trials and tribulations of writing one's first album. The same issue features a lengthy interview with Cris Williamson, the "best selling, yet least personally known of the lesbian musicians of the 1970's."

Like all magazines, the *Tide* had its share of advertisements. While announcements for women's bookstores, such as Magic Speller, Womansplace, and the Oscar Wilde Memorial Bookshop, appealed to literary appetites, ads for bars such as Sisters' Suds catered to those also interested in the party scene. Labyris Auto Repair promised "complete car care by women" and A Pair of Toucans Ethnic Folk Art offered "affordable handcrafts from around the world." Whatever the content of the advertisements, all shared the underlying objective of connecting women to women.

The *Tide* also published poetry and cartoon illustrations, which had been common media in the 1970's. While one woman's cartoon waxes humor on the lesbian proclivity to constantly "discuss the meaning of life," another woman's poem examines monogamy versus nonmonogamy. The overall tone of the magazine was both light and focused. An ad in a 1980 issue pleading for "Lily Tomlin for President" was juxtaposed with an article warning of right-wing power.

The "sex wars" of the 1980's saw lesbians disagreeing openly about the good and bad of pornography, and the *Tide* covered the story. The sex wars began when "propornography" or "pro-sex" lesbians started to reconsider the antipornography stance that has always been a platform of lesbian-feminist politics. Antipornography lesbians were repulsed by this move, considering it a mindless adoption of masculine sexuality and masculine attitudes toward women's bodies and thus a slap in the face of feminism.

The sex wars were highly charged, but the *Tide* still presented all sides to the story. In her article featured in the July, 1972, issue, Rita Goldberger's "Exploitation, Misrepresentation Must Stop" laments the media's portrayal of lesbians. She wrote,

> A friend of mine recently ripped off a copy of some sex-rag out of a broken news rack. . . . The article was so obviously phony that I almost laughed, except that I realized that such ideas represent the stereotyped image the straight world has of us, and these false images are being perpetuated and exploited by the sex-rags. . . . Our culture has a perverted and distorted image of lesbians. We are *not* sex objects—we are women, human beings. We must protest such representation!

In a later issue, Jeanne Cordova and Kerry Lobel accuse lesbian feminists of collaborating with the political right on the pornography and exploitation issue.

> A new trend has emerged—the anti-pornography movement. The movement to end pornography isn't a new one, but feminist involvement within it is. . . . In a patriarchal society, most of what is called "raising a family" is economic exploitation of women by men. Most of what is called "sex" is physical exploitation of women by men. And most of what is called "christianity" is spiritual exploitation of women by men.

Another hot issue that ignited controversy within the lesbian community was lesbian separatism. As with the pornography and exploitation debates, the *Lesbian Tide* was careful to include opinions from women of all schools of thought. A few of the social advertisements encouraged lesbians to integrate themselves among the larger community. One such ad proclaims, "Sisters and Brothers Together! Every Thursday Beginning July 13. Gentlemen escorted by a sister—Admitted Free! And a free beer or glass of wine for the groovy gal who brings him!" Another announcement states "Non-Separatist Lesbians: Join our established rural communes. Here women and men (primarily hetero) live and work in a gentle culture dedicated to equality, non-sexism, and the good life." Other establishments, conversely, promoted women-only space and thus were separatist.

### Significance

In a decade when lesbian writing was scarce, the *Lesbian Tide* afforded lesbians a forum for conversation, culture, and debate. Unfortunately, economics was always an issue for the magazine, funds were always scarce, and advertising, what little there had been, could not support the publication indefinitely. Cordova had no choice but to fold the *Tide*. In the May/June, 1980, issue, the *Tide* announced plans to suspend publication, citing that staff members were "tired, need[ed] a break, and wanted some time free of deadlines to review [their own] work and consider [their own] future." Publication had been expected to resume in November of that year, but it never did.

The *Tide* was part of a decade of rapid growth in lesbian politics and had untold influence on the lesbian community. It was at the forefront of a movement for lesbian rights when it published in-depth articles on issues that still are discussed and debated.

—*Christy Burbidge*

**FURTHER READING**

Crow, Barbara A. *Radical Feminism: A Documentary Reader.* New York: New York University Press, 2000.

Fejes, Fred, and Kevin Petrich. "Invisibility, Homophobia, and Heterosexism: Lesbians, Gays, and the Media." *Critical Studies in Mass Communication* 10 (1993): 396-422.

Streitmatter, Rodger. *Unspeakable: The Rise of the Gay and Lesbian Press in America.* Winchester, Mass.: Faber and Faber, 1995.

Walters, Suzanna. *All the Rage: The Story of Gay Visibility in America.* Chicago: University of Chicago Press, 2002.

**SEE ALSO:** 1896: *Der Eigene* Is Published as First Journal on Homosexuality; June, 1947-Feb., 1948: *Vice Versa* Is Published as First Lesbian Periodical; 1953: *ONE* Magazine Begins Publication; 1967: *Los Angeles Advocate* Begins Publication; 1970: Amazon Bookstore Opens as First Feminist-Lesbian Book Shop; Nov., 1971: *The Body Politic* Begins Publication; 1973: Naiad Press Is Founded; Oct., 1974: *Lesbian Connection* Begins Publication; 1980: Alyson Begins Publishing Gay and Lesbian Books; Oct., 1981: Kitchen Table: Women of Color Press Is Founded; Jan., 1986: South Asian Newsletter *Trikone* Begins Publication; May, 1987: *Lambda Rising Book Report* Begins Publication.

## March, 1971
# LOS ANGELES GAY AND LESBIAN CENTER IS FOUNDED

*The Los Angeles Gay and Lesbian Center, the oldest and largest GLBT community center in the world, pioneered social, cultural, educational, and health programs and services—including those addressing HIV-AIDS—that laid the foundation for the formation of other GLBT centers around the United States and abroad.*

**ALSO KNOWN AS:** Gay Community Services Center

**LOCALE:** Los Angeles, California

**CATEGORIES:** Organizations and institutions; health and medicine; HIV-AIDS

**KEY FIGURES**

*Morris Kight* (1919-2003), gay rights activist and cofounder of the Center in Los Angeles

*Don Kilhefner* (b. 1939), psychologist, gay rights activist, and cofounder of the Center in Los Angeles

**SUMMARY OF EVENT**

Inspired by the community centers created by minority populations in the 1960's and the GLBT community center in San Francisco, which opened in 1966, the Los Angeles Gay and Lesbian Center (the Center) was founded in 1971. The opening of the Center was part of a wave of GLBT rights advocacy that hit many cities of the United States in the decade following New York City's Stonewall Rebellion of 1969.

The original name for the Center was the Gay Community Services Center (GCSC), which had been cofounded by gay activists Morris Kight and Don Kilhefner. Kight also founded, in 1969, the Los Angeles chapter of the Gay Liberation Front, and Kilhefner was a cofounder of the Radical Faeries in 1979. Closely affiliated with the GCSC from its beginning was the Gay Women's Services Center, and although the GCSC added "lesbian" to its name in 1984, the two finally merged in 1996 to form the current organization.

Relying solely upon private donations until 1974, the Center's early years addressed the most desperate and basic needs of the gay and lesbian community, such as housing, employment, and health care, and it pioneered a number of GLBT-oriented human service programs along the way.

The Center provided low-cost emergency housing for run-away and homeless youth, free counseling and support groups, and free or low-cost diagnosis and treatment of sexually transmitted diseases (STDs). These services were offered at little or no cost to people of any sexual orientation.

Upon seeking and acquiring government funding in 1974, the Center became the first organization in the United States with the word "gay" in its name to be awarded federal 501(c)(3) tax-exempt status. With these funds, the Center added more services to its cadre, including legal counseling, employment services, and assistance to former prison inmates.

With the Center's growth came drug and alcohol counseling in a safe and nonjudgmental environment. Men, women, and youth created a number of gender- and age-appropriate rap groups and participated in peer counseling. The Center provided women with referrals and resources on issues ranging from abortion and abuse to education and self-awareness. By the late 1970's, the Center served more than 200,000 people per year, a number that dramatically increased in the 1980's during the height of the HIV-AIDS crisis.

When AIDS was named as a "new" disease (first called GRID, or gay-related immunodeficiency) in 1981, Los Angeles was home to one of the three largest GLBT populations in the world and was, consequently, one of the cities hardest hit by the disease. When the Center's STD clinic program proved inadequate to address the quickly increasing medical needs of gay men, especially, the Center expanded its services to include counseling, prevention, referrals, and, when it became available, HIV testing. The Center also extended services for lesbians, added more beds in its youth shelter, and expanded its mental health services.

During the 1990's, the Center experienced exponential growth in its physical space, budget, and programs. The Center acquired a 44,000-square-foot building in 1992 and a 33,000-square-foot structure in 1996, providing space for increased social and cultural programming. The Center currently employs a full-time staff of more than 250 individuals, owns five buildings in the Hollywood area of Los Angeles, has an annual budget exceeding $30 million, and serves an average of 18,000 visitors each month, making it not only the oldest but also the largest gay and lesbian community center in the United States.

## SIGNIFICANCE

The Center's comprehensive and innovative services have served as models for many of the gay and lesbian community centers throughout the United States and the world. During the 1970's, dozens of GLBT centers opened across the country, using the Center in Los Angeles as a guide.

From its founding, the Center has served an ethnically, economically, and sexually diverse population of both youth and adults, acknowledging their often very different needs. A number of pioneering services for youth, women, people of color, and seniors came out of this focus on inclusion.

The Center's STD clinic also proved influential as it joined a small number of community health clinics in the 1970's that served the gay and lesbian population specifically. These clinics worked to test, treat, and educate the people they served about a variety of sexually transmitted diseases that existed at epidemic proportions in the GLBT community in the 1970's. Many of these early gay-health clinics were the first to respond to the HIV-AIDS crisis of the early 1980's. The large numbers of gays in Los Angeles and the Center's proximity to major medical research institutions also allowed the Center to play a major role in identifying and addressing the needs of people with HIV-AIDS and to set the standard for HIV- and AIDS-related services.

The Center's growth and innovation in services and programs for the GLBT community as a whole, including those who are HIV-positive, exemplifies the increased development of comprehensive centers for the gay and lesbian community in cities throughout the United States.

*—Catherine P. Batza*

## FURTHER READING

Burns, Richard, and Eric Rofes. "Gay Liberation Comes Home: The Development of Community Centers Within Our Movement." In *The*

*Sourcebook on Lesbian and Gay Healthcare*, edited by Michael Shernoff and William Scott. Washington, D.C.: National Lesbian and Gay Health Foundation, 1988.

Marcus, Eric. *Making Gay History: The Half Century Fight for Gay and Lesbian Equal Rights*. New York: HarperCollins, 2002.

National Association of Lesbian and Gay Community Centers. *National Directory of Lesbian & Gay Community Centers*. New York: Lesbian and Gay Community Services Center, 1996.

Osborne, Torie. *Coming Home to America: A Roadmap to Gay and Lesbian Empowerment*. New York: St. Martin's Press, 1996.

**SEE ALSO:** June 5 and July 3, 1981: Reports of Rare Diseases Mark Beginning of AIDS Epidemic; 1982: Lesbian and Gay Youth Protection Institute Is Founded; July, 1982: Gay-Related Immunodeficiency Is Renamed AIDS; Spring, 1984: AIDS Virus Is Discovered; May, 1988: Lavender Youth Recreation and Information Center Opens; 1994: National Association of Lesbian and Gay Community Centers Is Founded.

## June, 1971
# THE GAY BOOK AWARD DEBUTS

*The American Library Association's Gay Book Award, the first of a number of GLBT literary awards to emerge beginning in the 1970's, has evolved to reflect the ever-changing makeup of the GLBT community. The awards program is now called the Stonewall Book Awards and includes several categories.*

**ALSO KNOWN AS:** Stonewall Book Awards
**LOCALE:** Dallas, Texas
**CATEGORIES:** Literature; organizations and institutions

### KEY FIGURES

*Barbara Gittings* (b. 1932), lesbian rights activist and longtime coordinator of the ALA Task Force on Gay Liberation

*Alma Routsong* (1924-1996), author whose book *A Place for Us*, written under the pseudonym Isabel Miller, won the first Gay Book Award

*Israel Fishman*, gay rights activist and founder of the ALA Task Force on Gay Liberation

### SUMMARY OF EVENT

At the 1971 annual conference of the American Library Association (ALA), the Task Force on Gay Liberation presented its first Gay Book Award to Alma Routsong for her self-published novel, *A Place for Us* (1969). The book was later picked up by a mainstream publisher (and reissued as *Patience and Sarah*, first in 1972). The award's initial goal was to honor books that ALA task force members considered landmark publications in gay and lesbian literature. Early winning titles include *Lesbian/Woman* (1972) by Del Martin and Phyllis Lyon, *Sex Variant Women in Literature* (1974) by Jeannette Foster, and *Christianity, Social Tolerance, and Homosexuality* (1981) by John Boswell.

The grassroots, activist philosophy of the award's task force members in the first decade was reflected in the manner in which award recipients were judged and by the prizes that were given to the authors. Winners were chosen by consensus, and the whimsical prizes—often homemade items created by task force members—were emblematic of the authors and their works. Bestowing the award was an informal process. Some years no awards were given; in other years there were two or three winning titles in a given year.

In its second decade, the awards process became more formalized. In 1981, the task force created guidelines and established a separate committee to solicit nominations and choose winners. Although the Gay Book Award had been presented at ALA

*Lesbian activist Barbara Gittings, left, and novelist Alma Routsong offering "Free Kisses" for "Women Only" at the American Library Association conference in 1971.*

Lesbian, Bisexual, and Transgendered Round Table. Finally, in 2002, the name of the award changed to the Stonewall Book Award.

As the decades progressed, so did the number of GLBT-themed titles under consideration by the various book award committees. While the beginning of the 1970's saw only a handful of affirmative titles, by the 1980's, there were more than five hundred published works. More recent committees have had to choose among almost three times that amount.

In 1990, concurrent with this exponential growth in GLBT publishing, the book award expanded to recognize books in two "new" categories: nonfiction and literature. When the award name changed to the Stonewall Book Awards in 2002, the names of the categories changed as well. The nonfiction award became the Israel Fishman Award for Non-Fiction (named after the founder of the ALA Task Force on Gay Liberation) and the literature award was renamed the Barbara Gittings Literature Award for Fiction (after the longtime coordinator of the task force).

To qualify for the Stonewall Book Awards, books must be English-language works published the year prior to the announcement date. (For example, the 2004 winners must have been published in 2003.) Anyone may nominate titles for the award (as long as the nominators are not affiliated with the author or publisher of the title they are nominating). A geographically diverse committee of library personnel from various types of libraries reviews the nominations and selects the five finalists for each category. The committee then chooses the winners from among the five finalists with the runners-up being termed "honor books." The award winners and the honor books are announced during the

conferences since 1971, it did not become an "official" ALA award until fifteen years later. In 1982, task force coordinator Barbara Gittings tenaciously began petitioning ALA to bestow official status on the book award, and, in 1986, in her last official act as coordinator, she could finally announce her success. With its official status came more typical rewards for winning authors, including cash stipends and commemorative plaques.

Over the years, the name of the award has been changed several times, as its focus expanded and its parent body began to recognize the diverse backgrounds and identities of its patrons. In 1987, the Gay Book Award changed its name to the Gay and Lesbian Book Award; in 1994, it became the Gay, Lesbian, and Bisexual Book Award; and in 1999, it was named the Gay, Lesbian, Bisexual, and Transgendered Book Award. Also in 1999, the status of the award task force was changed to an awards' round table; it is now called the ALA Gay,

ALA's midwinter conference, which is held every January. The awards are presented to the winners during the ALA's annual conference, which is held every June.

Eighteen years after the first Gay Book Award was presented at ALA, other GLBT literary awards have emerged. In 1989, the Lambda Literary Foundation established the Lambda Literary Award, or "Lammy," as they have been affectionately dubbed. That same year the Publishing Triangle—the Association of Lesbians and Gay Men in Publishing— began its own awards program for lesbian and gay writers called the Triangle Awards.

## SIGNIFICANCE

The American Library Association's Stonewall Book Awards reflect the sensibilities, aspirations, and controversies associated with GLBT experiences and cultures throughout the post-Stonewall era. As sanctioned ALA awards, Stonewall Book Awards will ensure that library shelves around the United States will include GLBT-themed titles.

—*Ellen Greenblatt*

## FURTHER READING

Gittings, Barbara. "Gays in Library Land: The Gay and Lesbian Task Force of the American Library Association: The First Sixteen Years." In *Daring to Find Our Names: The Search for Lesbigay History*, edited by James V. Carmichael, Jr. Westport, Conn.: Greenwood Press, 2004.

Moore, Lisa. "A History of Publishing Pride." *Lambda Book Report* 11, nos. 9-11 (April, 2003): 38.

Preston, John. "Gay Lit Goes Mainstream: The Big Business of Publishing Gay Books." *The Advocate*, November 26, 1985, 51-54, 60.

Streitmatter, Rodger. *Unspeakable: The Rise of the Gay and Lesbian Press in America*. Winchester, Mass.: Faber and Faber, 1995.

**SEE ALSO:** July 4, 1855: Whitman Publishes *Leaves of Grass*; May 25, 1895: Oscar Wilde Is Convicted of Gross Indecency; 1924: Gide Publishes the Signed Edition of *Corydon*; 1939: Isherwood Publishes *Goodbye to Berlin*; 1947-1948: Golden Age of American Gay Literature; 1956: Baldwin Publishes *Giovanni's Room*; 1963: Rechy Publishes *City of Night*; 1974: *The Front Runner* Makes *The New York Times* Best-Seller List; 1975: First Novel About Coming Out to Parents Is Published; 1980-1981: Gay Writers Form the Violet Quill; May, 1987: *Lambda Rising Book Report* Begins Publication; June 2, 1989: Lambda Literary Award Is Created; 1993: Monette Wins the National Book Award for *Becoming a Man*.

## November, 1971
# *THE BODY POLITIC* BEGINS PUBLICATION

*One of the most influential and controversial North American publications for lesbians and gays,* The Body Politic, *began publishing in November of 1971. After several police raids, criminal charges, trials, and acquittals, as well as financial instability and increasing police harassment of the GLBT community in Toronto, Canada, the paper ceased publication at the end of 1986.*

**LOCALE:** Toronto, Ontario, Canada
**CATEGORIES:** Publications; organizations and institutions; civil rights; government and politics; laws, acts, and legal history; marches, protests, and riots

**KEY FIGURE**
*Jearld Moldenhauer*, conceived of *The Body Politic*

**SUMMARY OF EVENT**
The history of the founding of *The Body Politic* starts with GLBT community activism and politics. To coincide with the anniversary of the passing of Canada's Bill C-150 (which decriminalized private and consensual sex between those of the same gender) on August 28, 1969, Toronto Gay Action (TGA), an activist caucus that spun off the Community Homophile Association of Toronto (CHAT), organized a rally on Parliament Hill in Ottawa (August 28, 1971). A letter sent to the federal government a week earlier stated that the 1969 amendments had "done but little to alleviate the oppression of homosexual men and women in Canada. In our daily lives we are still confronted with discrimination, police harassment, exploitation, and pressures to conform which deny our sexuality." A formal brief, titled "We Demand," accompanied the letter.

Within a couple of weeks and back in Toronto, TGA members met in the basement of a counterculture hall on Sunday nights, invited by Jearld Mol-

denhauer (also a TGA member) to start a paper for gays and lesbians. Moldenhauer had written an article about the August 28 rally for the Toronto underground leftist tabloid *Guerilla*, but upon finding that the article had been heavily edited, he knew Toronto needed a distinctive gay voice, and its own periodical.

About two dozen people responded to the call for a meeting, and fifteen decided to form The Body Politic Editorial Collective, the political and (eventually legal) base responsible for the paper that was to be called *The Body Politic*, or *TBP*. The first issue, published in November, 1971, had twenty

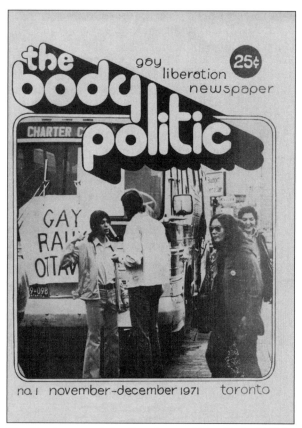

*The front page of the first issue of* The Body Politic, *November-December, 1971.* (Hudler Archives [Pride Library], University of Western Ontario)

## PINK TRIANGLE PRESS MISSION STATEMENT

We, the members and workers of Pink Triangle Press, are lesbians, gay men and people of good will. We carry on the work first undertaken by *The Body Politic*.

The outcome that we seek is this:

Gay and lesbian people daring together to set love free. Working to achieve our end, we use the published word. We earn in commerce the money that we need, mindful that money is not an end, but merely means.

"Gay and lesbian people." We have chosen as our public lesbians and gay men, but we bear in mind all those who challenge gender or bend the borders of desire.

"Daring together." The will and work to change our downcast state can only be our own. We engage our chosen public, rousing them singly and in numbers to think and act and grow and fill the world, to form a movement, fight for change and, in so doing, change themselves.

"Set love free." We honour lust and seek a world where sex is valued as a human trait, no more no less than any other, and all are free and equal, no matter whom they love.

"Engagement." We engage our chosen public—readers, listeners, clients and each other—as worthy equals, with respectful camaraderie. In all our work we do our best, so drawing out the best in others. We entice and we incite; we challenge and we lead.

"Communities." Through the customs of their people, the web of their associations, the output of their artists and the practice of their commerce, communities are made and know themselves. Through strife and argument they grow. Because communities give birth to movements, we nurture them.

"Words." Words are power and they always serve some purpose. Others use them to oppress us. We use them to express our lives. We assail the work of censors. Our drive is to arouse debate, to inform and to enlighten in a fair and honest way.

"History." Gay life was built from social circumstance by conscious will and daunting work. What came before is foundation, inspiration, a lesson and a warning. We seek to own our history: we learn and teach and guard it.

pages, sold for 25 cents, and was sold primarily through street hawking.

## SIGNIFICANCE

As the paper grew and gathered an internal reputation, it also gathered increasing scrutiny from the conservative provincial government and a local police force that, like many other law enforcement agencies, was not gay positive. In 1977, writer Gerald Hannon penned "Men Loving Boys Loving Men," an article that became the pretext for a police raid on the newspaper. Operation P, a joint Toronto and Ontario police unit set up to investigate pornography, raided the *TBP* offices on December 30, 1977, to collect evidence of an alleged crime. On January 5, 1978, the paper was charged under Section 164 of the criminal code: the "use of mails to transmit immoral, indecent and scurrilous material."

Despite the charge, *TBP* was acquitted the following year, and the government appealed. In what became a raucous few years for Toronto's gay and lesbian community, the police raided a number of bathhouses in 1978 and 1979. The largest raid came in February of 1981, which was a simultaneous attack on four bathhouses that saw the arrest of more than three hundred men. In May of the next year, the Toronto police's morality squad again visited *TBP* premises with a search warrant. On May 12, they charged the editorial collective with "publishing obscene material" after it ran an article in the April, 1982, issue titled "Lust with a Very Proper Stranger." Shortly after, there was a retrial of the 1978 charges, and, again, on June 15, *TBP* was acquitted. Later that year, *TBP* was acquitted on the May, 1982, charges.

Perhaps one of the largest victories for gays and lesbians in Canada was the passage of Bill 7 in the Ontario legislature in November of 1986, which added to the province's human rights code a prohibition against discriminating on the basis of a person's "sexual orientation." Yet, this event also had suggested to some of *TBP*'s members that the long and protracted struggle to this highly symbolic event meant that the political battle, as it was understood to that point, had ended. What would come next? Who would define the agenda? The paper's financial stability and political wherewithal were both in question. On December 16, 1986, the collective decided to cease publication. Its last issue came out in February, 1987.

—*Andrew Lesk*

**FURTHER READING**

Hannon, Gerald. "Men Loving Boys Loving Men." *The Body Politic* 39 (December, 1977/January, 1978).

Jackson, Ed, and Stan Persky. *Flaunting It! A Decade of Gay Journalism from "The Body Politic."* Vancouver, B.C.: New Star, 1982.

McLeod, Donald W. *Lesbian and Gay Liberation in Canada: A Selected Annotated Chronology, 1964-1975.* Toronto, Ont.: ECW Press, 1996.

Streitmatter, Rodger. *Unspeakable: The Rise of the Gay and Lesbian Press in America.* Winchester, Mass.: Faber and Faber, 1995.

Warner, Tom. *Never Going Back: A History of Queer Activism in Canada.* Buffalo, N.Y.: University of Toronto Press, 2002.

**SEE ALSO:** 1953: *ONE* Magazine Begins Publication; 1967: *Los Angeles Advocate* Begins Publication; Dec. 31, 1977: Toronto Police Raid Offices of *The Body Politic*; Feb. 5, 1981: Toronto Police Raid Gay Bathhouses; Jan. 1, 1988: Canada Decriminalizes Sex Practices Between Consenting Adults; Apr. 27, 1992: Canadian Government Antigay Campaign Is Revealed.

---

## 1972-1973
# LOCAL GOVERNMENTS PASS ANTIDISCRIMINATION LAWS

*Beginning in the early 1970's, a number of city governments in the United States—and Canada—passed ordinances protecting lesbians and gays from discrimination in areas such as employment, housing, and education. The municipal-level actions were soon followed by county- and state-level legislation prohibiting discrimination on the basis of sexual orientation.*

**LOCALE:** East Lansing, Michigan; San Francisco, California; Ann Arbor, Michigan; Toronto, Ontario, Canada

**CATEGORIES:** Civil rights; government and politics; laws, acts, and legal history

**SUMMARY OF EVENT**

Beginning shortly after the Stonewall Rebellion in New York City in 1969, a number of local governments in the United States began debating whether to amend their local civil rights ordinances to prohibit discrimination against people on the basis of sexual orientation (also referred to as "affectional preference" or "sexual preference" in some ordinances). Several municipalities and counties, and then states, have changed their laws.

The university town of East Lansing, Michigan, is generally credited with adopting, on March 7, 1972, the first such nondiscrimination policy. Under pressure from gay activists at Michigan State University but unable to muster enough votes to adopt a formal ordinance giving effect to this policy, the East Lansing city council settled for a policy that simply prohibited discrimination in city employment. On April 3, 1972, San Francisco passed a law prohibiting discrimination against gays and lesbians by city contractors. In July, Ann Arbor, Michigan, amended its civil rights ordinance to prohibit sexual orientation discrimination in a wide variety of arenas, including employment, housing, and public accommodations.

It seems that both San Francisco and New York City had administrative nondiscrimination policies for city employees in place before East Lansing did, but East Lansing was the first city council to hold a public vote on the issue of sexual orientation discrimination. A little more than one year later, East Lansing formally amended its human rights ordinance establishing the nondiscrimination policy in law and expanding its coverage to private as well as public employment and public accommodations. In October of 1973, Toronto became the first Canadian city to adopt a nondiscrimination ordinance.

Another dozen or so U.S. cities, including both college towns and major urban centers, passed similar ordinances in the remaining years of the 1970's. Some big cities, such as San Francisco and Minneapolis, Minnesota, adopted laws before 1975, while others, such as New York and Chicago, debated the issue for several years before their city councils finally adopted nondiscrimination ordinances.

Opposition to local ordinances began even before the first ordinances were passed. In several cities, bills were introduced but could not muster enough votes to pass. Religious groups in particular often were the leading opponents of such laws, though others, who believed that homosexuality was immoral, criminal, or an illness also argued against offering civil rights protection to gays and lesbians for living a "lifestyle" believed to be deviant.

In 1977, the backlash against nondiscrimination ordinances took on new momentum. Singer Anita Bryant led the charge against the actions of the Dade County Commission, which had adopted Florida's first nondiscrimination ordinance. The ordinance was repealed by a 2 to 1 vote in the first major referendum on GLBT rights in the United States. Referenda repealing GLBT rights ordinances in Wichita, Kansas; Eugene, Oregon; and St. Paul, Minnesota, quickly followed. Miami did not pass another GLBT rights ordinance again until 1998, and it again faced a referendum in 2002: In 2002, however, a little more than half the voters chose to retain the law.

This pattern continued throughout the 1980's, as a few cities and counties adopted ordinances and many cities tried unsuccessfully to adopt such laws. The 1980's also saw the first states to adopt nondis-crimination ordinances, beginning with Wisconsin in 1982. The 1980's and 1990's also saw intensive campaigns to repeal ordinances. In 1992, the voters of Colorado passed Amendment 2, which amended the state constitution to prevent local governments from adopting local nondiscrimination ordinances that would prohibit sexual orientation discrimination. The U.S. Supreme Court's 1996 decision in *Romer v. Evans* overturned Colorado's constitutional provision. In the first few years of the twenty-first century, more than two hundred city and county governments had ordinances or formal policies prohibiting discrimination on the basis of sexual orientation.

As of March, 2006, seventeen states and the District of Columbia had state laws protecting GLBT rights (and eight of these plus the District of Columbia also protect gender identity/gender expression), while another dozen or so states have executive orders covering state employees only. Executive orders, however, often last only as long as a sympathetic governor remains in office. Several states that had such executive orders lost them when new governors or hostile legislatures opposed to GLBT rights repeal or amend the previous executive order. Other states, including Delaware, have had hotly contested debates over several years about protecting GLBT rights but have failed to garner sufficient support to pass the nondiscrimination legislation.

The actual content and strength of these policies and ordinances can vary widely, however. Many of them simply prohibit the government from discriminating against its own employees. Others attempt to be as comprehensive as federal civil rights laws that prohibit discrimination in employment, housing, public accommodations, education, credit, and union practices. Some only allow a human rights commission at the local level the right to hear complaints and attempt to negotiate settlements, whereas others allow a given city to impose fines or allow individuals who feel their rights were violated to pursue private court actions. Formal complaints under such laws are infrequent, in part because civil complaints become public record; filing a complaint, then, is a form of "self-outing," which likely keeps many from filing in the first place.

## Significance

Social and cultural attitudes about lesbians and gays have changed through the years, partly because of the actions of numerous municipalities and state governments. Cities, counties, and states are beginning to see that discrimination against GLBT people is a *civil rights* issue. In response, they have adopted antidiscrimination ordinances and laws, even if limited in scope. The number of cities, counties, and states providing such coverage is relatively small, but about half the U.S. population lives in jurisdictions where sexual orientation discrimination is prohibited.

—*Charles W. Gossett*

## Further Reading

Button, James, Barbara Rienzo, and Kenneth D. Wald. *Private Lives, Public Choices*. Washington, D.C.: CQ Press, 1997.

Koppelman, Andrew. *The Gay Rights Question in Contemporary American Law*. Chicago: University of Chicago Press, 2002.

Murdoch, Joyce, and Deb Price. *Courting Justice:*

*Gay Men and Lesbians vs. the Supreme Court*. New York: Basic Books, 2001.

Riggle, Ellen, and Barry Tadlock, eds. *Gays and Lesbians in the Democratic Process*. New York: Columbia University Press, 1999.

Witt, Stephanie L., and Suzanne McCorkle. *Anti-Gay Rights: Assessing Voter Initiatives*. Westport, Conn.: Praeger, 1997.

**See also:** June 21, 1973: U.S. Supreme Court Supports Local Obscenity Laws; Aug., 1973: American Bar Association Calls for Repeal of Laws Against Consensual Sex; 1977: Anita Bryant Campaigns Against Gay and Lesbian Rights; Dec. 19, 1977: Quebec Includes Lesbians and Gays in Its Charter of Human Rights and Freedoms; 1978: Lesbian and Gay Workplace Movement Is Founded; Nov. 27, 1978: White Murders Politicians Moscone and Milk; Nov. 6, 1984: West Hollywood Incorporates with Majority Gay and Lesbian City Council; Apr., 2003: Buenos Aires Recognizes Same-Gender Civil Unions.

## March, 1972-March, 1973
# First Gay and Lesbian Synagogue in the United States Is Formed

*Six Jewish churchgoers, who felt disconnected with the established Jewish community because of their sexuality, formed Beth Chayim Chadashim, a GLBT synagogue in Los Angeles, the first in the United States and the first GLBT synagogue to become a member of the Union of American Hebrew Congregations. Also, the synagogue was the first religious congregation to write a gender-neutral prayer book, which eventually served as a model for Reform Judaism.*

**Also known as:** Metropolitan Community Temple

**Locale:** Los Angeles, California
**Categories:** Religion; organizations and institutions

## Key Figure

*Janet Marder*, first ordained rabbi to serve Beth Chayim Chadashim

## Summary of Event

Judaism is a dispersed religion that includes three branches—Reform, Conservative, and Orthodox. The Reform movement of Judaism is the most receptive and is committed to gender issues and inclusive language. In the early 1970's, a fear of and hostility toward gays and lesbians in society in general was not uncommon, and organized religion was certainly no safe haven. In fact, many people felt unable to practice their Judaism in a synagogue for fear of being outed as gay or lesbian to family or employers.

There were no organized Jewish places of worship in the early 1970's that provided outreach to the GLBT community. This would change, however, as six individuals who were Jewish investigated their common bonds at a meeting at the Metropolitan Community Church (MCC) in Los Angeles. (MCC is a nationwide church whose stated mission, since 1968, has been to provide outreach to gays, lesbians, bisexuals, transsexuals, and transgender persons specifically.) Ultimately, the six wanted to bring together and balance their Jewish religion and their sexuality. They began to worship together at MCC, forming a group called the Metropolitan Community Temple. Later, they met in other venues, including group-member's homes, a dance studio, and, after a fire at MCC, the Leo Baeck Temple in Los Angeles.

Encouraged by Reverend Troy Perry, minister of MCC, the Jewish group discussed organizing a synagogue. They had a difficult time attracting a rabbi to their new synagogue, however, so the worshipers led their own Sabbath services. Rabbinical interns from Hebrew Union College would later come to lead the group.

In 1973, in order to distinguish itself from MCC, the Metropolitan Community Temple took the name Beth Chayim Chadashim (BCC), which means "house of new life" in Hebrew. The name is symbolic of the giving of new life to GLBT Jews, who had no religious home to call their own. BCC wrote religion's first gender-neutral prayer book, which eventually served as a model for all of Reform Judaism.

In 1974, the synagogue became the first GLBT synagogue to become a member of the Union of American Hebrew Congregations (UAHC), which is the umbrella organization of the Reform movement. Rabbi Erwin Herman, then director of the Pacific Southwest Council of UAHC, encouraged the synagogue to pursue membership in the organization.

In 1977, the synagogue purchased a permanent building; it then hired its first rabbi, Janet Marder, in 1983. Their first full-time rabbi was Denise Eger (hired in 1989), and Lisa Edwards served as a rabbinic intern in 1991. From 1992 to 1994, Marc Blumenthal served as the rabbi. Edwards, after her ordination, joined BCC as the rabbi in 1994, and she has remained in that position for more than twelve years.

## SIGNIFICANCE

At its inception, the idea of a GLBT synagogue was innovative, radical, hotly debated, and unsupported by most Reform Judaism leaders. Since the formation of Beth Chayim Chadashim, approximately thirty other GLBT synagogues have formed in the United States. BCC was soon followed by Congregation Beth Simhat Torah in New York City, Sha'ar Zahav in San Francisco, Beth Ahava in Philadelphia, and Beth Mishpaha in Washington, D.C.

As mainstream synagogue membership becomes more blended, gay and lesbian synagogues may fall out of favor. Synagogues with a predominantly GLBT membership have straight, gay, or lesbian rabbis, just as synagogues with a mostly traditional membership have gay or lesbian rabbis. Clearly, the gay or lesbian rabbi in a GLBT synagogue does not have the same burden as a gay or lesbian rabbi in a traditional synagogue of convincing his or her congregation that he or she comes as a spiritual leader with no other agenda.

As society continues to accept lesbians, gays, bisexuals, and transgender persons, the lines of distinction between who is homosexual or bisexual or who is heterosexual begin to blur. Furthermore, it is the presence of an educational component, and not the rabbi's sexual orientation, at a given synagogue that often determines its attractiveness to, especially, parents of school-age children. Parents, GLBT or not, with children tend to be drawn to synagogues with a Hebrew school.

In 1980, the World Congress of Gay, Lesbian, Bisexual, and Transgender Jews: Keshet Ga'avah (rainbow of pride) was formed and currently boasts sixty-five member organizations worldwide. The congress conducts conferences and workshops around the world on issues relative to GLBT Jews.

The Reform and Reconstructionist movements have been at the forefront of change and inclusiveness within Judaism. Conservative synagogues vary in their level of acceptance. As of the early years of the twenty-first century, no Conservative GLBT synagogues existed. Though there are gay and lesbian Conservative rabbis, they are not ordained if they are known to be gay or lesbian. The Orthodox movement does not train women as rabbis, and, currently, it does not allow out gays in leadership roles.

The impact of the formation of BCC is simultaneously monumental and incremental. It was a monumental event in that BCC was the first to consider breaking from the accepted constraints of Judaism, as it had been known. Forming the first GLBT synagogue did not come without resistance from established Jewish leaders, yet BCC garnered support in places it had not fathomed. Membership into the UAHC, specifically, marked a huge step that paved the way for the formation of other GLBT synagogues. BCC's formation is an incremental event in that gay and lesbian rabbis still need to consider if they will be out as gay or lesbian and if "straight" congregations will accept them.

—*Amy L. Besnoy*

## FURTHER READING

Alpert, Rebecca T., Sue Levi Elwell, and Shirley Idelson, eds. *Lesbian Rabbis: The First Generation*. New Brunswick, N.J.: Rutgers University Press, 2001.

Balka, Christie, and Andy Rose, eds. *Twice Blessed: On Being Lesbian or Gay and Jewish*. Boston: Beacon Press, 1989.

Jewish and Queer Youth Web site. http://www.jqyouth.org/.

Lamm, Norman. "Judaism and the Modern Attitude to Homosexuality." In *Encyclopedia Judaica Yearbook*. Jerusalem: Encyclopedia Judaica, 1974.

Raphael, Lev. *Journeys and Arrivals: On Being Gay and Jewish*. Boston: Faber and Faber, 1996.

Shneer, David, and Caryn Aviv, eds. *Queer Jews*. New York: Routledge, 2002.

*Trembling Before G-d*. Documentary video recording. Directed by Sandi Simcha Dubowski. New York: New Yorker Video, 2001.

**SEE ALSO:** Oct. 6, 1968: Metropolitan Community Church Is Founded; June 25, 1972: First Out Gay Minister Is Ordained; Oct. 9-12, 1998: First International Retreat for Lesbian and Gay Muslims Is Held; Mar. 7, 2004: Robinson Becomes First Out Gay Bishop in Christian History; Nov. 29, 2005: Roman Catholic Church Bans Gay Seminarians.

## March 22, 1972-June 30, 1982
# EQUAL RIGHTS AMENDMENT FAILS STATE RATIFICATION

*The Equal Rights Amendment would prohibit discrimination on account of gender. Despite winning congressional approval, the proposed amendment was not ratified by the required two-thirds majority of the states, in part because critics feared that protecting against gender discrimination would confuse gender distinctions and, therefore, legitimize homosexuality.*

**LOCALE:** United States

**CATEGORIES:** Government and politics; laws, acts, and legal history; feminism; civil rights; organizations and institutions; religion

**KEY FIGURES**

*Alice Paul* (1885-1977), suffragist, founder of the National Woman's Party, and author of the Equal Rights Amendment

*Emanuel Celler* (1888-1981), longtime Democrat and representative from New York City, 1922-1972

*Phyllis Schlafly* (b. 1924), conservative Republican attorney from Illinois, founder of Stop ERA, and founder of the Eagle Forum

**SUMMARY OF EVENT**

Women won the seventy-year-battle to get voting rights with the passage of the Nineteenth Amendment to the U.S. Constitution in 1920. Feminist activists debated their next step for women's equality. Alice Paul, a suffragist leader, suggested that equal treatment for men and women be guaranteed in the Constitution. In 1923, she wrote the Equal Rights Amendment (ERA), which states, simply, that, "Equality of rights under the law shall not be denied or abridged by the United States or by any State on account of sex."

The proposed ERA drove a deep wedge among former suffragists. Even though Paul's newly formed National Woman's Party (NWP) arranged for the amendment to be introduced into Congress by Kansas Republican senator Charles Curtis in 1923, most politically active women opposed it. They feared that it would remove laws that benefited women, especially the protective labor laws that reformers (including Paul) had worked so hard to obtain. Also, this remarkable unanimity among women's groups showed their reluctance to venture into new and more radical solutions to women's inequality.

For decades, only the small NWP membership worked to promote the ERA, but with little success. While both the Republican and Democratic parties voiced support for the amendment in their platforms, many members of Congress were hesitant to oppose organized labor and liberal political groups. The rise of the Civil Rights movement and the rebirth of feminism in the 1960's breathed life into the ERA.

When Congress debated the Civil Rights Act of 1964, the NWP persuaded Democratic representative Howard Smith of Virginia to sponsor an amendment adding "sex" to Title VII, the section prohibiting discrimination in employment. Smith, a conservative and no friend of progressive legislation, may have intended the amendment as a joke that would emphasize the silliness of civil rights and kill the bill. However, the act passed into law along with Title VII. Protective labor laws, which typically prohibited women from holding certain jobs and from working at night, were abolished by the legislation.

| FIFTEEN STATES THAT FAILED TO RATIFY THE EQUAL RIGHTS AMENDMENT | | |
|---|---|---|
| Alabama | Illinois | North Carolina |
| Arizona | Louisiana | Oklahoma |
| Arkansas | Mississippi | South Carolina |
| Florida | Missouri | Utah |
| Georgia | Nevada | Virginia |

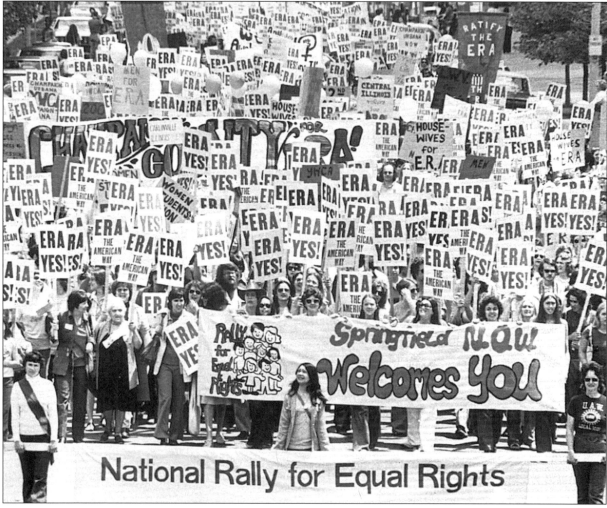

*Thousands march in 1976 in Springfield, Illinois, in a sea of white signs and banners, calling for the passage of the Equal Rights Amendment.* (AP/Wide World Photos)

With the issue of protective legislation now moot, many women's organizations came to support the ERA, which would have been the 27th amendment to the Constitution. The National Organization for Women (NOW), one year after its founding, endorsed the amendment in 1967 and took the leadership of the ERA fight from the nearly extinct NWP.

Before Congress could vote on the ERA, the bill had to pass out of committee. Emanuel Celler, a liberal New York Democrat and chairman of the powerful House Judiciary Committee, had refused to allow a hearing on the ERA for twenty-three years. Many of Celler's Brooklyn constituents were for-

mer garment district workers who staunchly opposed the ERA on grounds of protective legislation, and so he catered to their wishes.

In 1970, Democratic representatives Edith S. Green of Oregon and Martha W. Griffiths of Michigan outflanked Celler and freed the ERA from committee. Green held hearings on legislation to expand prohibitions against sex discrimination in education that expanded into a public discussion of general discrimination against women and the need for equal rights. Griffiths used a parliamentary maneuver to get a House vote on the ERA. On March 22, 1972, the Senate approved the ERA by a vote of 84 to 8, and it was sent to the states. Six states ratified the amendment within two days (Hawaii ratified within hours) and by the middle of 1973, the amendment seemed well on its way to adoption with 30 of the needed 38 states having ratified.

The debate over the ERA changed when passage appeared imminent, as conservatives and religious fundamentalists launched a grassroots campaign aimed at all things deemed to be unnatural and immoral. Phyllis Schlafly, founder of Stop ERA, portrayed the amendment as a threat to "family values" and traditional relationships between men and women. She saw women not as equals to men but as a gendered class that enjoyed certain protections and differential treatment. She argued that the ERA would permit men to evade their special responsibilities as men, such as being drafted into the military, and would allow women to escape their destiny as mothers. She added that the ERA would erase sexual differences and thereby legitimize homosexuality. (Schlafly's eldest son, John Schlafly, an attorney who works with his mother's Eagle Forum, was outed as gay in 1992.)

When it seemed apparent that the ERA would not meet the 1979 deadline for ratification, supporters gained an extension from Congress until June 30, 1982. No other proposed amendment has ever received an extension. The exception did not help the ERA.

## SIGNIFICANCE

Many reasons exist for the failure of the Equal Rights Amendment, most important, the inability of its supporters to realize the strength of the opposition. The conservative movement in the United States had been growing, partly as a backlash to the lesbian and gay and women's rights movements of the 1960's and 1970's. The defeat of the ERA demonstrated the political power of conservatism.

Some analysts blamed the amendment's defeat on the prominence of lesbians within the women's movement. Conservatives had made reference to "homosexuals" and homosexuality to argue that the legislation would mandate sameness between the sexes and therefore absurdity and danger. Fears were also raised that the ERA would permit gays and lesbians to legally marry and even to adopt chil-

dren. However, primarily, the defeat involved two clashing world views and belief systems.

The social base of feminism grew after the defeat of the amendment, partially *because of* the defeat. The new feminists of the 1960's and 1970's mobilized a mass movement to promote the amendment and then continued to use that mass to promote other goals. The effort to remove inequality has been slow and often piecemeal, however, whereas an amendment to the Constitution would have offered immediate protection to each citizen of every state, regardless of gender.

—*Caryn E. Neumann*

## FURTHER READING

Berry, Mary Frances. *Why ERA Failed: Politics, Women's Rights, and the Amending Process of the Constitution.* Bloomington: Indiana University Press, 1986.

Hoff-Wilson, Joan, ed. *Rights of Passage: The Past and Future of the ERA.* Bloomington: Indiana University Press, 1986.

Mathews, Donald G., and Jane Sherron De Hart. *Sex, Gender, and the Politics of ERA.* New York: Oxford University Press, 1990.

Phelan, Shane. *Sexual Strangers: Gays, Lesbians, and Dilemmas of Citizenship.* Philadelphia: Temple University Press, 2001.

Rimmerman, Craig A., Kenneth D. Wald, and Clyde Wilcox, eds. *The Politics of Gay Rights.* Chicago: University of Chicago Press, 2000.

Steiner, Gilbert Y. *Constitutional Inequality: The Political Fortunes of the Equal Rights Amendment.* Washington, D.C.: Brookings Institute, 1985.

**SEE ALSO:** May 1, 1970: Lavender Menace Protests Homophobia in Women's Movement; May 1, 1970: Radicalesbians Issues "The Woman Identified Woman" Manifesto; Jan. 22, 1973: *Roe v. Wade* Legalizes Abortion and Extends Privacy Rights; June 27, 1974: Abzug and Koch Attempt to Amend the Civil Rights Act of 1964; July 3, 1975: U.S. Civil Service Commission Prohibits Discrimination Against Federal Employees; 1977: Anita Bryant Campaigns Against Gay and

Lesbian Rights; 1978: Lesbian and Gay Workplace Movement Is Founded; Nov. 7, 1978: Antigay and Antilesbian Briggs Initiative Is Defeated; Sept. 21, 1996: U.S. President Clinton

Signs Defense of Marriage Act; Dec. 20, 1999: *Baker v. Vermont* Leads to Recognition of Same-Gender Civil Unions; Nov. 18, 2003: Massachusetts Court Rules for Same-Gender Marriage.

## June 25, 1972
# First Out Gay Minister Is Ordained

*William R. Johnson became the first out gay person to be ordained as a minister by a mainstream Christian denomination, the United Church of Christ in San Francisco.*

**Locale:** San Francisco, California
**Category:** Religion

**Key Figure**
*William R. Johnson* (b. 1946), ordained minister
of the United Church of Christ

**Summary of Event**
The Christian church has long struggled with acceptance and tolerance of gay, lesbian, and bisexual Christians. In the twentieth century, as homosexuality came to be seen as a sexual orientation and not merely one's participation in homosexual acts, the church had been challenged to determine the appropriate role of gay, lesbian, and bisexual Christians in the life of congregations. This was particularly difficult since the Bible does not explicitly address the issue of sexual orientation or the existence of gays, lesbians, and bisexuals. Perhaps nowhere did the issue become more complicated for the church than in the matter of whether to ordain out gay, lesbian, and bisexual persons to the ministry or to the priesthood of the Roman Catholic Church.

No doubt, there have been ordained homosexual ministers and priests since the beginning of Christianity. However, these persons have been forced to be silent publicly about their sexual orientation. In some liberal traditions out of the mainstream, there were a few ministers who became public about be-

ing gay, lesbian, or bisexual after their ordinations. One of the earliest ministers to do so was the Reverend James Stoll, who came out as gay while serving as a Unitarian Universalist minister in 1969. However, it is the Reverend William R. (Bill) Johnson who holds the distinction of being the first out gay person to be ordained by a mainline Christian denomination.

As a seminarian, Johnson came out publicly at the Pacific School of Religion on November 11, 1970, during a public forum on homosexuality and the church. Word of Johnson's affirmed sexual orientation spread quickly to members and congregations of the United Church of Christ (UCC), including to the local church where Johnson was working in a paid position as a Sunday school teacher as part of his training. The pastor of the church subsequently telephoned Johnson to inform him that it was no longer possible for him to be on the church's staff.

Having lost the income from this job, Johnson faced the threat of being unable to finish his seminary education. Genevieve Macliver was an elderly member of the Community UCC in San Carlos, California, where Johnson had served as a youth minister and as an interim associate minister earlier in his seminary years. Macliver believed that Johnson's sexual orientation should not prohibit him from becoming ordained. She arranged for a scholarship that enabled Johnson to continue his seminary education. In part because of this assistance, Johnson was able to continue his studies and complete his master of divinity degree in 1971.

The Reverend Henry Hayden, pastor of the Community UCC in San Carlos during this era, also

## "WE ARE ONE BODY IN CHRIST"

Whereas, the Apostle Paul said that, as Christians, we are many members, but we are one body in Christ (Rom. 12:4), and Jesus calls us to love our neighbors as ourselves (Mk. 12:31) without being judgmental (Mt. 7:1-2) nor disparaging of others (Lk. 18:9-14); and

Whereas, recognizing that many persons of lesbian, gay and bisexual orientation are already members of the Church through baptism and confirmation and that these people have talents and gifts to offer the United Church of Christ, and that the UCC has historically affirmed a rich diversity in its theological and Biblical perspectives; and

Whereas, the Tenth through Fourteenth General Synods have adopted resolutions encouraging the inclusion, and affirming the human rights, of lesbian, gay and bisexual people within the UCC; and

Whereas, the Executive Council of the United Church of Christ adopted in 1980 "a program of Equal Employment Opportunity which does not discriminate against any employee or applicant because of . . . sexual orientation"; and

Whereas, many parts of the Church have remained conspicuously silent despite the continuing injustice of institutionalized discrimination, instances of senseless violence and setbacks in civil rights protection by the Supreme Court; and

Whereas, the Church has often perpetuated discriminatory practices and has been unwilling to affirm the full humanness of clergy, laity and staff with lesbian, gay and bisexual orientation, who experience isolation, ostracism and fear of (or actual) loss of employment; and

Whereas, we are called by Christ's example, to proclaim release to the captives and set at liberty the oppressed (Lk. 4:18); . . .

Therefore, the Fifteenth General Synod of the United Church of Christ encourages a policy of non-discrimination in employment, volunteer service and membership policy with regard to sexual orientation; encourages association conferences and all related organizations to adopt a similar policy; and encourages the congregations of the United Church of Christ to adopt a non-discrimination policy and a Covenant of Openness and Affirmation of persons of lesbian, gay or bisexual orientation within the community of faith.

*Source:* United Church of Christ, 1985 resolution, "Calling on UCC Congregations to Covenant as Open and Affirming." http://www.ucc.org/men/open.html.

---

played a critical role in Johnson's journey to ordination. Hayden's pastoral leadership enabled the Community UCC congregation to remain resolutely supportive of Johnson and to weather the criticism it was receiving from within the UCC and beyond.

The Ecclesiastical Council of the Golden Gate Association, a grouping of UCC congregations of the Northern California and Nevada Conference, held an official meeting on April 30, 1972, to determine whether it was appropriate to ordain Johnson. In the course of the discussion and debate, no one questioned Johnson's qualifications for the ministry in personal terms. The meeting, in effect, became a forum to determine whether or not it was appropriate to ordain out gays and lesbians at all. In addition to moral concerns about homosexuality, there had been a real fear that Johnson's ordination would endanger the UCC's relationship with other Christian churches. A majority vote was required

for Johnson's ordination. Of the ninety-six persons present and eligible to vote, sixty-two voted yes for ordination and thirty-four voted no.

On June 25, 1972, Johnson was ordained by the Golden Gate Association, and Bonnie Ploeger, moderator of the Golden Gate Association, presided. The ordination sermon was delivered by the Reverend Dr. James Clark Brown, who was the pastor of the First Congregational Church of San Francisco. The Reverend L. William Eichhorn gave the charge to the minister at the ordination ceremony, stating,

I charge you, Bill Johnson, to remember, to continue to choose *life* means to choose *authenticity*— to somehow be authentic to both the United Church of Christ and that communion and your gay brothers and sisters, who you have already been loyal and faithful to. So, Bill Johnson, I charge you to choose life.

## SIGNIFICANCE

Johnson's ordination and leadership had an immediate impact within the UCC. He would soon found the UCC Gay Caucus in 1972 (which became the UCC Coalition for Lesbian, Gay, Bisexual & Transgender Concerns) and served as its national coordinator from 1972 to 1977. In 1983, this coalition introduced to the UCC Synod the concept of the Open and Affirming Church Program, which the Synod adopted in 1985. When a congregation votes to be "open and affirming," they are declaring publicly that gay, lesbian, bisexual, and transgender people are welcome in the life and ministry of the church. More than four hundred UCC congregations are open and affirming.

In 1991, the General Synod of the UCC declared that it "boldly affirms, celebrates and embraces the gifts of ministry of lesbian, gay and bisexual persons." In 1999, the UCC created an endowed scholarship fund for out GLBT seminarians studying to become UCC parish ministers. In April, 2000, this fund was named the William R. Johnson Scholarship Fund. In 2004, more than two hundred out GLBT persons had been serving as ordained UCC ministers.

The impact of Johnson's ordination also spread beyond the UCC to the broader community of faith. In addition to the UCC, Reform Judaism and the Unitarian Universalist Association have numerous policies that are supportive of lesbian, gay, and bisexual clergy, some of which date back two or even three decades. The Episcopal Church has officially deemed that sexual relations are appropriate only in the context of a heterosexual marriage, but each diocese is able to decide for itself on the controversial issue of ordination. On January 10, 1977, the Episcopal Diocese of New York made Reverend Ellen Marie Barrett the first out lesbian to be ordained as a minister (priest) by a mainline Christian denomination.

Europeans have been the most responsive to the idea of ordination for out GLBT persons, and more than twenty different Christian denominations in Europe allow GLBT individuals to become ordained. Today, most mainline religious denominations in the United States still prohibit sexually active lesbians, gays, and bisexuals from ordination, but they will often allow ordination if they are committed to celibacy.

—*Lara Hoke*

## FURTHER READING

Gomes, Peter J. *The Good Book: Reading the Bible with Mind and Heart*. San Francisco, Calif.: HarperSanFrancisco, 2002.

Johnson, William R. "Protestantism and Gay and Lesbian Freedom." In *Positively Gay: New Approaches to Gay and Lesbian Life*, edited by Betty Berzon and Frank Barney. Berkeley, Calif.: Celestial Arts, 2001.

McNeill, John J. *The Church and the Homosexual*. Boston: Beacon Press, 1993.

Rhodes, Mike. *A Position of Faith*. Rhodes Films, 1973. Documentary film on the ordination of the Reverend William R. Johnson.

Righter, Walter C. *A Pilgrim's Way: The Personal Story of the Episcopal Bishop Charged with Heresy for Ordaining a Gay Man Who Was in a Committed Relationship*. New York: Random House, 1998.

White, Mel. *Stranger at the Gate: To Be Gay and Christian in America*. New York: Simon & Schuster, 1994.

Wink, Walter, ed. *Homosexuality and Christian Faith: Questions of Conscience for the Churches*. Minneapolis, Minn.: Augsburg Fortress, 1999.

**SEE ALSO:** Oct. 6, 1968: Metropolitan Community Church Is Founded; Mar., 1972-Mar., 1973: First Gay and Lesbian Synagogue in the United States Is Formed; Oct. 9-12, 1998: First International Retreat for Lesbian and Gay Muslims Is Held; Mar. 7, 2004: Robinson Becomes First Out Gay Bishop in Christian History; Nov. 29, 2005: Roman Catholic Church Bans Gay Seminarians.

## November 7, 1972
# JORDAN BECOMES FIRST BLACK CONGRESSWOMAN FROM THE SOUTH

*Texan Barbara Jordan was elected to the U.S. House of Representatives, becoming the first African American woman to represent a Southern state. Her relationship with life partner Nancy Earl became public knowledge after Jordan's death in 1996.*

**LOCALE:** Austin, Texas
**CATEGORIES:** Civil rights; government and politics

**KEY FIGURES**
*Barbara Jordan* (1936-1996), political leader
*Nancy Earl*, Jordan's life partner

**SUMMARY OF EVENT**

Pathbreaking political leader Barbara Jordan was first elected to the U.S. House of Representatives in 1972 and served three terms. Publicly silent about her private life, she rarely discussed her health and never mentioned her long-term relationship with Nancy Earl. Upon Jordan's death, the *Houston Chronicle* identified Earl as Jordan's "longtime companion," and Jordan also was "outed" in *The Advocate* newsmagazine.

Jordan was born on February 21, 1936, in Houston, Texas. She graduated from Phyllis Wheatley High School and received degrees from Texas Southern University and Boston University. After passing the bar exam in Texas in 1959, she practiced law and first ran for the Texas House of Representatives in 1962. Losing that and a subsequent 1964 race, she won the 1966 race for state Senate and became the first African American woman in Texas to hold a seat there. She served in the Texas Senate from 1967 to 1973.

In addition to being elected president pro tem of the Texas Senate and becoming the first African American to preside over a state governing body, she is also credited with the passage of the 1971 re-districting act, which drew a new House district of central Houston. Easily defeating opponents in the primary and general elections, she won the seat in November of 1972 and left the Texas legislature for Washington, D.C., taking her seat officially on November 7.

In Congress, Jordan made an early name for herself during the House Judiciary Committee's Nixon deliberations. Her opening statement began,

Earlier today we heard the beginning of the Preamble to the Constitution of the United States, We, the people. It is a very eloquent beginning. But when that document was completed on the 17th of September in 1787, I was not included in that "We, the people." I felt somehow for many years that George

*Representative Barbara Jordan addresses the Democratic National Convention on July 12, 1976.* (Library of Congress)

## JORDAN'S KEYNOTE SPEECH BEFORE THE 1976 DEMOCRATIC NATIONAL CONVENTION

Now we must look to the future. Let us heed the voice of the people and recognize their common sense. If we do not, we not only blaspheme our political heritage, we ignore the common ties that bind all Americans. Many fear the future. Many are distrustful of their leaders, and believe that their voices are never heard. Many seek only to satisfy their private work—wants; to satisfy their private interests. But this is the great danger America faces—that we will cease to be one nation and become instead a collection of interest groups: city against suburb, region against region, individual against individual; each seeking to satisfy private wants. If that happens, who then will speak for America? Who then will speak for the common good?

This is the question which must be answered in 1976: Are we to be one people bound together by common spirit, sharing in a common endeavor; or will we become a divided nation? For all of its uncertainty, we cannot flee the future. We must not become the "New Puritans" and reject our society. We must address and master the future together. It can be done if we restore the belief that we share a sense of national community, that we share a common national endeavor. It can be done.

There is no executive order; there is no law that can require the American people to form a national community. This we must do as individuals, and if we do it as individuals, there is no President of the United States who can veto that decision.

to divert my energy to something different and to move away from demands which are all-consuming." She also had multiple sclerosis. Upon her retirement from politics, Jordan joined the faculty of the University of Texas at Austin and served on several different corporate boards. She worked to raise money for Democratic candidates and causes. In 1992, at President Bill Clinton's request, Jordan returned to politics, delivering the keynote address at the Democratic National Convention that year. She was awarded the Presidential Medal of Freedom in 1994 by Clinton.

Jordan lived with Nancy Earl in the home they built together in Austin. In addition to caring for Jordan through her struggle with leukemia and multiple sclerosis, Earl saved Jordan's life in 1988 after Jordan lost consciousness in their backyard swimming pool. Earl has rarely commented publicly on her relationship with Jordan.

Washington and Alexander Hamilton just left me out by mistake. But through the process of amendment, interpretation and court decision I have finally been included in "We, the people."

Jordan's comments garnered much publicity.

The next year, Jordan worked for expansion of the Voting Rights Act—an act that would include Texas. Despite opposition to the act in Texas and in the District of Columbia, Jordan prevailed. In 1976, she became the first black woman selected by a major political party for a keynote address. At the Democratic National Convention she declared, famously, "Who will speak for the common good?" Placed on the list of vice presidential possibilities for presidential candidate Jimmy Carter, Jordan declined nomination, and she later declined Carter's offer to make her the U.S. ambassador to the United Nations.

Jordan announced that she would retire from politics in 1979, saying that her reasons were "predicated totally on my internal compass directing me

### SIGNIFICANCE

Barbara Jordan, a formidable orator and defender of civil rights, is remembered for her intellect and her commitment to justice. In 1990, she was inducted into the National Women's Hall of Fame and, in 1994, she served as chair of the United States Commission on Immigration Reform. She received a total of thirty-one honorary doctorates. It is difficult to reconcile this legacy with her decision in 1986 to refuse to cosponsor federal GLBT rights legislation on the grounds that discrimination on the basis of sexual orientation is not equivalent to discrimination on the basis of race or ethnicity. However, she consistently spoke of tolerance and of building community.

Once described by *The Washington Post* as "the first black woman everything," Jordan accomplished another first, even after her 1996 funeral.

She was laid to rest at the Texas State Cemetery, the first African American woman to be buried there.

—*Stephen Paul Whitaker*

**FURTHER READING**

Fenno, Richard F. *Going Home: Black Representatives and Their Constituents.* Chicago: University of Chicago Press, 2003.

Jordan, Barbara, and Shelby Hearon. *Barbara Jordan: A Self-Portrait.* Garden City, N.Y.: Doubleday, 1979.

LaVerne, MacCain Gill. *African American Women in Congress: Forming and Transforming History.* New Brunswick, N.J.: Rutgers University Press, 1997.

Mendelsohn, James. *Barbara Jordan: Getting Things Done.* Brookfield, Conn.: Twenty-First Century Books, 2000.

Rogers, Mary Beth. *Barbara Jordan: American Hero.* New York: Bantam Books, 2000.

**SEE ALSO:** 1975: Gay American Indians Is Founded; 1975-1983: Gay Latino Alliance Is Formed; Apr., 1977: Combahee River Collective Issues "A Black Feminist Statement"; Nov. 18-21, 1977: National Women's Conference Convenes; Oct. 12-15, 1979: First National Third World Lesbian and Gay Conference Convenes; Oct. 12-15, 1979: Lesbian and Gay Asian Collective Is Founded; 1981: *This Bridge Called My Back* Is Published; Oct., 1981: Kitchen Table: Women of Color Press Is Founded; 1982: Lorde's Autobiography *Zami* Is Published; Sept., 1983: First National Lesbians of Color Conference Convenes; 1987: Anzaldúa Publishes *Borderlands/La Frontera*; 1987: *Compañeras: Latina Lesbians* Is Published; 1990: United Lesbians of African Heritage Is Founded; Jan., 2006: Jiménez Flores Elected to the Mexican Senate.

## 1973
# BROWN PUBLISHES *RUBYFRUIT JUNGLE*

*Rita Mae Brown's* Rubyfruit Jungle *was significantly different from earlier novels addressing lesbian lives. It likely was the first novel that made it clear that being lesbian is a good thing.*

**LOCALE:** Plainfield, Vermont
**CATEGORIES:** Literature; publications

**KEY FIGURES**

*Rita Mae Brown* (b. 1944), novelist
*June Arnold* (1926-1982), writer and a cofounder of Daughters, Inc., publisher of *Rubyfruit Jungle*
*Parke Bowman*, attorney and a cofounder of Daughters, Inc.

**SUMMARY OF EVENT**

Rita Mae Brown's first novel, *Rubyfruit Jungle* (1973), burst upon a lesbian community at a time when the newly awakened consciousness of lesbians had no literature to match their self-image. The 1969 Stonewall Rebellion in New York City had brought homosexuality not only to the often horrified eyes of the general public but also to the newly opened eyes of individual, and often isolated, lesbians and gays across the United States. Suddenly it seemed possible to a silent and marginal lesbian and gay community, consisting largely of individuals and couples who believed they were "the only ones," that they could find both a voice to speak their existence and a space within the heterosexual world in which to be visible to one another and to the larger world.

Into this historical moment exploded *Rubyfruit Jungle*, which has been called the mother of lesbian coming-out novels. It was first issued in paperback by Daughters, Inc., a small Plainfield, Vermont, women's press established in 1973 by writer June Arnold and her partner, lawyer Parke Bowman, to publish high-quality fiction by women. In the year of *Rubyfruit Jungle*'s publication, Daughters, Inc., also published Arnold's *The Cook and the Carpenter: A Novel by the Carpenter* (1973) and Blanche McCrary Boyd's *Nerves* (1973), now lesbian classics, albeit of a different sort from *Rubyfruit Jungle*.

Lesbian readers responded instantly and enthusiastically to *Rubyfruit Jungle*. Its outspoken, totally out heroine, Molly Bolt, was what every lesbian wanted to be—bold, sharp-witted, self-made, and unafraid of her sexuality in all its manifestations. Mainstream media were slower to respond. *Book World* reviewed the novel, as did several alternate publications, including *The Village Voice*. The novel's most significant reviews were in *Ms.* magazine (June, 1974), which included it among four others in a review of Daughters, Inc.'s, first-year offerings, and in the lesbian-feminist publication *Off Our Backs*, but at the time neither periodical was widely read. Major review outlets ignored Brown's work.

*Rita Mae Brown and her famous cat Sneaky Pie Brown, 1994.* (© Mark Homan)

Readers, however, loved the book and bought it. *Rubyfruit Jungle* rapidly sold seventy thousand copies, becoming Daughters best seller. This ongoing demand brought the book to mainstream attention, and after a bidding war in which Daughters held out for the best possible offer, in 1977, Bantam bought the book rights for $250,000 and issued an initial press run of 250,000 copies, soon to be increased to more than one million. Since that time the book has been in print.

Once *Rubyfruit Jungle* entered mainstream media, it reached a new audience. As a Bantam offering, it got an extensive and favorable review in *The New York Times*. The novel also was optioned for a 1979 film, but the film was never made.

## SIGNIFICANCE

Possibly the single most important reason *Rubyfruit Jungle* caused such an immediate and ongoing stir among both lesbian and heterosexual readers was that it filled a place in English-language literature that had been conspicuously vacant. Certainly there had been a "literature of homosexuality," but that literature largely presented the then-standard view of homosexuality as an aberration—albeit God-given—whose expression brought only unhappiness.

The model for this literature was Radclyffe Hall's *The Well of Loneliness* (1928), perhaps the most widely read fictional account of a homosexual life, in which Stephen Gordon "manfully" drives her lover Mary Llewellyn into the arms of heterosexual normality. Although Gordon is a successful writer, and although both she and her creator stoutly maintain that "the invert" is a child of God and therefore should be accepted and loved, the entire narrative force of the novel moves inexorably toward unhappiness in love and failure in relationships.

So too with the drugstore novels of the 1950's and 1960's. In books like the series written by Ann Bannon or Paula Christian, there was a lot of love and a lot of sex, and lesbians read the books avidly, but relationships were never completely successful. Even well-written art novels like those of Gail Wilhelm launched their protagonists into a sea of feeling in which "we too are drifting."

It was not impossible, of course, to imagine a better fictional world for lesbians and gays. That imagining, however, was largely confined to realms not directly accessible to the readers of the books. For instance, the delightfully romantic *Patience and Sarah* (1973; originally published in 1969 as *A Place for Us* by Alma Routsong under the pseudonym Isabel Miller) is set in a distant past and located on an unpeopled frontier, and the protagonists' lives are lived virtually alone and self-reliant. Bertha Harris's *Lover* (1976) has been variously described as nonlinear and surreal, and its nontraditional attempt to establish what Harris herself called a new genre made it, along with its near-contemporary Monique Wittig's, *Les Guerilleres* (1969), unreadable for many readers.

Arnold's *The Cook and the Carpenter* confused and even angered some readers because of its pronoun avoidance, which made it impossible to determine the sex of the main characters. Elana Nachmann's *Riverfinger Women* (1974) was a fantasy, Joanna Russ's *The Female Man* (1975) was science fiction, and Sally Miller Gearhart's *Wanderground* (1978) was set in a dystopian future. Although these and other contemporaneous novels presented a newly positive view of lesbian life, that life remained inaccessible to the people who read them.

Not so with *Rubyfruit Jungle*. Its protagonist Molly Bolt is loosely patterned on Rita Mae Brown. An illegitimate adopted child in the redneck South, Molly discovers at an early age both her poly-

morphous sexuality and her inclination to defy authority and custom. She questions adult authority, follows her inclinations, eschews limiting attachments, and overcomes an industry's hostility to become a filmmaker. At the end of the novel, Molly remains jobless, mentorless, without a significant relationship, and uncertain of her next step in life. One might say that *Rubyfruit Jungle* leaves Molly no better off, really, than Stephen Gordon was at the end of *The Well of Loneliness*, but there is a key difference that readers immediately perceived and that drove the book's success, both when it appeared and now. Molly Bolt has a finely developed sense of self and a conviction that she is valuable and lovable *as she is*—as a lesbian. It was this consciousness, this assertion of the value of being lesbian, that made *Rubyfruit Jungle* Daughters, Inc.'s, signal success and has given it an ongoing life as a lesbian classic.

Daughters, Inc., however, went out of business in 1977, the same year Bantam bought the rights to *Rubyfruit Jungle*. *Rubyfruit Jungle* continues to be *the* modern coming-out novel; Molly Bolt's audacious happiness has replaced Stephen Gordon's dignified doom as The Lesbian Story.

*—Loralee MacPike*

### FURTHER READING

Brown, Rita Mae. *Rubyfruit Jungle*. 1973. Anniversary ed. New York: Bantam Books, 1988.

Douglas, Carol Anne. "*Rubyfruit Jungle*." *Off Our Backs* 4, no. 2 (January 31, 1974).

Forrest, Katherine V. "The Evolution of a Revolution in Lesbian Literature." *Harvard Gay & Lesbian Review* 3, no. 2 (Spring, 1996).

Harris, Bertha. Introduction to *Lover*. New York: Arno Press, 1993.

Klemesrud, Judy. "An Underground Book." *The New York Times*, September 26, 1977, p. 38.

Webb, Marilyn. "A Publishing House Is Born." *Ms.* 11, no. 12 (June, 1974): 35-38.

**SEE ALSO:** 1903: Stein Writes *Q.E.D.*; 1928: Hall Publishes *The Well of Loneliness*; 1956: Foster Publishes *Sex Variant Women in Literature*; June, 1971: The Gay Book Award Debuts; 1973: Naiad

Press Is Founded; 1975: Rule Publishes *Lesbian Images*; 1981: Faderman Publishes *Surpassing the Love of Men*; 1981: *This Bridge Called My Back* Is Published; Oct., 1981: Kitchen Table: Women of Color Press Is Founded; 1982: Lorde's Autobiography *Zami* Is Published; 1985: Lesbian Film *Desert Hearts* Is Released; 1986: Paula Gunn Allen Publishes *The Sacred Hoop*; 1987: Anzaldúa Publishes *Borderlands/La Frontera*; 1987: *Compañeras: Latina Lesbians* Is Published; June 2, 1989: Lambda Literary Award Is Created.

## 1973
# NAIAD PRESS IS FOUNDED

*Life partners Barbara Grier and Donna McBride built Naiad Press from a home-based vanity press into the leading publisher of lesbian books.*

**LOCALE:** near Kansas City, Missouri
**CATEGORIES:** Publications; literature

**KEY FIGURES**

*Barbara Grier* (pseudonym, Gene Damon; b. 1933), cofounder of Naiad Press and life partner of Donna McBride
*Donna McBride*, cofounder of Naiad Press and life partner of Grier
*Anyda Marchant* (pseudonym, Sarah Aldridge; b. 1911), helped found Naiad Press
*Muriel Crawford* (b. 1925), helped found Naiad Press, and life partner of Marchant

**SUMMARY OF EVENT**

In the years immediately following the Stonewall uprising of 1969, affirmative lesbian literature was scarce and often difficult to find. Mainstream publishers rarely published positive lesbian-themed fiction, which meant authors were forced to self-publish their novels.

It was in this context that two lesbian couples began Naiad Press. Anyda Marchant and her life partner Muriel Crawford approached Barbara Grier and her life partner Donna McBride with a manuscript and $2,000 in startup money. The couples first became acquainted through Grier and Marchant's work on *The Ladder*, the first national lesbian periodical. Grier was the last editor of the magazine, which ceased publication in the fall of 1972, and Marchant was a contributor. Although the cofounders of the press place Naiad's birthday at the beginning of 1973, it was not until 1974 that their first book, *The Latecomer*, was actually published under Marchant's pen name, Sarah Aldridge. Both Grier and McBride continued to work full-time jobs, devoting evenings and weekends to Naiad. Running the business from their home near Kansas City, Missouri, the couple spent the next six years building the press's list one title at a time.

At the time of Naiad's inception, marketing lesbian books was a difficult proposition. Most mainstream bookstores did not carry "alternative" literature, and, although women's bookstores were beginning to sprout up in the wake of the women-in-print movement, they were few and far between and consequently largely inaccessible to the majority of lesbians. Additionally, the social stigma attached to lesbianism meant that many potential readers were closeted and isolated. Naiad was able to reach these readers through direct mailings based upon a list of 3,800 addresses gathered over many years by Grier and her colleagues at *The Ladder*. As Naiad grew, so did the list. In 1982, the press was sending out several mailings each year to more than 10,000 addresses, and by 1998 the mailing list had grown to 26,000.

In 1980, the couple moved to Tallahassee, Florida, where McBride became assistant director at the Leon County Public Library. The two continued to run Naiad out of their garage in their spare time until 1982, when Grier became Naiad's first full-time employee in January and McBride quit her library job to follow suit six months later. Although at first both took substantial cuts in pay from their regular jobs, throughout the next two decades the couple's hard work and tireless dedication transformed Naiad into the world's largest lesbian press. In the video *Lesbian Tongues*, Grier comments on Naiad's phenomenal growth from home-based business into a million-dollar-plus enterprise: "I love the idea that lesbian money literally is keeping Naiad Press growing like crazy."

Over the years, Naiad not only has introduced readers to a wide variety of authors of lesbian-themed genres—including romance, mystery, science fiction, and fantasy—but also has reintroduced lesbian literary and pulp classics to new generations by reissuing works such as Gertrude Stein's *Lifting Belly* (wr. 1915-1917; reissued 1989), Jeannette Foster's *Sex Variant Women in Literature* (1956; reissued 1985), and Ann Bannon's Beebo Brinker series (1962; reissued 1983, 1986, 2001). In 1985, Naiad garnered its biggest success and most notoriety when it published *Lesbian Nuns: Breaking Silence*, coedited by former nuns Rosemary Curb and Nancy Manahan. Selling the serial rights for this anthology to other publications, notably *Forum* (a Penthouse-owned magazine) not only broadened the book's audience and led to unheralded sales but also caused considerable controversy within the lesbian community.

Naiad has been recognized by the LGBT literary community, which has bestowed an American Library Association Gay Book Award (now Stonewall Book Award) and several Lambda Literary Awards on specific titles. Publishers Grier and McBride have been similarly honored. The couple received the Lambda Literary Foundation's 1991 Publisher's Service Award and Grier received the foundation's 2002 Pioneer Award.

Near the start of the twenty-first century, Naiad began to wind down its operations, publishing only a handful of new books each year, in preparation for Grier and McBride's eventual retirement. Fledgling publisher Bella Books took on many of Naiad's authors and bought out much of Naiad's inventory, thus ensuring the survival of Naiad's legacy when the press closed its doors on June 30, 2003.

## SIGNIFICANCE

During its thirty-year history, Naiad Press published almost five hundred titles. The press has achieved the goal of cofounder Barbara Grier to "[make] it possible that any lesbian, anywhere, any age, who comes out can walk into a bookstore and pick up a book that says 'of course you're a lesbian and you're wonderful!'"

—*Ellen Greenblatt*

## FURTHER READING

Greenblatt, R. Ellen. "Barbara Grier." In *Gay and Lesbian Biography*, edited by Michael J. Tyrkus. Detroit, Mich.: St. James Press, 1997.

Grier, Barbara. "Climbing 'The Ladder' to Success: Naiad Press." In *Happy Endings: Lesbian Writers Talk About Their Lives and Work*, edited by Kate Brandt. Tallahassee, Fla.: Naiad Press, 1993.

Grier, Barbara, and Rhonda J. Factor. "A Burning Love for Lesbian Literature." *Journal of Lesbian Studies* 5, no. 3 (2001): 87-94.

*Lesbian Tongues: Lesbians Talk About Life, Love, and Sex*. Video recording. Washington, D.C.: Pop Video, 1989.

**1973**
# NATIONAL GAY TASK FORCE IS FORMED

*The National Gay Task Force was the first major national organization dedicated to lesbian and gay civil rights. In addition to successfully pressuring the American Psychiatric Association in 1973 to remove "homosexuality" from its list of mental disorders, the group's work includes helping to repeal antisodomy laws, and, reflecting its mission to be politically active at the grassroots level, it established the first national gay crisis hotline and conducted the first national survey of homophobic violence.*

**ALSO KNOWN AS:** National Gay and Lesbian Task Force

**LOCALE:** New York, New York

**CATEGORIES:** Organizations and institutions; civil rights

## KEY FIGURES

*Bruce Voeller* (1934-1994), NGTF cofounder and first director

*Virginia Apuzzo* (b. 1941), former NGTF director

*Jeffrey Levi*, first NGTF lobbyist and former director

*Urvashi Vaid* (b. 1958), former NGLTF director

*Kerry Lobel*, former NGLTF director

*Matt Foreman*, NGLTF director beginning in 2003

## SUMMARY OF EVENT

The National Gay Task Force (NGTF) was the first national gay and lesbian civil rights advocacy organization. NGTF was founded in 1973 by a group of activists including former New York City health commissioner Howard Brown, Ron Gold, Nath Rockhill, and Bruce Voeller, the latter three of whom were involved in the Gay Activists Alliance.

NGTF has played an important role in many of the GLBT movement's key struggles. In its first year, the organization successfully pressured the American Psychiatric Association to stop classifying homosexuality as a mental disorder and lobbied the American Bar Association to support the repeal of sodomy laws. In 1975, the NGTF pressured the federal government to rescind its ban on employment of gays and lesbians and worked with Representative Bella Abzug (Democrat, New York) to introduce the first national gay rights legislation. The following year, NGTF worked to influence the policies of the Democratic Party, and in 1977, codirectors Voeller and Jean O'Leary were among the first GLBT leaders to discuss gay issues at the White House. The NGTF also supported local efforts, including the unsuccessful effort to defeat Dade County, Florida's, antigay ordinance led by singer and entertainer Anita Bryant.

After a period of decline in the late 1970's, NGTF, under director Virginia Apuzzo, turned its attention to antigay violence and then, in the early 1980's, to AIDS. In 1982, the organization initiated its Anti-Violence Project and went on to establish the first national gay crisis hotline and to conduct the first national survey of homophobic violence. In 1983, NGTF helped start two national advocacy coalitions, AIDS Action and National Organizations Responding to AIDS, and in 1984 it secured the first federal funding for community-based AIDS groups. At the same time, the NGTF supported more militant activism, such as the 1988 "die-in" staged by the AIDS Coalition to Unleash Power (ACT UP) outside the Food and Drug Administration building.

In keeping with the organization's increasing focus on federal-level work, in 1985 NGTF moved its headquarters from New York City to Washington, D.C. That same year, emphasizing its commitment to lesbian issues, the group changed its name to the National Gay and Lesbian Task Force (NGLTF). Under Jeffrey Levi's direction, the NGLTF renewed its efforts to repeal state sodomy laws following the U.S. Supreme Court's *Bowers v. Hardwick* ruling (1986). NGLTF helped organize the October, 1987, March on Washington, and members of its staff were among the seven hundred

## NATIONAL GAY AND LESBIAN TASK FORCE: STRATEGIES AND DIRECTIONS

The Task Force is the organization that builds grassroots political power of the LGBT community in order to attain complete equality. The following four Primary Strategies are employed by The Task Force to build political power for the LGBT community:

*Primary Strategies*
1. Strengthening state and local grassroots activists' power by building their capacity to organize and to initiate and respond appropriately and effectively to a range of political struggles
2. Arming activists with research, facts, and messages to advance complete equality and refute and expose the homophobic attacks against the LGBT community
3. Being the unwavering and uncompromising national voice within the LGBT movement, that consistently raises the interconnections between homophobia, transphobia, biphobia, sexism, racism, and classism
4. Acting as the movement's primary convener and coalition builder including working with non-LGBT allies

*Strategic Directions for the Task Force*
1. Expands the ability of local and state organizations to exercise political power
2. Uses strategically its power and presence in political arenas
3. Uses strategically its role as the principal convener within the movement

GLBT leaders arrested in a massive act of civil disobedience outside the Supreme Court. The NGLTF launched its Military Freedom Project in 1988, followed by the Families Project in 1989.

In the early 1990's, under director Urvashi Vaid, the NGLTF increasingly devoted itself to grassroots organizing—a shift that began in 1988 with the first annual Creating Change Conference, dedicated to training new movement leaders and promoting networking among activists. In 1992, NGLTF launched its Fight the Right Project, and staff members traveled widely to support local GLBT groups fighting antigay state and municipal legislation and ballot initiatives.

In the mid-1990's, NGLTF went through a period of internal struggle. Three directors (Torie Osborn, Peri Rude Radecic, and Melinda Paras) came and went in quick succession, and the organization's staff and budget decreased by half.

Nevertheless, in 1995, NGLTF launched its Policy Institute, envisioned as a think tank for the GLBT movement.

NGLTF experienced a resurgence in the latter half of the decade. Under the direction of Kerry Lobel, the organization rekindled its emphasis on local organizing, spearheading in March of 1999 Equality Begins at Home, a series of 350 coordinated public forums, demonstrations, and lobbying events in all fifty states. True to her politics of inclusion, Lobel oversaw the adoption of a new vision statement in 1997 that explicitly included bisexuals and transgender people.

In 2000, NGLTF appointed a controversial new director, Elizabeth Toledo, who had just divorced her husband and come out of the closet the year before. Toledo was succeeded in 2001 by Lorri Jean, who stabilized the organization's finances and, according to some, took the NGLTF in a more conservative direction. In April, 2003, NGLTF appointed Matt Foreman as its director, and Jean returned in 2003 to Los Angeles as the executive director of the Los Angeles Gay and Lesbian Center.

## SIGNIFICANCE

Along with the Human Rights Campaign (HRC), NGLTF remains one of the two primary national GLBT advocacy organizations. While HRC emphasizes Washington, D.C., politics and national legislation, NGLTF focuses on grassroots activism and coalition building. This emphasis has put NGLTF at the center of various controversies concerning the nature of the GLBT movement as a whole, controversies such as the relative value of moderate "insider" politics versus radical "outsider" activism. A recurring debate revolves around

*National Gay Task Force representatives participate in the annual pride parade in New York City in 1975.* (Hulton Archive/Getty Images)

whether the GLBT movement should focus on gay-specific identity politics or on broader, multi-issue social justice activism. The latest round of the debate took place in the fall of 2002, as left-leaning progressives successfully pressured NGLTF to take a stance against the then-impending invasion of Iraq, while more conservative individuals urged the organization to stick to GLBT issues. NGLTF also supports racial and economic justice, reproductive freedom, and abolition of the death penalty.

Over the years, NGLTF has periodically shifted its focus back and forth from national advocacy to local grassroots organizing—and from "insider" to "outsider" politics—and at times has tried with varying degrees of success to maintain a balance between the two. NGLTF now is widely regarded as the national organization representing the progressive wing of the GLBT movement. The NGLTF's

current vision statement, adopted in 1997, unequivocally positions the organization as "part of a broader social justice movement for freedom, justice and equality."

—*Liz Highleyman*

## FURTHER READING

D'Emilio, John. "Organizational Tales: Interpreting the NGLTF Story." In *The World Turned: Essays on Gay History, Politics, and Culture*. Durham, N.C.: Duke University Press, 2002.

D'Emilio, John, William Turner, and Urvashi Vaid, eds. *Creating Change: Sexuality, Public Policy, and Civil Rights*. New York: St. Martin's Press, 2000.

National Gay and Lesbian Task Force. "Task Force History." http://www.thetaskforce.org/aboutus/history.cfm.

Vaid, Urvashi. *Virtual Equality: The Mainstreaming of Gay and Lesbian Liberation*. New York: Anchor Books, 1995.

**SEE ALSO:** 1950: Mattachine Society Is Founded; 1952: ONE, Inc., Is Founded; 1955: Daughters of Bilitis Founded as First National Lesbian Group in United States; May 27-30, 1960: First National Lesbian Conference Convenes; Feb. 19-20, 1966: First North American Conference of Homophile Organizations Convenes; Apr. 19, 1967: First Student Homophile League Is Formed; Aug. 11-18, 1968: NACHO Formally Becomes the First Gay Political Coalition; July 31, 1969: Gay Liberation Front Is Formed; June 28, 1970: First Lesbian and Gay Pride March in the United States; Nov. 28, 1970: Del Martin Quits Gay Liberation Movement; Oct. 18, 1973: Lambda Legal Authorized to Practice Law; Mar. 5, 1974: Antigay and Antilesbian Organizations Begin to Form; 1977: Anita Bryant Campaigns Against Gay and Lesbian Rights; Apr. 22, 1980: Human Rights Campaign Fund Is Founded; 1989: Vaid Becomes Executive Director of the National Gay and Lesbian Task Force.

# 1973
# OLIVIA RECORDS IS FOUNDED

*A lesbian-feminist collective, which formed the company Olivia Records, provided recording opportunities for women and produced some of the first recordings to include the lyrics of out lesbian songwriters.*

**LOCALE:** Washington, D.C.
**CATEGORIES:** Economics; arts; feminism

**KEY FIGURES**
*Meg Christian* (b. 1946), cofounder of Olivia Records and a recording artist
*Cris Williamson* (b. 1947), recording artist
*Ginny Berson,*
*Judy Dlugacz,*
*Cyndi Gair,*
*Helaine Harris,*
*Kate Winter,* and
*Jennifer Woodul,* cofounders of Olivia Records

**SUMMARY OF EVENT**

In 1973, Cris Williamson performed a concert at Georgetown University in Washington, D.C. Meg Christian, a musician who had popularized Williamson's music among the local lesbian-feminist community, later invited her to do a radio interview on a show called *Sophie's Parlor*. During the interview, conducted by Christian and Ginny Berson, they discussed the challenges facing women artists in the mainstream recording industry. Williamson made an offhand suggestion that they start a women's record company.

Christian and Berson happened to be part of a group of lesbian feminists who were deciding how to put their politics into practice. Spurred by Williamson's suggestion, they decided to form Olivia Records, a company that would record music by and for women. They took the name for their company, Olivia, from the title of a 1949 lesbian pulp novel.

Although incorporated as a nonprofit organization, Olivia Records was run as a collective. The group was committed to creating a nonhierarchical organization that reflected feminist values. The collective initially included ten women, most of whom lived in Washington, D.C. After six months, the number had decreased to eight, including Berson, Christian, Judy Dlugacz, Cyndi Gair, Helaine Harris, Kate Winter, and Jennifer Woodul. The majority had been affiliated with The Furies, a radical lesbian-feminist organization.

Christian continued to tour, and she spread the

*Cris Williamson.* (Irene Young)

word about Olivia, leading to small donations for the recording company. Joan Lowe, the owner of a small recording company in Oregon, offered to put her own current projects on hold in order to engineer Olivia's first release, a single that featured Christian singing "Lady" by Carole King and Gerry Goffin and, on the flip side, Williamson singing "If It Weren't for the Music." Women did all the work on this record, with the exception of the pressing. They conceived of this first effort as a fund-raising strategy, sending copies out to selected individuals to solicit contributions. Although they raised only $250 in donations, they learned of many women who wanted to purchase the record. The revenue from mail-order sales and a loan allowed Olivia to cut Christian's first album, *I Know You Know*. The goal was to sell five thousand copies over the record's lifetime. They surpassed that goal within a few months and sold more than ten thousand copies

within the first year after the record's release.

When Olivia's collective decided to move the company to California, its membership decreased again. Christian, Berson, Dlugacz, Winter, and Woodul left their jobs and moved to Los Angeles, where they lived collectively in a shared house that also served as their office. Particularly during the first few years, Olivia was largely dependent on the revenue from Christian's concert tours.

In the summer of 1975, after raising $18,000, Olivia released its second album, Williamson's *The Changer and the Changed*. Given the success of Christian's *I Know You Know*, they hoped to sell ten thousand copies of this new release. Once again, their hopes were surpassed, as the album garnered critical acclaim. Olivia sold between 40,000 and 50,000 copies in its first year, and by 1988 they had sold more than 250,000 copies.

This early success spurred Olivia to continue its expansion, but subsequent recordings did not achieve the same level of success. In 1977, Olivia relocated to Oakland, California. By the end of 1978, with fourteen women in the collective, they faced serious financial difficulties. The combination of ambitious goals with a lack of business expertise left Olivia without enough money to produce more copies of *The Changer and the Changed*, its most popular recording. Following the advice of a consultant, Olivia went through a major reorganization and moved away from the collective model. Christian departed in 1984 to devote herself full-time to Syda Yoga, leaving Dlugacz as the only remaining founder. In 1995, Olivia ceased its recording activities, changed its name, and changed its product to vacation packages for lesbians. Olivia Records is now Olivia Cruises.

### SIGNIFICANCE

Olivia Records received a tremendous amount of positive feedback from women who connected with the music and heard their own lives reflected in lyrics for the first time. The number of records sold was remarkable for such a small company, as were the sold-out Carnegie Hall concerts that marked Olivia's tenth and fifteenth anniversaries. Olivia's recordings avoided sexist, racist, homophobic, and ageist imagery and were particularly notable for portraying lesbian relationships. Their messages empowered women and spurred activism for women's and lesbian rights. Olivia also engaged in their own creative activism, releasing *Lesbian Concentrate*, a compilation album responding to Anita Bryant's antigay and antilesbian crusade in the 1970's.

Olivia is notable as an example of lesbian-feminist collective organizing. The structure of the company was as integral to its members' activist goals as it was to the music. The collective envisioned creating an alternative workplace that would allow women to achieve financial independence in a nonoppressive environment. They advocated collective decision making, a nonhierarchical structure, sharing of skills with other women, and a system of compensation based on personal need. Olivia hoped to encourage women to spend their money within the community, thus building an independent financial base.

At times these efforts drew the criticism of women who believed that feminism and capitalism were fundamentally incompatible. Because of their commitment of accountability to their community, members of the collective often found themselves exhausted by the amount of energy required to defend their decisions. They held workshops and discussions where they accepted compliments but also received criticisms on topics ranging from their use of a capitalistic business model to their employment of a transsexual recording engineer.

Despite these criticisms, Olivia Records was an integral part of the women's music movement that comprised several small recording companies, distributors, and a festival circuit. They created opportunities for women musicians, contributed to the development of women's music, and deeply affected the lives not only of their members but of their listeners as well.

—*Kathleen Liddle*

## FURTHER READING

Crow, Margie, Margaret Devoe, Madeleine Janover, and Fran Moira. "The Muses of Olivia: Our Own Economy, Our Own Song." *Off Our Backs* 49, no. 9 (September 30, 1974): 2.

Dlugacz, Judy. "If It Weren't for the Music: Fifteen Years of Olivia Records, Part 1." *Hot Wire* 4, no. 3 (July, 1988): 28.

_____. "If It Weren't for the Music: Fifteen Years of Olivia Records, Part 2." *Hot Wire* 5, no. 1 (January, 1989): 20.

Harper, Jorjet. "Fifteenth Anniversary Bash: Olivia Records at Carnegie Hall." *Hot Wire* 5, no. 2 (May, 1989): 32.

Holden, Stephen. "Olivia Records Is a Success in 'Women's Music.'" *The New York Times*, November 4, 1983, p. C16.

Woodul, Jennifer. "From Olivia: What's This About Feminist Business?" *Off Our Backs* 6, no. 4 (June 30, 1976): 24.

**SEE ALSO:** Sept., 1975: Anna Crusis Women's Choir Is Formed; Aug. 20-22, 1976: Michigan Womyn's Music Festival Holds Its First Gathering; 1977: Anita Bryant Campaigns Against Gay and Lesbian Rights; 1981-1982: GALA Choruses Is Formed; June 6-June 20, 1981: San Francisco Gay Men's Chorus Concert Tour; Dec. 8, 1981: New York City Gay Men's Chorus Performs at Carnegie Hall; 1991: Stone Publishes "The Posttranssexual Manifesto"; 1992-2002: Celebrity Lesbians Come Out.

# January 22, 1973
# *ROE V. WADE* LEGALIZES ABORTION AND EXTENDS PRIVACY RIGHTS

*The U.S. Supreme Court established a pregnant woman's constitutional right to an abortion. The decision overturned abortion laws in most states and has occasioned decades of political controversy and litigation. Gays and lesbians have benefited from the reasoning in* Roe v. Wade *because the case has been used by some state courts to strike down sodomy or other statutes that impinge on private, same-gender sexual activities between consenting adults.*

**LOCALE:** Washington, D.C.
**CATEGORIES:** Laws, acts, and legal history; civil rights; feminism

## KEY FIGURES

*Norma Jane McCorvey* (b. 1947), plaintiff known as "Jane Roe"
*Sarah Weddington* (b. 1945), Roe's attorney
*Henry Wade* (1915-2001), district attorney of Dallas County
*Harry A. Blackmun* (1908-1999), associate justice of the United States and author of the Court's opinion
*Byron White* (1917-2002), associate justice of the United States and a dissenter

## SUMMARY OF EVENT

*Roe v. Wade* (1973) sprang from the attempt of "Jane Roe" (Norma Jane McCorvey) to terminate her pregnancy by means of abortion in Texas in 1970. Texas law forbade abortion except "for the purpose of saving the life of the mother." Roe's life was not endangered by her pregnancy. With the encouragement of her attorney, Sarah Weddington, Roe decided to challenge the Texas statute on constitutional grounds.

A federal district court suit was brought against Henry Wade, the district attorney of Dallas County, asking that he be ordered not to enforce the Texas abortion statute on the ground that it unconstitutionally interfered with a pregnant woman's right to personal privacy. The district court agreed with Roe, and Texas appealed to the U.S. Supreme Court. The case was first argued on December 13, 1971, reargued on October 11, 1972, and decided by the Court on January 22, 1973.

The fundamental issue in *Roe v. Wade* was whether "personal privacy" rights included the right of a woman to choose to have an abortion. By 1971, the Supreme Court had already extended the idea of "liberty" protected under the due process clause of the Fourteenth Amendment to include some marital and personal privacy rights. The most important precedent was *Griswold v. Connecticut* (1965), the Connecticut birth-control case. A Connecticut law forbade the dissemination of birth-control devices or information. The Court decided that married people have a constitutional right to receive and use contraceptive devices and information. The same right was extended to unmarried people in *Eisenstadt v. Baird* (1972). In these cases the Court assumed for the first time that there is a "zone of privacy" that protects private family and sexual decisions.

The Court's decision in *Roe v. Wade* was written by Justice Harry A. Blackmun for a 7-2 majority. Dissenting opinions were submitted by Justices William Rehnquist and Byron White. The majority held that a pregnant woman does have the right to an abortion on demand in the first trimester of pregnancy. In the second trimester, the state is free to place some restrictions on the right in order to protect the health of the mother. In the third trimester, after the child has "quickened," the state may have the power to prohibit abortion altogether.

The majority opinion balances the interests of the state governments against the personal privacy rights of women. The state's interest is to protect unborn life and the safety and health of pregnant

## *ROE V. WADE* (1973): KEY PASSAGES

*From the Court's opinion:* The principal thrust of appellant's attack on the Texas statutes is that they improperly invade a right, said to be possessed by the pregnant woman, to choose to terminate her pregnancy. Appellant would discover this right in the concept of personal "liberty" embodied in the Fourteenth Amendment's Due Process Clause; or in personal, marital, familial, and sexual privacy said to be protected by the Bill of Rights or its penumbras . . . ; or among those rights reserved to the people by the Ninth Amendment.

• The Constitution does not explicitly mention any right of privacy. In a line of decisions, however, . . . the Court has recognized that a right of personal privacy, or a guarantee of certain areas or zones of privacy, does exist under the Constitution. In varying contexts, the Court or individual Justices have, indeed, found at least the roots of that right in the First Amendment, in the Fourth and Fifth Amendments, in the penumbras of the Bill of Rights, in the Ninth Amendment, or in the concept of liberty guaranteed by the first section of the Fourteenth Amendment. . . . These decisions make it clear that only personal rights that can be deemed "fundamental" or "implicit in the concept of ordered liberty," . . . are included in this guarantee of personal privacy. They also make it clear that the right has some extension to activities relating to marriage, procreation, contraception, family relationships, and child rearing and education. . . . This right of privacy, whether it be founded in the Fourteenth Amendment's concept of personal liberty and restrictions upon state action, as we feel it is, or, as the District Court determined, in the Ninth Amendment's reservation of rights to the people, is broad enough to encompass a woman's decision whether or not to terminate her pregnancy. The detriment that the State would impose upon the pregnant woman by denying this choice altogether is apparent. Specific and direct harm medically diagnosable even in early pregnancy may be involved. Maternity, or additional offspring, may force upon the woman a distressful life and future. Psychological harm may be imminent. Mental and physical health may be taxed by child care. There is also the distress, for all concerned, associated with the unwanted child, and there is the problem of bringing a child into a family already unable, psychologically and otherwise, to care for it. In other cases, as in this one, the additional difficulties and continuing stigma of unwed motherhood may be involved. All these are factors the woman and her responsible physician necessarily will consider in consultation.

• We, therefore, conclude that the right of personal privacy includes the abortion decision, but that this right is not unqualified and must be considered against important state interests in regulation.

We note that those federal and state courts that have recently considered abortion law challenges have reached the same conclusion. A majority, in addition to the District Court in the present case, have held state laws unconstitutional, at least in part, because of vagueness or because of overbreadth and abridgment of rights.

In view of all this, we do not agree that, by adopting one theory of life, Texas may override the rights of the pregnant woman that are at stake. . . .

Our conclusion that Art. 1196 [the Texas statute] is unconstitutional means, of course, that the Texas abortion statutes, as a unit, must fall.

---

women. Roe's interest is what the Court called "the fundamental right of single women and married persons to choose whether to have children." By tying the right to an abortion to the right to choose whether to have children, Blackmun brought the case more squarely within the precedent established by *Griswold v. Connecticut*. The decision substantially increased women's autonomy both within and without the family.

The main dissenting opinion was submitted by Justice White. It argues that there is no constitutional warrant to establish a new constitutional right

that substitutes a balancing of the competing values by the Court rather than by state legislatures.

### SIGNIFICANCE

The immediate or direct effect of *Roe v. Wade* was to empower women to avoid having unwanted children. Since the Supreme Court made its decision, there have been millions of abortions in the United States, a fact often cited by opponents of the decision.

*Roe v. Wade* continues to be enormously controversial. Since the case was decided, there have been

constant efforts by its opponents to overturn it and
by its supporters to protect the rights it establishes.
The passions raised by this case have led to violence
and harassment. Several physicians have been shot
to death or beaten, and there have been many bombings and arson attacks at family planning clinics.
The issue has been before the Supreme Court in one
form or another in nearly every Court term since
1973. Because the decision in the case appeared to
many people to be political rather than judicial in
character, there have been many marches or demonstrations at the Supreme Court itself.

The reasoning of *Roe v. Wade* and the precedent
it established have often been cited, sometimes successfully, to support or establish other rights of personal privacy. Gays and lesbians have benefited
from *Roe v. Wade*, whose reasoning has been used
by some state courts to strike down sodomy or other
statutes that impinge on private, consensual, same-
gender sexual activities between adults. In fact, the
Supreme Court struck down state sodomy laws as
unconstitutional with its 2003 ruling in *Lawrence v.
Texas*.

—*Robert Jacobs*

**FURTHER READING**

Garrow, David J. *Liberty and Sexuality: The Right
to Privacy and the Making of Roe v. Wade*. Updated ed. Berkeley: University of California
Press, 1998.

Gorney, Cynthia. *Articles of Faith: A Frontline
History of the Abortion Wars*. New York: Simon
and Schuster, 2000.

Gruen, Lori, and George E. Panichas, eds. *Sex, Morality, and the Law*. New York: Routledge, 1997.

Hull, N. E. H., and Peter Hoffer. *Roe v. Wade: The
Abortion Rights Controversy in American History*. Lawrence: University Press of Kansas, 2001.

Rubin, Eva R. *Abortion, Politics, and the Courts:
Roe v. Wade and Its Aftermath*. New York: Greenwood Press, 1987.

Schwarzenbach, Sibyl A., and Patricia Smith, eds.
*Women and the United States Constitution: His-
tory, Interpretation, and Practice*. New York:
Columbia University Press, 2003.

Weddington, Sarah. *A Question of Choice*. New
York: Putnam, 1992.

**SEE ALSO:** Jan. 12, 1939: *Thompson v. Aldredge*
Dismisses Sodomy Charges Against Lesbians;
1952-1990: U.S. Law Prohibits Gay and Lesbian
Immigration; May 22, 1967: U.S. Supreme
Court Upholds Law Preventing Immigration of
Gays and Lesbians; June 21, 1973: U.S. Supreme
Court Supports Local Obscenity Laws; Aug.,
1973: American Bar Association Calls for Re-
peal of Laws Against Consensual Sex; Nov. 17,
1975: U.S. Supreme Court Rules in "Crimes
Against Nature" Case; 1981: Gay and Lesbian
Palimony Suits Emerge; 1982-1991: Lesbian
Academic and Activist Sues University of Cali-
fornia for Discrimination; 1986: *Bowers v.
Hardwick* Upholds State Sodomy Laws; May 1,
1989: U.S. Supreme Court Rules Gender-Role
Stereotyping Is Discriminatory; Dec. 17, 1991:
Minnesota Court Awards Guardianship to Les-
bian Partner; 1992-2006: Indians Struggle to
Abolish Sodomy Law; 1993-1996: Hawaii
Opens Door to Same-Gender Marriages; Sept.
21, 1993-Apr. 21, 1995: Lesbian Mother Loses
Custody of Her Child; Dec. 20, 1999: *Baker v.
Vermont* Leads to Recognition of Same-Gender
Civil Unions; June 28, 2000: *Boy Scouts of
America v. Dale*; June 26, 2003: U.S. Supreme
Court Overturns Texas Sodomy Law.

## June 21, 1973
# U.S. SUPREME COURT SUPPORTS LOCAL OBSCENITY LAWS

*By allowing local communities to set standards of obscenity, two U.S. Supreme Court decisions expanded the definition of materials that could be judged "obscene" and thus vulnerable to state repression and control. The decision impacts lesbians and gays because "community standards," and thus public morality, are often antigay and antilesbian and likely to define any material addressing homosexuality or bisexuality as "obscene."*

**ALSO KNOWN AS:** *Miller v. California*; *Paris Adult Theatre I v. Slaton*
**LOCALE:** Washington, D.C.
**CATEGORIES:** Laws, acts, and legal history; publications

### SUMMARY OF EVENT

In the landmark case of *Roth v. United States* (1957), the U.S. Supreme Court held that the First Amendment did not protect obscene materials. Thereafter, the problem became how to define "obscene," so that these materials could be regulated while protected materials, even pornographic ones, remained free. For a time, the explicit test was whether the publication was "utterly without redeeming social value," part of the 1966 definition in the "Fanny Hill" case, *Memoirs v. Massachusetts*. Because almost everything can be construed to have at least some social value, the *Memoirs* test was a liberal standard that allowed regulation of only the hardest-core obscenity.

With the addition of new, more conservative justices, the Court on June 21, 1973, enunciated a more restrictive standard in *Miller v. California*. This case arose when a dealer mailed an unsolicited advertisement for adult materials to a California citizen. In place of the *Memoirs* test, *Miller* announced a new test to define "obscene": The trier of fact must ask

(a) whether the average person, applying contemporary community standards, would find that the

work, taken as a whole, appeals to the prurient interest; (b) whether the work depicts or describes, in a patently offensive way, sexual conduct specifically defined by the applicable state law; and (c) whether this work, taken as a whole, lacks serious literary, artistic, political, or scientific value.

The third prong of the definition decreases the opportunity for a pornographic piece to be "saved" because of its contribution to society. Whereas under *Memoirs* the item would be protected if it had any social value at all, after *Miller* it must have "serious" value of a limited type. Although the second prong requires the forbidden acts to be described with specificity, in practice this standard has been very low, to the point that some judges find the state laws to be impermissibly vague.

It is upon the first prong, however, that debate continues to dwell. It establishes "community standards" as the test to find material obscene, narrowing the earlier practice. *Jacobellis v. Ohio* (1964) said that the standards of the *Roth* test were national, not state or local. (*Jacobellis* is also the case that contains Justice Potter Stewart's famous comment about obscenity, "I know it when I see it.") *Miller* expressly rejects this interpretation, allowing the jury to consider the standards of California instead.

Announced at the same time as *Miller* was another obscenity case, *Paris Adult Theatre I v. Slaton*. In *Paris*, an adult movie theater in Atlanta was prohibited from showing films the owner conceded were obscene. The defendant argued that because these films were shown only to consenting adults, their screening was protected. The argument highlights a significant legal difference between *Miller* and *Paris*: While *Miller* addressed the case of unwilling viewers of obscene materials, in *Paris*, everyone in the theater had paid to view the films in full knowledge of their content.

The Supreme Court had earlier, in *Stanley v. Georgia* (1969), held unconstitutional a Georgia

---

### *PARIS ADULT THEATRE I v. SLATON* (1973): KEY PASSAGES

*From the Court's opinion:* We categorically disapprove the theory, apparently adopted by the trial judge, that obscene, pornographic films acquire constitutional immunity from state regulation simply because they are exhibited for consenting adults only. This holding was properly rejected by the Georgia Supreme Court. Although we have often pointedly recognized the high importance of the state interest in regulating the exposure of obscene materials to juveniles and unconsenting adults, this Court has never declared these to be the only legitimate state interests permitting regulation of obscene material. The States have a long-recognized legitimate interest in regulating the use of obscene material in local commerce and in all places of public accommodation, as long as these regulations do not run afoul of specific constitutional prohibitions. . . . In particular, we hold that there are legitimate state interests at stake in stemming the tide of commercialized obscenity, even assuming it is feasible to enforce effective safeguards against exposure to juveniles and to passersby. Rights and interests "other than those of the advocates are involved." These include the interest of the public in the quality of life and the total community environment, the tone of commerce in the great city centers, and, possibly, the public safety itself. The Hill-Link Minority Report of the Commission on Obscenity and Pornography indicates that there is at least an arguable correlation between obscene material and crime. Quite apart from sex crimes, however, there remains one problem of large proportions aptly described by Professor Bickel: "It concerns the tone of the society, the mode, or to use terms that have perhaps greater currency, the style and quality of life, now and in the future. A man may be entitled to read an obscene book in his room, or expose himself indecently there. We should protect his privacy. But if he demands a right to obtain the books and pictures he wants in the market, and to foregather in public places—discreet, if you will, but accessible to all—with others who share his tastes, then to grant him his right is to affect the world about the rest of us, and to impinge on other privacies. Even supposing that each of us can, if he wishes, effectively avert the eye and stop the ear (which, in truth, we cannot), what is commonly read and seen and heard and done intrudes upon us all, want it or not." . . .

*Brennan's dissent:* If, as the Court today assumes, "a state legislature may act on the assumption that commerce in obscene books, or public exhibitions focused on obscene conduct, have a tendency to exert a corrupting and debasing impact leading to antisocial behavior," then it is hard to see how state-ordered regimentation of our minds can ever be forestalled. For if a State, in an effort to maintain or create a particular moral tone, may prescribe what its citizens cannot read or cannot see, then it would seem to follow that in pursuit of that same objective a State could decree that its citizens must read certain books or must view certain films. However laudable its goal—and that is obviously a question on which reasonable minds may differ—the State cannot proceed by means that violate the Constitution.

---

law that prohibited the private possession of obscene materials to be viewed in the privacy of one's home. In *Paris*, however, the Court rejected any extension of *Stanley* to support a claim that "obscene, pornographic films acquire constitutional immunity from state regulation simply because they are exhibited for consenting adults only." Because the state has an interest in "the quality of life and the total community environment," it could restrict commerce in activities that were reasonably believed to have unsavory secondary effects.

The more general significance of *Paris* perhaps rests in the dissent by Justice William J. Brennan. The original author of the *Roth* opinion, he had come to the reluctant conclusion that any attempt to define "obscenity" would be unconstitutionally

vague. Because obscenity that could be regulated could not be reliably separated from "other sexually oriented but constitutionally protected speech," the entire effort should be abandoned. "Booksellers, theatre owners, and the reading and viewing public" are provided no notice beforehand about what is criminally obscene and thus cannot act to avoid that material until it has been identified by a majority of the justices of the Supreme Court.

### SIGNIFICANCE

Reliance upon local community standards provided a new tool to antipornography crusaders. Once personal jurisdiction over a national distributor has been obtained through advertising or mail order, it becomes subject to the most restrictive local standards in the country. This has led to what has been called "the lowest common denominator" standard for sexually explicit materials, including materials showing same-gender sexuality.

The use of local community standards is not unlimited. While it has been judged appropriate to label an item "obscene," national standards continue to apply when determining whether a work lacks serious value (see *Pope v. Illinois*, 1987). Another limiting factor is the Court's practice of *de novo* review for material to determine if it is obscene, which undercuts the application of local community standards. The Court often avoids the direct conflict of substituting its own judgment in place of the findings of a local trier by focusing on the third, or national standard, prong.

The advancing edge of obscenity law will continue to be the issue of the community standard. If videos and other materials can be downloaded directly from the Internet, it is an unresolved question as to which "local community" standards should be applied to find the material obscene, perhaps undermining the settled definitions of *Miller*. Further, if these materials are distributed solely electronically, it is unlikely that the community secondary impacts that allowed regulation of obscene materials in *Paris* still apply.

*—James M. Donovan*

**FURTHER READING**

Hixson, Richard F. *Pornography and the Justices: The Supreme Court and the Intractable Obscenity Problem*. Carbondale: Southern Illinois University Press, 1996.

Marcuse, Ludwig. *Obscene: The History of an Indignation*. Translated by Karen Gershon. London: MacGibbon & Kee, 1965.

Strossen, Nadine. *Defending Pornography: Free Speech, Sex, and the Fight for Women's Rights*. New York: New York University Press, 2000.

## August, 1973
# AMERICAN BAR ASSOCIATION CALLS FOR REPEAL OF LAWS AGAINST CONSENSUAL SEX

*The American Bar Association's passage of a resolution calling for the repeal of all laws criminalizing noncommercial sexual conduct between consenting adults represented the organization's first step in a long internal struggle over support for gay and lesbian rights. The ABA did not support laws against sexual orientation discrimination until it passed a resolution in 1989.*

**LOCALE:** Chicago, Illinois
**CATEGORIES:** Laws, acts, and legal history; organizations and institutions; civil rights; crime

### SUMMARY OF EVENT

The American Bar Association (ABA) is the American legal profession's largest national organization. At its annual meeting in August, 1973, the ABA's house of delegates passed a carefully worded resolution that urged state legislatures to "repeal all laws which classify as criminal conduct any form of noncommercial sexual contact between consenting adults in private, saving only those portions which protect minors or public decorum."

Many time lines of GLBT history trumpet this rather cryptic and equivocal resolution under such headings as "ABA Recommends Repeal of State Sodomy Laws" or "ABA Urges States to Repeal All Sodomy Laws." The ABA's action is often listed in conjunction with the historic 1973 decision of the American Psychiatric Association to declassify homosexuality as a mental illness. However, the ABA's resolution was much more ambiguous and its impact far more limited.

Although the report of the ABA section that drafted the 1973 resolution focused on the repeal of sodomy laws (in addition to the repeal of laws relating to adultery and fornication), it is not entirely clear whether this focus was evident to all: The

word "sodomy" never actually appeared in the resolution. Nor was the resolution's impact very far-ranging. Indeed, it was not even included in the summary of the convention proceedings reported in the *ABA Journal*.

Moreover, the section's report made it clear that the purpose of the 1973 resolution was "neither to advocate nor condemn any particular form of sexual activity between consenting adults." The resolution was based on the Model Penal Code developed by the prestigious American Law Institute (ALI) in 1955 in an effort to modernize state legal codes. In calling for the decriminalization of sodomy laws, the ALI failed to demonstrate any support for homosexual rights. Rather, its recommendation (which passed by a narrow margin) was rooted in concerns that sodomy statutes reflected no valid governmental interest, required intrusive police investigations, were enforced in an arbitrary and discriminatory manner, and undermined public respect for the law because many Americans (both heterosexual and homosexual) engaged in sodomy.

### SIGNIFICANCE

Until 1962, when Illinois became the first state to repeal its statutes, all states had some form of sodomy laws. During the 1970's, twenty more states repealed their laws. However, the ABA played no active role in these campaigns. Although the ABA would become an advocate of GLBT rights in the 1990's, during the 1970's and 1980's it repeatedly voted down resolutions calling for antidiscrimination laws.

In 1975, two years after the purportedly groundbreaking 1973 resolution, the ABA's house of delegates voted 158-97 to table a more specific resolution calling for the organization to urge state legislatures to prohibit discrimination based on sexual orientation in employment, housing, and public accommodations. In 1976 an identical resolution was tabled as not being "germane to the purposes of the American Bar Association." Likewise, in 1980 the ABA's board of governors refused to support an amendment to the 1952 McCarran-Walter Immigration and Nationality Act. The amendment would have allowed gays and lesbians to enter the United States as out gays and lesbians and obtain citizenship.

In 1983 the ABA's section of Individual Rights and Responsibilities (IRR), which had sponsored all of these resolutions, created the Committee on the Rights of Gay People. Dan Bradley, president of the Federal Legal Services Corporation and the nation's highest-ranking out gay official, served as chair. Despite platform speeches by Bradley and Robert E. Bauman, a conservative Republican who took the occasion to acknowledge his homosexuality publicly, the ABA's house of delegates again rejected (158-134) a resolution calling for state legislatures to prohibit discrimination based on sexual orientation. The vote followed an emotional debate in which opponents condemned homosexuality as "a crime against nature" that contradicted "fundamental and basic moral laws."

Meanwhile, the ABA played *no* role in the pioneering antisodomy and gay-and-lesbian-rights cases brought at the state or national levels by other legal advocates. Despite its 1973 resolution, the ABA did not participate in the historic 1983 conference hosted by the Lambda Legal Defense and Education Fund and the American Civil Liberties Union (ACLU), whose purpose was to develop a national strategy for eradicating sodomy laws. Nor did the ABA participate in the subsequent Ad Hoc Taskforce to Challenge Sodomy Laws. Similarly, in 1986 the ABA failed to file an amicus curiae (friend of the court) brief opposing Georgia's sodomy laws in the infamous *Bowers v. Hardwick* (1986) case, in which the U.S. Supreme Court upheld the constitutionality of sodomy laws.

In July, 1985, after another emotional debate, the ABA's house of delegates narrowly defeated (161-152) another antidiscrimination resolution, despite the authors having bowed to ABA conservatives by explicitly refusing to endorse homosexuality. The failed resolution stated that the ABA, "consistent with its longstanding opposition to unjust deprivation of civil rights and without approving or endorsing homosexual activity, urges the Federal, state, and local governments" to prohibit discrimination based on sexual orientation.

In 1987, however, the ABA passed a resolution condemning hate crimes based on prejudice against the victim's race, religion, sexual orientation, or minority status. Then, in 1989, after a lengthy and acrimonious debate (and against the recommendation of its board of governors), the house of delegates finally passed an antidiscrimination resolution. By a vote of 251-121, the ABA called on federal, state, and local governments to "enact legislation, subject to such exceptions as may be appropriate, prohibiting discrimination on the basis of sexual orientation in employment, housing and public accommodations." Although the resolution did not define what exceptions would be allowed, a background report said the proposal "would not preclude certain standard exceptions frequently found in civil rights legislation," such as allowing discrimination in the case of owner-occupied rental housing or small companies.

In 1992, the National Gay and Lesbian Law Association (founded in 1988) became an officially affiliated organization with a seat in the ABA's house of delegates. During the 1990's the ABA passed several significant resolutions in favor of gay and lesbian rights. These included amending the ABA's law school standards to prohibit discrimination based on sexual orientation; urging local bar associations to study bias against gays and lesbians in the legal profession; and opposing restrictions on child custody, visitation, and adoption based on sexual orientation. In 2004, the ABA lobbied against the proposed constitutional amendment that would have banned same-gender marriage, although it had not officially endorsed gay and lesbian marriage.

In its amicus curiae brief on behalf of *Lawrence v. Texas* (2003), the landmark Texas case in which the Supreme Court finally struck down state sodomy laws as unconstitutional, the ABA proudly presented itself as having been at the forefront of the campaign for GLBT rights. However, the historical record reveals a far more ambivalent story. Activists suffered many defeats before they succeeded in changing the ABA's official policy and practices. In the end, the ABA's obscure 1973 resolution represented only a faltering first step, rather than a significant watershed, in the legal establishment's attitude toward gay and lesbian rights. Indeed, most historical accounts barely mention it.

—*L. Mara Dodge*

**FURTHER READING**

Cain, Patricia A. *Rainbow Rights: The Role of Lawyers and Courts in the Lesbian and Gay Civil Rights Movement.* Cambridge, Mass.: Westview Press, 2000.

Eskridge, William N. *Gaylaw: Challenging the Apartheid of the Closet.* Cambridge, Mass.: Harvard University Press, 1999.

Murdoch, Joyce, and Deb Price. *Courting Justice: Gay Men and Lesbians v. the Supreme Court.* New York: Basic Books, 2001.

Rubenstein, William B. *Cases and Materials on Sexual Orientation and the Law: Lesbians, Gay Men,* *and the Law.* 2d ed. St. Paul, Minn.: West, 1997.

_____. *Lesbians, Gay Men, and the Law.* New York: New Press, 1993.

**SEE ALSO:** May 6, 1868: Kertbeny Coins the Terms "Homosexual" and "Heterosexual"; 1885: United Kingdom Criminalizes "Gross Indecency"; Jan. 12, 1939: *Thompson v. Aldredge* Dismisses Sodomy Charges Against Lesbians; Sept. 4, 1957: The *Wolfenden Report* Calls for Decriminalizing Private Consensual Sex; 1961: Illinois Legalizes Consensual Homosexual Sex; Jan. 22, 1973: *Roe v. Wade* Legalizes Abortion and Extends Privacy Rights; Oct. 18, 1973: Lambda Legal Authorized to Practice Law; Nov. 17, 1975: U.S. Supreme Court Rules in "Crimes Against Nature" Case; 1986: *Bowers v. Hardwick* Upholds State Sodomy Laws; Jan. 1, 1988: Canada Decriminalizes Sex Practices Between Consenting Adults; 1992-2006: Indians Struggle to Abolish Sodomy Law; June 26, 2003: U.S. Supreme Court Overturns Texas Sodomy Law.

---

## Fall, 1973
# LESBIAN HERSTORY ARCHIVES IS FOUNDED

*The Lesbian Herstory Archives, an all-volunteer organization that preserves lesbian history, distinguishes itself from other archives by accepting material from all lesbians, not just the famous. Also, the archives maintains that its materials can be better cared for and preserved, and their accessibility better ensured, by entrusting them to other lesbians and not to academic or other professional archivists in an academic or other setting.*

**LOCALE:** New York, New York

**CATEGORIES:** Cultural and intellectual history; organizations and institutions; feminism

**KEY FIGURES**

*Joan Nestle* (b. 1940), archives coordinator, author, and professor at Queens College, 1960-1995

*Deborah Edel*, archives coordinator and psychologist

*Judith Schwarz*, archives coordinator

**SUMMARY OF EVENT**

In the fall of 1973, a few lesbian members of the Gay Academic Union, which had been meeting in New York City, formed a separate consciousness-raising group that conceived the idea of an archive for lesbian history. Joan Nestle and Deborah Edel served as the first coordinators of the newly founded Lesbian Herstory Archives (LHA) and were joined

---

### LESBIAN HERSTORY ARCHIVES: STATEMENT OF PRINCIPLES

- All Lesbian women must have access to the Archives; no academic, political or sexual credentials may be required for usage of the collection; race and class must be no barrier for use or inclusion.
- The Archives shall be housed within the community, not on an academic campus that is by definition closed to many women.
- The Archives shall be involved in the political struggles of all Lesbians.
- Archival skills shall be taught, one generation of Lesbians to another, breaking the elitism of traditional archives.
- The community should share in the work of the Archives.
- The Archives will collect the prints of all our lives, not just preserve the records of the famous or the published.
- Funding shall be sought from within the communities the Archives serves, rather than from outside sources.

---

by Judith Schwarz in 1978. They would continue in these roles assisted by a coordinating committee, volunteers, and occasional interns. LHA has always been an all-volunteer organization.

From the beginning, the organization's goal was to preserve material about lesbians in an environment controlled by lesbians. Seeing invisibility as a form of oppression, the organizers wanted to rectify the silence about lesbian lives that characterized mainstream archives. In particular, LHA sought to preserve and share the stories of any lesbian who wished to contribute materials. Nestle was especially concerned that the history of certain lesbian communities was fast disappearing, particularly the experiences of the working class butch/femme bar culture; Nestle wanted to preserve their memories.

The archives' initial collection consisted of personal papers and books donated by Nestle and Edel. Housed in their Upper West Side apartment's pantry beginning in 1974, LHA opened for community use in 1976. In 1980, the organization incorporated as a nonprofit organization using the name Lesbian Herstory Educational Foundation, Inc. Volunteers offered speaking engagements, first bringing samples of materials and later presenting slide shows. A series titled "At Home with the archives" featured monthly readings, talks, films, and presentations that drew audiences ranging from 10 to 150 people. LHA also began issuing a regular newsletter. Through these outreach efforts, the archives reached lesbians who later donated letters, photographs, diaries, and other items. The organization also built its volunteer base, in part through weekly "work nights" that welcomed anyone who wanted to assist with filing, sorting, and mailing.

The collection quickly filled the majority of Nestle's apartment. Some items were moved to offsite storage, making retrieval difficult. The crowded file drawers on site also posed challenges to visitors. Recognizing the need for more space, LHA began a fund-raising drive in 1985 to raise money for its own building. With the help of contributions and a bank loan, LHA purchased a four-story brownstone in Park Slope, Brooklyn. Lesbian architects and construction workers renovated it and made it wheelchair accessible. Three of the levels have been filled with archival materials, while the top floor holds a caretaker's apartment. LHA reopened in the new location in 1993. By June of 1996, the archives had paid off the building and held a mortgage-burning party to celebrate.

LHA's guiding principles emphasize that any lesbian may use the materials; however, no questions about sexual orientation are asked of visitors. Others may also use the collections, although certain items were contributed with the stipulation that no man ever see them. Although individuals must make an appointment to visit, no academic credentials are necessary. While materials at LHA have been used to create books, films, and artwork, they are also available simply for browsing. To facilitate community access, LHA is not located on an academic campus. In order to maintain autonomy, it does not accept any funding from mainstream or government sources. Rather, the organization is supported by grassroots fund-raising efforts and occasional grants from radical funding sources.

## SIGNIFICANCE

The Lesbian Herstory Archives began its collections before mainstream institutions had started to acknowledge the importance of preserving lesbian materials. In addition to asserting the significance of lesbian lives, the organization was notable for its approach. Rather than employing professional librarians or archivists, the coordinators taught themselves the archivists' craft, sometimes by trial and error. Part of the LHA mission has been accessibility to all lesbians, and they have understood that some women would be intimidated by a more traditional archive, which accounts for LHA's location in a neighborhood rather than on an academic campus.

Joan Nestle defended this approach when people such as Jim Monahan from Chicago's Gay Academic Union expressed disagreement. Monahan believed the preservation of lesbian and gay historical materials should take place within mainstream institutions, where academic experts could develop collections and only qualified researchers would be permitted to use them. LHA's position, in contrast, was that mainstream institutions had yet to acknowledge the importance of these materials and that even if such interest arose it might be considered only a fad. LHA maintained that its materials would be better cared for and their accessibility better ensured by entrusting them to other lesbians.

LHA houses more than twenty thousand books, twelve thousand photos, three hundred special collections, sixteen hundred periodicals, thirteen hundred subject files, and miles of film and video footage. Unlike many archives, LHA also accepts donations of objects such as posters, T-shirts, buttons, personal recordings, art, film, and memorabilia. While other archives are typically selective about what materials they add to their collections, LHA accepts any contribution from any lesbian. In addition to providing the community with access to the materials, LHA offers events and a safe place for women to gather.

—*Kathleen Liddle*

## FURTHER READING

Cohen, Mark Francis. "Neighborhood Report: Park Slope; In Lesbian Archive, Education and Sanctuary." *The New York Times*, April 7, 1996, p. 9.

Cvetkovich, Ann. *An Archive of Feelings: Trauma, Sexuality, and Lesbian Public Cultures.* Durham, N.C.: Duke University Press, 2003.

_____. "In the Archives of Lesbian Feeling: Documentary and Popular Culture." *Camera Obscura* 17, no. 1 (2002): 107-147.

Edel, Deborah. "Building Cultural Memories: The Work of the Lesbian Herstory Archives." In *The New Our Right to Love: A Lesbian Resource Book,* edited by Ginny Vida. New York: Touchstone Books, 1996.

Lesbian Herstory Archives. http://www.lesbian herstoryarchives.org.

Nestle, Joan. "The Will to Remember: The Lesbian Herstory Archives of New York." *Journal of Homosexuality* 34, nos. 3/4 (1998): 225-235.

Strock, Carren. "Three-Dimensional Herstory." *Ms.* 3, no. 1 (1992): 59.

Thistlethwaite, Polly J. "Building 'A Home of Our Own': The Construction of the Lesbian Herstory Archives." In *Daring to Find Our Names: The Search for Lesbigay Library History*, edited by James V. Carmichael, Jr. Westport, Conn.: Greenwood Press, 1998.

_____. "The Lesbian Herstory Archives." In *Gay and Lesbian Library Service*, edited by Ellen Greenblatt. Jefferson, N.C.: McFarland, 1990.

_____, ed. and comp. "An Activist's Guide to Lesbian History." http://manta.library.colostate .edu/research/gnl/NotJustPassingThrough _merge.pdf.

**SEE ALSO:** 1952: ONE, Inc., Is Founded; 1975: First Gay and Lesbian Archives Is Founded; Aug., 1991: Leather Archives and Museum Is Founded.

## October 18, 1973
# LAMBDA LEGAL AUTHORIZED TO PRACTICE LAW

*The Lambda Legal Defense and Education Fund, a nonprofit, public interest law firm for lesbians, gays, and people with HIV-AIDS, argues cases with the potential of establishing positive legal precedents. Authorized to practice law by the New York Court of Appeals, Lambda Legal also was the first gay rights organization to receive tax-exempt status from the U.S. government.*

**ALSO KNOWN AS:** Lambda Legal
**LOCALE:** New York, New York
**CATEGORIES:** Civil rights; government and
    politics; laws, acts, and legal history;
    organizations and institutions

### SUMMARY OF EVENT

Lesbians and gays have yet to obtain legal rights that parallel the legal rights of heterosexuals, people of color, and, to some extent, women and those with disabilities, in areas of housing and accommodation, education, employment, marriage rights, medical care, and hospital visitation. Prior to 1973, the year Lambda Legal Defense and Education Fund was permitted to practice law, the only organization with a national *gay* identity was the Mattachine Society. The group, in 1958, won a case against the U.S. postal service, which had restricted the mailing and receipt of gay-themed publications. The only organization of the time with a national *lesbian* identity was the Daughters of Bilitis.

During the social upheaval of the 1960's, many gay (and some lesbian) groups originated on campuses and in large cities across the United States. While these were very important social organizations, a concerted effort to address the legal rights denied to lesbians and gays seemed to be lacking, and no national organizing was being done to address legal issues.

The creation of Lambda Legal is historic, for its founding in 1973 filled a profound legal gap. Lambda would emphasize a number of major issues, including the need for legal representation by a counsel who understands lesbians and gays, the need to encourage lesbians and gays to enter the legal profession, and the need for, and impact of, activism in the legal arena.

The founding of Lambda Legal was in and of itself a legal battle to establish Lambda as a nonprofit organization. Lambda had been denied by a New York court the right to exist as a nonprofit legal organization on the grounds that its "stated purposes 'are on their face neither benevolent nor charitable, nor, in any event, is there a demonstrated need for this corporation.'" The court further stated that it "does not appear that discrimination against homosexuals, which undoubtedly exists, operates to deprive them of legal representation."

On October 18, 1973, after many battles, the original denial for nonprofit status was overturned by the New York Court of Appeals in the case *In re Thom.* In July of 1974, the Internal Revenue Service granted to Lambda Legal its tax-exempt status, the first gay and lesbian rights organization to receive tax-exempt status from the U.S. government. Lambda Legal, thus, was established as a legal nonprofit organization, and it adopted the following mission statement: "Lambda Legal is a national organization committed to achieving full recognition of the civil rights of lesbians, gay men, bisexuals, transgender people and those with HIV through impact litigation, education, and public policy work."

### SIGNIFICANCE

The Lambda Legal Defense and Education Fund has had a profound impact on the LGBT community and on those living with HIV or AIDS. Lambda Legal, now a well-established organization with a national headquarters, has a staff of more than eighty in four regional offices, and hosts of volunteer attorneys. Its goals are the same as they were in 1973: recognizing that lesbians and gays deserve the same human, civil, and legal rights as the general population.

Lambda has worked since its founding to gain for

the LGBT community fundamental human and legal rights, including fighting discrimination in housing and public accommodation, employment and domestic partnership, and the treatment and care of people with HIV-AIDS. Lambda also has argued cases involving U.S. immigration and asylum laws, international human rights for gays and lesbians, First Amendment issues, and legal benefits for survivors of the terrorist attacks of September 11, 2001, and the partners of those who died because of those attacks. Additionally, Lambda Legal represents clients who have been discharged or are facing discharge from the military, argues cases regarding the public funding of religious groups, represents clients who have faced transgender discrimination, and works on reproductive rights and adoption and family rights.

Because of the long history of discrimination against lesbians and gays, all of Lambda Legal's litigation is important, but a few cases have had a major impact, including the following: In 1981, the Department of Defense changed its policy of automatically giving lesbian or gay servicemembers a dishonorable discharge, regardless of the individual's service record, to a policy of honorably discharging a servicemember, barring any other circumstance that would warrant a discharge of less than honorable or general. In 1993, New York City became the largest municipality to offer domestic partnership benefits to its employees. In 1995, second-parent adoptions became legal in New York State.

In 2003, Lambda played a crucial role in the U.S. Supreme Court's decision in *Lawrence v. Texas*, which invalidated sodomy laws in the United States. Since the November 2, 2004, election, a great deal of Lambda's time and energy has been devoted to arguing for the legal right for lesbians and gays to marry and to challenging the bans against same-gender marriage approved in eleven states during this same election.

"Since 1973," its Web site states, "Lambda Legal has challenged [U.S.] courts and [the U.S.] constitutional system to open up the promise of liberty and equal treatment to lesbians, gay men, and people with HIV-AIDS. In the process, we have won significant victories both in and out of the courtroom. By widely publicizing our cases, we break the silence that has traditionally surrounded our lives and tell the real stories about ourselves."

—*Mary F. Stuck*

## FURTHER READING

Bernbach, Jeffrey M. *Job Discrimination II: How to Fight, How to Win*. Englewood Cliffs, N.J.: Voir Dire Press, 1998.

Cain, Patricia A. *Rainbow Rights: The Role of Lawyers and Courts in the Lesbian and Gay Civil Rights Movement*. Boulder, Colo.: Westview Press, 2000.

Curry, Hayden, Denis Clifford, and Frederick Hertz. *A Legal Guide for Lesbian and Gay Couples*. 11th ed. Berkeley, Calif.: Nolo Press, 2002.

Halley, Janet E. *Don't: A Reader's Guide to the Military's Anti-Gay Policy*. Durham, N.C.: Duke University Press, 1999.

Lambda Legal Defense and Education Fund. http://www.lambdalegal.org.

Nava, Michael, and Robert Dawidoff. *Created Equal: Why Gay Rights Matter to America*. New York: St. Martin's Press, 1995.

Pinello, Daniel R. *Gay Rights and American Law*. New York: Cambridge University Press, 2003.

"Same-Sex Marriage: A Selective Bibliography of the Legal Literature." Law Library, Rutgers School of Law. http://law-library.rutgers.edu/SSM.html.

**SEE ALSO:** Apr. 27, 1953: U.S. President Eisenhower Prohibits Federal Employment of Lesbians and Gays; 1972-1973: Local Governments Pass Antidiscrimination Laws; 1973: National Gay Task Force Is Formed; June 21, 1973: U.S. Supreme Court Supports Local Obscenity Laws; Aug., 1973: American Bar Association Calls for Repeal of Laws Against Consensual Sex; Apr. 6, 1991: Asian Lesbians and Gays Protest Lambda Fund-Raiser; June 26, 2003: U.S. Supreme Court Overturns Texas Sodomy Law.

# December 15, 1973
# HOMOSEXUALITY IS DELISTED BY THE APA

*The American Psychiatric Association removed "homosexuality" from its list of mental disorders, largely ending the social and cultural labeling of homosexuality as a disorder and disease and the labeling of lesbians and gays as mentally ill. The delisting has led to wider discussions of the origins not only of homosexuality but also sexuality in general.*

**LOCALE:** United States
**CATEGORIES:** Health and medicine; science; organizations and institutions; publications

**KEY FIGURES**
*Evelyn Hooker* (1907-1996), psychologist, conducted groundbreaking studies on sexuality and mental health
*Alfred Kinsey* (1894-1956), sexologist, conducted studies on sexual behavior and found all sexual expression normal and widespread
*Franklin Kameny* (b. 1925), gay rights activist who confronted, with Gittings, the APA
*Barbara Gittings* (b. 1932), lesbian rights activist who, with Kameny, confronted the APA and who exhibited material on lesbians and gays at APA conferences

**SUMMARY OF EVENT**
On December 15, 1973, the board of trustees of the American Psychiatric Association (APA) voted 13-0 with two abstentions to remove "homosexuality" from its list of mental disorders. The APA had included the classification in 1952. The 1973 vote effectively lifted the burden and stigma of the mental-illness label from gays and lesbians and laid the groundwork for the removal of "homosexuality" from international health typology.

The board's vote was followed by a vote of the entire APA membership, which supported the board of trustees' decision by 5,854 (58 percent) to 3,810 (37 percent). In 1992, "homosexuality" was removed from the list of mental disorders in the publi-

cation *International Statistical Classification of Diseases and Related Health Problems* (ICD), published by the World Health Organization, and from the diagnostic manuals of other national associations, such as the Chinese Psychiatric Association in 2001.

This vote was the culmination of years of work by GLBT rights advocates. In the mid-1960's, Franklin Kameny, a scientist by profession and president of the Mattachine Society of Washington, fought openly against the listing and confronted the APA in 1970. Kameny and others, including long-time lesbian activist Barbara Gittings, disrupted the annual APA conference in San Francisco and demanded that the APA include a panel on homosexuality at its next conference in 1971, which it did. The APA delisted "homosexuality" two years later.

The decision to delist was more than simply a scientific one. It was also a political and social decision that has had far-reaching implications in the United States and around the world. It laid the foundation for the movement to include those discriminated against because of "sexual orientation" as a protected group in civil rights laws.

The APA is a professional organization of physicians trained in psychiatry whose members represent not only the United States but other countries. The association publishes various professional journals and pamphlets, as well as the *Diagnostic and Statistical Manual of Mental Disorders*, better known as the DSM. The DSM codifies generally accepted psychiatric conditions and the guidelines for diagnosing those conditions. It is the most frequently used handbook in the United States in diagnosing mental disorders, and it is used in the training of all mental-health professionals, not just psychiatrists. This book has seen a fourth edition; hence, the most common reference to it in current literature is DSM-IV or, simply, DSM. Another version is the "Text Revision" of the DSM-IV, also known as the DSM-IV-TR. Although widely accepted among psychiatrists, psychologists, counselors, and other mental-health professionals, the manual has proved controversial in its past listing of certain characteristics as mental disorders, such as homosexuality.

The basis for labeling homosexuality a mental disorder and disease is found in the psychoanalytic professions. In 1896, Sigmund Freud began to publish his ideas on psychoanalysis. Psychoanalysis, dealing as it did with sexual urges that are often unconscious or subconscious, was frequently used in the "treatment" of homosexuality. Also, much psychoanalytic discussion was devoted to the issue of homosexuality as a paraphilia, or sexual disorder. For example, psychoanalysts theorized that either castration anxiety or a family with a dominant mother was the basis for male homosexuality.

The pathologizing of homosexuality increased the number of individuals placed in mental hospitals and in prisons, the places where studies concerning homosexuality in men were carried out. In addition to subjecting patients and prisoners to studies of sexuality, researchers attempted to use a variety of therapies to "cure" homosexuality specifically, including aversion therapy, nausea-producing drugs, castration, electric shock, brain surgery, and breast amputations.

The post-World War II era is considered the start of the movement by researchers and others to declassify homosexuality as a psychological disorder. Evelyn Hooker, a psychologist at the University of California, Los Angeles, carried out groundbreaking studies on nonpatient groups of gays in 1953 and revealed many misconceptions held by mental-health practitioners. In particular, Hooker's studies discovered that there was no specific psychopathology linked to homosexuality and that there was as much psychological diversity in the homosexually focused group as in the group that was heterosexually focused.

Similarly, Alfred Kinsey's reports, *Sexual Behavior in the Human Male* (1948) and *Sexual Behavior in the Human Female* (1953), also revolutionized thinking on sexuality, and on homosexuality. In particular, the reports found a high occurrence of same-gender sexual behavior in both men and women. Kinsey also developed a now-famous scale of hu-

man sexual behavior that measured, or ranked, behavior that is exclusively same-gender to that which is exclusively opposite-gender. The Kinsey Scale also includes gradations between extremes.

## Significance

Although the concepts of "curing homosexuality" or "homosexuality as a disease" have been, for the most part, dismissed by mental-health professionals, there persists a movement backed by the Christian Right in the United States that continues to regard homosexuality as a disorder, a disorder curable through "conversion" or "reparative" therapies. Later resolutions opposing such therapies on scientific and ethical grounds have been overwhelmingly passed by the American Psychiatric Association, American Counseling Association, and other mental-health professions.

In 2003, a gay person became the president of the American Counseling Association, the first out gay or lesbian person to be elected as the chief officer of a major mental-health professional group. His election occurred exactly thirty years after "homosexuality" was removed from the DSM as a mental disorder.

*—Mark Pope*

## Further Reading

Bayer, Ronald. *Homosexuality and American Psychiatry: The Politics of Diagnosis*. New York: Basic Books, 1981.

Hooker, Evelyn. "The Adjustment of the Male Overt Homosexual." *Journal of Projective Techniques* 21 (1957): 18-31.

Kameny, Frank. "Gay Liberation and Psychiatry." In *The Homosexual Dialectic*, edited by Joseph A. McCaffrey. Englewood Cliffs, N.J.: Prentice-Hall, 1972.

Kinsey, Alfred C., Wardell B. Pomeroy, and Clyde E. Martin. *Sexual Behavior in the Human Male*. Oxford, England: Saunders, 1948.

Kinsey, Alfred C., Wardell B. Pomeroy, Clyde E. Martin, and Paul H. Gebhard. *Sexual Behavior in the Human Female*. Oxford, England: Saunders, 1953.

Minton, Henry L. *Departing from Deviance: A His-*

*tory of Homosexual Rights and Emancipatory Science in America*. Chicago: University of Chicago Press, 2002.

**SEE ALSO:** May 6, 1868: Kertbeny Coins the Terms "Homosexual" and "Heterosexual"; 1869: Westphal Advocates Medical Treatment for Sexual Inversion; 1897: Ellis Publishes *Sexual Inversion*; May 14, 1897: Hirschfeld Founds the Scientific-Humanitarian Committee; 1905: Freud Rejects Third-Sex Theory; 1929: Davis's Research Identifies Lesbian Sexuality as Com-

mon and Normal; 1948: Kinsey Publishes *Sexual Behavior in the Human Male*; 1952: APA Classifies Homosexuality as a Mental Disorder; 1953: Kinsey Publishes *Sexual Behavior in the Human Female*; 1953-1957: Evelyn Hooker Debunks Beliefs That Homosexuality Is a "Sickness"; 1955: Daughters of Bilitis Founded as First National Lesbian Group in United States; 1971: Kameny Is First Out Candidate for U.S. Congress; Apr. 20, 2001: Chinese Psychiatric Association Removes Homosexuality from List of Mental Disorders.

## 1974
# BISEXUAL FORUM IS FOUNDED

*Bisexual researcher and medical doctor Fritz Klein created the Bisexual Forum as a support and discussion group that also helped his research into the life experiences of bisexuals. The forum was one of the first groups for bisexuals in the United States, opening the door for bisexuals in the closet.*

**LOCALE:** New York, New York
**CATEGORY:** Organizations and institutions

**KEY FIGURES**
*Fritz Klein* (b. 1932), Bisexual Forum founder
*Chuck Mishaan*, Bisexual Forum discussion
    leader

**SUMMARY OF EVENT**
In many ways, the bisexual movement's history mirrors that of the gay and lesbian rights movement, but on a smaller scale. Few homosexual or bisexual communities existed at the beginning of the twentieth century. Fifty years later, homophile groups such as the Mattachine Society and the Daughters of Bilitis (DOB) began to develop in the United States, but there were no organizations devoted exclusively to bisexuals.

Indeed, just as gays and lesbians felt compelled

to conceal their identities, even from friends involved with other counterculture movements, so too did bisexuals feel obligated to keep their bisexuality secret. Though bisexuals often joined groups such as Mattachine or DOB, they did so identifying as gays or lesbians. It was assumed by many gays and lesbians that bisexuals could pass as straight and "hide" behind their straightness, and heterosexuals generally assumed the opposite: that bisexuals were actually homosexuals.

The gay and lesbian liberation movement proved to be ideal for bisexuals wanting to express their own unique sexuality and for placing bisexuality in the larger framework of gay, lesbian, and transgender issues. Much activity in the gay rights movement of the late 1960's and early to mid-1970's flourished in cities such as New York, San Francisco, and Los Angeles. College and university towns also had some draw, especially those that had connections to the counterculture movement of the era. For example, the Sexual Freedom League at the University of California, Berkeley, hosted orgies for several years. These movements and communities encouraged sexual fluidity, and thus welcomed bisexuals. The early bisexual movement flourished, though, when gays and lesbians began to position themselves as strictly gay or lesbian. Bisexuality was often considered a defection from homosexuality, and bisexuals who needed a group identity initially had few resources because of the stigma.

Fritz Klein, who earned his medical degree in Switzerland in 1971 and became a board certified psychiatrist in 1976, created the Bisexual Forum in 1974. (Other sources have listed the founding as 1975, but Klein has confirmed that the correct year is 1974.) Klein, now considered a pioneer of the bisexual movement, found it difficult to locate resources on bisexuality for his research, so he founded the group as a discussion and support group and also as an aid to his research.

Meetings, held weekly at Klein's home on East 84th Street in New York City, were led most often by Chuck Mishaan, and, as was the case with most bisexual groups at the time, the Bisexual Forum focused primarily on bisexual married men. It would be some years before bisexual women gained ground with their own movement specific to women, or before bisexual groups of both genders began to form. An earlier group had formed, however, during the 1970's. The National Bisexual Liberation Group was founded in 1972, also in New York City.

## SIGNIFICANCE

Klein's book, *The Bisexual Option: A Concept of One-Hundred Percent Intimacy* (1978), represented groundbreaking research into bisexuality and presented the Klein Sexual Orientation Grid. Like Alfred Kinsey's famous scale, Klein's grid identifies an individual's behaviors as homosexual, heterosexual, or bisexual. Klein's grid, however, also allows for change in an individual over time and suggests that a person can be different sexualities at different times in their life.

As the HIV-AIDS epidemic swept into the United States in the early 1980's, and gay and bisexual men found themselves unfairly vilified and inaccurately blamed for spreading the disease to the mainstream population, bisexual groups turned to supporting those with HIV-AIDS. The Bisexual Forum in New York stopped meeting in 1982, but

the forum's founder went on to found a bisexual forum in San Diego that same year, which is still in existence.

—*Jessie Bishop Powell*

## FURTHER READING

Anderlini-D'Onofrio, Serena, ed. *Women and Bisexuality: A Global Perspective*. New York: Haworth Press, 2003.

Beemyn, Brett. *Creating a Place for Ourselves: Lesbian, Gay, and Bisexual Community Histories*. New York: Routledge, 1997.

_____. "The Silence Is Broken: A History of the First Lesbian, Gay, and Bisexual College Student Groups." *Journal of the History of Sexuality* 12, no. 2 (2003): 205-223.

Bisexual Foundation. http://www.bisexual.org.

Fox, Ronald C., ed. *Current Research on Bisexuality*. New York: Harrington Park Press, 2004.

Haeberle, Erwin J., and Rolf Gindorf. *Bisexualities: The Ideology and Practice of Sexual Contact with Both Men and Women*. New York: Continuum, 1998.

Klein, Fritz. *The Bisexual Option: A Concept of One-Hundred Percent Intimacy*. 2d ed. Binghamton, N.Y.: Haworth Press, 1993.

Mishaan, Chuck. "The Bisexual Scene in New York City." *Journal of Homosexuality* 11, nos. 1/2 (December, 1985): 223-226.

Rust, Paula C. Rodríguez, ed. *Bisexuality in the United States: A Social Science Reader*. New York: Columbia University Press, 2000.

Suresha, Ron Jackson, and Pete Chvany, eds. *Bi Men: Coming Out Every Which Way*. New York: Harrington Park Press, 2005.

SEE ALSO: May 6, 1868: Kertbeny Coins the Terms "Homosexual" and "Heterosexual"; 1905: Freud Rejects Third-Sex Theory; June 27-July 2, 1969: Stonewall Rebellion Ignites Modern Gay and Lesbian Rights Movement; June, 1990: BiNet USA Is Formed; Mar.-Apr., 1993: Battelle Sex Study Prompts Conservative Backlash.

# 1974
# *THE FRONT RUNNER* MAKES *THE NEW YORK TIMES* BEST-SELLER LIST

*The first gay-themed novel to make* The New York Times *best-seller list,* The Front Runner *helped open the door for publishers to promote other gay and lesbian books.*

**LOCALE:** New York, New York
**CATEGORIES:** Literature; publications

## KEY FIGURES

*Patricia Nell Warren* (b. 1936), author and editor
*John Hawkins*, literary agent

## SUMMARY OF EVENT

The manuscript of my novel *The Front Runner* happened to be in the right place at the right time in 1973, when the U.S. publishing industry was starting to promote gay- and lesbian-themed books openly. Since 1964, I had been working at *Reader's Digest* as a book editor. The digest staff reviewed virtually every English-language title, searching for material to condense. So I was positioned to see the trend develop.

After World War II, gay- and lesbian-themed fiction had emerged low key. Unwritten rules dictated how—and if—they would be presented, marketed, and published. One could not use the "G" word or "L" word on the cover. Big publishers positioned important works such as Gore Vidal's *The City and the Pillar* (1948) as "art." Or they stuck to safer subjects—like ancient times, as in Mary Renault's *Fire from Heaven* (1969). Under this policy, gay and lesbian pulp fiction had flourished since the 1950's. It was the small, hip, independent houses, notably Grove Press, that started publishing edgier works such as John Rechy's *City of Night* (1963).

In the early 1970's, as the post-Stonewall GLBT-rights movement gained momentum and more Americans realized that GLBT political issues were here to stay, the big publishers finally took a giant step. "Niche marketing" had been emerging, and

the "gay book niche" would likely be profitable. Initially, I think, publishers saw this market as a fuzzier, more generalized crossover phenomenon: anybody, gay or straight, who would buy a gay book. They did not see it as the certifiable GLBT-only demographic of today, complete with hard figures on spendable income.

In late 1972, in my own closet, I started writing *The Front Runner* on my lunch hours. It came out of my experiences as a long-distance runner. I had run into other closeted amateur athletes like myself and realized that the subject of gays in sports was a powerful one, still unexplored. I did not think of it as a "gay novel"—I merely hoped that many people would read it.

The book was completed by April, 1973. After literary agent John Hawkins read the manuscript, he told me, "This is a subject whose time has come. I don't think I'll have any trouble placing it." A week later, William Morrow bought the world English-language publishing rights. Significantly, Morrow was the last major U.S. trade publisher that was still independent, so it was free of any pressure from corporate bosses to reject such a book.

The hardcover edition came out in the spring of 1974, supported by Morrow's strong marketing campaign. Morrow was still paying lip service to the rules—the word "gay" was omitted from the blurb and ads. The book was log-lined simply as "a love story." Indeed, the cover art avoided any sexual suggestion—it simply showed a young athlete sitting on a locker room bench. Morrow wanted a dignified approach that avoided any comparison with pulp fiction. The ads ran in *The New York Times* and other mainstream media.

Because of this marketing support and because of the shock value of the theme (real-life athletes would not start coming out until David Kopay in 1975), the book went right onto *The New York Times* best-seller list, becoming the first gay-themed novel to do so. Though it appeared only briefly on the *Times* and *Los Angeles Times* lists, it stuck on the B. Dalton chain store list for some months. The book also had heavy sales to libraries, thanks to a good review in *Library Journal*.

Next came the paperback. Morrow had sold the English-language paperback rights to Bantam Books, which scheduled its mass-market U.S. edition for the spring of 1975. In a letter to my agent, Bantam confided that *The Front Runner* would be its first title to be openly mass-marketed as "gay."

Bantam had looked beyond the GLBT enclaves in big cities, where gay and lesbian (feminist) bookstores were clustered. They suspected, rightly, that there were closeted gay and lesbian people everywhere in the American heartland. They also noted the straight people with a potential interest, like parents of the many GLBT college students who were coming out (Parents and Friends of Lesbians and Gays, PFLAG—now called Parents, Families, and Friends of Lesbians and Gays—was already active). Bantam designed a marketing campaign to reach them. The word "gay" was in the back blurb. The front illustration went a daring step farther than the Morrow cover—it showed *two* athletes in that locker room, one wearing only a towel, and a hint of tension between the two. The picture sent a clear message.

The paperback not only went into chain bookstores but also on book racks in supermarkets, drugstores, airports, and other popular outlets. Gays and lesbians in the Midwest or the Deep South or rural areas of the West could find the book in a local store. Most amazing of all, GLBT people in the military were finding it in their local PX (post exchange), as I learned from a number of fan letters. Military book buyers ordered in bulk and initially paid no attention to the marketing message.

Bantam's strategy worked. The U.S. paperback sold millions of copies in seventeen printings. Bantam also published an edition for the United Kingdom that sold well throughout the Commonwealth market. In the mid-1980's, Penguin/Plume took over the paperback license and issued an additional eleven printings.

## Significance

Today many older women and men buttonhole me at events to describe their feelings on seeing that paperback cover for the first time. One young man from east Tennessee told me how he had bought an old car, and was clearing junk from under the seats, when he found a battered copy of the paperback hidden there. He told me, "All the feelings that I'd had about men for years suddenly crystallized around that book cover, and I knew I was gay."

Meanwhile, I was personally out too—not only on the long-distance running scene but on the *Reader's Digest* staff as well. Surprisingly, the conservative *Reader's Digest* seemed rather proud of my best-seller and wrote it up in the company magazine.

—*Patricia Nell Warren*

## Further Reading

Bergman, David. "American Literature: Gay Male, Post-Stonewall." In *Gay, Lesbian, Bisexual, Transgender, and Queer Encyclopedia*. http://www.glbtq.com/literature/am_lit3_gay_post_stonewall.html.

Warren, Patricia Nell. "Changes in the Wind." *The Advocate*, August 18, 1998, 37-38.

_____. *The Front Runner*. 1974. 20th anniversary paperback ed. Beverly Hills, Calif.: Wildcat Press, 1996.

**See also:** July 4, 1855: Whitman Publishes *Leaves of Grass*; May 25, 1895: Oscar Wilde Is Convicted of Gross Indecency; 1924: Gide Publishes the Signed Edition of *Corydon*; 1939: Isherwood Publishes *Goodbye to Berlin*; 1947-1948: Golden Age of American Gay Literature; 1956: Baldwin Publishes *Giovanni's Room*; 1963: Rechy Publishes *City of Night*; June, 1971: The Gay Book Award Debuts; 1975: First Novel About Coming Out to Parents Is Published; 1980-1981: Gay Writers Form the Violet Quill; May, 1987: *Lambda Rising Book Report* Begins Publication; June 2, 1989: Lambda Literary Award Is Created; 1993: Monette Wins the National Book Award for *Becoming a Man*.

## March 5, 1974
# ANTIGAY AND ANTILESBIAN ORGANIZATIONS BEGIN TO FORM

*In response to a growing GLBT rights movement in North America, conservative, mostly Christian groups organized into a wave of antigay and antilesbian political activism in Canada and the United States. The wave has continued into the twenty-first century, nearly unabated.*

**LOCALE:** Canada; United States

**CATEGORIES:** Organizations and institutions; marches, protests, and riots; government and politics; civil rights; religion

### KEY FIGURES

*Ken Campbell*, Canadian Baptist minister who founded antiabortion and antiobscenity campaigns

*Anita Bryant* (b. 1940), American entertainer who campaigned across North America against gay and lesbian rights

*Fred Phelps* (b. 1929), American pastor of Westboro Baptist Church in Topeka, Kansas

### SUMMARY OF EVENT

In the early 1970's, groups fighting for the civil rights of gays and lesbians saw the Christian Right develop antigay and antilesbian groups in response. One such organization in Canada, the Halton Renaissance Committee, formed in March of 1974 through the efforts of fundamentalist minister Ken Campbell. Angered by a speaking invitation extended by his daughters' school to members of the Hamilton-McMaster Homophile Association, Campbell initially withdrew his children from the school system, organized his neighbors, and refused to pay school taxes.

By 1978, Campbell had organized Renaissance International (now called Renaissance Canada), which sponsored American celebrity and antigay activist Anita Bryant—an entertainer who founded the 1970's "Save Our Children" campaign in

Florida—in a series of prayer rallies on a national tour. The tour, as well as fundamentalist Christian organizing and state repression of GLBT rights, fueled virulent homophobia following the murder of a Toronto shoeshine boy that was linked to "homosexual depravity." In the United States in the same time period, local antigay groups had coalesced into larger organizations, such as Christian Voice, Religious Round Table, and Moral Majority. In the United Kingdom, organizations, such as the Festival of Light, formed from similar origins.

By the 1980's, these evolving groups went beyond antigay activities to promote what they described as a "pro-family" agenda: Through mainstream organizations such as the Christian Coalition and the Promise Keepers, the groups would protest abortion, pornography, and any proposals to reintroduce the Equal Rights Amendment. Drawing on a particular form of homophobia, evangelical Christians drew on a socially conservative ideology to decry the supposed destruction of the nuclear family. More militant and homophobic evangelical groups, such as the Westboro Baptist Church of Topeka, Kansas, founded by Fred Phelps, are now monitored by the Southern Poverty Law Center in Atlanta, Georgia, as hate groups.

This evolving network of organizations made broad media appeals and overt forays into the political realm, but with mixed results. In 1989, Campbell described Renaissance International as a bankrupt religious charity and stopped his fight with Canada's revenue department over the organization's tax-exempt status and questionable participation in various election campaigns against progay candidates. The matter went all the way to Canada's Court of Appeal. In 1991, Campbell registered as a candidate in the Toronto mayoral election, to assist, he said, an antigay candidate in the defeat of two other candidates he classified as progay. In the United States, evangelicals are politically well organized. The late 1970's and early 1980's saw a significant increase in commercial religious broadcasting from these groups as well as involvement in various local and state antigay initiatives.

By the late 1990's, Campbell became director of Canada's Civilized Majority, a coalition of conservative religious groups that in 1998 produced an advertisement that protested a Canadian Supreme Court ruling that Alberta must protect gays and lesbians from discrimination. In 2000, the Ontario Human Rights Commission rejected a complaint that alleged the advertisement produced hatred and discrimination against gays and lesbians.

In 1999, Campbell publicly expressed support for the group Homosexuals Opposed to Pride Extremism (HOPE) and their participation in the 2000 Halton GLBT pride celebration. In the United States in 2004, various religious-right organizations, as well as President George W. Bush, clamored for a vote before the presidential election for an amendment to the U.S. Constitution that would define "marriage" as being between a woman and a man. While the vote did not transpire, the issue did prompt the passing of eleven state initiatives in November of 2004, banning lesbian and gay marriages, civil unions, or both.

## SIGNIFICANCE

The Halton Renaissance Committee continues to have a local, regional, and national impact as well as a relationship to the broader GLBT rights movement. In addition to continued involvement and intervention in local "morality" issues, the committee's successor organization represents a trend in social movement dynamics that typifies liberation struggles. For instance, in 1996, Renaissance Canada—successor to Renaissance International—protested the decision of Milton District High School in Ontario, Canada, to use Joyce Carol Oates's novel *Foxfire: Confessions of a Girl Gang* (1993) because of what opponents viewed as explicit sexual content. Campbell has claimed to have influenced book decisions in a number of cases involving several Canadian schools. In addition, the organization—and Campbell—had ties to a variety of other conservative pro-family organizations.

For the broader GLBT rights movement, the formation of groups such as Renaissance Canada may be a mixed blessing. On the one hand, they represent a conservative response to progressive reforms. On the other hand, they provide an opportunity for the revitalization of GLBT organizations and the potential for wider media exposure of pivotal GLBT rights issues. Extreme organizations such as those of Phelps and vitriolic rhetoric such as that produced by Campbell, often have the effect of mobilizing politically on *behalf* of GLBT rights. However, the emergence of these groups has also shifted the battle for GLBT rights from federal venues to venues at the local and state level, where regional cultural differences have made many battles difficult.

—*Stephen Paul Whitaker*

## FURTHER READING

Adam, Barry. *The Rise of a Gay and Lesbian Movement.* 1987. Reprint. New York: Twayne, 1995.

Rimmerman, Craig A., Kenneth D. Wald, and Clyde Wilcox, eds. *The Politics of Gay Rights.* Chicago: University of Chicago Press, 2000.

Smith, Miriam. *Lesbian and Gay Rights in Canada: Social Movements and Equality Seeking, 1971-1995.* Buffalo, N.Y.: University of Toronto Press, 1999.

Staggenborg, Suzanne. *Gender, Family, and Social Movements.* Thousand Oaks, Calif.: Pine Forge Press, 1997.

Werum, Regina, and Bill Winders. "Who's 'In' and Who's 'Out'? State Fragmentation and the Struggle over Gay Rights, 1974-1999." *Social Problems* 48, no. 3 (2001): 386-410.

Witt, Stephanie, and Suzanne McCorkle. *Anti-Gay Rights: Assessing Voter Initiatives.* Westport, Conn.: Praeger, 1997.

SEE ALSO: 1950: Mattachine Society Is Founded; 1952: ONE, Inc., Is Founded; 1955: Daughters of Bilitis Founded as First National Lesbian Group in United States; May 27-30, 1960: First National Lesbian Conference Convenes; Feb. 19-20, 1966: First North American Conference of Homophile Organizations Convenes; Apr.

19, 1967: First Student Homophile League Is Formed; Aug. 11-18, 1968: NACHO Formally Becomes the First Gay Political Coalition; July 31, 1969: Gay Liberation Front Is Formed; June 28, 1970: First Lesbian and Gay Pride March in the United States; Nov. 28, 1970: Del Martin Quits Gay Liberation Movement; 1973: National Gay Task Force Is Formed; Oct. 18, 1973: Lambda Legal Authorized to Practice Law; 1977: Anita Bryant Campaigns Against Gay and Lesbian Rights; Nov. 7, 1978: Antigay and Antilesbian Briggs Initiative Is Defeated; 1979: Moral Majority Is Founded; Apr. 22, 1980: Human Rights Campaign Fund Is Founded; Nov., 1986: Californians Reject LaRouche's Quarantine Initiative; Mar., 1987: Radical AIDS Activist Group ACT UP Is Founded; Mar.-Apr., 1993: Battelle Sex Study Prompts Conservative Backlash.

## June 27, 1974
# ABZUG AND KOCH ATTEMPT TO AMEND THE CIVIL RIGHTS ACT OF 1964

*U.S. representatives Bella Abzug and Edward Koch introduced a bill to amend the 1964 Civil Rights Act. Had the act passed, it would have prohibited discrimination on the basis of sexual orientation.*

**ALSO KNOWN AS:** Equality Act of 1974; Civil Rights Amendment Act of 1975
**LOCALE:** Washington, D.C.
**CATEGORIES:** Civil rights; government and politics; laws, acts, and legal history

### KEY FIGURES
*Bella Abzug* (1920-1998), New York City representative to Congress
*Edward Koch* (b. 1924), New York City representative to Congress and mayor of New York City, 1978-1989
*Robert Nix* (1905-1987), Philadelphia representative to Congress

### SUMMARY OF EVENT
On June 27, 1974, the fifth anniversary of the Stonewall uprising in New York City, two Democratic members of Congress representing New York City introduced at the federal level legislation that would make discrimination against lesbians and gays illegal. A month later, an African American congressman from Philadelphia, Robert Nix, also a Democrat, introduced a similar piece of legislation.

The Equality Act of 1974 was proposed as a broad-based amendment of the Civil Rights Act of 1964 that would prohibit discrimination in employment, housing, education, federal programs, and public accommodations on the basis of "sex, marital status, and sexual orientation." The original Civil Rights Act of 1964 had prohibited only sex (or gender) discrimination in employment and education, thus the word "sex" was included for the remaining categories.

Also around this time, a few cities had followed the lead of East Lansing, Michigan, and adopted local nondiscrimination ordinances, but no states had adopted such a law. The sponsors were well aware that the likelihood of the bill becoming law was nonexistent, but every legislative battle had to begin somewhere, and this battle became the first step on the national level.

Following the 1974 elections, seeing that representatives Bella Abzug, Edward Koch, and Nix had all managed to get reelected despite having introduced such a "radical" piece of legislation, two California congressmen from San Francisco and its suburbs, John Burton (a Democrat) and Paul McCloskey (a Republican), joined as sponsors of the proposed equality act. This time, however, the references to sex and marital status had been separated from the issue of sexual orientation and presented as a separate piece of legislation. In fact, the term "sexual orientation" itself had disappeared and been replaced by the term "affectional or sexual preference." Still, the proposed legislative strategy was the same, an amendment of all the relevant sections of the 1964 Civil Rights Act. To this end, the short name given the bill was the Civil Rights Amendment Act of 1975.

The middle and late 1970's was also the beginning of the presence in Washington, D.C., of gay and lesbian political organizations that focused on lobbying the legislative and executive branches. The bill was a key focus of their activities. Realizing passage was unlikely in the near term, the principal goal of the activists was to increase the number of legislators who would sign on as cosponsors; in this they were successful. While a disproportionate share of the cosponsors came from the New York City, San Francisco, and Los Angeles metropolitan areas, a few liberal members of Congress from the West and Midwest also signed on. Additionally, many members of the Congressional Black Caucus (CBC) served as cosponsors (for example, nine of the twenty-one sponsors of a 1977 version of the bill were from the CBC).

The bill was reintroduced in every Congress. From time to time there were changes made to the bill to reflect the impact of the wider social and cultural debates on civil rights in general and gay and lesbian rights in particular.

In 1977, for example, sections were added that prohibited the use of statistical disparities as proof of discrimination or the use of "quotas" as a remedy for any sexual orientation discrimination. In 1979, the term "orientation" returned instead of "preference," but because a number of high profile antigay and antilesbian referenda had taken place in the late 1970's, the sections prohibiting discrimination in education (including Title IX) and public accommodations were dropped from the bill. Proponents feared that a debate on having gay and lesbian teachers would prevent the bill from ever passing. In 1980 and 1982, the House Subcommittee on Employment Opportunities, chaired by Representative Augustus Hawkins, held public hearings on the bills, which provided some publicity for the issue but did not have much impact on moving the legislation forward.

Also in 1979, a companion bill was introduced in the U.S. Senate by Senator Paul Tsongas of Massachusetts. The Senate bill, however, focused exclusively on employment discrimination, until 1985, when Senator John Kerry of Massachusetts became the lead sponsor and returned to the bill all covered sections of the Civil Rights Act except those dealing with education.

For most of the 1980's, however, HIV-AIDS issues dominated the legislative agenda of gay and lesbian rights advocates and their allies. In the early 1990's, the issue of lesbians and gays in the military took over as the leading concern for many. In 1994, gay and lesbian activists, working with the Leadership Conference on Civil Rights, introduced a bill that no longer sought to amend the 1964 Civil Rights Act, but rather proposed a bill that would stand on its own and address only the issue of employment discrimination. The proposed bill, called the Employment Non-Discrimination Act (ENDA), continues to linger in Congress.

## SIGNIFICANCE

The approach advocated by Bella Abzug and Edward Koch to amend the 1964 Civil Rights Act came alive again briefly in the 2000 Democratic primary race, when Senator Bill Bradley indicated that he preferred the original approach to the ENDA strategy. However, Bradley's failure to gain the presidential nomination ended further discussion on that point. Most activists and politicians had come to believe that such a strategy, unsuccessful for twenty years, held no promise of success and posed actual danger to the provisions of the 1964 Civil Rights Act.

*—Charles W. Gossett*

## FURTHER READING

Feldblum, Chai. "The Federal Gay Rights Bill: From Bella to ENDA." In *Creating Change: Sexuality, Public Policy, and Civil Rights*, edited by John D'Emilio, William Turner, and Urvashi

Vaid. New York: St. Martin's Press, 2000.

Gross, Larry, and James D. Woods, eds. *The Columbia Reader on Lesbians and Gay Men in Media, Society, and Politics*. New York: Columbia University Press, 1999.

Hunter, Nan D., Courtney G. Joslin, and Sharon M. McGowan. *The Rights of Lesbians, Gay Men, Bisexuals and Transgendered People*. American Civil Liberties Union Handbook. 4th ed. Carbondale: Southern Illinois University Press, 2004.

Nava, Michael, and Robert Dawidoff. *Created Equal: Why Gay Rights Matter to America*. New York: St. Martin's Press, 1995.

**SEE ALSO:** Apr. 27, 1953: U.S. President Eisenhower Prohibits Federal Employment of Lesbians and Gays; June 27-July 2, 1969: Stonewall Rebellion Ignites Modern Gay and Lesbian Rights Movement; 1972-1973: Local Governments Pass Antidiscrimination Laws; 1973: National Gay Task Force Is Formed; June 21, 1973: U.S. Supreme Court Supports Local Obscenity Laws; Aug., 1973: American Bar Association Calls for Repeal of Laws Against Consensual Sex; Oct. 18, 1973: Lambda Legal Authorized to Practice Law; July 3, 1975: U.S. Civil Service Commission Prohibits Discrimination Against Federal Employees; 1978: Lesbian and Gay Workplace Movement Is Founded; Apr. 22, 1980: Human Rights Campaign Fund Is Founded; 1994: Employment Non-Discrimination Act Is Proposed to U.S. Congress; Sept. 21, 1996: U.S. President Clinton Signs Defense of Marriage Act.

## October, 1974
# *LESBIAN CONNECTION* BEGINS PUBLICATION

*In 1974, a feminist collective called Ambitious Amazons began publishing* Lesbian Connection, *the longest-running lesbian periodical in the United States. The periodical is a reader-driven source for not only information—such as where to stay when traveling—but also for the exchange of ideas on society, culture, and politics. Its letters section is one of the periodical's most popular sections.*

**LOCALE:** East Lansing, Michigan
**CATEGORIES:** Publications; feminism; organizations and institutions

### SUMMARY OF EVENT

In May of 1974, approximately three hundred women attended the Midwest Lesbian Conference and Music Festival in East Lansing, Michigan. Many women at the conference had never been part of such a large gathering of lesbians, and the experience led to the formation of several politically conscious feminist groups in the Lansing area. One group banded together as the Ambitious Amazons, with the goal of creating "a network of communication that would unite all lesbians on this continent." Their communication network would take the form of a national, bimonthly, lesbian newsletter called *Lesbian Connection.*

*LC*, or "Elsie," as *Lesbian Connection* is also called, was established during the heyday of the lesbian-feminist movement. Several other lesbian-feminist publications also started at this time, including *Lavender Woman, Amazon Quarterly*, and *Lesbian Tide*. Although these periodicals did not survive for long—generally because of a lack of adequate funding—*LC* remains in circulation, and it celebrated its thirtieth anniversary in 2004.

When the Ambitious Amazons decided to publish a national lesbian newsletter, they placed an advertisement in *Ms.* magazine (which was founded one year before, in 1973), and mailed flyers announcing their new publication to hundreds of lesbian, feminist, and gay groups across the United States. In their introductory letter, dated August 3, 1974, the Ambitious Amazons explained that they were a group of nine lesbians in their twenties, with political views ranging from separatism to integration. Their goal from the beginning was to create a free publication that enabled lesbians across the country to discuss their lives.

> "LESBIAN CONNECTION means communication," the Ambitious Amazons wrote in their introductory flyer. "We need feedback. Your ideas and reactions will comprise the most important part of this publication. Our purpose is to create a network of communication between lesbians in this country and in Canada; the rest is up to you. We are not yet in sight of a national lesbian community . . . but we are on our way."

The first issue of *LC*, published in October, 1974, was a ten-page, double-sided, 8.5 x 11 inch, mimeographed, and hand-stapled newsletter mailed to about four hundred addresses. The return address, to ensure anonymity for the recipient, was the fictitious "United Ministries in Higher Education"; the return address was later changed to the "Helen Diner Memorial Women's Center." *LC*'s premiere issue included reviews of Rita Mae Brown's *Rubyfruit Jungle* and the now-classic women's music album *Lavender Jane Loves Women*. Articles included a review of sodomy laws across the United States, an interview with a lesbian mother, and a report from a lesbian writers conference.

Advertisements and announcements in the first issue included an advertisement from the new Olivia Records introducing their first record, a 45 rpm record featuring Meg Christian and Cris Williamson. Like all future issues of *LC*, this first issue included numerous letters from readers, many expressing hope that the venture would be successful.

By the second issue, *LC*'s circulation tripled to twelve hundred and financial costs quickly became a concern, although the Ambitious Amazons remained committed to distributing the publication for free. Their budget for 1975 totaled $865.80 and was based on an expected eventual circulation of twenty-five hundred. Within one year, however, *LC* had five thousand subscribers, and rising printing and labor costs forced the Ambitious Amazons to ask for donations of $8 from each reader, "more if you can, less if you can't." By 2003, *LC* had reached a circulation of about twenty-five thousand, with production costs of approximately $70,000 per issue. *LC* still remains "free for lesbians," although the suggested subscription donation has now risen to $27.

From the beginning, *LC* was organized on feminist principles, including collective decision-making that remained exclusively in the hands of women, and a reliance on word-of-mouth and assistance from other women in advertising the publication. *LC* was staffed entirely by volunteers for the first seven years, and began to pay a few regular employees in 1981, with each worker receiving the same wage; in 2004, all paid staff still received the same hourly rate.

*LC* is now a journal-sized, twenty-eight-page publication with glossy covers and some color advertisements, and it continues to include readers' letters and responses, articles, and reviews. The "Festival Forum" provides a space for readers to discuss the dozens of women's music festivals that take place every year, and the "Contact Dykes" directory lists hundreds of women around the world who are willing to act as liaisons for lesbians traveling to their areas.

## SIGNIFICANCE

*LC* has made a significant impact on the lives of tens of thousands of lesbians living in North America, particularly those who live in areas where lesbians lack a visible local community. One of *LC*'s most important contributions to creating a national lesbian community has been its Contact Dyke network, which has established a network of lesbians around the world. As scholar, writer, and archivist Joan Nestle explained, "'Contact Dykes' became a wonderful service because it offered us 'safe houses' virtually everywhere in the country. It opened the whole country up to us!"

*LC* also provided a space for lesbians to create a virtual community for themselves well before the age of the World Wide Web. The articles, letters, and responses published in *LC*—all written by readers—make up a forum in which lesbian identity and meaning are created, challenged, and constituted through lively debate. Topics that have been discussed in the pages of *LC* include alcoholism, health issues, lesbian pregnancy and parenting, legal issues, sexuality, and transgenderism. As *LC* enters its fourth decade, it continues to be funded largely from donations and is still published by the Ambitious Amazons and the Helen Diner Memorial Women's Center, both under the aegis of the nonprofit Elsie Publishing Institute.

—*Malinda Lo*

**FURTHER READING**

Steiner, Linda. "The History and Structure of Women's Alternative Media." In *Women Mak-*

*ing Meaning: New Feminist Directions in Communication*, edited by Lana Rakow. New York: Routledge, 1992.

Streitmatter, Rodger. *Unspeakable: The Rise of the Gay and Lesbian Press in America*. Boston: Faber and Faber, 1995.

Zimmerman, Bonnie, ed. *Lesbian Histories and Cultures*. New York: Garland, 2000.

**SEE ALSO:** June, 1947-Feb., 1948: *Vice Versa* Is Published as First Lesbian Periodical; 1967: *Los Angeles Advocate* Begins Publication; 1970: Amazon Bookstore Opens as First Feminist-Lesbian Book Shop; May 1, 1970: Radicalesbians Issues "The Woman Identified Woman" Manifesto; 1971: *Lesbian Tide* Publishes Its First Issue.

## November 5, 1974
# NOBLE IS FIRST OUT LESBIAN OR GAY PERSON TO WIN STATE-LEVEL ELECTION

*Elaine Noble was elected to the Massachusetts General Assembly, making her the first out lesbian or gay individual to be elected as a state official in the United States. She served two terms and has been a model for lesbians and gays seeking political office.*

**LOCALE**: Boston, Massachusetts
**CATEGORY:** Government and politics

**KEY FIGURE**
*Elaine Noble* (b. 1944), first out lesbian state official

**SUMMARY OF EVENT**
Elaine Noble, born in New Kensington, Pennsylvania, obtained a BSA degree from Boston University and graduate degrees in speech and education from Emerson College and Harvard University. She

came out as a lesbian in the 1960's while teaching at Boston colleges and was a founding member of the Boston chapter of the Daughters of Bilitis. Later, she produced one of the first national gay and lesbian radio programs, the Gay Way. Noble also served as director of the Massachusetts Women's Political Caucus, lobbied the state legislature on behalf of women's issues, and further served on the Massachusetts governor's Commission on the Status of Women.

At a National Organization for Women conference Noble spoke against antilesbian sentiments within the group. In 1971, she addressed Boston's first official gay and lesbian pride march. She has distinguished herself in community work, addressing issues to many communities, and has a reputation for being tough, articulate, and outgoing.

Noble ran for the Massachusetts General Assembly from Boston's Back Bay district on a multi-

278

issue platform in 1974. Her campaign in the Democratic primary and in the general election was comprised of friends along with gay, lesbian, and heterosexual community activists. Many were new and inexperienced in the ways of Boston's old boys' political network. Noble's campaign was a true grassroots, amateur, political undertaking.

Noble's opponent in the general election was Joseph P. Cimino, co-owner of a chain of singles' bars known as Daisy Buchanan's. Noble, on the opposite side of the political spectrum, had been active with local residents trying to control the number of bars in the neighborhood. Stressing her community work, being outspoken for desegregation in Boston, and working to ease tensions rather than politicking helped Noble win the election on November 5, 1974.

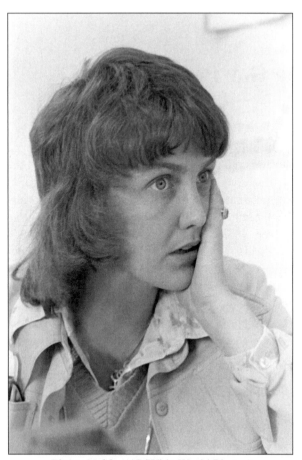

*Elaine Noble.* (AP/Wide World Photos)

Noble became the first lesbian state legislator in the United States and the second elected to public office in the nation. Kathy Kozachenko, also a lesbian, won a seat on the Ann Arbor, Michigan, city council earlier the same year. Ironically, Boston's gay and lesbian community did not wholeheartedly embrace Noble. Many, though, had ideas of what she should be and how she should lead.

During her two terms of office, Noble worked diligently on behalf of her constituents, regardless of their sexual orientation. In 1976, she supported statewide sodomy reform legislation that became inaccurately described as a gay rights bill. No other legislators stood to support or debate the bill. Noble requested a roll call vote be taken but could not obtain the minimum vote to approve the bill.

The following year, Noble was part of an LGBT delegation called to meet with officials of the administration of then-president Jimmy Carter. That same year, she, along with twenty-one other representatives and six state senators, sponsored the Massachusetts Public Service Employment measure. The bill would have provided employment protections to gays and lesbians at the state level. The measure stated merely that discrimination in Massachusetts civil service positions would be prohibited based on sexual orientation, but the bill was not passed in the Massachusetts legislature.

Noble's two terms of office did see major achievements for her and her Boston constituency. She helped deliver to her district funding for major street lighting programs and rent control and pro-tenant legislation, and she helped to establish an Equal Rights Amendment commission.

In 1978, Noble decided against running for a third term, a decision based, in part, on disillusionment, unrealistic and unrelenting demands from the lesbian and gay community, and a massive redistricting in Boston, which would put her at a disadvantage running against Barney Frank. She was caught between the demands of the legislative role and expectations of impatient activists. Noble created more scorn from lesbian-separatists by urging LGBT and women's involvement in electoral politics. As Noble stated, "I had not only more work, but got more flack, more criticism, more heartache

## HISTORY OF THE PRIDE INSTITUTE

Noble Associates, a health care consulting business, served as the catalyst for the Pride Institute, formed in 1986 by Elaine Noble and Ellen Ratner. The institute's goals are to affirm homosexuality as a valued way of life, to help patients understand the role of sexuality in drug and alcohol addictions, and to learn how to cope more effectively with heterosexual society. Each patient before discharge must make specific arrangements for continuing therapy, for medical care, and for attending local support organizations.

The institute has been the premiere drug and alcohol treatment center exclusively for the gay, lesbian, bisexual, and transgender communities, recognizing that GLBT individuals have unique treatment concerns, including issues of secrecy, societal rejection, and internalized homophobia. Each concern requires a targeted practitioner response geared to the individual and his or her rehabilitation.

The institute's programs provide each client with formal support and counseling. Similar to Alcoholics Anonymous, the agency employs twelve-step programs. Patients are required to admit the destructive roles of addiction, must seek help and support from others, and must develop a belief in a spiritual entity. Key to a client's recovery are the weekly group discussions that examine concerns specific to the lesbian and gay life course.

The Pride Institute has a proven track record of success with more than eight thousand "graduates." Studies by Yale University and the University of Pennsylvania show that graduates of the institute's programs are more likely to stay chemical free than are those who are clients of mainstream rehabilitation programs. Pride Institute services have expanded beyond Minneapolis, its first location, to Dallas, Texas; Fort Lauderdale/Key West, Florida; Chicago, Illinois; and New York City/New Jersey.

from the gay community than from the people who elected me." She also reminded people that a politician has to deal with a wide variety of issues in office, and that once one takes on a specific issue or set of issues, that focus can become a political death sentence.

Noble ran for the Democratic nomination for the U.S. Senate in 1980, but lost to political newcomer Paul Tsongas. She twice ran unsuccessfully for the Cambridge city council in 1991 and 1993. Outside the political arena, she worked in Boston mayor Kevin White's Office of Intergovernmental Affairs. She was entangled in an investigation of Mayor White's administration by the Federal Bureau of Investigation. Noble testified for nearly nineteen hours before a federal grand jury but was exonerated of any wrongdoing. The investigation, however, ended her political career.

Always the politician, she continued to fight behind the scenes for human rights causes. She played a pivotal role in helping gay Boston city councillor David Scondras obtain passage of the city's ban against discrimination based on a person's sexual orientation. She was also responsible for the creation of the Boston Gay Liaison Office, which provides a deputy mayor to the LGBT community.

During the early 1980's, Noble cofounded Pride Institute, an alcohol and drug treatment center in Minneapolis, Minnesota, serving LGBT clients. She also tried to establish similar centers in Waltham and Cambridge, Massachusetts, but was turned down. She also helped to establish the Pride Value Fund, a gay and lesbian investment fund.

### SIGNIFICANCE

Undoubtedly, Elaine Noble encouraged gays and lesbians to run for political office, including Minnesota state senator Alan Spears, Minnesota state representative Karen Clark, and others around the country. She also eloquently pointed out the demands of being not only the voice of the constituency but also, more important, the gay and lesbian community at large. In essence, she revealed the value and power of the LGBT vote.

—*Michael A. Lutes*

### FURTHER READING

Blasius, Mark. *Gay and Lesbian Politics: Sexuality and the Emergence of a New Ethic.* Philadelphia: Temple University Press, 1994.

Hertzog, Mark. *The Lavender Vote: Lesbians, Gay*

Men, and Bisexuals in American Electoral Politics. New York: New York University Press, 1996.

Mixner, David, and Dennis Bailey. Brave Journeys: Profiles in Gay and Lesbian Courage. New York: Bantam Books, 2000.

Phillips, Susan. "A Stormy Passage: The Noble Bill." The Advocate, June 27, 1977, 11-12.

Rayside, David. On the Fringe: Gays and Lesbians in Politics. Ithaca, N.Y.: Cornell University Press, 1998.

Rimmerman, Craig. From Identity to Politics: The Lesbian and Gay Movements in the United States. Philadelphia: Temple University Press, 2002.

Rowland, Craig. "Women in Politics: Elaine Noble." The Advocate, December 11, 1984, 34, 36-37.

Yeager, Ken. Trailblazers: Profiles of America's Gay and Lesbian Elected Officials. New York: Haworth Press, 1999.

**SEE ALSO:** 1971: Kameny Is First Out Candidate for U.S. Congress; 1972-1973: Local Governments Pass Antidiscrimination Laws; Nov. 7, 1972: Jordan Becomes First Black Congresswoman from the South; July 14, 1983: Studds Is First Out Gay Man in the U.S. Congress; Nov. 6, 1984: West Hollywood Incorporates with Majority Gay and Lesbian City Council; May 30, 1987: U.S. Congressman Frank Comes Out as Gay; Sept. 23, 1992: Massachusetts Grants Family Rights to Gay and Lesbian State Workers; May 24, 1993: Achtenberg Becomes Assistant Housing Secretary; Nov. 18, 2003: Massachusetts Court Rules for Same-Gender Marriage.

# 1975
# FIRST GAY AND LESBIAN ARCHIVES IS FOUNDED

*Jim Kepner amassed a collection of gay-related materials that are now a major part of one of the world's largest and most significant GLBT archival collections, the ONE National Gay & Lesbian Archives. Kepner is regarded by some as the first historian and archivist of gay and lesbian culture in the United States.*

**LOCALE:** Torrance, California; Los Angeles, California

**CATEGORIES:** Civil rights; cultural and intellectual history; organizations and institutions; publications

## KEY FIGURES

*Jim Kepner* (1923-1997), American collector, activist, writer, and educator

*W. Dorr Legg* (1904-1994), American activist, writer, and educator

## SUMMARY OF EVENT

Jim Kepner was born and raised in Texas by adoptive parents. When his father sought better work, Kepner moved with him in 1942 to San Francisco. While there, Kepner visited the public library but found no objective materials about homosexuality.

One of the earliest books on homosexuality remembered by Kepner is *Homosexuality in the Lives of the Great* (1930), a Haldeman-Julius Blue Book, which were small-format books issued in wrappers. It was the lack of materials in San Francisco's library, though, books and other works that he *knew* existed, that inspired Kepner to start his collection, which had been made up first of clippings about gay life in San Francisco during the time he lived there.

Kepner moved to Los Angeles in 1943, then to New York, then back to San Francisco, where he co-owned a bookstore with his friend Mel Brown; the store failed, however. Kepner then moved back to Los Angeles in 1951, to reside again with his friend in the Echo Park area of the city. Gay friends met there for informal discussions, and in 1952, Kepner attended his first meeting of the Mattachine Society.

Beginning in 1954, Kepner wrote articles under pseudonyms for Mattachine's *ONE* magazine, and he became the first journalist to have a gay news column, called "tangents, news & views" (printed in lower case letters) for which he collected further clippings, including those sent to him by readers.

The materials grew to include not only books but also printed ephemera, posters, and media materials. In 1975, Kepner announced the formation of the Western Gay Archives in his Torrance, California, apartment. At his crowded Lexington Avenue (Hollywood) apartment, a photograph shows him in front of a massive wall of books, sitting at a desk with more books and archival items in the foreground.

In 1979, Kepner's Western Gay Archives was incorporated as The Gay Archives: Natalie Barney/Edward Carpenter Library and opened in a storefront in Hollywood. The archives came to be known as the National Gay Archives, and then, after 1984, as the International Gay and Lesbian Archives (IGLA). After the rent at that location increased, IGLA moved to the Werle Building, a space provided by the city of West Hollywood. Kepner financed his archives by living frugally and by soliciting funds from the community. IGLA received a small amount of institutional funding only.

## SIGNIFICANCE

Jim Kepner's knowledge of gay and lesbian history was first put to use in publications and gay studies classes. With W. Dorr Legg (William Lambert Dorr Legg), Kepner founded in 1956 the ONE Institute of Homophile Studies, the first gay studies program in the United States, and issued its quarterly, beginning in 1958, the first such gay-studies publication in the country.

Kepner's writings for *ONE* magazine and other publications were collected in his book *Rough News, Daring Views: 1950's Pioneer Gay Journalism* (1998), and they show the breadth of his approaches to GLBT history. He simply wanted to present items of GLBT interest that had long been suppressed, but he also wanted to do so through thoughtful activism. His writings framed early GLBT debates about civil rights and in some cases, they still apply today.

Notable early collections acquired by Kepner include Manuel Boyfrank's (also known as Monwell Boyfrank) correspondence with Henry Gerber, who founded the Society for Human Rights in 1924, the first gay organization in the United States, and published the first American gay journal called *Friendship and Freedom*. Kepner also acquired, beginning in 1972, the records of the Los Angeles Gay and Lesbian Center from cofounder Morris Kight, and he collected art from Sidney Bronstein, who published in *ONE* magazine.

Kepner made his collection available to early GLBT researchers beginning about 1971, so he had a profound influence not only on those writing GLBT-liberation histories but also those who read these works. To take one example, Kepner had opened his files in 1971 to Jonathan Ned Katz, who published the comprehensive work *Gay American History* in 1976.

With his health getting worse, Kepner and those close to him began to seek more permanent housing for the archives. The University of California, Los Angeles (UCLA), one possible permanent location, declined the offer to house the archives because doing so would have been too expensive for the campus at the time. Also, Kepner had requested a staff position in "exchange" for the archives, but UCLA library policy did not allow for such an exchange.

In 1956, a ONE, Inc., report noted that its library "may well be . . . the most important contribution of ONE." The library was named the Blanche M. Baker Memorial Library, for a doctor and psychologist who was not a lesbian but was a ONE ally and speaker until her death.

The libraries of ONE Institute and IGLA (ONE/IGLA) merged in 1995, through the efforts of Walter Williams, an anthropology professor at the University of Southern California (USC) and others on the two boards. Housing, but not funding, has since been provided by USC. In 1996, the collection of Don Slater (and the Homosexual Information Center), which started with books and records originally housed by ONE until 1965, was added back to ONE/IGLA, the new name of the archives.

Kepner's vision statements always included the idea that his archive and library were not just for storage of material but were made up of "one of the richest and most usable informational tools the gay community has." He envisioned the archives with multiple purposes: fostering research and publication and sponsoring events.

Kepner's vision and life work is now part of ONE/IGLA. His vision is shared by the work of an active IGLA board seeking more ties with USC for permanent housing, seeking endowed funds for preservation and further cataloging of the books, and looking for funds to fully process the archival collections. The ONE Institute archives includes collections at the Werle Building in West Hollywood.

ONE celebrated its fiftieth anniversary in May of 2002. It remains the longest-lived American GLBT organization, housing collections begun by Kepner in 1942.

*—Dan Luckenbill*

**FURTHER READING**

Carmichael, James V., Jr. "'They Sure Got to Prove It on Me': Millennial Thoughts on Gay Archives, Gay Biography, and Gay. . . ." *Libraries & Culture* 35, no. 1 (Winter, 2000).

_____, ed. *Daring to Find Our Names: The Search for Lesbigay Library History*. Westport, Conn.: Greenwood Press, 1998.

Cvetkovich, Ann. *An Archive of Feelings: Trauma, Sexuality, and Lesbian Public Cultures*. Durham, N.C.: Duke University Press, 2003.

Gannett, Lewis, and William A. Percy, III. "Jim Kepner (1923-1997)." In *Before Stonewall: Activists for Gay and Lesbian Rights in Historical Context*, edited by Vern L. Bullough, Judith M. Saunders, and C. Todd White. New York: Harrington Park Press, 2002.

Hall, Richard. "Reclaiming Our Gay American Past: Jonathan Katz, Activist in the Archive." *The Advocate*, January 12, 1977, 19-21.

Kepner, Jim. *Rough News, Daring Views: 1950's Pioneer Gay Press Journalism*. New York: Haworth Press, 1998.

Legg, W. Dorr, David G. Cameron, and Walter L. Williams, eds. *Homophile Studies in Theory and Practice*. San Francisco, Calif.: GLB Publishers and ONE Institute Press, 1994.

Potvin, Ernie. "Kepner Remembered." In *ONE IGLA Bulletin* no. 5 (Summer, 1998).

_____. Subject Files, ONE National Gay & Lesbian Archives. Kepner's files contain mission statements, drafts of articles of incorporation, resumes, and more.

**SEE ALSO:** 1952: ONE, Inc., Is Founded; 1953: *ONE* Magazine Begins Publication; Fall, 1973: Lesbian Herstory Archives Is Founded; 1976: Katz Publishes First Lesbian and Gay History Anthology; Aug., 1991: Leather Archives and Museum Is Founded.

## 1975

# FIRST NOVEL ABOUT COMING OUT TO PARENTS IS PUBLISHED

*Laura Z. Hobson's best-selling novel,* Consenting Adult, *is the first fictional treatment of the experience of coming out as gay or lesbian to a parent, as told from the perspective of parents of lesbian or gay children. Hobson was inspired to write the novel after her son came out to her.*

**LOCALE:** New York, New York
**CATEGORIES:** Literature; publications

**KEY FIGURES**
*Laura Z. Hobson* (1900-1986), American writer
*Christopher Z. Hobson,* American scholar and
Hobson's son, whose coming out to his mother
inspired her to write *Consenting Adult*

**SUMMARY OF EVENT**
The opening page of Laura Z. Hobson's novel, *Consenting Adult* (1975), announced the book's controversial subject matter (parents struggling to accept their son as gay). It also showed that Hobson, at seventy-five years old, was using her fiction to tackle an issue of social justice.

> Dear Mama . . . I am a homosexual. I have fought it off for months and maybe years, but it just grows truer. . . . I know how much pain this will cause you, and shock too. But I can't keep it a secret from you any longer. . . .

Hobson was born Laura Keane Zametkin in 1900 in New York City to Russian-Jewish parents who were socially active, indeed radical. An impassioned writer early in her teens, Hobson (she married in 1930) wrote for newspapers and magazines for nearly twenty years before publishing her first novel, *The Trespassers* (1943), a scathing account of the injustices of the U.S. immigration system. Her second and most notorious work, *Gentleman's Agreement*, appeared in 1946; its searing portrait of the polite realities of anti-Semitism in the post-

World War II era was enduringly successful for the emerging, and soon notorious, author, permanently securing her status as one of the leading social-justice voices of mid-century American letters.

Later novels dealt with such topics as free speech and civil liberties (*First Papers*, 1964) and single motherhood (*The Tenth Month*, 1971), but Hobson's 1975 novel about parents dealing with the coming out of their gay son, *Consenting Adult*, stands out, however, as the author's most personal and enduringly relevant work.

Hobson traced the inspiration for *Consenting Adult* to her receipt of two letters from her younger son, Christopher. She received his first letter in 1958, when Christopher was an accomplished high school senior preparing to matriculate at Harvard University. In it, Christopher informed his mother of his homosexuality. The second letter arrived in 1970, when Christopher was nearly thirty and finishing his doctorate in English literature. In this second letter, Christopher, who had become deeply involved in the gay and lesbian rights movement, informed his mother that he was coming out as gay. For Laura Hobson, these two letters—the first from a teenage boy, the second from an adult man—marked the beginning and end points of a journey of acceptance for both parent and child. As she wrote in her memoir, *Laura Z.* (1983,1986), "for twelve years his secret had been my secret . . . and it [began] to occur to me that Christopher's life was not the only one that had been changed by the decision [to come out]."

In 1970, Hobson began the research that would ultimately be instrumental to the composition of *Consenting Adult*. She had read many novels about homosexuality. While appreciating the work of Mary Renault, Gore Vidal, and James Baldwin, among others, Hobson noted that "in all those books, one person had always been missing—a parent." With the novel's central character, Tessa

Lynn, acting as Hobson's acknowledged surrogate, Hobson began writing *Consenting Adult* to correct what she called the "orphanhood" of gay and lesbian characters in literature.

*Consenting Adult* received the best and most widespread reviews of Hobson's career. She had received "as many as eight or ten" letters per day from parents who identified with having a gay or lesbian child, from gays and lesbians inspired to write coming-out letters to their own parents, and (most numerous of all) from young people discovering that they too were gay or lesbian. Few of Hobson's fans could have known, however, that Christopher Hobson, whose own letters inspired his mother's novel, was less than pleased with *Consenting Adult*, and the novel's publication led to an extended period of estrangement between the author and her younger son.

Hobson's more-famous *Gentleman's Agreement* was made into an Oscar-winning film (1947), which had entered production even as Hobson's novel was still arriving in stores for the first time. *Consenting Adult*, however, struggled, despite constant interest from producers, to enter film or television production for nearly a decade. Finally, in February of 1985, barely one year before the author's death, ABC-TV broadcast the television movie *Consenting Adult*. The television adaptation updated the story by a decade, transplanted the action from New York City to Seattle, Washington, and featured actors Marlo Thomas and Martin Sheen, both of whom are social-justice advocates, as Tessa and Ken Lynn.

## SIGNIFICANCE

Laura Z. Hobson's *Consenting Adult* reframed the discourse that described the issues faced by families with gay and lesbian children. Rather than fixating on their son's sexuality as a solvable problem, Hobson's characters, Tessa and Ken Lynn, like Hobson herself, had to learn to accept their son and his homosexuality. The novel corrected an absence in gay and lesbian literature—a lack of parents or other family members—and it described the process by which one family member's coming out transforms the family as a whole.

*Consenting Adult* emerged as one of the first works to seriously and empathetically consider the experiences of individuals with gay or lesbian family members. The novel became a crucial touchstone in the early organizing efforts of groups such as Parents, Families, and Friends of Lesbians and Gays (PFLAG).

—*Brian Eugenio Herrera*

## FURTHER READING

Anderson, Robert W. "Parents and Friends of Lesbians and Gays (PFLAG)." In *Gay Histories and Cultures*, edited by George Haggerty. New York: Garland, 2000.

Bernstein, Robert A. *Straight Parents, Gay Children: Keeping Families Together*. 2d ed. New York: Thunder's Mouth Press, 1999.

Drucker, Jane. *Families of Value: Gay and Lesbian Parents and Their Children Speak Out*. New York: Insight Books, 1998.

_____. *Lesbian and Gay Families Speak Out: Understanding the Joys and Challenges of Diverse Family Life*. Reading, Mass.: Perseus, 2001.

Fairchild, Betty, and Nancy Hayward. *Now That You Know: A Parents' Guide to Understanding Their Gay and Lesbian Children*. 3d ed. San Diego, Calif.: Harcourt Brace, 1998.

Griffin, Carolyn W., and Marian J. Wirth. *Beyond Acceptance: Parents of Lesbians and Gays Talk About Their Experiences*. New York: St. Martin's Press, 1997.

Hobson, Laura Keane Zametkin. *Consenting Adult*. Garden City, N.Y.: Doubleday, 1975.

_____. *Laura Z: A Life*. New York: Arbor House, 1983. Reprint. New York: D. I. Fine, 1986. Contains an introduction by Norman Cousins and an afterword by Christopher Z. Hobson.

**SEE ALSO:** 1956: Baldwin Publishes *Giovanni's Room*; 1963: Rechy Publishes *City of Night*; 1973: Brown Publishes *Rubyfruit Jungle*; 1974: *The Front Runner* Makes *The New York Times* Best-Seller List; 1975: Rule Publishes *Lesbian Images*; 1981: Faderman Publishes *Surpassing the Love of Men*; 1981: Parents, Families, and Friends of Lesbians and Gays Is Founded.

**1975**
# GAY AMERICAN INDIANS IS FOUNDED

*Gay American Indians was created to support the indigenous peoples of all nations in North America who identify themselves as gay, lesbian, or two-spirit. The group, the first formal organization of lesbian and gay indigenous peoples, formed at a critical time for urban American Indians: a few years before the coming HIV-AIDS epidemic, which struck the San Francisco area with particular harshness.*

**LOCALE:** San Francisco, California
**CATEGORIES:** Civil rights; organizations and institutions; HIV-AIDS; race and ethnicity

**KEY FIGURES**
*Randy Burns* (b. 1955), Northern Paiute activist, author, and health care provider, cofounded Gay American Indians
*Barbara Cameron* (1954-2002), Lakota Sioux/ Hunkpapa activist and author, cofounded Gay American Indians

**SUMMARY OF EVENT**
American Indian cultures in the early historic period of European contact and documentation demonstrated and accepted a broader range of gender variation than typical of Euro-American societies of the time. This generalization holds for many North American tribal societies, though it must be recognized that the expression and meanings of different genders varied depending on regional, tribal, and linguistic conventions, which also changed through time.

With the influence of Christianity, government-enforced schooling, and other acculturating influences, traditional gender practices and understandings became stigmatized, which ensured that mid-twentieth century American Indians who identified themselves as gay or lesbian often were no longer accepted positively by their indigenous communities. This meant that large numbers of young people who wanted to express their nonhetero-

sexual gender identities in a supportive context found it necessary to migrate to urban centers, such as San Francisco, which had, and still has, a thriving and politically active gay and lesbian population. By the 1970's, San Francisco was home to an increasing number of American Indians, including an unknown percentage of individuals who had alternative gender expressions.

This was the context that led Randy Burns and Barbara Cameron, with a small group of friends, to found Gay American Indians (GAI), the first formal organization established in North America by and for gay and lesbian Native Americans. Within a year of its founding, the group had approximately thirty members from about twenty different tribes.

GAI provided support and practical assistance to young people new to the San Francisco area, and it served a social role for long-term community members. Reportedly, the organization had 150 members by the late 1970's, an indication of its importance to its constituents.

In the early 1980's, Will Roscoe, a researcher and writer, became involved with GAI, and with his assistance the Gay American Indian History Project was founded in 1984. By this time, the group numbered several hundred members and was still the only North American support organization for gay and lesbian American Indians.

By this time, AIDS was severely impacting the San Francisco gay community, although the effects on American Indians went unrecognized because the Centers for Disease Control were not collecting statistical data on indigenous people with HIV or AIDS. Instead, the indigenous were categorized as "white," "black," or "other." This meant that no intervention was offered to American Indians specifically, so there was no awareness that indigenous people living in San Francisco and other urban centers, with unique needs (as is the case with any group not part of the mainstream), were at risk for HIV-AIDS, as was the general population.

It was a huge shock to the GAI when one of its

members, Jodi Harry (a Miwok) was diagnosed with AIDS in 1987. The distress was compounded when he committed suicide soon after his diagnosis. Members of GAI grieved over his death and were sad that he had not requested support from the GAI community. Harry's death, however, had two positive consequences.

In 1988, when GAI members collaborated with Roscoe to produce *Living the Spirit: A Gay American Indian Anthology*, they made sure Roscoe included information about AIDS services in the endnotes of the book. In addition to providing agency contacts, the book also included a list of tribes with documented alternative gender roles, and it provided accounts of contemporary gender variation among American Indians. Burns wrote the book's preface, and many other GAI members contributed autobiographies, essays, short stories, and poems. *Living the Spirit* makes a powerful statement about the ongoing presence of alternatively gendered Indians and their feelings of continuity with their tribal histories.

In the year before *Living the Spirit*'s publication, GAI had established the Indian AIDS Project in memory of Jodi Harry and Herbie Jeans (a Navajo/Otoe), who died of AIDS complications. By 1988, this initiative formed the basis for the newly established American Indian AIDS Institute. Other gay and lesbian Indian organizations were formed in Minneapolis, Toronto, and New York City around the same time. All of these groups provided AIDS education and support services for their communities, which began to suffer the ravages of the illness.

Sadly, and despite more intervention and health education projects, the membership of GAI continues to be impacted by AIDS. Burns remembers that "at 65 plus deaths from AIDS," he "stopped counting." He continues to speak at memorial services for community members and is involved with promoting health initiatives for the indigenous of California. He and others involved with GAI celebrated the third decade since GAI's founding and hosted a writers conference of LGBT indigenous peoples in July of 2005. Also, Burns was the grand marshal of the 2005 San Francisco LGBT pride parade. GAI

disbanded as a formal organization in the late 1990's, however, and its records are archived at the GLBT Historical Society in San Francisco (www.glbthistory.org), ensuring the preservation of GAI's history.

## SIGNIFICANCE

Gay American Indians, the first formal organization for gay and lesbian American Indians, had a major impact on the lives of gay, lesbian, and two-spirit American Indians living in the San Francisco area. GAI provided an activist role model for other indigenous groups that followed its own formation, including the Bay Area American Indian Two-Spirits (BAAITS). BAAITS (www.baaits.org) hosted an international two spirit gathering in the summer of 2005.

—*Susan J. Wurtzburg*

## FURTHER READING

Allen, Paula Gunn. *The Sacred Hoop: Recovering the Feminine in American Indian Traditions*. 1986. New preface. Boston: Beacon Press, 1992.

Cameron, Barbara. "Gee, You Don't Seem Like An Indian from the Reservation." In *The Social Construction of Difference and Inequality*, edited by Tracy E. Ore. 2d ed. New York: McGraw-Hill, 2003.

Katz, Jonathan Ned. *Gay American History: Lesbians and Gay Men in the U.S.A.* Rev. ed. New York: Meridian Books, 1992.

Medicine, Beatrice. "Changing Native American Roles in an Urban Context and Changing Native American Sex Roles in an Urban Context." In *Two-Spirit People: Native American Gender Identity, Sexuality, and Spirituality*, edited by Sue-Ellen Jacobs, Wesley Thomas, and Sabine Lang. Chicago: University of Illinois Press, 1997.

Roscoe, Will. *Changing Ones: Third and Fourth Genders in Native North America*. New York: St. Martin's Press, 1998.

_____, ed. *Living the Spirit: A Gay American Indian Anthology*. New York: St. Martin's Press, 1988.

**SEE ALSO:** Jan.-June, 1886: Two-Spirit American Indian Visits Washington, D.C.; Oct. 12-15, 1979: First National Third World Lesbian and Gay Conference Convenes; Oct., 1981: Kitchen Table: Women of Color Press Is Founded; Sept., 1983: First National Lesbians of Color Conference Convenes; 1986: Paula Gunn Allen Publishes *The Sacred Hoop.*

## 1975
# RULE PUBLISHES *LESBIAN IMAGES*

*Jane Rule's* Lesbian Images *was the first nonfiction study of lesbian writers to be published in book form by a commercial publisher. The writers in Rule's collection share a common bond: They all wrote with a sensibility that came from their own experiences of having intense emotional and physical relationships with women.*

**LOCALE:** United States
**CATEGORIES:** Literature; publications

**KEY FIGURE**
*Jane Rule* (b. 1931), American writer

**SUMMARY OF EVENT**
In 1975, Jane Rule was an American-born author living in Canada and writing works of fiction. Earlier in her career, she had published three novels with lesbian content, but, as Judith Neimi notes, reviews of her work "amount[ed] to nothing more than popular prejudice elevated to aesthetic principle." One novel, however, *Desert of the Heart* (1964), first rejected by nearly two dozen publishers, became a hit film called *Desert Hearts* (1985), and is now a lesbian classic. The prejudice waned when Rule departed from her usual fictional fare to write a work of nonfiction, *Lesbian Images.*

*Lesbian Images* focuses on the lives and works of female authors. Luminaries such as Radcyffe Hall, Gertrude Stein, Willa Cather, Vita Sackville-West, Colette, and May Sarton are profiled along with Ivy Compton-Burnett, Elizabeth Bowen, Violette Leduc, Margaret Anderson, Dorothy Baker, and Maureen Duffy. Each of these authors shares common characteristics: They all were born in the nineteenth century and survived into the twentieth century, giving them a shared sense of history and social convention. Most important, however, each

*The cover of Rule's* Lesbian Images *(1975).* (The Crossing Press)

## "LOVE BETWEEN WOMEN"

From the ugly masochism of Violette Leduc to the lyric wonder of Margaret Anderson, from the moral earnestness of Gertrude Stein to the ambivalent cynicism of Colette, from the neutered sexuality of Ivy Compton-Burnett to the blatant sexual hunger of Vita Sackville-West, from the silence of Willa Cather to the confessions of May Sarton, the reality of lesbian experience transcends all theories about it. If this book astonishes simply by the number of women, and very gifted women, who have been concerned about love between women, it will have fulfilled its purpose, for no one can comfortably dismiss all those who find a place in these pages.

*Source:* Jane Rule, Preface to *Lesbian Images.*

of them wrote from personal experience about intense emotional and physical relationships among women.

Rule begins her book with a personal essay, and she tells her readers that she is lesbian. In the essay, she sets the tone for exploring the art of writing in relation to personal experience and historical context. *Lesbian Images*, she writes, was intended to be a "discover[y] of what images of lesbian women writers have projected in fiction, biography, and autobiography . . . ," and not concerned with the writers' literary styles. Rule examines "the interaction of these writers with their culture" and "how they [w]ere influenced by religious and psychological concepts and by their own personal experience in presenting lesbian characters."

Rule's introductory essay is followed by two chapters summarizing the laws, myths, and prejudices relating to homosexuality. Subsequent chapters recount the lives and published works of the surveyed authors. The chapters "Four Decades of Fiction" and "Recent Nonfiction" conclude the narrative portion of *Lesbian Images*.

## SIGNIFICANCE

Prior to the Stonewall Rebellion in 1969, publishers rarely published books about homosexuality unless the books could safely be called scientific or unless they projected a negative, unhappy outcome. Critical analyses of lesbian authors and literature were virtually nonexistent. The literature that existed was predominately written by men and was of questionable quality, difficult to obtain, or focused on a single author. Within this historical context the style and timing of Rule's book is critical.

The reception of *Lesbian Images* was mixed. Reviewers applauded Rule for including her personal story, although one reviewer found the inclusion embarrassing and another considered the entire work propaganda because of its positive portrayal of lesbians. Opinions regarding Rule's writing style were divided; some praised the work for its general-reader approach, while others criticized it as simplistic and nonscholarly. Regardless of reviewer opinion, it is evident that Rule's work was intended for the general reading public; it has been used frequently as a classroom text and remains in hundreds of libraries.

Rule's work was not the first lesbian authored exploration of lesbian literature; that distinction belongs to Jeannette H. Foster's *Sex Variant Women in Literature* (1956). Although scholarly in nature, Foster was forced to publish her manuscript independently and, as a result, her book was not widely available. Rule, however, was contacted by a commercial publisher and was commissioned to write *Lesbian Images*. Clearly, by the time Rule wrote her work, social attitudes toward homosexuality had shifted to the point where it was possible to publish works about homosexuality; publishers were actually seeking books to publish. Even Rule had agreed that the work could not have been published five years earlier.

The release of *Lesbian Images* also coincided with a strong lesbian presence in the women's movement. Because of the women's movement, national interest had been focused on women's issues. The appearance of Rule's work during this period ensured a wider audience than if the book had been published prior to the rise of 1970's feminism. Furthermore, *Lesbian Images* could withstand charges that it was politically motivated because Rule was not politically active at the national level in the women's movement.

Finally, 1975 was a watershed year for lesbian literature. The appearance of *Lesbian Images* was complemented by a new edition of Barbara Grier's bibliography *The Lesbian in Literature*, two works about lesbian author Djuna Barnes, and the reissue of Foster's *Sex Variant Women in Literature*, which by 1975 had become a classic.

In 1976, *Lesbian Images* had been reprinted for the British and Canadian markets and a paperback edition was released in the United States. The title has remained in print since its first publication. As a study of lesbian identity and character, *Lesbian Images* remains significant and stands as one of the earliest examples of queer literary theory and history.

—*Ellen Bosman*

## FURTHER READING

Foster, Jeannette H. *Sex Variant Women in Literature: A Historical and Quantitative Survey.* London: F. Muller, 1956.

Hancock, Geoffrey. "An Interview with Jane Rule." *Canadian Fiction Magazine* 23 (Autumn, 1976): 57-112.

Niemi, Judith. "Jane Rule and the Reviewers." *Margins* 8, no. 23 (1975): 34.

Rule, Jane. *Lesbian Images.* Garden City, N.Y.: Doubleday, 1975.

Schuster, Marilyn R. *Passionate Communities: Reading Lesbian Resistance in Jane Rule's Fiction.* New York: New York University Press, 1999.

_____. "Strategies for Survival: The Subtle Subversion of Jane Rule." *Feminist Studies* 7, no. 3 (Fall, 1981): 431-450.

Summers, Claude J., ed. *The Gay and Lesbian Literary Heritage: A Reader's Companion to the Writers and Their Works, from Antiquity to the Present.* New York: Holt, 1995.

Zimmerman, Bonnie. *The Safe Sea of Women: Lesbian Fiction, 1969-1989.* Boston: Beacon Press, 1990.

SEE ALSO: 1928: Hall Publishes *The Well of Loneliness*; 1956: Foster Publishes *Sex Variant Women in Literature*; June, 1971: The Gay Book Award Debuts; 1973: Brown Publishes *Rubyfruit Jungle*; 1981: Faderman Publishes *Surpassing the Love of Men*; 1981: *This Bridge Called My Back* Is Published; 1982: Lorde's Autobiography *Zami* Is Published; 1985: Lesbian Film *Desert Hearts* Is Released; 1986: Paula Gunn Allen Publishes *The Sacred Hoop*; 1987: Anzaldúa Publishes *Borderlands/La Frontera*; 1987: *Compañeras: Latina Lesbians* Is Published; May, 1987: *Lambda Rising Book Report* Begins Publication; June 2, 1989: Lambda Literary Award Is Created; June, 1992: Feinberg Publishes *Transgender Liberation*.

## 1975-1983
# GAY LATINO ALLIANCE IS FORMED

*Lesbian and gay Latino/as and Chicano/as formed a social and political alliance, creating visibility, identity, and shared space and inspiring the formation of similar organizations throughout the United States.*

**LOCALE:** San Francisco Bay Area and San Jose, California

**CATEGORIES:** Organizations and institutions; race and ethnicity; civil rights; government and politics; marches, protests, and riots

**KEY FIGURES**
*Diane Felix*, alliance cofounder
*Rodrigo Reyes*, alliance cofounder

**SUMMARY OF EVENT**

In 1975, sensing the need to organize socially and politically, gay Chicanos and Latinos and Chicana and Latina lesbians founded the Gay Latino Alliance (GALA) in the San Francisco Bay Area/San Jose. Bridging political consciousness of lesbian, gay, and Chicano/a liberation with social and cultural expression, GALA became a visible organization in San Francisco's then Latino-majority Mission District. The organization also became a Latino voice in gay and lesbian political and social life in the city. By placing itself in the racially and sexually diverse Mission District, GALA helped to negotiate conflicts between gay and lesbian whites with those of the broader Latino community in the San Francisco area.

The child of Texan migrant farmworkers, Rodrigo Reyes became one of the most visible figures in the organization from the beginning. Placing a classified ad in the *Bay Area Reporter* in October, 1975, Reyes piqued the interest of others who were also looking for ways to come together as Latinos and as gays and lesbians. In the city of San Jose, a one-hour drive south from San Francisco, Manuel Hernández Valadéz saw Reyes's ad and informed his friend, Jesús Barragán, who similarly was be-

coming politically conscious as a gay Chicano. One of the women who saw the ad was lesbian Chicana Diane Felix. Originally from the central California agrarian region of Stockton, a couple hours drive outside the Bay Area, Felix had been an active participant in the Chicano cultural and political movement of the period but faced homophobia after she announced she was lesbian.

GALA, along with a regional social and political movement, was just emerging. The organization brought together hundreds of participants through successful fund-raising dances with live salsa bands; loud, musical participation in gay freedom day parades; political forums against U.S. intervention in Central America and against the poor living conditions of gays and lesbians in Cuba; and personal accounts of being gay/lesbian and Latino/Latina in both the gay/lesbian and Latino press. The money GALA raised was earmarked for Mission District community organizations, including the Latino newspaper *El Tecolote*.

Even though GALA tried to carry out cogender organizing, it was unable to create a safe space for most lesbians. Felix, for example, consistently fought to address women's needs in the organization and to create a women's social and political space. Felix and other women created a women's component to GALA, whose members worked in coalition with other lesbians of color in the region and nationally. On one occasion, GALA's women's component wanted to host a women-only dance to raise funds to travel to a women's conference in Puerto Rico. Many of the men in GALA opposed the move and tried to crash the dance.

**SIGNIFICANCE**

As racial minorities, gay and lesbian Latinos and Latinas often face discriminatory practices within the white GLBT community, such as having to show more than one form of identification to gain entry into a particular club. Influenced by countercultural, civil rights, and protest movements, GALA's struggles went hand in hand with the fight for racial justice, against police brutality, and for educational access. Some GALA members also organized in multiracial coalitions, such as the coalition with San Francisco's Third World Gay Caucus in the late 1970's or with organizations for lesbians and feminists of color. GALA also participated in the historic March on Washington for Lesbian and Gay Rights in 1979. Coalitions from Texas, California, and the East Coast—together with representatives from Latin America—convened days before the march at Howard University in Washington, D.C., to participate in the First National Third World Lesbian and Gay Conference.

Unresolved struggles between women and men, animosities between Chicano and Puerto Rican men, and plain burnout led to GALA's demise. The start of the first openly gay Latino bar in the Latino district also played a role in shifting attention away from the organization's politicized social events to the new private commercial space for alcohol consumption and leisure, especially for men. Nevertheless, GALA had a major impact.

In the 1980's, numerous Latina/Latino organizations took form throughout the United States. Even though GALA had disappeared by 1983, Los Angeles's Gay and Lesbian Latinos Unidos (GLLU) formed in 1981, and a subcommittee, Lesbianas Unidas (LU), formed in 1983, becoming an independent group the following year. In 1984, Denver had Ambiente Latino and Las Mujeres Alegres, while Houston had a Gay Hispanic Caucus. In New York, a group of Latina lesbians created Las Buenas Amigas in November of 1986, emerging out of the African American lesbian organization Soul Sisters, which had welcomed Latinas. Many of these and other organizations, including San Francisco's Mujerío in the late 1980's and early 1990's, organized transnationally with LGBT activists in Puerto Rico, Nicaragua, Venezuela, and other countries in Latin America.

GALA was an early example of a movement where women and men of color charted new political territory. They challenged superficial and stereotypical depictions of "exotic" Latinos and "passive" Latinas. They also challenged the homophobia in their own Latino communities, religious intolerance, and, to some degree, their own sexism against women.

The different Latino national groups that were represented in the organization, predominantly Chicano and Puerto Rican, also signaled an effort to appreciate racial and ethnic differences while trying to overcome divisions and animosities. Developing a new language of lesbian and gay liberation in English and in Spanish, GALA reshaped the meaning of what it means to be Latina or Latino and queer.

—*Horacio N. Roque Ramírez*

### FURTHER READING

Anonymous (Diane Felix). "Understanding the Gay Latino: Part II." *El Tecolote* 6, no. 10 (July, 1976): 9.

De la Garza, Luis Alberto C., and Horacio N. Roque Ramírez. "Queer Community History and the Evidence of Desire: The Archivo Rodrigo Reyes, a Gay and Lesbian Latino Archive." In *The Power of Language: Selected Papers from the 2nd REFORMA National Conference*, edited by Lillian Castillo-Speed and the REFORMA Publications Committee. Englewood, Colo.: Libraries Unlimited, 2001.

Leyva, Yolanda. "Breaking the Silence: Putting Latina Lesbian History at the Center." In *The New Lesbian Studies: Into the Twenty-First Century*, edited by Bonnie Zimmerman and Toni A. H. McNaron. New York: Feminist Press, 1996.

Reyes, Rodrigo. "Latino Gays: Coming Out and Coming Home." *Nuestro Magazine*, April, 1981, 42-45, 64.

Roque Ramírez, Horacio N. "'That's *My* Place': Negotiating Gender, Racial, and Sexual Politics in San Francisco's Gay Latino Alliance, 1975-1983." *Journal of the History of Sexuality* 12, no. 2 (April, 2003): 224-258.

*¡Viva 16!* Written, produced, and directed by Valentín Aguirre and Augie Robles. 21st Century Aztlan Productions, 1994. Video recording.

**SEE ALSO:** 1969: Nuestro Mundo Forms as First Queer Organization in Argentina; 1975: Gay

American Indians Is Founded; Oct. 12-15, 1979: First National Third World Lesbian and Gay Conference Convenes; 1981: *This Bridge Called My Back* Is Published; Sept., 1983: First National Lesbians of Color Conference Convenes; 1987: Anzaldúa Publishes *Borderlands/La Frontera*; 1987: *Compañeras: Latina Lesbians* Is Published; 1987: VIVA Is Founded to Promote Latina and Latino Artists; Oct. 14-17, 1987:

Latin American and Caribbean Lesbian Feminist Network Is Formed; 2002: Sylvia Rivera Law Project Is Founded; June 19, 2002: Gays and Lesbians March for Equal Rights in Mexico City; Oct. 4, 2002: Transgender Teen Gwen Araujo Is Murdered in California; Apr., 2003: Buenos Aires Recognizes Same-Gender Civil Unions; Jan., 2006: Jiménez Flores Elected to the Mexican Senate.

## July 3, 1975
# U.S. Civil Service Commission Prohibits Discrimination Against Federal Employees

*The U.S. Civil Service Commission, functioning as the federal government's human resources department until 1978, had a prolonged record of antigay and antilesbian discrimination in its hiring and retention practices. Through court challenges and changes in public attitude, the policy was halted in 1975.*

LOCALE: Washington, D.C.
CATEGORIES: Government and politics; civil rights; laws, acts, and legal history

KEY FIGURES
*Franklin Kameny* (b. 1925), U.S. Army Map Service astronomer
*Bruce Scott*, employee of the U.S. Department of Labor
*Clifford Norton*, NASA budget analyst
*Donald Hickerson*, employee of the U.S. Department of Agriculture

SUMMARY OF EVENT
The U.S. Civil Service Commission served as the central personnel agency for the federal government from 1883 until 1978. Following passage of the Civil Service Reform Act of 1978, the commission became the Office of Personnel Management. The commission had a long history of terminating homosexual employees (and barring them from employment), dating to at least the 1950's and the McCarthy era. The government feared Communist infiltration, and also feared that homosexuals, considered by many to be part of a powerful, well-educated, and highly placed "secret society," also posed a threat to American morals and values.

The Civil Service Commission relied heavily upon the U.S. Senate document "Employment of Homosexuals and Other Sex Perverts in Government" (1950) to formulate its regulations regarding gay and lesbian applicants and employees. First, agency officials stated that fellow employees would not tolerate working with homosexuals. Second, because it was believed that a scandal would erupt if known homosexuals were allowed to work in federal positions, the commission thought it necessary to exclude homosexuals on grounds of workplace efficiency and public trust. From the 1950's until 1975, an estimated five thousand gay and lesbian employees were terminated by the Civil Service Commission. This figure does not include those not hired because of their sexual orientation.

Franklin Kameny, who had been fired by the Civil Service Commission in 1957, advocated a series of test cases in the courts that challenged the commission's discriminatory practices. The first challenge appeared in 1965, when Bruce Scott, a former Labor Department employee, filed suit (*Scott v. Macy*, 1965, 1968). The Court of Appeals overruled his commission disqualification, but the commission stood steadfast against the ruling. Scott refiled the case and won again three years later.

Another victory came with the landmark decision in *Norton v. Macy* (1969). In the opinion written by Judge David Bazelon, Clifford Norton's sexual orientation was irrelevant to his employment and therefore he never should have been discharged. Bazelon wrote that the federal government did not have the authority to enforce morals. Discriminatory practices against gays fail to uphold U.S. standards of liberty, privacy, and diversity. Furthermore, the government failed to provide a rational basis for how this discharge promoted an efficiency of service. A clear relational test must exist for determining whether a person could be terminated for homosexual or other behavior deemed immoral. While the ruling was a huge leap forward, it did not offer unqualified support for gay and lesbian employee rights. Overall, it had a minor impact on the commission's policies and the courts.

In the post-Stonewall decade of the 1970's, changing social opinions began to make the Civil Service Commission's exclusion of gays and lesbians less acceptable. The LGBT community moved aggressively against federal employment policies. The courts took a more progressive and activist approach concerning gay and lesbian rights. The federal government, however, remained recalcitrant and slow to reform hiring practices.

On December 20, 1971, the American Civil Liberties Union filed a class-action lawsuit against the commission and the U.S. government, demanding a stop to the discriminatory job dismissals of lesbian and gay federal employees. The suit requested a permanent injunction against the Civil Service Commission and the government from investigations of sexual activities of federal employees or those applying for employment. Employment disqualification based solely on sexual orientation should be considered unlawful.

By October, 1973, it was clear that the Civil Service Commission had to change its policies regarding gay and lesbian employees. As a result of the

class-action lawsuit, named *Society for Individual Rights and Hickerson v. Hampton* (also known as *S.I.R. v. Hampton*), the commission's antigay exclusionary policy was overturned, and a permanent injunction placed against further implementation. Presiding Judge Alphonso J. Zirpoli became the first judge to recognize gays and lesbians as a "class" under the law. Individuals could not be denied federal employment merely on the basis of his or her homosexuality.

Within two months of the court decision the Civil Service Commission proposed in the *Federal Register* a set of new rules on hiring. Although the commission approved the final version of the regulations in late summer of 1973, it did not release them pending detailed guidelines, clarified by *S.I.R. v. Hampton*. As published, the changes would require hiring officials to use a case-by-case checklist to determine applicant suitability for federal employment. The regulations stated that a rational connection must be drawn between a person's homosexual conduct and job performance before dismissal or denial of employment. Any differentiation between heterosexual and homosexual employees is unallowable. Most important, the new checklist would come to provide an objective, verifiable, legal tool in case of court challenge.

Under the new guidelines, grounds for dismissal include conduct that is criminal, dishonest, infamous, or notoriously disgraceful. However, the nature of the job, content and seriousness of outside conduct, and that conduct's potential impact on job performance, are allowable factors in reviews regarding the employment suitability of job candidates.

In the light of the *Norton*, *Scott*, and *S.I.R.* court rulings against the U.S. Civil Service, the three-member commission had few other options than to change its discriminatory policy toward lesbians and gays. Through July 3, 1975, however, the commission held resolute on the matter, believing *Norton*, *Scott*, and *S.I.R.* applied to individuals involved in litigation only and not to "homosexuals" as a blanket category. On a quiet July 4 holiday weekend in 1975, out of the media limelight, the commission adopted the revised employment suitability regulations. Still adhering to old taboos, however, "sensitive" positions in agencies such as the Federal Bureau of Investigation (FBI), the Central Intelligence Agency (CIA), and the U.S. military would be exempt from antidiscriminatory measures.

The Civil Service Reform Act of 1978 completely overhauled the federal civilian personnel system, and the Civil Service Commission was replaced by the Office of Personnel Management. The reform act carried forward antidiscriminatory standards the courts established in rulings in *Norton*, *Scott*, and *S.I.R.* The new law prohibited personnel practices that discriminate against any employee or applicant whose behavior or conduct does not adversely affect the job performance of the individual or of others. On May 28, 1998, President Bill Clinton issued Executive Order 13087, prohibiting discrimination based on sexual orientation in federal civilian employment.

## Significance

Similar to other civil rights advances, it was the federal courts as well as progressive thinking that engendered changes in the case of lesbian and gay federal workers. If the U.S. government, as one of the largest employers in the country, failed to stop antigay hiring practices, who or what would motivate private companies to not follow the government's lead and institute their own antidiscriminatory practices? As the courts have ruled, homosexuals are no more nor less capable of performing government work than are heterosexuals.

—*Michael A. Lutes*

## Further Reading

"ACLU Suit Fights Federal Dismissals for Homosexuality." *The New York Times*, December 21, 1971, p. 26.

Aikens, David. "Gay Is Now OK in 2.6 Million Federal Jobs." *The Advocate*, July 30, 1975.

_____. "U.S. Asks Job Rules Keyed to Performance." *The Advocate*, January 2, 1974.

Causey, Michael. "Changes Proposed in Rules on Hiring." *Washington Post/Times Herald*, December 4, 1973, p. B13.

Federal GLOBE: Gay, Lesbian, Bi, and Transgender Employees of the Federal Government. http://www.fedglobe.org.

"Federal Judge Orders United States to End Hiring Ban." *The Advocate*, December, 1973.

Green, Stephen. "Homosexuals Win Job Rights." *Washington Post*, July 4, 1975, p. A1.

"Homosexuals' U.S. Job Rights Upheld." *Los Angeles Times*, July 4, 1975, p. A17.

Jasiunas, J. Banning. "Is ENDA the Answer? Can a 'Separate but Equal' Federal Statute Adequately Protect Gays and Lesbians from Employment Discrimination?" *Ohio State Law Journal* 61 (2000): 1529.

Johnson, David. "Homosexual Citizens: Washington's Gay Community Confronts the Civil Service." *Washington History* (Fall/Winter, 1994-1995): 44-63.

Lewis, Gregory. "Lifting the Ban on Gays in the Civil Service: Federal Policy Toward Gay and Lesbian Employees Since the Cold War." *Public Administration Review* 57, no. 5 (September/October, 1997): 387-395.

"Shedding Blinders." *The New York Times*, July 16, 1975, p. 32.

Winfeld, Liz. *Straight Talk About Gays in the Workplace: Creating an Inclusive, Productive Environment for Everyone in Your Organization.* 3d ed. New York: Harrington Park Press, 2005.

SEE ALSO: Apr. 27, 1953: U.S. President Eisenhower Prohibits Federal Employment of Lesbians and Gays; 1972-1973: Local Governments Pass Antidiscrimination Laws; June 27, 1974: Abzug and Koch Attempt to Amend the Civil Rights Act of 1964; 1978: Lesbian and Gay Workplace Movement Is Founded; June 2, 1980: Canadian Gay Postal Workers Secure Union Protections; Dec. 4, 1984: Berkeley Extends Benefits to Domestic Partners of City Employees; Nov. 8, 1988: Oregon Repeals Ban on Antigay Job Discrimination; May 1, 1989: U.S. Supreme Court Rules Gender-Role Stereotyping Is Discriminatory; Sept. 29, 1991: California Governor Wilson Vetoes Antidiscrimination Bill; Sept. 23, 1992: Massachusetts Grants Family Rights to Gay and Lesbian State Workers; 1994: Employment Non-

Discrimination Act Is Proposed to U.S. Congress; Apr. 2, 1998: Canadian Supreme Court Reverses Gay Academic's Firing; July, 2003: Singapore

Lifts Ban on Hiring Lesbian and Gay Employees; July, 2003: Wal-Mart Adds Lesbians and Gays to Its Antidiscrimination Policy.

## September, 1975
# ANNA CRUSIS WOMEN'S CHOIR IS FORMED

*The Anna Crusis Women's Choir, the longest-running feminist chorus, was formed out of a combined vision of artistic expression and social change. A lesbian and gay choral movement, which has flourished around the United States and the world since the 1970's, represents one of the largest elements of the LGBT rights movement at the grassroots level.*

**LOCALE:** Philadelphia, Pennsylvania
**CATEGORIES:** Arts; organizations and institutions; feminism

**KEY FIGURES**
*Catherine Roma* (b. 1948), founder of Anna Crusis
*Jane Hulting*, music director since 1984

**SUMMARY OF EVENT**
The early 1970's saw a burgeoning women's music movement that included lesbian-feminist community choruses. Many of these choruses developed out of the needs of women sharing a vision of social change. While working on issues that included the ERA (Equal Rights Amendment), reproductive health and freedom, workplace equity, gay and lesbian rights, and international peace, many also wanted a supportive community and a place to sing and celebrate their work and vision. Of these early choruses, the oldest in continuous existence is Philadelphia's Anna Crusis Women's Choir, started by Catherine Roma in September of 1975. Anna Crusis is now considered a grandmother chorus for the LGBT choral movement.

One of the largest contingents of the grassroots LGBT social movement around the world has been the LGBT choral movement, which developed out of the civil rights and lesbian and gay rights movements' impulses for social change and artistic expression during the 1960's. While community choruses have historically played a variety of roles in many different social movements, the LGBT choral movement has proven to be a compelling medium in addressing the particular types of oppression faced by LGBT people.

As a grassroots movement that addresses issues of gender and sexuality, various elements that have developed into the LGBT choral movement came out of a response to different aspects of sex and gender oppression. In general, women's groups organized out of largely feminist, often lesbian concerns and therefore have a mix of lesbians, bisexual women, heterosexual women, and sometimes women who are transgender, while men's choruses—which developed later, often out of a gay-pride milieu—consist mostly of gay men. Mixed-gender choruses have a later history that marks the coming together of gays, lesbians, bisexuals, and transgender people, often with straight allies to create social change.

Emblematic of the desire to envision the world differently, the name "Anna Crusis" was chosen as a feminist play on the musical term, *anacrusis*, a Greek word that describes an "upbeat" or "feminine" entrance to a sung phrase. As explained on the choir's Web site,

Physically, it [*anacrusis*] may be described as the precise moment of anticipation and exhilaration which occurs as a singer takes a quick, deep breath before vocalizing. The choir finds the phrase fit-

## COMPOSING WOMEN

Music by women composers, ignored for many years, began to be unearthed by directors and musicologists. Some works were easily discarded because the texts proved to be inappropriate; either they reflected Judeo-Christian principles or were meant for "unchanged voices" (boys), or for children. There has been a dearth of dramatic, moving, and, of course, feminist texts set to music for the mature women's chorus. The women's choral movement has begun to change this situation and suitable works have been discovered and performed, and many choruses have commissioned contemporary women composers to write for them.

*Source:* Catherine Roma, "Brief History: Women's Choral Movement." http://www.musechoir.org/history.htm.

ting for the purpose of defining ourselves in relation to music, a philosophy of feminism, and the joy of performing.

Exploring the interrelationship between art and social change in order to develop a consistent philosophy and action was and continues to be taken on as a challenge by feminist choruses. Indeed, feminist choruses are generally less hierarchical and more likely to run by some version of consensus than most men's or even mixed choruses.

An obvious place to merge theory and practice is in choice of music. As Roma writes in "Brief History: Women's Choral Movement" (www.musechoir.org/history.htm), "The repertoire of women's choruses is one of the most unusual characteristics of the whole movement."

Like many feminist choirs, Anna Crusis began by focusing on music that celebrated women. Under the directorship of Jane Hulting since Roma left in 1983, it continues that tradition today, often through collaborations and commissions.

Not all women's choruses within the LGBT choral movement articulate a strongly feminist vision. Indeed, geography, historical context, and a variety of factors affect the sense of purpose of any chorus. As Roma notes,

Some [choruses] begin when a group of women gather to sing, others are founded by a single woman director, or by a group of planners; in still other cases, a men's chorus in the area proves anxious to have a partner chorus. Women's choruses vary in structure: some use clear democratic majority rule, while others operate by consensus. Some choruses choose to stay a certain size, while others put no limit on how many may join. Some hold auditions; others are open to any woman who wants to sing. Some sing a popular-style repertoire, while others sing a wide variety of music. Some have no trouble deciding what to wear for concert garb; others have their most heated debates over dress.

Anna Crusis's mission remains strongly feminist in its vision not only of striving for musical excellence but also for

social change, with a special focus on music by, for and about women and their lives. The choir values and seeks diversity and inclusion in its membership, audiences and musical selection. While honoring their common ground, members also work to respect and learn from their differences in sexual orientation, racial and cultural heritage, age, class, and spiritual expression. The choir supports, empowers and uplifts its audiences and its members in their struggle for justice, peace and equality.

While choruses in the LGBT choral movement generally articulate a balance between artistic excellence and a mission of social change, the extent of the change desired and emphasis given to this part of the mission varies widely. Feminist choruses such as Anna Crusis and Muse, also founded and directed by Roma, remain at the forefront in the push for social change through excellence in music.

### SIGNIFICANCE

The lesbian-feminist choral movement has had its own substantial impact on the repertoire of choral music available for soprano and alto voices as well as on the LGBT movement as a whole. In meeting with the often larger and wealthier men's choruses through the development of larger umbrella organizations such as the Gay and Lesbian Association of

Choruses (GALA Choruses), lesbian feminists have influenced the nature of the movement and sustained ongoing conversations that continue to impact musical repertoire, organizational practices, and visions for the larger GLBT movement.

*—Julia Balén*

**FURTHER READING**

Barkin, Elaine, and Lydia Hamessley, eds. *Audible Traces: Gender, Identity, and Music*. Los Angeles: Carciofoli, 1999.

Brett, Phillip, Elizabeth Wood, and Gary C. Thomas. *Queering the Pitch: The New Gay and Lesbian Musicology*. New York: Routledge, 1994.

Gay and Lesbian Association of Choruses. http://www.galachoruses.org/.

Gordon, Eric. "GALA: The Lesbian and Gay Community of Song." *Choral Journal* 30, no. 9 (1990): 25-32.

Hadleigh, Boze. *Sing Out! Gays and Lesbians in the Music World*. New York: Barricade Books, 1998.

McLaren, Jay. *An Encyclopaedia of Gay and Lesbian Recordings: An Index of Published Recordings of Music and Speech Expressing Themes Relevant to Gay Men and Lesbians*. Limited ed. Amsterdam: J. McLaren, 1992.

Roma, Catherine. "Choruses, Women's." In *Lesbian Histories and Cultures*, edited by Bonnie Zimmerman. New York: Garland, 2000.

_____. "Women's Choral Communities: Singing for Our Lives." *Hotwire* 8, no. 1 (January, 1992): 36.

Vukovich, Dyana. "The Anna Crusis Women's Choir." *Women and Performance: A Journal of Feminist Theory* 4, no. 1 (1986): 50-63.

**SEE ALSO:** 1973: Olivia Records Is Founded; Aug. 20-22, 1976: Michigan Womyn's Music Festival Holds Its First Gathering; 1981-1982: GALA Choruses Is Formed; June 6-June 20, 1981: San Francisco Gay Men's Chorus Concert Tour; Dec. 8, 1981: New York City Gay Men's Chorus Performs at Carnegie Hall; 1992-2002: Celebrity Lesbians Come Out.

---

**November 17, 1975**

# U.S. SUPREME COURT RULES IN "CRIMES AGAINST NATURE" CASE

*In* Rose v. Locke, *the U.S. Supreme Court overturned a lower appeals court opinion, finding that the sexual act of cunnilingus, whether between heterosexuals or homosexuals, could be considered a violation of Tennessee's "crimes against nature" law. The ruling encouraged a broad interpretation of sodomy laws in Tennessee and throughout the United States.*

**ALSO KNOWN AS:** *Rose v. Locke*
**LOCALE:** Knox County, Tennessee
**CATEGORIES:** Laws, acts, and legal history; civil rights; government and politics

**KEY FIGURES**

*William J. Brennan* (1906-1997),
*Thurgood Marshall* (1908-1993), and
*Potter Stewart* (1915-1985), associate justices of the United States
*Charles Galbreath*, Tennessee appeals court judge

**SUMMARY OF EVENT**

In Tennessee, in the early 1970's, support for sodomy laws had been waning. A proposed comprehensive criminal code revision in 1973 would have abrogated common-law crimes and repealed the sodomy law, establishing the age of consent at six-

---

## *ROSE V. LOCKE* (1975)

*Majority opinion:* Respondent seems to argue . . . that because some jurisdictions have taken a narrow view of "crime against nature" and some a broader interpretation, it could not be determined which approach Tennessee would take, making it therefore impossible for him to know if 39-707 ["crime against nature" code] covered forced cunnilingus. But even assuming the correctness of such an argument if there were no indication which interpretation Tennessee might adopt, it is not available here. Respondent is simply mistaken in his view of Tennessee law. As early as 1955 Tennessee had expressly rejected a claim that "crime against nature" did not cover fellatio, repudiating those jurisdictions which had taken a "narrow restrictive definition of the offense."

*Dissenting opinion:* No specter of increasing caseload can possibly justify today's summary disposition of this case. The principle that due process requires that criminal statutes give sufficient warning to enable men to conform their conduct to avoid that which is forbidden is one of the great bulwarks of our scheme of constitutional liberty. The Court's erosion today of that great principle without even plenary review reaches a dangerous level of judicial irresponsibility. I would have denied the petition for certiorari, but now that the writ has been granted would affirm the judgment of the Court of Appeals or at least set the case for oral argument.

---

teen years old. This new code, however, was never adopted by the Tennessee legislature. Because of this near miss, the conservative courts felt the need to reassert the importance of such laws.

A Tennessee man, named by the court as "Locke," entered the apartment of a female neighbor late at night, saying that he needed to use the woman's telephone. Soon after entering, he threatened her with a butcher knife, demanded that she disrobe, and twice performed cunnilingus upon her against her will. Among other charges, Locke was later convicted in Knox County's criminal court of having committed a "crime against nature," a violation of the criminal code of Tennessee. He was subsequently sentenced to between five and seven years in prison.

Then, a series of appeals began. In Locke's first appeal to the Tennessee State Court of Criminal Appeals, Locke's attorneys asserted that the Tennessee statute does not specifically reference cunnilingus as a "crime against nature." Further, they claimed that the statute was "unconstitutionally vague." This appeal failed, and the Supreme Court of Tennessee refused to review the case. Later, the Knox County District Court reconsidered the appeal and again ruled against Locke.

In 1975, however, Locke's luck began to change. He appealed to the Sixth Circuit Court of Appeals, which validated his constitutional challenge. Believing that the statutory phrase "crimes against nature" could not "in and of itself withstand a charge of unconstitutional vagueness," and being unable to find any Tennessee opinion previously applying the statute to the act of cunnilingus, the Court of Appeals held that the statute failed to give Locke "fair warning." The judges decided that the fair warning requirement embodied in the Due Process Clause prohibited the states from holding an individual "criminally responsible for conduct which he could not reasonably understand to be proscribed." (Locke's sexual assault of his neighbor was a different charge entirely, and was not under question in this case.)

In 1975, the State of Tennessee appealed to the U.S. Supreme Court. In this final case (decided on November 17) the judgment of the Sixth Circuit Court of Appeals, which found in Locke's favor, was reversed. After much deliberation, Locke's conviction was upheld, and the Court's decision was definitive. First, the Court ruled that cunnilingus is covered by Tennessee's "crimes against nature" statute, even though it is not expressly mentioned there. According to the ruling, the Due Process Clause requires only that the law should give sufficient warning that persons may conduct themselves so as to avoid forbidden acts. With this standard in mind, the Court judged that the phrase "crimes against nature" is not "unconstitutionally vague." Locke could have discovered easily what acts were considered "crimes against nature" and could thus have avoided those acts.

Supreme Court justices Thurgood Marshall, Potter Stewart, and William J. Brennan wrote the dissenting opinion. They asserted that U.S. courts have consistently interpreted offenses referred to as "crimes against nature" as dealing specifically with anal sex. They further asserted that the Court of Appeals accurately ruled that, "courts have differed widely in construing the reach of 'crimes against nature' to cunnilingus." The statute, therefore was sufficiently vague as to have confused the public and specifically Locke.

## SIGNIFICANCE

*Rose v. Locke* had been strengthened by *Bowers v. Hardwick* (1986) by allowing states to liberally interpret and enforce their sodomy laws. This method of interpreting vague "crimes against nature" statutes remained available to state courts until *Lawrence v. Texas* in 2003. Broadening the scope of these statutes, however, would prove to be their downfall. From the beginning, this case contradicted public opinion and behavior. In his dissenting opinion at one of the state appeals, Tennessee judge Charles Galbreath noted that a study published in *Playboy* magazine, at the time, revealed that for adults under thirty-five years old, 90 percent approved of cunnilingus.

Though Locke remained the only person prosecuted by this interpretation of the law, and the charges against him were considered by some to be more heinous than his "crime against nature," the ruling increased, virtually, the number of individuals who could be prosecuted under this statute. For example, any person, regardless of their sexual orientation or their gender, could be prosecuted as a result of the Court's ruling. Also, the practice of cunnilingus within heterosexual marriage in general was not considered by any of the courts, revealing the distinct double standard of such statutes. The question arose as to why an act was a "crime against nature" for some people and a "right of marriage" for others.

*Rose v. Locke* also influenced many decisions from the 1970's through the 1990's. Many of these cases had little to do with sexuality, but rather questioned the "vagueness" of certain laws and statutes. Among the circuit court decisions citing *Rose v.*

*Locke* were *Mark Mueller and James I Stopple v. Michael Sullivan, Secretary of Wisconsin Department of Corrections* (1998) responding to a vague antifraud statute, and *Hope Clinic v. Ryan, James E.* (1999), dealing with a vague law concerning so-called partial-birth abortion. At the U.S. Supreme Court level, *Whalen v. United States* (1980) and *Marks v. United States* (1977) both cited *Rose v. Locke* in the same manner.

—*Daniel-Raymond Nadon*

## FURTHER READING

Ball, Howard. *The Supreme Court in the Intimate Lives of Americans: Birth, Sex, Marriage, Childbearing, and Death*. New York: New York University Press, 2002.

Gruen, Lori, and George E. Panichas. *Sex, Morality, and the Law*. New York: Routledge, 1997.

Moran, Leslie J. *The Homosexual(ity) of Law*. New York: Routledge, 1996.

Murdoch, Joyce, and Deb Price. *Courting Justice: Gay Men and Lesbians v. Supreme Court*. New York: Perseus Books, 2001.

Painter, George. "The Sensibilities of Our Forefathers: The History of Sodomy Laws in the United States." 2001. http://www.sodomylaws.org/sensibilities/tennessee.htm.

Pinello, Daniel R. *Gay Rights and American Law*. New York: Cambridge University Press, 2003.

*Rose v. Locke*, 423 U.S. 48 (1975). http://laws.findlaw.com/us/423/48.html.

Rubenstein, William B. *Cases and Materials on Sexual Orientation and the Law: Lesbians, Gay Men, and the Law*. 2d ed. St. Paul, Minn.: West, 1997.

_____. *Lesbians, Gay Men, and the Law*. New York: New Press, 1993.

SEE ALSO: May 6, 1868: Kertbeny Coins the Terms "Homosexual" and "Heterosexual"; 1885: United Kingdom Criminalizes "Gross Indecency"; Jan. 12, 1939: *Thompson v. Aldredge* Dismisses Sodomy Charges Against Lesbians; Sept. 4, 1957: The *Wolfenden Report* Calls for Decriminalizing Private Consensual Sex; 1961: Illinois Legalizes Consensual Homosexual Sex; Jan. 22, 1973: *Roe v. Wade* Legalizes Abortion and Extends Privacy Rights; Aug., 1973: American Bar Association Calls for Repeal of Laws Against Consensual Sex; Oct. 18, 1973: Lambda Legal Authorized to Practice Law; 1986: *Bowers v. Hardwick* Upholds State Sodomy Laws; Jan. 1, 1988: Canada Decriminalizes Sex Practices Between Consenting Adults; 1992-2006: Indians Struggle to Abolish Sodomy Law; June 26, 2003: U.S. Supreme Court Overturns Texas Sodomy Law.

## 1976
# KATZ PUBLISHES FIRST LESBIAN AND GAY HISTORY ANTHOLOGY

*The publication of the first major compilation in English of documentary sources on gays and lesbians in the United States, from colonial times to the early 1970's, helped to establish the legitimacy of gay and lesbian historical research.*

**LOCALE:** New York, New York
**CATEGORIES:** Cultural and intellectual history; literature; publications

**KEY FIGURE**
*Jonathan Ned Katz* (b. 1938), gay rights activist and historian

**SUMMARY OF EVENT**

The question of the demonstrable existence and value of gay and lesbian history is an important one, because knowing one's history is critical to the coming-out process for individuals. Also, documenting gay and lesbian history provides a verifiable historical grounding and framework for the GLBT rights struggle, a framework that had been ill-defined within the field of history in the United States in the mid-1970's, when Jonathan Ned Katz compiled, edited, and published the anthology *Gay American History: Lesbians and Gay Men in the U.S.A., a Documentary History* (1976).

Lesbian and gay history that had been recognized dealt almost exclusively with famous public figures, such as the Emperor Hadrian. It also was recognized by those activists who had some prior knowledge not only of same-gender civil rights campaigns but also of the destruction of the first homosexual rights movements. For example, attempts by the Nazis to discredit the work and findings of sexologist Magnus Hirschfeld on homosexuality was part of a larger campaign of domestic repression leading up to World War II. The Nazis closed Hirschfeld's clinic, the Institut füer Sexualwissenschaft, in 1933.

Academic research on homosexuality at the dissertation level (a subject that had been discouraged because of the imputed damage it would do to a graduate student's academic career) was barely beginning to be accepted at U.S. universities; only two projects by 1976—in history and in political science—addressed at some level same-gender sexuality. Among the grounds used to justify resistance to scholarly inquiry into homosexuality was the absence of a collection of identified and verified primary source texts that could serve as the core of a new field of study.

The appearance of *Gay American History* forever changed the landscape of gay and lesbian historical research and laid the foundations for the crystallization of LGBT studies as a separate academic field. Katz began his research in 1971 while he was a member of New York City's Gay Activist Alliance, with the assumption that the unknown and often deliberately suppressed historical record of the lives of gay and lesbian Americans did exist and could be recovered. Katz wanted to close the gap left by international surveys of sexual history. His initial researches led him to conceive of the idea of presenting the subject first in visual form, in this case as the topic of a play. *Coming Out! A Documentary Play About Gay Life and Liberation in the U.S.A.* premiered in June, 1972. It wove together accounts of men and women drawn to their own gender from the seventeenth century to then-contemporary newspaper coverage of the movements for gay and lesbian rights, demonstrating for the first time on the American stage the realities of the gay and lesbian past.

Katz had gathered his documentary sources by 1975. For his introduction to *Gay American History*, he reviewed philosophical treatments of and approaches to homosexuality and homosexuals in historical writing, and was sure to include works in the collection that had a philosophical focus on gay and lesbian liberation. He emphasized how a historical identity for gays and lesbians had been established in the struggle to create a positive and balanced self-image.

The work itself is divided into six sections and covers some four centuries. Subjects include the legal status and social repression of homosexuals between 1566 and 1976, the history of approaches to "treating" homosexuality by the psychiatric and psychological professions between 1884 and 1974, and the history of women who passed as men between 1872 and 1920.

In the realm of primary sources, the collection includes colonial Spanish documents from 1566, documentation ranging in date from 1528 to 1976 on the variety of social roles played by male and female homosexuals in Native American cultures, records of intimate same-gender relationships between 1779 and 1932, and modes of resistance by individuals as well as the first organizations that challenged legal and social limits and oppression. Among the notable discoveries made by Katz in this last section was the charter issued in 1924 by the State of Illinois to Chicago's Society for Friendship and Freedom, the first short-lived homosexual rights group in the United States.

Katz noted that because his research had been conducted independently, it is free of the limitations imposed by the academic establishment. The model set by *Gay American History* was followed by Katz's *Gay/Lesbian Almanac* (1983) and later compilations, such as the collection edited by Robert Ridinger of gay and lesbian speeches and rhetoric, *Speaking for Our Lives* (2004).

## SIGNIFICANCE

The publication of *Gay American History* effectively shattered the idea that lesbians and gays in the United States, and around the world, were social deviants without a place in history. The work demonstrated that lesbians and gays—and homosexuality—always had been present, even if marginalized or unrecognized. The collection's primary documents inspired the growth of gay and lesbian historical research and helped lead to the founding of gay and lesbian archives, where similar sources could be collected and preserved.

*—Robert Ridinger*

## FURTHER READING

Hall, Richard. "Reclaiming Our Gay American Past: Jonathan Katz, Activist in the Archive." *The Advocate*, January 12, 1977, 19-21.

Katz, Jonathan Ned. *Coming Out! A Documentary Play About Gay Life and Liberation in the U.S.A.* New York: Arno Press, 1975.

_____. *Gay American History: Lesbians and Gay Men in the U.S.A., a Documentary History.* New York: Crowell, 1976. Rev. ed. New York: Meridian, 1992.

_____. *Gay/Lesbian Almanac: A New Documentary in Which Is Contained, in Chronological Order, Evidence of the True and Fantastical History of Those Persons Now Called Lesbians and Gay Men.* New York: Harper & Row, 1983.

National Museum & Archive of Lesbian and Gay History. *The Lesbian Almanac.* New York: Berkley Books, 1996.

Ridinger, Robert B., ed. *Speaking for Our Lives: Historic Speeches and Rhetoric for Gay and Lesbian Rights (1892-2000).* New York: Harrington Park Press, 2004.

Wright, Les K. "Jonathan Ned Katz." In *Gay and Lesbian Biography*, edited by Michael J. Tyrkus. Detroit, Mich.: St. James Press, 1997.

## 1976-1990
# ARMY RESERVIST BEN-SHALOM SUES FOR REINSTATEMENT

*After Sgt. Miriam Ben-Shalom had confirmed to a reporter that she was lesbian, she was discharged from the U.S. Army Reserve. She sued for reinstatement and was readmitted by the courts, but the Army refused the court's orders until 1988. She served one more year but lost her bid to reenlist, a case that reached the U.S. Supreme Court in 1990. Her battle with the military and courts makes her the first out lesbian or gay service person to be reinstated to the U.S. armed forces for any length of time after being discharged as lesbian or gay.*

**LOCALE:** Wisconsin
**CATEGORIES:** Military; civil rights; laws, acts, and legal history

### KEY FIGURES
*Miriam Ben-Shalom* (b. 1948), U.S. Army Reserve drill sergeant
*Leonard Matlovich* (1943-1988), U.S. Air Force sergeant and Vietnam veteran
*Terence Evans*, U.S. district court judge who ruled, in 1980, that Ben-Shalom's discharge was illegal
*Harlington Wood, Jr.*, federal appeals court judge who authored the final decision, in 1989, that prohibited Ben-Shalom's reenlistment

### SUMMARY OF EVENT
After Sgt. Leonard Matlovich began his battle to win reinstatement after the U.S. Air Force discharged him in 1975 because he was gay, U.S.

Army Reserve drill sergeant Miriam Ben-Shalom took notice. An out lesbian, Ben-Shalom was one of the first two female drill sergeants in the 84th Training Division of the Army Reserve. She had been wondering at the time why she, too, had not been discharged because of her sexual orientation.

Ben-Shalom had earned bachelor's and master's degrees at the University of Wisconsin and had served in the Israeli army before completing drill sergeant school with the U.S. Army. After her training, she was asked by a reporter about her sexuality. She answered honestly, and her commanding officer then sought her discharge. Ben-Shalom was discharged in 1976 and then sued for reinstatement. She had won her case, was refused reentry by a noncomplying Army, continued her legal fight, and then finally won reinstatement in 1987. In late 1988, with the Army still refusing to comply with the court's order, she began serving the remaining year of her service obligation after the court threatened the Army with contempt of court. She then tried to reenlist but the Army refused to reenlist her; she sued, then lost her U.S. Supreme Court case, *Ben-Shalom v. Marsh*, in 1989.

At the same time as Ben-Shalom's battle, Matlovich continued his fight against the Air Force. In 1978, the U.S. Court of Appeals ruled his discharge illegal, and in September of 1980, a federal judge ordered his reinstatement and awarded him back pay. Rather than comply, the Air Force worked out a costly settlement with Matlovich; he accepted and dropped the case because he felt it better to end with a victory and believed the conservative Supreme

Court would have been unlikely to rule in his favor.

Ben-Shalom, however, continued to pursue her case. She had not been discharged for homosexual *conduct*, but rather because she *stated* she was lesbian. For this reason, her discharge was listed as honorable. Moreover, Ben-Shalom's case was based on her First Amendment right to free speech and due process. In May of 1980, five months before the more well-known Matlovich decision, the U.S. District Court in Chicago ruled Ben-Shalom's discharge unconstitutional according to the First, Fifth, and Ninth Amendments. Judge Terence Evans also noted that one's sexual orientation should not be subject to government interference, whether in the armed forces or elsewhere. His statements demonstrated that gays and lesbians in the military deserve the constitutional protection of free speech, among other rights. The Army refused to reinstate Ben-Shalom, in spite of Judge Evans's orders, though it dropped its appeal in the case.

After being denied reinstatement by the Army, Ben-Shalom filed suit to force Army compliance. The Court of Appeals in Chicago repeated the orders to reinstate Ben-Shalom in 1987, and, in 1988, after the court threatened the Army with heavy fines for contempt of court if it continued to fail to comply, Ben-Shalom was allowed to resume her position as a drill sergeant and finish her term of service, which ended in 1989. She then tried to reenlist, and the Army refused. She sued once more, and the lawsuit landed in the Court of Appeals. A three-member panel led by Judge Harlington Wood, Jr., found in the Army's favor. Wood had reasserted a long-standing military claim, that the presence of out gays and lesbians would imperil military morale and discipline. It did not matter to Wood that Ben-Shalom had been reinstated earlier and that she served with distinction without imperiling morale and discipline. Wood had relied on the military regulation that authorized discharge because of an individual's statements that demonstrated a tendency toward homosexual conduct or statements that one is homosexual or bisexual. The Army still had no evidence of "lesbian contact." The Supreme Court refused to hear Ben-Shalom's appeal in 1990, and her costly bid for reenlistment was denied. With lit-

tle outside support, she was left to pay off a heavy legal debt.

## SIGNIFICANCE

Although she ultimately lost her bid for reenlistment, Miriam Ben-Shalom's reinstatement in 1988 was a key victory for gays and lesbians in the military. Judge Evans's reinstatement orders were upheld in 1987. It was on the point of reenlistment that Ben-Shalom lost. Thus, the Army had been forced to reinstate Ben-Shalom for roughly one year, the time left on her service contract. Her successful presence in the Army for that time challenges the argument that out gays and lesbians would undermine morale among the troops. Moreover, she had been the first lesbian or gay person to win reinstatement, five months ahead of Matlovich, and she had pursued the case through higher courts and won. Though she had been denied by the Supreme Court reenlistment as an out lesbian, she exposed military hypocrisy in a way Matlovich was unable to do because he had settled his case before the Air Force faced a legal challenge.

*—Jessie Bishop Powell*

## FURTHER READING

Belkin, Aaron, and Melissa Sheridan Embser-Herbert. "A Modest Proposal: Privacy as a Flawed Rationale for the Exclusion of Gays and Lesbians from the U.S. Military." *International Security* 27, no. 2 (2002): 178-197.

Bérubé, Allan. *Coming Out Under Fire: The History of Gay Men and Women in World War Two.* New York: Free Press, 1990.

Cain, Paul D. *Leading the Parade: Conversations with America's Most Influential Lesbians and Gay Men.* Lanham, Md.: Scarecrow Press, 2002.

Don't Ask, Don't Tell, Don't Pursue Digital Database, Stanford University Law School. http://dont.stanford.edu.

Humphrey, Mary Ann. *My Country, My Right to Serve: Experiences of Gay Men and Women in the Military, World War II to the Present.* New York: HarperCollins, 1990.

Rimmerman, Craig A. *Gay Rights, Military Wrongs: Political Perspectives on Lesbians and*

*Gays in the Military*. New York: Garland, 1996.

Servicemembers Legal Defense Network. *Conduct Unbecoming: Annual Reports on "Don't Ask, Don't Tell, Don't Pursue, Don't Harass."* 1994-2003. http://www.sldn.org.

———. *Survival Guide: A Comprehensive Guide to "Don't Ask, Don't Tell, Don't Pursue, Don't Harass," and Related Military Policies*. 4th ed. Washington, D.C.: Author, 2003.

Shilts, Randy. *Conduct Unbecoming: Lesbians and Gays in the U.S. Military—Vietnam to the Persian Gulf*. New York: St. Martin's Press, 1993.

**SEE ALSO:** 1912-1924: Robles Fights in the Mexican Revolution; Mar. 15, 1919-1921: U.S. Navy Launches Sting Operation Against "Sexual Perverts"; July 3, 1975: U.S. Civil Service Commission Prohibits Discrimination Against Federal Employees; May-Aug., 1980: U.S. Navy Investigates the USS *Norton Sound* in Antilesbian Witch Hunt; May 3, 1989: *Watkins v. United States Army* Reinstates Gay Soldier; 1990, 1994: *Coming Out Under Fire* Documents Gay and Lesbian Military Veterans; Aug. 27, 1991: *The Advocate* Outs Pentagon Spokesman Pete Williams; Oct., 1992: Canadian Military Lifts Its Ban on Gays and Lesbians; Nov. 30, 1993: Don't Ask, Don't Tell Policy Is Implemented; Jan. 12, 2000: United Kingdom Lifts Ban on Gays and Lesbians in the Military.

## August 20-22, 1976
# MICHIGAN WOMYN'S MUSIC FESTIVAL HOLDS ITS FIRST GATHERING

*Founded in 1976 and continuing as an annual event, the week-long Michigan Womyn's Music Festival is one of the largest gatherings of lesbians in the world, featuring performances from women musicians and artists, hundreds of workshops, and sharing of lesbian and feminist culture. The festival helped pave the way for the mainstream success of women's music festivals such as Lilith Fair and Ladyfest.*

**LOCALE:** Mt. Pleasant, Hesperia, and Hart, Michigan

**CATEGORIES:** Cultural and intellectual history; arts; organizations and institutions; feminism

**KEY FIGURES**

*Lisa Vogel*, co-organizer of the first festival and long-time producer

*Kristie Vogel*, co-organizer of the first festival

*Boo Price*, coproducer of the festival, 1976-1994

**SUMMARY OF EVENT**

Drawing from the hippie movements of the 1960's as well as from radical politics, 1970's lesbian feminism advocated a women-centered culture separate from the rules of patriarchal society. At the same time, women's music was growing in popularity, with artists such as Alix Dobkin and Maxine Feldman proudly singing about loving women and living as lesbians. Olivia Records, founded by ten women in 1973, produced and distributed women's music albums that were sold at women's music festivals across the United States.

The first Michigan Womyn's Music Festival took place over the weekend of August 20-22, 1976, in Mt. Pleasant, Michigan, with an audience of approximately two thousand women. Organized by Kristie Vogel, Mary Kindig, and Lisa Vogel under the name We Want the Music Collective, the first festival offered camping, food, and performances for a ticket price of $20.00. Performers included Dobkin, Feldman, Meg Christian, Holly

Near, and Margie Adam—all of whom hailed from the growing women's music genre and would become popular performers on the women's festival circuit.

The early Michigan festivals were characterized by inexperience in combination with determination to produce an entirely woman-run program. Boo Price, who coproduced the festival from 1976 to 1994, was instrumental in bringing a more professional production ethic to the festival. Despite inclement weather—tornadoes visited the festival in its second year—producers and festival-goers alike were drawn to the spirit of the woman-centered community.

Describing the early years of the Michigan festival, Price explains,

> There was an ecstatic quality to these first years of gatherings, punctuated by acts of social defiance: letting menstrual blood flow freely, throwing off shirts or all clothing, taking on male-identified jobs such as trench digging, tent stake sledging, stage rigging, tractor driving. Most of festival culture in the early days was the result of doing it all ourselves.

Although the festival was begun as a collective, it soon became apparent that it would need to be run as a business, and by 1979 the name of the founding organization had been changed to We Want the Music Company. From 1977 to 1981 the festival was held in Hesperia, Michigan, and Lisa Vogel, who had been only eighteen at the time the festival began, assumed a leadership role. In 1982, Lisa and Kristie Vogel took on the responsibility of signing for loans to buy 650 acres of land in Hart, Michigan, in order to provide a permanent home for the festival. Thereafter, the festival was held on this privately owned and largely undeveloped land, which remains unused for most of the year.

After the festival was moved to Hart, coproducers Price and Lisa Vogel spearheaded efforts to create a more organized festival culture that was inclusive of all women. The Womyn of Color Tent was founded in 1983 to provide a space where only women of color were allowed to gather. The tenth

festival, in 1986, was the first festival in which women from outside the United States were invited to greet the entire audience at the opening ceremony. To make the festival wheelchair-accessible, concrete paths were laid in some areas, and by 1988 water and electrical systems had been installed to make hot showers available to campers. In addition, hundreds of workshops were offered to teach women about everything from feminist activism to drumming and stilt-walking.

The Michigan festival, like many women's music festivals, has been punctuated by several controversies, beginning with its decision from the first year not to admit men; later it was decided that boys over the age of five would be restricted to a camp separate from the main portion of the festival. Concerns about sadomasochism (S/M) were raised in the late 1980's and 1990's, with many women arguing that S/M was inappropriate because it involved violence against women, while others argued that consensual sexual expression was their right. Beginning in 1994, transgender activists protested the festival's policy of admitting only women born as women through the establishment of Camp Trans (www.camp-trans.org), a separate camp located less than a mile from the original Michigan festival's main gate. Their desire to open the Michigan Womyn's Music Festival to male-to-female transgender individuals has been viewed by many long-time festival-goers as a threat to the temporary safe space for women who have "survived girlhood."

Throughout the 1980's until the mid-1990's, festival attendance ranged from five thousand to eight thousand women, peaking in the mid-1990's at about nine or ten thousand. Thereafter, attendance declined; 2004, the twenty-ninth year, saw approximately four thousand festival-goers. Lisa Vogel, who has been with the festival since the first year, continues to act as the festival's producer.

## SIGNIFICANCE

The Michigan Womyn's Music Festival, along with the dozens of other women's music festivals that sprang up across the United States in the 1980's, was a major catalyst for the growth of the women's music business. The festivals provided space for musicians to perform and build an audience; enabled women's music distribution companies such as Olivia Records, Ladyslipper, and Goldenrod to flourish; and provided opportunities for many women to learn sound engineering and professional production techniques—skills that many women were denied by a male-dominated field.

Although the heyday of the women's music festival circuit may have passed, Michigan and the other women's music festivals paved the way for the mainstream success of Lilith Fair, which toured the United States from 1997 to 1999. Newer festivals such as Ladyfest, a series of grassroots-produced art and music festivals for younger queer women that are often held in urban locations, also followed in the tradition of Michigan.

Finally, the legacy of Michigan is certainly felt by the thousands of women who have spent time on the land. Many call the land "home" and feel that the week of the festival is the one time of the year when they can truly be free to be who they are without fear of violence or judgment. The Michigan Womyn's Music Festival has indeed become a legend in lesbian culture.

*—Malinda Lo*

**FURTHER READING**

Faderman, Lillian. *Odd Girls and Twilight Lovers: A History of Lesbian Life in Twentieth-Century America*. New York: Penguin, 1991.

Kearney, Mary Celeste. "The Missing Links: Riot Grrrl—Feminism—Lesbian Culture." In *Sexing the Groove: Popular Music and Gender*, edited by Sheila Whiteley. New York: Routledge, 1997.

Lewis, Deborah R. "The Original Womyn's Woodstock." In *The Woman-Centered Economy*, edited by Loraine Edwalds and Midge Stocker. Chicago: Third Side Press, 1995.

Morris, Bonnie J. *Eden Built by Eves: The Culture of Women's Music Festivals*. Los Angeles: Alyson, 1999.

Rothblum, Esther, and Penny Sablove, eds. *Lesbian Communities: Festivals, RV's, and the Internet*. New York: Harrington Park Press, 2005.

Sandstrom, Boden C. "Performance, Ritual, and Negotiation of Identity in the Michigan Womyn's Music Festival." Unpublished Ph.D. dissertation. University of Maryland, 2002.

_____. "Women's Music: Passing the Legacy." In *Women's Culture in a New Era: A Feminist Revolution?*, edited by Gayle Kimball. Lanham, Md.: Scarecrow Press, 2005.

**SEE ALSO:** May 27-30, 1960: First National Lesbian Conference Convenes; May 1, 1970: Radicalesbians Issues "The Woman Identified Woman" Manifesto; 1973: Olivia Records Is Founded; Sept., 1975: Anna Crusis Women's Choir Is Formed; 1981-1982: GALA Choruses Is Formed; 1992: Transgender Nation Holds Its First Protest; 1992-2002: Celebrity Lesbians Come Out; Apr. 24, 1993: First Dyke March Is Held in Washington, D.C.

**1977**

# ANITA BRYANT CAMPAIGNS AGAINST GAY AND LESBIAN RIGHTS

*Voters in Dade County, Florida, led by entertainer Anita Bryant and her "Save Our Children" campaign, repealed a gay and lesbian rights law by a two-to-one margin. The original ordinance is generally viewed as the focal point for the backlash against gay and lesbian rights in the United States in the late 1970's and early 1980's.*

**LOCALE:** Dade County, Florida
**CATEGORIES:** Laws, acts, and legal history; civil rights

**KEY FIGURES**
*Anita Bryant* (b. 1940), entertainer and a spokesperson for the Florida Orange Growers Association
*Jerry Falwell* (b. 1933), Baptist minister and leader of the conservative Moral Majority

**SUMMARY OF EVENT**
After the Stonewall Rebellion in New York City in 1969 triggered more than a decade of gay and lesbian revolution, antigay crusaders began to mobilize to protest GLBT-rights activism and its successes. In 1977, Dade County, Florida, passed an ordinance protecting gays and lesbians against discrimination based on sexual orientation.

Anita Bryant, a singer and a runner-up in the 1959 Miss America pageant (and later spokesperson for the Florida Orange Growers Association), launched a campaign to repeal the ordinance primarily prompted by her Southern Baptist upbringing and heavily conservative morals. Bryant was a relentless crusader, and she was quickly surrounded by friends and supporters. Focusing their efforts on stereotypes and prejudices surrounding homosexuality, the group named itself Save Our Children and used fears of child molestation and gays "recruiting" children to join their ranks to spark voters to repeal the ordinance by a 69 to 31 percent vote.

Featured on the June 6, 1977, cover of *Newsweek*, Bryant became a national figure, and popular Baptist preacher Jerry Falwell joined her crusade. Indeed, around the country, antigay campaigners rallied around Bryant to protest gay rights legislation. For example, California State senator John V. Briggs attempted unsuccessfully to pass an antigay initiative that would have prevented gay and lesbian teachers from teaching in California schools. Bryant's supporters called themselves the Religious, or Christian, Right, and, in 1979, Falwell formed the Moral Majority, with the specific goal of promoting conservative Christianity in politics. The conservative fundamentalist Christian agenda espoused by the Moral Majority included antiabortion and antigay campaigns, the reinstatement of prayer in public schools, and the addition of creationism (a Bible-based counterview of evolution) to public school curricula. In the 1980 elections, the Moral Majority successfully lobbied in favor of conservative candidates. Falwell led the Moral Majority until 1987, and the group disbanded in 1989.

White supremacist groups generally endorsed antigay politicians and causes, and violence often accompanied their activities. Antigay sentiment ran so high that, in 1979, former San Francisco city and county supervisor Dan White was sentenced to less than eight years in prison for his 1978 assassination of gay San Francisco city and county supervisor Harvey Milk and San Francisco mayor George Moscone. Gay rights activists retaliated with rioting.

In this reactionary atmosphere, gay rights initiatives around the country began to encounter defeat, and gay rights activists found themselves regularly struggling against the antigay crusaders at the polls. However, Bryant and the Religious Right also inadvertently sparked a new wave of GLBT-rights organizing, as their highly visible stance drew attention to the gay rights debate. Gay rights activists accused Bryant of promoting bigotry and repression, and gay rights advocates turned out as often as did antigay campaigners to fight for control at the ballot box.

## SIGNIFICANCE

The impact of Anita Bryant's campaign on her personal life was swift and negative. She went on tour, campaigning against homosexuality, the same year that Save Our Children effected the overturn of the Dade County ordinance. However, her crusade devastated her career. In Des Moines, Iowa, gay rights protesters "creamed" her in the face with a pie, a tactic that gained popularity in the fight against the Moral Majority. The controversy surrounding Bryant led the Florida Orange Juice Growers Association to drop her as their spokesperson in 1980, due to a nationwide orange juice boycott organized by gay rights activists. Bryant was divorced in the same year and used much of her own money trying to promote her cause. Because of her divorce, many of her Christian conservative allies reviled her as a sinner. By the time of her 1990 remarriage, her popularity had waned, and by 2001 she had filed for bankruptcy in two states.

Bryant's social impact can still be felt in the presence of vocal antigay celebrities who use a strong conservative Christian stance to denounce homosexuality. Bryant herself has largely withdrawn from the battle, insisting that there is a distinction between hating homosexuality and hating homosexual individuals. (Homosexuals, she feels, can be "saved" from their "sinful" behavior.) Religious conservatives launched programs to "cure" gays and lesbians of their homosexuality, and these programs and their descendants persist to the present. However, there are also vocal gay rights protesters among modern celebrities, including lesbian talk-show hosts and comedians Ellen Degeneres and Rosie O'Donnell, who now lives in Florida.

The impact of Bryant's campaign on national politics had been enormous. Conservative leaders were largely in favor of the Moral Majority. In Florida, legislation was soon passed outlawing adoption by gays and lesbians. In 2004, the Eleventh Circuit Court of Appeals upheld the legislation. Twenty-one years after Bryant's Save Our Children campaign, gay rights activists succeeded in bringing about the equal treatment legislation Bryant had initially succeeded in overturning when, in 1998, Miami-Dade County passed an antibias ordinance. In 2002, a conservative Christian group calling itself SAVE Dade attempted to overturn the ordinance just as Bryant and her followers had done in 1977. However, a vocal activist group, No to Discrimination/SAVE Dade, successfully prevented a repeat of Bryant's earlier success.

—*Jessie Bishop Powell*

## FURTHER READING

Bryant, Anita. *The Anita Bryant Story: The Survival of Our Nation's Families and the Threat of Militant Homosexuality*. Nashville, Tenn.: Revell, 1977.

Button, James W., Barbara Ann Rienzo, and Kenneth D. Wald. *Private Lives, Public Conflicts: Battles over Gay Rights in American Communities*. Washington, D.C.: CQ Press, 1997.

Howard, John. *Men Like That: A Southern Queer History*. Chicago: University of Chicago Press, 1999.

Moran, Leslie J. *Sexuality and the Politics of Violence and Safety*. New York: Routledge, 2004.

**SEE ALSO:** 1972-1973: Local Governments Pass Antidiscrimination Laws; Mar. 5, 1974: Antigay and Antilesbian Organizations Begin to Form; Nov. 7, 1978: Antigay and Antilesbian Briggs Initiative Is Defeated; 1979: Moral Majority Is Founded; Nov., 1986: Californians Reject LaRouche's Quarantine Initiative; Nov. 3, 1992: Oregon and Colorado Attempt Antigay Initiatives; Mar.-Apr., 1993: Battelle Sex Study Prompts Conservative Backlash.

## April, 1977
# COMBAHEE RIVER COLLECTIVE ISSUES "A BLACK FEMINIST STATEMENT"

*An African American lesbian-feminist group called the Combahee River Collective issued "A Black Feminist Statement," addressing the connections among racial, sexual, heterosexist, and classist oppressions. The statement has become foundational for feminists of all backgrounds and is core reading in women's studies and other college courses.*

**LOCALE:** Boston, Massachusetts
**CATEGORIES:** Race and ethnicity; feminism; publications

### SUMMARY OF EVENT

The origins of the Combahee River Collective lie in the black women's movement, which was formed in response to the neglect and oppression many black women were experiencing from both the Civil Rights movement and the women's movement. Racism had worked against black women in the women's movement led by white women, while sexism had worked against them in the Civil Rights movement, which was headed mostly by men.

Many feminists believed that the specific concerns of black women should be secondary to the concerns of women in general, regardless of race or ethnicity. Since the women's movement was made up of primarily white women, white women's concerns were addressed. Similarly, members of many black civil rights groups gave secondary importance to women and paid little mind to women's rights, let alone feminism, forces the groups felt threatened their antiracist directives. Out of a growing frustration with this marginalization, a group of black feminists formed the National Black Feminist Organization (NBFO) in 1973 to address the specific concerns of black women.

In 1974, shortly after the first eastern regional conference of the NBFO, a black feminist group outside Boston was formed for political organizing.

Initially, the group met to determine only what resources were available to them and to continue the politics of consciousness-raising and emotional solidarity they felt would enhance their lives. They also decided to form their own independent collective because of disagreements with what they considered the classist and unfocused position of the NBFO. They became known as the Combahee River Collective, named after the river in South Carolina where Harriet Tubman led one of the first military engagements in U.S. history planned and executed by a woman. Tubman freed more than eight hundred enslaved blacks.

Despite trouble in their earlier years with internal conflict, the group grew in numbers and esteem. "In the process of consciousness-raising, actually life-sharing, we began to recognize the commonality of our experiences and, from that sharing and growing consciousness, to build a politics that will change our lives and inevitably end our oppression." Eventually the group became not only a study group but also an important political organization for African American women.

The collective promoted equality through sisterhood and cooperation. Their initial politics were derived from the belief that "black women are inherently valuable, that our liberation is a necessity not as an adjunct to somebody else's but because of our need as human persons for autonomy." In addition to the oppression caused by race and gender, the collective also sought to address the concerns of lesbians and women in the "lower" working classes. They recognized that issues of sexual orientation, imperialism, and class position were also contributing to the oppression of African American women. Thus, utilizing the techniques of identity politics, the collective asserted a socialist ideal of equality for all peoples.

In April, 1977, the collective put forth a political manifesto called "A Black Feminist Statement."

## From "A Black Feminist Statement"

We are a collective of Black feminists who have been meeting together since 1974 . . . involved in the process of defining and clarifying our politics, while . . . doing political work within our own group and in coalition with other progressive organizations and movements. . . . [W]e see Black feminism as the logical political movement to combat the manifold and simultaneous oppressions that all women of color face.

1. *The Genesis of Contemporary Black Feminism*

[W]e find our origins in the historical reality of Afro-American women's continuous life-and-death struggle for survival and liberation. . . . As Angela Davis points out, Black women have always embodied an adversary stance to white male rule and have actively resisted its inroads upon them and their communities. . . . Black, other Third World, and working women have been involved in the feminist movement from its start, but both outside reactionary forces and racism and elitism within the movement itself have served to obscure our participation. . . . Black feminist politics also have an obvious connection to movements for Black liberation, particularly those of the 1960's and 1970's. . . . It was our experience and disillusionment within these liberation movements, as well as experience on the periphery of the white male left, that led to the need to develop a politics that was anti-racist, unlike those of white women, and anti-sexist, unlike those of Black and white men. There is also undeniably a personal genesis for Black feminism. . . . However, we had no way of conceptualizing what was so apparent to us, what we *knew* was really happening. . . . Our development must also be tied to the contemporary economic and political position of Black people. . . . [A] handful of us have been able to gain certain tools as a result of tokenism in education and employment which potentially enable us to more effectively fight our oppression. . . . [A]s we developed politically we addressed ourselves to heterosexism and economic oppression under capitalism.

2. *What We Believe*

Our politics evolve from a healthy love for ourselves, our sisters and our community which allows us to continue our struggle and work. This focusing upon our own oppression is embodied in the concept of identity politics. . . . [T]he most profound and potentially most radical politics come directly out of our own identity . . . [t]o be recognized as human, levelly human, is enough. . . . Although we are feminists and Lesbians, we feel solidarity with progressive Black men and do not advocate the fractionalization that white women who are separatists demand. . . . We struggle together with Black men against racism, while we also struggle with Black men about sexism. . . . We are socialists because we believe that work must be organized for the collective benefit of those who do the work and create the products, and not for the profit of the bosses. . . . We need to articulate the real class situation of persons . . . for whom racial and sexual oppression are significant determinants in their working/economic lives. . . .

*Source:* Combahee River Collective, "The Combahee River Collective Statement: Feminist Organizing in the Seventies and Eighties." 1977.

This declaration has since become one of the defining documents of not only the black women's movement but also the women's movement in general, and it represents one of the earliest attempts at combating multiple, interlocking oppressions. The following outlines the guiding force of the collective:

The most general statement of our politics at the present time would be that we are actively committed to struggling against racial, sexual, heterosexual, and class oppression and see as our particular task the development of integrated analysis and practice based upon the fact that the major systems of oppression are interlocking.

This statement was critical because many people believed that multifocused, strategic action was the only way to address multiple forces of oppression. A coherent theory was needed to address the simultaneous effects of racism, sexism, heterosexism, and classism. The manifesto was one of the first steps toward developing this theory.

### Significance

The black women's movement has powerfully impacted the lives of African American women who have been neglected by other civil rights movements. Black feminists have raised awareness about the interrelatedness of sexism and racism, and heterosexism and classism, in the struggles for racial and sexual equality. Most important, black feminists have shed light on the specific struggles endured by black women and given solidarity and voice to those traditionally silenced or silent. The Combahee River Collective's successes at consciousness-raising have been widely acclaimed.

Although the Combahee River Collective was disbanded in 1980, "A Black Feminist Statement" has continued to influence feminists, academics, civil rights leaders, and social reformers. The statement represents the earliest attempt by an African American feminist group to produce a manifesto. The document has become mandatory reading for students of the Civil Rights movement and for feminist and women's studies.

—*Michael Ryan*

**FURTHER READING**

Collins, Patricia Hill. *Black Feminist Thought: Knowledge, Consciousness, and the Politics of Empowerment.* New York: Routledge, 1990.

_____. *Fighting Words: Black Women and the Search for Justice.* Minneapolis: University of Minnesota Press, 1998.

Combahee River Collective. "A Black Feminist Statement." In *All the Women Are White, All the Blacks Are Men, but Some of Us Are Brave*, edited by Gloria Hull, Patricia Bell Scott, and Barbara Smith. Old Westbury, N.Y.: Kitchen Table: Women of Color Press, 1983.

Giddings, Paula J. *When and Where I Enter: The Impact of Black Women on Race and Sex in America.* New York: HarperCollins, 1984.

Naples, Nancy A. *Community Activism and Feminist Politics: Organizing Across Race, Class, and Gender.* New York: Routledge, 1998.

Wallace, Michele. "A Black Feminist's Search for Sisterhood." *Village Voice*, July, 1975, 6-7.

**SEE ALSO:** July 2-Aug. 28, 1963: Rustin Organizes the March on Washington; May 1, 1970: Radicalesbians Issues "The Woman Identified Woman" Manifesto; Nov. 7, 1972: Jordan Becomes First Black Congresswoman from the South; 1981: *This Bridge Called My Back* Is Published; Oct., 1981: Kitchen Table: Women of Color Press Is Founded; 1982: Lorde's Autobiography *Zami* Is Published; Sept., 1983: First National Lesbians of Color Conference Convenes; 1990: United Lesbians of African Heritage Is Founded.

## November 18-21, 1977
# NATIONAL WOMEN'S CONFERENCE CONVENES

*A majority of delegates to the national women's conference, the first nationwide conference of its kind since the Seneca Falls Convention of 1848, voted to support a "sexual-preference" resolution. The resolution gave lesbians the support of the women at the conference and the visibility they had been denied in the women's movement.*

**ALSO KNOWN AS:** International Women's Year Conference

**LOCALE:** Houston, Texas

**CATEGORIES:** Feminism; organizations and institutions

**KEY FIGURES**

*Barbara Jordan* (1936-1996), congresswoman from Texas, delivered the keynote address

*Patsy Mink* (1927-2002), congresswoman from Hawaii, proposed conference with Bella Abzug

*Bella Abzug* (1920-1998), congresswoman from New York, presiding officer of conference, proposed conference with Mink

*Jean O'Leary* (1948-2005), presented the sexual-preference proposal, later member of President Jimmy Carter's National Advisory Committee for Women

*Betty Friedan* (1921-2006), feminist, educator, writer, cofounder of the National Organization for Women, and speaker at conference

*Phyllis Schlafly* (b. 1924), conservative Republican attorney from Illinois, founder of Stop ERA, founder of the Eagle Forum, and antifeminist and antilesbian activist

### SUMMARY OF EVENT

In 1974, President Gerald Ford signed an order creating a National Commission on the Observance of International Women's Year. One year later, Congressmembers Bella Abzug and Patsy Mink proposed that a national women's conference be held as part of the U.S. bicentennial celebration.

*Bella Abzug.* (Library of Congress)

Federal money was earmarked for fifty state conferences to elect delegates to a national conference planned for November 18-21, 1977, in Houston, Texas.

After learning of the conference, lesbian activist Jean O'Leary, who at the time was co-executive director of the National Gay Task Force in Washington, D.C., alerted Los Angeles lesbian activist Diane Abbitt about the importance of the state conferences for lesbians. Abbitt, Jeanne Cordova, Bobbi Bennett, and others began planning for lesbian representation, visibility, and advocacy at the conferences, at the state and national levels. The California State Conference was held at the University of Southern California (USC) in June of 1977.

At USC, lesbians worked in alliance with heterosexual women to elect what came to be called the Orange Slate: pro-choice, pro-lesbian, and pro-ERA (Equal Rights Amendment). Those who endorsed these issues and other progressive measures became known as the "pro-plan" group, or faction. The name of the Orange Slate was coined as a reference to singer and Florida orange juice spokesperson Anita Bryant, who had led a successful campaign to rescind an LGBT rights statute in Dade County, Florida. John V. Briggs, a state senator who wanted to be governor of California, thought he could do something similar and had managed to place a proposition on the California state ballot that, if it had passed, would have prevented the hiring of lesbian and gay teachers and the firing of those already teaching.

A second group of delegates at the Houston conference was led by antifeminist and antilesbian activist Phyllis Schlafly (who is also the mother of a gay son), representing what came to be called the "pro-life, pro-family" faction. Schlafly's supporters would hold a "counter-conference" on Saturday, November 19, at a location five miles from the national conference venue.

Displaying a newly acquired penchant and skill for Roberts Rules of Order, the Lesbian Caucus and their straight allies at the USC conference managed to elect thirteen out lesbians to the California delegation, including Abbitt, Cordova, Bennett, Marilyn Murphy, Lillene Fifield, Phyllis Lyon, and Del

## DECLARATION OF AMERICAN WOMEN (1977)

We are here to move history forward.

We are women from every State and Territory in the Nation.

We are women of different ages, beliefs and lifestyles.

We are women of many economic, social, political, racial, ethnic, cultural, educational and religious backgrounds.

We are married, single, widowed and divorced.

We are mothers and daughters.

We are sisters. . . .

We speak in varied accents and languages but we share the common language and experience of American women who throughout our Nation's life have been denied the opportunities, rights, privileges and responsibilities accorded to men. . . .

We do not seek special privileges, but we demand as a human right a full voice and role for women in determining the destiny of our world, our nation, our families and our individual lives. . . .

We are entitled to and expect serious attention to our proposals.

We demand immediate and continuing action on our National Plan by Federal, State, public, and private institutions so that by 1985, the end of the International Decade for Women proclaimed by the United Nations, everything possible under the law will have been done to provide American women with full equality.

The rest will be up to the hearts, minds and moral consciences of men and women and what they do to make our society truly democratic and open to all.

We pledge ourselves with all the strength of our dedication to this struggle "to form a more perfect Union."

*Source:* Handbook of Texas Online. http://www.tsha.utexas.edu/handbook/online.

in leadership positions had not been open for debate.

More than two thousand elected delegates and more than eighteen thousand observers had converged on Houston for the National Women's Conference (NWC). Lesbians whose issues had been silenced at the International Women's Year Conference in Mexico in 1975 were extremely visible in Houston. Also, 1977 marked the first time that a significant number of women of color were delegates at a nationwide U.S. women's conference. While most women of color delegates were not lesbians, many were supportive of lesbian rights.

The opening ceremonies included the arrival of a lighted torch, which had been carried by runners to Houston from Seneca Falls, New York, site of the first women's rights convention in 1848. The keynote address was delivered by Congresswoman Barbara Jordan, who at the time was not out as a lesbian. Musician Margie Adam, who was out, led the delegates in a hearty rendition of her song, "We Shall Go Forth!" Delegates then prepared to address the issues in the proposed National Plan of Action, which contained twenty-six planks or proposals ranging from health care to affirmative action to sexual orientation. The twenty-third plank, called the "sexual-preference resolution," called for legislation to eliminate discrimination based on "sexual and affectional" preference. It also called for reform of penal codes that restricted sexual relations between consenting adults and for the prohibition of practices that were prejudicial toward lesbian mothers. Lesbians from various delegations and their heterosexual allies worked overtime to get the resolution passed.

For those attending as observers, a $5 admission

Martin. Out lesbian activists elected in other state conferences included Charlotte Bunch from Washington, D.C., and Betty Powell, Eleanor Cooper, and Ginny Apuzzo from New York.

Lesbians were ecstatic about attending the national conference, but as one member of the Lesbian Caucus noted, "I was pleased that the Lesbian Caucus presented such a unified, strong front, but I was upset [that] we were not able to form a coalition with Third World women due to our lack of sensitivity to their needs." In the excitement, inclusiveness was at times left behind. Some of those who attended the USC and the Houston conferences felt that the women who had been elected as lesbian delegates had self-selected from specific social and political networks and that, in Houston, an agenda set by a few

## Friedan on the Lesbian Rights Resolution

I am Betty Friedan, delegate at large. I am known to be violently opposed to the lesbian issue in the woman's movement, and in fact I have been. This issue has been used to divide us too much. It has been seized on by the enemies of women's equality and it has alienated many. As someone who has grown up in middle America—as someone who grew up in Peoria, Illinois, and as someone who has perhaps loved men too well—I have had trouble with this issue, as have many other women who grew up as I have. We have all made mistakes in our focus on this issue, but we have all learned. Now my passionate priority is ratification of the Equal Rights Amendment or we will lose all we have fought for in the last 15 years. And because I know, as you know, that despite what our right-wing reactionary enemies say, there is nothing whatsoever in the Equal Rights Amendment that will give any protection to homosexuals, I believe that we must help the women who are lesbians be protected in their own civil rights. And in the historic unity of this day, and because we will need every ounce of all our efforts in the next 13 months to get the Equal Rights Amendment ratified, I suggest that you waste no further time in debating this issue and join with me in voting support of the resolution on sexual preference.

*Source:* Betty Friedan speech transcript, National Women's Conference, November 18-21, 1977, Houston, Texas. Distinguished Women in Government lecture series (Hayward, Calif.: Tape Services Unlimited, 1978).

fee allowed one to visit the vendor area, attend workshops, and view the proceedings from the gallery. Supporters of various issues mingled and performed street theater outside the Albert Thomas Convention Hall. At one point there was an altercation between white supremacists and a large group of women. The women pushed the supremacists away from the convention hall and back into the street. Homophobic and nonfeminist delegates, including Schlafly and her supporters, were vastly outnumbered.

On Sunday evening, November 20, delegate Jean O'Leary read the sexual-preference resolution; speakers on the pros and cons of the proposal followed. Government security officers became concerned after hearing that lesbians would revolt if the proposal was not passed. One conference official assured the officers that no revolt was imminent.

Just before the vote on the lesbian-rights resolution, National Organization for Women representative Betty Friedan, who in 1969 had used the phrase "lavender menace" to describe what she believed

was the menacing effect lesbians had on the women's movement, spoke in favor of the lesbian-rights resolution and apologized for her past comments. It was an emotional moment.

In spite of opposition from Schlafly and friends, a majority of the two thousand mostly heterosexual women voted to support their lesbian sisters. After the proposal passed, observers in the bleachers and those standing behind a large "Lesbian Rights" banner, joyfully shouted "Thank you sisters!" and released thousands of balloons that said "We are Everywhere!" The vote was not binding, it was simply advisory, yet it was a key moment in lesbian history. Lesbians had gained invaluable visibility. The word "lesbian" began to appear in major newspapers and for some who had fought so long for lesbian rights, there was a brief moment when lesbian sexuality seemed socially acceptable.

### Significance

Activist Judy Freespirit, who had attended the conference, remembered watching one newscaster mention, "in a matter of fact way," that lesbians were present at the conference. Struck by the lack of judgment in his words and voice, Freespirit and some of her friends who were watching the newscast then cried. Freespirit also noted that the National Women's Conference marked the first time in history that large numbers of out lesbians had mingled with straight women in an intensely political and emotional environment. Freespirit would come to believe that many heterosexual women had shed their ignorance, fear, and lesbophobia, and that these changes were some of the most important and long-lasting effects of the conference.

U.S. president Jimmy Carter later appointed Jean O'Leary to the National Advisory Committee for

Women (NACW), which was chaired by Bella Abzug. In January of 1979, after the committee challenged Carter's "economic priorities," Carter dismissed Abzug as chair, and more than half the committee resigned in protest.

—*Yolanda Retter*

**FURTHER READING**

Cottrell, Debbie Mauldin. "National Women's Conference, 1977." Handbook of Texas Online. http://www.tsha.utexas.edu/handbook/online.

Grasberg, Lynn. "Thousands Flock to L.A. to Block Bryant Takeover." *Common Sense*, July, 1977.

Jay, Karla. *Tales of the Lavender Menace: A Memoir of Liberation*. New York: Basic Books, 1999.

Kenney, Anne R. "The Papers of International Women's Year, 1977." *American Archivist* 42 (July, 1979).

"National Women's Conference in Houston, 1977." Jo Freeman. http://www.jofreeman.com/photos/IWY1977.html.

*The Spirit of Houston, the First National Women's Conference: An Official Report to the President, the Congress, and the People of the United States*. Washington, D.C.: Government Printing Office, March, 1978.

**SEE ALSO:** May 27-30, 1960: First National Lesbian Conference Convenes; May 1, 1970: Lavender Menace Protests Homophobia in Women's Movement; Mar. 22, 1972-June 30, 1982: Equal Rights Amendment Fails State Ratification; June 25, 1972: First Out Gay Minister Is Ordained; Nov. 7, 1972: Jordan Becomes First Black Congresswoman from the South; Jan. 22, 1973: *Roe v. Wade* Legalizes Abortion and Extends Privacy Rights; 1977: Anita Bryant Campaigns Against Gay and Lesbian Rights; Oct. 12-15, 1979: First National Third World Lesbian and Gay Conference Convenes; Sept., 1983: First National Lesbians of Color Conference Convenes.

---

## December 19, 1977
# QUEBEC INCLUDES LESBIANS AND GAYS IN ITS CHARTER OF HUMAN RIGHTS AND FREEDOMS

*Canada's second largest province, Quebec, amended its Charter of Human Rights and Freedoms to add lesbians and gays to the list of those persons protected, thus becoming the first jurisdiction in North America to protect its citizens against discrimination in employment, housing, and public accommodation on the basis of sexual orientation.*

**LOCALE:** Montreal, Quebec, Canada
**CATEGORIES:** Laws, acts, and legal history; civil rights

**KEY FIGURE**
*Marc-André Bédard*, minister in the separatist Parti Québécois

**SUMMARY OF EVENT**
In 1975, the province of Quebec, Canada, passed legislation establishing its Charter of Human Rights and Freedoms. At this time, the separatist Parti Québécois (PQ) moved that sexual orientation be added to the legislation; sexual orientation was not added. The liberal justice minister defended this omission, arguing that Canadian society was not ready to accept such an inclusion and further indicated that conferring legitimacy on homosexuality was not within the bounds of human rights legislation. After consideration, the PQ acquiesced and accepted the liberal stance.

Soon, however, the political climate in Montreal changed dramatically, responding to numerous bathhouse raids in 1975 and 1976, as well as the

---

**FROM THE QUEBEC CHARTER OF
HUMAN RIGHTS AND FREEDOMS**

*Chapter I.1*: Fundamental Freedoms and Rights: Right to Equal
Recognition and Exercise of Rights and Freedoms

*Discrimination forbidden.*
10. Every person has a right to full and equal recognition and exercise of his human rights and freedoms, without distinction, exclusion or preference based on race, colour, sex, pregnancy, sexual orientation, civil status, age except as provided by law,
religion, political convictions, language, ethnic or national origin, social condition, a handicap or the use of any means to palli-
ate a handicap.

*Discrimination defined.*
Discrimination exists where such a distinction, exclusion or preference has the effect of nullifying or impairing such right.

---

antigay police "cleanup" of the city of Montreal for
the 1976 Olympics. In response to these and other
events, gay political groups such as the Coalition
Against Repression and the more influential Association pour les Droits des Gais du Quebec (ADGQ,
or Association for Gay Rights in Quebec) were
founded. The ADGQ quickly presented a brief to
the Commission des Droits de la Personne du Quebec (CDPQ, or Commission on Individual Rights in
Quebec) demanding the inclusion of sexual orientation in Quebec's Charter of Human Rights and
Freedoms.

In July, 1977, the Human Rights Code review
committee's report, *Life Together*, responded to
this demand and recommended that sexual orientation be added to the code. This groundbreaking and
well-publicized event created a swift and negative
reaction. A volatile political climate developed
from a collective homophobic hysteria. Soon, Canada would experience a rash of incidents equating
homosexuality with pedophilia and blaming a homosexual for the sexual assault and murder of
twelve-year-old Emmanuel Jacques. Anita Bryant
imported into Ontario her "Save Our Children"
campaign, and criminal charges had been filed
against TBP Publications for publishing Gerald
Hannon's 1977 essay "Men Loving Boys Loving

Men" in the magazine *The Body
Politic*. A stunned gay and lesbian community mobilized
quickly against this hysteria.

Public opinion began to turn
again in October, 1977, when police raided Truxx, a popular
Montreal bathhouse. That night,
138 men were arrested, and there
were allegations of police brutality at the next night's protests.

The PQ, known for its progressive image, feared that angry
community response and widespread condemnation of the raid
and subsequent police action
would cause unwelcome publicity. As a result, the ADGQ secured a commitment from the
Quebec Human Rights Commission to recommend
a sexual orientation amendment to the charter, a
gesture the government immediately embraced.
Acting without hesitation, PQ minister Marc-André
Bédard introduced Bill 88 on December 7, 1977,
which added a sexual orientation amendment to the
charter. To avoid publicity, the PQ rushed the bill
through the legislative process. It was passed immediately after its final reading, ten minutes before
midnight on December 15, 1977. Bill 88 was signed
into law four days later, without fanfare, making
Quebec the first jurisdiction in North America to
pass human rights legislation prohibiting discrimination on the basis of sexual orientation.

## SIGNIFICANCE

The impact of the legislation would not be seen for
many years. It is ironic that the early victories of the
ADGQ would slow the advancement of gay and lesbian rights in Quebec. This came about for three important reasons.

First, almost immediately after the passage of the
amendment to the code, the effectiveness of the law
was challenged. In November, 1977, just after the
Truxx raid and before the amendment of the Charter
of Human Rights and Freedoms, the ADGQ had requested a room rental from the school board. The

Commission des Ecoles Catholiques de Montreal (CECM, or Montreal Catholic School Commission) had refused. In a deliberate test of the new provisions, one month later, the ADGQ again requested a room from the school board. At first, the board agreed to rent the room but two months later reneged on its decision citing its effects on the education of children. The ADGQ immediately filed a complaint with the CDPQ; a CDPQ inquiry found that the school board's action was discriminatory. However, the CDPQ commissioners disagreed. They called for exceptions to the provision, explaining that discrimination could be justified by, among other things, the religious and educational goals of a nonprofit organization.

Second, and surprisingly, the impact of the Quebec charter on other provincial governments was minimal. All other provinces ignored the historic legal change in Quebec and none chose to follow suit. Even in Atlantic Canada, where Halifax's Gay Alliance for Equity organized to support a similar amendment throughout the 1970's and early 1980's, Nova Scotia's laws remained unchanged.

Third, the ADGQ did not maintain its established political power in Quebec, and it eventually disbanded in the mid-1980's. Furthermore, the ADGQ did not provide an organizational base for Quebec's other ongoing gay rights organization. Aside from AIDS organizing, state-directed lesbian-and-gay rights activism did not occur during the 1980's. The true exemplary impact of the Quebec charter's sexual orientation clause was clearly seen when the Canadian Charter of Rights and Freedoms adopted a similar provision in Ottawa in 1982. The time had come.

—*Daniel-Raymond Nadon*

## FURTHER READING

Charter of Human Rights and Freedoms, Quebec. http://www.canlii.org/qc/laws/sta/c-12/20050513/whole.html.

Lahey, Kathleen A. *Are We "Persons" Yet? Law and Sexuality in Canada*. Buffalo, N.Y.: University of Toronto Press, 1999.

MacDougall, Bruce. *Queer Judgements: Homosexuality, Expression, and the Courts in Canada*. Buffalo, N.Y.: University of Toronto Press, 2000.

McLeod, Donald W. *Lesbian and Gay Liberation in Canada: A Selected Annotated Chronology, 1964-1975*. Toronto, Ont.: ECW Press/Homewood Books, 1996.

Smith, Miriam. *Lesbian and Gay Rights in Canada: Social Movements and Equality Seeking, 1971-1999*. Buffalo, N.Y.: University of Toronto Press, 1999.

Warner, Tom. *Never Going Back: A History of Queer Activism in Canada*. Buffalo, N.Y.: University of Toronto Press, 2002.

**SEE ALSO:** 1972-1973: Local Governments Pass Antidiscrimination Laws; June 21, 1973: U.S. Supreme Court Supports Local Obscenity Laws; Aug., 1973: American Bar Association Calls for Repeal of Laws Against Consensual Sex; 1977: Anita Bryant Campaigns Against Gay and Lesbian Rights; Nov. 27, 1978: White Murders Politicians Moscone and Milk; Nov. 6, 1984: West Hollywood Incorporates with Majority Gay and Lesbian City Council; Dec. 4, 1984: Berkeley Extends Benefits to Domestic Partners of City Employees; Apr., 2003: Buenos Aires Recognizes Same-Gender Civil Unions.

**December 31, 1977**
# TORONTO POLICE RAID OFFICES OF *THE BODY POLITIC*

*Police in Toronto raided the editorial offices of the influential Canadian gay newspaper* The Body Politic, *charging staff members with distributing obscene material after they published an article on intergenerational sex. The article, "Men Loving Boys Loving Men," was the opening salvo of a several-year battle with police, the courts, and the media.*

**LOCALE:** Toronto, Ontario, Canada

**CATEGORIES:** Publications; laws, acts, and legal history; civil rights; marches, protests, and riots; organizations and institutions

**KEY FIGURES**

*Gerald Hannon*, author of the controversial article, *The Body Politic* treasurer, charged by Canadian authorities

*Ken Popert*, president of *The Body Politic*, charged by Canadian authorities

*Ed Jackson*, secretary of *The Body Politic*, charged by Canadian authorities

*Roy McMurtry*, attorney general of Ontario, 1975-1985

*Claire Hoy*, columnist for the *Toronto Sun* and a vocal critic, who urged the Ontario crown attorney to charge *The Body Politic*

**SUMMARY OF EVENT**

On December 31, 1977, members of Operation P, a joint Toronto and Ontario police unit set up to investigate pornography, raided the offices of *The Body Politic* (*TBP*), removing twelve boxes of materials and later charging *TBP* staff with possessing and distributing obscene material. Police had been informed of an article, "Men Loving Boys Loving Men," published in the December, 1977/January, 1978 issue of *TBP*.

The article's author, Gerald Hannon, had interviewed men who had engaged in sex with boys. In a nonjudgmental tone, Hannon wrote about his discussions with men such as "Simon," a thirty-three-

year-old primary school teacher with a twelve-year-old lover, a student in his class. Hannon acknowledged that Simon was "exactly the person families most worry about," as Simon described forming "sexual, loving relationships with boys" in all four of the schools in which he had taught. Simon admitted that his sex acts with boys "form a kind of sex education"; Simon said that he wanted to "liberate" his "kids a little bit and help them find their own sexual direction."

*Toronto Sun* newspaper editors and its columnist, Claire Hoy, informed Toronto police about the article. Hoy, a vocal critic of *TBP*, wrote a column (the first of many critical columns), which appeared in the December 22 edition of the *Sun*, titled "Our Taxes Help Homosexuals Promote Abuse of Children." The piece also condemned Ontario arts funding for *TBP*. The first week of 1978, the paper was charged under Section 164 of the criminal code: the "use of mails to transmit immoral, indecent and scurrilous material."

The following day, a defense fund was started to aid *TBP*. San Francisco city and county supervisor Harvey Milk soon called for a tourist boycott of Toronto. On January 5, 1978, the Ontario crown attorney charged *TBP* and staff members Ken Popert, Ed Jackson, and Gerald Hannon with possessing and distributing obscene material, and they were tried the following month. Beginning one year later, in January of 1979, was a series of trials, acquittals, and retrials of *TBP*.

In the ruling of February 14, 1978, *TBP* and its directors were acquitted of obscenity charges. On March 6, 1979, the attorney general's office announced that it would appeal the acquittal, citing errors in law made by the trial judge, and on February 29, 1980, *TBP*'s 1979 acquittal was set aside and a new trial was ordered. Attempts by *TBP* to overturn this decision failed, and in May of 1982, *TBP* was again on trial.

On June 15, 1982, though, the court again acquitted *TBP* of all charges. Hoping to overturn this second acquittal, the attorney general appealed the decision but the court rejected the application in September of 1983. On October 15, with the passing of the deadline for any further appeals by the attorney general, *TBP*'s six-year legal fight came to an end.

A look at events taking place before the *TBP* raid can help to place the actions of the attorney general and Toronto police, as well as the media coverage, into context. The raid and subsequent media attention show that there existed a growing anxiety about the visibility of Toronto's gay and lesbian community and a fear of gay and lesbian teachers and gay-positive education in the schools. On July 21, 1977, the Ontario Human Rights Commission had suggested for the first time that sexual orientation be protected from discrimination. Toronto newspapers were generally favorable, but they also argued that schools should be exempt so as to prevent homosexual teachers from promoting their "lifestyle." The "Save Our Children" campaign of American antigay activist Anita Bryant in Florida, who feared "what they [homosexuals] can do to our children as role models in teaching," had been slated to visit Toronto in January of 1978.

About six months before Bryant's planned visit, a twelve-year-old named Emanuel Jaques, a shoe-shine boy working on Toronto's Yonge Street, had disappeared. Days later, on August 1, Jaques's body was found. He had been murdered after being sexually assaulted by four men. Jaques's murder strengthened calls to cleanup Yonge Street, an area dominated by sex-related businesses, and to crack down on gays in Toronto because they threatened young people.

## SIGNIFICANCE

As Toronto newspapers debated human rights protections for gays and lesbians (but not gay and lesbian teachers) and Toronto citizens expressed outrage over Jaques's murder, *TBP* had published its piece on "men loving boys." Writer Gerald Hannon noted that the "man-boy" story, which had been written months before Jaques was killed, also had seen a delay in its publication, as the timing would have been ill-conceived. Hannon concluded that "the cli-

mate will never be right" and "the tide must be resisted, the discussion must be opened up."

The Jaques murder was politically useful to city and police officials, who chose to close Yonge Street sex shops in favor of "legitimate businesses"; the shops could be closed without question. After *TBP* ran the controversial article, Toronto police initiated a campaign of harassment, raids, and entrapment against the gay community. The police action culminated in a series of bathhouse raids on February 5, 1981, in which hundreds of men were arrested. Yet the lesbian and gay community made it known they had seen enough. With the rallying cry of "No More Shit," three thousands gays, lesbians, and supporters protested the following night, and four thousand took to the streets the next night as well. Soon, the Toronto lesbian and gay community began a concerted effort to end years of police harassment and public insult. Many would come to describe those nights of protest as "Toronto's Stonewall."

On December 16, 1986, the collective decided to cease publication of *The Body Politic*, citing financial and other reasons. The last issue came out in February of 1987.

*—Michael E. Graydon*

## FURTHER READING

Canadian Lesbian and Gay Archives. http://www.clga.ca/. Extensive collection of related materials on the raid and the newspaper in general.

Hannon, Gerald. "Men Loving Boys Loving Men." *The Body Politic* 39 (December, 1977/January, 1978). Reprinted in *Flaunting It! A Decade of Gay Journalism from the Body Politic*, edited by Ed Jackson and Stan Perksy. Vancouver, B.C.: New Star, 1982.

Kinsman, G. *The Regulation of Desire: Homo and Hetero Sexualities.* 2d rev. ed. Montreal, Ont.: Black Rose Books, 1996.

McLeod, Donald W. *Lesbian and Gay Liberation in Canada: A Selected Annotated Chronology, 1964-1975.* Toronto, Ont.: ECW Press, 1996.

Ng, Y. *Ideology, Media, Moral Panics: An Analysis of the Jaques Murder.* Unpublished master's thesis. Centre for Criminology, York University, Canada, 1981.

Streitmatter, Rodger. *Unspeakable: The Rise of the Gay and Lesbian Press in America*. Winchester, Mass.: Faber and Faber, 1995.

Warner, Tom. *Never Going Back: A History of Queer Activism in Canada*. Buffalo, N.Y.: University of Toronto Press, 2002.

**SEE ALSO:** Nov., 1971: *The Body Politic* Begins Publication; 1977: Anita Bryant Campaigns Against Gay and Lesbian Rights; Dec. 19, 1977: Quebec Includes Lesbians and Gays in Its Charter of Human Rights and Freedoms; Feb. 5, 1981: Toronto Police Raid Gay Bathhouses; Jan. 1, 1988: Canada Decriminalizes Sex Practices Between Consenting Adults.

## 1978
# HARRY BENJAMIN INTERNATIONAL GENDER DYSPHORIA ASSOCIATION IS FOUNDED

*The Harry Benjamin International Gender Dysphoria Association was founded to create standards of care for individuals with gender identity disorders. The association's formation led to a cohesive treatment community for transsexuals and transgender individuals seeking care in a supportive and understanding environment.*

**LOCALE:** Minneapolis, Minnesota

**CATEGORIES:** Transgender/transsexuality; health and medicine; science; organizations and institutions

**KEY FIGURES**

*Harry Benjamin* (1885-1986), endocrinologist and gerontologist who studied transsexuality

*Paul A. Walker*,

*Jack C. Berger*,

*Richard Green*,

*Donald R. Laub*,

*Charles L. Reynolds, Jr.*,

*Leo Wollman*, and

*Jude Patton*, founders of the association

*Sheila Kirk*, with Patton, the first transsexual to join the association's board

**SUMMARY OF EVENT**

The Harry Benjamin International Gender Dyspho-ria Association, Inc. (HBIGDA), opened its doors in 1978 to establish care standards for transsexuals and to foster international collaboration on ideas about servicing those with special concerns about gender identity. Initial help for the group came from individuals such as Paul A. Walker, Jack C. Berger, Richard Green, Donald R. Laub, Charles L. Reynolds, Jr., Leo Wollman, and Jude Patton. The association was named for Harry Benjamin, a noted doctor in the field.

Benjamin, a gerontologist and endocrinologist, had become interested in the field of treating transsexuals—those who have an overwhelming sense that their gender is different from which they are known. Benjamin, known by clients for his kindness and understanding, was one of the first to work with transsexuals, and he treated more than fifteen hundred individuals in his career. His groundbreaking book, *The Transsexual Phenomenon*, was published in 1966. Benjamin, an advocate of the use of scientific method, also challenged those working with transsexuals to use dispassionate and compassionate listening rather than treatment based on emotional biases: "Our emotions are the very essence of life, and they are indeed the source of all that makes life worth living. But for science and logic, they are bad companions."

Prior to the emergence of HBIGDA, there was

---

**FROM *STANDARDS OF CARE FOR GENDER IDENTITY DISORDERS* (2001)**

*Chapter IX. The Real-Life Experience*

The act of fully adopting a new or evolving gender role or gender presentation in everyday life is known as the real-life experience. The real-life experience is essential to the transition to the gender role that is congruent with the patient's gender identity. Since changing one's gender presentation has immediate profound personal and social consequences, the decision to do so should be preceded by an awareness of what the familial, vocational, interpersonal, educational, economic, and legal consequences are likely to be. Professionals have a responsibility to discuss these predictable consequences with their patients. Change of gender role and presentation can be an important factor in employment discrimination, divorce, marital problems, and the restriction or loss of visitation rights with children. These represent external reality issues that must be confronted for success in the new gender presentation. These consequences may be quite different from what the patient imagined prior to undertaking the real-life experiences. However, not all changes are negative.

*Parameters of the Real-Life Experience.* When clinicians assess the quality of a person's real-life experience in the desired gender, the following abilities are reviewed:

1. To maintain full or part-time employment;
2. To function as a student;
3. To function in community-based volunteer activity;
4. To undertake some combination of items 1-3;
5. To acquire a (legal) gender-identity-appropriate first name;
6. To provide documentation that persons other than the therapist know that the patient functions in the desired gender role.

*Real-Life Experience versus Real-Life Test.* Although professionals may recommend living in the desired gender, the decision as to when and how to begin the real-life experience remains the person's responsibility. Some begin the real-life experience and decide that this often imagined life direction is not in their best interest. Professionals sometimes construe the real-life experience as the real-life test of the ultimate diagnosis. If patients prosper in the preferred gender, they are confirmed as "transsexual," but if they decided against continuing, they "must not have been." This reasoning is a confusion of the forces that enable successful adaptation with the presence of a gender identity disorder. The real-life experience tests the person's resolve, the capacity to function in the preferred gender, and the adequacy of social, economic, and psychological supports. It assists both the patient and the mental health professional in their judgments about how to proceed. Diagnosis, although always open for reconsideration, precedes a recommendation for patients to embark on the real-life experience. When the patient is successful in the real-life experience, both the mental health professional and the patient gain confidence about undertaking further steps.

*Source:* Harry Benjamin International Gender Dysphoria Association.

---

little in the way of a cohesive movement for the treatment of what had been considered gender identity "problems." From 1965 to 1967, clinics had been started at Johns Hopkins University, the University of Minnesota, and the University of California, Los Angeles. These clinics were initially supported by some financial aid from philanthropist Reed Erickson (1917-1992), a female-to-male transsexual.

Gradually, treatment options were discussed at annual, international symposiums. In 1978, about forty centers in the Western world performed gender reassignment surgeries. As the United States grew more conservative, however, these clinics began to come under fire, and many transsexuals themselves felt that the clinics did not understand them.

during this time doctors at a symposium devised a specialty group to form the HBIGDA. Their aim was to plan how professionals could best help those seeking assistance with what the medical profession calls "gender dysphoria." In 1979, HBIGDA issued its first version of *Standards of Care for Gender Identity Disorders* (SOC), an ongoing working document that service providers can use as a guide to care.

The SOC has been updated and has gone through various versions over the years. While not all clients agree with the SOC, and HBIGDA has no enforcement power with providers, the document does offer a benchmark. Client groups frequently lobby HBIGDA with their concerns about consumer issues and problems with care. In 1997, the first community members, Sheila Kirk (a transgender surgeon) and Jude Patton (a transsexual), joined the board of HBIGDA. In 2000, the group devised ethics guidelines for providers.

HBIGDA publishes *The International Journal of Transgenderism*. Professionals in all areas contribute to the journal, which contains topics touching on psychiatry, endocrinology, surgery, psychology, sexology, counseling, sociology, and the law. Association members meet at biennial conferences.

The evolving mission of HBIGDA kept the basic theme of its founding, but it has become more knowledgeable in subsequent years. Many of the association's efforts still focus on health issues, such as promoting sexual health, transgender medicine and research, sexually transmitted diseases, training for allied health professionals, and optimal access to health care.

Increasingly, the association's role has become more social, addressing issues such as intersex identity and ethics for practitioners, as well as promoting sound and ethical research, fighting stigma and discrimination, and enhancing social tolerance for gender diversity. Importantly, HBIGDA began to tackle issues of changing laws, social policies, and religious views. HBIGDA looks to other cultures for helpful clues, and it has fostered a climate for professionals where old methods pass on and new ones emerge.

In part because of the work of HBIGDA, transsexuals have more options today. In the realm of language the term "transgender," which also is used by the association, encompasses gender's complexity and does not imply a "disorder," as is often the case with terms such as "gender dysphoria" or "gender dysphoric." Although "transgender" has been embraced as a term of self-identification by many individuals, especially those who live ambiguously

gendered lives, others find the term problematic as a sort of catch-all category that denies the specific experiences of those who, to take one example, reassign their gender through surgical means.

## SIGNIFICANCE

HBIGDA has played a large role in the care of transsexuals, and it's research in the field has been used for fighting for legal rights. Its continuously updated protocols for care have become the standard for therapy; there now are time limits for each of the steps in diagnosis and therapy. The rules help to guide a correct choice for surgery and hormone treatments by excluding other diagnosis types, such as homosexuality, psychosis, personality disorders, brain lesion, and transvestitism.

HBIGDA and its conferences have paved the way for international, cross-disciplinary interaction regarding research and services for the welfare of transsexuals. The association was responsible in part for a major change in the psychiatric guidebook, *Diagnostic and Statistical Manual of Mental Disorders* (DSM), which added "gender identity disorder" as a diagnosis in 1980.

*—Jan Hall*

## FURTHER READING

Benjamin, Harry. *The Transsexual Phenomenon.* New York: Julian Press, 1966. Available at http://www.symposion.com/ijt/benjamin/.

Gilbert, Michael, ed. *International Journal of Transgenderism* 4, no. 3 (July/September, 2000). Special issue, "What Is Transgender?" http://www.symposion.com/ijt/index.htm.

Harry Benjamin International Gender Dysphoria Association. http://www.hbigda.org/.

Lev, Arlene Istar. *Transgender Emergence: Therapeutic Guidelines for Working with Gender-Variant People and Their Families.* New York: Haworth Clinical Practice Press, 2004.

Meyerowitz, Joanne. *How Sex Changed: A History of Transsexuality in the United States.* Cambridge, Mass.: Harvard University Press, 2002.

Standards of Care for Gender Identity Disorders, Version Six. 2001. http://www.hbigda.org/soc.cfm.

## 1978
# LESBIAN AND GAY WORKPLACE MOVEMENT IS FOUNDED

*The first gay and lesbian employee group in the United States formed in the late 1970's. By the early twenty-first century, the workplace movement had more than one hundred gay and lesbian employee networks pushing for change inside corporate America, spearheading major policy transformations and a rethinking of corporate culture.*

**LOCALE:** California
**CATEGORIES:** Organizations and institutions; economics; marches, protests, and riots

### SUMMARY OF EVENT

In 1978, the first-known gay and lesbian employee group formed inside a major corporation. During the next twenty-five years, more than one hundred such networks would spring up within *Fortune* 500 companies across the United States.

As the core of what activists now call the workplace movement, these networks have ushered in a sea change in corporate America. Ranging from a few people to as many as two thousand members, gay and lesbian employee groups typically share four main goals: to provide support and networking opportunities; to gain official corporate recognition; to educate management and other workers on sexual orientation issues; and to bring about gay- and lesbian-inclusive nondiscrimination policies, diversity training, and domestic-partner benefits.

Prior to internal corporate mobilization, gay and lesbian rights activists borrowed strategies from the Civil Rights movement to target the antigay and antilesbian employment policies of the federal government and civil service sector. With the Homophile League of New York staging the country's first gay and lesbian rights protest, which was held outside a military induction center in the early 1960's, by 1964 lesbians in dresses and gay men in suits were picketing outside the White House, the Pentagon, and other government buildings with signs condemning employment discrimination and demanding civil rights. Despite their bravery, very few tangible gains were made in the struggle for workplace equality. After the Stonewall Rebellion in New York City in June of 1969, however, in addition to targeting the homophobic policies of the state and mental health establishment, gay and lesbian activists set their sights on antigay and antilesbian corporate practices.

In the earliest known protest against a major company, activists in San Francisco, Los Angeles, and New York picketed ABC-TV in the spring of 1970 after a San Francisco station fired an employee who had joined the movement for gay and lesbian rights. Others decided to survey corporations about their policies. In 1970, FREE (Fight Repression of Erotic Expression), a rights group at the University of Minnesota, combined surveys with test cases to see if out gay and lesbian applicants would be turned down. In a letter accompanying the survey, the group promised to target discriminatory employers. After first mentioning research showing that homosexuality was not a mental disorder, the tone of the letter then quickly shifted to a co-optation of corporate discourse. Emphasizing that motivation and productivity suffer if employees have to remain closeted, the group argued that gay-

## AMERICAN AIRLINES: STATEMENT OF EQUAL OPPORTUNITY

It is the expressed policy of American Airlines to provide equal employment opportunity to all employees and applicants for employment without regard to age, race, sex, gender identity, color, religion, national origin, sexual orientation, citizenship status, disability or veteran status. . . .

All employees must be aware of and support the company's commitment to the principles of equal employment opportunity.

*Policy on Discrimination*

American Airlines is committed to the following principles: Employment decisions should not be based on race, sex, sexual orientation, age, religion, or other protected characteristics. People should not be treated differently because of personal characteristics that are not related to their ability to do a job, such as their race, sex, gender, gender identity, sexual orientation, age, religion, or disabilities. With few exceptions, individuals must be hired, promoted, disciplined, or fired because of their job-related skills and performance. People with similar skills and performance records should be treated equally.

*Policy on Unlawful Harassment*

American Airlines will not tolerate unlawful harassment or discrimination. The company is committed to providing a work environment for all employees free of unlawful harassment, including sexual harassment. American strictly prohibits harassment because of race, sex, gender, gender identity, religion, color, national origin, ancestry, mental or physical disability, medical condition, union or non-union affiliation, marital status, age, sexual orientation, or any other basis protected by federal, state or local law or ordinance.

American Airlines' unlawful harassment policy applies to all persons involved in the operations of the company and prohibits harassment by any employee of the company including supervisors and co-workers, as well as by any person doing business with or for the company. Management is responsible for ensuring that this policy is followed. Employees violating this policy—and managers who condone violations of this policy—may be terminated.

*Source:* American Airlines, 2002. http://www.aa.com.

and lesbian-inclusive policies would bring companies recruitment advantages.

Other gay and lesbian activists took a decidedly more aggressive approach. In the fall of 1971, when Pacific Telephone and Telegraph said it would not hire homosexuals, the Gay Activists Alliance picketed both PT&T and parent company AT&T. After two years of continued intransigence, activists staged a Good Friday zap action featuring a young gay man dragging a heavy "cross" made from a telephone pole, which he carried through downtown San Francisco to PT&T headquarters. Two weeks later, protesters held another rally, but to no avail. During that same summer of 1973, activists picketed and also passed out leaflets for six days outside Northwestern Bell in Minnesota after the AT&T subsidiary announced its antigay and antilesbian hiring policy on the front page of the local newspaper. Although the American Civil Liberties Union (ACLU) in Minnesota filed suit against parent company AT&T in 1973, it was not until May of 1974, with the lawsuit still pending, that Northwestern Bell rescinded its discriminatory policy. The change was preceded three days earlier by the passage of a gay and lesbian rights ordinance in Minneapolis. Shortly thereafter, AT&T changed its policy as well. Notably, the corporation had earlier settled a highly publicized class action suit for discrimination against women.

Despite such early victories, however, gays and lesbians were reluctant to mobilize *inside* companies, especially because on the outside, a handful of cities argued that antigay and antilesbian employment discrimination was perfectly legal (it remained so in most states as of mid-2006). The tentative pace of early corporate organizing also makes sense given the rise of the New Right in the late 1970's and its consolidation of power in the 1980's. It is hardly surprising, then, that by the end of that decade, the number of *Fortune* 1000 companies with gay and lesbian networks had barely reached two handfuls.

In the first half of the 1990's, however, with a more favorable political climate ushered in during Bill Clinton's successful run for president, workplace mobilization took off. New gay and lesbian employee groups sprang up in the *Fortune* 1000 at an average rate of ten per year, bringing the total number of networks to a critical mass of sixty by the start of 1995. The national marches on Washington, D.C., for gay, lesbian, and bisexual rights in 1987 and 1993, along with the emergence of media-savvy direct-action groups, such as ACT UP (AIDS Coalition to Unleash Power) in 1987 and Queer Nation in 1990, had also helped to energize and expand the ranks of the workplace movement. Once the mainstream media's spotlight on queer politics widened to include gay and lesbian employee activism, new networks spread across the country. With the HIV-AIDS epidemic adding tragic saliency to the lack of equitable benefits, including not only health insurance but even bereavement leave, the gay and lesbian media also began to focus more critically on corporate policies and practices at the start of the 1990's.

Mainstream press coverage of particularly blatant cases of discrimination also boosted mobilization. In early 1991, the Cracker Barrel restaurant chain issued a press release announcing its anti-gay and antilesbian employment policy, and eleven lesbian and gay employees were fired. Activists quickly issued calls for a boycott and staged demonstrations and sit-ins at various restaurant locations. Stories sympathetic to the protesters appeared on national news networks as well as on television programs such as *Oprah Winfrey*, *Larry King Live*, and *20/20*.

Cracker Barrel's crusade persuaded many gay and lesbian employee networks to join forces. In 1991, activists from several different companies organized the first two conferences in the country to focus on lesbian, gay, and bisexual issues at work. These conferences constituted a critical turning point for the workplace movement. The East Coast conference, which focused on educating corporate executives, generated considerable press attention, such that even business publications and personnel journals began to cover gay and lesbian issues generally and workplace activism in particular. The West Coast conference, called Out and Equal in the Workplace, was organized primarily for gays and lesbians and was so successful that it became an annual event. With early support from both the National Gay and Lesbian Task Force (NGLTF) and the Human Rights Campaign (HRC), the annual conferences quickly expanded, and in the first few years of the twenty-first century, they served as key mobilizers for the movement.

Other infrastructural supports contributing to the emergence and success of gay employee networks include e-mail listservs and Web sites focused on gay and lesbian issues in the workplace; local, regional, and national umbrella groups; and workplace projects launched by NGLTF in the early 1990's and HRC in 1995. In addition to its Business Council, whose members work with companies to achieve inclusive policies, the HRC Foundation provides invaluable resources through its WorkNet project. Along with many other useful tools, the WorkNet site (www.hrc.org/worknet) includes a searchable database containing information on employers in the corporate, educational, nonprofit, and government sectors, including whether or not they have gay-, lesbian-, and transgender-inclusive non-discrimination policies, diversity training, domestic-partner benefits, and GLBT employee groups.

The dawning of domestic partner benefits on the corporate horizon spurred many gays and lesbians to form workplace networks and to push harder for the benefits. When Lotus became the country's first major corporation to adopt equitable benefits in 1991, national newspapers began running stories about domestic-partner benefits. Inspired by this policy breakthrough, employee activists would eventually push numerous companies to follow along in Lotus's footsteps.

## Significance

Despite the backlash against LGBT rights occurring across the United States, the workplace movement has won remarkable policy success thus far. In 1990, just three corporations had offered family and bereavement leave for their lesbian and gay employees, and none provided health insurance coverage for domestic partners. By the middle of the 1990's, however, domestic-partner benefits had practically become a household phrase given their adoption by numerous big-name companies. As of June 1, 2006, more than 50 percent of *Fortune* 500 companies had instituted equitable benefits. Indeed, corporations far outpace educational, nonprofit, and government employers in offering these benefits.

Research tracking corporate policy change and workplace mobilization through 1999 reveals that, in the vast majority of cases, employers adopted equitable benefits only after facing internal pressure from gay and lesbian employee groups. Although some companies are now extending the benefits in the absence of such networks, the workplace movement deserves credit for spearheading these changes and for its still-central role in the continued transformation of corporate America.

—*Nicole C. Raeburn*

## FURTHER READING

Baker, Daniel B., Sean O'Brien Strub, and Bill Henning. *Cracking the Corporate Closet: The Two Hundred Best (and Worst) Companies to Work For, Buy From, and Invest in if You're Gay or Lesbian—and Even if You Aren't*. New York: Harper Business, 1995.

Krupat, Kitty, and Patrick McCreery, eds. *Out at Work: Building a Gay-Labor Alliance*. Minneapolis: University of Minnesota Press, 2001.

McNaught, Brian. *Gay Issues in the Workplace*. New York: St. Martin's Press, 1993.

Raeburn, Nicole C. *Changing Corporate America from Inside Out: Lesbian and Gay Workplace Rights*. Minneapolis: University of Minnesota Press, 2004.

Winfeld, Liz, and Susan Spielman. *Straight Talk About Gays in the Workplace: Creating an Inclusive, Productive Environment for Everyone in Your Organization*. New York: Amacom, 1995.

SEE ALSO: Apr. 27, 1953: U.S. President Eisenhower Prohibits Federal Employment of Lesbians and Gays; 1972-1973: Local Governments Pass Antidiscrimination Laws; June 27, 1974: Abzug and Koch Attempt to Amend the Civil Rights Act of 1964; July 3, 1975: U.S. Civil Service Commission Prohibits Discrimination Against Federal Employees; June 2, 1980: Canadian Gay Postal Workers Secure Union Protections; Dec. 4, 1984: Berkeley Extends Benefits to Domestic Partners of City Employees; Nov. 8, 1988: Oregon Repeals Ban on Antigay Job Discrimination; May 1, 1989: U.S. Supreme Court Rules Gender-Role Stereotyping Is Discriminatory; Sept. 29, 1991: California Governor Wilson Vetoes Antidiscrimination Bill; Sept. 23, 1992: Massachusetts Grants Family Rights to Gay and Lesbian State Workers; 1994: Employment Non-Discrimination Act Is Proposed to U.S. Congress; Apr. 2, 1998: Canadian Supreme Court Reverses Gay Academic's Firing; July, 2003: Singapore Lifts Ban on Hiring Lesbian and Gay Employees; July, 2003: Wal-Mart Adds Lesbians and Gays to Its Antidiscrimination Policy.

**July 3, 1978**

# U.S. SUPREME COURT DISTINGUISHES BETWEEN "INDECENT" AND "OBSCENE"

*The U.S. Supreme Court ruled that the Federal Communications Commission, or FCC, can restrict the broadcast of material that is "indecent," that is, broadcast material does not have to be "obscene" to be restricted or prohibited by the FCC. The ruling also set a legal precedent for the "valuing" of speech by the public.*

**ALSO KNOWN AS:** *Federal Communications Commission v. Pacifica Foundation*
**LOCALE:** Washington, D.C.
**CATEGORIES:** Civil rights; laws, acts, and legal history; arts

**KEY FIGURES**

*John Paul Stevens* (b. 1920), justice of the United States
*William Rehnquist* (b. 1924), chief justice of the United States
*William J. Brennan* (1906-1997), justice of the United States
*Harry M. Plotkin*, attorney for the Pacifica Foundation
*Joseph A. Marino*, chief counsel for the FCC
*George Carlin* (b. 1937), comedian and actor

**SUMMARY OF EVENT**
On October 30, 1973, the Pacifica Foundation radio station WBAI (99.5 FM) in New York City had broadcast comedian George Carlin's twelve-minute monologue "Seven Dirty Words" during a talk show discussing people's attitudes toward expletive language. Carlin's monologue consisted of seven four-letter words on sexual and excretory activities; words, he joked, that "you couldn't say on the public airwaves." Just before the broadcast, the disc jockey had asked listeners to turn the dial to another station if they believed such language offensive.

The Federal Communications Commission (FCC) received just one complaint about the Carlin monologue; the complaint came one month after the monologue from a New York City man who heard the broadcast while driving with his young son. In response, the FCC issued a declaratory order informing the Pacifica Foundation that it faced possible FCC sanctions. The order also clarified the FCC's definition of "indecent": "language that described, in terms patently offensive as measured by contemporary community standards for the broadcast medium, sexual or excretory activities and organs, at times of the day when there is a reasonable risk that children may be in the audience." Because WBAI aired the Carlin show at 2:00 P.M., a time when children were most likely to be listening, the FCC said it would fine WBAI if it received another complaint or complaints about the broadcast.

Pacifica petitioned the U.S. Court of Appeals to review the order. On March 30, 1976, Pacifica's attorney Harry M. Plotkin argued that the station was entitled to First Amendment protection from government censorship. The FCC's indecency standard went too far because it restricted the broadcast of artistic, political, literary, and scientific programs (in other words, programs considered to have "value"). Joseph A. Marino, counsel for the FCC, counterargued that the order neither attempted to censor indecent language nor limit valuable programming, but it did limit the broadcast of indecent language to times during the day when children were least likely to be listening.

A court of appeals overturned the FCC ruling on March 16, 1977. Despite FCC intentions, the court of appeals found that the direct effect of the order was to inhibit the free and robust exchange of ideas on a wide range of issues and subjects. The FCC had ignored both the Communications Act of 1934, which forbade the censoring of radio communications, and its previous decisions that left the question of programming content to the discretion of station owners. The FCC appealed the decision to the U.S. Supreme Court.

On July 3, 1978, the Supreme Court, in *Federal Communications Commission v. Pacifica Foundation*, ruled 5 to 4 in favor of the FCC. Justice John Paul Stevens, joined by Justice William Rehnquist, delivered the majority opinion of the Court. The Carlin monologue, as broadcast, was indecent and neither the First Amendment nor the Communications Act of 1934 prohibited the FCC from regulating such language. Although the First Amendment

generally protected the abridgement of free speech, not all forms of free expression were entitled to absolute constitutional protection. Radio and television broadcasts were subject to lesser First Amendment protection than other communication media because children could easily access radio and television broadcasts. Therefore, it was within the "public interest" of the FCC to regulate offensive programming.

Justice William J. Brennan delivered the dissenting opinion, in which he argued that the word "indecent" can be construed only to prohibit "obscene"

---

### FEDERAL COMMUNICATIONS COMMISSION V. PACIFICA FOUNDATION

*From the Court's opinion:* The Commission identified several words that referred to excretory or sexual activities or organs, stated that the repetitive, deliberate use of those words in an afternoon broadcast when children are in the audience was patently offensive, and held that the broadcast was indecent. Pacifica takes issue with the Commission's definition of indecency, but does not dispute the Commission's preliminary determination that each of the components of its definition was present. . . . Pacifica argues, however, that this Court has construed the term "indecent" in related statutes to mean "obscene." . . .

When the issue is narrowed to the facts of this case, the question is whether the First Amendment denies government any power to restrict the public broadcast of indecent language in any circumstances. For if the government has any such power, this was an appropriate occasion for its exercise.

The words of the Carlin monologue are unquestionably "speech" within the meaning of the First Amendment. It is equally clear that the Commission's objections to the broadcast were based in part on its content. The order must therefore fall if, as Pacifica argues, the First Amendment prohibits all governmental regulation that depends on the content of speech. Our past cases demonstrate, however, that no such absolute rule is mandated by the Constitution.

The classic exposition of the proposition that both the *content and the context of speech are critical elements of First Amendment analysis* is Mr. Justice Holmes' statement for the Court in Schenck v. United States . . . : "We admit that in many places and in ordinary times the defendants in saying all that was said in the circular would have been within their constitutional rights. But the character of every act depends upon the circumstances in which it is done. . . . The most stringent protection of free speech would not protect a man in falsely shouting fire in a theatre and causing a panic. It does not even protect a man from an injunction against uttering words that may have all the effect of force. . . .

[T]he constitutional protection accorded to a communication containing such patently offensive sexual and excretory language need not be the same in every context. . . . Words that are commonplace in one setting are shocking in another. To paraphrase Mr. Justice Harlan, one occasion's lyric is another's vulgarity.

In this case it is undisputed that the content of Pacifica's broadcast was "vulgar," "offensive," and "shocking." Because content of that character is not entitled to absolute constitutional protection under all circumstances, we must consider its context in order to determine whether the Commission's action was constitutionally permissible. . . .

It is appropriate, in conclusion, to emphasize the narrowness of our holding. . . . The Commission's decision rested entirely on a nuisance rationale under which context is all-important. . . . As Mr. Justice Sutherland wrote, a "nuisance may be merely a right thing in the wrong place, like a pig in the parlor instead of the barnyard." . . . We simply hold that when the Commission finds that a pig has entered the parlor, the exercise of its regulatory power does not depend on proof that the pig is obscene.

The judgment of the Court of Appeals is reversed.

speech, and not speech that is "indecent," as the majority opinion argued. Brennan argued that neither the capacity for the broadcast to intrude into unwilling listener's homes nor the presence of children in the listening audience offered enough justification for the Court to allow the FCC to inhibit the free exchange of ideas. Inhibition of speech is allowed, he argued, only if it is "obscene."

## SIGNIFICANCE

The Pacifica case established two legal precedents. First, it indirectly categorized "homosexual" speech as "low-value" speech: Speech whose worth depends on the value judgments of viewers and listeners. Second, it established that the government could restrict "low-value" speech when acting in the "public interest."

In 1986, the FCC had warned KPFK (90.7 FM), a Pacifica Foundation station in Los Angeles, that its broadcast of excerpts from *Jerker*, a play about two terminally ill men coping with AIDS, on its 10:00 P.M. program "I Am Are You?" constituted indecency. The excerpts from the play included a conversation describing anal intercourse and masturbation. Although the station had warned its listeners that the program would contain material offensive to some listeners, the FCC had concluded that any future broadcasts of such material would be actionable under its indecency standard.

In the summer of 2004, the FCC fined CBS television $550,000 for its Super Bowl halftime broadcast earlier that year of singer Janet Jackson baring part of her breast in a reported "wardrobe malfunction" also involving singer Justin Timberlake. The FCC also fined Clear Channel $1.75 million for several profanity-laced statements made during Howard Stern's radio talk show, which Clear Channel had broadcast nationwide.

These FCC actions have led many television and radio broadcasters to self-censor their GLBT-themed programming. For example, some viewers were unable to watch an October, 2004, broadcast of the public television program "In the Life" be-

cause the episode included a segment on the state of Texas's decision to purchase high school textbooks that carry an abstinence-only sex-education message alleging that condoms do not work in disease prevention. The show's distributors, American Public Television, warned stations to consult legal counsel if they planned to broadcast the program in prime time. Although the show's producers argued that Texas's book buying decision was national news, eleven public television stations chose to not air the show and so prevent potential FCC sanctions.

—*Jamie Patrick Chandler*

## FURTHER READING

Heins, Marjorie. *Not In Front of the Children: "Indecency," Censorship, and the Innocence of Youth.* New York: Hill and Wang, 2001.

Hunter, Brent Allen. "The First Amendment and Homosexual Expression: The Need for an Expanded Interpretation." *Vanderbilt Law Review* 47 (May, 1993).

Spitzer, Matthew Laurence. *Seven Dirty Words and Six Other Stories: Controlling the Content of Print and Broadcast.* New Haven, Conn.: Yale University Press, 1987.

## August 8, 1978
# INTERNATIONAL LESBIAN AND GAY ASSOCIATION IS FOUNDED

*The International Lesbian and Gay Association was established in a postwar era of increasing globalization to address human rights issues facing lesbian, gay, bisexual, and transgender individuals around the world.*

**ALSO KNOWN AS:** International Gay Association
**LOCALE:** Coventry, England
**CATEGORIES:** Organizations and institutions; government and politics

### KEY FIGURES

*Joseph Doucé* (1945-1990), Belgian-born Baptist preacher, director of the Centre du Christ Libérateur in Paris, France, and ILGA cofounder
*Jeff Dudgeon*, gay rights activist from Belfast, Northern Ireland, and ILGA cofounder

### SUMMARY OF EVENT

On August 8, 1945, the United States of America had ratified the Charter of the United Nations and became the third member nation to join the international organization. This act fulfilled the Wilsonian dream of an international tribunal to address concerns among nations. Thirty-three years later, on August 8, 1978, thirty men, attending a meeting of the Campaign for Homosexual Equality in Coventry, England, established the International Gay Association (IGA), later named the International Lesbian and Gay Association, or ILGA, in 1986.

The Campaign for Homosexual Equality (CHE) is an organization in Great Britain whose mission includes promoting legal and socioeconomic equality for bisexuals, gays, and lesbians. The group was originally named the North Western Homosexual Law Reform Committee (NWHLRC) when it was founded at Church House, Deansgate, Manchester, England on October 7, 1964, but it changed its name to the Campaign for Homosexual Equality in 1971.

CHE considered itself a democratic organization shunning the hierarchical leadership model favored by most mainstream groups.

One of the primary goals of the Coventry meeting was to pressure Amnesty International to address the oppression of sexual minorities around the globe. Amnesty International had been established in London in 1961 in response to Peter Berenson's "The Forgotten Prisoners," which he wrote after reading a report in the *London Observer* about two students in Portugal who had been arrested for toasting freedom in a Lisbon bar. Thirteen years later, in 1991, Amnesty International added gay and lesbian rights to its organizational mandate.

The 1978 CHE meeting in Coventry was remarkable for its diversity and vision. The men in attendance represented seventeen organizations from fourteen nations, mostly European. ILGA's founding members include Joseph Doucé, a gay Baptist preacher and director of the Centre du Christ Liberateur in Paris, and Jeff Dudgeon, a gay activist from Belfast, Northern Ireland.

The site of the meeting is itself an interesting nexus of historical coincidences that marked the coming of the postwar global era. By 1978, jet travel and telecommunications were revolutionizing the world as more and more Westerners and other global consumers accessed and used technology services. The net effect of technological advances annihilated distance and leveled space and time, establishing and expanding global markets. Globalization afforded greater opportunities for international contacts and raised awareness of human rights abuses around the world, including the abuse and oppression of GLBT persons.

### SIGNIFICANCE

Throughout its several decade tenure working to promote basic human rights for GLBT persons, the International Lesbian and Gay Association has been instrumental in identifying and raising awareness of human rights abuses against sexual minorities throughout the world. ILGA played a key role, for example, in lobbying the World Health Organization (WHO) to drop "homosexuality" from its list of illnesses in 1990. In 1985, ILGA had published its first *Pink Book*, a comprehensive census of the legal status of gays and lesbians around the globe.

Even with its excellent record of championing the cause of international gay and lesbian rights, ILGA has not escaped controversy. Both personal tragedy and political scandal have shaded ILGA's history since its creation in 1978. The brutal and mysterious 1990 killing in France of ILGA cofounder Doucé, was both a personal tragedy and a loss for ILGA's human rights work. In addition to his work with ILGA, Doucé's Centre du Christ Liberateur in Paris ministered to the needs of French sexual minorities. The Centre's advocacy for and provision of human support services to homosexuals, pedophiles, sadomasochists, and transsexuals could have marked Doucé as a target for political investigation by the Renseignements Généraux (RG), the intelligence gathering arm of the French national police.

According to numerous published accounts, the Centre du Christ Liberateur had been burglarized and under surveillance throughout the summer of 1990. On the evening of July 19, 1990, two plainclothed men who identified themselves as police officers arrived at Doucé's apartment, which he shared with his lover in Paris. The men asked Doucé to accompany them for questioning, and he was never again seen alive. Doucé's badly decomposed

> ## INTERNATIONAL LESBIAN AND GAY ASSOCIATION: AIMS AND OBJECTIVES
>
> 1. To work for the equality of lesbians, gay men, bisexuals and transgendered people and liberation from all forms of discrimination;
> 2. To promote the universal respect for and observance of human rights and fundamental freedoms, including the elimination of all forms of discrimination and also including the realisation of the specific provisions of the following international human rights instruments:
>    - The International Covenant on Civil and Political Rights
>    - The International Covenant on Economic, Social and Cultural Rights
>    - The International Convention on the Elimination of all Forms of Racial Discrimination
>    - The Convention on the Elimination of all Forms of Discrimination Against Women
>    - The Convention on the Rights of the Child
>
> To work towards these goals, ILGA shall:
> 1. Create a platform for lesbians, gay men, bisexuals and transgendered people internationally, in their quest for recognition, equality and liberation, in particular through the world and regional conferences;
> 2. Work towards equal representation in all regions for lesbians, gay men, bisexuals and transgendered people in our quest for recognition, equality and liberation;
> 3. Give locally initiated and determined support for our organisations in all parts of the world;
> 4. Collect information, conduct research, publish material and organise seminars, training, briefings and specialised conferences;
> 5. Offer facilities for co-ordination of activities and actions.

body was found in Rambouillet woods, southwest of Paris, in October.

Another political scandal has affected ILGA. In July, 1993, ILGA was granted nongovernmental organization (NGO) representative status with the United Nations (U.N.). In 1993 and 1994, sessions of the U.N. Sub-Commission on Prevention of Discrimination and Protection of Minorities included statements issued on behalf of ILGA. A 1994 session of the U.N. Commission on Human Rights also included statements made in the name of ILGA. However, in September, 1994, ILGA's consultative status with the U.N. was suspended after a protracted and determined effort by conservative U.S. senator Jessie Helms (R-NC) to revoke ILGA's privileges and standing. Helms objected to ILGA's status within the U.N. and its Economic and Social Council because the North American Man/Boy Love Association (NAMBLA) was a member of ILGA.

ILGA members then voted 214-30 to suspend the membership status of NAMBLA and two other groups (Project Truth/Free Will and Vereniging Martijn), deeming these organizations unqualified for membership status because their primary aim was to support or promote pedophilia. Despite revoking the three memberships, ILGA's applications for U.N. consultative status have been repeatedly rejected, the latest rejection coming in January of 2006.

*—Keith Carson*

**FURTHER READING**

Adam, Barry D., Willem Jan Duyvendak, and André Krouwel, eds. *The Global Emergence of Gay and Lesbian Politics: National Imprints of a Worldwide Movement.* Philadelphia: Temple University Press, 1999.

Hendriks, Aart, Rob Tielman, and Evert van der Veen, eds. *The Third Pink Book: A Global View of Lesbian and Gay Liberation and Oppression.* Buffalo, N.Y.: Prometheus Books, 1993.

International Lesbian and Gay Association. http://www.ilga.org.

LaViolette, Nicole, and Sandra Whitworth. "No Safe Haven: Sexuality as a Universal Human Right and Gay and Lesbian Activism in International Politics." *Millennium: Journal of International Studies* 23, no. 3 (1994): 563.

Ogilvie, Dayne. "NAMBLA Expelled from Rights Group." *Capital Xtra!,* July 15, 1994, p. 17.

Stychin, Carl, and Didi Herman, eds. *Law and Sexuality: The Global Arena.* Minneapolis: University of Minnesota Press, 2001.

Waaldijk, Kees, et al. *Tip of an Iceberg: Anti-lesbian and Anti-gay Discrimination in Europe, 1980-1990, a Survey of Discrimination and Anti-discrimination in Law and Society.* Utrecht, the Netherlands: International Lesbian and Gay Association, 1991.

**SEE ALSO:** Dec. 1, 1988: First World AIDS Day; 1989: Act Up Paris Is Founded; 1990: International Gay and Lesbian Human Rights Commission Is Founded; Sept. 16, 1994: U.N. Revokes Consultative Status of International Lesbian and Gay Association; June 17, 1995: International Bill of Gender Rights Is First Circulated; Oct. 9-12, 1998: First International Retreat for Lesbian and Gay Muslims Is Held; Nov., 1999: First Middle Eastern Gay and Lesbian Organization Is Founded.

**November 7, 1978**
# ANTIGAY AND ANTILESBIAN BRIGGS INITIATIVE IS DEFEATED

*California voters defeated a ballot initiative that would have barred lesbians and gays from teaching in public schools. The campaign against the Briggs Initiative mobilized the GLBT community into unprecedented political action.*

**ALSO KNOWN AS:** Proposition 6
**LOCALE:** California
**CATEGORIES:** Civil rights; government and politics; laws, acts, and legal history

**KEY FIGURES**

*John V. Briggs* (b. 1930), California Republican state senator and initiative sponsor
*David Goodstein* (1932-1985), activist, publisher, cofounded Concerned Voters of California
*Harvey Milk* (1930-1978), San Francisco supervisor and activist
*David Mixner* (b. 1946), activist, political consultant
*Ronald Reagan* (1911-2004), former U.S. president, governor of California

**SUMMARY OF EVENT**

As GLBT activists obtained legal protections in some communities around the United States in the 1970's, religious conservatives began mobilizing to block and overturn these laws. Following Anita Bryant's successful "Save Our Children" campaign to repeal an antidiscrimination law in Dade County, Florida, in 1977, Bryant worked with California Republican state senator John V. Briggs to collect enough signatures in California to place a measure on the ballot that would bar homosexuals from teaching in public schools and allow teachers to be fired for "advocating, imposing, encouraging or promoting" homosexuality.

Briggs had been a state assembly member and was a state senator from 1977 to 1981. Although he focused his legislative efforts on insurance reform,

the death penalty, and decreasing government regulations, by 1977 he had become interested in what he believed was a decline in moral and family values. Briggs first submitted an initiative in 1977 banning lesbian and gay teachers, withdrew the original language, and then resubmitted the initiative with wording that eventually was approved. The initiative would go before the voters of California as Proposition 6.

By 1977, laws banning discrimination on the basis of sexual orientation had been passed in several California cities, including Berkeley, Cupertino, Mountain View, Santa Barbara, Santa Cruz, and San Francisco. As gay activists chalked up these local victories, they increased the salience of gay rights issues across the state and attracted the ire of religious conservatives, including Briggs and other conservative California politicians.

Also around this time, Bryant had mobilized religious conservatives to begin a number of campaigns to repeal local ordinances banning sexual-orientation discrimination. In addition to repeals in Florida, measures were successfully repealed in St. Paul, Minnesota; Wichita, Kansas; and Eugene, Oregon. Only one local repeal measure failed in 1977-1978, a proposal that appeared on the Seattle, Washington, ballot at the same time as the Briggs Initiative in California.

Briggs collected the required number of signatures (312,000) to place the measure before the voters in the November, 1978, election. The measure was the first GLBT-related measure on any statewide ballot. Briggs began his campaign for the measure in the heart of GLBT-friendly territory, San Francisco. He traveled the state arguing that homosexuals were using the public schools to recruit children to the GLBT movement. His efforts were channeled through a group he chaired called California Defend Our Children, whose executive director was the Reverend Lou Sheldon. Sheldon went on to form the Traditional Values Coalition and pay for the production of *Gay Rights, Special Rights*, a film used in anti-GLBT ballot initiative contests in the late 1980's and 1990's. Proponents ended up spending more than $1 million on the campaign.

GLBT activists immediately began mobilizing for the initiative's defeat. However, the first polls on the proposition showed voters supporting it 61 to 31 percent. Even the national GLBT newsmagazine *The Advocate* seemed pessimistic in June of 1978, suggesting that the measure might pass by a margin of 2-to-1 and that even San Francisco voters might support it.

The threat posed to the civil rights of gays by the Briggs Initiative, however, also helped to bring gays and lesbians into mainstream politics. Activists formed a statewide group called No on 6 that organized fund-raising campaigns, grassroots mobiliza-tion, and voting registration. With the help of enter-tainers and special events, GLBT groups were able to raise $1.3 million dollars to fight the initiative.

In San Francisco, activists held a Gay Freedom Day Parade that drew some 400,000 people. One participant, activist Cleve Jones, marched in the pa-rade carrying symbols of death camps to protest the Briggs Initiative. Likewise, the newly elected and out gay San Francisco supervisor Harvey Milk be-came a key opposition leader to the initiative, even debating Briggs in town-hall meetings and on tele-vision around the state. (Milk, along with San Fran-cisco mayor George Moscone, were murdered by Dan White later the same year.) Milk consistently and effectively made strong arguments against bringing the government into people's bedrooms and used the facts to demonstrate that child abuse was perpetrated mostly by heterosexuals and not homosexuals.

## FROM THE BRIGGS INITIATIVE

*Section 1.* One of the most fundamental interests of the State is the establishment and the preservation of the family unit. Consistent with this interest is the State's duty to protect its impressionable youth from influences which are antithetical to this vital interest. This duty is particularly compelling when the state undertakes to edu-cate its youth, and by law, requires them to be exposed to the state's chosen educational environment throughout their formative years.

A schoolteacher, teacher's aide, school administrator or counselor has a professional duty directed exclusively towards the moral as well as intellectual, social and civic development of young and impressionable students.

As a result of continued close and prolonged contact with schoolchildren, a teacher, teacher's aide, school ad-ministrator or counselor becomes a role model whose words, behavior and actions are likely to be emulated by stu-dents coming under his or her care, instruction, supervision, administration, guidance and protection.

For these reasons the state finds a compelling interest in refusing to employ and in terminating the employment of a schoolteacher, a teacher's aide, a school administrator or a counselor, subject to reasonable restrictions and qualifications, who engages in public homosexual activity and/or public homosexual conduct directed at, or likely to come to the attention of, schoolchildren or other school employees.

This proscription is essential since such activity and conduct undermines that state's interest in preserving and perpetuating the conjugal family unit.

The purpose of sections 44837.6 and 44933.5 is to proscribe employment of a person whose homosexual activi-ties or conduct are determined to render him or her unfit for service. . . .

*Section 2.* The governing board of a school district shall refuse to hire as an employee any person who has en-gaged in public homosexual activity or public homosexual conduct should the board determine that said activity or conduct renders the person unfit for service. . . .

*Section 3.* In addition to the grounds specified in Sections 44932, 44948 and 44949, or any other provision of law, the commission of "public homosexual activity" or "public homosexual conduct" by an employee shall subject the employee to dismissal upon a determination by the board that said activity or conduct renders the employee unfit for service. Dismissal shall be determined in accordance with the procedures contained in this section. . . .

While Milk focused on grassroots organizing, some individuals, such as David Mixner, an adviser to Los Angeles mayor Tom Bradley, came out as gay to friends and coworkers. Mixner helped organize fund-raising dinners with the social elite and Hollywood celebrities. At one such dinner, activists raised $40,000 to fight the measure, which at the time was a single-event record in California. Mixner also helped to organize a benefit concert with folk singers Joan Baez and Harry Chapin. Mixner and others formed the first GLBT political action committee in the country, the Municipal Elections Committee of Los Angeles (MECLA), to raise money to defeat the measure. Mixner felt compelled to fight the measure even though some in the GLBT community believed it would be a loss, and even though no heterosexual political consultants would take on the campaign.

Another GLBT activist, David Goodstein, was a controversial leader in the movement, but he helped found Concerned Voters of California in 1977, which existed solely to defeat the Briggs Initiative. Concerned Voters of California was credited by some as having coordinated much of the statewide effort against the initiative.

Mixner, a Democrat, and several gay Republicans, helped convince former California governor Ronald Reagan, in a private meeting, to oppose the initiative. Mixner helped develop the argument that the initiative was a real threat to free speech and could easily be abused. These arguments seemed to convince Reagan, who argued that existing laws protected children and that the measure might be used by students to blackmail teachers: "I don't approve of teaching a so-called gay lifestyle in our schools," Reagan wrote, "but there is already adequate legal machinery to deal with such problems if and when they arise. . . . [W]hat if an overwrought youngster, disappointed by bad grades, imagined it was the teacher's fault and struck out by accusing the teacher of advocating homosexuality? Innocent lives could be ruined."

Reagan also argued that "Whatever else it is, homosexuality is not a contagious disease like the measles. Prevailing scientific opinion is that an individual's sexuality is determined at a very early age and that a child's teachers do not really influence this," and that the measure had "the potential of infringing on basic rights of privacy and perhaps even constitutional rights." Reagan's words were risky; he was gearing up for a 1980 campaign for the presidency, and many credit his public opposition as a key force in turning public opinion against the measure. Others spoke against Proposition 6 as well, including California governor Jerry Brown, U.S. president Jimmy Carter, entertainer Bob Hope, state teachers associations, the *Los Angeles Times*, unions, and religious leaders.

On November 7, 1978, the measure failed 42 to 58 percent, and did not pass even in some of the most conservative California counties, including Orange County, Briggs's base. The defeat of the measure was credited to many factors, including the mobilization of the GLBT community and the support of political elites. It is also clear, though, that Democrats, union members, and minority groups strongly opposed the measure.

## SIGNIFICANCE

The mobilization of the GLBT community in California and around the country convinced many activists to publicly announce their sexual orientation and to form new political groups. For example, before the Briggs Initiative of 1978, there were dozens of GLBT interest groups in various cities around the state, but none at the state level. During the campaign, a number of lesbian and gay groups formed and a number of out politicians were elected to local offices.

Indeed, the gay Log Cabin Republicans organization credits its founding to the mobilization of GLBT conservatives against the Briggs Initiative. Log Cabin has gone on to form a national group heavily involved in congressional and presidential politics.

MECLA continued to be a powerhouse in California elections into the 1980's, raising thousands of dollars for GLBT-friendly candidates. MECLA founders, including David Mixner, went on to form new groups and raise funds for GLBT-friendly candidates in national elections. In fact, Mixner has worked on more than seventy-five election campaigns, including Bill Clinton's campaign in 1992 for the presidency, where Mixner was senior campaign adviser. The largest GLBT political action committee in the country, the Human Rights Campaign, modeled itself after MECLA in the early 1980's and has since raised millions of dollars for candidates running for national office.

Because of the successful repeal of gay-civil-rights measures throughout the country in 1977 and 1978, and because Oklahoma and Arkansas had passed laws banning lesbians and gays from teaching in public schools, the passage of the Briggs Initiative likely would have led to similar measures throughout the country. Following the defeat in California, Anita Bryant and Briggs fell out of the limelight.

The mid-1980's saw new California ballot initiatives targeting GLBT people, beginning with a 1985 initiative pushed by Lyndon LaRouche that would have mandated the quarantine of HIV-positive individuals and those *suspected* of being HIV-positive. That measure, Proposition 64, failed in November of 1986.

—*Donald P. Haider-Markel*

## FURTHER READING

Adam, Barry D. *The Rise of a Gay and Lesbian Movement*. Rev. ed. New York: Twayne, 1995.

Haider-Markel, Donald P., and Kenneth J. Meier. "Legislative Victory, Electoral Uncertainty: Explaining Outcomes in the Battles over Lesbian and Gay Civil Rights." *Review of Policy Research* 20, no. 4 (2003): 671-690.

Hollibaugh, Amber L. "Sexuality and the State: The Defeat of the Briggs Initiative and Beyond." In *My Dangerous Desires: A Queer Girl Dreaming Her Way Home*. Foreword by Dorothy Allison. Durham, N.C.: Duke University Press, 2000.

Rimmerman, Craig A. *From Identity to Politics: The Lesbian and Gay Movements in the United States*. Philadelphia: Temple University Press, 2002.

Shilts, Randy. *The Mayor of Castro Street: The Life and Times of Harvey Milk*. New ed. New York: St. Martin's Press, 1988.

Thompson, Mark, ed. *The Long Road to Freedom: "The Advocate" History of the Gay and Lesbian Movement*. New York: St. Martin's Press, 1994.

Vaid, Urvashi. *Virtual Equality: The Mainstreaming of Gay and Lesbian Liberation*. New York: Anchor Books, 1995.

SEE ALSO: 1972-1973: Local Governments Pass Antidiscrimination Laws; June 21, 1973: U.S. Supreme Court Supports Local Obscenity Laws; Mar. 5, 1974: Antigay and Antilesbian Organizations Begin to Form; June 27, 1974: Abzug and Koch Attempt to Amend the Civil Rights Act of 1964; July 3, 1975: U.S. Civil Service Commission Prohibits Discrimination Against Federal Employees; 1977: Anita Bryant Campaigns Against Gay and Lesbian Rights; 1978: Lesbian and Gay Workplace Movement Is Founded; Nov. 27, 1978: White Murders Politicians Moscone and Milk; 1979: Moral Majority Is Founded; Apr. 22, 1980: Human Rights Campaign Fund Is Founded; Nov., 1986: Californians Reject LaRouche's Quarantine Initiative; Nov. 8, 1988: Oregon Repeals Ban on Antigay Job Discrimination.

## November 27, 1978
# WHITE MURDERS POLITICIANS MOSCONE AND MILK

*Former San Francisco supervisor Dan White clandestinely entered San Francisco City Hall and murdered Mayor George Moscone and Supervisor Harvey Milk, one of the first openly gay elected officials in the United States.*

**LOCALE:** San Francisco, California

**CATEGORIES:** Crime; civil rights; marches, protests, and riots

**KEY FIGURES**

*Harvey Milk* (1930-1978), member of San Francisco's board of supervisors

*George Moscone* (1929-1978), mayor of San Francisco

*Dan White* (1946-1985), former supervisor who murdered Milk and Moscone

*Dianne Feinstein* (b. 1933), San Francisco board of supervisors president, acting mayor after Moscone's murder, and U.S. senator

**SUMMARY OF EVENT**

On the morning of November 27, 1978, Dan White, a former police officer and firefighter who also had been a San Francisco city and county supervisor, entered San Francisco's City Hall through a basement window, avoiding security screening at the building's main entrances. White made his way to the office of Mayor George Moscone and shot and killed him with a revolver.

He then reloaded his weapon with highly lethal dumdum (hollow point) bullets and walked into Supervisor Harvey Milk's office. Wishing to avoid a confrontation, Milk ushered White into White's former office, which he had vacated ten days earlier after resigning from the board of supervisors. White positioned himself between Milk and the door, drew his revolver from his jacket, and fired five times at Milk, killing him instantly.

White, a San Francisco native, had been a respected member of both the police and fire departments of the city. Raised as a devout Roman Catho-

lic, he had married and become a father. He had given up his regular job upon his election to the board of supervisors as the representative for District 8. He was characterized as rigid, homophobic, self-righteous, and ultraconservative. Immediately before the shootings, he had complained that he could not support his family on the $9,600 annual supervisors' salary and then used the low salary as an excuse to resign from the board less than two weeks earlier.

The underlying cause of his resignation, however, was his opposition to San Francisco's gay rights bill, which had been introduced by Harvey Milk and passed by a board vote of ten to one; White made the only dissenting vote. Mayor Moscone, who was dedicated to equal rights for all citizens, signed the bill into law as soon as the board had voted.

This legislation, protecting gays and lesbians from job discrimination and unequal treatment before the law, was heralded by San Francisco's large GLBT community, which soon after participated in a Gay Freedom Day Parade that attracted some 400,000 people. White had attempted to stop the march, but his efforts were futile.

White soon resigned from the board of supervisors, only to regret almost immediately that he had done so. He urged the mayor to reappoint him, but Moscone refused. White, who was said to have been overstimulated from having eaten too much junk food, murdered the mayor, then murdered Milk. The bullets White used to kill Milk were bullets designed to explode inside a person's body after being shot.

Dianne Feinstein, then-president of the board of supervisors and the acting mayor after Moscone's death, announced the murders. The shocked city, still dealing with the aftermath of the Jonestown massacre in Guiana, South America, in which many San Franciscans had died, went into a state of deep mourning. By evening, thirty thousand people marched along Market Street and then gathered for

*Supervisor Harvey Milk and Mayor George Moscone signing San Francisco's gay and lesbian rights bill in April, 1977. Milk and Moscone were assassinated a year and a half later by Dan White.* (AP/Wide World Photos)

a candlelight vigil in memory of the two victims.

Five months later, White was tried for first degree murder. His act was premeditated. Nevertheless, sympathy for the accused murderer was widespread. City police and firefighters raised more than $100,000 for White's defense fund. The impaneled jury consisted mostly of white, working-class people; out gays and lesbians, blacks, and members of other ethnic groups were systematically excluded. Prosecutors reduced the charges against White to voluntary manslaughter in order to secure conviction. White's attorney had argued the so-called "Twinkie" defense, alleging that White was so stimulated by the high sugar and high carbohydrate foods he had consumed the night before the murders that he could not be held responsible for his actions. He was found guilty and was sentenced to seven years and eight months but, with time off for good behavior, served just short of five years. On

the day of the verdict, May 22, 1979, San Francisco's GLBT community clashed with police in what was called the "White Night" riots, burning many police vehicles and breaking into City Hall, causing more than $1 million in damage.

Dan White left San Francisco for Los Angeles on his release from prison, but found that Los Angeles did not want him. He returned to San Francisco and, on October 21, 1985, attached a garden hose to the exhaust pipe of his 1970 Buick Le Sabre and took his own life.

### SIGNIFICANCE

The protests by San Francisco's GLBT community that followed the sentencing of Dan White to just seven years in prison, although violent in themselves, nevertheless marked a new activism against violence motivated by hatred of GLBT people, and they helped to raise Harvey Milk, who knew he was a possible target for murder, to the status of an icon within the GLBT community. The Dan White murder case is just one instance of the violence and threat of violence faced by GLBT people. Many less-visible murders and other hate crimes against GLBT persons have received far less, if any, media attention.

—*R. Baird Shuman*

**FURTHER READING**

Krakow, Kari. *The Harvey Milk Story.* Illustrated by David Gardner. Ridley Park, Pa.: Two Lives, 2001.

Marcus, Eric. *Making History: The Struggle for Gay and Lesbian Equal Rights.* New York: HarperCollins, 1992.

Ridinger, Robert B. Marks. *The Gay and Lesbian Movement: References and Resources.* New York: G. K. Hall, 1996.

Shilts, Randy. *The Mayor of Castro Street: The Life and Times of Harvey Milk.* New ed. New York: St. Martin's Press, 1988.

*The Times of Harvey Milk.* San Francisco, Calif.: Black Sands Productions, 1984. Academy-award winning documentary film.

**SEE ALSO**: June 30-July 1, 1934: Hitler's Night of the Long Knives; 1972-1973: Local Governments Pass Antidiscrimination Laws; June 21, 1973: U.S. Supreme Court Supports Local Obscenity Laws; Aug., 1973: American Bar Association Calls for Repeal of Laws Against Consensual Sex; Dec. 19, 1977: Quebec Includes Lesbians and Gays in Its Charter of Human Rights and Freedoms; Nov. 6, 1984: West Hollywood Incorporates with Majority Gay and Lesbian City Council; Dec. 4, 1984: Berkeley Extends Benefits to Domestic Partners of City Employees; Apr., 2003: Buenos Aires Recognizes Same-Gender Civil Unions.

## 1979
# MORAL MAJORITY IS FOUNDED

*An elite group of political strategists, headed by the evangelical minister Jerry Falwell, organized the Moral Majority to rally conservative Christian voters in support of the Republican Party and against, especially, GLBT rights.*

**LOCALE:** Lynchburg, Virginia
**CATEGORIES:** Organizations and institutions; government and politics; religion

**KEY FIGURES**

*Jerry Falwell* (b. 1933), evangelical minister with both radio and television ministries
*Richard Viguerie,*
*Howard Phillips,* and
*Paul Weyrich,* aides to Barry Goldwater in his 1964 presidential campaign
*Robert Billings* (1927-1995), former director of the White House Liaison Office

*Ed McAteer,* Religious Round Table founder and head of the sales department of Colgate-Palmolive

**SUMMARY OF EVENT**

There was a time when right-wing Americans would not dare to utter the word "homosexual" in public debate. After World War II and long presidential reigns (from Democrat Franklin D. Roosevelt's four-term presidency to the end of Democrat Harry Truman's administration in 1952), these citizens had chafed at the domination of Democrats in the White House and what they viewed as godless humanism and socialism taking over America.

The public's attitudes about gays and lesbians changed in the period from 1947 to 1950, during the investigation and trial of Alger Hiss as a Soviet spy, with revelations that Hiss's accuser, journalist Whittaker Chambers, had "homosexual tendencies."

Through 1954, the Hiss affair sparked witch hunts by Republican Wisconsin senator Joseph McCarthy, who aimed to expose communists and homosexuals in government. Eventually, Congress ended McCarthy's hearings, but the harm had been done. Rightwing religion could talk openly about "homosexual immorality" and link it with "red subversion."

In 1956, Jerry Falwell, an obscure but charismatic thirty-three-year-old evangelical minister, started a church in Lynchburg, Virginia. By 1967, he had a flock of thousands and his own radio show called *The Old Time Gospel Hour*. Soon, he was preaching nationwide through radio affiliates and television. Although he was a fundamentalist Christian, Falwell became known for his willingness to make common cause with Catholics, Jews, charismatics, and Moonies.

Segments of the Christian Right were growing into a labyrinth of nonprofits, political action committees, think tanks, and lobbyist groups. Organizers were skilled with the media and excelled at long-term strategizing. Whenever they faced Internal Revenue Service regulations prohibiting political activity by nonprofits, they often started a new one. Traditional tithing (donating 10 percent of one's income to one's church) garnered additional millions, some of which were available for political use.

During the 1964 presidential campaign, the New Right had supported Barry Goldwater against Democratic incumbent Lyndon B. Johnson. Goldwater lost, and the 1960's saw the United States experiencing a liberal mood and the questioning of authority. After the 1969 Stonewall Rebellion in New York City, the gay and lesbian rights movement roared into high gear. At first the New Right's reaction to this was somewhat ad hoc. In 1977, singer and entertainer Anita Bryant led a successful attack against a gay rights ordinance in Florida, which was followed by the unsuccessful antigay Briggs Initiative (which Bryant had also supported) in California the next year. Falwell launched his own antigay career by helping Bryant.

In 1979, when the Moral Majority appeared, it constituted the first formal attack on gay and lesbian rights. Falwell is often credited with founding the Moral Majority, but the idea and the name originated with an elite in-group of strategists. After the Nixon/Watergate scandal that put Democrats back in the White House from 1977 to 1981, the New Right had been desperately looking for a new doorway back to power. Three men who had worked on the Goldwater campaign—Richard Viguerie, Howard Phillips, and Paul Weyrich—met with former White House liaison Robert Billings and Ed McAteer, the Religious Round Table founder and the head of sales for Colgate-Palmolive.

This core group believed it could have a major influence on the Republican Party by capitalizing on the fears that conservative Americans of various religions had harbored since the 1940's. *Roe v. Wade* legalized abortion in 1973; gay activists were getting sodomy laws struck down. The group believed that Americans who were upset about these issues would join the Republican Party and vote for Ronald Reagan. To achieve this goal, a new national nonprofit organization was needed. Falwell was brought into the meetings, evidently because of his ability to network other religions.

According to conservative commentator Barbara Aho,

> Weyrich proposed that if the Republican Party would take a strong stand against abortion, the large Catholic voting bloc within the Democratic Party would be split. . . . [T]he term "Moral Majority" was coined to represent the ecumenical bloc of voters that would be led by the Rev. Falwell. . . . Startup cash was provided by the Coors family, while Viguerie, their direct-mail guru, used the old Goldwater mailing list to launch a massive fundraising effort. Sales wizard McAteer became the head of public relations.

### SIGNIFICANCE

Initially, the Moral Majority played a prominent role during Reagan's 1980 election, mobilizing churches and registering voters. By 1986, Falwell was claiming 500,000 contributors and a mailing list of six million. Yet the Moral Majority was just a storefront member of a bigger nonprofit with bluechip membership and more money. This was the

Council on National Policy (CNP), founded in 1981. The CNP kept a low profile—no public meetings. Its secret membership, when discovered by researchers, proved to be a right-wing roster, from billionaire Howard Ahmanson to the American Center for Law and Justice. Falwell served on the CNP board for a time. Despite differences in ideologies—fundamentalist, Jewish, Catholic, Mormon, Moonie—its members worked for consensus on ways to influence policy. Stopping gay and lesbian rights was one of those issues.

The Reagan era ended amid scandal, and Falwell had run the Moral Majority and other enterprises into debt. The Reverend Sun Myung Moon quietly gave Falwell a $3.5 million bailout, but this could not rescue the Moral Majority. The Internal Revenue Service had revoked its tax-exempt status. Falwell closed it down in 1989, and its work was taken over by the Christian Coalition. After Democrat Bill Clinton had recaptured the White House, Falwell mailed fund-raising letters to those on his old list asking whether he should reactivate the Moral Majority. The answer was evidently negative.

Through the Clinton years in the 1990's, Falwell continued to behave as if he still ran the Moral Majority, but his homophobia grew more poisonous—even some Christian supporters of Falwell found it distasteful. Canada's religion network, Vision TV, which carried Falwell's *Gospel Hour*, started censoring his remarks. In 1999, gay clergyman Mel White tried the ecumenical approach, hoping to persuade Falwell to stop preaching hatred. At first, Falwell agreed to work with White. However, after the terrorist attacks of September 11, 2001, this promise was conveniently forgotten as Falwell publicly accused gays and lesbians of helping to cause the terrorist attacks by "throwing God out." In 2004, Falwell created a new organization, the Faith and Values Coalition, with a platform as conservative as that of the Moral Majority fifteen years earlier.

*—Patricia Nell Warren*

## FURTHER READING

Harding, Susan Friend. *The Book of Jerry Falwell: Fundamentalist Language and Politics*. Princeton, N.J.: Princeton University Press, 2000.

Hixson, William B., Jr. *Search for the American Right Wing: An Analysis of the Social Science Record, 1955-1987*. Princeton, N.J.: Princeton University Press, 1992.

Shupe, Anson, and William A. Stacey. *Born Again Politics and the Moral Majority: What Social Surveys Really Show*. New York: Edwin Mellen Press, 1982.

Snowball, David. *Community and Change in the Rhetoric of the Moral Majority*. New York: Praeger, 1991.

Urofsky, Melvin I., and Martha May, eds. *The New Christian Right: Political and Social Issues*. New York: Garland, 1996.

SEE ALSO: Mar. 5, 1974: Antigay and Antilesbian Organizations Begin to Form; 1977: Anita Bryant Campaigns Against Gay and Lesbian Rights; Nov. 27, 1978: White Murders Politicians Moscone and Milk; Apr. 22, 1980: Human Rights Campaign Fund Is Founded; Nov., 1986: Californians Reject LaRouche's Quarantine Initiative; Mar.-Apr., 1993: Battelle Sex Study Prompts Conservative Backlash; Mar. 7, 2004: Robinson Becomes First Out Gay Bishop in Christian History; Nov. 29, 2005: Roman Catholic Church Bans Gay Seminarians.

## 1979-1981
# FIRST GAY BRITISH TELEVISION SERIES AIRS

*Gay Life became the first gay-focused series commissioned for British television. It not only laid the groundwork for the development of other GLBT-themed shows and characters but also introduced gay and lesbian concerns to the general public and helped to politicize the GLBT community in the United Kingdom.*

**LOCALE:** London, England
**CATEGORIES:** Cultural and intellectual history; arts

**KEY FIGURE**
*Michael Attwell*, British television actor and *Gay Life* producer

**SUMMARY OF EVENT**
During the early years of television in the United Kingdom, as in other countries, characters in sitcoms and dramas were portrayed as exclusively heterosexual. With the so-called sexual revolution in the 1960's came an increase in visibility for lesbians and gays. Slowly, gay characters began appearing on British television, although most were presented as stereotypical quick-with-a-comeback salesclerks or hairstylists with no sense of sexuality.

As the 1970's came to a close, gays and lesbians began looking for media that would inform, inspire, and connect them as a community. *Gay News*, the United Kingdom's first gay newspaper, began publishing in 1972, but television still remained closed to characters who were clearly gay or lesbian and to gay subject matter. Michael Attwell, a British producer and actor, sought a remedy.

In 1979, London Weekend Television commissioned the first ever gay series for British television: *Gay Life*, a newsmagazine format that focused both on stories of triumph and on daily social injustices. For the first time gays and lesbians could see their lives represented on the small screen more accurately; one episode, for example, featured the preju-

dicial attitude of British security services against lesbians and gays. Following the show's airing, community groups began to form, looking for social change.

The eleven-part series was broadcast well after the "family hour" in 1980 and 1981, however: 11:30 P.M. on Sundays. Still, Attwell was lauded for his contributions to furthering positive gay imagery on television. The average audience for *Gay Life* was 350,000, which was a strong enough rating to encourage producers to look at future gay-themed programming.

Although there had been gay characters on television before Attwell's program, there had not been such an open and honest portrayal of contemporary gay life. Public demand for similar programming grew, and, by 1988, ITV's Channel 4, a commercial station, began a series by and for gays and lesbians called *Out on Tuesday*. Throughout the 1980's, British soap operas, notably BBC's *EastEnders* and Channel 4's *Brookside*, presented gay couples as part of their regular programming. Though not immediately accepted by the general public, these characters became tolerated as television began to more accurately reflect Britain's diversity.

Gay characters were rarely allowed to show physical affection on British television, however. Even the most innocuous kiss became the subject of protests outside television studios. Because of this, many of the "groundbreaking" gay characters were nothing more than variations of the sexless eunuchs represented in the 1950's and 1960's. Gay characters could be open about their sexual orientation but could not be sexual. Without this complexity, the shows seemed "flat" and remained attached to secondary storylines.

Lesbian characters, on the other hand, seem to have been less scrutinized and less restricted. In 1990, *Oranges Are Not the Only Fruit* and *Portrait of a Marriage* drew large audiences, and lesbian couples appeared on both *Brookside* and *East-Enders*. In 1993, the soap opera *Emmerdale* introduced Zoe Tate, a lesbian veterinarian who proved very popular with audiences, and she still appears on the program. In fact, the actor who plays her has won numerous audience awards.

The HIV-AIDS epidemic brought pressure during the 1990's to depict more honest and complex portrayals of gays and lesbians. In response, the BBC introduced the series *Gaytime TV* from *Gay Life* producer Attwell. *Gaytime TV* offered a show that was more cutting-edge and flashy than the traditional newsmagazine show *Gay Life*, and though it received criticism from both the GLBT community and general audiences for sometimes being too superficial, it lasted four seasons because it addressed contemporary concerns and issues.

By the end of the 1990's, television fully embraced GLBT individuals as part of the social diversity it wished to reflect. GLBT topics were discussed openly on news programs and talk shows; gay characters appeared on numerous sitcoms and soap operas. British television had incorporated gays in almost every facet of programming; however, it still chose to show a fairly antiseptic portrayal of gay life.

Challenging political correctness was Channel 4's *Queer as Folk*, which first aired in 1999. This unapologetic, in-your-face drama featuring frank and graphic sex stretched the bounds of what had been shown on television previously and became so popular it spawned both a sequel and a successful cable-TV version in the United States. Two years later, the equally LGBT-focused *Metrosexuality* also proved a popular audience favorite. Suddenly, there was little about the gay experience, if anything, that could not be portrayed on television.

## SIGNIFICANCE

While British television had traditionally presented gay characters as oddities and nonsexual beings, the 1990's saw a sharp shift in focus. GLBT television stations, programs featuring solely gay characters, and a more vocal and discerning GLBT audience forced British producers to show representations that were more varied and nuanced than before.

The 1979 through 1981 airing of *Gay Life* allowed British audiences to see "real" gays and les-

bians. The general public saw a more human side to GLBT lives and introduced TV viewers to the daily stigmatization and discrimination faced by GLBT individuals. Also, the program helped increase the demand for GLBT characters on television and united gays and lesbians from around Great Britain politically, an activism sparked, in part, by the HIV-AIDS epidemic.

*Gay Life* also used numerous GLBT artists as directors, producers, and members of its production crew, many of whom have gone on to create or develop other GLBT programming. Indeed, Attwell, who introduced a fresh and youth-oriented style to gay programming on BBC2, continues to be one of Britain's most successful and respected television producers. Having laid the groundwork for regular programming that serves the needs of the GLBT community and informs the viewing public, *Gay Life* is regarded as one of the most important gay programs ever produced for television.

*—Tom Smith*

## FURTHER READING

Capsuto, Steven. *Alternate Channels: The Uncensored Story of Gay and Lesbian Images on Radio and Television, 1930's to the Present.* New York: Ballantine Books, 2000.

Gauntlett, David. *Media, Gender, and Identity: An Introduction.* New York: Routledge, 2002.

Howes, Keith. *Broadcasting It: An Encyclopaedia of Homosexuality on Film, Radio, and TV in the UK, 1923-1993.* London: Cassell, 1993.

Keller, James R., and Leslie Stratyner, eds. *The New Queer Aesthetic on Television: Essays on Recent Programming.* Jefferson, N.C.: McFarland, 2006.

McNair, Brian. *Striptease Culture: Sex, Media, and the Democratization of Desire.* New York: Routledge, 2002.

Sanderson, Terry. *Mediawatch: The Treatment of Male and Female Homosexuality in the British Media.* London: Cassell, 1995.

SEE ALSO: 1930's-1960's: Hollywood Bans "Sexual Perversion" in Films; Mar. 7, 1967: CBS Airs *CBS Reports: The Homosexuals*; Oct. 31, 1969:

*Time* Magazine Issues "The Homosexual in America"; June 5 and July 3, 1981: Reports of Rare Diseases Mark Beginning of AIDS Epidemic; 1985: GLAAD Begins Monitoring Media Coverage of Gays and Lesbians; 1985: Lesbian Film *Desert Hearts* Is Released; July 25, 1985: Actor Hudson Announces He Has AIDS; 1988: *Macho Dancer* Is Released in the Philippines; 1992-2002: Celebrity Lesbians Come Out; Mar. 21, 2000: Hollywood Awards Transgender Portrayals in Film; Sept. 7, 2001: First Gay and Lesbian Television Network Is Launched in Canada; Mar. 5, 2006: *Brokeback Mountain, Capote,* and *Transamerica* Receive Oscars.

## October 12-15, 1979
# First March on Washington for Lesbian and Gay Rights

*More than 100,000 people converged on the National Mall for the first March on Washington for Lesbian and Gay Rights. The event encouraged and embraced racial and gender diversity within the lesbian and gay movement and showed that lesbians and gays—representing a variety of backgrounds—could come together at the national level.*

**Locale:** Washington, D.C.
**Categories:** Marches, protests, and riots; civil rights; organizations and institutions

### Summary of Event
On October 14, 1979, more than 100,000 people gathered at the National Mall in Washington, D.C., to take part in the first March on Washington for Lesbian and Gay Rights. The march was the main event of four days of conferences, meetings, lobbying, and social gatherings, which brought together gays, lesbians, bisexuals, transgender (GLBT) persons, and their supporters from nearly every state in the United States.

The march was held at the end of a decade that saw a growing movement against GLBT people. In 1977, entertainer Anita Bryant began her "Save Our Children" campaign in Florida, which led to the repeal of one of the country's first gay-civil-rights laws. On November 27, 1978, the first out elected official, Harvey Milk, had been assassinated in San Francisco along with San Francisco's mayor, George Moscone. The killer, Dan White, received a lenient sentence. Also in 1978, the Briggs Initiative was introduced to voters in California, which, if it had passed, would have required the firing of all gay and lesbian teachers in the state. Although this initiative was narrowly defeated, it sparked a mobilization against the gay and lesbian community car-

*Logo for the first National March for Lesbian and Gay Rights.* (Courtesy: Lesbian, Gay, Bisexual & Transgender Community Center Archive)

---

**REMEMBERING THE MARCH, TWENTY-FIVE YEARS LATER**

*The following statements come from participants of the first lesbian and gay march on Washington, D.C., and were compiled by the National Gay and Lesbian Task Force to commemorate the 1979 event.*

"What is most memorable to me was the power of being in the company of thousands of gays and lesbians who were passionate about our cause—to be accepted and acknowledged as citizens of our country with all the equal rights and opportunities that we deserve."

"It was such a wonderful, if not spiritual experience. Even though there was close to a million people, the atmosphere was so welcoming and you felt like one big family. I have never felt such a welcoming experience since. My favorite part was riding the escalator up from the subway and everyone who had already arrived was welcoming those who were on the way. Upon the conclusion of the march, I was motivated to make a difference, happy, yet depressed that I had to leave that wonderful experience. I would have to say that it was the turning point for me in feeling confident who I was as a person. Now that I have children, I would love to have them [have the kind of] life altering experience as the March in Washington was to me."

"I had only just recently graduated from the idea that I was the only man in the world who felt like I did for other men. I now thought maybe there might be a couple hundred guys like me. Then I went to Washington and I was blown away to realize that I was really part of a world-wide brother and sisterhood. I was liberated and I could not be turned back."

"I abandoned classes at Wake Forest early for the lonely drive to DC. Scared, hopeful, nervous—I'd never seen a person I knew to be gay but all that was about to change. I was far too afraid to join in. Instead inched along with the marchers sitting at the corners of buildings and on the edges of bushes pretending to look for something and only casually glancing up at the throngs of marchers. I was afraid, but I was inside [and was] bubbling with my newfound excitement. There were my people. There was my tribe! I've never been alone again thanks to those, the bravest queers amongst us!"

*Source:* "25th Anniversary of the March on Washington—Thoughts and Reflections," National Gay and Lesbian Task Force media release (October 14, 2004). http://www.thetaskforce.org.

---

ried by the newly emerging Christian Right. These actions, combined with a nearly decade-long movement to build strong and political gay and lesbian communities, led to the national gathering for lesbian and gay rights in 1979.

Initially, several groups were reluctant to support the march for fear of sparking a backlash. Even after groups agreed to participate, there was intergroup conflict regarding how the march should be run, what type of tactics to use, and how to frame the issues. This conflict mirrored the schism that had grown among organizations in the broader gay and lesbian movement. Some organizations, such as the Mattachine Society and the Daughters of Bilitis, felt that the event should emphasize similarities between gays and lesbians and heterosexuals and should hold informative conferences instead of protests; they feared that anything more radical would alienate those who would otherwise support the rights of lesbians and gays. Other organizations, such as the Gay

Liberation Front and the National Coalition of Black Gays (NCBG), now the National Coalition of Black Lesbians and Gays (NCBLG), wanted to organize protests and other more disruptive activities to demand equal rights and protections under the law. In the end, however, there were no radical protests or acts of civil disobedience.

The march and rally had the following five formal demands:

1. Prohibit discrimination based on sexual orientation.
2. Repeal antigay legislation.
3. Urge then-President Jimmy Carter to sign a federal bill banning discrimination against gays and lesbians in the military and in federal government jobs.
4. Amend the Civil Rights Act of 1964 to include sexual orientation.
5. Create family protection laws.

The four-day event also included the first National Third World Gay and Lesbian Conference. Groups such as the NCBG and the D.C. Coalition of Black Gays had urged during the planning stage that organizations involved with the main march be racially balanced and diverse; and the main march was diverse.

Along with the march, rally, and the third world conference, there were workshops, legal forums, religious ceremonies, a lesbian and gay concert, dances, dinners, and other social events, all taking place peacefully; there were counterprotesters, however.

## SIGNIFICANCE

The 1979 March on Washington for Lesbian and Gay Rights was the first gathering—of this magnitude—of gays and lesbians. The sheer number of people with many common experiences created an atmosphere of celebration.

Several groups and organizations grew out of this event, including the National Black Lesbian & Gay Leadership Forum and the National Gay Rights Advocates (NGRA). An organization dealing with immigration issues for lesbians and gays was founded in Los Angeles soon after. Also, the D.C.-based Gay and Lesbian Parents Coalition emerged to support, educate, and advocate on behalf of gay and lesbian parents. The year following the march saw the founding of the Human Rights Campaign Fund (now the Human Rights Campaign), the National Association of Black and White Men Together, as well as several other lesbian and gay organizations.

The 1979 March on Washington had been one of the first such gatherings to be organized with attention to racial diversity. The NCBG helped plan the march, and it organized the third world conference, a gathering of gays and lesbians of color that had far-reaching implications, including the formation of several groups concentrating on issues facing gays and lesbians of color.

—*Jenn Rosen*

## FURTHER READING

Bernstein, Mary. "Celebration and Suppression: The Strategic Uses of Identity by the Lesbian and Gay Movement." *American Journal of Sociology* 103 (1997): 531-565.

D'Emilio, John, William B. Turner, and Urvashi Vaid, eds. *Creating Change: Sexuality, Public Policy, and Civil Rights*. New York: St. Martin's Press, 2000.

LeVay, Simon, and Elisabeth Nonas. *City of Friends: A Portrait of the Gay and Lesbian Community in America*. Cambridge, Mass.: MIT Press, 1995.

Morgan, Thomas. "National Gay Rights March, Counter Events Set Here." *The Washington Post*, October 12, 1979, p. C4.

Saslow, James. "A Monumental March Marks a Big Moment in Gay History." *The Advocate*, November 29, 1979, 7-9.

Sears, James T. *Rebels, Rubyfruit, and Rhinestones: Queering Space in the Stonewall South*. New Brunswick, N.J.: Rutgers University Press, 2001.

SEE ALSO: July 2-Aug. 28, 1963: Rustin Organizes the March on Washington; Aug., 1966: Queer Youth Fight Police Harassment at Compton's Cafeteria in San Francisco; June 27-July 2, 1969: Stonewall Rebellion Ignites Modern Gay and Lesbian Rights Movement; June 28, 1970: First Lesbian and Gay Pride March in the United States; 1977: Anita Bryant Campaigns Against Gay and Lesbian Rights; Nov. 7, 1978: Antigay and Antilesbian Briggs Initiative Is Defeated; Nov. 27, 1978: White Murders Politicians Moscone and Milk; 1979: Moral Majority Is Founded; Oct. 12-15, 1979: First National Third World Lesbian and Gay Conference Convenes; Oct. 11, 1987: Second March on Washington for Lesbian and Gay Rights; Apr. 24, 1993: First Dyke March Is Held in Washington, D.C.; Apr. 25, 1993: March on Washington for Gay, Lesbian, and Bi Equal Rights and Liberation; June, 1994: Stonewall 25 March and Rallies Are Held in New York City; June 19, 2002: Gays and Lesbians March for Equal Rights in Mexico City.

## October 12-15, 1979
# FIRST NATIONAL THIRD WORLD LESBIAN AND GAY CONFERENCE CONVENES

*The first national conference of third world lesbians and gays was held concurrently with the first March on Washington for Lesbian and Gay Rights. The conference, which brought together for the first time lesbian and gay people of color at the national level, also marked a significant historical moment: coalition building among various ethnic minorities.*

**ALSO KNOWN AS:** "When Will the Ignorance End: The Coming Together of Asians, American Indians, Latins and Blacks"
**LOCALE:** Washington, D.C.
**CATEGORIES:** Race and ethnicity; organizations and institutions; civil rights; feminism; marches, protests, and riots

**KEY FIGURES**
*Audre Lorde* (1934-1992), black feminist poet and educator
*Aura L. Beteta*, general consul of Nicaraguan consulate, San Francisco
*Tana Loy*, Chinese American representative of Lesbian and Gay Asian Collective
*Michiyo Fukaya* (Margaret Cornell; b. 1953), Japanese European poet and activist

**SUMMARY OF EVENT**
The first National Third World Lesbian and Gay Conference took place from October 12 to 15, 1979, at Harambee House, a then-new black-owned hotel next to Howard University in Washington, D.C. Organized by the National Coalition of Black Gays (NCBG), the conference drew more than five hundred registered participants and one hundred observers from across the nation and abroad, demonstrating for the first time in U.S. history the wide diversity of races, ethnicities, and nationalities that comprise the gay and lesbian population. Women made up 55 percent of the participants, and an estimated 20 percent were white. The conference, ti-

tled, "When Will the Ignorance End: The Coming Together of Asians, American Indians, Latins and Blacks," although focused especially on the concerns of people of color, made it clear in early publicity for the event that no one would be excluded from the gathering.

Black lesbian-feminist poet Audre Lorde gave the keynote speech, addressing the conference theme. She applauded the audience for its "power of vision" and for coming together, declaring also that ignorance about lesbian and gay people would end "when each one of us begins to seek out and trust the knowledge deep inside us." She celebrated the "wonderful diversity of groups within this conference, and a wonderful diversity between us within those groups." She said, "That diversity can be a generative source, a source of energy fueling our visions of action for the future."

Lorde attacked the homophobia within ethnic communities, suggesting that "historically, all oppressed peoples have been taught to fear and despise any difference among ourselves, since difference had been used against us so cruelly." She suggested, however, that among the lessons the audience can learn is that "we cannot separate our oppressions, nor yet are they the same. That not one of us is free until we are all free . . . difference must not be used to separate us, but to generate energy for social change at the same time as we preserve our individuality." She added, "What we dare to dream today we can work to make real tomorrow. Visions point the way to make the possible real." She concluded, "What we are doing here this weekend can help shape our tomorrows and a world. We are going to turn that beat totally around."

Political awareness and an air of militancy marked the conference as well, with workshops discussing racism and sexism. Participants also heard solidarity statements from socialist supporters in Mexico, as well as a statement from Aura L. Beteta, the general consul of the Nicaraguan consulate in

San Francisco, who sent "revolutionary Sandinista greetings." Beteta said, "May from your conference be born a movement that identifies, that unites and struggles with liberation movements of all oppressed people."

Tana Loy, a Chinese American lesbian representing the new Lesbian and Gay Asian Collective, which had formed that weekend at the conference, said in her plenary presentation, "Who's the Barbarian?," that Asian lesbians and gays should not avert each other's eyes, but instead, having met at the conference, "run toward each other." The conference culminated in a dance at the hotel ballroom, where many white supporters joined in, including gay poet Allen Ginsberg.

On Sunday, two hundred conferees marched down Georgia Avenue, in the heart of a black neighborhood of D.C. About one dozen Asian American lesbians and gays marched through Chinatown behind a sign declaring "We're Asians, Gay & Proud," while chanting the same slogan. They joined the main march on Washington, parading behind the Native American contingent and their sign, "First Gay Americans." Chants included, "Third World: We Must Be Heard!" "Third World: Liberation!" "Third World: We Will Be Heard!" A conferee chosen by the Lesbian and Gay Asian Collective, Michiyo Fukaya, a lesbian poet from Vermont who is of mixed European and Japanese origin, addressed some 100,000 celebrants gathered at the Washington Monument that day, speaking on "Living in Asian America."

## SIGNIFICANCE

The conference pierced the myth that there are no lesbians and gays who are also people of color. In one weekend, hundreds of lesbian and gay people of color gathered and marched visibly and proudly to affirm their sexual identities as well as their races and ethnicities. The gathering also marked a significant historical moment: coalition building among various ethnic minorities, presaging the later efforts at coalition work during the HIV-AIDS crisis and the havoc and devastation it wreaked on the same communities.

The conference and march empowered the lesbian and gay people of color who attended, and the impact was immediate. Soon after, the NCBG organized a meeting for lesbian and gay people of color with officials at the White House. The NCBG had been disregarded by the National Gay Task Force after that group failed to invite the NCBG to earlier White House meetings; NCBG, however, vowed to never repeat the mistake, and it did not.

In addition, caucuses that formed at the conference were soon established nationally. These new groups included the Latin American Lesbian and Gay Men's Coalition, Lesbian and Gay Asian Collective, Gay Asians Toronto, the Committee of Gay Black Men in Atlanta, as well as additional chapters of NCBG in Philadelphia and New York City. Student groups were formed on two black campuses—Howard University and Norfolk State University—and a stronger Gay American Indians developed.

The conference had been ignored by mainstream media but had received coverage by the alternative press. Audre Lorde's keynote address was reprinted in *Off Our Backs* (a feminist publication) and in *Gay Insurgent: A Gay Left Journal*, which also published Michiyo Fukaya's address and the plenary speech by Tana Loy. *Gay Insurgent* also printed conference resolutions from the Third World Women's Caucus, Freedom Socialist Party, Radical Women, and the Immigration Workshop. It also published photographs of participants from Mexico, the Latin American Lesbian and Gay Men's Caucus, the Jewish Caucus, and the NCBG. *Blacklight*, NCBG's publication, also covered the conference in two subsequent issues, including one devoted to photographs from the gathering.

—*Daniel C. Tsang*

## FURTHER READING

Constantine-Simms, Delroy, ed. *The Greatest Taboo: Homosexuality in Black Communities*. Los Angeles: Alyson, 2001.

Fukaya, Michiyo. "Living in Asian America: An Asian American Lesbian's Address Before the Washington Monument." *Gay Insurgent: A Gay Left Journal* no. 6 (Summer, 1980): 16.

Lorde, Audre. "I Am Your Sister: Black Women Organizing Across Sexualities." Freedom Organizing Pamphlet Series 3. Latham, N.Y.: Kitchen Table: Women of Color Press, 1985.

Loy, Tana. "Who's the Barbarian? An Asian American Lesbian Speaks Before the Third World Conference." *Gay Insurgent: A Gay Left Journal* no. 6 (Summer, 1980): 15.

Moraga, Cherríe L., and Gloria E. Anzaldúa, eds. *This Bridge Called My Back: Writings by Radical Women of Color.* 3d ed. Berkeley, Calif.: Third Woman Press, 2001.

Ratti, Rakesh, ed. *A Lotus of Another Color: An Unfolding of the South Asian Gay and Lesbian Experience.* Boston: Alyson, 1993.

**SEE ALSO:** May 27-30, 1960: First National Lesbian Conference Convenes; 1969: Nuestro Mundo Forms as First Queer Organization in Argentina; 1975: Gay American Indians Is Founded; Apr., 1977: Combahee River Collective Issues "A Black Feminist Statement"; Oct. 12-15, 1979: First March on Washington for Lesbian and Gay Rights; Oct. 12-15, 1979: Lesbian and Gay Asian Collective Is Founded; 1981: *This Bridge Called My Back* Is Published; Sept., 1983: First National Lesbians of Color Conference Convenes; 1987: Anzaldúa Publishes *Borderlands/La Frontera*; 1987: Asian Pacific Lesbian Network Is Founded; Oct. 14-17, 1987: Latin American and Caribbean Lesbian Feminist Network Is Formed; 1990: United Lesbians of African Heritage Is Founded; Dec., 1990: Asian Lesbian Network Holds Its First Conference.

---

## October 12-15, 1979
# LESBIAN AND GAY ASIAN COLLECTIVE IS FOUNDED

*The Lesbian and Gay Asian Collective was the first international group organized by and for lesbian and gay Asians. Although short-lived, the collective, which came together at the First National Third World Lesbian and Gay Conference, empowered its members to organize for lesbian and gay civil rights at the local level and inspired the formation of GLBT Asian groups in later years.*

**LOCALE:** Washington, D.C.
**CATEGORIES:** Organizations and institutions; marches, protests, and riots; race and ethnicity

**KEY FIGURES**
*Richard Fung*, cofounder of the collective
*Tana Loy*, cofounder of the collective
*Michiyo Fukaya* (Margaret Cornell; b. 1953), Japanese European poet and activist

**SUMMARY OF EVENT**
The Lesbian and Gay Asian Collective, the first group of its kind anywhere in the world, was formed during the First National Third World Lesbian and Gay Conference, which was held October 12-15, 1979, in Washington, D.C. The collective, made up of lesbian and gay Asian activists from North America, emerged from a gay Asian caucus at the national conference, which had been meeting at Harambee House, a black-owned hotel next to Howard University. The collective, which included Asians from not only the United States but also Canada, was organized to last a short time only.

An announcement about the group's formation in *Gay Insurgent: A Gay Left Journal* (Summer, 1980) stated the group's goals succinctly: "There is as yet no agreed upon organizational structure; and no statement of principles to guide our group. But we all agreed that we wanted to end our isolation with the majority white gay movement, and to reach out to other Asian Americans and Asian Canadians." The announcement provided a contact postal address in Philadelphia, and it suggested that Boston-area readers contact the previously formed group, Boston Asian Gay Men and Lesbians. It also suggested that Canadian readers contact a Third

World conference participant who was from Toronto—Richard Fung, who would later be well known as an independent filmmaker documenting the Asian GLBT movement. Fung formed Gay Asians Toronto, the first gay Asian group in Canada, after the conference in Washington, D.C.

A black-and-white photograph (taken on October 13, 1979) in the same issue of *Gay Insurgent* shows participants of the first meeting of the Lesbian and Gay Asian Collective at the Third World conference. In addition to the four men and six women seen sitting in a circle, there were about one dozen or so more present at the formation of the collective.

One collective member, Chinese American Tana Loy, had been chosen by the collective to represent the group and address the Third World conference during a plenary session. Her speech, "Who's the Barbarian?" suggested that Asians, newly empowered by the conference, should no longer avoid each other's eyes when meeting in public, but, instead, should "run toward each other."

About one dozen members of the collective joined the first March on Washington for Gay and Lesbian Rights that Sunday, October 14, preceded by a historical march through D.C.'s predominantly black neighborhood and through Chinatown, the first time Asian lesbians and gays had openly marched through these neighborhoods. The group marched behind a large banner declaring "We're Asians, Gay & Proud," while chanting the same slogan. The collective's marchers, along with the banner, also appear on the cover of the Summer, 1980, issue of *Gay Insurgent*. At the Washington Monument, Michiyo Fukaya, a lesbian poet of mixed European and Japanese origin from Vermont, addressed some 100,000 celebrants after the march, speaking on "Living in Asian America." *Gay Insurgent* also reproduced the speeches by Loy and Fukaya.

## SIGNIFICANCE

The First National Third World Lesbian and Gay Conference served as a beacon for groups such as the Lesbian and Gay Asian Collective, bringing like-minded individuals together for a weekend of politicking and organizing. The larger conference also shattered the myth that there are no people of color who are also lesbian or gay. The collective was part of a weekend where hundreds of lesbian and gay people of color gathered and marched visibly and proudly to affirm their sexual identities as well as their races and ethnicities. Lesbian and Gay Asian Collective members would keep in touch with each other after the conference for a few years, but the group eventually dissolved as members continued their involvement with local civil rights organizing.

*—Daniel C. Tsang*

## FURTHER READING

Fukaya, Michiyo. "Living in Asian America: An Asian American Lesbian's Address Before the Washington Monument." *Gay Insurgent: A Gay Left Journal* no. 6 (Summer, 1980): 16.

Lorde, Audre. "I Am Your Sister: Black Women Organizing Across Sexualities." Freedom Organizing Pamphlet Series 3. Latham, N.Y.: Kitchen Table: Women of Color Press, 1985.

Loy, Tana. "Who's the Barbarian? An Asian American Lesbian Speaks Before the Third World Conference." *Gay Insurgent: A Gay Left Journal* no. 6 (Summer, 1980): 15.

Moraga, Cherríe L., and Gloria E. Anzaldúa, eds. *This Bridge Called My Back: Writings by Radical Women of Color.* 3d ed. Berkeley, Calif.: Third Woman Press, 2001.

Ratti, Rakesh, ed. *A Lotus of Another Color: An Unfolding of the South Asian Gay and Lesbian Experience.* Boston: Alyson, 1993.

SEE ALSO: 1969: Nuestro Mundo Forms as First Queer Organization in Argentina; 1975: Gay American Indians Is Founded; Oct. 12-15, 1979: First March on Washington for Lesbian and Gay Rights; 1981: *This Bridge Called My Back* Is Published; 1982-1991: Lesbian Academic and Activist Sues University of California for Discrimination; Sept., 1983: First National Lesbians of Color Conference Convenes; 1987: Asian Pacific Lesbian Network Is Founded; 1987: VIVA Is Founded to Promote Latina and Latino Artists;

Oct. 14-17, 1987: Latin American and Caribbean Lesbian Feminist Network Is Formed; 1990: United Lesbians of African Heritage Is Founded; Dec., 1990: Asian Lesbian Network Holds Its First Conference; Oct. 9-12, 1998: First International Retreat for Lesbian and Gay Muslims Is Held; Nov., 1999: First Middle Eastern Gay and Lesbian Organization Is Founded.

# 1980
# ALYSON BEGINS PUBLISHING GAY AND LESBIAN BOOKS

*Alyson Publications, founded in 1980, is the largest and oldest publisher dedicated to books focusing on gays, lesbians, bisexuals, transgender persons, and their families. The company helped to energize and inspire the early years of GLBT publishing.*

**LOCALE:** Boston, Massachusetts
**CATEGORIES:** Publications; economics; cultural and intellectual history; literature

**KEY FIGURE**
*Sasha Alyson*, founder of Alyson Publications, activist, and author of children's books

**SUMMARY OF EVENT**

In 1977 in Boston, Sasha Alyson had founded Carrier Pigeon, a distributor for small progressive and feminist publishers in the United States and in Great Britain. Two years later, Alyson decided to start his own publishing company to fill gaps in the publishing industry, and in 1980, Alyson Publications was officially founded when it published its first books. The company's early titles examined social, health, and environmental issues. Also in 1980, the company published *Young, Gay, and Proud!*, a book that set the stage for its successful future. Drawing on his experience working for small presses, Alyson built a company recognized still as the largest and oldest publisher of GLBT-themed books.

From its inception, Alyson Publications wanted to increase the quantity and diversity of GLBT literature. *Young, Gay, and Proud!* dealt with coming-out issues for gay and lesbian teenagers. Subsequent titles similarly addressed GLBT audiences who were historically underrepresented in literature. The release of Joseph Beam's edited collection *In the Life: A Black Gay Anthology* (1986) marked one of the first times that the writings of African American gay men were brought together for publication. Marcy Adelman addressed the lives of older lesbians in her book *Long Time Passing: Lives of Older Lesbians* (1986), while Heinz Heger brought to light the persecution of gays and lesbians in Nazi Germany in his book *The Men with the Pink Triangle: The True, Life-and-Death Story of Homosexuals in the Nazi Death Camps* (1980).

In 1990, under the new imprint of Alyson Wonderland, the company began publishing books for the children of gay and lesbian parents. In 1992, Alyson estimated that his company had published twelve of the eighteen existing children's picture books featuring gay or lesbian characters. Although they received praise from gay and lesbian couples with children, the books were attacked from other quarters. The school boards of four New York City boroughs rejected a board of education curriculum guide because it included the books *Heather Has Two Mommies* (1989) by Lesléa Newman and Diana Souza, *Daddy's Roommate* (1990) by Michael Willhoite, and *Gloria Goes to Gay Pride* (1991) by Lesléa Newman and Russell Crocker. Meanwhile, the Oregon Citizen's Alliance (OCA) spoke out against *Heather Has Two Mommies*, *Daddy's Roommate*, and *The Duke Who Outlawed Jelly Beans* (1991) by Johnny Valentine and Lynette Schmidt. Although the OCA initially planned to remove copies of *Heather Has Two Mommies* from the Eugene,

Oregon, public libraries, it backed down after receiving negative publicity.

In 1992, Alyson announced his intention to sell the company because he wanted to devote more time to AIDS activism. In May of 1994, Alyson hired Alistair Williamson to take over management of the company. Williamson, who had previously served as an editor at the Harvard Business School Press, wrote the first article on coming out in the workplace ever published by the *Harvard Business Review*.

While Alyson continued his involvement with decision making and editing, he was able to shift much of his attention to other causes. In 1995, Liberation Publications, Inc. (LPI), a Los Angeles company that publishes several magazines, including *The Advocate* and *Out*, purchased Alyson Publications. In addition to retaining the Alyson Publications and Alyson Wonderland imprints, LPI added Advocate Books as a third imprint.

## Significance

Sasha Alyson is widely credited for encouraging the publication of books written by, for, and about GLBT people. Alyson Publications increased the amount and variety of GLBT-themed material, paying particular attention to underrepresented populations, including teenagers and younger children. In addition to the books published for adult audiences, Alyson championed some of the first—and most popular—books for children of gays and lesbians. The company even operated a pen-pal program for children and youth who were gay, lesbian, or questioning their sexuality. Through these publishing activities, Alyson expanded the representations of GLBT people and added impetus to a burgeoning GLBT publishing industry.

Despite the controversies over the content of its children's books, especially those in public libraries, the company continues to publish titles in multiple genres appropriate for various age groups. Alyson Publications has about two hundred titles in print and continues to publish about twenty-five titles per year, appropriate for various age groups and spanning multiple genres.

Alyson Publications also has been active in the GLBT community. In 1988, it solicited essays about what an average person could do to fight AIDS. Contributors included actors Whoopi Goldberg and Elizabeth Taylor and former U.S. surgeon general C. Everett Koop. The writings were pulled together for a ninety-six-page book called *You Can Do Something About AIDS*; 1.3 million copies of the book were distributed free in bookstores across the United States.

Alyson's many other accomplishments include founding *Bay Windows* in 1983, a gay and lesbian newspaper serving the Boston area. He has written a number of children's books under the pseudonym Johnny Valentine. After selling Alyson Publications, he opened a GLBT travel company called Alyson Adventures.

—*Kathleen Liddle*

## Further Reading
Barber, Karen. "Letter from Boston." *Lambda Book Report* 4, no. 9 (March/April, 1995): 8-10.
Gleason, Katherine. "Not in Front of the Children." *Lambda Book Report* 3, no. 6 (September, 1992): 6.
Graham, Renee. "A Strong Voice for Gay Lit Is Moving On." *Boston Globe*, June 8, 1992, p. 30.
Moore, Lisa. "A History of Publishing Pride." *Lambda Book Report* 11, nos. 9-11 (April, 2003): 38.
Preston, John. "Gay Lit Goes Mainstream: The Big Business of Publishing Gay Books." *The Advocate*, November 26, 1985, 51-54, 60.
Streitmatter, Rodger. *Unspeakable: The Rise of the Gay and Lesbian Press in America*. Winchester, Mass.: Faber and Faber, 1995.

See also: July 4, 1855: Whitman Publishes *Leaves of Grass*; May 25, 1895: Oscar Wilde Is Convicted of Gross Indecency; 1924: Gide Publishes the Signed Edition of *Corydon*; 1939: Isherwood Publishes *Goodbye to Berlin*; 1947-1948: Golden Age of American Gay Literature; 1956: Baldwin Publishes *Giovanni's Room*; 1963: Rechy Publishes *City of Night*; June, 1971: The Gay Book Award Debuts; 1974: *The Front Runner* Makes *The New York Times* Best-Seller List; 1975: First Novel About Coming Out to

## 1980-1981
# GAY WRITERS FORM THE VIOLET QUILL

*The Violet Quill, a short-lived but ultimately successful and significant writing group, helped change the world of publishing and literature. Violet Quill members helped create an open environment in which it was acceptable to write about gay topics in a way that did not compromise true gay experiences.*

**LOCALE:** New York, New York
**CATEGORIES:** Literature; publications; organizations and institutions

**KEY FIGURES**
*Christopher Cox*,
*Robert Ferro*,
*Michael Grumley*,
*Andrew Holleran* (b. 1943),
*Felice Picano* (b. 1944),
*Edmund White* (b. 1940), and
*George Whitmore* (b. 1945), writers and members of the Violet Quill

**SUMMARY OF EVENT**
During the year 1980 to 1981, a group of gay writers came together in New York City to form a writing group called the Violet Quill. The group members' dialogues and writings would change the face of gay literature in the United States. The group consisted of seven men: Christopher Cox, Robert Ferro, Michael Grumley, Andrew Holleran, Felice Picano, Edmund White, and George Whitmore. While their combined efforts would together change the arena of gay publishing, they brought both common goals and individual purpose to the group.

The men of the Violet Quill met formally on only eight occasions over the course of one year. The revolving gatherings were held in members' homes and included readings from one another's manuscripts or journals and, on a lighter note, servings of dessert, which became more lavish with each gathering. Generally, two people would read at each meeting, receiving comments from other members.

Ferro, Grumley, and Holleran had met while attending the University of Iowa's Writers' Workshop. The remaining members became acquainted through various New York literary circles. The common denominator of the group was that they were all out gay writers who were having similar struggles in dealing with their own literature and the world of publishing. They were ambitious in their fields and open in their sexuality, a mix that was not easily accepted. They were writing a new type of gay literature, without apologies, in a post-Stonewall era.

It could be said that the eight meetings of the group were the least important part of the Violet Quill. In fact, this group had been given its name even before the occasion of its first meeting. The members' common struggles solidified an alliance before they came together on their own. They asked questions of themselves and others, such as, How do we represent a gay culture that is not subversive of the dominant discourse? and, How do we create gay characters that are true to our own experience and still have our work published by the mainstream not familiar with those experiences? Although they had a common goal, they did not always share a collective thought. Scholar David Bergman noted that the group,

*Edmund White, "May 16, 1996."* (Jill Krementz/Courtesy of Allen and Unwin)

shared several impulses: a desire to write works that reflected their gay experiences, and specifically, autobiographical fiction; a desire to write for gay readers without having to explain their point of view to shocked and unknowing heterosexual readers; and finally, a desire to write . . . in a selection of the language really used by gay men.

## SIGNIFICANCE

The Violet Quill did much to change the way that publishers and the general public felt about gay literature. However, change was not always easy to see, nor was change seen immediately. Some gay writers would come to criticize the impact of the group in the literary arena, claiming that the members of the Violet Quill had actually blocked the doors to the publishing world. Despite the criticism,

the future would show that the group had had a positive influence.

After the existence of the Violet Quill, each group member was able to publish his work. Edmund White (who had actually published prior to the group's formation) would go on to become one of the most influential writers of the 1980's and 1990's—gay or straight. The literary world in New York ran in relatively small circles, and publishers knew of the Violet Quill and its goals. In an era when the grassroots gay and lesbian rights movement was just beginning, these men were able to bang on doors and demand that publishers pay attention to their work. The outcome, if not full acceptance, was at least the ability to publish. Books and stories may not have been published in their raw original form, but gay characters were emerging from the oppression of previous decades.

The men in the Violet Quill helped pave the way for a future in which other men and women would be able to write with their authentic voices. The result was not only the publication of gay-themed literature but the creation of a new genre. The efforts of the Violet Quill helped lead the way to a proliferation of gay and lesbian literature, to the existence of gay and lesbian publishing houses, and to the wide topical reach of GLBT literature.

—*N. Y. Gulley*

## FURTHER READING

Bergman, David. *The Violet Hour: The Violet Quill and the Making of Gay Culture.* New York: Columbia University Press, 2004.

_____, ed. *The Violet Quill Reader: The Emergence of Gay Writing After Stonewall.* New York: St. Martin's Press, 1994.

Herren, Greg. "Felice Picano: Sex, Lies, and Manuscripts." Review of Picano's *The Book of Lies*, *Lambda Book Report* 8, no. 4 (1999).

Holleran, Andrew, and Felice Picano. "Telling the Truth in Fiction." *James White Review* 16, no. 4 (1999): 5-11.

Picano, Felice. "On the Real Violet Quill Club." In *Queer Representations: Reading Lives, Reading Cultures*, edited by Martin Duberman. New York: New York University Press, 1997.

_____. "The Real Violet Quill Club." *Harvard Gay & Lesbian Review* 2, no. 2 (1995): 5.

White, Edmund. "Out of the Closet, onto the Book-shelf." *The New York Times Magazine*, 1991, 22-26.

**SEE ALSO:** July 4, 1855: Whitman Publishes *Leaves of Grass*; May 25, 1895: Oscar Wilde Is Convicted of Gross Indecency; 1924: Gide Publishes the Signed Edition of *Corydon*; 1939: Isherwood Publishes *Goodbye to Berlin*; 1947-1948: Golden Age of American Gay Literature; 1956: Baldwin Publishes *Giovanni's Room*; 1963: Rechy Publishes *City of Night*; June, 1971: The Gay Book Award Debuts; 1974: *The Front Runner* Makes *The New York Times* Best-Seller List; 1975: First Novel About Coming Out to Parents Is Published; 1980: Alyson Begins Publishing Gay and Lesbian Books; May, 1987: *Lambda Rising Book Report* Begins Publication; June 2, 1989: Lambda Literary Award Is Created; 1993: Monette Wins the National Book Award for *Becoming a Man*.

# April 22, 1980
# HUMAN RIGHTS CAMPAIGN FUND IS FOUNDED

*The Human Rights Campaign Fund was established as a political action committee to raise funds for candidates for public office who would be supportive of gay and lesbian civil rights. The organization's founding came at a time when conservative lobbying groups, such as the Moral Majority, were busy establishing their own presence in Washington, D.C.*

**ALSO KNOWN AS:** Human Rights Campaign
**LOCALE:** Washington, D.C.
**CATEGORIES:** Organizations and institutions; government and politics

## KEY FIGURE

*Steve Endean* (1948-1993), gay rights lobbyist and Human Rights Campaign Fund founder

## SUMMARY OF EVENT

In the late 1970's, groups such as the National Conservative Political Action Committee and the Moral Majority had much success supporting and influencing conservative political candidates. It became obvious that for the protection of gay and lesbian rights, lobbyists also had to work for gay and lesbian causes. In 1978, Steve Endean founded the Gay Rights National Lobby and went to Washington, D.C., to serve as its director. Some contributors, however, had been reticent to contribute to a political action committee with the word, "gay" in its name. For that reason, some fund-raising organizations chose names such as "Legal Foundation for Personal Liberties." Finally, on April 22, 1980, Endean founded the Human Rights Campaign Fund (HRCF), a name designed to allow donors to contribute without specifically funding a group with "gay" or "lesbian" in its name; however, the goal was the same as that of Endean's earlier project: political lobbying for lesbians and gays. The HRCF, based in Washington, D.C., had the broader appeal of "human rights." The HRCF attracted an advisory board of well-known individuals, including singer and songwriter Joan Baez, feminist activist and writer Gloria Steinem, and Civil Rights activist and former Atlanta mayor Andrew Young.

During 1980 the HRCF registered with the Federal Election Committee and made its first contribution. The HRCF supported Representative Jim Weaver (D-Oregon), who went on to defeat a Moral Majority supported conservative candidate. Also in 1980 the Fund mailed its first nationally distributed gay-focused fund-raising letter, with the support of playwright Tennessee Williams. In 1985 the Fund merged with the Gay Rights National Lobby, and in 1995, the organization changed its name to the Human Rights Campaign (HRC) and adopted the current "equal sign" logo. By 1998 the HRC's political action committee had contributed more than $1 million to more than two hundred congressional candidates.

In 1982 the HRCF had incorporated and drafted bylaws that made clear the purpose of advancing the cause of gay and lesbian civil rights "by supporting and educating candidates for federal elective office." It held a major fund-raiser in New York City at the Waldorf Astoria hotel and its keynote speech, given by former vice president Walter Mondale, was covered on *Nightline* (ABC-TV). By November of 1982 the HRCF had raised $800,000 and had become the seventeenth largest independent political action committee in the United States. It also had a great success rate for the candidates it supported, with 81 percent of HRCF-backed candidates winning their elections.

In 1989 the HRCF reorganized, becoming a membership organization as well as a political action committee (PAC). The HRCF would become a PAC for the "promotion of the social welfare of the gay and lesbian community, by drafting, supporting and influencing legislation and policy at the federal, state and local level." In June of that year, HRCF's membership had grown to twenty-five thousand.

In 1992 the HRC backed its first presidential candidate, Bill Clinton, and one year later it took on the National Coming Out Day project. In August, 2000, Elizabeth Birch, the organization's director, addressed the Democratic National Convention. Birch was the first leader of a national gay and lesbian organization to address a convention of a major political party in the United States.

## SIGNIFICANCE

The Human Rights Campaign Fund was the first national lobbying organization supporting gay and lesbian rights, founded to counter the efforts of the New Right, which had been forming political action committees as well. HRCF mobilized gays and lesbians and encouraged many to contribute to the organization as it assisted gays, lesbians, and allies who were running for political office. The HRC remains dedicated to educating citizens and politicians alike on GLBT issues and concerns.

HRCF's founder, Steve Endean had stepped down from the HRCF during some power struggles in the mid-1980's, but he continued to be politically active, supporting gay and lesbian rights until his death in 1993. The Philanthrofund, a national philanthropic organization, has established an endowed fund in Endean's honor. The Endean fund provides support for activism and the study of public policy related to the GLBT community.

The HRC also has a number of current issues on its agenda, including the protection of GLBT families (working for the rights of same-gender couples); marriage; workplace discrimination; health (HIV-AIDS, lesbian health); hate crimes (expanding federal hate crimes legislation to include crimes based on sexual orientation, gender, and disability); transgender issues; immigration; military; privacy issues; and judicial nominations.

From its small beginnings in 1980, the Human Rights Campaign has moved into the national political arena and has remained a formidable force on Capitol Hill: its name and logo are widely recognized, it commands respect when speaking out on a wide variety of issues, and it is successful during elections, both with ballot measures and with the candidates it endorses.

The fund's financial supporters include *The Advocate* and *Out* magazines, American Airlines, Chase, Citigroup, Deloitte. hotels.com, IBM, Mitchell Gold and Bob Williams Co., Nike, Olivia Cruises and Resorts, Prudential Financial, Replacements, Ltd., Shell Oil, Showtime, Volvo Cars of North America, and Washington Mutual. While some of these are obvious supporters of the gay and lesbian political cause (*The Advocate, Out,* Olivia), others (Citigroup, IBM, Shell Oil, Volvo) are mainstream companies.

—*Mary Ware*

## FURTHER READING

Endean, Steve, and Vickie Eaklor. *Bringing Lesbian and Gay Rights into the Mainstream*. Binghamton, N.Y.: Haworth Press, 2006.

Human Rights Campaign Foundation. *The State of the Workplace for Gay, Lesbian, Bisexual, and Transgender Americans, 2005-2006.* http://www.hrc.org.

Mohr, Richard D. *Gays/Justice.* New York: Columbia University Press, 1988.

Rimmerman, Craig, Kenneth Wald, and Clyde Wilcox, eds. *The Politics of Gay Rights.* Chicago: University of Chicago Press, 2002.

**SEE ALSO:** Feb. 19-20, 1966: First North American Conference of Homophile Organizations Convenes; 1971: Kameny Is First Out Candidate for U.S. Congress; 1973: National Gay Task Force Is Formed; Oct. 18, 1973: Lambda Legal Authorized to Practice Law; Mar. 5, 1974: Antigay and Antilesbian Organizations Begin to Form; June 27, 1974: Abzug and Koch Attempt to Amend the Civil Rights Act of 1964; 1978: Lesbian and Gay Workplace Movement Is Founded; Nov. 7, 1978: Antigay and Antilesbian Briggs Initiative Is Defeated; 1979: Moral Majority Is Founded; Oct. 11, 1988: First National Coming Out Day Is Celebrated; July 26, 1990: Americans with Disabilities Act Becomes Law; 1994: Employment Non-Discrimination Act Is Proposed to U.S. Congress.

## May-August, 1980
# U.S. NAVY INVESTIGATES THE USS *NORTON SOUND* IN ANTILESBIAN WITCH HUNT

*The U.S. Navy attempted to purge women believed to be lesbian from their assignments on the USS* Norton Sound. *Navy officials used coercion and fabricated testimony in their investigations. The American Civil Liberties Union defended the women in a case that was unique because the accused spoke out against the charges and because the case received widespread media attention.*

**ALSO KNOWN AS:** Norton Sound Eight
**LOCALE:** Port Hueneme and Long Beach, California
**CATEGORIES:** Military; civil rights; government and politics; laws, acts, and legal history

### KEY FIGURES
*Helen Teresa Wilson,* servicewoman, who named twenty-four shipmates on the USS *Norton Sound* as lesbian
*Alicia Harris,* African American servicewoman, discharged from the Navy

*Wendi Williams,* African American servicewoman, discharged from the Navy
*Carole Brock,* white servicewoman, accused, brought case to the attention of the National Organization for Women
*Tangela Gaskins,* African American servicewoman, retained in the Navy
*Barbara Lee Underwood,* white servicewoman, retained in the Navy
*Susan McGreivy,* staff attorney for the American Civil Liberties Union of Southern California

### SUMMARY OF EVENT
In the late 1970's, the military began to enlist women at an accelerated pace to compensate for a decline in the number of male recruits. When the United States entered a recession in 1980 and more male recruits became available, the military's regulations and procedures against gays and lesbians tightened.

The formal investigation aboard the USS *Norton Sound* of women believed to be lesbian was begun by the Naval Investigative Service (NIS), when the ship's commander, James Seebirt, was on leave. The officer responsible for the investigation was known to oppose the Navy's Women at Sea program (which assigned women to ships for the first time). The Women at Sea program was only a year and a half old when the NIS started its investigation.

On May 16, 1980, an NIS agent questioned servicewoman Helen Teresa Wilson about an incident of drug dealing and loan-sharking on the *Norton Sound*; she was also asked if she knew of lesbians on board ship. Wilson accused twenty-four of the ship's sixty-one women (including all but one of the African American women). Her accusations were based solely on the women's attitudes, appearance, and behavior, such as using endearing terms when talking to women, sitting close to them, looking "masculine," or defending homosexuals when the topic came up in conversation.

The next move by the NIS was to call in the thirty-eight servicewomen not named by Wilson and ask them to check off, on a roster of all the ship's women, anyone they believed to be lesbian. Again, although none of them had witnessed any sexual encounters, twenty-nine women were named. Those whose names were checked most often were interrogated by NIS agents.

Later, gay journalist Randy Shilts conducted extensive interviews and gathered a variety of documents on the *Norton Sound* incident. He discovered that NIS investigators employed a variety of coercive techniques. First, women were asked explicit, suggestive questions or were told that since the NIS already had evidence against them, they should simply confess. Some were told that if they did not sign statements against their shipmates, their leave could be delayed, they could be court-martialed for withholding evidence, or they themselves could be investigated as lesbians.

The Navy began its formal investigation with twenty-four women. Carole Brock, a twenty-two-year-old Engineman Second Class, and other accused servicewomen, met with Johnnie Phelps of the Los Angeles chapter of the National Organization for Women (NOW). Phelps, a veteran of World War II, arranged a meeting of the women with Su-

san McGreivy, an attorney with the American Civil Liberties Union (ACLU) specializing in lesbian and gay rights. The ACLU held a press conference on June 13 to announce that if the Navy discharged the women without hearings (as the women had been told could happen), the ACLU would take the incident to federal court. On June 20, Commander Seebirt announced that charges against eleven of the women had been dropped. The charges against the remaining eight were changed to misconduct, a lesser charge that would allow them an administrative hearing.

Later known as the "Norton Sound Eight," the women did not refrain from going public with their experiences; they and attorney McGreivy welcomed media attention to expose the Navy's tactics. The servicewomen appeared on the TV shows *Phil Donahue* and *Today*, were supported by a fundraiser hosted by producer Norman Lear and actor Ed Asner at a Hollywood disco, and were grand marshals for the San Francisco Gay Freedom Parade.

The hearings, which were held on board the ship, began on August 4 before a three-member administrative panel. Administrative hearings had no rules of evidence, so prosecutors were allowed to present hearsay and unsworn testimony. Evidence submitted by prosecution witnesses included seeing a servicewoman reading a book about homosexuality, seeing a card from one servicewoman to another signed "Love, Tange" (Tangela Gaskins), and hearing that one servicewoman attended "gay night" at a Los Angeles amusement park.

Five of the twelve servicewomen whose statements were the foundation of the Navy's case said that the NIS altered or invented parts of their statement. Somewhat more substantial was the testimony of three witnesses who said they had seen Alicia Harris and Wendi Williams touching and caressing each other in a public area of the ship during the day.

For Gaskins's and Barbara Lee Underwood's defense, attorneys called as witnesses men who had engaged in sex with them—including Gaskins's fiancé and Underwood's supervisor, a petty officer first class. No such witnesses were available for

Harris and Williams, though. Hearings were held on only four of the Norton Sound Eight. The Navy recommended retention for Gaskins and Underwood and an honorable discharge of the two African American women (Harris and Williams). On August 21, the Navy announced it had dropped charges on the remaining four because of insufficient evidence.

## SIGNIFICANCE

The *Norton Sound* incident was one of many witch hunts against lesbians in the 1980's. Similar incidents occurred on the USS *Gompers* (earlier in 1980), the USS *Yellowstone* (1988), and the USS *Grapple* (1988), and at the Parris Island Marine Corps Recruit Training Depot (1986-1988). From 1980 to 1990, an average of fifteen hundred servicemembers per year were discharged for homosexuality; 23 percent were women, although women comprised only 10 percent of all servicemembers. The NIS's techniques of coercion and intimidation in the *Norton Sound* incident had been used for years by military special intelligence units, according to Susan McGreivy.

Unlike other military witch hunts, the *Norton Sound* incident received widespread media attention, with daily coverage in California newspapers and broader coverage by magazines, television, and national newspapers. Also, unlike other incidents, the accused women resisted and talked openly about the case. Because of their persistence, combined with the pressure of publicity and support from the ACLU, the Navy's attempted purge of twenty-four servicewomen resulted in two discharges, two retentions, and twenty dropped charges.

*—Glenn Ellen Starr Stilling*

## FURTHER READING

Lindsey, Robert. "Navy Sends More Women to Sea, Despite Problems." *The New York Times*, June 29, 1980, p. 14.

McGreivy, Susan. "*Norton Sound* Case Shows Investigators Rely on Intimidation and False Evidence." *Civil Liberties*, June, 1981.

Servicemembers Legal Defense Network. *Conduct Unbecoming: Annual Reports on "Don't Ask, Don't Tell, Don't Pursue, Don't Harass."* 1994-2003. http://www.sldn.org/.

_____. *Survival Guide: A Comprehensive Guide to "Don't Ask, Don't Tell, Don't Pursue, Don't Harass," and Related Military Policies*. 4th ed. Washington, D.C.: Author, 2003.

Shilts, Randy. *Conduct Unbecoming: Gays and Lesbians in the U.S. Military*. 1994. New ed. New York: St. Martin's Griffin, 2005.

_____. "The Ship That Dare Not Speak Its Name." *Village Voice*, September 24-30, 1980, p. 13-14, 16, 63.

SEE ALSO: 1912-1924: Robles Fights in the Mexican Revolution; Mar. 15, 1919-1921: U.S. Navy Launches Sting Operation Against "Sexual Perverts"; July 3, 1975: U.S. Civil Service Commission Prohibits Discrimination Against Federal Employees; 1976-1990: Army Reservist Ben-Shalom Sues for Reinstatement; May 3, 1989: *Watkins v. United States Army* Reinstates Gay Soldier; 1990, 1994: *Coming Out Under Fire* Documents Gay and Lesbian Military Veterans; Aug. 27, 1991: *The Advocate* Outs Pentagon Spokesman Pete Williams; Oct., 1992: Canadian Military Lifts Its Ban on Gays and Lesbians; Nov. 30, 1993: Don't Ask, Don't Tell Policy Is Implemented; Jan. 12, 2000: United Kingdom Lifts Ban on Gays and Lesbians in the Military.

## June 2, 1980
# CANADIAN GAY POSTAL WORKERS SECURE UNION PROTECTIONS

*The Canadian Union of Postal Workers ratified a contract with Canada Post and the Canadian Treasury that includes a nondiscrimination clause protecting gay and lesbian employees, the first time federal employees, in any country, received such protection. The contract served as a catalyst for subsequent progressive measures regarding the civil rights of GLBT individuals in Canada.*

**LOCALE:** Ottawa, Canada
**CATEGORIES:** Civil rights; government and
   politics

### SUMMARY OF EVENT

On June 2, 1980, the Canadian Union of Postal Workers (CUPW) ratified a contract with Canada Post and the Canadian Treasury Board that provided coverage under the union's antidiscrimination code for gay and lesbian postal workers, marking the first time any federal government department provided these protections for lesbian and gay employees.

The seeds for federal reform in Canada were sown in 1967 by then-Justice Premiere Pierre Trudeau. Shortly before Christmas of that year, he proposed amendments to the criminal code of Canada, relaxing laws against homosexuality. Trudeau stated "there's no place for the state in the bedrooms of the nation. What's done in private between adults doesn't concern the Criminal Code."

Shortly after Trudeau's 1969 election as prime minister, amendments to the criminal code were passed, decriminalizing homosexuality nationwide. The Parti Québécois that was elected in 1976 approved inclusion of sexual orientation under the Quebec Charter of Human Rights and Freedoms, making Quebec the first Canadian province to pass a civil rights law for gays and lesbians. A broader national attempt was proposed by the Canadian Human Rights Commission in 1979. Their proposal

stated sexual orientation should be added to the Canadian Human Rights Act. One year later, Canadian member of parliament (MP) Pat Carney gave first reading in the House of Commons to Bill C-242, an Act to Prohibit Discrimination on Grounds of Sexual Orientation. The legislation, however, did not pass. The issue of sexual orientation also became the focus of collective labor agreements in both the public and private sectors across the nation.

It had been four years since the CUPW had participated in contract-bargaining with Canada Post and the Treasury Board. Issues up for negotiation were wages and working conditions in the 1980 collective agreement. The CUPW proposed to amend Article 5 of its contract to provide antidiscrimination protections for not only lesbians and gays but also left-handed employees and anyone holding a union position. The union's rationale for adding sexual orientation under Article 5 was to bring the worker's organization in line with advances made during the twentieth century that recognized individual rights.

At conciliation hearings, Canada Post and the Treasury Board argued against inclusion of the antidiscrimination provision, stating there was no problem or need. Both governmental bodies claimed that gays and lesbians were already covered by the Public Service Staff Relations Act, the Canadian Human Rights Act, and the Anti-Discrimination Bureau of the Public Service Commission— claims that were incorrect.

In the final conciliation board report offered to the CUPW and Canada Post, chairperson Germain Jutras agreed to the union's antidiscrimination proposal. Jutras stated, "We cannot see why employees should be discriminated against on account of their sexual orientation." He further added that a person's sexual orientation "has nothing to do with their work and concerns the private life of the employee." While the union supported the final ver-

---

### From an Act to Amend the Canadian Human Rights Act

Whereas the Government of Canada affirms the dignity and worth of all individuals and recognizes that they have the right to be free from discrimination in employment and the provision of goods and services, and that that right is based on respect for the rule of law and lawful conduct by all; And whereas the Government recognizes and affirms the importance of family as the foundation of Canadian society and that nothing in this Act alters its fundamental role in society; Now, therefore, Her Majesty, by and with the advice and consent of the Senate and House of Commons of Canada, enacts as follows:

1. *Section 2* of the Canadian Human Rights Act is replaced by the following:

Purpose 2. The purpose of this Act is to extend the laws in Canada to give effect, within the purview of matters coming within the legislative authority of Parliament, to the principle that all individuals should have an equal opportunity to make for themselves the lives that they are able and wish to have, consistent with their duties and obligations as members of society, without being hindered in or prevented from doing so by discriminatory practices based on race, national or ethnic origin, colour, religion, age, sex, sexual orientation, marital status, family status, disability or conviction for an offence for which a pardon has been granted.

2. *Subsection 3(1)* of the Act is replaced by the following:

Prohibited grounds of discrimination. For all purposes of this Act, the prohibited grounds of discrimination are race, national or ethnic origin, colour, religion, age, sex, sexual orientation, marital status, family status, disability and conviction for which a pardon has been granted.

---

sion of the report, the employer stood silent on the issue.

On May 20, 1980, extensive negotiations began on the new contract. Postmaster General Andre Ouellet, CUPW president Jean-Claude Parrot, and Dennis McDermott, president of the Canadian Labour Congress, hammered out the final details of the collective agreement. The union insisted that the final version of the conciliator's report was the minimum package they would accept. Canada Post and the Treasury Board agreed, and the contract was ratified on June 2.

Under Article 5 (No Discrimination) of the Agreement Between Canada Post Corporation and the CUPW, prohibitions against discrimination based upon sexual orientation are clearly defined. The agreement reads,

> It is agreed that there shall be no discrimination, interference, restriction, coercion, harassment, intimidation, or stronger action exercised or practised with respect to an employee by reason of age, race, creed, colour, national origin, political or religious affiliation, sex, sexual orientation, or membership or activity in the Union.

### Significance

Agreement by the Canadian federal government to the 1980 postal contract acted as a catalyst for continuing progressive measures across Canada regarding antidiscrimination based upon sexual orientation. Among these measures was the Canadian Charter of Rights and Freedoms (Section 15), which came into force on April 15, 1987. It declared,

> Every individual is equal before and under the law and has the right to the equal protection and equal benefit of the law without discrimination based on race, national or ethnic origin, colour, religion, sex, age, or mental or physical disability.

In a unanimous ruling in May of 1995, the Supreme Court of Canada stated that these provisions also shall be applied to the category of sexual orientation. On June 20, 1996, Bill C-33 was signed into law by royal assent, adding "sexual orientation" as a protected status under the Canadian Human Rights Act.

*—Michael A. Lutes*

## Further Reading

Lahey, Kathleen A. *Are We "Persons" Yet? Law and Sexuality in Canada*. Buffalo, N.Y.: University of Toronto Press, 1999.

MacDougall, Bruce. *Queer Judgements: Homosexuality, Expression, and the Courts in Canada*. Toronto, Ont.: University of Toronto Press, 2000.

Pierceson, Jason. *Courts, Liberalism, and Rights: Gay Law and Politics in the United States and Canada*. Philadelphia: Temple University Press, 2005.

"Posties First Federal Employees to Win Protections for Gay Workers." *The Body Politic* no. 65 (August, 1980), p. 13.

Smith, Miriam. *Lesbian and Gay Rights in Canada: Social Movements and Equality Seeking, 1971-1999*. Buffalo, N.Y.: University of Toronto Press, 1999.

**See also:** 1885: United Kingdom Criminalizes "Gross Indecency"; Aug. 26, 1969: Canada Decriminalizes Homosexual Acts; 1972-1973: Local Governments Pass Antidiscrimination Laws; Aug., 1973: American Bar Association Calls for Repeal of Laws Against Consensual Sex; Dec. 19, 1977: Quebec Includes Lesbians and Gays in Its Charter of Human Rights and Freedoms; Jan. 1, 1988: Canada Decriminalizes Sex Practices Between Consenting Adults; Dec. 30, 1991-Feb. 22, 1993: Canada Grants Asylum Based on Sexual Orientation; Apr. 27, 1992: Canadian Government Antigay Campaign Is Revealed; Oct., 1992: Canadian Military Lifts Its Ban on Gays and Lesbians; Apr. 2, 1998: Canadian Supreme Court Reverses Gay Academic's Firing; June 17, 2003, and July 19, 2005: Canada Legalizes Same-Gender Marriage.

## 1981
# Faderman Publishes *Surpassing the Love of Men*

*Lillian Faderman placed lesbian cultures in Western Europe and North America into their historical contexts in a groundbreaking and ambitious book called* Surpassing the Love of Men, *considered by many the first major academic work in lesbian history.*

**Locale:** New York, New York

**Categories:** Literature; cultural and intellectual history; publications; feminism

**Key Figure**

*Lillian Faderman* (b. 1940), author and professor of literature and creative writing

**Summary of Event**

Lillian Faderman's *Surpassing the Love of Men: Romantic Friendship and Love Between Women from the Renaissance to the Present* (1981) is a lesbian history, the first of its kind, that shows how les-

bian cultures in Western Europe and North America changed over time and place. The work maintains that any woman-identified woman from the sixteenth century to the present in the West could be considered lesbian. To Faderman, genital sexual expression alone was too modern and too limiting in describing the experiences of those European and American women in the past who had derived most, if not all, of their emotional, romantic, and intimate life from other women.

While her work is present-minded in reconstructing lesbian pasts with inspiration from the women's and gay and lesbian rights movements of her own time, she was careful not to use a sexualized, psychoanalytic straitjacket in describing eighteenth and nineteenth century realities.

Expanding upon earlier research by Carroll Smith-Rosenberg, Faderman celebrated female romantic friendships as lived by literary and academic women and as portrayed in contemporary literature,

## LILLIAN FADERMAN

Lillian Faderman is a true Renaissance woman who has overcome many obstacles and detours to become a prize-winning founder of the academic discipline of gay and lesbian studies. She was born in 1940 in New York City to a working-class Latvian Jewish mother whose family would be murdered during the Holocaust. Her mother was single, and she raised her daughter Lilly with the help of her own sister Rae. Mother and aunt guided and inspired Lilly to avoid their fate and to find a man while it still counted. For Lilly, this conformity required acting and self-invention, at both of which she excelled.

Gradually realizing that she preferred women erotically to men, she bounced back from early mistakes such as her conventional marriage as a teenager to an older doctor, who turned out to be both gay and alcoholic. Abandoned by her husband and having to support herself in part by becoming a pinup girl and stripper, she earned a bachelor's degree in English from the University of California, Berkeley, in 1962 and a doctorate in literature from the University of California, Los Angeles, in 1967. After being hired at Fresno State University, she quickly became head of its school of humanities in 1972 and then an assistant vice president for academic affairs soon after.

While a busy college official, she still found time to have a child, Avrom, who was born in 1975. She escaped the administrative grind to produce the two formative works for which she is best known: *Surpassing the Love of Men* (1981) and *Odd Girls and Twilight Lovers* (1991).

particularly before the popularization of psychoanalyst Sigmund Freud in the 1920's.

Faderman recast familiar literary and elite figures within a feminist perspective, showing that the Ladies of Llangollen—Lady Mary Wortley Montagu, Marie Antoinette, and the Bluestockings, among others—were not weird pariahs who needed male guidance. Instead, they were anchored and energized by strong friendships and partnerships with each other and without male interference. Faderman showcases an exemplary "Boston marriage," that is, a long-term, domestic, committed relationship between two women, the widowed Annie Fields and author Sarah Orne Jewett, from 1881 to Jewett's death in 1909. In a "marriage" that was completely respectable and accepted at the turn of the twentieth century, Fields and Jewett inspired each other as they bonded, lived, and traveled together without male companionship.

Faderman shows the contemporary indifference to, but also support for, such relationships from the eighteenth century through World War I, especially if they did not involve extreme cross-dressing or subversive political activity that might challenge male supremacy and heterosexuality. Since Georgian and Victorian societies considered women, particularly those of the middle classes, asexual if they were without men, most people reassured themselves that female romantic friends of a certain class and refinement could not be of a sexual nature.

Before the 1920's, people had surmised that single women living together were simply women who had not found the right men, or they were virtuous, secular "nun" types doing community service and were married to their work. These scenarios might have described the experiences of some women, but for others the supposition provided a convenient cover for a whole range of behaviors and feelings that, if discovered, could have brought down on them the full weight of the law and of public opinion. Contemporaries did not think to ask, and romantic friends were not about to tell.

Faderman argues that this hands-off arrangement began to unravel in the 1920's, but she notes that even before World War I there were three main preconditions for the fall of the "golden age" of the romantic friendship. One, the rise of feminism in the late nineteenth century had unleashed a backlash against suffragists and an anxiety about strong women of any sort. Two, scientists had by this time categorized independent women as members of a "third" and even more dangerous sex. Three, avant-garde French writers, such as Pierre Louys, explored and exposed the sexual potential of female romantic friendships in their verse and prose.

To Faderman, Freud and psychoanalysis made

deteriorating conditions for women-identified women worse, marking, perhaps, a fourth condition that helped lead to the end of romantic friendships between women. The popularization of Freud after 1920 sexualized everything, including what people thought was going on within female romantic friendships. "Homosocial" suddenly and automatically meant "homosexual," which was being diagnosed at this time as a psychiatric disorder, a well of loneliness to which one was consigned.

These changes also led to what has been termed a "compulsory heterosexuality" from birth; even juvenile crushes on members of the same gender that were tolerated and even expected just twenty years earlier were now thought to lead directly to adult depravity. For example, love letters between Fields and Jewett published by Fields in 1911 without censorship were heavily censored in 1922 by a male editor, who believed he needed to preserve the reputations of the women given the changes in cultural mores.

World War II and its need for women in the military and women's civilian labor (the government's "Rosie the Riveter" campaign) brought about the growth of lesbian subcultures. After the war—and after the temporary acceptance of "strong" women who were needed for the war effort—however, psychoanalysts renewed their efforts to keep independent and especially lesbian women in their place.

The 1950's and 1960's represented an especially bad time to be lesbian in the United States, as the hateful crescendo of psychoanalysis had combined with the McCarthy era's fight against alleged internal enemies to American values; these supposed villains included lesbians. Yet the pain of this oppression led to the cultural gains of the homophile movement, to the butch-femme working-class milieu, and to pulp fiction's inadvertent consciousness-raising, with its ubiquitous lesbian themes. Then, as authorities and customs came under attack in the late 1960's, the Civil Rights movement, second-wave feminism, the lesbian and gay rights movement, and humanistic psychology all contributed to rid lesbian sexuality and popular perceptions of lesbians of any lingering Freudian self-hatred.

Indeed, lesbian feminists during the 1970's tried their own separatist utopias and reconstructions of society along less-hierarchical grounds. The failure of these more radical experiments led to what Faderman characterized as the Sapphic moderation of the 1980's, which was less political in nature, implying at times more adventuresome sexual practices. These continual changes and the increasing fragmentation of lesbian identities, Faderman wrote, underscore that "sexuality is often a social construct—a product of the times and of other factors that are entirely external to the 'sexual drive.'"

## SIGNIFICANCE

*Surpassing the Love of Men* was the forerunner in the academic field of lesbian history. The work rejected essentialist or static characterizations of lesbians, and reflected the cultural feminism popular in the 1970's.

Faderman's next great opus, *Odd Girls and Twilight Lovers: A History of Lesbian Life in Twentieth-Century America* (1991), chronicles the accommodation and resistance of lesbians to periodic bouts of official oppression stemming from psychiatry and the national security state. The sexual revolution of the 1920's stigmatized and pigeonholed romantic friendships as homosexual and thus sick, but it also stimulated a greater awareness among women about the sexual potential of their relationships. The labeling and segregation had led ironically to more, not less, female same-gender loving.

—*Charles H. Ford*

## FURTHER READING

Faderman, Lillian. *Naked in the Promised Land: A Memoir.* New York: Houghton Mifflin, 2003.
_____. *Odd Girls and Twilight Lovers: A History of Lesbian Life in Twentieth-Century America.* New York: Columbia University Press, 1991.
_____. *Surpassing the Love of Men: Romantic Friendship Between Women from the Renaissance to the Present.* New York: William Morrow, 1981.
McCullough, Kate. *Regions of Identity: The Construction of America in Women's Fiction, 1885-1914.* Stanford, Calif.: Stanford University Press, 1999.

Mamet, David. *Boston Marriage*. New York: Vintage Books, 2000.

Smith-Rosenberg, Carroll. "The Female World of Love and Ritual: Relations Between Women in Nineteenth-Century America." *Signs: Journal of Women in Culture and Society* 1, no. 1 (Autumn, 1975): 1-29.

Vicinus, Martha. "'They Wonder to Which Sex I Belong': The Historical Roots of Modern Lesbian Identity." In *The Lesbian and Gay Studies Reader*, edited by Henry Abelove, Michele Aina Barale, and David Halperin. New York: Routledge, 1993.

**SEE ALSO:** 1928: Hall Publishes *The Well of Loneliness*; 1956: Foster Publishes *Sex Variant Women in Literature*; June, 1971: The Gay Book Award Debuts; 1973: Brown Publishes *Rubyfruit Jungle*; 1975: Rule Publishes *Lesbian Images*; 1981: *This Bridge Called My Back* Is Published; 1982: Lorde's Autobiography *Zami* Is Published; 1986: Paula Gunn Allen Publishes *The Sacred Hoop*; 1987: Anzaldúa Publishes *Borderlands/La Frontera*; 1987: *Compañeras: Latina Lesbians* Is Published; May, 1987: *Lambda Rising Book Report* Begins Publication; June 2, 1989: Lambda Literary Award Is Created.

## 1981
# GAY AND LESBIAN PALIMONY SUITS EMERGE

*Following the 1976 success of the first palimony suit, former partners of famous gays and lesbians attempted to extend the principle to include their own dissolved relationships.*

**LOCALE:** Los Angeles, California
**CATEGORIES:** Laws, acts, and legal history; civil rights

**KEY FIGURES**
*Billie Jean King* (b. 1943), professional tennis player
*Marilyn Barnett*, former domestic partner of King
*Liberace* (1919-1987), pianist and popular entertainer
*Scott Thorson*, former domestic partner of Liberace
*John-Michael Tebelak*, director of the musical *Godspell*
*Richard Hannum*, former domestic partner of Tebelak

**SUMMARY OF EVENT**
The word "palimony" entered the public vocabulary in 1976, when the California Supreme Court handed down its decision in *Marvin v. Marvin*. In *Marvin*, Michelle Triola, the unmarried cohabitating partner of Hollywood actor Lee Marvin, won the right to sue to have an oral agreement of support enforced.

Until *Marvin*, courts generally refused to enforce such agreements, viewing them as contrary to public policy. Without benefit of marriage, the contract looked too much like the exchange of sexual services for financial security—that is to say, like prostitution. The *Marvin* court challenged this assumption when it held that a contract between unmarried partners could be enforced, unless the agreement was explicitly based on an exchange for sexual services. The court also concluded that even when sexual services were part of the contract, any portion of the contract severable from this barred agreement could still be enforced.

*Marvin* argued that some cohabitation agreements did not necessarily require the performance of sexual services but could instead be contracts concerning property that the couple accumulated through their mutual efforts. While the parties could not contract to pay for the performance of sexual services, they could agree either to pool their earnings and hold all property acquired during the relationship in common or to maintain each party's earnings and property as the earner's separate property.

The reasoning of the *Marvin* court would have broad implications for gay and lesbian couples, as events of 1981 demonstrated. A sea change in domestic law began on April 28, 1981, when thirty-two-year-old Marilyn Barnett filed a lawsuit against tennis star Billie Jean King. Invoking the palimony doctrine of *Marvin*, Barnett claimed that she was entitled to part of King's property for the years she had spent in a lesbian relationship with King.

At first denying the relationship, King later confirmed that she and Barnett had indeed been lovers, although she denied "feel[ing like a] homosexual." After generating much publicity that called public attention to gay and lesbian relationships, the suit was dismissed on November 19, 1982. The suit failed not least because the two women did not cohabit in the sense of *Marvin*. At no time during the relationship did King and Barnett so completely intermingle their lives as to be an economic unit.

By that time, however, a California appeals court had already ruled against what became known as "galimony," or gay palimony. In *Jones v. Daly* (1981), the court rejected the claim of a surviving male partner to a share of his deceased lover's estate. In short, the court could find no part of the agreement between the two men "severable" from the taint of sexual considerations, and thus none of it was enforceable.

Suits of this kind were not unique. At the same time that Barnett made her claim against King, Richard Hannum was suing his former companion John-Michael Tebelak—who conceived and directed the musical *Godspell*—this time in a New York court. This case, however, was overshadowed by more notorious suits, such as that of Scott Thorson against the showman Liberace. In October of 1982, Thorson, then twenty-three years old, sued Liberace for $113 million. Thorson claimed that he had a "personal services agreement" with the enter-

tainer that was broken when Liberace evicted Thorson from his mansion. The suit was settled in 1987 for a mere $95,000.

## SIGNIFICANCE

The tally of cases attempting to take advantage of the opportunities opened by *Marvin* is at best inconclusive. Later cases would score spotty successes, both in California, where the *Marvin* doctrine would best apply (see *Whorton v. Dillingham*, 1988) and in other states, such as Georgia (see *Crooke v. Gilden*, 1992). Some states—such as Texas in *Zaremba v. "Van Cliburn"* (1997)—allowed limited forms of same-gender couple palimony suits, but only if the agreement between the parties had been in writing, unlike *Marvin*, which contemplated enforcing oral or implicit agreements as well.

Despite initiating a line of cases that has today made same-gender marriage a reasonable goal, classic palimony cases are currently rare. Among the variables resulting in this decline, not least would be the fundamental changes in the wake of the HIV-AIDS scourge. Many Americans, who once viewed gay and lesbian relationships as necessarily "meretricious," are in growing numbers recognizing that same-gender relationships are sincere emotional commitments that should be honored by society.

A wider range of mechanisms to legitimize relationships available to twenty-first century gays and lesbians has also contributed to the dearth of classic palimony cases. Domestic partnerships, even when largely symbolic in their explicit grant of rights and protections, confer a degree of legitimacy that merely living together does not.

Not only are there more kinds of formal relationship arrangements; there also are new causes of action on which to base a suit seeking fair treatment beyond the palimony arguments. Marc Christian, for example, sued the estate of actor Rock Hudson for intentional misrepresentation and deliberate exposure to HIV (see *Aetna Casualty & Surety Co. v. Sheft*, 1993). Christian was awarded $14.5 million. Finally, the central tendency of present suits between former partners arguably deals more with child custody and other family law issues than with the simple property quarrels palimony was designed to address.

—*James M. Donovan*

## FURTHER READING

Oliver, Brooke. "Contracting for Cohabitation: Adapting the California Statutory Marital Contract to Life Partnership Agreements Between Lesbian, Gay, or Unmarried Heterosexual Couples." *Golden Gate University Law Review* 23 (1993): 899-972.

Parr, Gavin M. "What Is a 'Meretricious Relationship'? An Analysis of Cohabitant Property Rights Under *Connell v. Francisco*." *Washington Law Review* 74 (1999): 1243-1273.

"Same-Sex Marriage: A Selective Bibliography of the Legal Literature." Law Library, Rutgers School of Law. http://law-library.rutgers.edu/SSM.html.

Thorson, Scott. *Behind the Candelabra: My Life with Liberace*. New York: E. P. Dutton, 1988.

SEE ALSO: July 25, 1985: Actor Hudson Announces He Has AIDS; 1986: *Bowers v. Hardwick* Upholds State Sodomy Laws; Dec. 17, 1991: Minnesota Court Awards Guardianship to Lesbian Partner; 1992-2002: Celebrity Lesbians Come Out; 1993-1996: Hawaii Opens Door to Same-Gender Marriages; Sept. 21, 1993-Apr. 21, 1995: Lesbian Mother Loses Custody of Her Child; Sept. 21, 1996: U.S. President Clinton Signs Defense of Marriage Act; Dec. 20, 1999: *Baker v. Vermont* Leads to Recognition of Same-Gender Civil Unions; Apr., 2003: Buenos Aires Recognizes Same-Gender Civil Unions; June 17, 2003, and July 19, 2005: Canada Legalizes Same-Gender Marriage; June 26, 2003: U.S. Supreme Court Overturns Texas Sodomy Law; Nov. 18, 2003: Massachusetts Court Rules for Same-Gender Marriage; Nov. 18, 2004: United Kingdom Legalizes Same-Gender Civil Partnerships.

## 1981
# PARENTS, FAMILIES, AND FRIENDS OF LESBIANS AND GAYS IS FOUNDED

*Jeanne Manford wrote to the* New York Post *and publically proclaimed her love for her gay son, helping to launch the first organization of parents, families, and friends of lesbians and gays in the United States, a group that remains active into the twenty-first century.*

**ALSO KNOWN AS:** PFLAG; Parents and Friends of Lesbians and Gays; Parents FLAG

**LOCALE:** New York, New York; Washington, D.C.; Los Angeles, California

**CATEGORIES:** Civil rights; organizations and institutions

### KEY FIGURES

*Morton Manford* (1950-1992), founder of Gay People at Columbia University

*Jeanne Manford*, Morton Manford's mother, who started the first support group for parents of gays and lesbians in 1973

*Adele Starr*, president of the first PFLAG office in Los Angeles and GLBT rights advocate

### SUMMARY OF EVENT

In New York City in 1972, three years after the city's Stonewall Rebellion and the birth of the modern GLBT rights movement, Morton Manford, a gay activist, had been brutally assaulted at a rally as police stood by and failed to protect him. Television cameras had captured Morton's assault and his parents watched helplessly as their son was beaten in the streets.

Morton survived the assault and emerged from the violence with a new outspoken ally, his mother.

Jeanne Manford, a New York school teacher, thought nothing of it when she wrote a letter to the editor of the *New York Post* in April, 1972, expressing outrage at the attack on her son and about police inaction. She wrote, "I have a homosexual son, and I love him." Her letter caught the attention of other parents. Jeanne recalled being surprised by the overwhelming response, but added, "I guess it was the first time a mother ever stood up publicly and said, 'Yes, I have a homosexual child.'"

Morton and Jeanne walked together in the 1972 New York City gay and lesbian pride parade. As they marched, the crowds cheered wildly, with Jeanne hoisting a sign with the words, "Parents of Gays: Unite in Support for Our Children." Thousands of gays and lesbians lining the parade route cheered so loudly that Jeanne thought the cheers were for someone else, but the cheers and cries of the crowd were for her. Her simple sign gave hope to countless gays and lesbians, and it also started a movement. Jeanne remembers telling Morton as they walked in the parade that "she hoped some day that this would become a national movement, but that was just a dream. I never imagined we would reach so many people."

Jeanne, overwhelmed by positive response, held the first support group for parents of gay and lesbian children in March, 1973, at the Metropolitan Duane Methodist Church in Greenwich Village. The twenty or so people who attended shared stories and

*PFLAG members and supporters march in the 1983 pride parade in New York City, two years after the national organization's founding.* (Hulton Archive/Getty Images)

support. The meeting flourished, and later, parents began calling Jeanne from all over the country.

In 1976, the Manfords encouraged parents Adele Starr and Larry Starr to start a similar meeting in Los Angeles, and in March of the same year, Adele launched the Los Angeles group. Soon more groups formed in other parts of California and in Arizona, Colorado, Illinois, Kansas, Massachusetts, Washington State, and Washington, D.C. During the mid-1970's, many of these same parents met at the Manfords' house in New York to discuss organizing a national group. Later, parents from across the country gathered in Washington, D.C., in 1979, at the first National March for Gay and Lesbian Rights. Adele had addressed the historic crowd and noted that the march was being held in the "year of the child" and that a group of about twenty-five parents had met and organized to plan the national organization.

Two years later, in a two-day meeting, thirty people in Adele's home in Los Angeles created the bylaws and articles of incorporation for a national organization that was to be called Parents FLAG (Federation of Parents and Friends of Lesbians and Gays). Adele remembers, according to the PFLAG Web site, that, "We . . . had pizza and drank beer . . . and formed the national organization" with a five-member board and Adele as president. In 1982, with twenty groups around the country, PFLAG was incorporated and granted nonprofit status, and for the next six years, the national office was located in the Starrs' living room.

## SIGNIFICANCE

From Jeanne Manford's letter to the *New York Post*, to a church in New York City, to Adele Starr's living room, to a national office in Washington, D.C., PFLAG grew from the love, commitment, and outrage of parents who believed that family support and advocacy could transform the world for their gay and lesbian children and ultimately for tens of thousands of other families.

The dream evolved into an international organization that has nearly five hundred chapters, at least one in every state and several countries, and serves two hundred thousand members. Just as the gay, lesbian, and bisexual rights movement has expanded to include those who are transgender or intersexed, PFLAG, too, has evolved with the times. In 1993, the organization restructured and created an affiliation process for chapters, elected board seats, and changed its name to Parents, Families and Friends of Lesbians and Gays.

PFLAG transformed the world of sexual and gender identity by shattering the familial silence surrounding having a gay, lesbian, bisexual, transgender, or intersexed (GLBTI) child or loved one. PFLAG has created a supportive space for parents, families, friends, and GLBTI people. The organization has a national presence at every GLBT march on Washington, participates in local pride events, and is active in opposing the anti-GLBT movement. PFLAG rightfully takes its place next to the many heroes of movements toward civil justice for all people.

*—Jennifer Self*

## FURTHER READING

Anderson, Robert W. "Parents and Friends of Lesbians and Gays (PFLAG)." In *Gay Histories and Cultures*, edited by George Haggerty. New York: Garland, 2000.

Bernstein, Robert A. *Straight Parents, Gay Children: Keeping Families Together*. Rev. and updated ed. New York: Thunder's Mouth Press, 2003.

Clark, Don. *Loving Someone Gay*. 4th ed. Berkeley, Calif.: Celestial Arts, 2005.

Drucker, Jane. *Lesbian and Gay Families Speak Out: Understanding the Joys and Challenges of Diverse Family Life*. Reading, Mass.: Perseus, 2001.

PFLAG. *Be Yourself: Questions and Answers for Gay, Lesbian, Bisexual, and Transgender Youth*. http://www.pflag.org.

_____. *Faith in Our Families: Parents, Families, and Friends Talk About Religion and Homosexuality*. http://www.pflag.org.

_____. *Our Daughters and Sons: Questions and Answers for Parents of Gay, Lesbian, and Bisexual People*. http://www.pflag.org.

Siegel, Laura, and Nancy Lamkin Olson, eds. *Out*

*of the Closet, into Our Hearts: Celebrating Our Gay Family Members.* San Francisco, Calif.: Leyland, 2001.

**SEE ALSO:** June 28, 1970: First Lesbian and Gay Pride March in the United States; 1975: First Novel About Coming Out to Parents Is Published; Oct. 12-15, 1979: First March on Washington for Lesbian and Gay Rights; Oct. 11, 1987: Second March on Washington for Lesbian and Gay Rights; Oct. 11, 1988: First National Coming Out Day Is Celebrated; Apr. 25, 1993: March on Washington for Gay, Lesbian, and Bi Equal Rights and Liberation; June, 1994: Stonewall 25 March and Rallies Are Held in New York City.

# 1981
# *THIS BRIDGE CALLED MY BACK* IS PUBLISHED

*This Bridge Called My Back is a key political text for lesbian feminists, especially lesbian feminists of color. It was one of the earliest multiethnic anthologies that analyzed multiple and interlocking forms of oppression from a feminist perspective. Also, the work was influential in creating global or Third World feminism.*

**LOCALE:** Watertown, Massachusetts
**CATEGORIES:** Publications; feminism; race and ethnicity; literature; civil rights; cultural and intellectual history

**KEY FIGURES**
*Cherríe Moraga* (b. 1952), coeditor of *This Bridge Called My Back*
*Gloria Anzaldúa* (1942-2004), coeditor of *This Bridge Called My Back*

**SUMMARY OF EVENT**
The first edition of *This Bridge Called My Back: Writings by Radical Women of Color* was published in 1981 by Persephone Press. The anthology, however unremarkable it might have seemed to the popular media at the time, represented a critical liberatory moment for women of color in the women's movement. Although women of color from Sojourner Truth to Pauli Murray had been present in feminist organizing, their historical and political contributions have been underacknowledged in

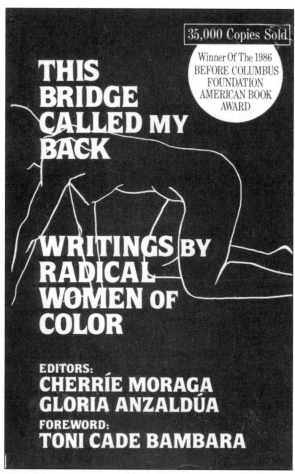

*The cover of* This Bridge Called My Back *(1981).* (Kitchen Table: Women of Color Press)

women's studies classrooms and by feminist organizations.

White feminists at the time had not been prepared to talk about racism within the women's movement. While *This Bridge Called My Back* was neither the first nor last collection of writing to bring women of color together to discuss racism and classism in the women's movement, the anthology has become a touchstone for women, including Third World feminists and lesbians of color, who identify with a number of marginalized identities.

In their introduction to the first edition, Cherríe Moraga and Gloria Anzaldúa wrote that they created *This Bridge Called My Back*

to "reflect an uncompromised definition of feminism by women of color in the US." The book was organized into six sections, which the editors felt were areas of concern for Third World feminists. Although each section focused on the intersection of multiple oppressions (including sexuality), the section most relevant to lesbians of color was the fourth, "Between the Lines: On Culture, Class, and Homophobia." The writings in this section focus on "the cultural, class, and sexuality differences that divide women of color," and contain incisive critiques of Third World communities and white feminists, written by distinguished scholars such as Barbara Smith, Beverly Smith, Merle Woo, and Cheryl Clarke.

## SIGNIFICANCE

There are at minimum three ways that the publication of *This Bridge Called My Back* has influenced the development of feminist, lesbian, and antiracist theories. First, authors expanded the conventional Western and feminist notions of lesbianism and lesbian identities. The work of Moraga and Anzaldúa, for example, like other lesbians of color, was politically daring because it not only challenged the sex-

---

### "HOW IT ALL BEGAN"

What began as a reaction to the racism of white feminists soon became a positive affirmation of the commitment of women of color to our *own* feminism. Mere words on a page began to transform themselves into a living entity in our guts. Now, over a year later, feeling greater solidarity with other feminists of color across the country through making of this book, we assert:

*This Bridge Called My Back* intends to reflect an uncompromised definition of feminism by women of color in the U.S.

We named this anthology "radical" for we were interested in the writings of women of color who want nothing short of a revolution in the hands of women—who agree that that *is* the goal, no matter how we might disagree about the getting there or the possibility of seeing it in our own lifetimes. We use the term in its original form—stemming from the word "root"—for our feminist politic emerges from the roots of both our cultural oppression and heritage.

*Source:* Cherríe Moraga and Gloria Anzaldúa, "Introduction," *This Bridge Called My Back*. 2d ed. (New York: Kitchen Table: Women of Color Press, 1982).

---

ism of men of color and the racism of feminists but also discussed the sexuality of women of color in frank terms.

In many of the communities of color, often deeply influenced by religious traditions, such as Catholicism and Christianity, it was taboo to discuss sexuality. In one example, Merle Woo, in her "Letter to Ma," asks her mother to understand why "your daughter has turned into a crazy woman who advocates not only equality for Third World people, for women, but for gays as well." Woo continues: "Please don't shudder, Ma, when I speak of homosexuality. Until we can all present ourselves to the world in our completeness, as fully and beautifully as we see ourselves naked in our bedrooms, we are not free."

These types of statements ran counter to the commonly held belief that women of color were somehow betraying their ethnic roots by embracing "white" lesbianism. Instead, women of color asserted in *This Bridge Called My Back* that their lesbianism was part of their heritage—an inextricable component of their ethnic and political identities. This declaration allowed lesbians of color to gain personal validation and political capital by organizing locally and internationally. For example, the Asian Lesbian Network would be organized in Bangkok in 1990, and in 1993, Gloria Wekker would write about the culturally specific form of same-gender love in the African Diaspora known as *mati-ism*.

A second way *This Bridge Called My Back* influenced the development of feminist, lesbian, and antiracist theories was how it critiqued lesbian separatism. Some lesbian-feminist authors, such as Marilyn Frye, Mary Daly, and the women of Radicalesbians, had redefined lesbianism as a political act that entailed the rejection of and separation from men. Lesbian-separatist writings were often utopian in nature and tended toward a gynocentric and ecocentric spirituality. However, lesbians of color were critical of this utopian vision, arguing that it perpetuated racism and classism in several ways: Lesbian separatists, the women of color argued,

could be racist as well. Also, dividing women of color from the men of color in their community was believed to be racist because it interfered with the collective fight against racism. In the Combahee River Collective's "A Black Feminist Statement" of 1979, reprinted in *This Bridge Called My Back*, the collective stated,

> Although we are feminists and Lesbians, we feel solidarity with progressive Black men and do not advocate the fractionalization that white women who are separatists demand.... We must also question whether lesbian separatism is an adequate and progressive political analysis and strategy, even for those who practice it, since it so completely denies any but the sexual sources of women's oppression, negating the facts of class and race.

*This Bridge Called My Back* set the stage for a number of similar anthologies that would follow, such as *Making Face, Making Soul/Haciendo Caras*, *This Bridge We Call Home*, and *Colonize This!* Theoretical resonances can be found in the later works of renowned scholars such as Bell Hooks and Patricia Hill Collins and poet-writer Audre Lorde, whose works draw not only from Western feminists but also from socialist texts and the politics of colonialism and Third World liberation. Their works also develop a nuanced analysis of the forces of sexism, racism, and homophobia, as well as of Western imperialism, capitalism, ethnocentrism, and the issues of religion, color, and nationality. This tradition in feminist writings still flourishes in the twenty-first century.

—*Blaise Astra Parker*

---

### "LA GÜERA"

In this country, lesbianism is a poverty—as is being brown, as is being a woman, as is being just plain poor. The danger lies in ranking the oppressions. *The danger lies in failing to acknowledge the specificity of oppression.* The danger lies in attempting to deal with oppression purely from a theoretical base. Without an emotional, heartfelt grappling with the source of our own oppression, without naming the enemy within ourselves and outside of us, no authentic, non-hierarchical connection among oppressed groups can take place.

When the going gets rough, will we abandon our so-called comrades in a flurry of racist/heterosexist/what-have-you panic? To whose camp, then, should the lesbians of color retreat? Her very presence violates the ranking and abstraction of oppression. Do we merely live hand to mouth? Do we merely struggle with the "ism" that's sitting on top of our own heads?

The answer is: yes. I think first we do; and we must do so thoroughly and deeply. But to fail to move out from there will only isolate us in our own oppression—will only insulate, rather than radicalize us.

*Source:* Cherríe Moraga, "La Güera," in *This Bridge Called My Back*. 2d ed. (New York: Kitchen Table: Women of Color Press, 1982).

---

### FURTHER READING

Alaniz, Yolanda, and Nellie Wong, eds. *Voices of Color*. Seattle, Wash.: Red Letter Press, 1999.

Anzaldúa, Gloria. *Borderlands/La Frontera: The New Mestiza*. San Francisco, Calif.: Spinster's Ink/Aunt Lute Books, 1987.

———, ed. *Making Face, Making Soul/Haciendo Caras: Creative and Critical Perspectives by Feminists of Color*. San Francisco, Calif.: Aunt Lute Foundation Books, 1990.

Anzaldúa, Gloria, and AnaLouise Keating, eds. *This Bridge We Call Home: Radical Visions for Transformation.* New York: Routledge, 2002.

Gil-Gomez, Ellen M. *Performing La Mestiza: Textual Representations of Lesbians of Color and the Negotiation of Identities.* New York: Garland, 2000.

Hernández, Daisy, and Bushra Rehman, eds. *Colonize This! Young Women of Color on Today's Feminism.* Emeryville, Calif.: Seal Press, 2002.

Lorde, Audre. *Zami: A New Spelling of My Name.* Freedom, Calif.: Crossing Press, 1982.

Moraga, Cherríe, and Gloria Anzaldúa, eds. *This Bridge Called My Back: Writings by Radical Women of Color.* Watertown, Mass.: Persephone Press, 1981.

Short, Kayann. "Coming to the Table: The Differential Politics of 'This Bridge Called My Back.'" *Genders* 19 (1994).

Smith, Barbara, ed. *Home Girls: A Black Feminist Anthology.* New York: Kitchen Table: Women of Color Press, 1983.

Thompson, Becky. "Multiracial Feminism: Recasting the Chronology of Second Wave Feminism." *Feminist Studies* 28, no. 2 (2002).

**SEE ALSO:** 1928: Hall Publishes *The Well of Loneliness*; 1956: Foster Publishes *Sex Variant Women in Literature*; June, 1971: The Gay Book Award Debuts; 1973: Brown Publishes *Rubyfruit Jungle*; 1975: Rule Publishes *Lesbian Images*; 1981: Faderman Publishes *Surpassing the Love of Men*; 1982: Lorde's Autobiography *Zami* Is Published; 1986: Paula Gunn Allen Publishes *The Sacred Hoop*; 1987: Anzaldúa Publishes *Borderlands/La Frontera*; 1987: *Compañeras: Latina Lesbians* Is Published; May, 1987: *Lambda Rising Book Report* Begins Publication; June 2, 1989: Lambda Literary Award Is Created.

## 1981-1982
# GALA CHORUSES IS FORMED

*Leaders from twelve lesbian, gay, and mixed-gender choruses gathered to form GALA Performing Arts Groups, which soon became the Gay and Lesbian Association of Choruses, or GALA Choruses. The organization includes more than two hundred member choruses from around the world with more than ten thousand singers.*

**ALSO KNOWN AS:** GALA Performing Arts Groups; Gay and Lesbian Association of Choruses
**LOCALE:** Chicago, Illinois
**CATEGORIES:** Arts; organizations and institutions

## KEY FIGURES
*Jay Davidson* (b. 1947), general manager, San Francisco Gay Men's Chorus, first president of the GALA board
*Gary Miller*, director, New York City Gay Men's Chorus, second president of the GALA board

## SUMMARY OF EVENT
During the course of the early and mid-1970's, many largely lesbian-identified feminist choruses developed around the United States, followed by gay-identified men's choruses and lesbian and gay mixed-gender choruses in the late 1970's. The "grandmother" chorus, Anna Crusis, which is still in existence, formed in Philadelphia in 1975. It was followed by Calliope in Minneapolis and the Los Angeles Community Women's Chorus in 1976. The Stonewall Chorale in New York, which began in December of 1977 as the Gotham Male Chorus, changed its name when women joined in 1979. Both Artemis Singers in Chicago and the San Francisco Gay Men's Chorus formed in 1978, followed

*West Coast Singers, based in Los Angeles, California, is the third oldest lesbian and gay mixed-gender chorus in the United States. It was formed in 1983.* (Courtesy, West Coast Singers)

in 1979 by Windy City Gay Chorus, Gay Men's Chorus of Los Angeles, Seattle Men's Chorus, and the Montrose Singers, which later became the Gay Men's Chorus of Houston.

Even though these choruses developed locally, like so many other community choruses they looked to larger organizations for support. They found little interest in their concerns, however, from conservative organizations such as the American Choral Directors Association. In the interest of developing their own support networks, directors, managers, and members from lesbian and gay choruses and bands across the country developed newsletters, shared music ideas, and sometimes even sent each other flowers for opening nights. In some of the larger cities, lesbian and gay performing arts umbrella organizations, such as San Francisco's Golden Gate Performing Arts and Chicago's Toddlin' Town Performing Arts, had developed to combine resources for choruses, bands, and theater groups.

In early 1981, concurrent with the development of the feminist Sister Singers Network, members of the Windy City Gay Chorus invited directors and managers of gay and lesbian choruses and bands to Chicago for a weekend to exchange ideas about forming an organization at the national level. Participants from twelve choruses met in Chicago in May, 1981, the first meeting in which the idea for the association was discussed. The Gay and Lesbian Association of Performing Arts Groups was formed out of this meeting, becoming the Gay and Lesbian Association of Choruses (GALA) in 1982.

The group immediately set several goals, including, one, to produce a large choral festival for September, 1983, in New York City, a festival eventually named Come Out And Sing Together (COAST). Two, in preparation for the larger festival, the group produced a smaller regional festival in San Francisco in the summer of 1982, called the West Coast Choral Festival, held in conjunction with the first-planned Gay Games. Three, the group planned another meeting of the managers and directors in San Francisco during the 1982 West Coast Choral Festival.

For this 1982 meeting in San Francisco, bands and other performing arts groups were again invited, but for the second time only choruses showed up. Out of this meeting came three more decisions. The group agreed to change its name from GALA Performing Arts to GALA Choruses; it was to seek incorporation as a tax-exempt organization based in California; and it decided to meet once again in New York, after the COAST Festival, to elect its first board of directors.

The Stonewall Chorale opened the first national GALA festival in 1983 at the Lincoln Center for the Performing Arts in Manhattan. A total of fourteen choruses performed for each other in an atmosphere of mutual support, a quality that sets GALA choral festivals apart from others, which are largely focused on competition. This approach, which emphasizes affirmation, respect, support, and networking over judgment, has created, in the words of a GALA founding member, Dennis Coleman, "a tremendous synergy" that has played a role in the organization's rapid and consistent growth. The LGBT choral movement remains, arguably, one of the largest components of the LGBT movement in the world.

GALA sponsored festivals every three years until 1992, when the interval between festivals was changed to four years; leadership conferences and regional festival would be held between festivals. From the original 14 choruses that sang in the first festival, the GALA festival in 2004 in Montreal had 163 choruses and 5,800 registered delegates from around the world, but mostly from North America. The week-long festival included international premiere performances of youth and transgender choruses and stand-up comedy with Lily Tomlin.

## SIGNIFICANCE

GALA's member choruses, which now number more than two hundred, with more than ten thousand singers, continues to support artistic and organizational development of gay, lesbian, bisexual, and transgender choruses, which are collectively changing the face of choral music through commissioning and performing new works. Through original commissions of new choral works, new arrangements of everything from classical to popular tunes, and by performing some songs with a twist—some would argue, "queering" them—the LGBT choral movement has developed a repertoire of popular "anthems" that include "We Are Everywhere," "Everything Possible," and "Love Worth Fighting For."

According to GALA's Web site, "more than 600,000 individuals purchase tickets to one or more member concerts per year and the combined audiences of member choruses through community appearances and television and radio broadcasts exceeds 5,000,000 individuals. Among the television networks that have aired performances of GALA Choruses members are ABC, BBC, CBS, Fox, NBC, and PBS."

GALA's member choruses have shared the stage with the likes of Maya Angelou, Natalie Cole, Michael Fienstein, Jerry Hadley, Marilyn Horne, Bobby McFerrin, Bette Midler, Liza Minelli, Mark Morris, Holly Near, Bernadette Peters, Roberta Peters, Mary Redhouse, Diane Schuur, and Frederica von Stade, and have performed for presidents, queens, and other leaders of state at major national events and in major venues, including the Kennedy Center in Washington, D.C., Carnegie Hall in New York City, Disney Concert Hall in Los Angeles, Boston Symphony Hall, and symphony halls in San Francisco, Seattle, Dallas, and Denver.

By engaging a traditionally conservative art form, LGBT choruses produce a social presence that resists the stereotypes of LGBT people as solely antisocial, deviant, or hypersexualized. The 2008 GALA festival is planned for Miami, Florida.

—*Julia Balén*

## FURTHER READING

Brett, Phillip, Elizabeth Wood, and Gary C. Thomas. *Queering the Pitch: The New Gay and Lesbian Musicology*. New York: Routledge, 1994.

Gay and Lesbian Association of Choruses. http://www.galachoruses.org/.

Gordon, Eric. "GALA: The Lesbian and Gay Community of Song." *Choral Journal* 30, no. 9 (1990): 25-32.

Hadleigh, Boze. *Sing Out! Gays and Lesbians in the Music World*. New York: Barricade Books, 1998.

McLaren, Jay. *An Encyclopaedia of Gay and Lesbian Recordings: An Index of Published Recordings of Music and Speech Expressing Themes Relevant to Gay Men and Lesbians*. Limited ed. Amsterdam: Author, 1992.

**SEE ALSO:** 1973: Olivia Records Is Founded; Sept., 1975: Anna Crusis Women's Choir Is Formed; Aug. 20-22, 1976: Michigan Womyn's Music Festival Holds Its First Gathering; June 6-June 20, 1981: San Francisco Gay Men's Chorus Concert Tour; Dec. 8, 1981: New York City Gay Men's Chorus Performs at Carnegie Hall; 1992-2002: Celebrity Lesbians Come Out.

## February 5, 1981
# TORONTO POLICE RAID GAY BATHHOUSES

*Toronto police conducted a massive raid on gay bathhouses and arrested nearly three hundred men, the largest mass arrest of gay men in North America. The protests and demonstrations that followed came to be known as the Canadian Stonewall.*

**LOCALE:** Toronto, Ontario, Canada
**CATEGORIES:** Marches, protests, and riots; civil rights

### KEY FIGURE

*Brent Hawkes*, senior pastor at the Metropolitan Community Church in Toronto, who staged a hunger strike to protest police abuse of gays

### SUMMARY OF EVENT

At 11:00 P.M., February 5, 1981, after a reported six months of investigation, 160 plainclothes and uniformed Toronto police officers, armed with crowbars and hammers, raided four of Toronto's gay bathhouses. Police entered the Club Baths, the Romans II Health and Recreation Spa, the Richmond Street Health Emporium, and the Barracks. They knocked down doors and walls, smashed through windows and mirrors, broke into private cubicles rented by patrons, and caused significant damage. The bathhouses sustained more than $35,000 in damages and the Richmond Street Health Emporium never reopened.

The men found within the bathhouses were subjected to verbal abuse, repeated taunts, and hostile searches. Two hundred fifty-three men were arrested and charged as "found-ins," that is, people found without lawful excuse in a "common bawdy house," a term in the Canadian criminal code referring to a place where prostitution or indecent acts take place. Fourteen others faced minor drug charges. In addition, twenty employees at the bathhouses were charged with running a common bawdy house. While not the first antigay police action in Canada's history, the massive and brutal po-

lice raid, and the largest mass arrest in Canada since the October Crisis of 1970 (mass protest against the Canadian War Measures Act), rallied lesbians and gays in Toronto.

The night following the raids, a crowd of fifteen hundred angry demonstrators gathered in downtown Toronto and began a march down Yonge Street. With loud whistles, chants such as "we shall overcome" and "stop the cops," and signs reading "Gay Rights Now" and "Fag Power," the crowd expressed its rage toward the police and their actions. Traffic was disrupted, some property was vandalized, and several people were injured. As the large group gathered momentum, police formed a phalanx outside the 52 Division headquarters to prevent the protesters from entering the stationhouse where the men arrested the night before had been held.

Lesbian and gay activists were encouraged to continue their fight. Three years earlier, in response to a bathhouse raid, only four hundred people had protested. This much larger gathering was a sign that people were fed up with police abuse. In the days that followed, organizations and individuals condemned the raids and called for a review of police action. The Metropolitan Toronto Board of Police Commissioners sat through emotional public testimony from representatives of churches, political parties, and civil liberties groups. On February 14, the five-member board decided to not investigate the police raids. The commissioners had found that the raids constituted legitimate police action.

Community anger and resentments grew. On February 20, 1981, a few thousand demonstrators rallied in Toronto's Queen's Park. Many straight people joined the gay community to protest the brutality of the police; the police force had often been accused of poor relations with many of Toronto's minority groups. Speakers voiced their outrage about the raids and called for human rights protections for gays and lesbians. The Reverend Brent Hawkes, senior pastor at the Metropolitan Community Church, began a hunger strike. He had said that, "No longer will we stand idly by while the politicians ignore us, the police abuse us and the right wing lie about us." Once again, protesters marched to the 52 Division of the Toronto Police Service to protest the bathhouse raids and call for an independent inquiry.

In the months that followed, Toronto's existing gay and lesbian organizations grew in size and strength, and new ones formed. A Right to Privacy Committee created a defense campaign for those charged in the raids. Of the men arrested, 249 were found not guilty. Antiviolence street patrols were initiated to fight local harassment. Another rally, the Gay Freedom Rally, held on March 6, pushed for faster action. On March 12, Hawkes ended his hunger fast when the Toronto City Council began an investigation into relations between the police and gays. A study on how to improve relations between the gay and lesbian community and police was finally funded in July. Released in September, the report, *Out of the Closet: Study of Relations Between Homosexual Community and Police*, legitimized the gay community and recommended a permanent committee to encourage dialogue between the police and gays.

## SIGNIFICANCE

Although the bathhouse raids are sometimes referred to as Toronto's Stonewall, the gay and lesbian rights movement and the campaign for human and civil rights was established well before the raids. The first gay march took place in August, 1971, timed to coincide with the second anniversary of the omnibus bill that decriminalized private consensual homosexual activity between individuals over the age of twenty-one. *The Body Politic*, a gay and lesbian newspaper formed in 1971 and in circulation until 1987, was politically aggressive and a constant voice for equal rights.

The raids, however, did give momentum to and foster support for the rights of Canadian gays and lesbians. While lesbian and gay activism grew, the police would not back down. On June 16, 1981, police entered the Back Door Gym and Sauna and the International Steam Bath and arrested twenty-one men on bawdy house charges. A large demonstration on June 20 again followed the arrests. Another raid took place at the Back Door on April 20, 1983. Many more protests would be needed for real change to occur.

Real change finally began to take shape in the mid-1980's. Canada's legal climate has since become more favorable, and discrimination claims based on sexual orientation now receive fair hearings.

—*Ira Tattelman*

## FURTHER READING

Canadian Lesbian and Gay Archives. http://www.clga.ca.

Coalition for Gay Rights in Ontario. *Who Are These People and What Do They Want!* Toronto, Ont.: Author, 1981.

Jackson, Edward, and Stan Persky, eds. *Flaunting It! A Decade of Gay Journalism from "The Body Politic."* Toronto, Ont.: New Star and Pink Triangle Press, 1982.

Woods, William J., and Diane Binson, eds. *Gay Bathhouses and Public Health Policy*. New York: Harrington Park Press, 2003.

**SEE ALSO:** Nov. 17, 1901: Police Arrest "Los 41" in Mexico City; Mar. 15, 1919-1921: U.S. Navy Launches Sting Operation Against "Sexual Perverts"; 1933-1945: Nazis Persecute Homosexuals; June 30-July 1, 1934: Hitler's Night of the Long Knives; June 27-July 2, 1969: Stonewall Rebellion Ignites Modern Gay and Lesbian Rights Movement; Dec. 31, 1977: Toronto Police Raid Offices of *The Body Politic*; Nov. 27, 1978: White Murders Politicians Moscone and Milk; May-Aug., 1980: U.S. Navy Investigates the USS *Norton Sound* in Antilesbian Witch Hunt; Jan. 1, 1988: Canada Decriminalizes Sex Practices Between Consenting Adults.

## June 5 and July 3, 1981
# Reports of Rare Diseases Mark Beginning of AIDS Epidemic

*Reports of Kaposi's sarcoma and* pneumocystis carinii *pneumonia among gay men appeared in* The New York Times *and in a medical newsletter, marking the first years of the AIDS epidemic. Two weeks before the "official" reports, however, came an article in the* New York Native, *a gay newspaper, about rumors of a new disease among gay men.*

**Locale:** Los Angeles and San Francisco, California; New York, New York
**Categories:** HIV-AIDS; health and medicine; science; literature

### Summary of Event

The summer 1981 editions of the *Morbidity and Mortality Weekly Report* (*MMWR*), the newsletter of the Centers for Disease Control, reported a number of unusual medical discoveries and hinted at a new disorder of unknown origin. In a July 3, 1981, article, doctors in New York and San Francisco reported the diagnosis of twenty-six gay men with a rare form of cancer called Kaposi's sarcoma (KS). Prior to 1981, the cancer afflicted only a small population of elderly Ashkenazi Jewish or Italian men, culminating in lesions on the legs and feet, spreading to internal organs after many years, and rarely causing death. In the new cases reported in the *MMWR*, however, young gay men showed lesions on the torso, neck, or face, and the cancer spread quickly to the internal organs and often resulted in death.

Less than one month before the July 3 report, the June 5, 1981, edition of the *MMWR* told of five young, previously healthy, gay men who had been treated in Los Angeles for a rare form of pneumonia called *pneumocystis carinii* pneumonia (PCP), thought only to appear in those with a weakened immune system. The July 3 article hypothesized a relationship between homosexuals and KS, PCP, and a variety of other strange illnesses that had befallen

a small number of gay men in the thirty months prior to the article's publication.

Also on July 3, *The New York Times* and the *Los Angeles Times* reported these findings, although they each buried the story in the last pages of the papers' first sections. In the following days, many major newspapers across the country carried the story. This first week in July, 1981, marked the initial reports of what was to become the AIDS epidemic. No mention of KS, PCP, or any other AIDS-related news made it into any major newspapers for at least the next year. The gay press, which at this time consisted of dozens of magazines and weekly newspapers across the country, provided only slightly better coverage in New York, San Francisco, and Los Angeles—the three cities with most of the first cases.

While sparse, the reports of gay newspapers in these cities often provided the only source of information about the early epidemic to those outside medical circles. The *New York Native*, the major gay newspaper for New York City, offered the best coverage of the epidemic's beginnings and early years. Pre-dating the first *MMWR* article by two weeks, the *New York Native* carried the news story "Disease Rumors Largely Unfounded" by Lawrence D. Mass, a medical doctor, in the May 18, 1981, issue that discussed rumors of a new disease among gay men in New York. In the July 27 issue, Mass wrote his first feature article on the disease, "Cancer in the Gay Community."

More than six months after the first *MMWR* report, in January, 1982, doctors and scientists dubbed the new disease "gay-related immunodeficiency," or GRID, only to rename it "acquired immunodeficiency syndrome," or AIDS, in July. By 1983, doctors in more than twenty-five states encountered patients with KS, PCP, or other rare diseases that had been added to the growing list of illnesses associated with AIDS. Modes of transmis-

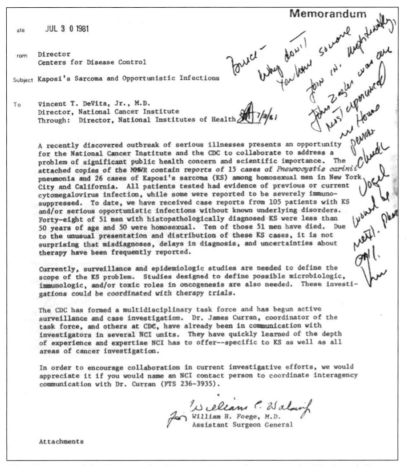

*The director of the Centers for Disease Control wrote to the National Cancer Institute on July 30, 1981, requesting collaboration on studies of Kaposi's sarcoma. The memo is an early instance of federal-level involvement in what would turn out to be the AIDS epidemic.* (National Institutes of Health)

sion and prevention, as well as effective forms of medication, remained largely unidentified by scientists until the mid-1980's.

## SIGNIFICANCE

The first reports of Kaposi's sarcoma and *pneumocystis carinii* pneumonia went largely unnoticed. Only a handful of doctors and the most observant of gay men took note of the articles. Most major gay newspapers around the country reported less than one dozen stories related to KS, PCP, or AIDS in 1981 and 1982 combined. Not until 1983, when the numbers of those infected with the disease topped one thousand, did a larger readership look for the

start of the epidemic. Political activists, AIDS activists, and historians have linked the lack of media coverage during the early years of the epidemic to societal homophobia. Many have argued that homophobia and lack of interest are responsible for the government's slow response to the AIDS epidemic in research funding and education, a delay that resulted in the spread of the disease.

Even with the lack of attention from the mainstream press, these early reports of KS and PCP mark the beginning of the most deadly epidemic in modern human history. The mysterious and complex nature of the diseases presented in the *MMWR* article proved to be trademarks of AIDS, especially in the 1980's.

As doctors and scientists struggled to understand the disease, people with AIDS or those thought to have AIDS found themselves the center of many heated public debates. By the mid-1980's, panic gripped the country over the disease and its transmission and prevention. Politicians, community leaders, and parents of schoolchildren argued about where people with AIDS could go, what they could do, and with whom they could interact. A variety of political groups, including the radical political-action group ACT UP, formed as a result of these efforts to limit the civil rights of people with AIDS.

Scientists—and even the general public, mainly those in the developed world—now understand the modes of transmission and prevention of HIV-AIDS, and they have successfully manufactured a number of effective medications. However, cures for the infection HIV, the virus believed most likely to cause AIDS, and for AIDS itself remain elusive, and testing and treatment is often unavailable in developing countries. At the end of 2003, an estimated 38 million people worldwide lived with HIV and 20 million people worldwide, including more than 500,000 in the United States, have died from AIDS through the first years of the twenty-first century.

—*Catherine P. Batza*

**FURTHER READING**

Andriote, John-Manuel. *Victory Deferred: How AIDS Changed Gay Life in America*. Chicago: University of Chicago Press, 1999.

Fee, Elizabeth, and Daniel Fox. *AIDS: The Making of a Chronic Disease*. Los Angeles: University of California Press, 1992.

Gottlieb, Geoffrey J., and A. Bernard Ackerman. *Kaposi's Sarcoma: A Text and Atlas*. Philadelphia: Lea & Febiger, 1988.

Mass, Lawrence D. "Larry Mass Looks Back on Twenty-Five Years of AIDS Reporting, Activism." *Gay City News*, May 1-7, 2006. http://www.gaycitynews.com/gcn_522/larrymasslooksback.html.

Parker, James N., and Philip M. Parker, eds. *The Official Patient's Sourcebook on Kaposi's Sarcoma*. San Diego, Calif.: Icon Health, 2003.

Patton, Cindy. *Sex and Germs: The Politics of AIDS*. Boston: South End Press, 1985.

Shilts, Randy. *And the Band Played On: Politics, People, and the AIDS Epidemic*. New York: St. Martin's Press, 1987.

**SEE ALSO:** Feb. 5, 1981: Toronto Police Raid Gay Bathhouses; July, 1982: Gay-Related Immunodeficiency Is Renamed AIDS; Spring, 1984: AIDS Virus Is Discovered; Oct. 9, 1984: San Francisco Closes Gay Bathhouses and Other Businesses; July 25, 1985: Actor Hudson Announces He Has AIDS; Sept., 1986: AZT Treats People with AIDS; 1987: Shilts Publishes *And the Band Played On*; Mar., 1987: Radical AIDS Activist Group ACT UP Is Founded; June 27, 1988: Report of the Presidential AIDS Commission; Dec. 1, 1988: First World AIDS Day; June 25, 1993: Clinton Appoints First AIDS Czar.

## June 6-June 20, 1981
# SAN FRANCISCO GAY MEN'S CHORUS CONCERT TOUR

*The San Francisco Gay Men's Chorus, the first men's chorus to identify as gay, toured eight U.S. cities just as news of HIV-AIDS—first called a "gay cancer"—was hitting the press. The group's founding inspired the formation of several other gay men's choruses throughout the United States.*

**LOCALE:** Dallas, Texas; Lincoln, Nebraska; Minneapolis, Minnesota; Detroit, Michigan; Boston, Massachusetts; New York, New York; Washington, D.C.; Seattle, Washington
**CATEGORIES:** Arts; organizations and institutions; cultural and intellectual history; HIV-AIDS

**KEY FIGURES**
*Jon Reed Sims* (1947-1984), founder of the chorus
*Dick Kramer*, first artistic director of the chorus
*Jay Davidson* (b. 1947), founding general manager of the chorus and first president of the GALA Choruses board

**SUMMARY OF EVENT**
The San Francisco Gay Men's Chorus (SFGMC), the first men's chorus to identify itself as gay, toured eight U.S. cities in the summer of 1981, just two-and-a-half years after its first meeting. It could be argued that choral music as a form of resistance to oppression was in the air because the tour happened in the same year that Sister Singers Network and the Gay and Lesbian Association of Choruses

(GALA Choruses) began taking form.

The formation of SFGMC followed a growing wave of new, mostly lesbian-feminist choruses, such as Anna Crusis (Philadelphia, 1975), the Los Angeles Community Women's Chorus (1976), and the first of the movement's mixed-gender, gay and lesbian choruses, the Stonewall Chorale in New York (which began in December of 1977 as the Gotham Male Chorus and changed its name when women joined in 1979).

SFGMC came into being through the visionary action of Jon Reed Sims, a musician who had successfully organized the San Francisco Gay Freedom Day Marching Band & Twirling Corps for the Gay Pride Day parade (June, 1978). While the band and twirling corps decided to continue performing beyond the parade, Sims expanded his vision for gay performing arts by placing flyers around San Francisco to start a men's chorus with plans to pass the director's torch to someone else as soon as possible. Reportedly, more than one hundred men showed up for the first rehearsal on Monday, October 30, 1978. As a program from April, 1980, explains,

> Four weeks later [after the first rehearsal], Dick Kramer, the present director, attended his first Monday rehearsal. It was the night of the shocking double-murder of Harvey Milk and George Moscone. Those members who showed up that evening experienced an unplanned, emotional and hastily rehearsed debut, as they sang a hymn by Mendelssohn on the steps of City Hall following the spontaneous candlelight procession of thousands of mourners that gathered there.

The chorus's impromptu performance at this historic event provided for the group a sense of its own sociohistorical importance from the start.

Under Kramer's direction, the chorus went on to gain critical acclaim in its hometown, and in 1981, it produced its own national tour in conjunction with the Bay Area Women's Brass Quartet. Beginning on June 6, the groups traveled to Dallas, Minneapolis, Lincoln, Detroit, New York, Boston, Seattle, and Washington, D.C., using music, as noted in their calls for financial support, as a "cultural and social bridge between our community and the community at large, fostering knowledge, understanding, and sensitivity across social and sexual categorizations." It was hoped that the national tour would provide a "significant contribution to the efforts of gay people to eliminate fears and prejudices that stand in the way of their open participation in our culture."

Indeed, news reports from the tour, which ended on June 20, indicate both the depth of the fears and prejudices, as well as evidence of the chorus's success in breaking through them. In Dallas, the Ramada Inn decided to relocate the group from its centrally located hotel to a hotel on the outskirts of the metropolis in a primarily Baptist town, Mesquite. The *Dallas Morning News* refused to run the chorus's ad, programs for the show never were delivered, and a local preacher chastised the city for renting the performance hall to the group, threatening a protest. Even without the expected protesters, the numbers in the hall were less than anticipated.

In Detroit, a news crew covering the event turned its cameras on the audience members, many of whom reportedly ducked in fear. In Nebraska, the CBS-TV affiliate, KOLN-KGIN, canceled the chorus's scheduled appearance on the morning show. The First Plymouth Congregational Church board, however, voted to rent space to the chorus for its performance, and community members filled it to standing room only. Letters to the editor in response aired the range of arguments for and against both the church's and the station's actions, creating open discussion of issues that had clearly been closeted.

Indeed, throughout the tour, music critics praised the quality of the performances while letters to newspaper editors in tour cities and to the chorus proclaim both the prejudices and the profound impact that the chorus's performances produced. For example, Brother Joseph A. Izzo of Catholic University of America in Washington, D.C., wrote to *The Washington Post*, "By the beauty of their music they can bridge the gap of misunderstanding, heal the wounds that have been inflicted upon us for many centuries and demonstrate to the Jerry Falwells and the Moral Majority types that we are real human beings, not moral misfits."

The praiseworthy quality of the performances and the stature of some of the performance venues, including the Kennedy Center in New York City, proved instrumental in moving the group and its issues beyond mere curiosity and into the national light. As music critics across the country agreed, SFGMC could not be easily dismissed because they were good, and also because they were reviving an art form that had waned. As *Boston Globe* music critic, Richard Dyer, wrote, "The sound of massed male voices . . . is not one we hear much anymore." The mix of message and medium that came out of the tour proved strategic in a manner that became more apparent, as homophobia reached fevered pitches with the coming of HIV-AIDS. The pride that came from singing and from listening to the group—especially because it was making music through this particular art form—countered, in a way, oppressive social forces against gays and lesbians.

The financial cost of the tour to the chorus and its members had been substantial. To pay for the more than $300,000 price tag, several members took out second mortgages on their homes, with the promise they would be paid back by the end of the tour. In fact, the "tour debt" was not fully paid off until early 1991, just shy of ten years later.

### SIGNIFICANCE

While the significance of the San Francisco Gay Men's Chorus tour has been much debated, what is clear is that the tour inspired those in tour cities and surrounding areas to come out and sing. Choruses who mark the tour as the inspiration for their own formation include the Gay Men's Chorus of Washington, D.C., Twin Cities Gay Men's Chorus, and the Boston Gay Men's Chorus. Dallas, New York, and Seattle already had gay-identified men's choruses. Los Angeles and Chicago soon followed with their own choruses. The tour also had reverberations beyond the LGBT community because of its "outness," scope, venues, quality performances, and community outreach.

—*Julia Balén*

### FURTHER READING

Attinello, Paul. "Sims, John Reed." In *Baker's Biographical Dictionary of Twentieth-Century Classical Musicians*, edited by Laura Kuhn. New York: Schirmer/Macmillan, 1997.

Brett, Phillip, Elizabeth Wood, and Gary C. Thomas. *Queering the Pitch: The New Gay and Lesbian Musicology*. New York: Routledge, 1994.

Gay and Lesbian Association of Choruses. http://www.galachoruses.org.

Gordon, Eric. "GALA: The Lesbian and Gay Community of Song." *Choral Journal* 30, no. 9 (1990): 25-32.

Hadleigh, Boze. *Sing Out! Gays and Lesbians in the Music World*. New York: Barricade Books, 1998.

McLaren, Jay. *An Encyclopaedia of Gay and Lesbian Recordings: An Index of Published Recordings of Music and Speech Expressing Themes Relevant to Gay Men and Lesbians*. Limited ed. Amsterdam: Author, 1992.

San Francisco Gay Men's Chorus. http://www.sfgmc.org.

**SEE ALSO:** 1973: Olivia Records Is Founded; Sept., 1975: Anna Crusis Women's Choir Is Formed; Aug. 20-22, 1976: Michigan Womyn's Music Festival Holds Its First Gathering; 1981-1982: GALA Choruses Is Formed; Dec. 8, 1981: New York City Gay Men's Chorus Performs at Carnegie Hall; 1992-2002: Celebrity Lesbians Come Out.

# October, 1981
# KITCHEN TABLE: WOMEN OF COLOR PRESS IS FOUNDED

*Kitchen Table: Women of Color Press was the first publishing house in North America devoted exclusively to publishing works by not only women of color but also lesbian women of color.*

**LOCALE:** New York, New York
**CATEGORIES:** Publications; literature; publications; race and ethnicity; feminism

## KEY FIGURES

*Barbara Smith* (b. 1946), African American essayist, artist, activist, editor, and publisher
*Audre Lorde* (1934-1992), West Indies-born poet, essayist, novelist, activist, and teacher
*Cherríe Moraga* (b. 1952), Chicana poet, playwright, essayist, editor, teacher, and activist

## SUMMARY OF EVENT

By the late 1970's, the schisms among social justice movements were becoming increasingly apparent. Sexism in the antiracism movement and racism in the women's movement required that many women of color make painful choices about where to place their allegiances. Homophobia in both realms, however, kept lesbians unwilling to renounce the critical importance of their sexual identity from making a choice.

From this void a new political movement emerged. Lesbians of color would come together to share the stories of their lives—those experiences discussed traditionally around the kitchen table—and apply these common stories to other social movements. Denouncing a single-issue approach, the women came to understand how oppressions intersect and to understand the significance and relevance of multiple identities.

Writing was a primary tool for articulating this critique of current social norms and for promoting a new consciousness of the lived reality of women and lesbians of color. Writers Barbara Smith and Audre Lorde each explored this concept and helped shape the Combahee River Collective's "A Black Feminist Statement" (1980), which critiqued the status quo. The statement by the collective, a group made up of lesbian-feminist African American women that formed in 1974, has become a lesbian and feminist manifesto and is widely read in women's studies and lesbian and gay studies courses.

By 1980, Lorde and Smith thought about forming a publishing house to address the dearth of publishing options available to women of color. With Cherríe Moraga and others, they formed the Kitchen Table Collective and announced the founding of the Kitchen Table: Women of Color Press at the Women in Print conference in 1981. Kitchen Table's mission was to commit to publishing the writing of Third World women across race, culture, sexuality, and class in order to promote the freedom of all people.

Kitchen Table first distributed and reprinted Cheryl Clarke's self-published poetry collection, *Narratives: Poems in the Tradition of Black Women* (1983), and published *Cuentos: Stories by Latinas* (1983), edited by Alma Gómez, Cherríe Moraga, and Mariana Romo-Carmona. They also distributed books published by feminist presses, including a now-classic anthology called *This Bridge Called My Back: Writings by Radical Women of Color* (1981), edited by Moraga and Gloria Anzaldúa. Published by Persephone Press, *This Bridge Called My Back* consisted of writing by black, Native American, Asian American, and Latina women and was the first published anthology devoted to the works of women of color. When Persephone closed its doors in 1983, just weeks before completing an anthology edited by Smith (*Home Girls: A Black Feminist Anthology*), Kitchen Table took over, published *Home Girls*, and issued a second edition of *This Bridge Called My Back*.

Kitchen Table published for sixteen years, producing titles such as *A Comrade Is as Precious as a Rice Seedling* (Mila D. Aguilar, 1987), *Healing Heart: Poems, 1973-1988* (Gloria T. Hull, 1989), and *Seventeen Syllables and Other Stories* (Hisaye Yamamoto, 1988). The rights to *Seventeen Syllables* eventually were purchased by Quality Paperback Book Club, thus becoming the first book by a lesbian-feminist press to be sold to a major publisher of book-club books. Kitchen Table also created the Freedom Organizing series, a series of short, affordable pamphlets designed to make key political statements and perspectives more widely available. Titles in the series include *The Combahee River Collective Statement* (Combahee River Collective, 1985) and *I Am Your Sister: Black Women Organizing Across Sexualities* (Audre Lorde, 1986).

Kitchen Table's community service has included sending free books to people in prison and in psychiatric institutions, and to people with HIV-AIDS. It distributed its titles at conferences, book readings by people of color, and other venues traditionally overlooked by the women's movement. Books by Kitchen Table were intended to be read by women and men of all races and sexualities so that active readers could confront and thus enrich their communities by telling about what they read.

Kitchen Table operated for thirteen years without a stable operating budget or a salaried managing editor. Between 1981 and 1995, Barbara Smith was the constant presence that kept the press going, although the press did not support her financially. In 1994, the Kitchen Table advisory board joined with the Union Institute's Center for Women to form what was called a Transition Coalition to promote better financial stability for the press. The first managing director was hired that year and Smith left the press in 1995 to pursue her own writing full time.

Despite a successful grant-writing campaign between 1994 and 1996, the press closed in 1997. This closing reflected a national trend, spurred by the emergence of megastores such as Barnes and Noble and Borders and online booksellers such as Amazon.com, during which 35 percent of the feminist presses folded between 1997 and 2000.

## SIGNIFICANCE

Kitchen Table's most concrete legacy is the mainstreaming of the writing, perspectives, and experiences of women of color. Both *Home Girls* and *This Bridge Called My Back* have become part of the standard curriculum in many college and university courses, and both texts were picked up by other presses when Kitchen Table closed. A new edition of *Home Girls* was published in 2000 by Rutgers University Press and a third edition of *This Bridge Called My Back* was published in 2002 by Third Woman Press.

Of central significance to this legacy is the lesbian leadership at Kitchen Table, a leadership that infused coalition politics with much of its strength. Through the wisdom of lives lived under multiple forms of oppression, and a fierce allegiance to all aspects of their identity, the women of Kitchen Table demonstrated that social change can and must be comprehensive. Furthermore, lesbians willing to articulate a need for men in their political and personal lives provided a bridge into the complex challenges and powerful transformations of this political approach.

Within feminism, this multicultural, multi-issue approach is sometimes referred to as third wave feminism. This terminology documents the influence of Kitchen Table. "The third wave" has been used as part of the title of several recent anthologies addressing the intersections of feminism and racism.

—*Diana Kardia*

## FURTHER READING

Moraga, Cherríe L., and Gloria E. Anzaldúa, eds. *This Bridge Called My Back: Writings by Radical Women of Color*. 3d ed. Berkeley, Calif.: Third Woman Press, 2001.

Short, Kayann. "Coming to the Table: The Differential Politics of *This Bridge Called My Back*." *Genders* 19 (1994).

Smith, Barbara. *The Truth That Never Hurts: Writings on Race, Gender, and Freedom*. New Brunswick, N.J.: Rutgers University Press, 1998.

_____, ed. *Home Girls: A Black Feminist Anthology*. New ed. New Brunswick, N.J.: Rutgers University Press, 2000.

Thompson, Becky. "Multiracial Feminism: Recasting the Chronology of Second Wave Feminism." *Feminist Studies* 28, no. 2 (2002).

SEE ALSO: 1970: Amazon Bookstore Opens as First Feminist-Lesbian Book Shop; 1973: Naiad Press Is Founded; Apr., 1977: Combahee River Collective Issues "A Black Feminist Statement"; 1980: Alyson Begins Publishing Gay and Lesbian Books; 1981: *This Bridge Called My Back* Is Published; 1982: Lorde's Autobiography *Zami* Is Published; Sept., 1983: First National Lesbians of Color Conference Convenes; 1990: United Lesbians of African Heritage Is Founded.

## December 8, 1981
# NEW YORK CITY GAY MEN'S CHORUS PERFORMS AT CARNEGIE HALL

*The New York City Gay Men's Chorus became the first gay musical group to perform at Carnegie Hall. One year later, Meg Christian and Cris Williamson became the first out lesbians to perform there. With the chorus's founding came a surge of gay and lesbian choral groups and the founding of the umbrella organization, GALA Choruses, which stages an international festival with hundreds of choruses and thousands of singers every four years.*

**LOCALE:** New York, New York
**CATEGORIES:** Arts; cultural and intellectual history; organizations and institutions

### KEY FIGURE
*Jon Reed Sims* (1947-1984), founder of the San Francisco Gay Freedom Day Marching Band and Twirling Corps, the San Francisco Gay Men's Chorus, Golden Gate Performing Arts, the orchestra Lambda Pro Musica, and the San Francisco Lesbian and Gay Men's Community Chorus

### SUMMARY OF EVENT
Only two years after it was established, the New York City Gay Men's Chorus (NYCGMC) made its debut at Lincoln Center's Avery Fisher Hall and then Carnegie Hall, on December 8, 1981. *New York Times* music critic Theodore W. Libbey, Jr., who noted that the concert had been sold out, considered the singers "impressive" "glowing," and

"vibrant." The amateur vocal ensemble continued to earn the respect of music critics and not only became a musical force, commissioning new works, but also became for many the "face" and "voice" of out gay men.

There exists a long history of community-based theatrical and musical ensembles, some formed to celebrate a municipality, others to empower the marginalized: religious groups, abolitionists, suffragists, temperance movements, unions, and ethnic or racial groups. Shortly after the Stonewall Rebellion in 1969, one of the earliest GLBT groups was established by composer Roberta Kosse. Originally formed to perform her compositions, her lesbian chorus performed from 1971 to 1980. Performing in the first three New York City Gay Liberation Day parades, the Victoria Woodhull All-Women's Marching Band (established 1973) was not exclusively lesbian, but its theme song was "When the Dykes Go Marching In." One of the oldest ongoing lesbian or gay choruses is the Anna Crusis Women's Choir, formed in 1975 in Philadelphia. As the modern gay and lesbian rights movement gained more momentum, other vocal ensembles began to appear: The Gotham Male Chorus (established 1977) changed its name to the Stonewall Chorale in 1979 when women joined the ensemble, making it the nation's first lesbian and gay chorus.

When founded in 1978 by Jon Reed Sims, the San Francisco Gay Men's Chorus was the first to proclaim its gay identity publicly in the group's name. A twelve-city tour in 1981 had the effect of inspiring many other individuals to organize same-gender or mixed choruses in their own communities. (The same year NYCGMC appeared at Carnegie Hall, the San Francisco Gay Men's Chorus garnered its first "mainstream" validation when a *San Francisco Chronicle* music critic proclaimed its work "superb.") When Gay Games I was held in San Francisco the next year, fourteen choruses met for the first West Coast Choral Festival, an event that led to the formation of the GALA Choruses Network. Incorporated to achieve nonprofit status, the umbrella organization's name was changed to GALA Choruses.

The first National Gay and Lesbian Choral Festival, held in 1983 in New York City with twelve choruses, featured pieces commissioned to out composers Libby Larson and Ned Rorem. GALA Choruses still produces international festivals every four years; Festival VIIe was held in Montreal, Canada, in 2004 with more than 160 choruses from the United States, Canada, England, Ireland, Germany, and Australia and with six thousand delegates in attendance. International membership in GALA Choruses has grown to ten thousand singers in more than two hundred choruses.

While membership in GALA is open to gay, lesbian, and mixed choruses, the bulk of the member choirs are composed of gay men. A parallel organization, Sister Singers Network (established 1981), was formed to facilitate communication and support for women's and lesbian vocal ensembles. Now consisting of forty-five member choruses, the network promotes and produces regional, national, and international women's choral festivals.

One reason for the relatively low number of lesbian choruses is that the common musical style in lesbian culture is of the folk/pop genres, rarely choral or traditional in nature. The abundant lesbian musical repertoire is identified by much more original music than is the gay repertoire and is more likely to be performed by a solo woman at the keyboard or with a guitar. Olivia Records was formed in 1973 not only to promote women's music, especially lesbian-feminist songwriters, but also to change the very nature of the recording industry.

Distributing music made by and for women, the label gave voice to many singers and songwriters until Olivia shifted focus in the 1990's to cruises and resorts. Although "womyn's" music concerts peaked in the 1970's and 1980's, other independent music labels and distribution companies, such as Goldenrod and Ladyslipper Music, continue to produce and distribute lesbian music.

To celebrate the tenth anniversary of Olivia, founder Judy Dlugacz booked the prestigious Carnegie Hall for a concert by Meg Christian and Cris Williamson in 1983. Given that Williamson's *The Changer and the Changed* (1975) had sold more than 45,000 copies in its first year of release, Dlugacz was convinced that the market for lesbian music was bigger than anyone had realized. The Carnegie Hall event sold out three months in advance and resulted in a record album that is still sold today.

Seven marching bands united in 1982 to form the Lesbian and Gay Bands of America (LGBA) to network and promote community band music. In addition to performing at three Gay Games, member bands have merged to participate in two marches on Washington and in President Bill Clinton's inaugural parade in 1993.

While many GLBT marching bands, drill corps, and choral ensembles have enjoyed broad-based audience support—in part because they operate within traditional community-based performing arts groups—acceptance has not always been easy. GALA Choruses members won a lawsuit in 1986 to allow their organizations to use the word "gay" in their names when performing at conventions of the American Choral Directors Association.

## SIGNIFICANCE

Early ensembles were novelties in the sense that they were groups of out gay men or lesbians, or both, who provided a visual example of the "gay community." By raising their collective voices in song, the troupes also provided "an affirmation that society is possible," according to cultural historian Jacques Attali. Music reflects the social order, and the fact that the choruses are polished, professional, rehearsed, "quality" ensembles gives the lie to myths that gays and lesbians are degenerate, subhuman, or otherwise incompetent.

As part of the twenty-fifth anniversary season of the New York City Gay Men's Chorus, the organization established the Youth Pride Chorus, which made its debut at Carnegie Hall in June, 2003. Continuing the dual mission of being a social as well as an artistic force, the young people's ensemble was envisioned as a public display of the gay community providing mentorship to gay young adults between the ages of fourteen and twenty-one.

In 2004, the NYCGMC consisted of 250 voices. The group performed three concerts in either Avery Fisher Hall or Carnegie Hall, continuing the tradition it started in 1981.

—*Bud Coleman*

## FURTHER READING

Attinello, Paul. "Authority and Freedom: Toward a Sociology of the Gay Choruses." In *Queering the Pitch: The New Gay and Lesbian Musicology*, edited by Philip Brett, Elizabeth Wood, and Gary C. Thomas. New York: Routledge, 1994.

Galtney, Smith. "All Together Now." *Out*, December, 2003, 50.

Gordon, Eric A. "GALA: The Lesbian and Gay Community of Song." *Choral Journal* 9, no. 30 (1990): 25-32.

Hadleigh, Boze. *Sing Out! Gays and Lesbians in the Music World.* New York: Barricade Books, 1998.

Libbey, Theodore W., Jr. "Music: New York City Gay Men's Chorus at Carnegie Hall." *The New York Times*, December 10, 1981, p. C14.

Shapiro, Amy. "A Chorus of Activism." *The Advocate*, October 11, 2004.

Wise, Matthew W. "Choruses and Marching Bands." In *Gay Histories and Cultures: An Encyclopedia*, edited by George E. Haggerty. New York: Garland, 2000.

SEE ALSO: 1973: Olivia Records Is Founded; Sept., 1975: Anna Crusis Women's Choir Is Formed; Aug. 20-22, 1976: Michigan Womyn's Music Festival Holds Its First Gathering; 1981-1982: GALA Choruses Is Formed; June 6-June 20, 1981: San Francisco Gay Men's Chorus Concert Tour; 1992-2002: Celebrity Lesbians Come Out.

# 1982
# LESBIAN AND GAY YOUTH PROTECTION INSTITUTE IS FOUNDED

*The founding of the Institute for the Protection of Lesbian and Gay Youth, which inspired the first high schools for gay and lesbian teens, confronted the accusation that gay and lesbian teachers were a threat to children and instead pointed out that the real threats in the schools were the social and cultural norms against homosexuality and other differences among students.*

**ALSO KNOWN AS:** Hetrick-Martin Institute
**LOCALE:** New York, New York
**CATEGORY:** Organizations and institutions

## KEY FIGURES

*Steve Ashkinazy*, original board member of the Institute for the Protection of Lesbian and Gay Youth, or IPLGY, and cofounder of Harvey Milk High School

*Emery Hetrick*, cofounder of IPLGY

*Joyce Hunter*, director of clinical services for IPLGY and cofounder of Harvey Milk High School

*Damien Martin* (1933-1991), cofounder and managing director of IPLGY

## SUMMARY OF EVENT

In 1952, the top two justifications for dismissing a teacher in the United States were the accusations that the teacher in question was a card-carrying member of the Communist Party or was lesbian or gay. While the Civil Rights and other movements of the 1960's and 1970's ushered in unprecedented freedom and visibility for lesbian and gay adults, the domain of children remained a highly reactive and moralized territory, drawing the ongoing fire of political and religious conservatives.

Some exceptions existed, though. In 1975, the Chicago board of education gave public school teachers permission to answer student's questions about homosexuality, and the San Francisco school board agreed to include information on homosexuality in the district's sex education curriculum in 1977. The national climate, however, was represented more accurately by Anita Bryant's 1977 "Save Our Children" campaign in Florida, which garnered 70 percent of the local vote to repeal Dade County's antidiscrimination clause that protected gays and lesbians. A 1978 initiative in California, sponsored by John V. Briggs, was defeated, but a similar proposal passed that same year in Oklahoma, thus allowing for the firing of any teacher advocating, encouraging, or otherwise promoting homosexuality.

Faced with ongoing accusations that homosexuals would both recruit and assault children, revolutionary gay activists responded to the ways in which these accusations and state initiatives threatened the civil rights of adults, but they shied away from direct interventions with and support of children. In large part, this left LGBT youth unprotected against harassment, violence, and rejection in their schools, communities, and homes.

In 1979, a New York youth had been gang-raped and beaten at a youth shelter and was subsequently evicted from the same shelter because he was gay. The rape, beating, and eviction was soon discussed at political meetings in New York and came to the attention of Emery Hetrick, a psychiatrist, and Damien Martin, a New York University professor. The couple organized the Institute for the Protection of Lesbian and Gay Youth (IPLGY), a group of professionals, primarily social workers and psychiatrists, who met to find ways to provide services to gay and lesbian youth. The organization would confront the charge made by Bryant and others that homosexuals were a threat to children, and point out instead that the real threat came from the conservative norms that put LGBT children at such risk.

Hetrick and Martin organized a major conference on gay and lesbian youth for social service professionals. This conference and other social service interventions also led by them drew the attention of a wealthy patron who provided $50,000 to establish a formal office. By 1983, they had established social service contracts with the city's Youth Bureau and Division for Youth and immediately began serving clients. In 1984, IPLGY provided services to one hundred youth in person and many others through

---

### BILL OF RIGHTS FOR LESBIAN, GAY, BISEXUAL, AND TRANSGENDER STUDENTS (1990)

1. The right to attend schools free of verbal and physical harassment; where education, not survival, is the priority.
2. The right to attend schools where respect and dignity for all is a standard set by the board's of education and enforced by every school administrator.
3. The right to have access to accurate information about themselves, free of negative judgment and delivered by adults who not only inform them, but affirm them.
4. The right to positive role models, both in person and in the curriculum.
5. The right to be included in all support programs that exist to help teenagers deal with the difficulties of adolescence.
6. The right to legislators who guarantee and fight for their constitutional freedoms, rather than ones who reinforce hate and prejudice.
7. The right to a heritage free of crippling self-hate and unchallenged discrimination.

*Source:* Virginia Uribe. Friends of Project 10. http://project10.org.

## MODEL ANTI-HARASSMENT POLICY FOR SCHOOLS

The [_____] School District is committed to providing all students with a safe and supportive school environment. Members of the school community are expected to treat each other with respect. Teachers and other staff members are expected to teach and to demonstrate by example that all members of the community are entitled to respect.

Harassment of a student by another student or by a teacher or other staff member is a violation of school policy. This includes (but is not limited to) harassment based on race, national origin, marital status, sex, sexual orientation, gender identity, religion, or disability. Punishable harassment is conduct, including verbal conduct, (1) that creates (or will certainly create) a hostile environment by substantially interfering with a student's educational benefits, opportunities, or performance, or with a student's physical or psychological well-being; or (2) that is threatening or seriously intimidating.

Sexual harassment is a form of harassment that also violates school policy. Punishable sexual harassment is an unwelcome sexual advance or sexual conduct, including verbal conduct, (1) that is tied to a student's educational benefits, opportunities, or performance, or to a student's physical or psychological well-being; (2) that creates (or will certainly create) a hostile environment by substantially interfering with a student's educational benefits, opportunities, or performance, or with a student's physical or psychological well-being; or (3) that is threatening or seriously intimidating.

To prevent harassment in the first instance, staff members should teach—teach why harassment is wrong and teach that tolerance and respect are essential to a free society. In response to an act of harassment, staff members should intervene immediately to stop the harassment and, if appropriate, should punish the harassment promptly, consistently, and proportionately to the seriousness of the act. But the response should not end there; rather, staff members should deter future harassment with continuing lessons of tolerance and respect.

*Note:* Schools should develop and publicize rules that explain how harassment can be reported and how reports of harassment will be handled. In some cases, schools are required to do so by federal law. These rules should require staff to report harassment to a designated school official; should prohibit retaliation against anyone who reports harassment; and, to the extent possible, should protect the confidentiality of anyone who is involved in a report of harassment.

*Source:* American Civil Liberties Union. http://www.aclu.org/lgbt/youth/.

telephone counseling. Those numbers tripled the following year as IPLGY developed after-school and hot meals programs, classes, group activities, and performances. IPLGY also became the first organization in New York City to start an AIDS- and HIV-prevention education program for adolescents. In 1988, IPLGY was renamed the Hetrick-Martin Institute.

Two staff members, Joyce Hunter and Steve Ashkinazy, noticed that many of their clients were not attending school. New York City board of education policy allowed for an on-site teacher at agencies with twenty-two or more clients who had dropped out of education. IPLGY would hire a teacher in 1985 and announce the opening of Harvey Milk High School (HMHS), a school for at-risk LGBT youth. The school served twenty students its first year and was devoted to providing education and support to students facing significant harassment in other New York City schools, with the goals of reintegrating them into their schools or providing them the opportunity to obtain their high school diploma. The student composition in 2003 consisted of close to one hundred students, 75 percent of whom were African American and Latino or Latina. Graduation rates at HMHS have averaged 95 percent. In 2003, HMHS was granted "full-school" status by the city, and was granted $3.2 million to renovate and expand its physical structure.

Outside New York City around this time, other events related to LGBT youth also had been unfolding. In a small town in Rhode Island, Aaron Fricke went to court to win the right to take a male date to his high school prom in 1980. Fricke chronicled this experience in a 1981 book called *Reflections of a Rock Lobster: A Story About Growing Up Gay*. Also in 1980, Alyson Publications published *Young, Gay, and Proud!*, edited by Sasha Alyson, and began collecting submissions for a subsequent book called *One Teenager in 10: Writings by Gay and Lesbian Youth* (1983), edited by Ann Heron. The first annual conference of the Gay Father's Coalition, later named the Family Pride Network, met in 1980. In 1982, Byton High School, a short-lived and small gay high school, was established in Philadelphia and graduated four students in 1983.

Educator Virginia Uribe surveyed the ten largest school districts in the United States for her doctoral dissertation in psychology and discovered a scarcity of resources for LGBT students. In 1984, catalyzed by these results and by her own experience with an out gay student who dropped out of school because of harassment, she designed Project 10, a Los Angeles Unified School District program of support services responding to the risks of suicide, alcohol and substance abuse, and HIV-AIDS among LGBT teenagers. Project 10 continues to serve youth in Los Angeles through the following services: a district resource center and program adviser; training workshops for administrators, counselors, teachers, and other staff members; on-site student support groups led by trained facilitators; assistance to school librarians; assistance to schools to comply with nondiscrimination policies; advocacy for LGBT student rights through task forces, parent groups, and community outreach programs; and networking with community agencies, parents, educational organizations, and teacher unions. Project 10 also sponsors an LGBT prom, a scholarship program, and a conference for LGBT youth.

In Massachusetts in 1988, Kevin Jennings, a young, gay high school teacher, began coming out to students and supporting their interests in establishing a student group they would call Gay-Straight Alliance. By 1990, he organized a conference of seventy lesbian and gay teachers and founded the Gay and Lesbian Independent School Teacher's Network. His efforts played a central role in the 1993 adoption of a Safe Schools program in Massachusetts that focused on supporting Gay-Straight Alliance student groups and providing training concerning LGBT youth to all teachers. His organization became the Gay, Lesbian, and Straight Education Network (GLSEN). By 2000, GLSEN became the fifth largest LGBT rights organization in the United States, with offices in New York, Chicago, Atlanta, San Francisco, and Washington, D.C., and ninety community-based chapters in more than forty states.

## Significance

Years after Hetrick and Martin responded to the need for services for LGBT youth, significant problems still exist in school settings and beyond. A 2003 GLSEN school-climate survey found that nearly 40 percent of LGBT youth had experienced physical violence at school, and four out of five LGBT students had been verbally harassed. The National Mental Health Association reported that 22 percent of LGBT respondents had skipped school in the month prior to the survey because they felt unsafe there, and that the average gay or lesbian student hears antigay and antilesbian slurs, including "homo," "faggot," and "sissy," about twenty-six times per day, or once every fourteen minutes. Less than 20 percent of LGBT youth report that they know of a supportive adult at their school, and LGBT youth are three times more likely than their peers to become high-school dropouts.

In 1991, New York's Children of the Rainbow curriculum was rejected because three pages out of five hundred included information about LGBT families. In 2000, the U.S. Supreme Court upheld the right of the Boy Scouts of America to oust leaders who were gay, and in a backlash response in Vermont, passage of marriage legislation was followed by a cut in funding to the state's youth services organization, Outright, and an 80 percent decrease in requests for presentations in high schools. In 2004, the positive portrayal of LGBT issues or LGBT people was still prohibited in schools in the states of Alabama, Arizona, Mississippi, Oklahoma, South Carolina, Texas, and Utah.

The 2004 State of the States report by GLSEN issued a failing grade to forty-two states based on an analysis of statewide laws that affect school safety and school environments for all students, and especially LGBT students. Its summary emphasizes that more than 75 percent of K-12 students are not protected by antidiscrimination legislation and that students were 40 percent more likely to skip school out of fear for their safety in contexts where no such protection was provided.

Although the situation for LGBT youth continues to be alarming, the positive changes made since the early 1980's have been significant. In 1979, statistics on antigay harassment and safety issues were not being compiled, and analyses were nonexistent. However, research on LGBT youth has escalated in the last several years.

Although books such as *Young, Gay, and Proud!* and *Heather Has Two Mommies* (written and self-published by Leslea Newman in 1989) were once the only resources of their kind, hundreds of books now exist for and about LGBT youth. Web resources provide even more information with articles, chat rooms, counseling, and networking through sites such as planetout.com, gayteens.org, outproud.org, younggayamerica.com, and youth resource.com. These sites have created an online community that reaches even rural youth.

Fueled with this wealth of information, advocates for LGBT youth have created school-based support programs in other cities (such as in St. Paul, Minnesota, and San Francisco, California) and Safe School programs have been passed in Massachusetts, Connecticut, California, and New Jersey. Adult advocates have stepped in to support Gay-Straight Alliance groups coming under fire in Utah, Oklahoma, and California. Youth service organizations exist in a multitude of cities across the country. Advocacy efforts have also harnessed the attention of the National Education Association, which supports LGBT curricular inclusion, teacher training, and gay-teen counseling.

By 2002, more than twelve hundred Gay-Straight Alliances had been formed, primarily by high school students, in nearly all fifty states. A host of other organizations have been created and run by teens and young adults. That these and other organizations are being conceived and run by LGBT and straight youth themselves may be the greatest change brought about in these times. No longer just victims, LGBT youth are becoming advocates for themselves and activists for us all.

—*Diana Kardia*

**FURTHER READING**

Baker, Jean M. *How Homophobia Hurts Children: Nurturing Diversity at Home, at School, and in the Community.* New York: Harrington Park Press, 2001.

Bass, Ellen, and Kate Kaufman. *Free Your Mind: The Book for Gay, Lesbian, and Bisexual Youth and Their Allies.* New York: HarperPerennial, 1996.

Huegel, Kelly. *GLBTQ: The Survival Guide for Queer and Questioning Teens.* Minneapolis, Minn.: Free Spirit, 2003.

Lipkin, Arthur. *Understanding Homosexuality, Changing Schools.* Boulder, Colo.: Westview Press, 2000.

Rich, Jason R. *Growing Up Gay in America: Informative and Practical Advice for Teen Guys Questioning Their Sexuality and Growing Up Gay.* Boston: Franklin Street Books, 2002.

Ryan, Caitlin. *Lesbian and Gay Youth.* New York: Columbia University Press, 1998.

**SEE ALSO:** Aug., 1966: Queer Youth Fight Police Harassment at Compton's Cafeteria in San Francisco; Mar., 1971: Los Angeles Gay and Lesbian Center Is Founded; 1975: First Novel About Coming Out to Parents Is Published; 1981: Parents, Families, and Friends of Lesbians and Gays Is Founded; May, 1988: Lavender Youth Recreation and Information Center Opens; 1994: National Association of Lesbian and Gay Community Centers Is Founded.

## 1982
# LORDE'S AUTOBIOGRAPHY *ZAMI* IS PUBLISHED

*In her groundbreaking autobiography,* Zami: A New Spelling of My Name, *African American writer and poet Audre Lorde reflects upon her childhood experiences in Harlem and upon lesbian life since the postwar period. The book helped to broaden understandings of the intersections of race, gender, class, and sexuality, and it has been noted for its telling details of lesbian relationships and sexuality.*

**LOCALE:** Freedom, California
**CATEGORIES:** Publications; literature; race and ethnicity; feminism; civil rights

**KEY FIGURE**
*Audre Lorde* (1934-1992), feminist poet, writer, and teacher

**SUMMARY OF EVENT**
Audre Lorde was the daughter of Caribbean immigrants. She graduated from Columbia University and Hunter College, went on to publish more than one dozen books of poetry and prose, and cofounded Kitchen Table: Women of Color Press. She was active in the Civil Rights movement in the 1960's, and promoted throughout her life institutions that celebrated African American culture. Lorde was a strong supporter for gay and lesbian rights and spoke at the first national march on Washington for lesbian and gay liberation, in 1979. She documented her fourteen-year battle against cancer in her award-winning books *The Cancer Journals* (1980) and *A Burst of Light* (1988).

Lorde's *Zami: A New Spelling of My Name* (1982) opens in Harlem during the Great Depression. Her colorful descriptions of the sights, sounds, and smells of 142nd Street re-create Upper Manhattan's vibrant mix of traditions and cultures from a child's perspective. Many of the book's early chapters are set in the apartment of Lorde's Caribbean immigrant parents. Lorde's mother, a power-

ful, private woman, maintained strong ties to the Caribbean island, Carriacou, where she was born, through her cooking, dress, mannerisms, and values. Her mother's nostalgia for home, a far-off place Lorde had not been to before writing *Zami*, drove Lorde's search for a home to call her own.

For much of her childhood, Lorde had felt like an outsider. She had not been close to her sisters, and her vision problems (she was considered legally blind when not wearing her glasses) and skin color kept her mostly white, Catholic schoolmates from accepting her. The larger societal structures of dis-

*The cover of Lorde's* Zami *(1982).* (The Crossing Press)

## FROM *ZAMI*

Every woman I have ever loved has left her print upon me, where I loved some invaluable piece of myself apart from me—so different that I had to stretch and grow in order to recognize her.... A year later, I finished library school. The first summer of a new decade was waning as I walked away from Seventh Street for the last time, leaving that door unlocked for whatever person came after me who needed shelter. There were four half-finished poems scribbled on the bathroom wall between the toilet and the bathtub, others in the window jambs and the floorboards under the flowered linoleum, mixed up with the ghosts of rich food smells.

The casing of this place had been my home for seven years, the amount of time it takes for the human body to completely renew itself, cell by living cell. And in those years my life had become increasingly a bridge and field of women. *Zami.*

Zami. A Carriacou name for women who work together as friends and lovers.

... There [Carriacou Island] it is said that the desire to lie with other women is a drive from the mother's blood.

*Source:* Audre Lorde, *Zami: A New Spelling of My Name*, 1982.

crimination rooted in pre-civil rights America echo throughout Lorde's retelling of her personal struggles for acceptance. The young Lorde's anger at a waitress's refusal to serve ice cream to her vacationing family at a cafe in Washington, D.C., helped to lay the foundation for her activism as an adult.

By high school, Lorde began to develop meaningful friendships and started to understand the importance of other women in her emotional, spiritual, and physical life. Her close relationship with Gennie, a free-spirited but troubled girl, ended tragically; the wounds resulting from this friendship discouraged Lorde from establishing an intimate bond with another person for quite some time.

Lorde's desire for independence and her ongoing search for identity informed her decision to leave home in her late teens. Independence came at a cost; Lorde worked hard to survive on the income generated from low-paying, back-breaking jobs. While her economic situation did not allow her much freedom, Lorde experienced her most mature and fulfilling relationship at this time in her life with a coworker, Ginger. Lorde gained confidence through this short-lived romance, which helped her

to come to terms with, then celebrate, her lesbian sexuality.

Lorde's growing disillusionment with the United States during the McCarthy era led her to Mexico, where she joined a group of like-minded, though more experienced, expatriates in the bohemian city of Cuernavaca. Her relationship with an older woman, Eudora, exposed her naïveté but also deepened her understanding of the skills necessary to make a relationship work.

For the remainder of the book, Lorde recounts her perceptions of the private parties and public haunts frequented by 1950's-era lesbians in New York. She entered into her most committed relationship with a schizophrenic woman named Muriel, a relationship notable for its devastating lows and its triumphant highs. The final relationship explored in the book, Lorde's love affair with an African American woman named Afrekete, brought Lorde's life to full circle and back to Harlem.

In the epilogue, Lorde explains the meaning of the book's title. She ended her search for identity by renaming herself Zami, a Carriacou name for "women who work together as friends and lovers."

### SIGNIFICANCE

*Zami* helped broaden the scope of second-wave feminist discourse through its open discussion of the intersections of race, class, gender, and sexual orientation. Lorde's firsthand account of the discrimination she faced in a racist and homophobic United States brought to light the need for a more nuanced discussion of difference within the often monolithic women's movement.

On the one hand, Lorde's *Zami* stands out for its celebration of lesbian relationships; the love between two women had rarely been described in such intimate and loving detail. On the other hand, Lorde does not shy away from critique in the book. For example, she exposes the roots of alcoholism within the lesbian community, a symptom of the self-loathing directly attributable to an atmosphere of intolerance. In addition, she frankly discusses the racial insensitivity of the mostly white lesbian community of lower Manhattan. Finally, Lorde candidly explores her discomfort with the butch/femme lesbian aesthetic, which she suggests only reconfirms gender stereotypes.

Lorde's exploration of the African American lesbian experience encouraged several other women of color to follow her lead and publish their own "biomythographies" in the 1980's. One such book is *Borderlands/La Frontera: The New Mestiza* (1987) by Mexican American lesbian author Gloria Anzaldúa.

Lorde's work continues to inspire women around the world. The existence of several grassroots organizations, such as the Atlanta-based Zami, an organization for lesbians of African descent, and the same-named Zami, based in Washington, D.C., an informal discussion and social group for black lesbians, bisexuals, and other women exploring their sexuality, demonstrates the powerful impact of Lorde's work.

*—Corinne Andersen*

## Further Reading

De Veaux, Alexis. *Warrior Poet: A Biography of Audre Lorde*. New York: W. W. Norton, 2004.

Hall, Joan Wylie, ed. *Conversations with Audre Lorde*. Jackson: University Press of Mississippi, 2004.

Lorde, Audre. *A Burst of Light: Essays*. Ithaca, N.Y.: Firebrand Books, 1988.

_____. *The Cancer Journals*. Argyle, N.Y.: Spinsters Ink, 1980.

_____. *I Am Your Sister: Black Women Organizing Across Sexualities*. New York: Kitchen Table: Women of Color Press, 1985.

_____.*Undersong: Chosen Poems, Old and New*. New York: W. W. Norton, 1992.

_____. *Uses of the Erotic: The Erotic as Power*. New York: Out & Out Books, 1978.

_____. *Zami: A New Spelling of My Name*. Freedom, Calif.: Crossing Press, 1982.

**See also:** Nov. 7, 1972: Jordan Becomes First Black Congresswoman from the South; 1975: Gay American Indians Is Founded; 1975-1983: Gay Latino Alliance Is Formed; Apr., 1977: Combahee River Collective Issues "A Black Feminist Statement"; Nov. 18-21, 1977: National Women's Conference Convenes; Oct. 12-15, 1979: First National Third World Lesbian and Gay Conference Convenes; Oct. 12-15, 1979: Lesbian and Gay Asian Collective Is Founded; 1981: *This Bridge Called My Back* Is Published; Oct., 1981: Kitchen Table: Women of Color Press Is Founded; Sept., 1983: First National Lesbians of Color Conference Convenes; 1986: Paula Gunn Allen Publishes *The Sacred Hoop*; 1987: Anzaldúa Publishes *Borderlands/ La Frontera*; 1987: *Compañeras: Latina Lesbians* Is Published; 1990: United Lesbians of African Heritage Is Founded.

## 1982-1991
# LESBIAN ACADEMIC AND ACTIVIST SUES UNIVERSITY OF CALIFORNIA FOR DISCRIMINATION

*Academic, writer, and activist Merle Woo twice filed suit against the University of California, Berkeley, after her contract as a lecturer at the university was not renewed. She argued that Berkeley failed to renew her teaching contracts in 1982 and in 1986, partly because of her radical politics, race, and gender. She won her first case and was reinstated in 1984. In 1986, again without a renewed contract, she filed suit once more but dropped the case in 1991 for health reasons.*

**LOCALE:** Berkeley, California
**CATEGORIES:** Laws, acts, and legal history; civil rights; race and ethnicity; feminism; organizations and institutions

**KEY FIGURE**
*Merle Woo* (b. 1941), writer, activist, and educator

**SUMMARY OF EVENT**

Merle Woo, a Korean-Chinese American lesbian, is a respected writer and social activist whose teaching contracts with the University of California, Berkeley, were not renewed, first in 1982 and again in 1986. Woo contended she was targeted by a conservative university administration for her radical views and her support of various student protests and causes. In 1984, she filed suit against the university in an unfair labor practice action, and was represented in court by the American Federation of Teachers (AFT).

Woo then spent much of the 1980's in a series of protracted legal proceedings over whether the university, on two occasions, had violated her free speech rights and discriminated against her on the basis of race, gender, sexuality, and political ideology. Woo eventually won the unfair labor practices case in 1984, received an out-of-court settlement,

and negotiated a union arbitration deal with Berkeley, brokered by the AFT. However, in 1986, the university failed to renew her contract once again, and she filed a lawsuit, again for unfair labor practices. The case was still in the courts in 1991, but Woo dropped the suit after she was diagnosed with breast cancer.

Woo had been a Marxist and lesbian-feminist critic teaching courses in Asian American studies, women's studies, and queer studies at Berkeley. Before Berkeley, she taught at San Francisco State University. Also, she was a leader of the group Radical Women and with the Freedom Socialist Party during an increasingly conservative decade in national politics.

On November 4, 1980, in a stunning upset of incumbent President Jimmy Carter, former California governor Ronald Reagan was elected president of the United States by 50.7 percent of the electorate to Carter's 41 percent. Reagan had run on a decidedly conservative platform of supply-side economics, tax cuts, abortion opposition, small government, and a strong military.

The so-called Reagan revolution was embraced and celebrated by the grassroots political efforts of the Christian Right and by conservative activists such as Richard Viguerie, who had founded the *Conservative Digest* in 1975. The Moral Majority, established by the Reverend Jerry Falwell in 1979, was instrumental in grassroots activism on behalf of conservative causes, especially among Christian evangelicals and fundamentalists. Conservatives, and conservative Christians, had a major part in Reagan's election.

To radical academics and social activists, the 1980 election marked a watershed year. Reagan's provocative, conservative rhetoric on nuclear weapons, relations with the Soviet Union, abortion, welfare, and government spending was antithetical to radical causes. It was within this changed, conservative context that Woo, while at Berkeley, found herself studying sexist images of Asian American women as demure, invisible, silent, and subordinate model minorities. Woo's work and writings examined the ways that distortions around difference and identity caused enlightened individuals to make generalizations about diversity that lead to discrimination, prejudice, and stereotyping.

If Woo hoped to expose the cultural and social constructions that supported oppression, conservatives, and particularly Reagan, were exacerbating such distortions. In his second term as governor of California (1971-1975), Reagan had introduced a series of welfare reforms that tightened eligibility requirements for welfare benefits and required the able-bodied to work rather than collect general assistance.

In the 1980's, Reaganomics—the White House's economic policy of tax cuts and domestic spending cuts—gutted social programs aimed primarily at helping the mentally ill, disabled, unemployed, urban poor, and working classes. In one speech, Reagan infamously noted the case of a Chicago "welfare queen" caught driving a Cadillac paid for with $150,000 ripped off from the government using aliases, false addresses, fake social security cards, and fictional dead husbands. The story had been a fabrication; but it made an indelible impression on public sentiment.

While the Republican right wing was seen as demonizing and denigrating the poor and disadvantaged, Woo was advocating for increasing child support, demonstrating against legislation to slash affirmative action, and shaming the medical establishment and pharmaceutical industry so that they would support research and treatment for breast cancer victims. Woo's criticism of the widening gap between the rich and poor, the dismantling of the social safety net, and the clampdown on free speech rights placed her at odds with conservative university administrators; they considered her a threat. Here again, her activism and ideology collided with the political agenda of California's governing hierarchy. (As governor of California from 1967 to 1975, Reagan had raised student fees at state colleges and universities and then sent state police to campuses to monitor and contain student protests.)

## SIGNIFICANCE

Merle Woo ultimately won her first discrimination case, and the message the University of California, Berkeley, sent to free thinkers, radical academics, and social critics was clear: The state was willing to invest its vast resources, time, and wealth in quieting criticism and silencing dissent.

Woo's resiliency and perseverance serve as models of academic freedom and campus free speech. In the 1990's, she became active in organizing lecturers and students in support of student democracy and maintaining a focus on lesbians and women of color in the women's studies department at San Francisco State University.

Woo is a socialist, feminist author, and teacher who remains focused on the project of developing multi-issue alliances to expose and escape the distortions around difference and identity. She has also taught women's studies at San Jose State University and remains an important radical voice in American academia. Her teaching philosophy is based on the celebration of the unique gifts that each student, "men and women/brown black yellow jewish white/gay and straight" brings to the learning experience. Her pedagogical approach seeks to kindle the natural, creative spark that gives voice to individual students. Woo encourages her students "[t]o take flight/using the words/that give us wings." She asks,

> What is language after all
> but the touching and uplifting
> one to the others:
> scenes
> poems
> dreams
> our own natural imagery . . .

*—Keith Carson*

## FURTHER READING

Cullen-DuPont, Kathryn, ed. *American Women Activists' Writings: An Anthology, 1637-2002*. New York: Cooper Square Press, 2002.

Thompson, Becky. "Multiracial Feminism: Recasting the Chronology of Second Wave Feminism." *Feminist Studies* 28, no. 2 (2002).

Wang, L. Ling-chi, Henry Yiheng Zhao, and Carrie L. Waara, eds. *Chinese American Poetry: An Anthology*. Santa Barbara, Calif.: Asian American Voices, 1991.

Wong, Nellie, Merle Woo, and Mitsuye Yamada. *Three Asian American Writers Speak Out on Feminism*. San Francisco, Calif.: SF Radical Women, 1993.

Woo, Merle. "Forging the Future, Remembering Our Roots: Building Multicultural, Feminist, Lesbian, and Gay Studies." In *Tilting the Tower: Lesbians, Teaching, Queer Subjects*, edited by Linda Garber. New York: Routledge, 1994.

_____. "Letter to Ma." In *This Bridge Called My Back: Writings by Radical Women of Color*, edited by Cherríe L. Moraga and Gloria E. Anzaldúa. 3d ed. Berkeley, Calif.: Third Woman Press, 2001.

_____. "Three Decades of Class Struggle on Campus: A Personal History." In *Legacy to Liberation: Politics and Culture of Revolutionary Asian Pacific America*, edited by Fred Ho, et al. San Francisco, Calif.: AK Press, 2000.

_____. *Yellow Woman Speaks: Selected Poems*. Expanded ed. Seattle, Wash.: Radical Women, 2003.

**SEE ALSO:** May 1, 1989: U.S. Supreme Court Rules Gender-Role Stsereotyping Is Discriminatory; Sept. 23, 1992: Massachusetts Grants Family Rights to Gay and Lesbian State Workers.

---

**February 25, 1982**

# WISCONSIN ENACTS FIRST STATEWIDE GAY AND LESBIAN CIVIL RIGHTS LAW

*Wisconsin became the first state to enact a gay, lesbian, and bisexual civil rights law, adding the term "sexual orientation" to the state's list of prevailing civil rights statutes. The law's effects exceeded the state's borders.*

**ALSO KNOWN AS:** Chapter 112 of the Wisconsin Statutes

**LOCALE:** Wisconsin

**CATEGORIES:** Civil rights; government and politics; laws, acts, and legal history

### KEY FIGURES

*David Clarenbach*, state representative from Madison

*Lloyd Barbee*, state representative from Milwaukee

*Lee Dreyfus*, governor of Wisconsin, 1979-1983

## SUMMARY OF EVENT

During the 1970's, a number of forward-thinking states began consideration of civil rights measures for gays and lesbians. States such as New York, Minnesota, California, Massachusetts, Oregon, Colorado, Hawaii, and Wisconsin introduced gay and lesbian rights bills in their legislatures. None of these bills were approved, however, and state policy changes moved at a slow pace.

The first attempt to reform Wisconsin statutes to provide legal protections for gay and lesbian residents occurred in 1975. Assembly Bill (AB) 269 was introduced by Representative Lloyd Barbee, an African American Milwaukee legislator, and Representative David Clarenbach, a twenty-one-year-old freshman legislator from Madison. The omnibus sex reform bill gathered interest because of its radical approach toward a wide variety of sexual issues at the state level.

Key proposals contained in the legislation were

the following: repeal of all laws prohibiting consensual sexual acts, which shall be defined as private matters not punishable by criminal law; legalization of same-gender marriage; repeal of all abortion and obscenity statutes; age of consent to be lowered to age fourteen; legalization of prostitution; and incest among adults no longer illegal.

Clarenbach also introduced an amendment to AB 209, which further protected against discrimination in housing based upon sexual orientation, income, religion, ancestry, disability, or educational status. He further introduced similar amendment provisions to AB 358 for legal protections against discrimination in public accommodations. Clarenbach's amendments to bill 358 were rejected by a wide majority in the judiciary committee.

During the same session of the legislature, Representative Barbee delayed revision of the Wisconsin criminal code in hopes of establishing gay and lesbian rights through a backdoor policy move. Both Barbee and Clarenbach wanted to include a change in the state criminal code that would make a distinction between public and private and gay and lesbian sex acts, stipulating punishment only for *public* sex acts between those of the same gender. The move did not succeed.

Clarenbach introduced the gay and lesbian rights measure into every session of the general assembly from 1975 to 1981, but he did not bring it to a vote until he was sure it would pass. He acknowledged the measure required some softening up and the education of those in opposition. In the intervening years he lined up the needed votes for approval. The question at hand concerning gay and lesbian rights, according to Clarenbach, was, How does one create an atmosphere of political security for elected politicians who are in favor but who do not want the political risks associated with it? Clarenbach publicly stated he had high praise for those legislators' fortitude.

Clarenbach's approach contained four key parts: present the measure as consistent with the traditions of the progressive state of Wisconsin; defuse religious dissent by acquiring mainline religious endorsements; present the civil rights measure as a bipartisan proposal; and political support would be the responsibility of gay and lesbian activists across the state. After his attempt to repeal Wisconsin's antisodomy law failed by one vote, Clarenbach decided to push forward the civil rights measure. He believed that time was running out to pass the bill. He thought he would have one session of the assembly only to do so.

Joining Clarenbach in support of the measure was four colleagues from Milwaukee. All four were from "politically safe" districts in the city. Sponsors of the bill (AB 70) focused attention on Wisconsin's liberal and progressive traditions toward civil rights, and also that the two largest cities in the state, Madison and Milwaukee, already had antidiscrimination laws on the books. The National Gay and Lesbian Task Force provided additional resources.

Gay and lesbian activists and their supporters framed the debate around the issue of whether antigay and antilesbian discrimination should be tolerated in Wisconsin; they did not frame the issue around the morality of homosexual behavior. To avoid religious dissent, gay and lesbian activists gathered endorsements from mainline religious groups—Protestant and Roman Catholic—most notably the Roman Catholic Archdiocese of Milwaukee and the American Baptist Church. The thrust was to lessen inroads by the conservative group, Moral Majority, which was attempting to prevent the bill's passage. To keep the bill from being viewed as a "Democratic" endeavor, Republican legislators were sought out as sponsors. While the number of Republicans supporting the legislation was small, those supporters were front and center. Other possible sources of discontent were co-opted in the effort.

To achieve passage of such a law, Clarenbach pointed out that one needs not just gay and lesbian activists, their supporters, and alliances on the outside; one also needs a government insider who has the determination, strength, and stamina to do the "dirty" work and get the job done. As a politician in the government one has to be prepared to engage colleagues in rational debate, to educate the less knowledgeable, and to bargain away political favors.

The strategy was successful, despite a close vote.

The bill passed the state assembly, the more conservative of the two legislative chambers, in a 49-45 vote. To achieve a compromise in the senate, the Committee on State and Local Affairs and Taxation proposed an amendment be added to the measure that stated affirmative action was not necessary regarding sexual orientation statutes. The measure passed the upper house on February 13, 1982, by a vote of 19-13, following a vote of nonconcurrence with the assembly bill version. The assembly then accepted by vote the senate language.

Before signing the bill into law, Wisconsin Republican governor Lee Dreyfus wanted to be assured by the state legislature that the law would not include gays and lesbians under affirmative action guidelines. An amendment was attached to the bill disclaiming affirmative action. Dreyfus signed the legislation into law on February 25, 1982. The bill became officially known as Chapter 112 of the Wisconsin Statutes. At the signing, Dreyfus stated "noninterference in people's private lives has always been a hallmark of the Republican philosophy." The governor also purportedly signed the measure immediately to avoid rising political sentiment to veto it. Ironically, the bill passage happened in an election year and was not an issue in either the gubernatorial or legislative races that year.

After seven years of debate and public education, Wisconsin had passed the first statewide gay and lesbian civil rights law in the United States. The new law as passed simply added the category "sexual orientation" to prevailing state civil rights statutes. It was presented in discussions solely as a civil rights law, not as a progay and pro-lesbian rights law, thus garnering support from a wide variety of state special interest groups.

The bill prohibited discrimination based upon an individual's sexual orientation in employment, housing, and public accommodations. "Sexual orientation" is defined under Wisconsin state law as "heterosexuality," "homosexuality," "bisexuality," "having a history of such a preference," or "being identified with such a sexual preference." The prohibition against discrimination further includes the state civil service, state contractors, and state national guard, and it includes administrative rules

promulgated by state agencies. The primary source of enforcement would be the Equal Rights Division of the Department of Industry, Labor, and Human Relations, other state and federal agencies, and the courts.

The passage of the gay and lesbian civil rights law was significant especially because Wisconsin is a mostly rural, conservative, midwestern state with many traditional values. It was the home of U.S. Senator Joseph McCarthy, who conducted "fag hunts" in the early 1950's. At the same time, Wisconsin embraced and fostered the progressive movement, developing many socially progressive programs in the early part of the twentieth century. Undoubtedly, it was through the political sentiments of progressivism that AB 70 came into existence.

Anthony Earl, a Democrat, assumed the office of Wisconsin governor in 1982. It was his responsibility to implement the newly passed gay and lesbian civil rights law. He developed the Governor's Council on Lesbian and Gay Issues to assist in enforcing the legislation and in making recommendations on other gay- and lesbian-related issues. He appointed an out gay man, Ron McCrea, as his press secretary. Under Earl's administration, the Wisconsin legislature also decriminalized gay sex by repealing the state sodomy statute in 1983.

In the first year of the law, only one hundred people had filed complaints with the Equal Rights Division. The majority of the filings concerned employment and public accommodation issues. This low number reflects perhaps the public's not knowing that the law existed. Lack of knowledge of the law in rural locations of Wisconsin was widespread among heterosexuals, as well as gays and lesbians. A bigger fear of retaliation and openness about their sexual status lurked in the minds of many people who considered filing complaints, diminishing the likelihood of filing.

Employers also became more sophisticated in their techniques to disguise discrimination in employment practices, given that antigay and antilesbian discrimination is harder to prove than other forms of discriminatory practices. Furthermore, the public accommodations section was weakened by leaving prosecution up to local district attorneys.

The impact of a gay and lesbian civil rights law is diminished when a state judicial system does not fully implement that law. There was an early need to infuse the whole state bureaucracy with the legislative principles.

To overcome these and other barriers, gay and lesbian activists cooperated with the Equal Rights Division in publishing a brochure called the "Rights of Gay People." Former Republican governor of Wisconsin Warren Knowles made several public service announcements concerning equal rights legislation, including sexual orientation coverage. Media around the state tried to get the word out about the civil rights guidelines as well.

## Significance

State government supporters of gay and lesbian rights stated that the law has had both profound and positive effects in Wisconsin. It has boosted the self-esteem of gay and lesbian residents, and it has given them legal recourse in matters pertaining to employment, housing, and accommodation in the public and private sectors. It has given all sexual minorities across the state legitimacy and credibility. The burden was no longer on gay and lesbian citizens to justify their existence, but instead was on the actions of the person who was discriminating.

The subtle message embedded in the passage of AB 70 was not so much that gay and lesbian citizens have legal remedy to fight discrimination, but rather that the governing body of the state of Wisconsin decided that society ought to protect an undervalued population, in this case, lesbians, gays, and other sexual minorities.

The passage of the Wisconsin gay and lesbian civil rights bill has provided inspiration for organizing, motivating, and coalescing community leaders. It further motivated community activists in Milwaukee and Madison to propose legislation barring discrimination by local governments and businesses against unmarried couples (those registered as domestic partners or those partnered in civil unions), regardless of sexual orientation. This type of legislation, if passed, would fill a void in the state statute regarding gay and lesbian family law. However, in November, 2006, Wisconsin voters were set to vote on a proposal to ban not only same-gender marriage but also civil unions in the state, an obvious setback if passed.

The political clout of gay and lesbian residents of Wisconsin has been strengthened. The impact of the law has exceeded the boundaries of the state, serving in a direct or indirect capacity as a model for other states. Since 1982, more than one dozen states have passed or issued executive orders outlawing discrimination toward gays and lesbians, providing either full or partial coverage under civil rights guidelines.

—*Michael A. Lutes*

## Further Reading

Anderson, Scott. "Wisconsin Assemblyman David Clarenbach: The Inside Track." *The Advocate*, July 22, 1982, 23.

Egerton, Brooks. "AB70 Anniversary: Gay Rights in Theory: Discrimination Still the Practice." *Out!*, March, 1983, 1-3.

Freiberg, Peter. "First State Gay Rights Law Three Years Later." *The Advocate*, September 3, 1985, 12-13.

McCrea, Ron. "Dairy State Looks at Sex Laws." *The Advocate*, May 21, 1975, 8.

Van der Meide, Wayne. *Legislating Equality: A Review of Laws Affecting Gay, Lesbian, Bisexual, and Transgendered People in the United States.* New York: Policy Institute of the National Gay and Lesbian Task Force, 2000.

"Wisconsin First State to Pass Gay Rights Law." *The Advocate*, April 1, 1982, 9.

See also: 1972-1973: Local Governments Pass Antidiscrimination Laws; 1973: National Gay Task Force Is Formed; Nov. 5, 1974: Noble Is First Out Lesbian or Gay Person to Win State-Level Election; July 3, 1975: U.S. Civil Service Commission Prohibits Discrimination Against Federal Employees; 1979: Moral Majority Is Founded; 1981: Gay and Lesbian Palimony Suits Emerge; Nov. 8, 1988: Oregon Repeals Ban on Antigay Job Discrimination; Dec. 17, 1991: Minnesota Court Awards Guardianship to Lesbian Partner; Sept. 23, 1992: Massachusetts

Grants Family Rights to Gay and Lesbian State Workers; Nov. 3, 1992: Oregon and Colorado Attempt Antigay Initiatives; 1993-1996: Hawaii Opens Door to Same-Gender Marriages; 1994: Employment Non-Discrimination Act Is Proposed to U.S. Congress; Sept. 21, 1996: U.S. President Clinton Signs Defense of Marriage Act; Dec. 20, 1999: *Baker v. Vermont* Leads to Recognition of Same-Gender Civil Unions; June 26, 2003: U.S. Supreme Court Overturns Texas Sodomy Law; Nov. 18, 2003: Massachusetts Court Rules for Same-Gender Marriage.

## July, 1982
# GAY-RELATED IMMUNODEFICIENCY IS RENAMED AIDS

*GRID, or gay-related immunodeficiency, was renamed AIDS, or acquired immunodeficiency syndrome, by medical researchers to better reflect that the disease is not exclusive to gay men. Still, intense public paranoia shadowed the disease. It was not until actor Rock Hudson's death in 1985 from AIDS-related complications that the United States saw major political and governmental concern and action. Discrimination, misinformation, and public denial about the disease, however, have persisted into the twenty-first century.*

**LOCALE:** United States; France

**CATEGORIES:** HIV-AIDS; health and medicine; science; civil rights; government and politics; marches, protests, and riots; organizations and institutions

### KEY FIGURES

*Larry Kramer* (b. 1935), American dramatist, early AIDS activist, and a cofounder of Gay Men's Health Crisis

*Luc Montagnier* (b. 1932), French researcher at the Pasteur Institute in Paris, who, in 1983, identified the virus later named HIV as the retrovirus behind the AIDS epidemic

*Robert Gallo* (b. 1937), American researcher, co-discoverer of HIV as the likely source of AIDS

*Randy Shilts* (1952-1994), American journalist, wrote on the political mismanagement that shaped the early years of the AIDS crisis

*Gaëtan Dugas* (1952/1953-1984), Québécois flight attendant, thought to be the first HIV-positive individual

*Rock Hudson* (1925-1985), American actor, whose death from AIDS-related complications in 1985 raised public awareness and concern for the disease

*Cleve Jones* (b. 1954), American gay rights activist, conceived of the AIDS Memorial Quilt

*Ronald Reagan* (1911-2004), U.S. president, 1981-1988

*Ryan White* (1971-1990), American hemophiliac teen, spokesperson for HIV-AIDS research and awareness

### SUMMARY OF EVENT

The AIDS crisis in North America began when the first cases of a rare form of pneumonia were reported in gay men starting in 1980. Those infected with the disease were treated as if they were at fault for their illness because of their "lifestyles," namely, their homosexuality. Initially called GRID (gay-related immunodeficiency), the disease seemed to affect mostly gay men and drug users. One popular but discriminatory belief was that the disease affected only the "3 h's"—homosexuals, heroin users, and Haitians. Doctors soon identified hemophiliacs as a fourth "h." As news spread of the disease's presence outside the groups initially identified, doctors felt that a name change was needed to better reflect the disease itself and also to help stem the tide of growing prejudice.

*Teenager Ryan White died from AIDS-related complications in 1990, six years after he was diagnosed HIV-positive. White, who had hemophilia, became an advocate for HIV-AIDS research and awareness. The Ryan White Comprehensive AIDS Resources Emergency (CARE) Act, (1990), is named for him.* (Hulton Archive/Getty Images)

At this time, public opprobrium swamped activism. The Christian Right, already driving the backlash against the 1970's gay rights revolution, mobilized its forces to argue that the disease was a punishment from God sent to wipe out homosexuals. Uncertainty about how the disease was actually spread led those who had AIDS to suffer additionally from emotional and physical isolation. People refused to drink from the same cups or even touch those who had the disease (or those *believed* to have the disease), and the public extended the stigma attached to anyone who fell into the identified groups.

In January, 1982, dramatist and gay rights activist Larry Kramer had formed Gay Men's Health Crisis (GMHC). Organized in New York City, the group had focused its attention on the practical needs of people living with AIDS seven months

before the AIDS acronym appeared. Volunteers headed up everything from counseling groups to therapy rounds. GMHC quickly set up patient treatments and a buddy program. One of the key reasons the group formed was the rise of a rare form of cancer called Kaposi's sarcoma among gay men. The medical field would soon determine that having a weakened immune system increased a person's susceptibility to other diseases and infections, including Kaposi's sarcoma.

The first congressional hearings on AIDS were held in April of 1982, focusing on Kaposi's sarcoma, called "gay cancer" at the time, and led to the release of just one million research dollars by the National Cancer Institute. The limited funding was symptomatic of the Reagan administration's apathy toward the disease. Throughout the 1980's, the Food and Drug Administration (FDA), the Centers for Disease Control (CDC), and National Institutes of Health (NIH) engaged in a turf war over who would get the meager funding, staff, and authority to conduct AIDS research.

In July, 1982, doctors at the CDC would change the early name of the disease, GRID, to AIDS. This same month, the first hemophiliac cases were reported. Hemophiliacs feared being associated with the same disease that afflicted gays, particularly as public venom surrounding the epidemic ran high. In 1982, the CDC reported around 900 documented AIDS cases. By the end of 1983, there were nearly 3,000 cases, and 1,283 people had died.

In 1987, Randy Shilts released an unprecedented exposé of the early years of the epidemic. His book, *And the Band Played On*, now a classic work on HIV-AIDS, attacks the Reagan administration for its total failure to address the epidemic, and it chronicles the disease's spread from the late 1970's until 1984. The book also promotes the theory that a single man, Canadian flight attendant Gaëtan Dugas, was responsible for the spread of AIDS in North America. It has since been determined, however, that Dugas was not the so-called "patient zero." The length of incubation for the virus is generally longer than was previously thought, meaning many of the people thought to have been infected by Dugas probably already had the virus. African in origin, the disease likely arrived in North America from a variety of sources simultaneously.

## SIGNIFICANCE

Actor Rock Hudson's death from AIDS-related complications was one of the factors that forced President Reagan to face the proportions of the crisis, even if he did so two years after Hudson died. Indeed, Hudson's homosexuality had long been a public "secret." He remained quite popular until his death, and it was his death that would finally attract nationwide attention to the AIDS epidemic.

By July, 1982, when the CDC coined the AIDS moniker, the Centers had become involved in research into the disease, though the funding battle made advances more difficult. One of the most important impacts of the new name for the disease was its identification as something that could not be isolated to one social group, making knowledge of the disease critical. However, the Reagan administration was not willing to release additional funding for AIDS research. It is not surprising, then, that it was not until 1984 that Robert Gallo identified HIV as the source of the disease, although he did so one year after French researcher Luc Montagnier made the same discovery. Gallo and Montagnier ultimately shared the Nobel Prize as codiscoverers of the virus because Gallo, although second to isolate and identify HIV, was the first researcher to publicly argue that a retrovirus (such as HIV) could be the source of AIDS.

This discovery of HIV as the source of AIDS was one of the most important impacts of AIDS research, and it became a cause of its own. As soon as researchers had identified HIV, scientists could identify the ways the virus spread and, hence, develop guidelines to help prevent its transmission.

Ultimately, knowing the virus could help find a cure. Again, government apathy played a heavy role in AIDS research in its early years, as drug companies charged exorbitant prices for the few AIDS and HIV medications they developed.

Gay and lesbian social activism, which had lost some of its momentum in the early 1980's, once more became a part of national politics. The need for AIDS activism became clear. Groups such as ACT UP (AIDS Coalition To Unleash Power) protested against drug companies, which overcharged for necessary medications. Persons with AIDS, and their friends and families, recognized how important it was to disseminate facts about AIDS and to fight misinformation and discrimination. Additionally, the GLBT community began to urge safer-sex practices to protect against the spread of HIV-AIDS. The combination of activism and scientific facts about the way the disease was spread combined to decrease discrimination and increase public awareness.

Largely because of widespread social activism at a time when government was apathetic toward the disease, social attitudes began to change. When Ryan White, a hemophiliac, was diagnosed with AIDS at the age of thirteen in 1984, he suffered intense isolation in his community of Kokomo, Indiana. Ultimately, his family moved to Cicero, Indiana, where White was greeted with respect. He died there in 1990. In the intervening years, White dedicated himself to AIDS awareness, drawing national attention and increasing AIDS activism.

In 1985, the same year Hudson died, the FDA finally licensed a test for HIV antibodies. This meant that individuals and the nation's blood supply could be screened for AIDS, drastically reducing the number of people exposed to the disease through blood transfusion and allowing early identification of the disease among its sufferers. Additionally, activist Cleve Jones organized an effort to display the names of one thousand San Franciscans who had died of AIDS. When he and others placed placards bearing those names on a wall after a candlelight march, the effect was much like a patchwork quilt. Jones went on to organize the NAMES Project Foundation, which generated the AIDS Memorial

Quilt. Also a long-term AIDS survivor, Jones has endeavored to keep the NAMES Project as nonpolitical as possible in order to avoid excluding from participating in the project those not comfortable with politics yet who mourn for the loss of a loved one to AIDS.

A key year for AIDS activism was 1987, a year in which Reagan would finally admit the proportions of the health crisis faced by the nation, and the CDC published its criteria for diagnosing AIDS. This year also marked the first display of the AIDS quilt. Also in 1987, ACT UP took militant action against the high cost of AIDS drugs and government indifference to the crisis. They staged a protest that shut down Wall Street in New York City, an action that drew worldwide attention. The same year, Reagan asked Surgeon General C. Everett Koop to research AIDS. Koop issued a strong document in favor of protecting against the spread of the disease by encouraging AIDS education, starting as early in life as possible, and the widespread use of condoms. Koop opposed mandatory testing without legal protection because he believed that such testing would discourage a person who had AIDS—or who believed he or she might be HIV-positive—from checking his or her status for fear of recriminations.

Ultimately, social activism has been the force most responsible for increasing awareness about the disease and for decreasing its stigma. Activism also has been responsible for a reduction in the number of new cases, more reasonable costs for AIDS drugs (though activism in this area persists and is still greatly needed), increased research into the disease, and a search for its cure. By the end of the 1980's, it was generally accepted that AIDS affected large portions of the world, leading to its status as a pandemic. The CDC estimates that, through 2002, 886,575 individuals had been diagnosed with AIDS in the United States, and 501,669 of them had died.

—*Jessie Bishop Powell*

## FURTHER READING

Auerbach, D. M., W. W. Darrow, H. W. Jaffe, and J. W. Curran. "Cluster of Cases of the Acquired Immune Deficiency Syndrome: Patients Linked by Sexual Contact." *American Journal of Medicine* 76 (1984): 487-492.

Behrman, Greg. *The Invisible People: How the U.S. Has Slept Through the Global AIDS Pandemic, the Greatest Humanitarian Catastrophe of Our Time.* New York: Free Press, 2004.

Kayal, Philip M. *Bearing Witness: Gay Men's Health Crisis and the Politics of AIDS.* Boulder, Colo.: Westview Press, 1993.

Levinson, Jacob. *The Secret Epidemic: The Story of AIDS and Black America.* New York: Pantheon, 2004.

Moss, Andrew R., D. Osmond, P. Bacchetti, J.-C. Chermann, F. Barre-Sinoussi, and J. Carlson. "Risk Factors for AIDS and HIV Seropositivity in Homosexual Men." *American Journal of Epidemiology* 125 (1987): 1035-1047.

Shilts, Randy. *And the Band Played On: Politics, People, and the AIDS Epidemic.* New York: St. Martin's Press, 1987.

White, Ryan, and Anne Marie Cunningham. *My Own Story.* New York: Dial Books, 1991.

**SEE ALSO:** June 5 and July 3, 1981: Reports of Rare Diseases Mark Beginning of AIDS Epidemic; Spring, 1984: AIDS Virus Is Discovered; July 25, 1985: Actor Hudson Announces He Has AIDS; Sept., 1986: AZT Treats People with AIDS; Mar., 1987: Radical AIDS Activist Group ACT UP Is Founded; June 27, 1988: Report of the Presidential AIDS Commission; Dec. 1, 1988: First World AIDS Day; 1989: Act Up Paris Is Founded; June 25, 1993: Clinton Appoints First AIDS Czar.

## August 28, 1982
# FIRST GAY GAMES ARE HELD IN SAN FRANCISCO

*A San Francisco physician and former Olympic athlete conceived of an international sports competition for out gay and lesbian athletes and teams. The event quickly became popular and stimulated the growth of sports organizations within gay and lesbian communities worldwide. The Gay Games are held every four years in cities around the world.*

**ALSO KNOWN AS:** Challenge 1982; Gay Olympics
**LOCALE:** San Francisco, California
**CATEGORIES:** Sports; organizations and institutions

**KEY FIGURES**
*Tom Waddell* (1937-1987), Olympic decathlete, physician, and Gay Games cofounder
*Mark Brown*, Gay Games cofounder
*Paul Mart*, Gay Games cofounder

**SUMMARY OF EVENT**
Lesbian and gay athletes competed in seventeen sports in Challenge 1982, the first Gay Games. The opening ceremonies, held on August 28, 1982, at Kezar Stadium in San Francisco, California, included carrying "the torch" into the stadium after it had crossed the United States with relays of runners from the site of the 1969 Stonewall Rebellion in New York City to San Francisco through Chicago, Illinois, and Salt Lake City, Utah. The games attracted the largest international public gathering of out gays and lesbians up to that time.

The idea for the Gay Games (originally conceived as the Gay Olympics) originated with Tom Waddell, a San Francisco physician who had competed as a decathlete in the 1968 Olympic Games in Mexico City, along with Mark Brown, Paul Mart, and a group of other friends in 1980. Their aim was to get past the limiting and stereotypical media images of gays and lesbians as marginal members of society, and to reframe the image of gay men as "sissies" who lacked physical strength or athletic

ability. (The media has depicted lesbian and gay culture as one of drag queens and leatherfolk only.) The group believed that by staging a gay and lesbian athletic event, with skilled athletes whose identities went well beyond their same-gender sexual orientation, they would help counter the stereotypes of gays and lesbians as being defined solely by their sexuality. As athletes, in this case, they were clearly something more.

The eight-day event included gay and lesbian athletes competing in all types of sports. The games, however, ran into early opposition from the International and U.S. Olympic Committees, which criticized the use of the word "Olympics" in the original name of the Gay Games. The Olympic Committees opposed the use of the word "Olympics" by Gay Games organizers, although other large sporting events, including those for special-education children (Special Olympics) and seniors, had been allowed to use the term in their official names. The Olympic Committees argued that they had been granted exclusive use of the term by the 1978 Amateur Sports Act. They also believed that having a separate "Gay Olympics" would imply that out gays and lesbians were unwelcome in the Olympic Games. In August, 1982, a U.S. district court judge in San Francisco issued a restraining order, subsequently reinforced by an injunction, that barred the use of the phrase "Gay Olympic Games."

Promoting the games as a serious sporting event initially went slowly, due in part to the failure of another large volunteer event in San Francisco earlier. The promotion gained momentum, however, as local athletes realized the event's potential for unprecedented competition and positive publicity for gays and lesbians in all types of sports. The level of outreach and inclusiveness shown by games organizers was unprecedented as well, with special effort made to reach as many women athletes as possible; six hundred women, nearly half of all athletes in the games, participated in all sporting events except wrestling. Furthermore, games organizers ex-

## FEDERATION OF GAY GAMES: CONCEPT AND PURPOSE

The purpose of the Federation of Gay Games is to foster and augment the self-respect of lesbians and gay men throughout the world and to engender respect and understanding from the nongay world, primarily through an organized international participatory athletic and cultural event held every four years, and commonly known as the Gay Games.

While particular emphasis is placed on these specific goals, it is a fundamental principle of the Federation of Gay Games that all activities conducted under its auspices shall be inclusive in nature and that no individual shall be excluded from participating on the basis of sexual orientation, gender, race, religion, nationality, ethnic origin, political belief(s), athletic/artistic ability, physical challenge, age, or health status.

*Source:* Federation of Gay Games. http://www.gaygames.com.

panded the age range for athletes, a move that countered the emphasis on youth by the Olympic Games. The Gay Games offered athletes in their third and fourth decades a chance to compete. Veteran athletes play a major part in many informal lesbian and gay sports teams and organizations in U.S. cities.

### SIGNIFICANCE

The Gay Games has helped unravel pervasive and longstanding myths about gays, lesbians, and sports: For gays, one myth has been that they are not sports-oriented and certainly not athletic. For lesbians, one myth is that they are one-sport athletes who play softball only. These beliefs reflect the values of an American sports culture unwilling to admit that the same-gender world of team sports and individual competitions also contain opportunities for same-gender emotional bonding. The first major and highly visible challenge to these stereotypes came with the publication of a memoir by professional football player David Kopay in 1977, who gave a frank account in *The David Kopay Story* of the professional and personal costs of being a closeted athlete in one of the three major sports in the United States. In the absence of out gay and lesbian athletes in any sport, the stereotypes would survive. The unquestioned assumption that there are no lesbian and gay athletes of sufficient skill and

ability to compete at the international level, let alone the Olympic Games, has been shattered, in part because of the Gay Games.

News of the games quickly spread outside the United States, with teams and individuals coming from nineteen different countries, including Australia, the Netherlands, and the United Kingdom. The roster of sporting events now include both the traditional events of the Summer Olympic Games—basketball, boxing, cycling, power lifting, soccer, softball, swimming and diving, tennis, track and field, volleyball, and wrestling—as well as events not commonly associated with Olympic competition, such as billiards, bowling, golf, physique, and rugby. The Gay Games also emphasizes personal health and fitness, a focus that would become significantly important in the early years of the HIV-AIDS pandemic, which had started about one year before the appearance of the first Gay Games.

More than ten thousand people attended the closing ceremonies on September 5, 1982. Writer Rita Mae Brown, who with fellow novelist Armistead Maupin served as master of ceremonies, told the assembled athletes that in their honor and integrity they represented the best that the gay and lesbian community could be. The Gay Games are held every four years. In addition to San Francisco, the games have been held in Vancouver, Canada; New York City; Amsterdam; Sydney, Australia; and Chicago. The games are scheduled for Cologne, Germany, in 2010.

—*Robert B. Ridinger*

### FURTHER READING

Davidson, Judy Louise. "The Wannabe Olympics: The Gay Games, Olympism, and Processes of Incorporation." Ph.D. dissertation, University of Alberta, Canada, 2003.

Kopay, David, and Perry Deane Young. *The David*

*Kopay Story: An Extraordinary Self-Revelation.* Foreword by Dick Schaap. 1977. Updated ed. New York: D. I. Fine, 1988.

Krane, Vikki, and Jennifer Waldron. "The Gay Games: Creating Our Own Sports Culture." In *The Olympics at The Millennium: Power, Politics, and the Games*, edited by Kay Schaffer and Sidonie Smith. New Brunswick, N.J.: Rutgers University Press, 2000.

Kulieke, Stephen, and Pat Califia. "In the True 'Olympic' Tradition: The Gay Games." *The Advocate*, October 10, 1982, 29-35.

Trefzger, Paul. "The Gay Olympic Games: San Francisco, 1982." *The Advocate*, August 5, 1982, 18-19.

Waddell, Tom, and Dick Schaap. *Gay Olympian: The Life and Death of Dr. Tom Waddell.* New York: Alfred A. Knopf , 1996.

SEE ALSO: 1994: Navratilova Honored for Her Career in Tennis; 1995: Athlete Louganis Announces He Is HIV-Positive; May 17, 2004: Transsexual Athletes Allowed to Compete in Olympic Games.

## July 14, 1983
# STUDDS IS FIRST OUT GAY MAN IN THE U.S. CONGRESS

*Gerry Studds came out as gay after he was censured by the U.S. House of Representatives on charges of sexual misconduct with a male congressional page. Studds's coming out made him the first gay member of Congress to do so and the first gay or lesbian officeholder at the national level.*

**LOCALE:** Washington, D.C.; Boston, Massachusetts

**CATEGORY:** Government and politics

**KEY FIGURE**

*Gerry Studds* (1937-2006), Democratic representative from Massachusetts, 1973-1996

**SUMMARY OF EVENT**

Gerry Studds served twelve terms in the U.S. House of Representatives between 1973 and 1996, representing southeastern Massachusetts. He was the first out gay member of Congress and a leader in issues concerning HIV-AIDS, women's health, civil rights, and the environment, and in maritime issues.

Studds was born in Mineola, New York, and was a namesake of distant ancestor Elbridge Gerry, who had been vice president under James Madison. Most of Studds's boyhood was spent in Cohasset, Massachusetts. He graduated from Yale University in 1959 and earned a master's degree in teaching two years later. His political ambitions were founded in 1960's Washington, D.C. He served as a foreign service officer with the U.S. Department of State and as a staff member with then-president John F. Kennedy's Domestic Peace Corps. He also was a congressional liaison for the Domestic Peace Corps. Opposition to the Vietnam War lead him into politics and a run for Congress in 1970.

In his 1970 campaign, Studds narrowly lost to a Republican incumbent. He spent the next two years learning the district's constituency. He studied the fishing industry and learned the Portuguese language of the local fishing community, earning their support. Studds won the 12th Congressional District in 1972, the first Democratic representative in more than fifty years. His devotion to a moral commitment in foreign policy captured the attention of many Republicans who became weary of Richard Nixon's handling of Vietnam. Little did voters know that they cast votes for the first gay U.S. congressmember.

After being sworn into office, Studds received assignments to the Merchant Marine and Fisheries and the Foreign Affairs Committees. Studds's leadership on the Merchant Marine and Fisheries Com-

## Studds's Statement to Congress

Mr. Speaker, all Members of Congress must cope with the challenge of initiating and maintaining a career in public office without destroying entirely the ability to lead a meaningful and emotionally fulfilling private life. It is not a simple task for any of us to meet adequately the obligations of either public or private life, let alone both. But these challenges are made substantially more complex when one is, as am I, both an elected official and gay.

The staff of the Committee on Standards of Official Conduct has spent more than 1 year, and hundreds of thousands of dollars on an investigation, the results of which were announced earlier today. The allegations which have been directed against me center on a brief relationship which began and ended 10 years ago. I do not seek to contest the existence of that relationship, which without question reflected a very serious error in judgment on my part.

I do not believe, however, that a relationship which was mutual and voluntary; without coercion; without any preferential treatment, express or implied; without harassment of any kind; which was private; and which occurred 10 years ago constitutes "improper sexual conduct" within the meaning of House Resolution 518, and as defined by the Committee on Standards of Official Conduct itself, in its report. . . .

But I have foremost in my mind the need to protect, to the extent it is still possible given the committee's action, the privacy of other individuals affected by these allegations. Those individuals have a right to personal privacy that would be inevitably and irremediably shattered if I were to insist on public hearings. It is apparent to me, after prolonged personal reflection, that the preservation of that right to privacy is more important than proving in public the validity of the points I have made.

Another consideration contributing to my decision is that I have an obligation to my constituents to perform to the best of my ability as a Member of Congress on issues of enormous importance and complexity. The demands on my time and energy, which a public fight on the issues raised by the committee's actions and procedures would require, would make it more difficult for me to do the job which I have elected to do.

Accordingly, I will not contest procedurally the course of action recommended by the Committee on Standards of Official Conduct.

In so doing, however, I repeat that in my judgment, the mutually voluntary, private relationship between adults, which occurred 10 years ago, should not—by any conceivable standard of fairness, rationality, rule or law—warrant the attention or action of the House of Representatives of the United States.

mittee was strongly felt, as he helped set a 200-mile ocean fishing limit and helped pass the Marine Mammal Protection Act.

While on the House Subcommittee on Health and Environment he advocated health-care reform, fought for expansion of AIDS-research funding, and ensured the availability of Taxol medication for ovarian and breast cancer treatment. More important, Studds never lost touch with his district and its needs. He visited every town several times a year, fielding questions and reporting on legislative votes. His congressional service was marked by hard work, honesty, and respect even from those who opposed him politically.

In 1983, Studds was forced to come out of the closet after public allegations were made that he had had a sexual relationship with a teenage boy, a seventeen-year-old congressional page, ten years prior. He was one of several members of Congress whose sexuality had been revealed. Among the others were Frederick W. Richmond (D-N.Y.), Robert E. Bauman (R-Md.), and Jon C. Hinton (R-Miss.).

The case against Studds that was prepared by committee counsel Joseph D. Califano and presented to the House Committee on Standards of Official Conduct, involved another representative as well: Daniel B. Crane (R-Ill.), a conservative Republican who had sexual relations with a seventeen-year-old female page. In Studds's case, the committee report stated the page traveled with Studds to Europe, accompanied him to restaurants, and visited the representative's home in Georgetown. Both Studds and the male page agreed that the relationship was consensual, that it did not involve coercion, threats, or preferential treatment.

On July 14, 1983, the House voted to censure both Studds and Crane, marking the first time House members had been censured for sexual misconduct. Surrounded by supporters, Studds publicly acknowledged his homosexuality and responded in the *Congressional Record* to allegations made against him. He affirmed his humanity as a gay man and stated that he had made an error in judgment by having the sexual relationship with the page.

While many viewed Studds's response as unrepentant and arrogant, it was in large part favorably received by his constituents. While one newspaper called for his resignation, most Cape Cod residents said it would not affect their support for Studds. Many House colleagues still viewed him as the most effective representative of the Massachusetts delegation.

The censure cost Studds the chairmanship of the House Coast Guard and Navigation Subcommittee, briefly, but he emerged relatively unblemished. He

*Gerry Studds, 1995.* (AP/Wide World Photos)

returned to Massachusetts soon afterward and held a series of town-hall discussions throughout the district. On January 31, 1984, he confirmed that he would run for re-election.

Studds was the first out gay man to run for re-election to Congress. (The first out gay man to run for Congress—but lose—was Franklin Kameny in 1971.) Studds's campaign was a bumpy ride for the six-term incumbent. Democratic primary challenger, Sheriff Peter Flynn of Plymouth County, Massachusetts, said the congressmember's sexual relationship with the male page was "an act of child molestation." Republicans, too, did not hesitate to raise the issue of homosexuality and "family values." However, Studds prevailed, and he again returned to his seat in Congress.

At the height of the HIV-AIDS crisis, in May of 1987, Representative Studds stated that the U.S. government should follow the lead of the United Kingdom, Sweden, and Switzerland and mail HIV-AIDS information to all U.S. citizens. Soon afterward, his office mailed the U.S. Surgeon General's explicit, thirty-six-page brochure on AIDS to all 268,000 households in his district. Studds urged other members of Congress to do likewise.

In the late 1980's, Studds lead the move to repeal the ban on gays and lesbians in the military. Near the end of 1989, two secret reports from the Defense Personnel Security Research and Education Center (1988, 1989), commissioned by the Pentagon, were leaked to Studds's office, and Studds quickly made them public. Both reports revealed that there was no conclusive evidence to support the ban and that the services should move to integrate gay and lesbian personnel. The reports flew in the face of standing military practice, but the Pentagon did not further engage in the policy debate.

Studds was one of a score of Democrats who decided to leave Congress in 1996. Studds told *The Washington Post* in October, 1995, that the Republican program left him somewhere between incredulous and nauseous. He would not leave, however, without one last fight against the Defense of Marriage Act (DOMA) that had been introduced by Representative Bob Barr of Georgia. Studds, along with Barney Frank (D-Mass.) and Steve Gunderson

(R-Wis.) led an attack against the proposed act, but they could not prevent DOMA from being passed (September 10, 1996).

## SIGNIFICANCE

Gerry Studds described himself as a "congressman who was gay," and not a "gay congressman." He believed one's sexual orientation is irrelevant to whether or not one succeeds in their profession. He argued that representatives need to focus on a wide variety of issues rather than be a crusader for one. A constituent's vote, he said, should not be based on whether they want a gay or lesbian person in Congress, but instead on whether or not that candidate could represent (or keep representing) them well.

Most important to Studds was that he wanted acknowledgment that his words and life had meaning to other people, and he wanted members of Congress to listen more carefully to gay and lesbian issues. As with Elaine Noble, the first lesbian elected to statewide office (Massachusetts, 1974), Studds was a pioneer and leader in gay and lesbian politics.

—*Michael A. Lutes*

## FURTHER READING

Bush, Larry. "Electing to Speak Out: Congressman Gerry Studds." *The Advocate*, September 15, 1983, 15, 52-53.

_____. "Personal Thoughts on Coming Out: Congressman Gerry Studds." *The Advocate*, October 29, 1983, 19-23.

Chibbaro, Lou. "Rep. Gerry Studds Becomes First Member of Congress to Come Out." *The Blade*, July 15, 1983, 1, 11.

Hertzog, Mark. *The Lavender Vote: Lesbians, Gay Men, and Bisexuals in American Electoral Politics.* New York: New York University Press, 1996.

Rayside, David. *On the Fringe: Gays and Lesbians in Politics.* Ithaca, N.Y.: Cornell University Press, 1998.

Walter, Dave. "Interview with Rep. Gerry Studds." *The Advocate*, September 23, 1985, 18-19.

Yeager, Ken. *Trailblazers: Profiles of America's Gay and Lesbian Elected Officials.* New York: Haworth Press, 1999.

SEE ALSO: 1971: Kameny Is First Out Candidate for U.S. Congress; Nov. 7, 1972: Jordan Becomes First Black Congresswoman from the South; May 30, 1987: U.S. Congressman Frank Comes Out as Gay; June 27, 1988: Report of the Presidential AIDS Commission; May 24, 1993: Achtenberg Becomes Assistant Housing Secretary; Nov. 30, 1993: Don't Ask, Don't Tell Policy Is Implemented; Sept. 21, 1996: U.S. President Clinton Signs Defense of Marriage Act; Jan., 2006: Jiménez Flores Elected to the Mexican Senate.